The Comanche Empire

THE LAMAR SERIES IN WESTERN HISTORY

The Lamar Series in Western History includes scholarly books of general public interest that enhance the understanding of human affairs in the American West and contribute to a wider understanding of the West's significance in the political, social, and cultural life of America. Comprising works of the highest quality, the series aims to increase the range and vitality of Western American history, focusing on frontier places and people, Indian and ethnic communities, the urban West and the environment, and the art and illustrated history of the American West.

RECENT TITLES

Vicious, by Jon T. Coleman
The Comanche Empire, by Pekka Hämäläinen
Frontiers, by Robert V. Hine and John Mack Faragher
Revolution in Texas, by Benjamin Heber Johnson
Emerald City, by Matthew Klingle
Murder in Tombstone, by Steven Lubet
Making Indian Law, by Christian W. McMillen
Fugitive Landscapes, by Samuel Truett
Bárbaros, by David J. Weber

FORTHCOMING TITLES

The War of a Thousand Deserts, by Brian Delay
The Bourgeois Frontier, by Jay Gitlin
Defying the Odds, by Carole Goldberg and Gelya Frank
The Far West in the Twentieth Century, by Earl Pomeroy
César Chávez, by Stephen J. Pitti
Geronimo, by Robert Utley

The Comanche Empire

Pekka Hämäläinen

Published in Association with The William P. Clements Center for Southwest Studies, Southern Methodist University

Yale University Press
New Haven & London

Published with assistance from the Louis Stern Memorial Fund.

Set in Electra type by Tseng Information Systems, Inc.
Printed in the United States of America.

The Library of Congress has cataloged the hardcover edition as follows:
Hämäläinen, Pekka, 1967–
The Comanche empire / Pekka Hämäläinen.
p. cm. — (The Lamar series in western history)
Includes bibliographical references and index.
"Published in association with the William P. Clements Center for Southwest Studies, Southern Methodist University."
ISBN 978-0-300-12654-9 (cloth : alk. paper)
1. Comanche Indians—History. 2. Comanche Indians—Government relations.
3. United States—History—19th century. 4. Mexico—History—To 1810.
I. William P. Clements Center for Southwest Studies. II. Title.
E99.C85.H27 2008
978.004′974572—dc22
2007041809

ISBN 978-0-300-15117-6 (pbk. : alk. paper)

A catalogue record for this book is available from the British Library.

This paper meets the requirements of ANSI/NISO Z39.48-1992 (Permanence of Paper).
It contains 30 percent postconsumer waste (PCW) and is certified by the Forest Stewardship Council (FSC).

11

CONTENTS

Acknowledgments

Several individuals and institutions helped me complete this book. I would like to thank Markku Henriksson, David Wishart, and John Wunder, who guided me into the world of academia, whose own scholarship has been an inexhaustible source of inspiration, and who have never failed to challenge me intellectually and otherwise. This book would not exist without the counsel and encouragement of David Weber. He has been a staunch supporter of my work and read the manuscript in its various stages, steering my formulations toward balance, precision, and clarity. Elliott West read the manuscript twice, improving it greatly with his keen insights and shrewd criticism. My debt to him is large.

A research fellowship at the William P. Clements Center for Southwest Studies at Southern Methodist University offered me a stimulating environment for revising and rethinking my work. The Clements Center's manuscript workshop brought together several prominent scholars to discuss my project. I am deeply indebted to the workshop participants—Edward Countryman, David Edmunds, Morris Foster, Todd Kerstetter, James Snead, Daniel Usner, Omar Valerio-Jiménez, David Weber, Elliott West, and John Wunder—for their critique and advice. I want to give a special note of thanks to Andrea Boardman for all her help during my stay at SMU. Subsequently, a generous two-year fellowship at the University of Helsinki's Collegium for Advanced Studies allowed me to write the bulk of this book in an intellectually lively setting. I would also like to thank Texas A&M University and the University of California, Santa Barbara, for financial support.

Many people have read all or parts of the manuscript and let me test my ideas in spirited conversations and debates. I am deeply grateful to Gary Clayton Anderson, Matthew Babcock, Ned Blackhawk, Guillaume Boccara, Colin

Calloway, Brian DeLay, Jason Dormandy, Ross Frank, Sarah Griffith, Andrew Isenberg, Ben Johnson, John Lee, Andrea McComb, Patrick McCray, Cecilia Méndez, Susan Miller, Jean Smith, Gabriela Soto Laveaga, Paul Spickard, Todd Wahlstrom, and Martina Will de Chaparro. Thomas Kavanaugh generously shared his vast knowledge of Comanche culture and history. There are also debts that dissolve into friendships forged in shared experiences: I was fortunate to write my first book while my good friends Mark Ellis, Mikko Saikku, and Sam Truett finished theirs. I could always rely on them for support and solid advice. I owe special thanks to Lee Goodwin, who shared her deep knowledge of archival depositories, located crucial documents, and engaged me in many sparkling historiographical discussions. She also read the manuscript with an unfailing eye for detail, saving me from many mistakes. Jennifer Mundy from the Special Collections Office of UCSB's Davidson Library offered invaluable assistance in retrieving obscure sources.

Several people at Yale University Press made the transformation of the manuscript into a book a delightful experience. My editor, Chris Rogers, immediately shared my vision for the book, and his perceptive editorial suggestions were immensely helpful during the final revisions. Laura Davulis and Jessie Hunnicutt steered the manuscript through production with reassuring aplomb, and Eliza Childs, my copyeditor, streamlined my prose and engaged me in fruitful discussions on style and syntax.

My greatest debt is to Veera Supinen who read and edited numerous versions of this book and often directed my thinking on new paths. Her intelligence, wisdom, and grace have sustained this project from its inception to conclusion.

INTRODUCTION

Reversed Colonialism

This book is about an American empire that, according to conventional histories, did not exist. It tells the familiar tale of expansion, resistance, conquest, and loss, but with a reversal of usual historical roles: it is a story in which Indians expand, dictate, and prosper, and European colonists resist, retreat, and struggle to survive.

At the dawn of the eighteenth century, the Comanches were a small tribe of hunter-gatherers living in the rugged canyonlands on the far northern frontier of the Spanish kingdom of New Mexico. They were newcomers to the region, having fled the political unrest and internal disputes in their old homelands on the central Great Plains, and they were struggling to rebuild their lives in a foreign land whose absorption into the Spanish world seemed imminent. It was here, at the advancing edge of the world's largest empire, that the Comanches launched an explosive expansion. They purchased and plundered horses from New Mexico, reinvented themselves as mounted fighters, and reenvisioned their place in the world. They forced their way onto the southern plains, shoved aside the Apaches and other residing nations, and over the course of three generations carved out a vast territory that was larger than the entire European-controlled area north of the Río Grande at the time. They became "Lords of the South Plains," ferocious horse-riding warriors who forestalled Euro-American intrusions into the American Southwest well into the late nineteenth century.[1]

The Comanches are usually portrayed in the existing literature as a formidable equestrian power that erected a daunting barrier of violence to colonial expansion.[2] Along with the Iroquois and Lakotas, they have been embedded in collective American memory as one of the few Native societies able to pose a significant challenge to the Euro-American conquest of North America. But the idea of a Comanche barrier leaves out at least half of the story. For in the mid-eighteenth century Comanches reinvented themselves once more, this time as a hegemonic people who grew increasingly powerful and prosperous at the expense of the surrounding societies, Indian and Euro-American alike. Gradually, a momentous shift took shape. In the Southwest, European imperialism not only stalled in the face of indigenous resistance; it was eclipsed by indigenous imperialism.

That overturn of power relations was more than a historical glitch, a momentary rupture in the process of European colonization of indigenous America. For a century, roughly from 1750 to 1850, the Comanches were the dominant people in the Southwest, and they manipulated and exploited the colonial outposts in New Mexico, Texas, Louisiana, and northern Mexico to increase their safety, prosperity, and power. They extracted resources and labor from their Euro-American and Indian neighbors through thievery and tribute and incorporated foreign ethnicities into their ranks as adopted kinspeople, slaves, workers, dependents, and vassals. The Comanche empire was powered by violence, but, like most viable empires, it was first and foremost an economic construction. At its core was an extensive commercial network that allowed Comanches to control nearby border markets and long-distance trade, swing surrounding groups into their political orbit, and spread their language and culture across the midcontinent. And as always, long-term foreign political dominance rested on dynamic internal development. To cope with the opportunities and challenges of their rapid expansion, Comanches created a centralized multilevel political system, a flourishing market economy, and a graded social organization that was flexible enough to sustain and survive the burdens of their external ambitions.

The Comanches, then, were an interregional power with imperial presence, and their politics divided the history of the Southwest and northern Mexico into two sharply contrasting trajectories. While Comanches reached unparalleled heights of political and economic influence, material wealth, and internal stability, the Spanish colonies, the subsequent Mexican provinces, and many indigenous agricultural societies suffered from a number of disruptions typical to peripheral regions in colonial worlds. Without fully recognizing it, the Spaniards, French, Mexicans, and Anglo-Americans were all restrained and overshadowed in the continent's center by an indigenous empire. That empire—its rise, anatomy, costs, and fall—is the subject of this book.

Great American Indian powers have captivated scholarly imagination since Hernán Cortés fought his way into Tenochtitlán and Francisco Pizarro marched into Cuzco. Over the years, historians and archaeologists have uncovered several imperialistic or quasi-imperialistic Native American polities that dominated other indigenous societies. The Aztecs, Incas, and other empire-builders in the precontact Americas come easily to mind, but one might, with a little more effort, also think of the Powhatans in early seventeenth-century Tidewater Virginia, Haudenosaunee—the Iroquois confederacy—in the seventeenth-century Northeast, or the Lakotas on the nineteenth-century northern plains.[3]

This book belongs to that genre while also stepping outside of it. Comanches, it shows, fought and subjugated other Native societies, but more important to their ascendancy was their ability to reduce Euro-American colonial regimes to building blocks of their own dominant position. Comanches achieved something quite exceptional: they built an imperial organization that subdued, exploited, marginalized, co-opted, and profoundly transformed near and distant colonial outposts, thereby reversing the conventional imperial trajectory in vast segments of North and Central America.[4]

Comanches, moreover, did that during the eighteenth and early nineteenth centuries, the high tide of imperial contestation when colonial powers jostled for preeminence across North America. The colonial Southwest was a setting for several dynamic and diverging imperial projects that converged and clashed in unexpected ways. As Spanish, French, British, and U.S. empires vied with one another over land, commerce, and raw materials, Comanches continued to expand their realm, profoundly frustrating European fantasies of superiority. The result was a colonial history that defies conventional wisdom. A longstanding notion has it that the course and contours of early American history were determined by the shifts in Euro-American power dynamics and the reactions of metropolitan headquarters in Madrid, London, Versailles, Mexico City, and Washington to those shifts. The Southwest, however, is a striking exception. Metropolitan visions mattered there, but they often mattered less than the policies and designs of Comanches, whose dominance eventually reached hemispheric dimensions, extending from the heart of North America deep into Mexico. Indeed, Comanche ascendancy is the missing component in the sweeping historical sequence that led to New Spain's failure to colonize the interior of North America, the erosion of Spanish imperial authority in the Southwest, and the precipitous decay of Mexican power in the north. Ultimately, the rise of the Comanche empire helps explain why Mexico's Far North is today the American Southwest.

Yet for all their strength and potential for expansion, Comanches never attempted to build a European-style imperial system. A creation of itinerant nomadic bands, the Comanche empire was not a rigid structure held together by a single central authority, nor was it an entity that could be displayed on a map as a solid block with clear-cut borders. Unlike Euro-American imperial powers, Comanches did not seek to establish large-scale settlement colonies, and their vision of power was not direct rule over multiple subject peoples. They did not publicize their might with ostentatious art and architecture, and they left behind no imperial ruins to remind us of the extent of their power. Preferring informal rule over formal institutions for both cultural and strategic reasons, Comanches nevertheless created a deeply hierarchical and integrated intersocietal order that was unmistakably imperial in shape, scope, and substance. The numerous Comanche bands and divisions formed an internally fluid but externally coherent coalition that accomplished through a creative blending of violence, diplomacy, extortion, trade, and kinship politics what more rigidly structured empires have achieved through direct political control: they imposed their will upon neighboring polities, harnessed the economic potential of other societies for their own use, and persuaded their rivals to adopt and accept their customs and norms.

To understand the particular nature of Comanche imperialism, it is necessary to understand how Comanche ascendancy intertwined with other imperial expansions—New Spain's tenacious if erratic northward thrust from central Mexico, New France's endeavor to absorb the interior grasslands into its commercial realm, and the United States' quest for a transcontinental empire. Comanches, to simplify a complex multistage process, developed aggressive power policies in reaction to Euro-American invasions that had threatened their safety and autonomy from the moment they had entered the southern plains. Indeed, the fact that Comanche territory, Comanchería, was encircled throughout its existence by Euro-American settler colonies makes the Comanches an unlikely candidate for achieving regional primacy. But as the Comanches grew in numbers and power, that geopolitical layout became the very foundation of their dominance. Their overwhelming military force, so evident in their terror-inspiring mounted guerrilla attacks, would have allowed them to destroy many New Mexico and Texas settlements and drive most of the colonists out of their borders. Yet they never adopted such a policy of expulsion, preferring instead to have their borders lined with formally autonomous but economically subservient and dependent outposts that served as economic access points into the vast resources of the Spanish empire.

The Comanches, then, were an imperial power with a difference: their aim was not to conquer and colonize, but to coexist, control, and exploit. Whereas more traditional imperial powers ruled by making things rigid and predictable, Comanches ruled by keeping them fluid and malleable.[5] This informal, almost ambiguous nature of Comanches' politics not only makes their empire difficult to define; it sometimes makes it difficult to see. New Mexico and Texas existed side by side with Comanchería throughout the colonial era, and though often suffering under Comanche pressure, the twin colonies endured, allowing Spain to claim sweeping imperial command over the Southwest. Yet when examined closely, Spain's uncompromised imperial presence in the Southwest becomes a fiction that existed only in Spanish minds and on European maps, for Comanches controlled a large portion of those material things that could be controlled in New Mexico and Texas. The idea of land as a form of private, revenue-producing property was absent in Comanche culture, and livestock and slaves in a sense took the place of landed private property. This basic observation has enormous repercussions on how we should see the relationship between the Comanches and colonists. When Comanches subjected Texas and New Mexico to systematic raiding of horses, mules, and captives, draining wide sectors of those productive resources, they in effect turned the colonies into imperial possessions. That Spanish Texas and New Mexico remained unconquered by Comanches is not a historical fact; it is a matter of perspective.

In this book I examine the Comanche power complex as part of an emerging transatlantic web that had not yet consolidated into an encompassing world economy. Seen from this angle, the eighteenth- and early nineteenth-century Southwest and Mexican North emerge as a small-scale world-system that existed outside the controlling grip of Europe's overseas empires. Comanchería was its political and economic nucleus, a regional core surrounded by more or less peripheral societies and territories whose fortunes were linked to the Comanches through complex webs of cooperation, coercion, extortion, and dependence. The world-system approach to history has often been criticized for being overly strict and mechanistic, which it is. I have used its spatial language and metaphors selectively but also advisedly, fully aware that they convey a certain kind of rigidity and permanence. Viewed against the backdrop of constantly shifting frontiers of North America, the intersocietal space the Comanches occupied and eventually dominated was marked by unusually hard, enduring, and distinctive power hierarchies.[6]

This Comanche-centric world was by no means self-contained; it was anchored from its inception to the broader colonial world through the strong administrative and economic networks among New Mexico, Texas, northern Mexican provinces, and Mexico City. But these institutional linkages often had less impact on the colonies' internal development than Comanche policies did; the troubled and convoluted history of New Mexico, Texas, Coahuila, and Nueva Vizcaya may have had as much to do with the Comanches as with the ebbs and flows of New Spain's imperial fortunes. In fact, the systemic connections between Comanchería and northern New Spain gave the Comanches a modicum of exploitative power over the Spanish empire as a whole. When New Mexico was founded at the turn of the sixteenth and seventeenth centuries, it was expected to fuel Spain's imperial veins with raw materials and laborers, but by the eighteenth century the colony was leaking so much wealth into Comanchería that it could survive only by continuous financial backing from Mexico City. Texas functioned through much of the late eighteenth and early nineteenth centuries as a money-draining, often tributary defensive province against Comanche expansion. By subsidizing its far northern frontier, then, the Spanish empire in effect drained itself to feed and fend off an indigenous empire.

Although I focus on a particular place in time in this book, my arguments engage in the broader debates about colonialism, frontiers, and borderlands in the Americas. Over the past three decades, historians have conceived entirely new ways of thinking about Native Americans, Euro-Americans, and their tangled histories. Moving beyond conventional top-down narratives that depict Indians as bit players in imperial struggles or tragic victims of colonial expansion, today's scholarship portrays them as full-fledged historical actors who played a formative role in the making of early America. Rather than a seamless, preordained sequence, the colonization of the Americas is now seen as a dialectic process that created new worlds for all involved. Indigenous societies did not simply vanish in the face of Euro-American onslaught. Many adjusted and endured, rebuilding new economies and identities from the fragments of the old ones. Indians fought and resisted, but they also cooperated and coexisted with the newcomers, creating new hybrid worlds that were neither wholly Indian nor European. By foregrounding indigenous peoples and their intentions in the story of early America, recent scholarship has reinvigorated a field that only a generation ago was suffocating under its parochial and mythologizing tenets.[7]

Significant as this revisionist turn has been, it is not complete. Too often the alterations have been cosmetic rather than corrective. Historians have sanitized vocabularies and updated textbooks to illuminate the subtleties of colonial encounters, but the broad outlines of the story have largely remained intact. Outside a cadre of Native and early American specialists, the understanding of Indian–Euro-American relations is still limited by what Vine Deloria, Jr., called "the 'cameo' theory of history": indigenous peoples make dramatic entrances, stay briefly on the stage, and then fade out as the main saga of European expansion resumes, barely affected by the interruption. With too few exceptions, revisionist historians have limited themselves to retelling the story of colonial conquest from the Indian side of the frontier. They have probed how Native peoples countered and coped with colonial expansion and have largely overlooked the other side of the dynamic—the impact of Indian policies on colonial societies. Such an approach reinforces the view of European powers as the principal driving force of history and tends to reduce indigenous actions to mere strategies of subversion and survival. To recover the full dimension of Indian agency in early American history, we must once again reevaluate the intersections among Native peoples, colonial powers, frontiers, and borderlands. We have to turn the telescope around and create models that allow us to look at Native policies toward colonial powers as more than defensive strategies of resistance and containment.[8]

This book offers new insights into that effort, and it does so by questioning some of the most basic assumptions about indigenous peoples, colonialism, and historical change. Instead of perceiving Native policies toward colonial powers simply as strategies of survival, it assumes that Indians, too, could wage war, exchange goods, make treaties, and absorb peoples in order to expand, extort, manipulate, and dominate. Instead of reading Indian dispossession back in time to structure the narrative of early America, it embraces the multiple possibilities and contingency of historical change. At its most fundamental level, it promotes a less linear reading of Indian-white relations in North America. After the initial contacts, when Indians usually held the upper hand over the invaders, the fate of indigenous cultures was not necessarily an irreversible slide toward dispossession, depopulation, and cultural declension. As the history of the Comanches illustrates, almost diametrically opposite trajectories were possible. Before their final defeat in the canyonlands of the Texas Panhandle in 1875, Comanches had experienced an astounding ascendancy from the margins of the colonial world into imperial prominence as a dominant people who thrived and expanded in the midst of Euro-American colonies for over a century.

The history of Indian–Euro-colonial relations, as we today understand them, is inseparable from the history of the frontier, which forms another theoretical thread of this study. Over the past fifteen years or so, the frontier has made a forceful reentry into the very center of North American historiography. Recast as a zone of cultural interpenetration, the frontier is finding new relevance among historians who not so long ago had rejected Frederick Jackson Turner's frontier thesis as an ethnocentric and narcissistic rendition of the European takeover of North America. Instead of Turner's binary dividing line between civilization and savagery—or as seedbed of American virtues—historians have reenvisioned the frontier as a socially charged space where Indians and invaders competed for resources and land but also shared skills, foods, fashions, customs, languages, and beliefs. Indian-white frontiers, new work has revealed, were messy, eclectic contact points where all protagonists are transformed—regardless of whether the power dynamics between them are evenly or unevenly balanced. This has brought the frontier closer to its rival concept, the borderland, which Herbert Eugene Bolton, the pioneering historian of Spanish North America, coined to challenge Turner's constricted Anglo-centric vision. Skepticism toward the nation-state as the main unit of historical analysis, a hemispheric vision, an appreciation of cultural and political mutability, and an emphasis on indigenous agency are the traditional strengths of borderlands history; today they are the strengths of frontier studies as well.[9]

This book makes use of several insights of new frontier-borderland studies. On a macrolevel, it shows how Comanches moved goods, ideas, and people across ecological, ethnic, and political boundaries, creating transnational (or transimperial) networks of violence and exchange that defied the more rigid spatial arrangements Euro-American powers hoped to implement in the Southwest. On a microlevel, it shows how Comanches forged intimate small-scale, face-to-face markets with Euro-Americans, creating nascent versions of what Daniel Usner has called "frontier exchange economies," self-sufficient trade systems that mostly existed outside of the burgeoning transatlantic economy. It describes how Comanches forced the colonizers to modify their aggressive ways and at the same time recalibrated some of their own practices to adjust to the Euro-American presence, engaging in the kind of process of mediation, mutual invention, and cultural production Richard White has called "the middle ground." Geopolitically, Comanches' Southwest would seem to fit into Jeremy Adelman's and Stephen Aron's recent redefinition of a borderland: it was a place where interimperial rivalries enhanced Native peoples' strategic options by permitting them to play off colonial powers against one another.[10]

And yet the new frontier-borderland studies can explain the world I am describing only partially. The Southwest depicted in this book is a violent and traumatic place where Natives and newcomers saw one another more as strangers and adversaries than as co-creators of a common world; it was only incidentally a place where frontier exchange economies or middle grounds could flourish. When Comanches and Euro-Americans met to discuss such contentious and conceptually slippery matters as war, peace, reciprocity, loyalty, and justice, they sometimes relied on creative and expedient misunderstandings that were so fundamental for the creation of middle grounds, but more often than not, they understood each other all too well and generally did not like what they saw. Euro-Americans deemed Comanches needy, pushy, oversensitive, and obstinate in their pagan beliefs, and in turn appeared greedy, arrogant, bigoted, and grotesquely boorish to Comanche sensibilities. In the end, most attempts at meaningful cross-cultural mediation crumbled against the insolence of Euro-Americans and the impatience of Comanches. Negotiating from a position of growing physical and political power, Comanches adopted an increasingly assertive stance toward colonial powers. Their foreign policy became less a matter of accommodating Euro-American expectations than rejecting, reforming, or simply ignoring them.[11]

Viewed broadly, the Southwest under the Comanche regime becomes a case study of alternative frontier history. From a Comanche point of view, in fact, there were no frontiers. Where contemporary Euro-Americans (as well as later historians) saw or imagined solid imperial demarcations, Comanches saw multiple opportunities for commerce, gift exchanges, pillaging, slave raiding, ransoming, adoption, tribute extracting, and alliance making. By refusing to accept the Western notion of sovereign, undivided colonial realms, they shredded Euro-American frontiers into their component parts—colonial towns, presidios, missions, ranches, haciendas, Native villages—and dealt with each isolated unit separately, often pitting their interests against one another. In the colonial Southwest, it was Comanches, not Euro-Americans, who mastered the policies of divide and rule.

Similarly, Comanches' assertive and aggressive policies toward Euro-Americans were only secondarily a borderland product. Comanches certainly benefited from their location between competing colonial regimes, but they had little in common with the Indians found in most borderland histories. Rather than marginalized people balancing between rival colonial regimes to enact minor alleviations in imperial policies, Comanches were key players who often forced the would-be colonizers to compete for *their* military support and goodwill and navigate *their* initiatives and intentions. In character and logic, the eighteenth- and early nineteenth-century Southwest was unequivocally a Comanche creation, an indigenous world where intercolonial rivalries were often mere surface disturbances on the deeper, stronger undercurrent of Comanche imperialism.

In popular imagination, the American Southwest before the United States takeover in 1848 is a study in imperial failure. The overstretched and stiflingly bureaucratic Spanish empire, with its North American headquarters in Mexico City, had spread its resources too thinly across the Western Hemisphere to affix its northernmost provinces firmly into its imperial structure. The French, while more resourceful than their myopic Spanish rivals, were too erratic and too preoccupied with Old World power politics, the British colonies, and Canadian fur trade to do anything imperially impressive with Louisiana or the western interior. The fledgling Mexican Republic was so fragile and fractious that it lost both New Mexico and Texas in less than three decades. Reduced to a caricature, the Southwest of the mainstream view appears a medley of politically weak and isolated Native tribes, exhausted empires, and dysfunctional republics, a fragmented world ripe to be absorbed by Anglo Americans who alone possessed the imagination, drive, and means to subjugate and control vast regions.[12] If weighed against such a background of imperial indifference and political impotence, Comanches' accomplishments would seem to diminish in significance: their ascendancy intersected with exceptional Euro-American vulnerability, and they became a dominant power by default.

I start with a different premise—far from an imperial backwater, the Southwest was a dynamic world of vibrant societies, and Comanches had to suppress and absorb vigorous imperial projects to achieve dominance—and draw on a string of pathbreaking studies that have given the history of the early Southwest a new look. Dismantling the long-standing stereotype of reactionary and unimaginative Spanish colonists, David Weber has demonstrated how high-ranking authorities in central Mexico and local officials in New Mexico, Texas, and Louisiana constantly and creatively modified the empire's frontier policies to extend Spanish claims and power into the heart of North America. That same political and strategic dynamism, Weber has further shown, defined the Mexican Southwest, although the infant republic lacked the resources and expansionist ambitions of the Spanish empire. Ross Frank has demonstrated that Bourbon-era New Mexico was more tightly integrated into New Spain's imperial centers and consequently more dynamic and prosperous than has been assumed, and Andrés Reséndez has revealed a robust Mexican nation-building project in the north after 1821. Ned Blackhawk has drawn attention to the Spaniards' enormous capacity to employ—and endure—violence in advancing their imperial interests. In revisiting the history of the Comanches, ethnohistorians like Morris Foster and Thomas Kavanagh have dispelled the stereotype of a simple hunting society by uncovering elaborate political systems, social institutions, trade networks, and pastoral herding economies. Together, these and other new studies have demolished the old image of the Southwest as a world of innately passive peoples, frozen in time and disconnected from the main currents of American history.[13]

Historians have also begun to create new syntheses that illustrate how this rediscovered human ambition, energy, and ingenuity shaped the evolution of cross-cultural relations in the Southwest. Gary Clayton Anderson has examined the region as a contested and culturally elastic meeting ground where many Native groups resisted conquest through ethnogenesis, by constantly reshaping their economies, societies, and identities. In a seminal study, James Brooks has recast the region as an ethnic mosaic connected by an intercultural exchange network that revolved around "kinship slavery" and blended indigenous and colonial traditions of servitude, violence, male honor, and retribution into a distinctive borderlands cultural economy. With such insights, the Southwest is now emerging as a vigorous world of enduring social subversion where Natives and newcomers remained roughly equal in power and where familiar dichotomies of Indians and Europeans, or masters and victims, often became meaningless.[14]

I also take a broad long-term look at intercultural relationships in the Southwest but draw a distinctive, two-pronged conclusion. I show how Comanches cooperated and compromised with other peoples but also argue that their relations with the Spaniards, Mexicans, Wichitas, and others remained grounded in conflict and exploitation. Comanchería's borders were sites of mutualistic trade and cultural fusion, but they were also sites of extortion, systematic violence, coerced exchange, political manipulation, and hardening racial attitudes. The key difference between the existing studies and this book centers on the question of power and its distribution. According to Brooks's landmark *Captives and Cousins,* for example, the intricate patterns of raiding, exchange, and captive-seizure knitted disparate peoples into intimate webs of interdependence, equalized wealth distinctions among groups, and worked against the emergence of asymmetrical power relations. The Southwest he—and others—portrays was a place of nondominant frontiers where neither colonists nor Natives possessed the power to rule over the other. My argument, in a sense, is more traditional: such actions as raiding, enslaving, ethnic absorption, and even exchange generally benefit some groups more than they do others. In the Southwest, moreover, that process toward inequality was a cumulative one. Once the Comanches secured their territorial control over the southern plains in the mid-eighteenth century, they entered into a spiral of growing power and influence that stemmed from their ability to extract political and material benefits from the urban-based societies in New Mexico, Texas, and the Great Plains.[15]

The conspicuous differences between earlier studies and this book rise from different conceptual framing and scaling. Recent works on Indian–Euro-American relations in the Southwest—as in North America in general—share a particular focus: they look at events through a local lens, stressing individual and small-group agency over the larger structural forces. Suffused with subaltern interpretations, they tend to focus on the fringe peoples living on the frontiers' edges and trace how they engaged in cross-cultural dialogue and came together to form new hybrid communities, gradually shading into one another. Occupied with the local, the specific, and the particular, they are less concerned with the broader political, economic, and cultural struggles. Hierarchies of power, privilege, and wealth, while not ignored, are relegated to the background of the central story of cross-cultural cooperation and assimilation.[16]

In this book, in contrast, I examine the inhabitants of the Southwest in larger aggregates. While recognizing that ethnic and cultural boundaries were often porous, I look at those peoples as they identified and understood themselves: as distinct groups of Apaches, Comanches, Spaniards, French, Mexicans, and Anglo-Americans. With this shift in frame and focus, local arrangements may become somewhat blurred and lose some of their primacy, but the broader panorama opens a clearer view to the governing macroscale dynamics. It shows that the American Southwest, for all its wide-ranging cultural mixing, remained a polarized world where disparate ethnic groups clashed and competed bitterly with one another, where inequities of wealth and opportunity remained a tangible fact of life, and where resources, people, and power gravitated toward Comanchería.[17]

Besides adjusting the analytical scale, the reconstruction of Comanche power has entailed a basic visual reorientation. Instead of looking at events from colonial frontiers inward—a traditional approach that inevitably ties explanations to contemporary Western biases—this book looks at developments from Comanchería outward. Viewed from this angle, Comanche actions take on new shape and meaning. Acts that previously seemed arbitrary or impulsive fall into coherent patterns with their own internal logic and purpose. A foreign policy that previously appeared an opportunistic search for microlevel openings on white-controlled imperial frontiers now emerges as planned, synchronized, and domineering. We see how Comanches did not merely frequent colonial markets; they fashioned an imposing trading empire that mantled much of the Southwest and the Great Plains. They did not merely respond to political initiatives dictated from abroad, but actively sought and stipulated treaties. Far from being situational opportunists, they fused exchange, organized pilfering, and targeted destruction into a complex economy of violence, which allowed them to simultaneously enforce favorable trade agreements, create artificial demand for their exports, extort tribute payments from colonial outposts, and fuel a massive trade network with stolen horses, captives, and other marketable commodities. Seen from Mexico City, the far north often seemed chaotic and unsettling; seen from Comanchería, it appears nuanced, orderly, and reassuring.

Understanding Comanches' rise to power requires more than unearthing previously veiled patterns and structures: it also requires describing events and developments on Comanche terms. To capture the fundamental nature of the Comanche empire, we need to uncover meanings behind words, motives behind actions, strategies behind policies, and, eventually, the cultural order that drove it all. This, however, is a daunting task because the available sources do not readily lend themselves to deep cultural analysis. Euro-American colonial records, the documentary spine of this book, address virtually every aspect of Comanche political economy from warfare, exchange, and diplomacy to material production, slavery, and social relations, but although the records are rich in depiction and detail, the picture they yield is nevertheless the one-dimensional view of an outsider. Government reports, captivity narratives, travelers' journals, and traders' accounts tell us a great deal about Comanche actions but rarely shed light on the cultural motives behind those actions. Few contemporary observers possessed the analytical tools to understand the subtleties between Native and non-Native cultural logic, and even fewer possessed the ability—or the inclination—to write down what they learned. The available sources are thus almost invariably infected with gaps, accidental misreadings, and intentional misconstructions, leaving historians to work with material that is fragmentary at best and outright erroneous at worst.

In my endeavor to recover Comanche motives and meanings from the flawed evidence, I have employed an array of historical and ethnohistorical methods. I have prioritized accounts that recount, even in a mutated form, Comanche voice—while keeping in mind that that voice is recorded through a cultural colander and that it belongs often to privileged headmen, seldom to the poor and deprived, and virtually never to women and the young. I have cross-checked Spanish, French, Mexican, and Anglo-American documents against one another to create more stereoscopic and, arguably, more accurate portrayals of Comanche intentions and objectives. Throughout the writing process, I have compared historical documents to ethnographic data, processing Euro-American-produced materials through an ethnohistorical filter. This has involved a cautious use of "upstreaming" whereby one works back from more recent and more complete ethnological observations to decipher practices and behaviors of earlier periods. Even more reluctantly, I have sometimes relied on "side-streaming," deducing interpretations about Comanche cultural values from generalized models of Native societies of the Great Plains and other regions.[18]

This kind of methodological layering and rotation of viewpoints helps outline the broad contours of Comanche cultural order, but the resulting picture is still only an approximate one. Regardless of their origin, all colonial records are marred with similar deep-seated biases, while upstreaming runs the risk of presentism, tainting analysis with a sense of static timelessness; it assumes that Native peoples and their traditions have somehow been immune to modernity and have somehow remained unchanged through centuries of dispossession, population loss, and cultural genocide. Side-streaming threatens to submerge unique Comanche traits under crude blanket definitions of Indians in general and Plains Indians in particular. Shortcomings like these can produce what historian Frederick Hoxie has called "cookbook ethnohistory": complex cultures are collapsed into shorthand recipes, human behavior is reduced to a culturally or genetically determined reflex, and individual impulses become irrelevant. As an antidote against this kind of trivialization, Hoxie urges historians to describe societies in their own, inherently asymmetrical terms and create less linear stories that leave room for the surprising and the puzzling.[19]

Taking a cue from Hoxie, I have embraced rather than downplayed the contradictory aspects of Comanche behavior. The Comanches depicted in this book were empire-builders who did not possess a grand imperial strategy and conquerors who saw themselves more as guardians than governors of the land and its bounties. They were warriors who often favored barter over battle and traders who did not hesitate to rely on lethal violence to protect their interests. They were shrewd diplomats who at times eschewed formal political institutions and peacemakers who tortured enemies to demonstrate military and cultural supremacy. They were racially color-blind people who saw in almost every stranger a potential kinsperson, but they nevertheless built the largest slave economy in the colonial Southwest. Their war chiefs insulted, intimidated, and demeaned colonial agents with shockingly brutal words and gestures, but their peace leaders spoke eloquently of forgiveness, pity, and regret, using elaborate metaphors and ritual language to persuade their Euro-American counterparts. Above all, the Comanches were not a monolith obeying an unyielding cultural code but rather an assemblage of individuals with different and sometimes conflicting personalities, interests, and ambitions. They shared certain core values and objectives, but they also disagreed and quarreled over the methods, goals, and costs of their policies. The Comanche society, in short, was a complex one in which several standards of conduct coexisted simultaneously.

Historian Bruce Trigger has explained Native American behavior from a slightly different angle than Hoxie by focusing on the underlying mental processes of learning, judging, and reasoning. Assuming a middle course in the long, drawn-out debates over cross-cultural variations in human motivations, Trigger argues that while traditional cultural beliefs continued to shape Native American responses to European contact and colonialism, in the long run more universal pragmatic assessments and calculations came to play a dominant role. This kind of cognitive reorganization, Trigger maintains, occurred at all levels of behavior but was most visible in those areas that relate more directly to Indians' material well-being—technology and power. For Trigger, the outcome of colonial contact was not a makeover of Native Americans into "universal economic men," nor was it an unyielding persistence of otherness.[20]

Following Trigger, I pay particular attention to the changes that occurred over time in the underlying principles of Comanche behavior. The introduction of horses, guns, and other Old World technology arguably prompted Comanches to view their place and possibilities in the world in a different light, while close political and commercial interactions with colonial powers exposed them to the logic and laws of European diplomacy and the market. Comanches may have initially perceived European goods through the mold of their idiosyncratic traditions, but that did not prevent them from grasping the tremendous military and material advantages of horses, firearms, and metal—or from employing those advantages against Euro-Americans themselves. Similarly, like many other indigenous peoples, Comanches may have at first viewed the mounted, gun-using newcomers as all-powerful otherworldly beings, yet within years they learned to manipulate the Spaniards' all-too-human weaknesses to their own advantage. Within a generation or so after the first contact, Comanches had learned to distinguish between the motives and methods of the different colonial powers and to exploit those differences to advance their own political and economic agendas. Grounded in utilitarian calculations of self-interest, such behavior was rational in the sense most contemporary Euro-Americans and later historians would have understood the term.

And yet the yawning gulf separating Comanche and Euro-American cultural and mental worlds never disappeared—far from it. Regardless of their universal features, the actions and policies of Comanches remained embedded in a system of reality that was distinctly non-Western in nature. To the limited extent that it is possible to unveil the intentions that went into the actions of eighteenth- or early nineteenth-century Indians, it seems plain that the rationale of Comanche behavior remained worlds apart from that of Euro-Americans.

On the face of it, Comanche actions fell into unambiguous categories—trading, raiding, enslaving, and so forth—that were easily recognizable and understandable to contemporary Euro-Americans and modern historians alike. But the similarities are only skin deep; a more focused look reveals how Comanche actions time and again transcended familiar categories and defied easy labeling. Unlike Euro-Americans, Comanches did not separate trade from larger social relations but instead understood it as a form of sharing between relatives, either real or fictive. They considered theft a legitimate way of rectifying short-term imbalances in resource distribution rather than an antagonistic act that automatically canceled out future peaceful interactions. They killed, waged war, and dispossessed other societies, not necessarily to conquer, but to extract vengeance and to appease the spirits of their slain kin through dead enemy bodies. Capturing people from other ethnic groups did not necessarily signify a passage from freedom into slavery but a move from one kinship network to another. Even gift giving, the leitmotif of American Indian diplomacy, contained what appears at least on the surface a striking contradiction. Like most American Indians, Comanches considered gift exchanges a prerequisite for peaceful relations, yet they demanded one-sided gift distributions from Euro-American colonists, readily relying on violence if denied.[21]

Like many other imperial powers, then, Comanches employed aggressive power politics without necessarily considering their actions as such. They built a hierarchical intersocietal system with policies that were often geared toward securing gifts, conciliation, reciprocal services, and new relatives from peoples whom they may have considered as much kin and allies as strangers and enemies. Indeed, the fact that Comanches did things differently may well have been one of their greatest political assets. Their ability to move nimbly from raiding to trading, from diplomacy to violence, and from enslaving to adoption not only left their colonial rivals confused; it often left them helpless. Western insistence upon uniformity in principle and action, a disposition that manifested itself most clearly in centralized state bureaucracies, rendered their policies slow and heavy-handed in comparison to Comanches' strategic fluidity. Euro-Americans compartmentalized foreign relations into distinct, often mutually exclusive categories and found it exceedingly difficult to deal with peoples who refused to recognize such categories. Unable to dissect, classify, and comprehend the Comanches and their actions, colonial agents were also unable to contain them.

Herein lay the ultimate paradox. While initially Comanches adjusted their traditions, behaviors, and even beliefs to accommodate the arrival of Europeans and their technologies, they later turned the tables on Europe's colonial expansion by simply refusing to change. By preserving the essentials of their traditional ways—and by expecting others to conform to their cultural order—they forced the colonists to adjust to a world that was foreign, uncontrollable, and, increasingly, unlivable.

The chapters that follow tell two intertwined stories. The first story examines cross-cultural relations on the southern plains, in the Southwest, and in northern Mexico from the perspective of Comanches, exploring how this nation rose to dominance and how it constantly reinvented itself to sustain external expansion. The other story looks at events from the standpoint of the Spaniards, Mexicans, Apaches, and others who variously competed and cooperated with the Comanches but ultimately faced marginalization and dispossession in the

Comanche-controlled world. These two stories are woven into a single narrative thread, which in turn is embedded within the broader framework of Europe's overseas expansion. This contextual approach shows how local, regional, and global forces intersected to shape Comanche expansion and how Comanches both suffered and benefited from fluctuations and contingencies in the emerging transatlantic world. Comanche expansion lasted for a century and a half, but it was not a linear, uninterrupted process. There were surges, lulls, retreats, and regroupings, and the Comanche power complex went through repeated mutations, many of them epochs unto themselves. The chapters that follow are organized around those shifts and cycles, which both reflect and challenge the more traditional historical turning points in American history.

1

Conquest

They came to the plains from the west, slipping through the canyon passes of the Sangre de Cristo Range in small, roving bands. Like so many other Native groups of the age, the Numunu moved to the great continental grasslands seeking new opportunities, to build a new way of life around the emerging ecological triad of grasses, bison, and horses. They were few in number, possessed little wealth beyond a handful of mounts, and seemed indistinguishable from their more prominent allies, the Utes. New Mexico's Spanish officials noted their arrival to the southern grasslands in 1706 and wrote it off as a minor event. Yet by midcentury, the Numunu, then bearing the name Comanches, had unhinged the world they had almost unnoticeably entered.

Despite its modest beginnings, the Comanche exodus to the southern plains is one of the key turning points in early American history. It was a commonplace migration that became a full-blown colonizing project with far-reaching geopolitical, economic, and cultural repercussions. It set off a half-century-long war with the Apaches and resulted in the relocation of Apachería—a massive geopolitical entity in its own right—from the grasslands south of the Río Grande, at the very center of northern New Spain. The Comanche invasion of the southern plains was, quite simply, the longest and bloodiest conquering campaign the American West had witnessed—or would witness until the encroachment of the United States a century and a half later.

But the Comanche invasion was far more than a military conquest. As they made a place for themselves in the southern plains, Comanches forged a series of alliances with the adjacent Indian and European powers, rearranging the political and commercial geography of the entire lower midcontinent. Seen from another angle, the Comanche invasion was a momentous cultural experiment.

It brought destruction and death to many, but it also introduced a new, exhilarating way of life—specialized mounted bison hunting—to the Great Plains, irrevocably altering the parameters of human existence on the vast grasslands that covered the continent's center. Finally, Comanche arrival to the southern plains was a major international event: it marked the beginning of the long decay of Spain's imperial power in what today is the American Southwest. The Comanche conquest of the southern Great Plains was a watershed event that demolished existing civilizations, recalibrated economic systems, and triggered shock waves that reverberated across North America.

But Comanches were not the only expansionist people in the early eighteenth-century Southwest; their invasion overlapped with, crashed against, and eventually benefited from three other sweeping colonizing campaigns. In 1716, after several aborted colonizing attempts, Spain laid the foundation for a new outpost, Texas, on the southern edge of the Great Plains, thereby pinching the grasslands between the new colonial base and its older counterpart in New Mexico. This expansionist thrust was a reaction to another imperial venture. At the turn of the century, France built a series of forts on Biloxi Bay and along the lower Mississippi valley, creating a springboard for what they hoped would become a great western empire stretching across the plains and beyond.[1] And finally, as Spain and France jostled into position around the southern plains, a much longer history of conquest and colonization was culminating on the grasslands themselves. Just as they faced the Comanche assault, the Apaches solidified their control over the entire southern grasslands by simultaneously annihilating and absorbing the last of the Jumanos, a once-prominent nation of hunter-traders that vanished from the historical record by 1715.

Into this volatile and violent multipolar world came the Comanches, who found both ordeals and possibilities in its instability. They suffered from the escalating disorder, which complicated their adaptation to their new homeland, and they frequently faced more than one enemy group on their expanding borders. But the advantages far outweighed the drawbacks. The confluence of several colonizing projects meant that their rivals were often preoccupied with other challenges and therefore unable to organize effective resistance or, alternatively, willing to negotiate and form alliances with the invaders. Comanches also took advantage of the imperial rivalry between New Spain and New France, playing off the two powers against one another to extort concessions from both. In their quest to carve a living space out of a foreign territory, they had the inestimable advantage of invading an already colonized landscape where territorial arrangements were in a state of flux. And finally, Comanches arrived in the southern plains just as European technology—horses, guns, and iron tools—began to spread there in mass. As immigrants used to adjusting their ways to changing conditions, Comanches were able to harness the empowering potential of the new technology more fully than their Native rivals who tried to incorporate the innovations into their more established and more tradition-bound lifestyles. Comanches were invaders who made a place for themselves on the southern plains by raw force, but they were also opportunists who exploited a chaos that was only partially their own making.

Despite its far-reaching influence, the Comanche invasion of the southern plains has never been studied in a systematic fashion, and we understand its battles, protagonists, turning points, and underlying impulses only vaguely. Scholars have tended to sketch the invasion with broad, impressionistic strokes, which inadvertently has promoted the eighteenth-century view of Comanches as land-hungry militarists who randomly pushed ahead until reaching the natural limits of expansion. In this chapter I will show, by contrast, that the Comanche conquest of the southern plains was a long and complex process that evolved through several stages and was fueled by a variety of forces ranging from geopolitics and commercial interests to defensive concerns and kinship politics. In traditional historiography, the early West stands alone, set apart from the East by its lack of high imperial stakes, climatic battles, and rich diplomatic history. The pages that follow make clear that such things were an integral part of the colonial West as well.

The Comanches entered recorded history in 1706, when residents of Taos pueblo in the far northern corner of New Mexico sent word to the Spanish governor in Santa Fe that the village was expecting an imminent attack from Ute Indians and their new allies, the Comanches. The attack did not materialize, however, and the report, along with the people it introduced to written history, was soon forgotten. Two decades later, as Comanches made their presence felt across New Mexico's northern borderlands as fierce but elusive raiders, Spanish officials were fervently gathering information about them. One of those officials was Brigadier Pedro de Rivera who, while inspecting New Mexico in 1726, attempted to piece together a coherent account of these "very barbarous" people whose "origin is unknown." Rivera's remarks, covering only a few lines, make up the first ethnographic account of Comanches, who emerge as brutal, seminaked slave raiders who "make war on all nations" and always travel "in battle formation." Rivera also learned, apparently from a Comanche captive, that their ancestors had begun their exodus to the New Mexican frontier from a land that lay three hundred leagues northwest of Santa Fe. In Spanish imagination, this put the Comanche place of origin in the fabled kingdom of Teguayo, a land of great riches and the birthplace of the Aztecs.[2]

Rivera's terse report bears a startling similarity to modern academic views of Comanche origin. Most scholars today believe that the Comanches are part of the Uto-Aztecan-speaking people, who in the early sixteenth century occupied an enormous territory stretching from the northern Great Plains and the southern Plateau deep into Middle America. This Uto-Aztecan supremacy was the result of two sweeping migrations and conquests that had began centuries earlier. Sometime in the early second millennium, large numbers of Uto-Aztecan speakers moved southward from a place they called Aztlán and the Spanish knew as Teguayo, somewhere in the deserts of the Great Basin or the Southwest. They traced the arc of the Rocky Mountains and Sierra Madres into the central valley of Mexico, where they built the vast Aztec empire that in 1500 towered over most of Central America. At the same time as the ancestors of the Aztecs migrated southward, another branch of Uto-Aztecans, the Numic people, left their core territory in the southern Sierra Nevada and moved to the east and north. A severe drought in the thirteenth century had vacated large tracts of the interior West, allowing the Numic people to expand into deserted lands. They drove east and northeast until, by 1500, they dominated much of the southern Plateau, eastern Great Basin, and central and northern Rocky Mountains. This Numic expansion was spearheaded by the Shoshones, the parent group of the Comanches, who came to occupy much of the northeastern Great Basin all the way to the edge of the Great Plains.[3]

Gradually, Shoshones settled down and adjusted to the varied environment of the Great Basin, Rocky Mountains, and Great Plains. They lived by a finely choreographed yearly cycle, combining hunting and fishing with intensive gathering. They spent most of their time in the mountains and meadows of the semiarid Basin, camping beside lakes and marshes; hunting antelope, deer, and mountain sheep with bows and arrows; catching salmon in the Snake and Salmon rivers; and harvesting nuts, roots, and other wild foods. In winters, however, they often journeyed through the South Pass to the eastern side of the Rocky Mountains where, in a deep, well-wetted erosional furrow between the mountains and the grasslands, they found multitudes of bison, elk, and other big game to hunt as well as superb shelter against the cold. These seasonal migrations brought the Shoshones to the fringes of the plains but probably not beyond. The dry period that had begun in the thirteenth century had plunged the plains' vast bison herds into a sharp decline, discouraging the Shoshones from entering. In fact, the decrease in animal populations was so drastic that most plains people had sought refuge from the bordering regions, using the grasslands only for seasonal hunts.[4]

Shoshones had built a flourishing and eclectic culture that belies the traditional image of the brutal, impoverished existence of Basin peoples; and yet over the course of the sixteenth century, they abandoned the Basin for the Great Plains. This migration was apparently triggered by a climate change, the beginning of the Little Ice Age, which ended the long dry spell and brought colder temperatures and higher rainfall. As steady rains once again nourished the grasslands, allowing the ailing bison herds to recover, humans began to move back, first in trickles, then in masses. What followed was one of the greatest migrations in the history of North America. As if pulled into a vacuum, people flowed in from the Rocky Mountains, northern woodlands, and the Mississippi valley, turning the plains into an agglomeration of migration trails. This human tide consisted mainly of groups that had lived on the plains before the great drought, but some of the immigrants were newcomers. Among those newcomers were the Shoshones.[5]

Building on their century-old tradition of seasonal transmontane migrations, more and more Shoshones filtered through the South Pass onto grasslands in the early seventeenth century, elbowing the Kiowas and other nations eastward to the Black Hills region. By midcentury a distinct branch of Plains Shoshones had emerged. Occupying the northwestern plains between the South Platte and upper Yellowstone rivers, these eastern Shoshones morphed into typical plains hunters who shaped their diet, economy, and culture around the habits of bison. They lived as nomads, following their migrant prey on foot, moving their belongings on small dog travois, and sheltering themselves with light, easily transportable skin tipis. In hunting bison, they alternatively surrounded the animals, ran them onto soft ice or deep snow, or drove them off steep precipices. These communal hunts absorbed a lot of time and energy and required careful planning, but astounding returns rewarded the efforts. The Vore site, a precontact buffalo jump near the Black Hills, contains partial remains of ten thousand bison, even though people used the site only once every twenty-five years or so. Hundreds of similar, if smaller, sites in the Shoshone range testify to a burgeoning economy and a flourishing way of life.[6]

But prosperity did not translate into stability. Sometime in the late seventeenth century, the Shoshones suddenly splintered into two factions and left the central plains. Possibly seduced by larger and denser bison populations above the Yellowstone valley, the bulk of the people migrated onto the northern plains, where they were dragged into prolonged wars with the southward moving Blackfeet and Gros Ventres—wars that were still raging on when the first Canadian fur traders entered the northern plains in the 1730s.[7] A smaller faction headed south and disappeared from archaeological record for several years. They reemerged in the early eighteenth century in Spanish records as Comanches, one of the many Native groups living along New Mexico's borderlands.

It is not entirely clear why these proto-Comanches split off from the main Shoshone body, abandoned their lucrative bison-hunting economy on the central plains, and migrated several hundred miles into an unfamiliar territory, but pressure from other Native groups seems to have played a role. In the late seventeenth century, the Apaches, up till then a minor presence on the central plains, began to build mud houses and irrigate fields along the region's river valleys. Apaches thrived in their new villages, which soon dotted the entire central grasslands from the Dismal to the Republican River, compressing the Shoshones' domain from the south and east and forcing them to extract subsistence from a shrinking realm. The encroachment of Apaches may have also introduced European diseases, which caused devastation among the Shoshones, who had not yet been exposed to the deadly alien microbes. This kind of scenario is supported by Comanche and Shoshone traditions, which maintain that Comanches broke off from the parent group after a dispute over game and an assault by a smallpox epidemic.[8]

This sketch casts Comanches as exiles fleeing escalating violence in their homelands, but there is another possible motivation behind the separation from their Shoshone relatives: their southern exodus may have been an attempt to gain a better access to the Spanish horses that had just begun to spread northward from Spanish New Mexico in large numbers. The Pueblo Revolt of 1680 in New Mexico and the subsequent banishment of Spanish conquerors from the colony had left large numbers of horses to Pueblo Indians, who embarked on a vigorous livestock trade with the surrounding Indians in the grasslands and the mountains. Supplied by Pueblo traders, the ancient Rocky Mountain trade corridor carried horses northward, bringing the animals among the Shoshones around 1690. Boosted by their suddenly enhanced ability to move, hunt, and wage war, some Shoshone bands invaded the bison-rich northern plains; the others, the ancestors of the Comanches, followed the horse flow back to its ultimate source in New Mexico. This scenario, too, is substantiated by the Shoshones who remembered that the Comanches "left them and went south in search of game and ponies."[9]

Once on the move, the proto-Comanches probably tracked the front range of the Rockies to the south, skirting the Apache villages on the open plains farther east. But while preventing clashes with the Apaches, that route took the migrants into the home territory of the powerful Utes, who ranged between the Sawatch Mountains in the west and the Colorado Front Range in the east. The encounter between the two groups probably took place in the closing years of the century, and it marked the beginning of a relationship that would profoundly change them both. Yet the only clue to what actually occurred is a single word, *kumantsi*, the Ute name for the newcomers. By conventional reading, the word means "enemy," or "anyone who wants to fight me all the time," suggesting that the first contact was a violent one. However, a more recent interpretation holds that *kumantsi* refers to a people who were considered related yet different, and it suggests an encounter of another kind: rather than a clash between two alien peoples with sharp reflexes for violence, it was a reunion of two Numic-speaking peoples, who probably originated from the same Sierra Nevada core area, had taken different routes during the sprawling Numic expansion, and now, despite centuries of physical separation, found a unifying bond in their persisting linguistic and cultural commonalities.[10]

Building on those commonalities, Comanches and Utes formed by the early years of the eighteenth century a long-standing military and political alliance that remained an essential part of Comanches' power base until the mid-eighteenth century. Cemented by intermarriage and kinship ties, the alliance offered compelling strategic advantages for both. Utes were locked in an on-and-off war with the Navajos over raiding and trading privileges in northern New Mexico and were eager to obtain Comanches' military assistance in their efforts to keep the numerically superior Navajos in the west and farther away from New Mexico. Utes also needed Comanches' military aid in their conflicts with the Indians of Tewa, Tano, Jémez, Picurís, and Keres pueblos, who had seized Spanish weapons, armor, and horses during the Pueblo Revolt and encroached into Ute territory to hunt deer, elk, and bison. In return, Utes shared with Comanches their land, their horses, and their knowledge of the political and ecological intricacies of the Spanish borderlands.[11]

As the union solidified, Comanches turned their course west and crossed the Front Range into Ute territory.[12] There, in the eastern Colorado Plateau, they entered a period of spectacular change, reinventing themselves within a few years technologically, economically, militarily, and socially. Living with and learning from their Ute allies, they adjusted to their new homeland, an ecological patchwork that extended from the Great Plains–Rocky Mountain foothills ecotone across the densely forested Sangre de Cristo and Jémez ranges, featuring snow-covered alpine mesas, deep, glacier-carved valleys, spruce-fir, juniper, and pine forests, and semiarid grass and shrublands.

The diverse environment supported an equally diverse economy. Utes and Comanches spent the fall, winter, and early spring in small bands, hunting antelopes; trapping jack rabbits; and gathering berries, nuts, and yampa roots. In the spring, the scattered bands congregated into larger units and traveled eastward to the upper Arkansas River valley, where they hunted bison and lived as tipi-dwelling plains nomads. Summer was the main season for warfare and raiding, witnessing Ute-Comanche squadrons moving into Navajo country and northern New Mexico. Utes also introduced Comanches to New Mexican markets, and soon the two allies were regular visitors at Taos and San Juan where, under temporary truces, they bartered robes, meat, and Navajo slaves for maize, horses, pottery, and cotton blankets at great fall fairs. Although most Utes and Comanches followed this general yearly pattern, there were significant variations among different bands. It was probably here in the Great Basin that the Comanches began to distinguish among three broad subdivisions, whose names evoke diversifying economic and dietary frontiers: Yamparikas (Yap Eaters), Kotsotekas (Buffalo Eaters), and Jupes (People of Timber).[13]

While initiating Comanches into the complexities of their new home territory, Utes also ushered them into a new technological age. They provided their new allies with horses as well as the knowledge of how to use them in transportation, hunting, and warfare. By the 1710s, only a generation after obtaining their first horses, Comanches were lashing northern New Mexico with uncontainable mounted raids. But the raids were only the most visible manifestation of a profound material revolution that came with horses. A horse could carry two hundred pounds on its back and drag up to three hundred pounds on a travois, four times as much weight as a large dog could move, and it could cover at least twice the distance in a day. With the rise of equestrianism, Comanches could transport more hides, meat, and household utensils, and they could search for prey over a wider range and kill the animals more effectively. Their reach of trade was multiplied, as was their ability to wage war, plunder, and defend themselves. In almost an instant, the world became smaller and its resources more accessible.[14]

Behind these practical advantages, however, was an even more fundamental change. More than a mere hunting and transportation tool—a bigger and stronger dog—the horse represented a new way to tap energy. Dogs used plants, the most prolific reserve of processed solar energy available for animals and humans, only indirectly, by consuming the flesh of herbivorous animals their owners fetched and fed them. Horses, in contrast, drew their strength directly from plant life, allowing their masters to eliminate one arduous phase in their search for power. A conduit between immense, abstract solar energy and concrete, immediately available muscle power, the horse redefined the realm of the possible, bringing Comanches a step closer to the sun, "the primary cause of all living things."[15]

Utes also introduced Comanches to European crafts. Having traded regularly in New Mexico since the 1680s, Utes had accumulated enough guns and metal tools to pass some of them on to their Comanche allies, who now moved, literally overnight, from the Stone Age to the Iron Age. Although Comanches used the new technology to replace their traditional tools and elaborate on their old techniques, not to realign their basic economic system, it was a momentous leap nonetheless. Iron knives, awls, needles, and pots were more durable and effective than their stone, bone, and wooden counterparts, making the daily chores of hunting, cutting, scraping, cooking, and sewing faster and easier. Spanish laws prohibited the sale of firearms to Indians, but the ban was widely ignored in New Mexico's trade fairs, especially in the northern parts of the province. The few guns available at the fairs were cumbersome and fragile flintlocks, but they nevertheless profoundly changed the nature of intertribal warfare. Firearms allowed Comanches to kill, maim, and shock from the safety of distance and to inflict wounds that the traditional healing arts of their enemies were unaccustomed to treating. And like horses, firearms gave Comanches access to an unforeseen source of energy—gunpowder—further expanding the world of new possibilities.[16]

With Ute assistance, Comanches incorporated themselves into the emerging slave raiding and trading networks on New Mexico's borderlands. By the time Comanches arrived in the region, commerce in Indian captives was an established practice in New Mexico, stimulated by deep ambiguities in Spain's legal and colonial system. Although thousands of Pueblo Indians lived within the bounds of the Spanish-controlled New Mexico, strict restrictions prohibited their exploitation as laborers. *Encomienda* grants of tributary labor, the economic keystone of early Spanish colonialism in the Americas, were abolished in New Mexico in the aftermath of the Pueblo Revolt. The *repartimiento* system of labor distribution continued, allowing the colonists to pool and allot Pueblo labor for public projects, but that system operated on a rotating basis, making Indian laborers a communal rather than a personal resource. Most Pueblo Indians, furthermore, were at least superficial Christian converts, whose exploitation was strictly regulated under Spanish law. Eager to obtain personal slaves to run their kitchens, ranches, fields, and textile workshops—and to reinforce their fragile sense of honor and prestige—Spanish elite turned to captive trade in *indios bárbaros*, savage Indians. Spanish laws specifically prohibited the buying, selling, and owning of Indian slaves, but the colonists in New Mexico cloaked the illegal traffic as *rescate* (ransom or barter), whereby they purchased captive Indians from surrounding nomadic tribes, ostensibly to rescue them from mistreatment and heathenism. In theory, these ransomed Indians were to be placed in Spanish households for religious education, but in practice many of them became common slaves who could be sold, bought, and exploited with impunity.[17]

Utes had first entered New Mexico's slave markets as commodities seized and sold by Spanish, Navajo, and Apache slave raiders, but the allied Utes and Comanches soon inserted themselves at the supply end of the slave traffic. When not raiding New Mexico for horses, Utes and Comanches arrived peacefully to sell human loot. Their raiding parties ranged westward into Navajo country and northward into Pawnee country to capture women and children, but their main target were the Carlana and Jicarilla Apache villages in the upper Arkansas basin at the western edge of the southern plains. Traffic in Apache captives mushroomed in New Mexico. By the late seventeenth century, the people in New Mexico possessed some five hundred non-Pueblo Indian captives and were emerging as major producers of slave labor for the mining camps of Nueva Vizcaya and Zacatecas; they even sent slaves to the tobacco farms in Cuba. By 1714 slave trade had become so widespread in New Mexico that Governor Juan Ignacio Flores Mogollón saw it necessary to order all Apache captives baptized before taken to "distant places to sell." Many of those Apaches were purchased from Utes and Comanches, whose mutually sustaining alliance had put them in a position of power over their neighboring Native societies.[18]

By the early eighteenth century, the Ute-Comanche coalition dominated the northern borderlands of New Mexico. The allies shut off Navajos from the prime trading and raiding locales in New Mexico and treated the colony itself as an exploitable resource depot. They alternatively traded and raided in northern New Mexico, sometimes bartering slaves and hides for horses, maize, and metal goods, sometimes making off with stolen livestock and foodstuffs. Spain's shallow imperial control of its northern frontiers could not keep the villages united, and the region began to disintegrate socially and politically. Utes and Comanches traded and intermarried with the Native inhabitants of Ojo Caliente, San Juan, and Picurís—many of whom were former slaves of theirs—while at the same time raiding Taos, Cochití, and other settlements for plunder. By 1716 Ute and Comanche raiders had so exhausted northern New Mexico's horse reservoirs that the settlers were not able to "march out in defense."[19]

Short of men and money, Spanish officials in Santa Fe were powerless against these exploitative policies. Voicing their growing frustration, one official demanded in 1719 that "war should be made upon the Ute nation and Comanche nations, who, always united, have been committing robberies of horseherds in the name of peace."[20] But by the time the Spaniards started to take cognizance of the threatening situation in the far northern frontier, Utes and Comanches had begun to shift their ambitions elsewhere—to the vast grasslands opening to the east.

Comanches had discovered unexpected riches and opportunities in their adopted homeland, but the same forces that helped them prosper in the valleys and mountains of the southern Rockies also pushed them out of the region. The more tightly they geared their lives around mounted hunting, slave trade, and European markets, the more they felt the pull of the great eastern grasslands. By the 1720s, a mere generation after their arrival, they were gone. It might be tempting to imagine that the Comanche exodus onto the southern plains was inspired by the endless horizons and unlimited opportunities opening to the east, but it is more likely that the migration—which also pulled several Ute bands away from their mountain homelands—began as extended slave raids. As the attacks of Comanche and Ute slavers intensified around the turn of the century, the Jicarillas and Carlanas sought refuge deeper on the plains and abandoned their old campgrounds at the headwaters of the Arkansas and along the foothills of the Rocky Mountains. Rather than bringing relief from raids, however, the retreat drew Comanche and Ute slavers into the very heart of Apachería. Tracking the fleeing Jicarillas and Carlanas to the plains, Comanches and Utes turned the upper Arkansas basin into a war zone. In 1706 a Spanish expedition led by Juan de Ulibarrí encountered near the Arkansas valley a small group of Penxaye Apache refugees who were trying "to join all the rest [of the Apaches] who live along those rivers and streams in order to defend themselves together from the Utes and Comanches." Ulibarrí also learned that Comanches and Utes had recently attacked two Apache villages near the headwaters of the Purgatoire River, more than a hundred miles south of the Arkansas corridor. When assessing the Comanche-Ute invasion in 1719, New Mexico Governor Antonio Valverde y Cosío wrote that the allies were drawn into the upper Arkansas valley and the outlying plains "by the interests they have in robbing the enclosures that exist in the rancherías [villages] of the Apaches."[21]

By the time Valverde penned his report, the transitory slave raids of Comanches and Utes had already escalated into a full-blown colonizing project, which was aimed at carving out a new home territory in the plains and displacing the resident Apaches. Behind that shift in purpose was a shift in vision: if opportunities for slave raiding had drawn Comanches and Utes to the open plains, a promise of a new life made them stay there. During their extended forays into Apachería, Comanches and Utes came to realize the plains' immense possibilities for a mounted way of life. The Spanish horses they had pilfered in New

Mexico and then rode onto the plains found a nearly perfect ecological niche on the southern grasslands. Descendants of the North African Barb stock, the resilient, smallish Spanish mounts had been bred to survive in desert conditions, to live entirely off grass, and to cover enormous distances between water sources. They were, in other words, pre-adapted for life on the relatively arid southern plains, whose thick layer of buffalo and grama grasses provided an abundant, year-round supply of forage, and whose scattered streams and playa lakes yielded sufficient water for the hardy desert animals.[22]

It was this auspicious match between horses and the plains environment that lured Comanches and Utes out of the mountains. The deeper they pushed onto the grasslands and the longer they stayed there, the more their horses flourished, growing rapidly in numbers. This in turn allowed Comanches and Utes to transform the plains' most immediately striking bounty, the seemingly inexhaustible bison herds, into an accessible and predictable resource. Moving their belongings on horseback, the newcomers could follow and find the dispersed, ever-moving herds with relative ease and, once they reached them, bring down the large beasts from the safety of horseback. Liberated and empowered by the horse, the Comanches and Utes moved to the plains to organize their lives around the bison.[23]

The possibilities of mounted bison hunting were the plains' primary attraction, but there was another enticement: commerce. When Comanches acquired manufactured goods from New Mexico and the Utes in the late seventeenth century, they soon found themselves in a quandary. Impressed by the efficiency and durability of the new weapons, tools, and utensils, they were anxious to obtain more, but northern New Mexico, with its limited reserves of manufactured goods, failed to meet their needs. The plains, on the other hand, bristled with commercial opportunities, which centered on the upper Arkansas valley, the Comanche entryway to the grasslands. When Comanches followed the river valley to the east, they stepped into an ancient, vigorous trading niche. Stretching between the urban centers along the Río Grande and the farming villages of the southern prairies, the Arkansas valley had for centuries been a major entrepôt of trade, a transition point where plains hunters bartered hides and meat for maize and other village products in east and west. By the time Comanches arrived in the Arkansas valley, moreover, its potential had already been discovered in French Louisiana. French merchants began westbound journeys soon after 1700, trading guns and metal to Apaches, and turning the Arkansas channel into a major artery of colonial commerce.[24]

Responding to various economic incentives, Comanches and their Ute allies moved in masses to the southern plains during the second and third decades of the eighteenth century. The result was a drawn-out and deadly conflict with the many Apache groups, whom Spaniards knew as Palomas, Cuartelejos, Penxayes, Carlanas, Sierra Blancas, Jicarillas, Pelones, and Lipans, and who controlled the entire western plains south of the Platte River. These Apaches had little to do with the later stereotype of the plains Apaches as a doomed, feeble people incapable of resisting the Comanche onslaught. By the time that the wars with the Comanches erupted, in fact, the Apaches were in the midst of an expansionist burst of their own.

If the Comanche expansion was fueled by the shift to bison-centered equestrian hunting and consequent economic specialization, the Apache expansion was driven by a contrasting process of economic diversification. Like Comanches, Apaches had expanded their horse herds during the Pueblo Revolt, when the Pueblo Indians seized Spanish horses and traded them to other Native groups, but unlike Comanches, only a few Apache groups specialized in mounted hunting. While experimenting with more intense equestrianism, Apaches also accelerated their conversion to agricultural production. Many Apache bands had practiced light farming for generations, but it was not until the turn of the seventeenth century that agriculture permeated the Apache way of life. Shaken by a series of droughts that decimated bison herds and inspired by the expertise of Pueblo farmers who had sought refuge in Apachería during the second Pueblo uprising in 1696, Apache groups across the plains took up systematic farming. They built small irrigation works in streambeds, lined river valleys with flat-roofed mud houses, and began to cultivate crops of maize, beans, squash, watermelons, and pumpkins. The new hybrid economy required a careful seasonal balancing of farming and hunting, but its rewards were compelling. Profusely supplied with proteins and carbohydrates, the Apaches enjoyed a steady population growth in an environment where droughts and European microbes constantly threatened the viability of Native societies.[25]

Internal strength translated into external expansion. On the central plains, the Cuartelejo and Paloma Apaches kept the Pawnees out of western hunting ranges, and farther south, around the Big Bend of the Arkansas and the forks of the Red River, the Jicarillas, Carlanas, and Sierra Blancas forced the Wichitas to move their villages out of prime bison range. The main course of Apache expansion was south of the Red River, where the Lipans clashed with the Jumanos, ethnically diverse seminomadic hunters and farmers who had built a bustling long-distance trade network between the Río Grande and the Caddo villages on the southern prairies. Apache-Jumano wars raged until the mid-1710s when the Jumanos, weakened by disease and droughts, moved into Spanish missions or joined the Lipans. From then on, the Apaches possessed a virtual monopoly over the western hunting ranges below the Platte as well as on the Spanish markets in eastern New Mexico and western Texas. Their various bands traded regularly at Taos, Pecos, La Junta, and San Antonio, bringing in hides, skins, and Caddo captives. During the dry spells that repeatedly scourged the Southwest, interrupting trade and diplomacy, they raided the same settlements for maize and livestock. Spanish officials responded with punitive campaigns, which were frequently transformed into slave raids, and Franciscan priests pleaded with the Apaches to embrace Catholicism and mission life, but both met with little success.[26]

By entering the southern plains, therefore, Comanches set themselves on a collision course with another expanding people, entangling themselves in a war that raged for more than half a century across the entire southern plains. Comanche-Apache wars are often depicted as a primal Hobbesian struggle for land fueled by ethnic hatred, but they began as a strategic contest over specific locations and resources. The main contention point was the control of river valleys. Both groups needed these precious zones for their survival, which gave rise to a war over microenvironments. During warm seasons, Apaches needed the stream bottoms for their maize fields and irrigation systems while Comanches needed them for the grass and low-saline water they provided for their growing horse herds. The contest became even fiercer in winters when both groups became utterly dependent on the river valleys, the only places on the open plains that offered relief from the harsh elements. The bluffs and cutbanks gave shelter against blizzards, the dense groves of cottonwood yielded fuel for heating and supplementary forage for horses, and the streams provided reliable water at a time when the rains often dwindled almost to nothing.[27]

Intertwined with this conflict over river bottoms was a commercial rivalry over New Mexico's markets and food exports. After committing to full-time hunting on the plains, Comanches could no longer concentrate on gathering with the same intensity they had maintained in the mountains. They continued to collect berries, nuts, fruit, and root vegetables, but gathering no longer formed a major economic activity; one estimate suggests that Comanches lost two-thirds of their plant lore upon moving to the grasslands. The corollary of this economic streamlining was a chronic nutritional imbalance: the new bison-based diet was high in protein but desperately low in carbohydrates. An extremely high-protein and low-carbohydrate diet can be hazardous for pregnant women and fetuses, causing miscarriages, lowered birth weight, and cognitive impairment. If the protein intake exceeds 40 percent while the intake of both carbohydrates and fat drops—as could easily happen on the plains during late winters when bison's body fat plunged—the entire population could become susceptible to protein poisoning.[28] Comanches had two basic options in solving such dietary dilemmas.

One was to follow the Apache example and undertake streamside gardening, but this option was unfeasible because it would have tied them to a place and compromised their mobile military effectiveness. The second, and strategically sounder, alternative was to further intensify their hunting economy, eliminate the Apaches from New Mexican markets, and then exchange their surplus meat, fat, and hides for maize and other carbohydrate products at the Pueblo fairs. In essence, then, the Comanche-Apache wars were fought over carbohydrates.

It was because the conflict revolved around life's essentials—food, water, shelter—that the fighting became so unforgiving. By the late 1710s an all-out war had engulfed the upper Arkansas basin and was rapidly spilling over to the adjacent areas. Comanches soon dominated the war and kept up the pressure until the last Apache villages disappeared from the southern plains. They often operated as a single unit with their Ute allies, relying on combined force, whereas the numerous Apache villages tended to act independently. The Apaches were also divided. The Jicarilla, Carlana, and Sierra Blanca bands were caught in an on-and-off war with the Faraone Apaches, who had specialized in the late seventeenth century in captive and livestock raiding, attacking in all directions from their homelands in the Sandia Mountains. But the Apaches' main weakness was their mixed hunting and farming economy, which now, when they were at war with the Comanches and Utes, turned from an economic asset into a military liability. Tied to the soil at exact times of the year, Apache farmers were defenseless against their mounted rivals who turned the once-protective farming villages into deathtraps. Capitalizing on their long-range mobility, Comanches and Utes concentrated overwhelming force against isolated Apache villages, raiding them for crops and captives or obliterating them with devastating guerrilla attacks. As organized as they were mobile, Comanches were also proficient in defensive warfare, as one observer reported in the 1720s: "the nation of the Comanches . . . conserves such solidarity that both on the marches which they continually make, wandering like the Israelites, as well as in the camps which they establish where they settle, they are formidable in their defense."[29]

Comanches and Utes also used their mobility and range to sever Apaches' trade links. They attacked New Mexican fairs during Apache visits, disrupting the seasonal pattern of the commerce. In 1719 one Spanish official deplored how Comanches and Utes "go about together for the purpose of interfering with the little barter which this kingdom has with the nations which come in to ransom. They prevent their entrance and communication with us." At the same time on the opposite side of their shrinking domain, Apaches lost touch with Louisiana's French merchants, whose western operations were undercut by the monopolistic trade policies of the formidable Osages and the Wichita confederation—the

Tawakonis, Taovayas, Iscanis, and Kichais—who controlled the lands between the Mississippi valley and the Apache territory. The collapse of Apaches' trade network not only weakened their ability to repel the Comanche-Ute onslaught; it also left them vulnerable in their old rivalries with the Wichitas and Pawnees, rivalries that had intensified markedly around 1700 when Wichitas and Pawnees began to sell Apache captives to French traders.[30]

Caught between two violent fronts and cut off from their economic lifelines, Apaches lost their ability to muster effective resistance. Facing imminent collapse, Jicarillas fled to Taos where they asked for protection and, for the first time, pledged to accept Christianity. "I am, Sir, in a mission called San Gerónimo de los Taos," an astonished Father Juan de la Cruz wrote to the viceroy in 1719, "so close to heathenism, that, as is commonly said, we are shoulder to shoulder. A tribe of heathen Apache, a nation widely scattered in these parts . . . have come to ask for holy baptism." The Apache offer, exactly because it mixed strategic and religious elements, appealed to Spanish authorities, who in August held a war council in Santa Fe and decided to side with the Apaches and declare war on the Comanche-Ute bloc. A stronger Apache nation on the plains, the council reasoned, would shield New Mexico from Comanche and Ute raids, which had grown increasingly destructive during the preceding years. Above all, a Spanish-Apache coalition would protect New Mexico and the mining districts of northern Mexico against the anticipated French invasion—an old threat that had become acute with the outbreak of a European conflict, the War of the Quadruple Alliance, in late 1718. "It is necessary to hold this [Apache] nation," the viceroy instructed from Mexico, "because of the hostilities which the French have launched" and because "the Apache nation aided by ourselves could inflict considerable damage on the French and block their evil designs."[31]

So, in fall 1719, New Mexico Governor Valverde personally led an expedition of some six hundred presidial troops, militia, and Pueblo auxiliaries into the Arkansas valley, hoping to "curb the boldness" of Comanches and Utes and punish them for the "hostilities, murders, and robberies they have made upon this realm." Rather than curbing the momentum of Comanche-Ute expansion, however, the campaign revealed that the Spaniards had already missed their window of opportunity. Signs were ominous from the start. On their way to the Arkansas war zone, the Spaniards encountered several fleeing Jicarilla and Sierra Blanca bands. One group told the governor that Comanches and Utes "had killed many of their nation and carried off their women and children captives until they no longer knew where to go to live in safety," and another depicted an episode of an indigenous total war: "the Comanche and Ute enemies had attacked a ranchería of their nation, causing sixty deaths, carrying off sixty-four women and children, burning and destroying a little house in the shape of a tower which was there, and even the heaps of maize. There were none of their possessions that were not destroyed." Eager to obtain Spanish assistance, Jicarillas agreed to "receive the water of holy baptism" and loyally serve the governor whom they accepted as their "father." On his part, Valverde handed chocolate and tobacco to the refugees and recruited them as auxiliaries for his march toward the Arkansas. Adhering to long-standing Spanish laws, he did not even consider giving guns to Spain's new Indian allies.[32]

As the expedition drew closer to the river, they entered a wasteland of deserted Apache villages and burned maize fields the Comanche-Ute invasion had left in its wake. Apaches, Valverde noted, "live in constant alarm and at night they leave their houses and retire to the hills to insure their lives." Comanches and Utes, however, were nowhere to be found, and Valverde's idle expedition transformed into a mobile ritual ground where the Spaniards and Apaches tried to buttress their tentative alliance through Catholic ceremonies and ritual killings of mountain lions, wildcats, and bears. After weeks of futile search, the expedition learned from a band of several hundred Apache refugees that Comanches and Utes had sacked El Cuartelejo, a fabled Apache settlement a few miles north of the Arkansas valley. It was a devastating blow, for El Cuartelejo—"fortified building"—had become a key seat of Apache power in the late seventeenth century, when disgruntled Pueblo apostates escaped there and introduced the Apaches to horses and new farming techniques. A few days later a wounded Paloma chief brought more bad news. Along the Platte River, "on the most remote borderlands of the Apaches," the French had built "two large pueblos, each of which is as large as that of Taos," among the Pawnees. The French and Pawnees had then attacked the Palomas "from ambush while they were planting corn" and seized their lands. Adding insult to injury, the French had called the Spaniards "women" and encouraged the fleeing Palomas to bring them into Pawnee country to fight them. Valverde's expedition returned to Santa Fe after having spent some two months on the plains. By the year's end, as rumors transformed into reports, Spanish officials in Mexico City found themselves dealing with dispatches stating that there were six thousand Frenchmen within 180 miles of Santa Fe.[33]

In a roundabout way, the French penetration onto the central plains also affected the outcome of Comanche-Ute-Apache struggle over the Arkansas basin. Fearing that New Mexico was threatened by an imminent French invasion, Spanish officials redirected their efforts against the French-Pawnee coalition on the central plains, ignoring the Apache situation farther south. In June 1720, Lieutenant General Pedro de Villasur led forty-five presidial soldiers and sixty Pueblo auxiliaries north to oust the French from Pawnee country. The campaign was a fiasco: thirty-two soldiers, a third of the strength of the Santa Fe garrison, perished at the hands of the Pawnees and their Otoe allies. The Villasur catastrophe, coupled with a peace between Spain and France in Europe later that year, made Spanish officials reluctant to invest men and money to help the Apaches in what appeared more and more to be a lost cause. The officials debated for several years whether to build a presidio at El Cuartelejo or closer to New Mexico among the Jicarillas, but they took no action.[34]

As Spain's support faded so too did Apaches' hopes of maintaining a foothold in the Arkansas valley. By 1723 a series of Comanche attacks had eliminated what remained of their resistance. In November of that year a delegation of Jicarilla and Sierra Blanca chiefs reported at the Governor's Palace in Santa Fe that Comanches "had attacked them with a large number" and "with such daring and resolution that they killed many men, carrying off their women and children as captives." Desperate to obtain Spanish help, Apache chiefs made an unprecedented offer. While earlier only an occasional Apache band had accepted Christianity and vassalage to Spain, the chiefs now spoke of a sweeping political, religious, and cultural conversion, "pleading that the sacrament of holy baptism be administered to them together with all those of their rancherías," and promising "to come together to live in their pueblos in the same form in which the Christian Indians of this kingdom dwell." In return for their "entire docility," they petitioned the Spaniards to build a garrison at La Jicarilla, a large Sierra Blanca, Paloma, and Jicarilla village on the Canadian River, some 110 miles northeast of Santa Fe. The offer sent Spanish imaginations running. A belt of loyal sedentary Indians on New Mexico's eastern front, a rapidly convened war council concluded, would "serve as a bulwark for this kingdom, for its greater security from French arms." Moreover, the colonization of Apachería would allow Spain to extend its authority to the plains and create a barrier against the Comanches. "It will be wise to continue the conquest until all the enemy be exterminated," Juan de Olivan Revolledo, a royal inspector in Mexico City, wrote.[35]

In November 1723 Governor Juan Domingo de Bustamante rode out with fifty soldiers—more than half of Santa Fe's presidial troops—to inspect La Jicarilla. Apaches welcomed him with engravings of the Virgin Mary and renewed pledges of subordination. But the Comanches, alarmed by the possibility of a double war with both the Spaniards and the Apaches, stormed La Jicarilla in January of 1724 with the intention to destroy it. They besieged the village for four nights and five days and demanded that the Apaches give up all their women and children. When the Apaches relented, they opened fire on the men and threatened to eat their bodies, forcing them to flee. In March, upon learning about the battle, Bustamante led an expedition deep into Comanche territory and retrieved sixty-four captives. But whatever momentum Bustamante had managed to create evaporated when the officials in Mexico City failed to decide whether or not to colonize La Jicarilla. While Mexico City hesitated, Comanches lashed the Apache villages with relentless attacks, which culminated in a ferocious nine-day battle at El Gran Sierra del Fierro in the present-day Texas Panhandle.[36]

Beaten by the Comanches and Utes and abandoned by Spain, the Apaches vacated all the lands north of the Canadian River, which became the southern border of the Comanche-Ute domain. Some Jicarilla bands crossed the Sangre de Cristo Range to seek protection among the Navajos, while others crossed the Cimarron and Canadian rivers to the south, hoping to find refuge in the Llano Estacado, an extensive tableland of trackless plateaus, deep canyons, and playa lakes that encompasses modern-day eastern New Mexico and western Texas. Some Jicarillas also settled on the Río Trampas near Taos, where Franciscans built them a mission in 1733. When Governor Gervasio Cruzat y Góngora "cut off their trade in hides," however, the Jicarillas abandoned the mission. Some of their members reportedly "dispersed themselves among the Utes and Comanches."

The Palomas, Cuartelejos, and Sierra Blancas survived a while longer on the grasslands, buoyed by a short-lived truce that the French mediated in 1724 between them and the Osages, Pawnees, Iowas, Otoes, and Kansas. Three years later the French were reported to be moving with "a great force of Apaches of the nations Palomas, Cuartelejos, and Sierra Blancas to look for the Comanches (a people widely scattered because of the numerousness of their nation) to see if they could force them to leave these regions." Nothing came of that effort, however, and by the decade's end the Palomas, Cuartelejos, and Sierra Blancas had given up resistance and dispersed. Some sought shelter in the Pecos River valley beyond the Mescalero Escarpment, which still fell outside of Comanche reach, and by the 1730s the Apaches had developed close ties with Pecos. Others crossed the Canadian River and pushed deep into the Llano Estacado, following Jicarilla refugees who had fled before.[37]

If there was a pivotal event in Apaches' defeat, it was Spain's decision not to colonize La Jicarilla. The final decision on the colonization scheme had fallen on Brigadier General Pedro de Rivera who in 1724 had been sent as a special crown official to inspect northern New Spain's formal defenses. A newcomer to the frontier, Rivera took a critical look at New Mexico's Indian policy and found it lacking. Adopting a panoramic strategic view while at the same time making every effort to cut spending, he concluded that Spanish settlers and resources were already too thinly spread for launching further colonizing projects. "If every proposal for the foundation of presidios for reduction were acceded to," he warned, "the treasury of Midas would not suffice," and he urged New Mexicans rather to "conserve that which is acquired, to enjoy the fruit which has been cut, than to augment the dominions without any hope."[38]

Rivera's report had a lasting legacy in New Mexico, prompting the authorities to suspend further colonizing efforts on the plains and cut off military support to the Apaches. Turning inward, Spanish New Mexico focused on consolidating its hold over the Río Grande valley, its demographic, economic, and political heart. But for all its fiscal and strategic acumen, Rivera's report contained a massive miscalculation. By withdrawing from the plains, Spain left the door wide open for the Comanches, who within a generation would sweep through the southern plains and press against the entire length of Spain's far northern frontier from New Mexico's northern tip down to central Texas.

The conquest of the upper Arkansas basin in the 1720s marked the end of the first phase of Comanche expansion. Instead of riding the momentum into the Llano Estacado to pursue the already dislodged Apaches, Comanches halted their conquering campaign. The relentless war had sent the Apaches fleeing, but it had also fulfilled the Comanches' immediate territorial ambitions and economic needs. Temporarily satisfied, they concentrated on solidifying their hold on their new plains homeland for nearly a decade.[39]

Stretching from the Arkansas valley in the north to the Cimarron River in the south and from the Sangre de Cristo Mountains in the west to the plains-prairie ecotone at the ninety-eight meridian in the east, that home range provided a superb setting for Comanches' emerging equestrian hunting-based way of life. The sprawling, gently rolling meadows proliferated with pasture and bison, and the broad valleys of the Arkansas and Cimarron rivers provided water, firewood, and shelter for Comanches and their herds. The most valuable portion of the nascent Comanchería was the Big Timbers of the Arkansas, a thick grove of cottonwood trees stretching over some sixty miles downriver from the Purgatoire junction. Known to Spaniards as *La Casa de Palo*, "the house of wood," the Big Timbers was a winter haven for horses. The trunks of the cottonwoods formed sheltering walls against cold breezes and their bark and twigs provided an alternative source of food when grasses failed or were buried under snow. These were crucial advantages, for the plains winters could be vicious even in the south, exposing horses to hypothermia and starvation.[40]

With their herds flourishing in the shelter of the Big Timbers, Comanches completed the conversion to full-blown equestrianism with remarkable speed. They were still only partially mounted in the late 1720s, using both horses and dogs to move their belongings, but within a decade they had accumulated so many horses that they had to break into numerous small bands to accommodate their herds' foraging needs. A local residential band of one or more extended families, *nʉmʉnahkahnis*, became the basic social unit. These bands—or *rancherías* as Spaniards called them—could include anywhere from one to a few dozen *nʉmʉnahkahnis*, and their size ranged from twenty or thirty to several hundred people. Regardless of size, kinship was the fundamental unifying force: a ranchería was a social extension of a single headman, *paraibo*, whose kinship ties, political influence, and personal charisma held the unit together.[41]

By the 1730s, the Comanches had accumulated enough horses to put all their people on horseback, thus reaching the critical threshold of mounted nomadism. They adopted bigger travois and tipis and developed a practice of seasonal migrations conditioned by the availability of bison, horse pasturages, wood, and water. It was also the period when Comanches began to employ the mounted bison chase, which would later become the quintessential symbol of the material prosperity and cultural flamboyance of Plains Indian cultures. In its fully matured form, the chase was as dramatic as it was effective. Riding in full speed alongside a fleeing herd and firing arrows into selected animals, a group of hunters could bring down two to three hundred bison in a single chase that took less than an hour. It was enough to keep several hundred people sheltered, clothed, and nourished for more than a month.[42]

Comanches also seized the vacant trading niche that had opened in northern New Mexico after the Apache retreat. They restored their war-worn ties with Taos and established new links with the villages in the Chama district west of Taos. The villages soon became sites for closely regulated trade fairs, which attracted large numbers of Comanches who traveled annually to the mountain-nestled settlements, following the sheltering Purgatoire valley. The main hub of the burgeoning exchange was Taos, where Comanches came to barter during summer months under "peace of the market." Comanches found in the pueblo a ready clientele for their bison hides, tanned skins, dried meats, salt, and, above all, captives. Sitting in New Mexico's far northeastern corner, Taos lay beyond the effective reach of Spain's colonial authority, allowing its inhabitants to engage relatively freely in the officially prohibited captive trade. Slave traffic was well established by 1730, and in 1737 Governor Henrique de Olavide y Michelena tacitly approved it by ordering that the citizens should notify the proper officials before engaging in ransoming. Taoseños designated specific dates for the *rescate*, and Comanches brought in vast numbers of captives they had taken during long-distance slaving expeditions. By 1740 the human traffic had become so extensive that former Indian captives, *genízaros*, were granted permission to form their own community on the border because the Spaniards could not absorb all the captives into their households as laborers. In exchange for captives, Taoseños supplied Comanches with crucial necessities for their newly conceived plains life—carbohydrates, horses, metal tools, and guns. Comanches responded by quelling their raids everywhere in New Mexico, giving the colony a much needed respite from violence.[43]

The peace lasted on the plains until the closing years of the 1730s, when Comanches pushed onto the Apache lands south of the Cimarron valley. The immediate impetus for the renewed expansion was probably demographic. Comanches' successful shift to mounted hunting and nomadism, together with their practice of incorporating captive women and children into their families, sustained a rapid population growth, which may have exceeded the carrying capacity of their bounded territory. In 1740 one observer reported that the upper Arkansas valley alone was dotted by fifty to sixty Comanche camps, which together must have contained some ten thousand people. Those camps, moreover, had to live "scattered about, caring for the many horses they get from New Mexico." Comanches, it seems, had become too prosperous for the confines of the Arkansas basin.[44]

The reactivation of Comanche expansion was also tied to the borderlands' increasingly intricate requirements of exchange, production, and raiding. To sustain their lucrative trade in northern New Mexico, Comanches needed, first of all, a steady access to Apache slaves. Equally important, they had to refrain from plundering New Mexico for horses, lest they jeopardize their access to the colony's slave markets. Raiding Apache villages in the south brought a solution on both counts, yielding captives for exchange and horses for domestic use.

But warfare was never a purely material affair for Comanches whose motives to fight ranged from material and strategic to cultural and social; accordingly, it is likely that the new round of expansion had an internal sociocultural element. The consuming wars of the 1710s and early 1720s had probably accentuated the martial aspects of the Comanche culture, fostering a process that would in the late eighteenth century culminate in a rank society in which men could gain considerable social status through war exploits. Increasingly, the inner workings of the Comanche society required violent external action, creating a compelling dynamic that may have come into play in the late 1730s. With the cessation of the Apache wars more than a decade earlier, there had emerged a cadre of young warriors who lacked the military records of the previous generation and consequently found their road to social prestige closed. For those men the resumption of fighting may have been a welcome development that unlocked the frozen social hierarchy.[45]

Before the late 1730s, Comanche war parties were assaulting the Jicarillas and other Apache groups across the northern Llano Estacado, relying on the same tactics that had earlier served them so well farther north. Often cooperating with Utes, they overran Apache villages with quick surprise attacks, seizing women and children, destroying everything from dwellings to crops, and disrupting the carefully orchestrated farming cycle. The odds were tilted against the Apaches even more heavily than before, since Comanches had by now developed an advanced equestrian war machine. They fought with long metal-tipped spears and short bows that were specially designed for mounted warfare and shielded their mounts and their own bodies with thick leather armor. They moved flexibly between small-scale guerrilla raids aimed at plundering and massive frontal attacks aimed at destroying the enemy.[46]

Unable to hold off the Comanche onslaught on their own, the Apaches fled toward New Mexico, seeking protection in the vicinity of Taos, Picurís, Pecos, and Galisteo. Spanish officials, however, were unwilling to reenter Comanche-Apache wars, in part because they were following Rivera's advice of nonparticipation and in part because the first Family Compact between Spain and France seemed to have given New Mexico a measure of safety against French encroachments from Louisiana. Many Spanish colonists also profited handsomely from the rekindled Comanche-Apache wars, which brought more captives to their slave markets: the number of Apache baptisms in the colony more than doubled from the 1730s to the 1740s, jumping from 136 to 313. Yet, little by little, New Mexico was drawn into the conflict. Spanish officials avoided direct involvement, but the fact that they harbored Apache refugees near Pecos and other border towns put the colony on a collision course with the Comanches, who must have regarded the Spaniards as anything but neutral. Spanish authorities further alienated Comanches when they started to enforce the hitherto often ignored laws that prohibited Pueblo Indian trade with unconquered Indians. Their apparent aim was to exclude the Pueblos from the increasingly lucrative slave business, but their efforts also interrupted the critically important food trade between New Mexico and Comanchería, pushing Comanches to rely on raiding.[47]

On a more abstract level, Comanches and Spaniards clashed over the proper way of doing things on the frontier that both connected and separated them. When the two groups had first come in contact, their ideas of basic forms of cross-social interaction—cooperation, exchange, violence, loyalty—were nearly incomprehensible to one another. In the Comanche worldview, gifts, trade, and kinship were inexorably linked; they formed a central cultural metaphor that made peaceful relations and material exchange possible. Exchanges of gifts transformed strangers into fictive kinspeople and brought them into the familial circle where people provided for each other's needs and where goods circulated relatively freely, flowing from affluence toward deficiency. Trade was not a mechanism to create wealth but a means to seal attachments and a way to build social and political networks that protected their members against poverty and need.[48]

Spaniards, in contrast, made a clear distinction between social and economic ties. They, too, framed trade with social rituals but insisted that the actual mechanics of exchange should be governed by the logic of the market; the balance between supply and demand—not the buyer's relationship with the seller—should determine what was exchanged and at what rates. Spaniards believed that bargaining and fluid exchange rates were an essential part of trade for they helped determine the balance between supply and demand, whereas Comanches saw trade as a form of sharing between kinspeople who took care of each other's needs and therefore did not haggle. These were more than semantic differences. If Spaniards bargained for better prices, they acted as strangers, placing themselves outside the circle of kinship where sharing and exchange took place. And if they refused to participate in gift giving, they did not merely strip exchange from a decorative, trivial framing; they negated the very rationale that enticed Comanches to trade in the first place.

This cultural chasm narrowed in the 1720s and 1730s as Comanches met with Spanish merchants at Taos and other border towns, but a genuine, mutual compromise was still remote in the 1740s. For example, the practice of distributing political gifts had not been coded into New Mexico's official policy, which meant that the colonists' adherence to Native forms of diplomacy shifted from one governor and one *alcalde mayor* (district magistrate) to another, leaving Comanches variously confused, frustrated, and furious. At the fairs, Spanish traders exchanged gifts with Comanche visitors and participated in ceremonies and rituals, but they also violated Comanche codes of proper behavior by haggling over prices, pushing inferior commodities, and refusing to sell certain goods, such as guns.[49]

The tensions arising from disputes over political neutrality, trading privileges, and exchange protocols erupted into open hostilities in the early 1740s. Comanches and Utes launched a fierce raiding war on New Mexico, plunging the frontier above Albuquerque into a steep decline, and Spanish officials responded with sporadic punitive expeditions. The war took an unexpected twist in 1746, when Governor Joachín Codallos y Rabál learned about a startling threat: despite the escalating violence across the frontier, the inhabitants of Taos were rumored to be informing Comanches of the movements of Spanish troops. While shocking to Spanish authorities, this kind of collaboration was quite plausible in the fluid social milieu of Spain's far northern frontier. Having reaped great profits from Comanche commerce for years, many Taoseños may have concluded that maintaining close ties with the powerful Comanches was a better policy than yielding to the controlling measures and tribute demands of the provincial center. Betraying his anxiety over the alleged collaboration, Governor Codallos banned the Comanches from the Taos fairs in 1746 and decreed a mandatory death penalty for any Taoseño venturing more than a league from the pueblo without a license. The next year, after a flurry of Comanche attacks that nearly "destroyed the region of Abiquiú," Codallos finally put together a large-scale punitive expedition. Riding out with more than five hundred soldiers and Indian auxiliaries, he overpowered a large Ute and Comanche camp along the Chama River, slaying 107 people, carrying 206 into captivity, and seizing nearly one thousand horses.[50]

It was a shocking defeat, but the worst was yet to come. In the aftermath of the carnage, Comanches found themselves in a serious military crisis: routed by Spanish forces in the west, they faced mounting dangers in the north and east as well. In the north they had inherited the Apaches' on-and-off border conflict with the Skidi and Chaui (or Grand) Pawnees along the Loup River, a conflict that by the late 1740s had escalated into a bitter raiding war in which Pawnees plundered horses from Comanche rancherías and Comanches raided Pawnee villages for slaves and retribution. Comanches also clashed on the northern border with the Arapahoes, who ventured south from their central plains homelands to raid horses. But the situation was even more perilous in the east, where the Comanches clashed with the Osages, a powerful nation of hunters and horticulturists that dominated the tallgrass prairie borderlands between the lower Missouri and Arkansas rivers and had a secure access to French markets in the Illinois Country, or Upper Louisiana. Driven by the French demand for bison robes and slaves, empowered by French guns, and propelled by a rapid population growth, Osages had launched in the early eighteenth century a forceful expansion to the west and south. By the mid-1740s, they had forced all Wichita communities save two adjoining Taovaya villages to relocate from the middle Arkansas southward to the Red River, and their path onto the western buffalo plains and into the Comanche range appeared wide open.[51]

This was the Comanches' most critical hour on the southern plains. Their half-century expansion had drawn them into disastrous multifront wars that engulfed them on three sides. But the mid-1740s also saw Comanches reconfiguring their overall foreign political strategy in a way that allowed them to maneuver out of the military crisis. Eschewing war for diplomacy and treaty-making, they fashioned in rapid order an elaborate alliance network that not only stabilized their northern and eastern borders but also gave them access to weaponry with which they were able to turn their military fortunes in the west.

The cornerstone of that alliance system was an accord they formed in 1746 with the Taovayas, the strongest member of the Wichita confederation and the only Wichita tribe that still clung to the middle Arkansas valley region. Comanches had shared a border with Taovayas since their conquest of the upper Arkansas basin in the 1720s, but the two groups had had limited contact until the mid-1740s when symmetrical interests drew them together. The Comanche-Taovaya alliance was probably brokered by French agents who hoped to extend Louisiana's commercial reach to the west by pacifying the Arkansas channel, but it was in design and substance an indigenous creation. As a military union, the alliance allowed Comanches and Taovayas to join their forces to repel the unrelenting Osage forays from the east and north; as a commercial partnership, it complemented the resource domains of both groups. Comanches offered Taovayas horses, bison robes, and Apache captives, the bulk of which Taovayas resold to Louisiana, and Taovayas supplied Comanches with guns, powder, ammunition, and iron tools they obtained from French traders as well as with maize, beans, and squash they cultivated in their riverside fields. This symbiotic food trade was critical to Comanches who had lost their traditional source of carbohydrate products with their 1746 ban from the Taos fairs.[52]

The Comanche-Taovaya-French trading alliance turned the Arkansas valley into a busy commercial avenue, with Comanche and Taovaya trade convoys constantly moving back and forth. When traveling to Comanchería, Taovayas often escorted French traders, who had paddled to Taovaya villages in canoes before continuing on land toward Comanche rancherías. As the ties solidified, Comanche camps along the upper Arkansas valley began to take the shape of a trade center. In 1748 Spanish officials were alarmed to learn that thirty-three Frenchmen had visited the Comanches northeast of Taos and purchased mules with "plenty of muskets." Soon a wide variety of commodities circulated at the Comanche fairs. Spanish officials in New Mexico fretted about how the French carried in "rifles, gunpowder, bullets, pistols, sabers, coarse cloth of all colors" and returned to Louisiana with "skins of deer and other animals, horses, mules, burros, and a few Indian captives whom the Comanches have taken as prisoners from other tribes with whom they are at war." Spanish officials grasped the overall structure of the trade, but they underestimated the extent of the slave traffic. In 1753 the governor of Louisiana concluded that the colony held so many Apache slaves that it was becoming difficult to maintain the old trade and alliance network with the Apaches.[53]

Virtually overnight, the Comanche-Taovaya alliance shifted the balance of power in the Comanche–New Mexico war. Armed with French muskets, iron axes, and metal-tipped arrows and lances, Comanches reversed the momentum the Spaniards had enjoyed since 1747. Together with Utes, they hit Pecos and Galisteo with incessant attacks, delivering debilitating blows to the outlying villages; one report claimed that 150 Pecoseños died at Comanche hands between 1744 and 1749. Farther north in the Chama district, the terror of Comanche-Ute raids—which often were nocturnal—drove the settlers to abandon the recently established villages of Abiquiu, Ojo Caliente, and Quemado. By 1748 Comanches had gained the upper hand, and Governor Codallos reinstituted their trading privileges at Taos. Codallos was replaced the following year by Tomás Vélez de Cachupín, who made the Comanches New Mexico's foreign political priority: while fortifying Pecos and Galisteo with towers, gates, and entrenchments, he also began seeking peace with the Comanches and their Ute allies.[54]

This shift in Spanish policy was as much a reaction to Comanches' war-making as it was a response to their vigorous diplomacy, which had altered the strategic chemistry of the Southwest borderlands to Spain's disadvantage. The Comanche-Taovaya alliance had put New Mexico in a precarious geopolitical position by unlocking the southern plains for French merchants and, as Spanish officials saw it, French imperialism. In the late 1740s and early 1750s Spanish officials nervously monitored French activities on the plains and especially among the Comanches, whom Cachupín described as a "powerful tribe that dominates the others." The French, he continued, were gathering "practical knowledge of the land adjacent to our settlements which they freely travel by permission of the Comanches." The governor bitterly condemned the commercial operations of the French, whose livestock markets in Louisiana stimulated Comanche horse raiding in New Mexico. "The trade that the French are developing with the Cumanches by means of the Jumanes [Wichitas]," he warned, "will result in most serious injury to this province. Although the Cumanche nation carries on a like trade with us, coming to the pueblo of Taos . . . always, whenever the occasion offers for stealing horses or attacking the pueblos of Pecos and Galisteo, they do not fail to take advantage of it."[55]

The situation was humiliating to Cachupín, but his hands were tied by a delicate play-off dynamic: he could not punish the Comanches by banning them from the Taos fairs, since that risked losing the Comanche nation and, by extension, the southern plains entirely to the French orbit. While lamenting the "perverse nature" of the Taos fairs, Cachupín stressed throughout his tenure the importance of maintaining "friendship and commerce with the Comanche tribe, [and] diverting as much of it as possible from the French, because the Comanche tribe is the only one that could impede [French] access to that terrain and be the ruin of New Mexico." The governor found particularly troubling the gun trade chain that extended from Louisiana through the Taovayas to the Comanches; it had the potential, he argued, of becoming "our great detriment, especially since this kingdom is so limited in armaments and its settlers too poor to equip themselves and too few to sustain the burden of continuous warfare." Finally, Cachupín was loath to use force against the Comanches simply because New Mexico needed their trade for its economic well-being. With war, he insisted, "an extremely useful branch of trade would be lost and the French of New Orleans would acquire it in toto."[56]

Instead of pressuring the Comanches, then, Cachupín tried to win their loyalty by offering more goods and better terms of exchange at Taos. Born out of desperation, his decision turned the Taos fairs into frenzied events. "When the Indian trading embassy comes to these governors and their alcaldes," Fray Andres Varo reported in 1751, "all prudence forsakes them." Driven by an explosive mix of greed and fear, said Varo, the governor and other high-ranking officials amassed "as many horses as they can" and "all the ironware possible" for exchange with Comanches: "Here, in short, is gathered everything possible for trade and barter with these barbarians in exchange for buffalo hides, and, what is saddest, in exchange for Indian slaves, men and women, small and large, a great multitude of both sexes, for they are the gold and silver and the richest treasure of the governors, who gorge themselves first with the greatest mouthfuls from this table, while the rest eat the crumbs."[57]

But even more shocking to Varo was the Comanches' behavior at the fairs. Before handing over female captives, he reported, they "deflower and corrupt them in the sight of innumerable assemblies of barbarians and Catholics . . . saying to those who buy them, with heathen impudence: 'Now you can take her—now she is good.'" The horrified priest attributed such acts to Comanches' "unbridled lust and brutal shamelessness," but it is likely that the public rapes were a way to generate markets for captives. The serial rapes were a graphic forewarning of the horrors captive women would—at least supposedly—endure in Comanche hands should Spaniards refuse to ransom them. Brutality, in other words, helped legitimize slave markets in Spanish eyes. In 1751, indeed, the inspector of war in Mexico City called the New Mexican *rescate* a "laudable work" of "ransoming . . . the little Indian slaves." "By means of this exchange," the inspector reasoned, "these captive children can be educated and brought into the fold of this church, and if the traffic should discontinue, the Cumanches would kill them."[58]

In late 1751, two years into his term, Governor Cachupín desperately needed a breakthrough with the Comanches, whose play-off maneuvering, raiding-and-trading policy, and rough trading tactics were demoralizing the New Mexicans, from priests and officials to ordinary settlers and Pueblo Indians. But as much as New Mexico needed peace, Spanish officials were not accustomed to negotiating with Natives from a position of weakness. In November, however, an unexpected military coup removed political barriers from peace. After yet another Comanche attack on Pecos, this time by three hundred warriors, Cachupín chased the raiders with ninety-two troops, militia, and Indian auxiliaries and, with the help of *genízaro* scouts, besieged them in a box canyon on the Llano Estacado. It became a close-range pitched battle, something the Spaniards were familiar and comfortable with and the Comanches were not. The fighting lasted for hours and by nightfall the Comanches had no arrows or gunpowder left. Spanish soldiers set fire to the thicket and lashed the illuminated Comanches with volleys of musket fire "which brought on their ruin and destruction." One hundred twelve Comanches died and thirty-three surrendered. The survivors, Cachupín reported, wept "from pain" and made a wooden "holy cross, which they presented to me with great veneration, putting it to their lips and mine." The spectacular victory let the governor open negotiations with the Comanches from a more equal footing, and he wasted no time. He kept four women as hostages, but released all the other Comanches, sending them home with a gift of tobacco and an offer of peace. He promised the Comanches free trade in Taos and asked them to return all the Spanish captives they had carried off from Abiquiu in 1747.[59]

During the first half of the eighteenth century, Spanish officials rarely stopped to study the people who were frustrating their colonial ambitions in the Southwest, and in those few cases when they did write about the Comanches in any length, they invariably depicted them as barbarians with immense capacity for violence and minimum capacity for social order.[60] But now, in the first formal peace talks between the two peoples, a different image of the Comanches began to surface. Although the idea of Comanches as savages persisted, Spanish reports reveal a sophisticated Comanche political organization, complete with distinctive hierarchies, established procedures for broadly inclusive decision making, and effective communication systems.

In December 1751, when the survivors of the disastrous battle brought Cachupín's peace offer among the Comanches, the chiefs from various rancherías sent out messengers to summon a grand council. That council, apparently sponsored by a chief called Nimiricante (Man Eater?), became an arduous one. The chiefs of various rancherías debated heatedly over Cachupín's peace offer, struggling to reach consensus. One hurdle involved the fate of five Spanish captives—three women and two boys—whose return Cachupín had made a precondition for peace. Nimiricante's brother refused to give up one of the captive women he held, and Nimiricante intervened, ordering his brother to leave the council ground "or suffer their punishment." Eventually, the council reached an agreement and decided to make peace "and take advantage of the profit of the fairs." Chief El Oso (The Bear), depicted as "the little king of all of them," declared that he would bring his followers to Taos if the Spaniards "should not deny them the items that may please them." The council sent a message to "all the rancherías that they were to be friends of the Spaniards and do them no injury by stealing horses or committing other hostilities and that those who had Spanish women captives should turn them over to be returned."[61]

In spring 1752, several delegations of Comanche chiefs visited Governor Cachupín in Taos and Santa Fe, forging personal ties that sealed and symbolized good relations between societies. Cachupín sent each delegation home with gifts "because it is indispensable for these people" and released the four female hostages taken in the November battle. Yet, the process toward peace was tenuous, jeopardized by continuing Comanche raids. A delegation sent by El Oso apologized for the attacks, explaining that "some Comanches were so deceitful that, although their chiefs warned and counseled them, it was not sufficient to prevent such from committing crimes." Through these personal interactions and exchanges of gifts, captives, and words, Comanches and Spaniards gradually forged a peace that ended more than a decade of unrelieved violence.[62]

The final peace agreement—the first between Europeans and Comanches—was highly favorable for the latter. In return for their chiefs' personal promises to prevent their followers from raiding, Comanches received several important concessions. Cachupín granted them unrestricted access to Pecos fairs and the right to resume the *rescate* at Taos, a privilege that effectively quashed the attempts of New Mexican slave raiders to monopolize the slave traffic. Cachupín also issued a meticulous diplomatic protocol that catered to Comanche sensibilities. Under the new code, the New Mexico governor in effect became a mediator who maintained the peace through ceremonial acts and by protecting the Comanches against the greed and rough business tactics of the colonists. More broadly, the treaty recognized the Comanches as a sovereign nation—a concession Spaniards denied many smaller Native societies—thereby setting a precedent that Mexico, the Republic of Texas, and the United States would later follow. Cachupín sensed that peace for Comanches was not a static state of coexistence two parties agreed on once, but rather a tenuous condition that needed to be continuously reaffirmed through words and deeds. To appeal to this premise, he instructed New Mexico's governors to personally attend trade fairs, "sit down" with Comanche chiefs, "command tobacco for them," and use "various expressions of friendship and confidence which discretion and wisdom suggest to learn their desires." He even offered advice on gestures and appearances. "Exterior acts and circumstances of one's looks influence considerably the idea that they [Comanches] ought to form," he advised his successor. "You should introduce yourself with skill and with expressive words, maintain in your looks a mien, grave and serene, which they may observe and thus continue the faithful friendship." Finally, Cachupín specified how Spanish officials should minister to Comanche trading parties. Soldiers were to protect Comanche horse herds during fairs and governors should personally adjudicate any disputes. With an eye for detail, he ordered the settlers to keep any livestock they did not wish to trade outside town limits during fairs, for a refusal to sell could anger the Comanches. Without fully realizing (or admitting) it, Cachupín had begun adjusting Spanish trading practices to Comanche principles, which demanded that material possessions should flow freely among friends and allies. In Comanche culture, reluctance to share signified more than stinginess; it was tantamount to enmity.[63]

During the peace talks, moreover, Cachupín yielded to Comanche rule over the Great Plains east of New Mexico and cut back Spain's support to the Apaches. He persuaded the remaining Carlana, Cuartelejo, and Paloma villages to relocate from the open plains to the immediate vicinity of Pecos, thus clearing the northern Llano Estacado for Comanche use. Separated from the bison range by the Sangre de Cristo and Mescalero ranges, Carlanas, Cuartelejos, and Palomas managed from then on only sporadic hunts to the grasslands. They attached themselves so closely to Pecos that when they went for their brief hunting forays they often left their women and children behind in the town. When Bernardo de Miera y Pacheco, a soldier and mapmaker who had visited Comanchería several times, prepared in 1758 a map of the kingdom of New Mexico, he identified the buffalo plains east of the Pecos River as simply "tierra de Cumanches" and placed all Apache rancherías to the west of the Pecos valley. Those Apaches who did not seek refuge in New Mexico migrated to the south and east to join their Lipan cousins on the Texas plains. With the Apaches either clustered near Pecos or relocated south, the Comanches now controlled the entire western plains from the Arkansas valley down to the Red River.[64]

At the same time that Comanches made peace with New Mexico and usurped the Apache lands on the northern Llano Estacado, they also achieved vital diplomatic and military victories on their northern and eastern borders. By 1750 their detente with the Taovayas had carried them into an alliance with both the Skidi and Chaui Pawnees, close relatives of the Taovayas. These connections secured Comanches' northern border while also augmenting their ability to combat the Osages in the east. The Comanche-Taovaya-Pawnee alliance had a clear anti-

Osage stance. All three nations felt threatened by the Osages and sought to combine their forces against this nation whose war parties moved across a wide range stretching from the Missouri to the Canadian River. In 1751 the allied Comanches, Taovayas, and Pawnees launched a massive assault on their common enemy, killing twenty-two chiefs and delivering a devastating blow to the Osage nation.[65]

The joint war served Pawnees and Comanches better than it did Taovayas, whose isolated villages on the middle Arkansas bore the brunt of Osage attacks. Taovayas' resistance collapsed in 1757, and they retreated some two hundred miles south to the Red River, where they built new villages just west of the Cross Timbers, a north-south sliver of scraggy oaks stretching between the Red and Brazos rivers. To prepare for future Osage raids, the Taovayas built their grass houses close together and encircled their villages with deep trenches and thick, twelve-foot-tall wooden and earthen ramparts. Comanches, meanwhile, managed to keep their newly seized territory intact. Osages failed to edge onto the bison-rich shortgrass plains, and the Comanche-Osage border on the middle Arkansas, Cimarron, and Canadian rivers became a no-man's-land which both groups entered only reluctantly, risking death. Created by mutual fear, this neutral ground lasted well into the nineteenth century: when U.S. Army officials inspected the southern plains in the 1830s, they noted its existence.[66]

The treaty of 1752 between the Comanches and New Mexico had a mixed legacy. While it pacified the Comanche-Spanish relations and helped put an end to the protracted Comanche-Apache wars on the Llano Estacado, it also led to the collapse of the long-standing union between the Comanches and the Utes. The Comanche-Ute alliance was in shambles by the early 1750s, having lived out its usefulness in the fluid, rapidly changing world. Then other things happened—Cachupín retired, the French and Indian War broke out, a little captive boy rejected redemption—and the Comanche-Ute conflict exploded into a sprawling war that engulfed the borderlands.

The sources provide only fragmentary glimpses into deteriorating Comanche-Ute relations. The first signs of trouble surfaced in 1749, when a Ute band asked in Santa Fe for Spanish military support against the Comanches. And when Comanches opened peace talks with New Mexico two years later, they did so without the Utes, who began their own negotiations with Governor Cachupín, reaching a separate accord in 1752. By the end of that year, Spanish sources suggest, Comanches and Utes had clashed in several battles.[67]

That the Comanches' and Utes' half-century-old alliance would disintegrate just as their joint war against the Apaches and Spaniards came to an end was not a coincidence. The war, it appears, had been the glue that held the alliance together, and its end brought latent tensions to the surface. The main point of contention was access to New Mexico's markets, which suffered from a scarcity of trade goods, an affliction Comanches and Utes themselves had aggravated. Although constantly subsidized by Mexico City, New Mexico had grown increasingly poor during its long wars with the Comanches and Utes, and by the late 1740s the colony was facing difficulties in generating enough goods for all its Native customers. Clashes between Comanches and Utes at and around trade fairs ensued, prompting Cachupín to instruct his successor to carefully coordinate Comanche and Ute visits to Taos in order to avoid violent confrontations between the two.[68]

But Comanche and Ute interests had not only overlapped and clashed; they had also diverged. Unlike Comanches, Utes never fully committed to life on the plains; only one of their subtribes, the Muaches, made a serious effort to develop a plains culture. While Comanches quickly severed their ties to the Rocky Mountains, Utes continued to migrate seasonally between the mountains and the grasslands. They joined Comanches in raiding eastern New Mexico during the warm months but spent the cold season in the shelter of the Rockies. The detachment deepened further in the late 1740s and early 1750s when Comanches built their plains-oriented alliance network, an independent maneuvering that wrenched them away from their union with the Utes, who were not included in the new political arrangements with the French, Taovayas, and Pawnees. The Comanche alliance system shut off the Utes from the plains commerce and diplomacy, locking the two groups in contrasting foreign political trajectories. Comanches turned themselves into key players in the imperial drama that unfolded in the contested borderlands between the Río Grande and the Mississippi valley, a repositioning that set them increasingly apart—politically and geographically—from the more locally oriented Utes.[69]

Comanche-Ute conflict started out as a clash between two former allies but soon escalated into a major borderland war. Utes, while having tutored Comanches in equestrianism, now found themselves powerless against Comanche cavalry and in their distress solicited Spanish support and protection. Governor Cachupín managed to balance between the two groups without committing to either, but the tenuous peace did not survive his departure in 1754. The new governor, Francisco Marín del Valle, lacked his predecessor's grasp of multipolar cross-cultural diplomacy and allowed the critically important personal ties with Comanche leaders to unravel; Comanches would later lament that "they had come with their hearts full of kindness to establish peace but . . . that governor . . . never wished to hear them speak directly to him." Valle also limited Indian trade by issuing a *bando* that prohibited the sale of firearms, knives, and other weaponry. Alarmed by Comanches' growing horse wealth, a wealth that fueled their arms trade with French Louisiana, he prohibited the sale of breeding mares, studs, and donkeys and set a high price of fifteen hides for high-quality geldings.[70]

Before long, Comanches resumed raiding, pillaging Pecos, Galisteo, and other border villages for horses and captives. In response, Spaniards formed a loose anti-Comanche coalition with the Utes and refugee Apache bands residing on the New Mexico border. At the same time, however, Spaniards also kept their markets open for Comanches out of the fear that complete alienation would intensify their raids. The borderland war that gradually gathered force in the shadow of the sprawling Seven Years' War was thus a confusing multisided conflict in which the distinction between enemies and allies was often blurred and in which terror was a key weapon.

In spite of escalating Comanche raids, Taos continued to welcome Comanche traders, apparently with official Spanish approval; Fray Pedro Tamarón y Romeral reported how Comanche trade convoys came every year to Taos fairs, as did the governor of New Mexico and "people from all over the kingdom." To Tamarón's disgust, Comanches often paid for the maize and metal tools they received from Taoseños with horses and other goods they had stolen from other New Mexican settlements. When confronted about the raids, he noted, Comanche leaders claimed nonparticipation with vicious bravado. "'Don't be too trusting,"' one chief said. '"Remember, there are rogues among us, just as there are among you. Hang any of them you catch.'" Such statements did not necessarily reflect existing divisions in Comanche ranks. As the events that followed suggest, they seem to have been calculated rhetoric aimed at confusing Spanish officials and keeping the Taos markets open.[71]

The summer fair of 1760 in Taos was even more unruly than usual, featuring not only lively bartering but also a ritual dance in which the Taoseños displayed twenty-four fresh scalps. When the Comanches were about to depart, the townspeople, as if to test the sincerity of Comanche statements that the "rogue" raiders could be killed at will, revealed that the scalps had been taken from Comanches. The Comanches left the pueblo peacefully but returned with an enormous military force. In a remarkable display of unity and organization, a reported three thousand Comanche warriors attacked Taos with the apparent "intention of finishing" the pueblo. The attackers, failing to penetrate the town's thick walls, then launched a destructive raiding spree down the Taos valley. They burned twelve ranches near the Spanish village of Ranchos de Taos and sacked the local stronghold, the fortified hacienda of Pablo Francisco Villalpando, killing seventeen people and carrying fifty-six women and children into captivity. The region never fully recovered. When visiting the Taos valley sixteen years later, one observer noted "a number of ruins of very good ranchos."[72]

The following year, 1761, brought even more violence and turmoil. In December a Comanche embassy of fifty-eight tipis arrived in Taos to ransom some of the captives they had taken a year before. Led by their "principal man," Onacama, ten Comanche captains entered the pueblo to meet with Manuel del Portillo Urrisola, the interim governor. The talks collapsed when one of the captives, a nine-year-old boy, refused to leave his captors. Portillo seized the boy and the Comanche captains. Overcoming their guards, the Comanches struggled free and barricaded themselves in a stable inside Taos. Portillo ordered his troops outside the pueblo and, "invoking the Queen of Angels and men," unleashed them on the unwary Comanche camp. Among Portillo's force was a group of Utes who had pledged to fight with the Spaniards "until death."[73]

The result was one of the worst military catastrophes in Comanche history. Dazed by volleys of cannon and shotgun fire, the warriors fled the battle scene, leaving most of their women and children behind in the camp. Portillo led his men into pursuit, but the Ute warriors broke away and stormed the Comanche camp, carrying off "more than a thousand horses and mules and more than three hundred Comanche women, large and small." Portillo's troops meanwhile continued the chase until they reached "a place impossible to pass." There, he reported, "we kept killing Comanches. Those fields were covered with their bodies, for none of them were willing to surrender alive." He reported four hundred dead Comanches. Upon returning to Taos, he ordered the stable with the trapped Comanche chiefs inside it to be burned. Two captains came out. One was shot on the spot; the other escaped, wounded and bleeding.[74]

A Ute captive who was among the Comanches at that time but managed to escape later described the battle's aftermath in Comanchería. Overcome with horror and grief, the surviving Comanches, numbering only thirty-six, "set fire to everything they had, they killed all their herd of horses, they cut their ears, and they went fleeing." The pain engulfed everyone, but it must have been especially excruciating for those men whose wives, children, and relatives were among the dead or captured. According to Comanche social code, a man's honor depended on his ability to protect and expand his kinship network, and losing one's wife or children to enemies was a source of unbearable shame, resulting in a loss of masculine respect. Such a loss brought a social stigma that could only be removed by retrieving the relatives, by replacing them with the captors' women and children, or by symbolically covering the dead with enemy bodies. Massive grief and loss, in other words, demanded massive retribution.[75]

It was into this frontier chaos that Cachupín returned in January of 1762 for his second gubernatorial term. Shocked to find the peace he had so carefully built dead and alarmed by rumors that Comanches were preparing for a general war against the colony, he immediately released six Comanche women and sent them home "as ambassadors to their nation." Cachupín's detailed reports, which also include Comanche testimonies, provide a stereoscopic view into the complex negotiations that ensued. When the six female ambassadors arrived in Comanchería with the peace overture, they found the Comanches "in council discussing the safest means of making war upon the Spaniards." When learning about Cachupín's return to New Mexico, however, the council quickly adopted a new agenda. The chiefs and elders decided to send nine secondary chiefs, two of whom had the right to give "opinions in their government," to meet with the governor. Escorted by sixty warriors, the emissaries arrived a few weeks later in Taos, from where they were ushered to Santa Fe. Along the way, on Cachupín's orders, Spanish officials showered the Comanches with presents "so that they would understand our kindness and good faith." The emissaries arrived at the Governor's Palace carrying a tall cross, wearing smaller crosses on their necks, and "well armed with French rifles," delivering a mixed message that at once underscored Comanches' willingness to negotiate and their military power and international reach. Significantly, Cachupín recognized several of the nine chiefs from his previous term that had ended eight years earlier, which indicates that the Comanche political system was based on institutionalized leadership positions.[76]

Comanche emissaries opened the talks by listing grievances that ranged from Governor Portillo's unprovoked attack in 1761 to chaos at the Taos fairs and the restrictions on Comanche trade in New Mexico. Cachupín's response was a combination of remorse, reconciliation, and patent Spanish paternalism. He declared that the recent hostilities had violated, but not annulled, the bonds of friendship that had been established in 1752. Both sides, he regretted, "had acted in an insane manner in making war upon one another when they ought to have been the best of friends." He then laid out his peace proposal. He promised to restore Comanches' trading privileges and invited them to visit New Mexico "frequently, without fear or lack of confidence." He also suggested that both sides return their captives, thus deftly eliminating a fundamental cause behind borderland violence—the pain that arose from losing one's relatives into captivity and other peoples' kinship networks. Visibly satisfied, the Comanches promised to take the terms "before the notice of all their chiefs and principal men of the nation," and Cachupín lavished them with presents so that "they might smoke and consider well their resolutions in regard to my purposes."[77]

The Comanche response came some months later when another embassy—four chiefs, seven warriors, and ten women and children—arrived in Santa Fe. "Dispatched by the two superior chiefs" of their nation, the emissaries informed Cachupín that an order had been sent to "all rancherías of their tribe to hold a council and hasten the return of all Spaniards, large and small, whom they held prisoners." The four chiefs then requested that Cachupín return to each of them a captive, "some relative or his own woman whom perhaps they might find," so that they would have proof of his "estimation" for the Comanche nation. Cachupín ordered thirty-one women and children to be brought before the chiefs, each of whom then "selected the relation closest to him." These acts sealed the peace by transforming the violent, disruptive potential embedded in the captive institution into a cross-cultural bridge. As the chiefs reunited with their loved ones, restoring fractured kinship networks, a major cause behind the Comanche-Spanish conflict disappeared. As a result of this action, the governor later exulted, the chiefs showed "undeniable satisfaction and pleasure; all embraced me around the neck and gave me repeated thanks. They now said that their tribe had no reason any longer to fear or follow any other dictate than the observance of a real peace and firm alliance with the Spaniards."[78]

These proceedings—which mirrored and built on the negotiations ten years earlier—were more than peace talks: they were an attempt to create a political and cultural middle ground between two nations. When Cachupín painstakingly documented Comanche customs and political practices, he was not only quenching Spanish bureaucracy's thirst for detail; he was writing a manual for cross-cultural communication. And when he gratified Comanches with gifts, he was not merely trying to create goodwill; he was appealing to the Comanche belief that real peace could not exist without gifts, which turned enemies into friends and strangers into metaphorical kinspeople. Anticipating a profound shift in Spanish Indian policy that would reconfigure Spain's northern frontier in the 1780s, Cachupín had realized that peace with Indian nations depended on gifting and personal bonds rather than institutional ties. It required yielding dreams of cultural supremacy to the reality of cultural accommodation and exchange.[79]

But Spaniards were not the only ones making concessions. Equally eager for peace, Comanches too compromised, paving the way for deep, mutual accommodation. They did not insist on framing the alliance with fraternal kinship metaphors but accepted, at least on the surface, Cachupín's patriarchal notion that they had yielded to "obedience and vassalage to the great and powerful captain of the world, the king and lord of the Spaniards." This was a fictional interpretation that ignored the real balance of power on the ground, but it was a fiction shared by both sides, albeit for different reasons. For Cachupín, the patriarchal formulation was a political necessity, the only acceptable way he could justify to his superiors in Mexico City and Madrid an alliance with heathen savages. Comanches, too, interpreted the alliance through their own cultural prism. They expected persons in authority to be generous guardians, not autocratic rulers, and it is likely that they expected the king of Spain to be a benefactor who would provide them with presents, protect their trading privileges, and shield them against such atrocities as Governor Portillo's 1761 attack. Comanches also seem to have respected—if not accepted—the notion that New Mexico was not a collection of autonomous communities with whom they could maintain separate, even contradictory relations. For several years after the accord they refrained from their long-standing raiding-and-trading policy in New Mexico and maintained a universal peace with the province.[80]

Besides pacifying the Comanche–New Mexican border, the 1762 accord also sealed the outcome of the decade-long Comanche-Ute war. With Spaniards and Comanches now united, Utes could no longer rely on Spanish support in their struggle to maintain a foothold on the plains-mountain ecotone. The Muaches, the most plains-oriented band of the Utes, withdrew west and shifted their trading operations from Taos to Abiquiu and Ojo Caliente, both of which had been resettled in the 1750s. Abiquiu and Ojo Caliente were separated from Taos by the Río Grande and Chama River, which meant that the Muaches were now removed from Comanche range of interest. Muaches retreated deep into the mountain parks to join the other Ute bands, leaving New Mexico's eastern borderland for the Comanches, their former allies and kin who had grown out of their union.[81]

Contrary to Spanish hopes, the 1762 treaty did not stop Comanche expansion. At the time Comanches solidified their dominance over the grasslands east of New Mexico in the 1762 accord, the next—the third—distinctive phase of their expansion was already well on its way. In the early 1750s, with the wars of the previous expansionist phase still raging on the Llano Estacado, several Kotsoteka bands plunged south, crossing the vast table of the Edwards Plateau to the Balcones Escarpment, where the high plains dissolve into the lowlands of Texas. It was one of the most explosive territorial conquests in North American history. In less than a decade, the entire Texas plains—a huge spread of undulating hill country and plains stretching from the Pecos River in the west to the Cross Timbers in the east and from the Red River in the north to the Balcones Escarpment in the south—became a Comanche dominion. This expansionist burst turned the Comanches into a territorial superpower. The Comanchería that emerged

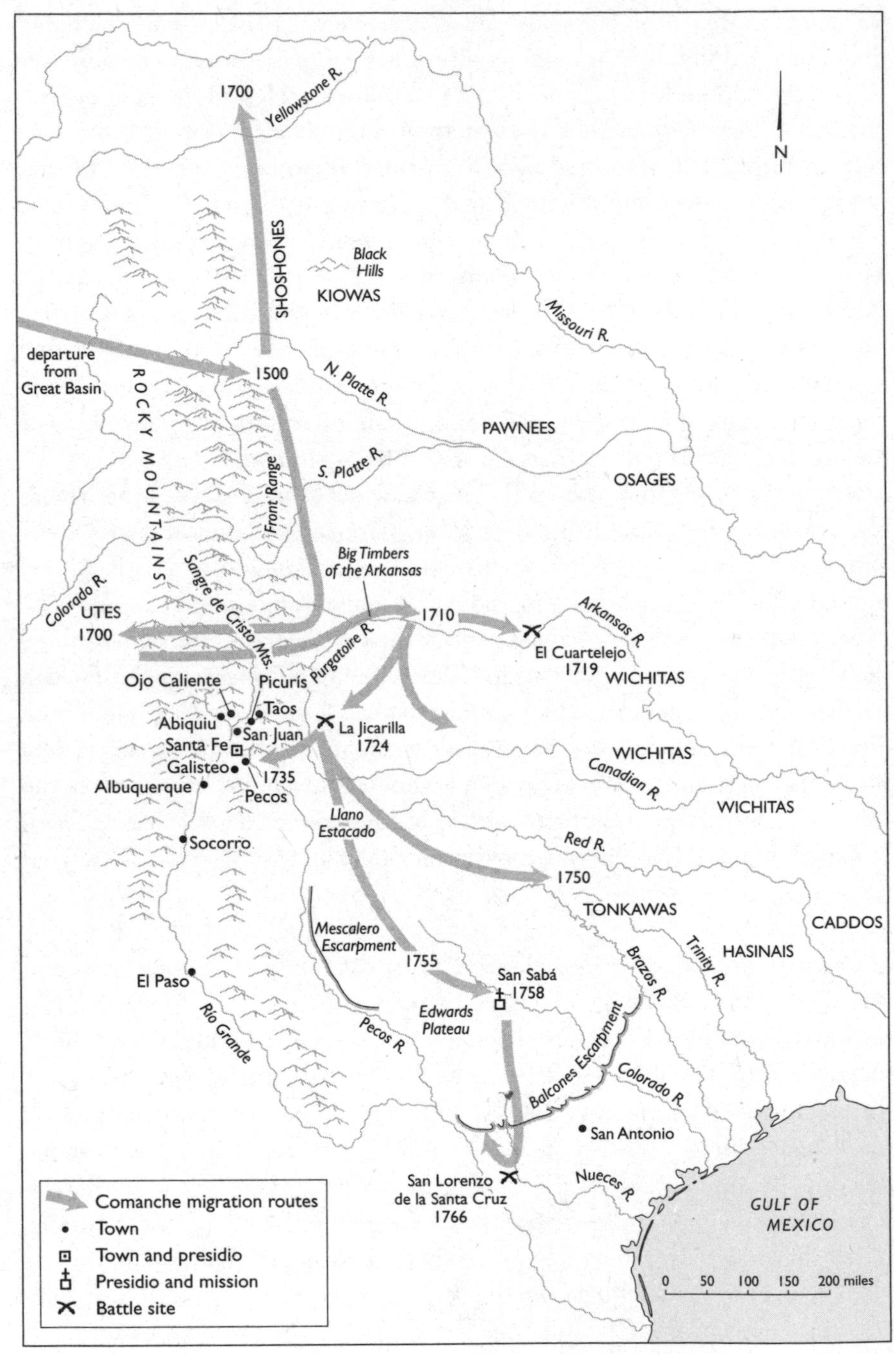

1. Comanche migrations and expansion. Map by Bill Nelson.

covered some quarter of a million square miles, casting a long shadow on European imperial designs in the continent's center.

The Comanche conquest of the Texas plains was fueled by several factors. In part, it was a repeat of the familiar dynamic. A need to expand their horse-and-bison economy had driven the Comanches to grasslands around 1700 and now, half a century later, the same need pushed them into the Texas plains. By the 1750s Comanches had completed their shift to mounted hunting and nomadism and in the process drastically simplified their economy. The mounted chase became the foundation of their economy, overshadowing other subsistence strategies. Gathering decreased, eating fish became a taboo, and fowl was reduced to an emergency food eaten only when other provisions failed. But now everything hinged on their ability to keep their horse herds large and growing, and it was this imperative that drew them south. Spanish Texas was dotted with horse-rich but often poorly manned missions, presidios, and civilian ranches, which were a reasonably easy prey for mounted guerrilla attacks. An even greater incentive were innumerable wild horses roaming in the hill country just north of the Texas frontier, perhaps more than one million in all, ready to be seized and tamed.[82]

The invasion may have also been motivated by changing geopolitics. The late 1740s witnessed the emergence of yet another anti-Comanche coalition—this time between Spanish Texas and Lipan Apaches. Since the founding of first permanent Spanish colonial settlements in San Antonio and Los Adaes in the late 1710s, Spaniards had been struggling with the Lipans who raided Texas for the European technology they could no longer acquire from New Mexican markets. It was a consuming on-and-off raiding war, characterized by Lipan livestock poaching, Spanish reprisals, and mutual captive seizing. But in 1749, after several aborted efforts, the two sides made peace in San Antonio in a three-day ceremony, which climaxed in a ritual burial of weapons, a live horse, and the war itself. The accord was prompted by the rising Comanche threat. Lipans, who had recently incorporated large numbers of Jicarilla refugees from the north, stated during the peace talks that they wanted Spanish support and weapons to fend off the Comanche war bands that had started to infringe upon their lands. Equally alarmed by Comanche expansion, Spanish officials seized the opportunity. By arming the Lipans, they reasoned, it would be possible to create a barrier between their young colony and the expansionist Comanches. Comanches, whose hunting and scouting parties had frequented the Texas plains since the early 1740s, were probably aware of the new threat from the outset.[83]

Finally, the Comanche sweep into the Texas plains may have been a response to a changing commercial geography. The expulsion of their Taovaya allies from the Arkansas to the Red River in the 1750s under Osage pressure prompted

French traders to refocus their operations from the Arkansas channel to the lower Red River, where an important trading satellite, Fort St. Jean Baptiste aux Natchitoches, had been established in 1716. This sudden shift in commercial gravity must have been a strong incentive for Comanches to relocate south as well, for they had grown heavily dependent on the French-Taovaya trade axis, their principal source of maize, guns, and metal.[84]

The Comanche invasion of the Texas plains unfolded on two levels—diplomatic and military. When they arrived in the Red River valley, Comanches first integrated themselves into the region's alliance network. They reestablished their trade relationship with the Taovayas, who then brought them in touch with the Tonkawas, a multiethnic group of nomadic hunters between the Colorado and Trinity rivers. Comanches also forged tentative ties with the Hasinai confederacy, the westernmost extension of Caddo people, who lived in large urban communities between the Ouachita and Neches rivers and made annual hunting excursions to the southern plains. This emerging coalition, which Spaniards would come to label as *Norteños*, was founded on shared foreign political interests. Taovayas, Tonkawas, and Hasinais—like Comanches—were alarmed by the Lipan-Spanish pact, which threatened to exclude them from Texas markets and leave them vulnerable against the Apaches. Taovayas and Hasinais were also engaged in a losing war with Lipans over hunting ranges and were eager to enlist the support of the formidable Comanches. Although Spanish officials would later blame French agents for promoting an anti-Spanish Norteño coalition, the immediate motivation for the Comanche-Taovaya-Tonkawa-Hasinai alliance was Spain's decision to ally with the Lipans at the exclusion of the other Native groups.[85]

Thus strengthened by new allies and arms, Comanches launched in the early 1750s a systematic offensive against the Lipans. It was a near repeat of the previous Comanche-Apache wars. Like their northern relatives, Lipans had gradually taken up small-scale riverside farming, which now undermined their ability to confront the wide-ranging Comanche war parties. Fixed to their fields and short of horses—a severe drought had devastated their herds in the 1740s—the Lipans were powerless to halt the Comanche advance. In 1755 they invited the Comanches to peace talks along the Guadalupe River. The two groups "sang together and touched weapons in token of friendship," but the peace did not last. Lipans then turned to Spaniards for military support, vowing to accept Christianity, give up their nomadic ways, and take on full-time farming. The offer was received excitedly by the colonists who, after decades of frustrating missionary efforts, could finally start fulfilling their assigned role within Spain's imperial system: turning nomads to neophytes and building a buffer zone of pacified Indian farmers to protect the silver mines of northern Mexico against foreign invasion. The construction of a new mission-presidio complex began in the spring of 1757 in the San Sabá valley.[86]

The San Sabá scheme epitomized in microcosm the kind of strategic miscalculations that had encumbered Spain's North American ventures from the outset. The first miscalculation involved the site itself, which at first glance seemed an auspicious choice. The San Sabá valley had a broad, irrigable bottom that was suitable for farming, and it had prospects of mining. Separated from the principal political and population center, San Antonio, by 135 miles, San Sabá also could have become a protective bastion for Texas deep on the interior plains. But that middle distance also meant that the mission-presidio complex would be an isolated outpost at the edge of Comanche range, where it stood defenseless in a conflict its very presence provoked. (Lipans, it seems, were fully aware of this: in June 1757 a massive party of some three thousand visited the construction site, but in the end only a few families stayed with the Franciscans; the rest, leaving, protested that the site was too close to Comanche territory.) San Sabá was also poorly designed for defense. To prevent sexual interaction and cohabitation between Spanish soldiers and Indian women, the friars had insisted that the presidio be built three miles upriver from the mission complex, which thus lay utterly exposed to attack. But perhaps the most serious miscalculation was financial. Although the mission was funded privately by a mining magnate, the presidio, designed to lodge four hundred people, absorbed men and funds that would have been needed elsewhere in poverty-stricken Texas. In the San Sabá scheme, then, Texas tied its limited resources in an improbable venture that virtually invited enemy assault.[87]

That assault came in March 16, 1758, when an estimated two thousand allied Comanches, Taovayas, Tonkawas, and Hasinais appeared at the gates of the San Sabá mission, announcing that "they had come with intention of killing the Apaches." The bulk of the force broke into the mission compound and began looting it and searching for Apaches, while the rest approached the presidio. When the presidial soldiers opened fire, the Indians retreated and gathered in and around the mission. Their faces "smeared with black and red paint," equipped with lances, cutlasses, helmets, metal breastplates, and "at least 1,000" French muskets, and led by a Comanche chief clad in a French officer's uniform, they set fire to the buildings—"so quickly that it seems probable that they were prepared in advance to do so," one soldier recalled—and gunned down those who failed to find shelter. The body count, made by the presidial soldiers who had been too terrified to confront the overwhelming Indian force, revealed eight casualties.[88]

If the loss of life was limited, the psychological aftermath was enormous. The attack was a military operation aimed at eliminating an enemy encroachment, but it was also a symbolic act laden with political messages. The attackers openly declared their nationality, perhaps to stake territorial claims or perhaps to proclaim that they were not afraid of Spanish reprisals, and their French weapons, by all accounts manifestly displayed, bespoke of far-reaching commercial and political connections. The violence itself, it seems, was staged for maximum impact. The attackers slaughtered oxen and other animals, destroyed church ornaments and sacred jewels and pictures, and overturned and beheaded the effigy of Saint Francis. They left behind stripped, scalped, eyeless bodies and placed the beheaded body of a friar on the church altar. If the intention was to use strategic violence to coerce the Spaniards to cut off their support to the Apaches, it worked. "Intent as they are on robbery and blunder," Father Manuel de Molina testified, "they will not desist from such activities, nor cease to carry out their diabolic schemes. Therefore I consider it impossible to reduce and settle these Apache Indians along the San Sabá, or for many leagues roundabout, even with the aid of the King's forces." The bare facts of the assault—the size of the coalition, its abundant French weaponry, its apparent organizational capacity—sent shock waves across Spanish Texas. The Indians were so superior "in firearms as well as in numbers," one officer declared, "that our destruction seems probable." Seeing French intrigue behind the attack, other officials feared that the attacks would be repeated as long as French traders and French guns poured west from Louisiana. The destruction of the San Sabá mission also left the Apaches demoralized, although none of their kin had died in the attack. Realizing that Spanish presidios and soldiers could not protect them on the plains, the Lipans began to retreat south and east and established new villages along the Colorado, Guadalupe, and Frio rivers on the edge of the grasslands.[89]

With the Lipans fleeing the plains and the San Sabá mission lying in ruins, Spaniards found themselves fighting a war that had lost its strategic rationale. But instead of seeking peace with the Norteños, the officials in Mexico City decided to continue the war. Motivated more by a desire to restore Spanish honor than tactical reasoning, they ordered the presidio of San Sabá to remain occupied. When Spanish officials convinced some Lipan bands to settle down in the vicinity of the presidio, Comanches responded with constant attacks. Then, in August 1758, Spanish authorities dispatched Colonel Diego Ortiz Parrilla, the desecrated commander of the San Sabá presidio, with 360 presidial soldiers and volunteers, 134 Apache scouts, and 42 other Indian auxiliaries to the north. Parrilla's force scored a sensational victory on the Clear Fork of the Brazos River, where it ambushed an isolated Tonkawa camp and killed 55 and captured 149 men, women, and children. Heady from the unexpected triumph, the party pushed ahead to the Red River valley, where they came upon the heavily fortified Taovaya village, which also hosted some Comanche bands. Parrilla ordered his troops into a frontal attack, but mounted Taovaya and Comanche warriors launched an equally organized countercharge, firing repeated volleys from horseback. Other Taovaya and Comanche men fired upon the attackers from the village's elevated palisades, pausing only to ridicule the bewildered troops. After four hours of futile attempts, and with the death toll rising at alarming rate, Parrilla ordered a retreat, leaving two bronze cannons behind.[90]

It was only in the wake of the Parrilla disaster that the Spaniards began to question the rationale of their anti-Comanche policy and the idea of an Apache barrier on the plains. In 1760, Texas Governor Ángel Martos y Navarrete suspended campaigns against the Norteños, who responded in kind, halting their attacks on the Apaches and Texas. Two years later, Franciscans established two unauthorized missions, San Lorenzo de la Santa Cruz and Nuestra Señora de la Candelaria del Cañon, on the upper Nueces River. Situated almost ninety miles south of San Sabá, the missions provided an asylum for the Apaches far from Comanche domain.[91]

But the realignment of Texas's frontier policy remained incomplete, for the colony still kept troops at the San Sabá presidio and even provided military escorts for Apache hunting parties onto the plains. Spaniards also harbored Apaches near San Antonio, which prevented the Norteños from trading in the villa. The indecisiveness of Texas officials nearly destroyed their colony. Incensed by the continuing support to their enemies, Comanches and their allies began a fierce raiding war. They attacked Apache villages and Spanish settlements relentlessly, creating a broad, triangle-shaped shatterbelt extending from the San Sabá to San Antonio and the Nueces missions. The attacks culminated in January 1766, when four hundred Comanches, Taovayas, Tonkawas, and Hasinais sacked San Lorenzo, sending the Lipans fleeing in panic; after the assault not "a single Indian" remained in the mission. Although the campaign ended in disaster when the returning Norteños ran into a Spanish ambush and suffered heavy casualties under cannon fire, the massive show of force quashed Lipan hopes of maintaining a foothold even at the outskirts of the plains. Within a year, all Lipans had retreated to the coastal plains of Texas, the deserts around the Río Grande valley, and the mountains of Coahuila, where they joined their Natagé cousins to build a new economy on poaching Spanish villages and ranches in southern Texas, Nueva Vizcaya, and Coahuila. The Apache diaspora from the plains was now complete, and a largely depopulated hundred-mile-wide buffer zone separated the Apache realm from the southern border of Comanchería.[92]

With the destruction of San Lorenzo mission, Texas's frontier strategy had come to a dead end. Yet, true to the pattern, it took an outside intervention to nudge long-standing practices and policies on a new course. That intervention came in 1767 when marqués de Rubí extended his famous two-year inspection tour of northern New Spain's frontier defenses to Texas. Like Pedro Rivera in New Mexico forty years earlier, Rubí found in Texas a battered, overstretched colony struggling under Comanche pressure. Comanches and their allies, he discovered, were "bordering our settlements, which are weak, ill-placed, and incapable . . . of making opposition to a torrent of enemies who in reality are appreciable in strength and number." And like Rivera, Rubí offered some drastic solutions. Determined to stamp out the "credulity and the shameful indulgence" of Texas officials with a strong measure of realpolitiks, he urged them to seek peace with the powerful Comanches and dissolve the "unfortunate" Lipan alliance, which only provoked Comanche aggression against Texas. If necessary, Rubí advised, Texas should consider "the total extermination" of the Lipans, who had taken up raiding in southern Texas while at the same time "spoon-feeding us with their deceitful friendship and supposed desire to be reduced."[93]

Rubí's proposals did not receive official crown approval until 1772, but the officials in Texas promptly put them in practice. In 1769, at Rubí's recommendation, they finally removed the presidio from the San Sabá River and adopted a conciliatory policy toward the Comanches. Much after the fact, Spaniards began to reenvision their plains borderlands as a bipolar world where there were two great powers, the Comanches and Spain, and no room for the ailing Apache nation.[94]

"We shall have, it is undeniable, one day the Nations of the North as neighbors; they already are approaching us now," Rubí warned in 1768, trying to advocate the removal of the Apaches from the plains that separated Texas from the expanding Comanchería. Rubí's warning was as pertinent as it was dated: by the time he filed his report, Comanches had already arrived at the Texas border, and their realm was staggering in size.

With the Lipans beaten and routed, the Comanches controlled almost all of the southern plains, flanking and fencing off Spain's far northern frontier nearly across its entire arc. Western Comanchería, the domain of the Yamparika, Jupe, and Kotsoteka divisions, pressed against New Mexico from Taos down to Albuquerque. Eastern Comanchería, primarily a Kotsoteka realm, was separated from San Antonio, the main population center of Texas, by the distance of one day's ride. Rather than the seat of a grand colonization project, San Antonio

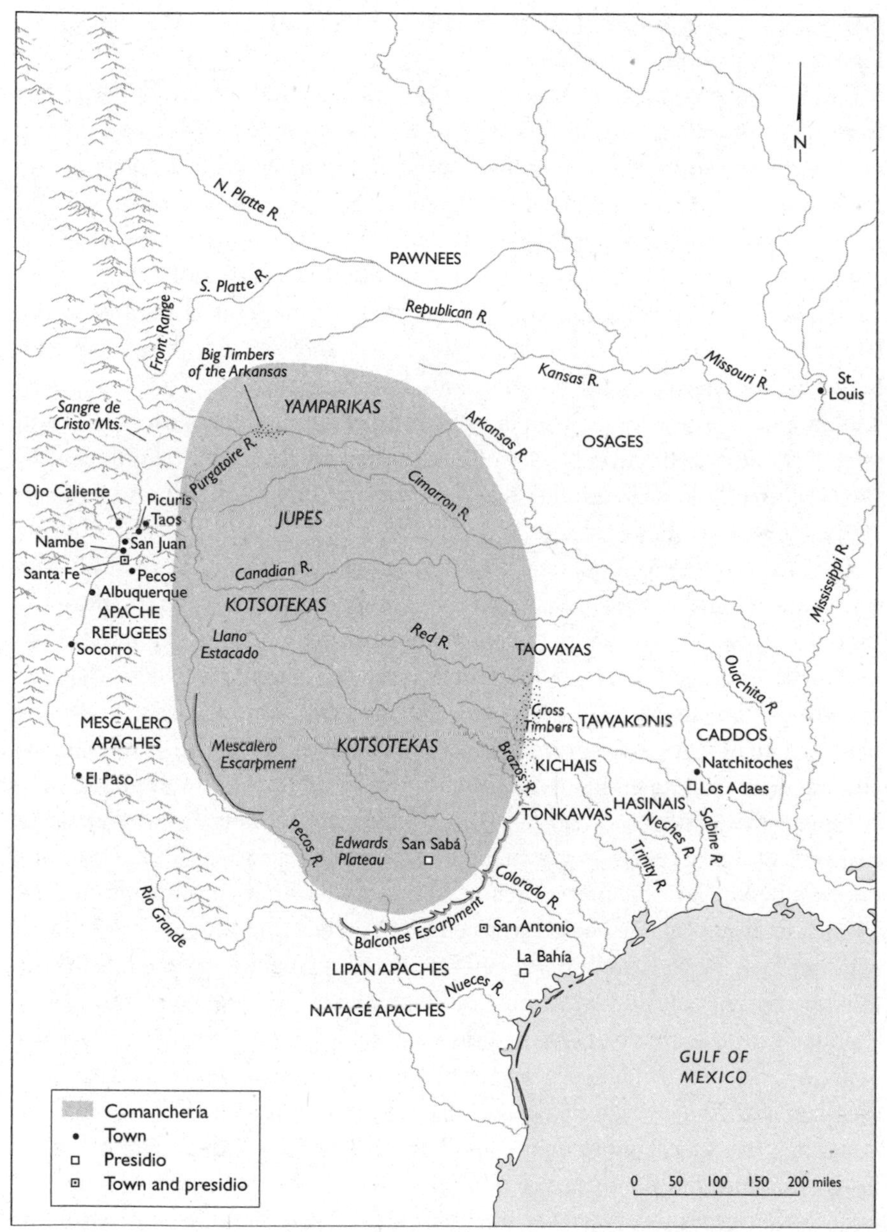

2. Comanchería in the 1760s. Map by Bill Nelson.

had become the frontline on a Spanish frontier that had caved in at the center, folding itself around Comanchería.

Comanche colonization, moreover, had dislocated thousands of Apaches from the Great Plains south and west of the Río Grande, where they joined other Apache groups in raiding Spanish villages, haciendas, and ranches. By midcentury the Apaches had forged an immense war zone that stretched 750 miles from northern Sonora through Nueva Vizcaya to Coahuila, posing a severe threat to northern New Spain's mining districts. Rubí's ultimate goal had been a solid northern frontier anchored in New Mexico and Texas, but by the late 1760s the sister colonies had become narrow and isolated ribbons pinched between two rapidly expanding indigenous dominions. Indeed, if Spanish troops and travelers wanted to reach Santa Fe from San Antonio, they struck *south* and circled to their destination by way of Saltillo in southeastern Coahuila and El Paso in the middle Río Grande valley, carefully skirting the newfound Comanchería and the transplanted Apachería.[95]

When those new geopolitical realities suddenly dawned on Spanish officials—and when the officials in Texas and New Mexico compared the stunning success of their Native rival to their own failures to extend Spanish authority to the North American interior—the Comanches and their colonizing campaign became the objects of intense scrutiny. To many Spanish observers, analyzing the Comanches' ascendancy from obscurity into regional dominance was also an exercise in excruciating self-criticism. In the far north, more completely than anywhere else, Spaniards had failed in the critical prerequisite of their colonial project—preventing large-scale diffusion of European technology among nonconquered, nonsedentary Indians. Across the northern frontier from New Mexico to Texas, Spanish colonists faced Comanches who fought on horseback with flintlock muskets and iron-tipped lances, using Spanish technology to contain Spanish imperialism. That techno-military turn, coupled with Comanches' assumed intrinsic cruelty, explained the Comanche rise to dominance in Spanish minds. In 1778 Miera y Pacheco offered a typical assessment in a series of map legends. "This nation is very warlike and cruel," read one of the legends, describing the Comanches, while another depicted the Comanche colonization of the southern plains as epic military conquest: "They acquired horses and weapons of iron, and they have acquired so much skill in handling both that they surpass all nations in agility and courage. They have made themselves the lords of all the buffalo country, seizing it from the Apache nation, which formerly was the most widespread of all known [Native nations] in America. They have destroyed many nations of them [Apaches], and those which remain they have pushed to the frontiers of our King's provinces."[96]

Accounts such as this capture an elemental truth: Comanches were superior fighters who had matched and then surpassed Spaniards in mounted combat. Their swift, wide-ranging guerrilla attacks, refined during the protracted wars against the Apaches, wreaked havoc against Spanish settlers and soldiers who preferred to fight in closed places and in tightly organized formations. Extraordinarily mobile, Comanches could strike unexpectedly and distract and disable their enemy with seemingly unorganized individual charges before abruptly breaking off and riding hard for dozens of miles into safety. If chased, they scattered across the trackless grasslands, forcing their pursuers to choose among multiplying targets. Yet the explanations that emphasize raw fighting ability alone miss a fundamental point: Comanches' overwhelming military power stemmed from a dynamic economic, social, and cultural core. Beneath the martial surface were adaptable people who aggressively embraced innovations, subjecting themselves to continuous self-reinvention.

Comanches' power complex was much more than a military creation; it was also, and indeed primarily, a political construction. Their colonization of the southern plains was a military enterprise built on astute and pragmatic diplomacy. As they swept across the southern plains, Comanches forged a series of strategic alliances, which buttressed their own strength while leaving their competitors variously defenseless and divided. They defeated the Apaches and their Spanish allies in several successive wars, and in all those wars they fought with powerful allies of their own. They sustained their long-standing union with the Utes for decades, only to detach themselves from the alliance in the 1750s, when the collapse of Apache resistance on the Llano Estacado turned Utes from useful allies into rivals. Exploiting existing rifts among Spanish colonists and their subject peoples, Comanches nurtured close ties with Taoseños, who supplied them with horses and weapons even when an open war raged between New Mexico and Comanches. Twice, in the early 1750s and in the early 1760s, Comanches also negotiated highly favorable peace treaties with New Mexico, blending diplomatic persuasion with the threat of violence to force the Spaniards to modify their aggressively paternalistic frontier policy toward a more accommodative approach.

The pinnacle of Comanches' diplomacy was the sweeping alliance network they forged in the early 1750s with the Taovayas, Skidi and Chaui Pawnees, Tonkawas, Hasinais, and French Louisiana. That cluster of alliances turned the nascent Comanchería from an isolated, militarized landscape into a nexus point of multiple trade routes while leaving the Apaches and Spaniards politically and commercially marginalized. It gave Comanches an access to guns, powder, lead, and other European goods and allowed them to play the Spaniards off against their French rivals. It also enabled them to mobilize large multinational military campaigns, which crushed the remains of Apache resistance and forced New Spain to accept a new geopolitical order on its northern borderlands.

But Comanche ascendancy was also rooted in economics: there was a direct link between territorial expansion and productive power. As the first people on the plains to fully commit to mounted nomadism and hunting, Comanches enjoyed a decisive advantage: they could exploit the vast reserves of bioenergy stored in the plains' bison herds more thoroughly than any of their competitors. By reinventing themselves as mounted bison hunters, Comanches dramatically simplified and intensified their economy; few societies in history have relied so totally on a single food source, and few have experienced such a sudden increase in total caloric intake as the early eighteenth-century Comanches did. This in turn made possible a rapid and sustained population growth, the single most important factor behind the Comanchenization of the southern plains.

Though punctuated by several lulls, the Comanche-Apache conflict was a drawn-out, half-century-long war of attrition in which the linkages among demography, production, and military power became increasingly pronounced. Where Apache population growth stagnated and then turned into a sharp decline, the Comanches grew rapidly in numbers, even while absorbing major losses. They suffered repeated and devastating losses to war—most notably in 1747, 1751, and 1761 when Spanish troops engaged war bands traveling with families and forced them into pitched battles—and yet the population growth continued unabated. According to one estimate, there were fifteen hundred Comanches in 1726 (probably an underestimation), but by 1750 their population seems to have exceeded ten thousand and was probably approaching fifteen thousand. For Apaches, Comanche invasion must have appeared like a swelling, unstoppable human tide that swept the southern plains, brushing aside their way of life with its sheer force of momentum.[97]

But if full-time equestrianism offered such obvious economic, demographic, and military advantages, why did only the Comanches make the shift? Why did the Apaches cling to their fields and villages even after it had become clear that their commitment was pushing their plains civilization into oblivion? At least part of the answer can be found in the two groups' divergent evolutionary trajectories and the resulting differences in their attitudes toward innovations and culture change. When the Comanche-Apache wars erupted in the early eighteenth century, the Apaches were in the midst of a long process of transforming themselves into agricultural people. Having begun at the turn of the sixteenth and seventeenth centuries, this process had gathered considerable force in the early eighteenth century. By then, the farming complex—its distinctive annual cycle, labors, social relations, beliefs, and ceremonies—had permeated the very core of the Apache culture, making a return to full-time nomadism and hunting all but unthinkable. External political pressures further narrowed Apaches' options, for every Spanish offer of military assistance against the Comanche onslaught was contingent on the premise that they give up even part-time hunting, settle down for good, and become full-time farmers.[98]

For Comanches, in contrast, the equestrian shift was nearly effortless. Viewed broadly, equestrianism represented to them merely a stage in an expedited evolutionary continuum that had witnessed them migrating from the central plains to the southern Rocky Mountains and, in the space of a few years, transforming themselves from stone-and-bone-using pedestrian hunters into horse-mounted, gun-and-metal-using slave and livestock raiders and traders on the Spanish borderlands. Against this backdrop, the shift to full-blown mounted nomadism on the southern plains was less a cultural revolution than a phase in a great adaptive spurt. Already remolded by a sweeping migration, the Comanches entered the southern plains as an extraordinarily adaptive people ready to exploit the possibilities of a mounted way of life to the full.

In the end, then, the dazzling equestrian maneuvers and fearsome guerrilla attacks that fired the contemporary imagination were simply an application of overwhelming economic and demographic power made available by adaptive fluency. Athanase de Mézières, a French and later Spanish career officer who observed the changing power relations on the southern plains at close range, noted as much in 1770. Instead of stressing military prowess as the building blocks of Comanche ascendancy, he listed prosaic economic factors ranging from manpower and economic independence to pasturelands and animal bounty. For him, the Comanche conquest of the southern plains was a case of demographic and economic imperialism. Comanches, he concluded, "are scattered from the great Missuris River to the neighborhood of the frontier presidios of New Spain. They are a people so numerous and so haughty that when asked their number, they make no difficulty of comparing it to that of the stars. They are so skillful in horsemanship that they have no equal; so daring that they never ask for or grant truces; and in the possession of such a territory that, finding in it an abundance of pasturage for their horses and an incredible number of cattle which furnish them raiment, food, and shelter, they only just fall short of possessing all of the conveniences of the earth, and have no need to covet the trade pursued by the rest of the Indians whom they call, on this account, slaves of the Europeans, and whom they despise."[99]

2

New Order

In February 1763 the world's greatest powers gathered in Paris to untangle a global chaos they had created. The summit was convened to terminate the virulent Seven Years' War that had raged for eight years over three continents, but it became an imperial reordering of unparalleled scale. Humbled by a series of defeats, France ceded all its possessions in North America and saw its American empire reduced to a few sugar islands in the Lesser Antilles, tiny fishing bases off Newfoundland, and a foothold in Guyana. Britain, whose army and fleet had scored victories from Manila to Montreal, won Canada, Grenada, and Senegal, emerging as the world's paramount colonial empire. Spain, a late arrival to the war, had suffered one humiliating loss after another as France's ally, but two interlinked transactions allowed it to actually expand its imperial presence in North America. It ceded Florida to Britain in Paris but balanced that loss with the 1762 Treaty of Fontainebleau in which Spain gained Louisiana from Louis XV, who was eager to get rid of the money-draining colony. And so, with a few casual incisions of diplomatic surgery, North America received a new imperial face. New France was stamped out, British dominion expanded to the north, south, and west, and the Spanish frontier leaped eastward. The complex colonial collage of old was replaced with a symmetrical division into British East and Spanish West along the Mississippi watershed.

The Treaty of Paris reconfigured the global balance of power and streamlined colonial North America, but its makers suffered from a striking tunnel vision. Acknowledging only claims to land of European nation-states, they utterly ignored the realities of indigenous power on the ground. The Indian nations in the Great Lakes region and the Ohio Country bitterly objected to the new order, insisting that the French had no right to give Britain lands that were under Indian control. The British then provoked a massive pan-Indian uprising, Pontiac's War, by claiming possession to the entire eastern half of North America, by treating Indians as conquered subjects, and by building unauthorized forts on their lands.[1]

A similar neglect and disregard of Native presence and power took place in the Southwest, where Spain won vast paper claims to the interior. At the same time that Britain and France had won and lost enormous colonial claims across North America during the French and Indian War, Comanches had completed their own sweeping campaign of conquest, which by the early 1760s made them the masters of the entire western Great Plains south of the Arkansas River. When Louis XV surrendered Louisiana to Carlos III in 1762, the transfer was, in effect, imaginary. By European reasoning, the treaty gave Spain all lands between the Mississippi valley and the Río Grande, but the real Spanish possessions formed a mere edging to a much larger geopolitical entity, Comanchería, which stretched six hundred miles north of Texas and four hundred miles east of New Mexico.

Ignoring that reality—as well as the warnings marqués de Rubí and other frontier officials had made about the rising Comanche power—Spanish policymakers set out to create a cohesive colonial domain out of their suddenly swollen North American possessions. Embellishing their frontier policy with French-styled strategies, they moved to pacify and ultimately absorb the *indios bárbaros* of the interior plains through treaties and trade.[2] But because Spanish officials failed to take cognizance of the Comanche ascendancy, their attempts were destined to fail. Ignored and massively underestimated, Comanches continued their decades-long expansion, but with a new set of ambitions. If earlier their aim had been to colonize the game-rich grasslands of the southern Great Plains, they now moved to bend the bordering regions—New Mexico, Texas, the lower Mississippi valley, and the northern Great Plains—to their own uses. By the late 1770s, less than two decades after the Treaty of Paris, Spain's imperial system in North America had become hollow. Rather than New Spain absorbing the southern plains into its imperial body, Comanches had reduced the Spanish borderlands to a hinterland for an imperial system of their own.

In 1762, the year Spain won the vast territory between the Mississippi valley and the Río Grande in the Treaty of Fontainebleau, the Spanish kingdom of New Mexico entered into treaty relations with the Yamparikas, Jupes, and Kotsotekas, who formed the powerful western branch of the Comanche nation. In Spanish minds, the treaties complemented one another perfectly. The Treaty of Fontainebleau granted Spain a nominal claim over North America's lower midsection, while the Comanche treaty turned the people who occupied those lands into Spain's loyal allies. New Mexico Governor Tomás Vélez de Cachupín, the

Spanish signatory of the Comanche treaty, succinctly articulated the Spanish interpretation: the accord had attached the Comanches to the Spanish empire as the king's compliant vassals.[3]

Such optimism was not unwarranted. France's expulsion ended French contraband trade and political scheming on the southern plains, giving Spain more sway over the region and its Native inhabitants. Moreover, New Mexico was now western Comanches' only reliable source of European goods, and Spanish policymakers had a reason to expect dependence to translate into compliance. That compliance was the key to Spain's imperial ambitions. There were no Spanish settlements on the interior grasslands, but if Spanish authorities could command the western Comanches, they could also claim control over the vast southern plains. In Spanish designs, the Comanches were masters of the southern plains and the Spaniards were masters of the Comanches.

But that grand imperial vision was founded on an illusion, for the assumption of Comanche compliance proved premature. Comanches had entered the 1762 treaty expecting Spanish presents and protection, but they rejected all restrictions on their autonomy and kept seeking trade and allies anywhere they could. And so instead of welding themselves to New Mexico as subordinates, western Comanches launched in the late 1760s a vigorous diplomatic and commercial expansion on the Great Plains, forging a far-reaching trade and alliance network that in time dwarfed Spain's imperial arrangements in mid-North America. Sustained by their growing wealth and power, Comanches yanked themselves free from New Mexico's economic grip and then went to war.

This reorientation of Comanche foreign policy rested on the geostrategic centrality of the upper Arkansas basin, the heart of early Comanchería. A superb hunting niche framed by two major agricultural spheres—the Río Grande valley and the southern prairies—the upper Arkansas was primed for commercial prominence. Comanches had capitalized on the Arkansas' centrality since the 1740s, when they forged exchange ties with the Taovayas and the French in the east. From the 1760s on, however, Comanches increasingly focused their commercial activities to the northern and central plains, where the diffusion of horses had opened fresh commercial opportunities.

The spread of the horse frontier across the Great Plains revealed yet another natural advantage of the upper Arkansas basin: it marked the northern limit for intensive horse husbandry on the continental grasslands. The climate became increasingly adverse for horses above the Arkansas, turning noticeably harsher north of the Platte River and outright hostile above the Missouri. The long and cold northern winters took a heavy toll on foals and pregnant mares, and the vicious blizzards could literally freeze entire herds on their hooves. Such hardships kept most northern tribes chronically horse-poor: only a few groups beyond the Arkansas valley managed to acquire enough animals to meet basic hunting and transportation needs. To the south of the Arkansas, however, winters were considerably milder, posing few limitations on animal husbandry. This meant that western Comanches could raise horses with relative ease and then export them to a vast perennial deficit region—a prerogative that gave them trading power that was rivaled on the plains only by the Mandans' and Hidatsas' celebrated trading villages on the middle Missouri River.[4]

As the various Native groups on the central and northern plains acquired their first horses around midcentury, they quickly began to look south to Comanchería to build up their herds. In the course of the 1760s and 1770s, western Comanches incorporated many of those groups into an expanding exchange circle. They opened trade relations with the Pawnees, Cheyennes, and Kiowas, who ranged on the western plains between the Arkansas River and the Black Hills, and with the Ponca, Kansa, and Iowa farmers along the lower Missouri, Kansas, and Des Moines rivers. Recent converts to equestrianism, all these groups coveted horses and were willing to travel hundreds of miles to the Arkansas valley to obtain them. They incorporated these trade journeys into their semiannual hunting expeditions, traveling along established trails that led from the Republican and Kansas rivers to the Great Bend of the Arkansas, which was only a few days' journey away from the Big Timbers, the favorite camping ground of western Comanches.[5]

While extending their commercial reach onto the northern plains, western Comanches continued to trade actively on their other fronts. They visited the Taos fairs and restored the ties with the Wichitas that had been severed in 1757 when the Taovayas fled from the Arkansas River. Now traveling to western Comanchería from their new villages on the middle Red and Brazos rivers, Taovayas traded garden produce as well as high-quality guns, which they obtained from wide-ranging British contraband traders operating out of the numerous British posts that emerged on the east bank of the Mississippi after 1763. As a dramatic example of the volume of this trade, a Taovaya trading party sold seventeen horseloads of guns to western Comanches in a single transaction in 1768. The three-way commerce among Comanches, Taovayas, and British thrived well into the 1770s. According to a 1776 Spanish account, western Comanches received quantities of rifles, pistols, munitions, iron hatchets, and metal utensils from Taovayas, who in turn acquired these goods from the lower Mississippi valley. Comanches also traded with Spanish Louisiana's French merchants who took advantage of the colony's weak border controls and kept venturing to the far western plains. One exasperated Spanish observer reported in the late 1760s how "the French come into their [western Comanches] rancherías and live there for years."[6]

Over the course of the 1760s and 1770s, western Comanches turned the upper Arkansas valley into the nodal point of a multifaceted commercial network that linked together numerous peoples and markets. Absorbing trade from several distinctive economic and ecological regions, they built an exceptionally comprehensive import structure. In exchange for horses and mules, they received manufactured goods—guns, powder, ammunition, spearpoints, knives, kettles, and textiles—from five colonial markets: from British Canada by way of the Mandan and Hidatsa villages and Pawnee and Cheyenne middlemen; from Illinois (or Spanish Upper Louisiana) via Kansa, Ponca, Iowa, and Kiowa intermediaries; from Spanish Lower Louisiana and British West Florida through itinerant Franco-Spanish merchants or the Taovayas; and from Spanish New Mexico by way of Taos. Intertwined in this trade in livestock and manufactured goods was an active commerce in locally produced subsistence goods. Pueblos, Wichitas, Pawnees, Poncas, Kansas, and Iowas all traded in maize, beans, and squash in exchange for Comanches' luxurious, high-quality bison robes and hides.[7]

The rise of the western Comanche trade center in the upper Arkansas basin marked a profound change in the commercial architecture on the Great Plains and in the Southwest. Until the mid-eighteenth century, major arteries of long-distance commerce were latitudinal, running from the farming villages of the eastern tallgrass prairies to the bison hunters' realm on the western shortgrass steppes, and from there to the Rockies and beyond. This began to change with the rise of the upper Arkansas basin as the main redistribution point of horses from the Southwest to the central and northern plains. Commerce was realigned along a south-north axis and repositioned around two gravitational points: the Mandan and Hidatsa villages on the middle Missouri River and the western Comanche rancherías on the upper Arkansas. When Estevan Rodriguez Miró, the acting governor of Louisiana, in 1785 collected the accumulated Spanish knowledge of Indian nations of the interior, he noted this realignment: "all the wealth of the Indians on the Missouri consists in having many horses which they get from the Laytanes [Comanches]."[8]

Out of this restructured commercial geography other important changes emanated. One was a shift in the Native American arms race that was escalating on the Great Plains. Initially, in the early eighteenth century, Comanches had been largely cut off from the burgeoning trade in European weaponry in the continent's center. Large quantities of guns, lead, and metalware flowed onto the grasslands from the north and east, from the French and British outposts in

Canada and the Mississippi valley. In contrast, the Spaniards in New Mexico and Texas were reluctant to sell guns to Indians, fearing that those weapons might be turned against themselves if the Natives allied with France or Britain for an attack against Spanish colonies. This disparity in the patterns of diffusion gave the northern and eastern plains tribes a decisive military edge—something that Comanches painfully learned in their early wars with the Pawnees and Osages. But the rise of the upper Arkansas trade center allowed western Comanches to break free from the gun embargo. By channeling vast numbers of horses to the northern and eastern Great Plains, they managed to create a substantial inflow of firearms. Alarmed Spanish officials reported as early as 1767 that the western Comanches were better armed than Spanish troops.[9]

Before long, in fact, western Comanches accumulated such quantities of guns and other manufactured goods that they could start exporting them. Domingo Cabello y Robles, governor of Texas, reported in the 1780s that western Comanches sold guns, powder, balls, lances, cloth, pans, and large knives to their eastern relatives on the Texas plains, who in turn supplied western Comanches with horses and mules, some of which were then traded to Wichitas, Pawnees, Cheyennes, Kiowas, Kansas, and Iowas. Moreover, in a reversal of the typical roles of colonial trade, western Comanches started to sell guns and other manufactures to Spanish New Mexico. Such a trade was first mentioned in 1760 by Bishop Pedro Tamarón y Romeral who wrote that Comanches sold muskets, shotguns, munitions, and knives at Taos. Fifteen years later the trade had become a routine. When visiting the town's summer fair in 1776, Fray Francisco Atanasio Domínguez was struck by Comanches' export stock, which included tin pots, hatchets, shot, powder, pistols, and "good guns." The gun trade, Domínguez noted, had become established enough to be based on fixed rates: "If they sell a pistol, its price is a bridle." In exchange for the precious manufactured items, Comanches received special equestrian and hunting gear, such as bridles and *belduques*, broad butchering knives, which were available only in New Mexico. Western Comanches, it seems, were creating a multilevel commodity flow that furnished them with imported staples, such as maize and horses, as well as with more specialized manufactured products.[10]

But the inverse trade in guns and other European commodities only hints at a much more profound shift in Comanche-Spanish relations: western Comanchería had began to replace New Mexico as the paramount economic, political, and military power center in the Southwest.

The embryonic common ground of political and cultural accommodation that New Mexico Governor Tomás Vélez de Cachupín and western Comanche chiefs had cultivated after the 1762 treaty crumbled almost immediately after 1767, when Cachupín left office. The change in Comanche-Spanish relations could hardly have been more drastic: during the decade that followed, Comanches lashed New Mexico with more than a hundred attacks,[11] turning the Río Grande valley into one of the most violent places in early America. Mixing small hit-and-run guerrilla raids with massive destroy-and-plunder operations, they killed and captured hundreds of settlers, stole thousands of horses and mules, slaughtered countless sheep and cattle, and left dozens of villages burned and abandoned. When Pedro Fermín de Mendinueta, Cachupín's unfortunate successor, retired in 1777, New Mexico was a broken colony.

To an extent, Spaniards had themselves to blame for the turmoil. Governor Mendinueta lacked his predecessor's political instincts and diplomatic proficiency and ignored the social and political protocols that were critical for maintaining peace with the Comanches. Mendinueta also failed to carry on Cachupín's successful maneuvering among New Mexico's neighboring Indian nations. Eager to pacify the colony's southern border and safeguard the Chihuahua Trail, the umbilical cord that linked New Mexico to central Mexico by way of Chihuahua, he focused his energies on forging an alliance with the Natagé and Sierra Blanca Apaches, letting the all-important personal ties to Comanche leadership corrode. A mere year into his tenure, Mendinueta had lost touch with Comanches and was beginning to question their "reliability." Fearing that Comanche war parties might invade the heart of New Mexico from the north, through "the weak frontier of Ojo Caliente," he stationed fifty troops on the San Antonio Mountains, fifteen miles north of Abiquiu and twenty-five miles southwest of Taos. It was an ill-calculated move that alienated the Comanches further. The troops threatened Comanches' access to Ojo Caliente fairs, where they had traded since the 1730s, and undercut northern New Mexico's status as an open realm that could be entered and exited unhindered.[12]

A climatic shift in the early 1770s inflamed the already volatile situation. In spring 1771, after three years of escalating raiding, Mendinueta succeeded in negotiating a truce with the western Comanches, securing New Mexico a much needed respite. But then a severe drought struck the Southwest, taking a heavy toll on New Mexico and straining the delicate peace. As the rains failed and crops died, Pueblo farmers grew reluctant to share their dwindling stores with the Comanches, which in turn triggered one of the oldest dynamics of hunter-farmer relations in the Southwest: unable to get what they needed through barter, Comanches relied on plunder. Mendinueta's truce did not last beyond the first dry months in the summer of 1772.[13]

But the most compelling impulses fueling Comanches' raiding in New Mexico stemmed from their commercial ascendancy on the plains. It was not a coincidence that the raiding war erupted at the same time as the western Comanches turned the upper Arkansas basin into a major trading point to the north. The seemingly limitless horse markets on the northern plains created an almost insatiable demand for southern horses—a demand western Comanches tried to meet almost single-handedly with stolen New Mexican stock. Moreover, the new trading allies supplied Comanches with a range of European commodities, lessening their reliance on New Mexico's markets and allowing them to raid the colony without fearing Spain's commercial sanctions.

Comanche raids on Spanish and Pueblo Indian horse herds in the late 1760s and 1770s generated the first of many wholesale property transfers that marked the Comanche-colonial relations into the mid-nineteenth century. In 1757, according to an official census, New Mexico possessed more than seven thousand horses, but by the mid-1770s Comanche raiders had moved the bulk of that animal wealth into their own camps and market circuits. In 1775 Mendinueta reported that New Mexico did not have enough horses for effective defense, pleading with the viceroy to send fifteen hundred animals from Nueva Vizcaya, lest "desolation will follow." A royal council in Mexico City promptly granted the request, but for unknown reasons the viceroy failed to deliver the animals. A year later New Mexican troops were deemed "useless" as they did not have enough horses to mount even token retaliatory expeditions.[14]

Meanwhile, horses proliferated in Comanchería. In the 1770s and 1780s many western Comanche rancherías possessed more than two horses per capita, which indicates a substantial surplus, since plains nomads needed only an average of one horse per capita for basic hunting and transportation needs. For example, a western Comanche family of eight needed one or two running horses for hunting and warfare, three to five riding animals for women and children, and two or three pack horses to move the tipi and other belongings. Such a family was likely to have possessed approximately eight extra animals that could be traded away at any time.[15]

The burgeoning horse wealth enhanced western Comanches' trading power, but it also gave them yet another reason to raid New Mexico—captive seizure. The rapidly growing horse herds, together with probable negative demographic effects of the drought years, increased the demand for imported labor in Comanchería. Since most Apache villages had retreated below the Río Grande and beyond easy reach from Comanchería, Comanches turned on New Mexico. The Comanche–New Mexico border became a slaving frontier. In many of their recorded attacks on New Mexico, Comanches took or tried to take captives, usually women and children working in fields or tending livestock. Some of these captives were returned to New Mexico for ransom—Spanish bureaucracy established in 1780 a formal *limosna* (alms) fund to facilitate such rescues—and some were sold to the Wichitas, Pawnees, and French. But Comanches also absorbed large numbers of captives into their workforce as horse herders and hide processors, thereby initiating a process that in the early nineteenth century would see the emergence of a large-scale slave economy in Comanchería.[16]

By the late 1770s, New Mexico began disintegrating under the weight of Comanche violence. The combined effect of raids and drought sapped the colony's energy, pushing it into a steep decline. In 1766 Nicolás de Lafora, the engineer of the marqués de Rubí expedition, had envisioned New Mexico as an "impenetrable barrier" against hostile Indians, but only a decade later this strongest of Spain's North American colonies had been reduced to a captive territory, where horseless troops watched in passive frustration as Comanche raiders destroyed towns and drained ranches, and where impoverished settlers subsisted on roasted hides, old shoes, and "the vellum from the saddletrees." Age-old settlement patterns broke down as violence and horror uprooted families and entire communities. In 1776, with Comanches storming into the colony "by all routes," New Mexicans lived "in such a state of terror that they sow their lands like transients and keep going and coming to the place where they can live in less fear." But finding such places was virtually impossible amidst the shifting coordinates of terror: in 1777 and 1778 alone, Comanches killed or captured almost two hundred New Mexicans.[17]

Over time, as communities dispersed and disappeared, large sections of New Mexico were left desolate. Along a hundred-mile stretch of the Río Grande valley numerous farms and villages vanished as panicked *pobladores* (settlers) sought refuge in Taos, Santa Fe, and Albuquerque. The situation was especially critical in an area bounded by Picurís, Ojo Caliente, Nambé, and Santa Clara. Using the Ojo Caliente valley as an entryway, Comanches hit this prosperous region with incessant attacks. The fifty troops Governor Mendinueta had stationed near Abiquiu proved wholly inadequate, leaving the region's mixed-descent communities "exposed to the sacrifice of inhumanity and fury of the enemies." Settlers began to flee the region, stirring alarm in Santa Fe. Fearing that the heart of northern New Mexico would become vacant, Mendinueta ordered the settlers to reoccupy and rebuild the villages or have their lands confiscated. That threat, spiced with admonitions of the fleeing settlers as "pusillanimous and cowards," had little effect. Settlers continued to pour out, risking losing their lands or simply relinquishing their titles. One of them, Diego Gomes, offered what was a common reason: five of his relatives had been killed in "his presence" and "he was not able to prevent it." By the late 1770s, the entire region between the Río de Ojo Caliente and Río Grande lay deserted, "destroyed by hostile Comanches" as a Spanish map explained. On the eastern side of the Río Grande, the outlying Las Trampas de Taos, Las Truchas, and Chimayó were repeatedly abandoned and resettled, which crippled the local economy. Picurís stood "isolated and therefore indefensible against the continuous incursions which the Comanche enemy is making."

Another zone of intense raiding emerged farther south, covering central New Mexico from Pecos in the east to Jémez in the west and to Tomé in the south. As in the north, Comanche raiders were after horses, captives, and food, but here strategic considerations gave their forays added intensity: Pecos, Albuquerque, and other central New Mexican towns still maintained political and commercial ties with Jicarillas, Carlanas, and other Apache groups, thus provoking aggressive assaults. Worse still, Comanches were not the only Indians raiding central New Mexico. While Comanches pushed in from the east and northeast, Mimbreño Apaches and the allied Gileños and Navajos invaded the region from the northwest, west, and southwest.[18]

Besieged by Indian enemies, central New Mexico began to cave in. In 1779, according to a Spanish map, *frontera y entradas de los enemigos Cumanchis*, "the frontier and entrances of enemy Comanches," extended to Pecos and Galisteo, exposing the heart of New Mexico to plundering. Small villages were next to defenseless. A single raid on Tomé, apparently provoked by the refusal of one of its citizens to give up his daughter to a Comanche chief, nearly stripped the village of its male inhabitants. But not even the bigger fortified villages could escape devastation. Pecos, the colony's eastern stronghold, was cramped and claustrophobic. The village was surrounded by fertile farmlands "in all the four principal directions," but as Fray Domínguez reported in 1776, the fields "are of no use today because this pueblo is so very much besieged by the enemy." The settlers tried to raise corn in small dry-land fields near the town walls, but the drought kept their harvests poor. "What few crops there usually are do not last even to the beginning of a new year from the previous October," Domínguez wrote, "and hence these miserable wretches are tossed about like a ball in the hands of fortune." A bastion of nearly one thousand people in the early eighteenth century, Pecos was reduced by 1776 to a hamlet of one hundred families, a dozen horses, and eight cows. A few years later only eighty-four families remained.[19]

Nearby Galisteo faded even faster. "Most of the year," Domínguez wrote, the war-weary and drought-ravaged inhabitants "are away from home, now the men alone, now the women alone, sometimes the husband in one place, his wife in another, the children in still another, and so it all goes. Comanche enemies and great famine because of the droughts are the captains who compel them to drag out their existence in this way. The former have deprived many of them of their lives and all of them of their landed property. The latter drives them to depart." Eighty families had called Galisteo home in 1760, but sixteen years later only forty-one families remained, trying to eke out a living without a single horse or cow. Fatally crippled, the village vanished from census records in the early 1780s.[20]

Spain's response to this devastation was conspicuously weak. Comanches' two raiding spheres were separated by a relatively peaceful twenty-mile belt, and at the center of that belt stood Santa Fe, its garrison utterly incapable of repressing the escalating violence. The Governor's Palace simply kept a toll of the mounting damage around it, and its grotesque imperial décor—strings of dried enemy Indian ears hanging in its portal—now mocked Spain's pretensions of dominance over indigenous communities. For the more than one hundred raids Comanches launched on New Mexico in the late 1760s and 1770s, Santa Fe dispatched only sporadic punitive expeditions into Comanchería, and only once, in 1774, did they manage to inflict major damage.[21]

In September of that year six hundred presidial and militia troops led by an experienced frontier officer, Captain Carlos Fernández, surprised and surrounded a large Comanche ranchería in a wooded enclosure 125 miles from Santa Fe. What followed was an orgiastic outburst of revenge and looting. The troops "poured in an unremitting fire to destroy" the cornered Comanche camp. "As shot and shell has no respect for sex or age," Mendinueta later reported, they killed nearly three hundred men, women, and children. The Spaniards took more than one hundred captives and confiscated "a thousand beasts of burden of all kinds," which were promptly "divided among those present, who also took possession of the tipis and the rest of the spoils of the enemy." The captives, as Mendinueta explained, were "maintained in accord with what was ordered by His Majesty in his new royal regulation." For adult men, this probably meant slavery in Mexican mines or Caribbean plantations, while the women and children were likely turned over to missionaries for religious instruction and later adopted into Spanish households as servants. But Comanches' ability to absorb losses was greater than Spain's ability to inflict them, and the battle had no effect on the larger balance of power. As Viceroy Antonio María de Bucareli reported only a year later, "the barbarous Comanches appear to overcome the injuries received. . . . In place of teaching them lessons, the punishment can have exasperated them and thus be the motivating reason for their uniting to seek the vengeance to which they are accustomed."[22]

Spain's failure to ward off the Comanches stemmed from a number of weak-

3. Southern plains and Southwest in the 1770s and early 1780s. Map by Bill Nelson.

nesses, some of them inbuilt, some inflicted by the Comanches. During the 1770s much of northern New Spain below the Río Grande became a battle zone, where Spanish soldiers waged a losing war against several loosely allied Apache tribes, many of them refugees of the Comanche wars. Having turned raiding into a profitable economy, Apaches pilfered horses, cattle, and captives and destroyed towns, haciendas, ranches, farms, and mines from Sonora to southern Texas. The turmoil stretched the resources of New Spain to the limit, undermining its ability to sustain the northern provinces. Desperately underfunded, New Mexico was left to fight the well-armed Comanches with some 100 presidial troops, 600 guns, and 150 pistols. Most settlers could not afford to buy powder and shot. To protect the exposed colony, Governor Mendinueta urged his subjects to consolidate in larger and more compact and defensible communities and pleaded with Mexico City to authorize a new presidio near Taos. Both attempts failed. The wealthier settlers refused to congregate near or within towns, clinging to the Hispanic tradition of living close to their fields, and the Taos presidio conflicted with the new policy of military retrenchment recommended by marqués de Rubí.[23]

In 1779, Bernardo de Miera y Pacheco was ordered to prepare a map showing the New Mexican settlements "in their present condition." The picture was bleak. Miera y Pacheco added to his map a long legend, part of which reads as follows: "[the villages are] extremely ill arranged, with the houses of the settlers of whom they are composed scattered about a distance from one another. Many evils, disasters, and destruction of towns, caused by the Comanche and Apache enemies who surround said province, killing and abducting many families, have originated from this poor arrangement." That decentralized layout—which both reflected and facilitated Comanche raids—also caught the eye of Fray Juan Augustín de Morfí, who assessed New Mexico's military and economic condition in the closing years of the 1770s. Morfí reported widespread destruction and depopulation in eight districts. Only the more compact Santa Fe had escaped devastation, but the capital had become a veritable refugee center as fear cleared the countryside: it "comprised two hundred and seventy-four families with one thousand nine hundred and fifteen souls of all ages, sexes, and conditions, having been augmented progressively by the settlers at the cost of the depopulating frontier where the workers, not being able to withstand the invasions, abandoned the ranches where they were cultivating and took refuge in the capital."[24]

By the seventh year of his term, writing despairing reports to his superiors seems to have become a numbing routine for Governor Mendinueta. In a letter to Viceroy Bucareli, dated September 30, 1774, he described in a blunt, methodological manner the latest Comanche raiding spree in the province.[25] There had been five raids during the previous eight weeks. The first had occurred on June 22 when Comanches killed two Indians near Picurís, and in the next attack on the following day Comanches ran off the horse herd of Nambé pueblo. A more destructive raid took place on July 27 when a massive force of "more than one thousand Comanches" invaded the Chama district, "reaching as far as the pueblos of Santa Clara, San Juan, and three other districts of Spaniards." Comanches killed seven people, took three captives, slaughtered twenty-five head of cattle, and stole more than three hundred horses during this wide-ranging raid. On August 15, some one hundred Comanches attacked Pecos, killing seven men and two women and carrying off seven captives, "all of whom were working in their maize fields." One hundred fourteen militia and presidial troops and Indian auxiliaries rode out from Santa Fe, surprising a large Comanche ranchería some 150 miles east of the capital. They kept the Comanches under siege and fire "until the evening prayer, when they retired in such good order that the enemy did not dare to molest them." The last Comanche raid of the summer, possibly a retaliation, followed three days later when one hundred warriors struck Albuquerque, killing five, capturing four, stealing "a body of horses," and slaughtering four hundred sheep.

Mendinueta listed the attacks, death tolls, and material losses in almost detached detail, noting with grim relief that "the barbarians" "killed only seven of our people" in one of the raids, but the most curious part of his report is a brief remark at the end: "On the 27th of the month of June, sixty groups of this same nation [Comanches] entered the pueblo of Taos in peace, and, during the trading, they ransomed six Indians, male and female, and traded some one hundred and forty animals, two guns, and a large quantity of meat and salt." Again, what is striking about the remark is its matter-of-fact tone. The governor expresses no surprise over the fact that Comanches, in the midst of the devastating raiding spree, would conduct peaceful trade at Taos.

By the mid-1770s, in fact, such blending of violence and trade had become commonplace on the New Mexico–Comanche border. Two years earlier, for example, Comanches had raided Picurís five and Galisteo four times, besieged Pecos with five hundred warriors, and scorched maize fields around Ojo Caliente. Yet, as Mendinueta reported, they "did not find it inconvenient to present themselves peacefully at Taos" and barter for "bridles, awls, knives, colored cloth, and maize." Similarly, during a five-month period in the winter of 1771–72, Comanches carried out six raids in northern New Mexico and sent six trade convoys to Taos, sometimes arriving to the fairs only a few days after attacking other towns. Sometimes the raiding and trading parties arrived in chorus, convincing Mendinueta that they were part of a "crafty stratagem." On May 31, 1768, six Comanche chiefs rode to Taos carrying a white flag and announcing that a larger party would come to the pueblo on June 2 with a captive to ransom. On that day four hundred Comanches did indeed arrive in Taos where they "were provided with muskets and munitions." But Comanches had also "dispatched one hundred men to attack Ojo Caliente, confident that, at the news of peace and trade they had announced at Taos, the people [of Ojo Caliente] would attend" the Taos fair. Only a propitious intervention by Spanish troops saved the village from attack.[26]

This policy of alternating raiding and trading marks the beginning of Comanches' cultural ascendancy over New Mexico. Capitalizing on their military superiority, Comanches divided the colony into distinct zones where they could simultaneously plunder horses, mules, and captives; purchase maize and other commodities that were difficult to obtain through raiding; and circulate stolen New Mexican goods for profit. More abstractly, this raiding-and-trading strategy epitomizes how New Mexico fell captive to alien cultural rules. Like most North American Indians, Comanches understood hostile and friendly acts differently from Europeans. They saw trade and theft not as mutually exclusive acts but as two expressions of a broad continuum of reciprocity. Raiding, when not aimed at killing, was not the antithesis of exchange but an alternative to it, a culturally sanctioned way to circulate material goods when peaceful exchange was not an option. Whenever a group failed to trade sufficient amounts of goods to its allies—whether due to internal problems or environmental reversals—those allies could carry out periodic raids without canceling the partnership.

This kind of fluidity had defined intergroup relations in the Southwest for centuries, and Comanches' raiding-and-trading policy is best seen as an elaboration of this ancient theme. In the 1760s and 1770s New Mexicans struggled with a number of hardships—Navajo and Apache attacks, drought, and overall economic stagnation—that undermined their ability to carry out trade. Comanches, by contrast, were experiencing sustained economic growth and needed horses to fuel their burgeoning trade. From their standpoint, the expected and accepted response to such a situation was to rely on theft in order to ensure continuous circulation of goods.[27]

Such logic was alien to Spaniards who saw trade and theft as mutually exclusive acts that canceled one another out. The thriving trade between Comanches and Taoseños in the midst of escalating violence represented therefore an acute embarrassment to Spanish officials, who had been assigned to keep New Mexico unified and intact. Not only were they unable to defend the frontier against "barbarous onslaughts," they could not even prevent their own subjects from interacting with the enemy who was slowly consuming the colony. Against the bloody background that was the New Mexican frontier, the Taos fairs seemed like a perverse display of Comanches' cultural supremacy and Spaniards' degeneration into savage decadence. By simply allowing the trade to continue, New Mexico seemed to be succumbing to an alien cultural order.

Comanches' raiding-and-trading policy violated the basic tenet of the Spanish imperial project, the notion that New Spain constituted a single, undivided colonial realm. Comanches, it seems, conceived Taos not as part of the larger Spanish-controlled New Mexico but as a separate community following autonomous policies. After all, except for one violent episode in 1761, Taoseños had nurtured their relations with Comanchería for generations, remaining neutral in the recurrent wars that erupted between Spaniards and Comanches. Such a behavior was a compelling sign of loyalty and affinity to Comanches, who determined group identity not by race or law but through the behavior of flesh-and-blood human beings. Some Spaniards, too, saw Taos as a virtual Comanche satellite. Rumors of an anti-Spanish Taoseño-Comanche coalition, first heard in the late 1740s, resurfaced in the troubled 1770s. Taos had incorporated the surrounding Hispanic settlers, who sought protection in the pueblo from Comanche raids, but that had little effect on the town's loyalties. Mendinueta complained how the Comanches who visited Taos for trade could easily "learn our decisions," while others scolded the Taoseños' willingness to cater to Comanche trade customs (there was no bargaining over prices, which were fixed). Visitors deplored the widespread popularity of the Comanche language in northeastern New Mexico and abhorred the *pobladores*' coarse Spanish, lewdness, and propensity to go about nude—in European imagination a telltale sign of savage degeneration.[28]

It was therefore with considerable unease that Mendinueta tried to explain to his superiors New Mexico's peculiar relationship with the Comanches. His 1771 letter to Viceroy Bucareli was uncharacteristically emotional:

> The alternate actions of this nation at the same time, now peace, now war, demonstrate their accustomed faithlessness. . . . Since it is impossible to . . . limit their freedom so that they do not do as they fancy, I have adopted the policy of admitting them to peace whenever they ask for it and come with their trade goods and of waging war whenever they assault our frontiers and commit plunder. From war alone, all that results is loss of life and property, but from the alternate this poor citizenry gains some good, as occurred at the last two fairs, or *rescates*. . . . Indeed at little cost they brought nearly 200 horses and mules, 12 muskets with ammunition, and a considerable number of buffalo hides, essential in this kingdom and profitable to trade in Nueva Vizcaya, as well as some Indian captives who are added to the body of Our Holy Faith.[29]

While emphasizing Comanches' "accustomed faithlessness" and New Mexico's inability to "limit their freedom," Mendinueta's report also reveals a more fundamental reason behind his decision to allow Comanche enemies to trade in New Mexico: he could and would not cancel the trade because New Mexico needed it for its very survival. Mendinueta himself admitted as much in 1769, when he wrote that Comanche fairs were the lifeline that protected New Mexico from economic collapse. Mendinueta wrote this at a time when a clash between Comanches and Spanish troops had temporarily interrupted Comanche trade in Taos. Poverty and distress spread immediately across northern New Mexico, forcing the governor to admit that the only solution was to reopen trade with Comanches.[30]

This is a startling concession from a high-ranking Spanish official that not only betrays New Mexico's humiliating dependence on Comanche commerce but also reveals the colonists' deeply conflicted attitude toward the Comanches themselves. Similar ambivalence perturbed Fray Domínguez who in 1776 deplored the "barbarity," "insolence," and "execrable extreme of evil" of Comanches while in the same breath marveling at the assortment of goods those "indomitable beasts" brought to Taos markets. There were "guns, pistols, powder, balls, tobacco, hatchets, and some vessels of yellow tin" as well as "buffalo hides, 'white elkskins,' horses, mules, buffalo meat, pagan Indians (of both sexes, children and adults) whom they capture from other nations." This was in fact nearly an exhaustive list of the imports New Mexicans needed and desired but could not obtain through New Spain's imperial supply lines. Not surprisingly, the fairs were extremely popular, reminding Domínguez of "a second-hand market in Mexico, the way people mill about." In 1776 so many New Mexican merchants attended the Taos fair that the governor was forced to halt government operations until they had returned to their home villages.[31]

On the face of it, New Mexico's dependence on Comanche commerce stemmed from the colony's inbuilt economic handicaps—its relative marginality in Spain's Caribbean-centered imperial system and its isolation from Atlantic trade channels. After more than a century of slave traffic, New Mexico's Spanish elite had also come to rely on a steady importation of Indian captives, who ran their kitchens, tilled their fields, tended their animals, and met their sexual needs. In 1776, when Comanche raids had nearly depleted the colony's horse and mule reserves, New Mexicans were still willing to pay Comanches "a she-mule and a scarlet cover" or "two good horses" for the most valuable human commodity, "an Indian girl from twelve to twenty years old."[32] More immediately, however, the dependence was a product of Comanche policies. Comanches not only exploited New Mexico's economic weakness but actively exacerbated it to their own advantage. The relentless raids in the 1760s and 1770s served a double function: they supplied Comanches' economy with plunder while stimulating artificial demand for their exports in New Mexico.

The stealing and selling of horses was central to this dynamic of simultaneous exchange and exploitation. As Comanches depleted New Mexico's domestic herds during the 1770s, they also embarked on an active horse and mule trade in Taos, often selling the villagers the very animals they had pilfered elsewhere in New Mexico. It soon became a large-scale business: the aforementioned 1774 transaction of 140 horses, for example, amounted to almost 10 percent of the 1,500 horses Governor Mendinueta would ask for the next year to restock New Mexico's wasted herds. Comanches used strategic violence to create demand for other exports as well. They drove back New Mexican hunting parties from the plains and slaughtered cattle and sheep, depriving the province of animal protein and robes; they torched pastures and fields and destroyed irrigation systems and crop caches across New Mexico, disrupting the traditional agricultural cycle. "The land is fertile," Fray Morfí noted in 1778 of the Albuquerque district, "although it does not produce what it could because of insufficient cultivation for lack of oxen and leisure, the [threat of] enemies not permitting them to absent themselves from the villages for various tasks. Thus the land lies fallow." The raids were particularly hard on the widely dispersed Hispanic ranches and farms. Morfí remarked how the Hispanic settlers "dare not go out and work the land, or if they do, they become victims of their indolence, because the swiftness and daring of their enemy [allows them to] penetrate the villages at will, due to their disorderly layout."[33]

Comanches thus had New Mexico in an economic stranglehold, which, together with the prolonged drought, brought the colony's subsistence system near collapse, triggering periodic bouts of starvation. That devastation in turn ensured that Comanches could use the colony as a market outlet for their surplus bison products and, conversely, maintain a steady inflow of crucial commodities from the impoverished New Mexicans whose only way to fend off cold and starvation was often to barter some of their meager possessions—horses, mules, metal, even maize—for Comanches' bison meat, fat, robes, and hides. Just how dependent New Mexico had become on Comanches' meat and hides dawned on Juan Bautista de Anza, Mendinueta's successor, in 1780 when he tried to persuade his subjects to support the construction of a supply line to Chihuahua City. The settlers, Anza reported to the viceroy, "are resolved not to form a cordon to cooperate because the present year does not fall in with the formal trading for hides with the pagans, carried on every two years. This affair stimulates and makes up the largest part of the trade in this province."[34]

Seemingly haphazard, the strategy of slotting peaceful exchanges between nearly constant raiding was highly sophisticated, allowing Comanches to simultaneously plunder and purchase New Mexico's resources and push their own products on the colony. It was an exploitative, essentially colonial relationship, the essence of which was captured by the ever-candid Fray Domínguez in an offhand remark: "Whether they are at peace or at war, the Comanches always carry off all they want, by purchase in peace and by theft in war." The painful and ambiguous relationship left a lasting imprint on shared New Mexican cultural consciousness. This impression is captured and dramatized by the conquest romance of "Los Comanches," a traditional folk play that probably originated in the late eighteenth or early nineteenth century and is still performed today in many villages and pueblos of northern New Mexico.[35]

There are two distinctive variations of "Los Comanches." One emphasizes the mutualistic, supportive aspects of Comanche–New Mexican relations and depicts the two peoples as potential allies and fictive kinspeople, bound together by a nexus of economic, social, and cultural transactions. In this version, a group of Comanches led by their chief, El Capitán, enter a New Mexican pueblo, seeking an image of El Santo Niño, the Christ Child. They break into one of the houses, seize the sacred image, and force their way out of the village. During the dash, however, El Capitán is separated from his daughter, La Cautiva, who is taken captive by the villagers. Once they realize this, the Comanches turn back, reenter the pueblo, and meet the villagers at the main plaza. An elaborate sequence of ritual and redemption commences. El Capitán and the head of the pueblo agree on the terms of exchange, and the Comanches surrender the Christ Child. The villagers in turn offer the Comanches food, wine, and cash. Finally, they return his beloved daughter to El Capitán, but they do so only after the chief promises to visit the village again for trade.

This version of "Los Comanches" underlines the need for and the persistence of cross-cultural transfers in a world structured and defined by mutual violence. Comanches, as depicted in the drama, represent to New Mexicans enemies and strangers who nevertheless become loyal, esteemed allies through a ceremonial bestowal of material gifts and reciprocal return of captives. The play's overarching motif is the fundamental interdependence of the two groups, and its moral thrust emanates from a sensitive process of intersocietal reconciliation and emergent understanding between two antagonistic peoples. The drama culminates in the redemption of La Cautiva and El Capitán's promise of future trade.[36]

Another variation of "Los Comanches" offers a strikingly different image of Comanches and their relationship with New Mexico. Celebrating Carlos Fernández's shocking victory over the Comanches in 1774, this version of the play emphasizes and elaborates Comanches' bellicosity and power and New Mexicans' mixed emotions of horror, disgust, anguish, and envy. Rather than pagans who instinctively gravitate toward the Christ Child, Comanches now emerge as irredeemable savage heathens who must be exterminated for New Mexico to survive. The focus of the drama is Comanches' material wealth, which they had largely accumulated by plundering New Mexico. That wealth, at this moment of New Mexican triumph, becomes an object of unbridled greed. Here, the relationship between Comanches and New Mexicans is openly exploitative and, unlike the parallel version of the play, allows no possibility for accommodation or coexistence. Mesmerized by their tormenters' affluence, the impoverished but suddenly victorious New Mexicans go on a killing and looting spree of their own. Barriga Duce, a Spanish camp follower, describes the battle from a distance:

Let them die, the more the better,
There will be more spoils for me.
Soft tanned skins of elk and beaver,
What a comfort they will be.
Meat of buffalo in abundance,
Everything that one might need,
I will fill my larder plenty,
I have many mouths to feed.
My good wife shall want for nothing,
She shall cook a gorgeous meal.
. . . .
Ah, at last I've reached their treasure,
There is plenty here indeed.
Sugars, fruits, and meats, and jellies,
What a life these heathens lead.
Everything to tempt the palate,
What a feast, fit for a king.
I shall eat and then I'll gather,
I'll not leave a single thing.
. . . .
Give no quarter, comrades, smite them,
Do your duty, have no fear,
Strike them, without mercy,
Strike them, smite them, without mercy. . . .[37]

A symbolic rendition of a complex and controversial past, "Los Comanches" is open to many interpretations, and historians have used its moral messages to make a range of arguments about cross-cultural relations in the Southwest borderlands. James Brooks, for example, has made powerful use of the first version of the romance, employing it as a window into a disorienting once-was world in which the familiar dichotomies between exchange and violence or masters and victims had become vague, almost meaningless.[38] Perhaps the most essential fact about "Los Comanches," however, is the very existence of the two contrasting versions. The parallel versions evoke New Mexicans' struggle to come to grips with their capitulation to the exploitative, manipulative, and divisive power policies of the Comanches. They are an attempt of an increasingly powerless people to understand their place in a volatile world over which they possessed little control.

The 1770s witnessed a dramatic expansion of Comanche power in New Mexico, but the decade also saw the emergence of two other Comanche raiding domains around the colony. The first of these domains lay to the north and west of New Mexico, extending across the Rockies toward Ute territory. Sporadically at first, and then with growing intensity, Comanche war bands followed the Arkansas River to its source, sidestepping New Mexico's northern tip into Ute country. The forays may have started soon after the breakdown of the Comanche-Ute alliance in the 1750s, and they probably began as plundering expeditions aimed at seizing slaves and horses. Over time, however, the raids escalated into a sustained expansion that carried several Comanche rancherías deep into Ute territory. Comanche population, which was growing explosively in the late eighteenth century, possibly exceeded the southern plains' carrying capacity, thus creating a compelling impulse for renewed expansion. It is also possible that the invasion of Ute lands was an attempt to weaken the alliance that had developed between the Utes and northwestern New Mexico in the 1750s and 1760s. That alliance, born out of mutual fear of Comanches, revolved around a lucrative trade in Abiquiu, a trade that each year brought hundreds of Ute visitors to the colony, thus compromising Comanches' unhindered access to their raiding and trading domains in northern New Mexico.[39]

In 1776 two Franciscan friars, Francisco Atanasio Domínguez and Silvestre Vélez de Escalante, led a meandering exploring expedition around the Colorado Plateau and toward the Pacific, hoping to locate usable routes linking New Mexico to newly colonized California. The friars expected to find in the northwest lands that were ready for Spanish colonies and missions, but instead they entered a volatile world enveloped in Comanche violence. Domínguez's and Escalante's observations revealed a drastically shifted balance of power between the Comanches and Utes. A map prepared by the expedition's cartographer, Bernardo de Miera y Pacheco, shows two clusters of Comanche rancherías between the Front Range of the Rockies and the Green River in present-day east-central Utah. The map also places a Yamparika ranchería on the western side of the Green River, where it stood separated from Comanchería proper by four hundred miles of rugged mountains, deep canyons, and thick forests. Those Comanche rancherías may have been temporary outposts for long-distance raids, but they may also have been more permanent settlement colonies signifying actual territorial takeover. Fray Domínguez labeled the lands east of the Green River simply as the "territory of the Comanches Yamparicas."[40]

Deep in the Colorado Plateau, the Green River formed the ancient heart of Ute territory. By the mid-1770s, however, many Ute bands had retreated west to the Utah Lake valley, where the Domínguez-Escalante expedition found them in desperate straits. Terrified of the wide-ranging Comanche war bands, they were unable to conduct hunts and suffered from starvation. Hoping to gain access to Spanish horses, metal, and protection, they begged the Franciscans to come and build permanent houses among them and they promised to "live as the tatas [friars] . . . taught them." Moved by their suffering and apparent willingness to convert, Domínguez and Escalante offered them salvation in Jesus Christ. They taught them to chant "Jesús-Maria" and promised them eternal life in Heaven, free from the Comanche heathen who "cannot enter Heaven, but go to Hell, where God punishes them, and where they will burn forever like wood in the fire." In the meanwhile, on Earth, Utes should wait patiently while the friars acquired authorization for a mission project. The project never materialized.[41]

Simultaneously, yet another phase of Comanche expansion across the Southwest was gathering momentum. Since their withdrawal to the southern Llano Estacado and the Río Grande valley in the 1750s, the Apaches had had little contact with the western Comanches, whose territory centered on the northern Llano Estacado and the upper Arkansas basin. Denied access to the buffalo plains, various Apache bands—whom the Spaniards now knew collectively as the Mescaleros—began raiding Spanish settlements in Coahuila, Nueva Vizcaya, southern New Mexico, and southwestern Texas, slowly building a new economy on livestock poaching and herding. The relocated Apaches also forged commercial ties with more marginal Spanish settlements, and at times these ties matured into local alliances that saw Apaches, socially marginalized Hispanics, and fugitive slaves trading, intermarrying, and joining their forces in attacking Spanish outposts. By the late 1770s, the Apaches seemed to have developed a secure way of life in their new southern homelands.[42]

But then the western Comanches launched another offensive. In 1776 Comanches came upon and attacked a Mescalero village near the headwaters of the Colorado River and reportedly killed three hundred families. Two years later Spaniards encountered several fleeing Mescalero bands near the Organ Mountains in southern New Mexico, and soon Apaches began arriving in El Paso and lamenting that Comanches had invaded their lands in the Sierra Blanca Range.[43] The far-ranging Comanche bands may have been raiding parties seeking horses and captives to supply Comanchería's growing pastoral economy and booming slave traffic in Taos or they may have been seek-and-destroy attacks aimed at eliminating the Mescaleros from Comanchería's southwestern border. But these southbound expeditions also anticipated an expansion that in the early nineteenth century would carry Comanches to the Río Grande and deep into northern Mexico.

At the same time that western Comanches realigned New Mexico and its surrounding regions to serve their interests, eastern Comanches imposed a similar Comanche-centric order on the Texas borderlands. Like their western kindred, eastern Comanches achieved this by breaking off old alliances while forming new ones, by aggressively seeking trade and resources, and by blocking their rivals from markets. And like western Comanches, they used Spain's colonial outposts simultaneously for trading and raiding, although they did so in a much larger geopolitical frame: they raided one Spanish frontier—Texas—to fuel their trade in another—Louisiana. The broader canvass also meant that eastern Comanches' ascendancy was more a convoluted process than that of their western relatives. Before establishing their hegemony in Texas by the late 1770s, eastern Comanches had endured repeated shifts in Spain's frontier policy, faced challenges from several Spanish-Indian coalitions, and absorbed the disruptive repercussions caused by the collapse of two colonial empires.

Since the early 1750s, eastern Comanches had fought Lipan Apaches and Spanish Texas side by side with Taovayas, Tonkawas, and Hasinais, a collaboration that culminated in the 1758 sacking of the San Sabá mission. But like the Comanche-Ute union, the Comanche-Taovaya-Tonkawa-Hasinai coalition lasted only as long as the wars against the Lipans and Spaniards did. Eastern Comanches preserved their alliance with Taovayas, who supplied them with essential European goods and farming produce, but Tonkawas and Hasinais possessed less economic weight and consequently had more tenuous relations with Comanches.

Tonkawas' ties with Comanches unraveled during the 1760s, paralleling their declining power in the changing colonial world. Never populous, Tonkawas became increasingly marginalized after 1763, when Spanish officials moved to buttress Texas against the British, who had began to fortify the Mississippi valley.

Tonkawas had raided Texas for decades, exhausting the colonists' patience. With the British threat looming, Spaniards cancelled Tonkawas' trading privileges and persuaded the Wichitas, who maintained a fluctuating alliance with Texas, to discipline them. Isolated and impoverished, Tonkawas retreated from their traditional homelands on the middle Brazos and Trinity rivers toward the Gulf Coast—and farther away from Comanches. There are no records of Comanche-Tonkawa interactions after the late 1760s, and soon Tonkawas were reported to be "disliked and even abhorred as vagabonds" by their former allies. They forged a tenuous alliance with the Lipans, another refuge group dislodged by Comanche expansion, but failed to maneuver out of their marginal position. In the early nineteenth century the Tonkawas lived in pitiful conditions along the lower Guadalupe River, unable to hunt bison "out of fear of meeting the Comanches."[44]

The collapse of Comanche-Hasinai relations, too, was caused by the allies' diverging fortunes. In the early eighteenth century Hasinais were the most powerful of the Caddoan peoples who lived in large riverside towns on the southeastern prairies between the Ouachita and Neches rivers. They occupied a gateway position between the lower Mississippi valley and the southern plains, controlling the east-west commerce in European and indigenous goods, but they were greatly weakened by two unwelcome imports of colonial trade: alcohol and epidemics. Hasinais lost their pivotal position around midcentury, when the Wichita tribes—Kichais, Tawakonis, Iscanis, Guichitas, and Taovayas—moved in from the north and built large villages on the Red, Brazos, Trinity, and Sabine rivers, just west of Hasinai range. The Wichita villages became commercial citadels that Spanish merchants from Texas, Franco-Spanish peddlers from Louisiana, and British contraband traders from the Mississippi valley frequented. Hasinai-Comanche relations collapsed soon after. Hasinais lost their connection with Comanches and with that their access to the bison-rich shortgrass plains. Caught in a spiraling decline, they were eclipsed by the Kadohadachos, their northeasterly relatives, whose confederated villages at the Great Bend of the Red River emerged as the new center of the Caddo universe.[45]

While their relations with Tonkawas and Hasinais dissolved, eastern Comanches' alliance with the Taovayas continued to flourish. The two groups shared hunting ranges and periodically joined forces to keep Lipan hunting parties out of the southern plains, but commerce was the heart of their union. Comanche-Taovaya trade linked together several economic systems. Taovaya farmers raised large crops of maize and squash on the sandy beds of the Red River and sold much of their surplus to Comanches in exchange for dried meat, hides, and Apache captives. The food and slave trades were complemented by a growing exchange in colonial goods. Comanches lived near south-central Spanish Texas, whose ranches and farms had so many horses that they sometimes had to be shot as a nuisance. Taovayas had close ties to Louisiana, whose rapidly growing population had a secure access to various manufactures through its Atlantic links but suffered from such a serious shortage of livestock that its economic growth was hindered. The asymmetries between Comanches' and Taovayas' respective resource domains stimulated a vigorous cross-borderland trade. Comanches pilfered horses from Texas and carried them to Taovaya villages, and wide-ranging Louisiana traders then hauled the animals to Natchitoches, Atakapas, Opelousas, Pointe Coupeé, and Bayou Teche. Louisiana's transfer from France to Spain in 1763 did not disturb this trade, for many French traders stayed on to become Spanish subjects and continued their operations with southern plains Indians.[46]

Comanche-Taovaya trade took place mostly beyond direct European observation, but developments at the terminal points of the raiding-and-trading chain demonstrate that the system was thriving. Comanche horse raiding in Texas escalated steadily in the late 1760s and 1770s. "Made proud by their great number, and led by their propensity to steal," one Spanish official wrote in 1770, Comanches "let few seasons pass without committing bloody outrages." And if Spanish officials in Texas failed to curb Comanche raids, Spanish officials in Louisiana were equally powerless to stop the importation of stolen Spanish stock to the colony. In 1770 Louisiana Governor Alejandro O'Reilly tried to eliminate the economic incentive behind Comanche raids in Texas by prohibiting the import of horses and mules from the plains, but his decree had little effect except turning the livestock trade into a lucrative smuggling business. O'Reilly also outlawed the enslavement and sale of Indians in Louisiana, again with limited results. The flow of Apache slaves from Comanchería to Taovaya villages and Louisiana continued uninterrupted through the 1770s.[47]

In spite of its overall vitality, the trade arrangement had a serious flaw from the Comanches' perspective. As gateway traders, Taovayas controlled the flow of goods to and from the Mississippi valley. Louisiana's French and Spanish traders, British contrabandists from West Florida, and Caddo middleman traders all frequented their villages, bringing in guns, metal tools, and textiles. Making the most of their key position, Taovayas supplied Comanches generously with produce from their fields but carefully regulated the circulation of guns, powder, and ammunition, the bulk of which they reserved for their own use to keep the well-armed Osages at bay. Taovaya trading policy left Comanches economically marginalized—one observer noted that they often had to settle for petty trading in knives, glass beads, and other "trifles"—but it also violated the kinship-based exchange protocol, which obliged wealthier allies to be generous and share possessions with their poorer partners. By limiting Comanches' access to their guns, lead, and bullets, even if they did so under duress, Taovayas denied Comanches' social worth as allies and friends.[48]

Comanches also agonized over the Taovayas' mounting political weight in Texas. In 1768, spurred by marqués de Rubí's report, Texas was moving toward a placatory stance toward Comanches, but that development faltered the following year when Spain consolidated its administrative system in lower Louisiana. From there on, Spanish policymakers concentrated on forging a tight alliance with Taovayas and other members of the Wichita confederacy, which, when viewed from the double vantage point of Texas and Louisiana, appeared the key Native power of the southern plains, as they had political and commercial ties to both colonies. Spanish officials made the nearly five-thousand-strong Wichita confederacy the focal point of an ambitious three-stage frontier strategy. First, they sought an alliance with the Wichita villages on the Red, Trinity, Brazos, and Sabine rivers in order to create a protective barrier for Texas and northern Mexico against a possible British invasion from the Mississippi valley. Spaniards also planned to use Wichita allies against the Lipans, who were obtaining guns from British West Florida and raiding in Texas with such ferocity that the colony was in danger of being cut off from the rest of New Spain. The final part of the plan involved employing the Wichitas as a barrier to shield Texas and Louisiana against the Osages' southward thrust, which had accelerated during the 1760s when the French and Indian War drove fragments of several eastern groups—Sauks, Foxes, Kickapoos, Shawnees, Delawares, and others—across the Mississippi valley into the northern Osage territory in the Ozarks. Pressured in the north, Osages pushed south, turning the Red River valley into "a pitiful theater of outrageous robberies and bloody encounters."[49]

Spain's gravitation toward the Wichitas gained momentum in 1769, when Athanase de Mézières was appointed lieutenant governor of the strategically sensitive Natchitoches district on the Texas-Louisiana border. A former French officer and Indian trader and now one of New Spain's most practiced frontier agents, de Mézières's arrival opened a new chapter in Spain's Indian policy. Drawing on both French and Spanish frontier tactics, he blended force and diplomacy to fashion a firm alliance with the Wichitas. He first established formal ties with the Kadohadachos and persuaded them to put the Wichitas in a trading boycott. Next, in October 1770, he sponsored a summit with several Wichita headmen at Gran Caddo, the principal Kadohadacho village on the lower Red River. He declared that the French had been "erased and forgotten" and asked the chiefs to pledge loyalty to the king of Spain. He then drew attention to the Wichitas precarious position "in the midst of four fires"—Spaniards, Comanches, Osages, and Lipans—"which, raising their horrible flames, would reduce them to ashes as easily as the voracious fire consumes the dry grass of the meadows," and proposed that the Wichitas make peace with the Lipans and pressure them to stop interacting with the British and raiding into Texas. As an incentive, he offered French-style frontier policy—licensed traders, lucrative trade, and liberal gifts. Eager to secure Spanish support and weapons against the Osages who were being supplied by illegal gun traffickers on the Arkansas, Wichitas acceded to de Mézières's propositions. By 1771, all five member groups of the Wichita confederation—Taovayas, Tawakonis, Kichais, Iscanis, and Guichitas—had declared allegiance to Spain.[50]

This was a severe blow to eastern Comanches. Regional geopolitics had been suddenly repositioned on a Texas-Louisiana-Wichita axis, and they found themselves dangerously isolated in a world where linkages conferred power. Spanish Texas, de Mézières believed, was now protected by a cordon of loyal Wichitas who kept the Comanches in check. "It seems difficult for them to commit the robberies and perfidies which formerly they were in the habit of doing," he wrote, "when they know that on their return they cannot escape the vigilance of their enemies, if perchance they should escape them during their entry." Excluded from negotiations, Comanches were in danger of becoming pawns in Spanish-Wichita diplomacy. In October 1771 Taovayas ratified a treaty with Spain in Natchitoches and pledged to use their influence to pressure Comanches to stop raiding in Texas. Should Comanches fail to comply, Taovayas would "suspend all communication and intercourse with them and consider them as enemies." Taovayas and other Wichitas were liberally compensated for transferring their loyalties. Spanish officials in Texas promised them regular gifts and authorized traders from San Antonio and Natchitoches to visit their villages.[51]

Comanches, meanwhile, witnessed their options narrowing as Spanish policies hardened. In the winter of 1771–72 Spanish troops captured seven Comanches—six women and a girl—and took them to San Antonio. Governor Juan Maria Vicencio, barón de Ripperdá, decided to use the captives to force the Comanches to stop raiding. He sent two of the captives to Chief Povea, the supposed head chief of the eastern Comanches, but held the other women and the girl as hostages to ensure that the Comanches remained peaceful. A few weeks later a Comanche delegation arrived in San Antonio, led by a woman carrying a white flag. The woman was the mother of the captive girl, and most of the emissaries were relatives of the captives held by Ripperdá. The governor released one woman and the girl but refused to free the three remaining women on the grounds that they had already been baptized and could not be returned. The Comanches made a desperate attempt to liberate the women, but Spanish soldiers recaptured them. The Comanche party fled the town but was attacked by the Lipans, who killed seven men and captured four women, including the mother and the daughter. The Lipans sold the women to Ripperdá, who deported them to missions and labor camps in Coahuila.[52]

Just how far to the margins of the shifting colonial world they had fallen became painfully clear to eastern Comanches during the next two years. In July 1772 Chief Povea accompanied a Wichita peace envoy to San Antonio, hoping to retrieve the captive women and establish peace with the colony. Governor Ripperdá invited Povea to a council but then publicly harangued the chief by displaying the white flag that the Comanches had used to feign truce. Povea promised to prevent his own band from raiding in Texas, but Ripperdá made no promise to return the captives. Povea's delegation—which included the husband of one captive woman—returned home distressed and humiliated.[53]

But Ripperdá had also seen in Povea's visit an opportunity to establish formal ties with the eastern Comanches and draw them under Spanish influence. It was possible to "subjugate the Camanche," he wrote to the viceroy, by making them to "love us through continual intercourse." In spring 1773 he dispatched a Louisiana trader, J. Gaignard, to establish contact with eastern Comanche rancherías and chart the region's commercial prospects. Ascending the Red River, Gaignard arrived in the twin Taovaya villages in the fall, but that was as far as he made it. Taovayas allowed him to meet with Comanche emissaries in their villages—and under their supervision—and Gaignard presented Comanche chiefs a blanket "to cover the blood which has been shed on the roads" and knives to "stop up the crooked trail." But when Gaignard tried to continue upriver to visit Comanche rancherías, Taovayas stopped him in his tracks. Their motives to do so seem apparent. A broad Comanche-Spanish alliance not only posed a threat to Taovayas' favored status in Spanish Texas but also would have cancelled their access to stolen Spanish stock through Comanche raiders. Taovayas' economic prosperity depended on keeping the Spaniards and Comanches isolated and, preferably, at war. When Gaignard left the Taovaya villages after six months of frustrated efforts to continue to Comanchería, he left behind a strained Comanche-Taovaya alliance.[54]

Facing deepening isolation, eastern Comanches began to distance themselves from their alliance with the Wichitas and adopted a more aggressive stance toward the confederation. They began a sustained trade war to grind down the Wichita cordon and extend their own commercial and political reach to Spanish Texas and Louisiana. Raiding and looting, they gradually forced their way deep into the Wichita realm, reaching by the late 1770s the lower Brazos River near Bosque Creek, almost one hundred miles east of Comanchería proper. In 1778 de Mézières reported that the Tawakonis and Iscanis were being constantly raided by Comanches "who have settled in large numbers on the same river, the Brazos, so that there is nothing for them to do but to withdraw themselves or, in conjunction with the neighboring [Wichita] nations, take serious action against so deadly a pest."[55]

Such "serious action" was not possible for the Wichitas, however, because they were entangled in wars on other flanks as well. In the north, they faced the formidable and expansionist Osages. Harassed in the north by the Sauks and Foxes and blocked in the west by the Comanches, Osages shifted to the south and moved to monopolize hunting, raiding, and trading privileges across the prairie belt between the Missouri and Red rivers. In the south, the Wichitas were engaged in a sporadic raiding war with the Lipans, whose attempts to carve out a larger foothold in the Texas borderlands were failing. Appalled by their continuing raids in Texas, Governor Ripperdá deemed the Lipans undependable and set out to isolate them politically and economically. When in 1773 Lipan delegates approached the Hasinais, Ripperdá interfered. Pressured by Ripperdá, Bigotes, the leading Hasinai negotiator, publicly beheaded four Lipan emissaries. Lipans retaliated with fierce attacks on the Spaniards and all their allies, including the Wichitas.[56]

The three-front war depleted Wichitas' power, undermining their ability to fight back the Comanches. Comanches stepped up their attacks against the Wichitas even as they continued to visit their villages for trade. De Mézières noted in 1778 how Comanches, "in the guise of friends, make them repeated visits, always with the purpose of stealing." Wichitas, he continued, tolerated the assaults with curious passivity: "These . . . insults they pretend not to notice, lest they should make other enemies, when they already have too many." Seeking protection in numbers, Wichitas congregated into larger villages, only to expose themselves to a much greater threat than war. In 1777 and 1778 a virulent epidemic, perhaps smallpox, struck the Wichitas twice, spreading devastation in the crowded villages. The Wichitas lost nearly one-third of their population, including many head chiefs, and they collapsed into poverty and political disarray.[57]

The epidemic had spared the mobile Comanches, who in its wake reduced the weakened Wichitas to virtual vassalage. They subjected them to "unceasing incursions and insults" and yet continued to visit the Taovaya and Tawakoni villages on the Red and Brazos rivers to barter for guns, ammunition, and salt. In 1780 Taovaya Chief Qui Te Sain complained in a letter to Louisiana Governor Bernardo de Gálvez about the Comanches "who happen to be our neighbors, but who shed our blood and steal our horses daily." "Much too embarrassed" to visit the governor personally, Qui Te Sain sent an urgent plea: "My father, we are deprived of everything, and have neither hatchets, nor picks, nor powder, nor bullets to defend from our enemies."[58]

As Wichitas' strength dissipated, Comanches usurped their trading niche between the Texas plains and the Mississippi valley. In 1777 Governor Ripperdá asked Louisiana officials to keep their subjects from trading with the Comanches who raided in Texas, and the following year de Mézières reported that the Comanches are "now masters in the region which must be crossed to get to the banks of this large-volumed river [Mississippi]." As before, Louisiana merchants continued to ignore the province's trade laws and ventured to the western plains with loads of guns, powder, and balls. "While our troops ignore or pay little attention to the correct use of their muskets," Teodoro de Croix, the commanding general of the recently founded Commandancy General of the Interior Provinces of the North, agonized in 1778, "the Indians strive with emulation to manage them dexterously." Croix also fretted over the activities of British traders "who lose no opportunity to introduce themselves among the Indians" of the Texas plains.[59]

The collapse of Wichita power also opened the door for closer relations between eastern Comanches and Spanish Texas. In 1777 de Mézières suggested that Texas should make every effort to draw the Comanches—who in his view "excel all the other nations in breeding, strength, valor, and gallantry"—into a coalition against the Osages, whose raids threatened to obliterate the Arkansas Post, a strategically critical fort near the Mississippi and Arkansas confluence. Spain faced even graver problems in the south, where Apache war bands ravaged Coahuila and Nueva Vizcaya; in the latter province alone Apaches had destroyed 116 haciendas, killed and captured nearly 2,000 people, and stolen more than 68,000 head of livestock from 1771 through 1776. To stop the devastation, Commanding General Croix organized a council of war in Chihuahua City, which decided to declare a general war on the Apaches and solicit military support among the Comanches and Wichitas. In spring 1778 de Mézières toured among the Wichitas, who voiced their "hatred" toward the Lipans. He then extended a peace overture to Comanches by releasing one Comanche captive.[60]

But the planning and implementation of policies did not always mesh easily on the disjointed Texas frontier. In May 1778, apparently unaware of the peace process, the settlers of Bucareli, a small trading community on the Trinity River, mistook a Comanche peace delegation for a war party and killed several of its members. Comanches retaliated by sacking the town. Unfazed, Spanish officials pressed on with the peace plan, but three events in 1779 nullified their efforts. First, King Carlos III rejected the planned Spanish-Comanche-Wichita campaign against the Apaches on the grounds that a genocidal war had no place on an enlightened state's agenda. Then, in late August, de Mézières fell off his horse and died of his injuries, leaving the plan without an overseer. Last, in mid-December, news of Spain's involvement in the American Revolutionary War against Great Britain reached Texas—along with orders to cut down spending. Within months, then, Texas was deprived of three prerequisites of a successful Indian policy—a common enemy around which to erect an alliance network, the funds for gifting, and a top official fluent in cross-cultural diplomacy—and it lost its brief window to reach a concord with the Comanches.[61]

The collapse of Spanish-Comanche rapprochement could hardly have come at a worse time for Texas, occurring just as eastern Comanches secured their position as the trade gateway to the Mississippi valley. Infuriated by Spaniards' failure to deliver gifts to ritually cover the deaths of the Bucareli incident, and coveting horses and mules with which to fuel their growing trade, eastern Comanches launched a raiding war in Texas. Highly mobile and seemingly unpredictable in their actions, their war parties were everywhere and nowhere, attacking villages, missions, ranches, and farms all across Texas only to disappear into the forbidding vastness of Comanchería. Governor Cabello feared that the Comanches were about to annihilate San Antonio and its missions and presidio, and the settlers named Comanche raiders' staging area, a ridge near the Guadalupe and Colorado rivers, El Monte del Diablo. Facing limited resistance from the overwhelmed local militias and the eighty presidial troops, Comanches raided as far east as Bucareli and as far south as Laredo on the lower Río Grande. Their war parties also fell upon Indian tribes all across Texas, attacking Lipans, Hasinais, Tonkawas, Bidais, Mayeyes, Cocos, Akokisas, Taovayas, Tonkawas, and Kichais and preventing these smaller groups from joining together in anti-Comanche alliances. In 1779 Comanches sacked a large Lipan camp in the San Sabá valley—now the main Comanche entryway into Texas—killing more than three hundred people and carrying many into captivity. The Comanche onslaught also exposed Texas to attacks from other Indian groups. With troops tied to the Comanche front, Texas could not fight the Karankawa raiders along the Gulf Coast, nor could it oppose Osages' expansion toward Natchitoches. Lipans, Natagés, and Mescaleros raided settlements in southern Texas virtually unopposed.[62]

Mirroring the concurrent developments in New Mexico, eastern Comanche raids reduced Texas to a captive territory. Its population dropped by 10 percent between 1777 and 1784, from 3,103 to 2,828. Bucareli was abandoned; countless missions, ranches, and farms were stripped of horses; and fields were left untended. The attacks peaked in 1780 and 1781, which in Croix's words saw "incessant attacks of the Comanches, so horrible and bloody that, if they continue with the same steadfastness, the desolation of the province will be consequent, irremediable and immediate, and (as the governor believes) very few vassals of the king may remain to contemplate this misfortune." Croix described a wasteland: "The province is overrun with these Indians, now alone, or as allies of the Nations of the North; at the moment not a foot of land is free of hostility. Its fruits of the field are despoiled, cattle ranches and farms that the happy days of peace had built up are rapidly being abandoned, and the settlers in terror taking refuge in the settlements, nor do they venture to leave the neighborhood without a troop escort." Watching his colony wasting away, Governor Cabello was reduced to buying respites from destruction by handing out any available goods to Comanche chiefs. Croix approved the policy after the fact, sending the pitiful advice that the gifts should be handed out in such a fashion that the Indians "may not be given cause for conceit or arrogance nor acquire our gifts as if we had been forced to give them." By 1781, Croix had accepted that peace with the Comanches would be possible only if Spaniards began annual gift distributions at San Antonio.[63]

The raids were more than simple plundering excursions; they were also an instrument of power politics that helped restructure Texas and its borderlands for further exploitation. In 1780 Comanche pillaging forced Texas ranchers to suspend their vitally important livestock drives to Louisiana. This deprived Texas of a major source of imports just as Spain's involvement in the American Revolutionary War began to generate material shortages throughout the empire, but it was a boon for the Comanches themselves: the cessation of drives fueled the demand for their horses and mules in Louisiana, where animals were needed for the Spanish and Patriot troops fighting the British along the Gulf Coast. Like western Comanche raids in New Mexico, eastern Comanche raids in Texas served a double function: they yielded valuable goods while also creating markets for those plundered goods.[64]

The decline of Spanish power in Texas and its borderlands was astoundingly precipitous. As late as 1778 Spaniards were still dreaming of a great imperial future for Texas. Commanding General Croix proposed that Texas build a series of outposts among the Taovayas on the Red River, which would mark the northern limit of effective Spanish rule in the continent's center. "This new line would be the palladium of war," he envisioned, "but from it to the interior of our now distant frontier there would be no enemies, and the provinces which now suffer hostilities would experience prosperity." Even the usually cautious de Mézières had been widely optimistic about the prospects of colonizing the Taovaya country. "It is certain that if this place comes to be settled," he predicted, "it will be one of the most important [Spanish colonial outposts], both at present and in the future, because it is the master-key of the north, where the friendly nations will be dealt with through their [Taovayas'] mediation, the unfriendly, such as the Comanches and the Osages, will be won over, or, with the help of the friendly nations, conquered." A Spanish colony on the middle Red River, he believed, could also be turned into a buffer "where any new enterprise or invasion of the neighboring English will be prevented" and an interimperial nerve center "where prompt and easy communication will be had with Natchitoches, Ilinoeses, New Mexico, and Bejar."[65]

Only a few years later, however, an almost diametrically contrasting geopolitical pattern had emerged. Texas was sliding into political and economic paralysis, and it was the Comanches who extended their sphere of authority to the coveted Red River valley and among the Taovayas. They usurped much of the Wichita commerce along the Red and Brazos rivers and extended their camping and hunting grounds south toward the lower Brazos valley. They incorporated large numbers of Taovaya warriors into their raiding parties, which sent Spanish officials into speculating that the Comanches had spawned a large anti-Spanish coalition that could obliterate the entire colony. By the early 1780s, the terror of Comanche assaults had become so entrenched on the Texas frontier that when a smallpox epidemic brought about a sudden hiatus in violence in late 1781, it stirred greater anxiety than the actual attacks. The years 1782 and 1783 passed in Texas with relative peace on the frontier—and rampant rumors of an imminent Comanche invasion.[66]

That the Comanches held a large sector of Spain's far northern frontier in a state of siege in the late 1770s reflected the fact that Spaniards had not been able to envision such a possibility in the first place. As Spanish strategists scrutinized the new imperial order created by the 1763 Treaty of Paris, they made a fateful miscalculation. Convinced that the main threat to New Spain came from the suddenly magnified British territories, they channeled money and men to those places where the two empires brushed against one another. By 1770, as a result, the Spanish empire had expanded into Alta California to fend off the British from North America's Pacific shores, turned lower Louisiana into a buffer colony against British West Florida, and buttressed the newly established St. Louis to shield upper Louisiana against the far-ranging British fur traders from the Ohio valley and Canada. Then, in 1776, in an unprecedented effort to foster military defenses and economic growth in the far north, King Carlos III placed all northern provinces of New Spain under a new, semiautonomous administrative entity, the Commandancy General of the Interior Provinces. On a map, the Interior Provinces were a prodigious creation, encompassing eight large provinces shielded by a continuous frontier stretching from the Pacific Coast through New Mexico and Texas to the Mississippi valley.

That frontier was a cartographic illusion. While maps were being drawn, the geopolitical ground kept shifting. In Sonora, Nueva Vizcaya, and Coahuila, at the heart of northern New Spain, the grand empire was slowly caving in. The Apaches—Gileños, Mescaleros, Natagés, and Lipans—many of them banished from the Great Plains by the Comanches, were forging a new Apachería in the midst of Spanish settlements. The situation was even more critical farther north in New Mexico and Texas, which served as New Spain's first line of defense. As Spain fortified the outer edges of its elongated North American realm, Comanches continued their expansion in the interior, drawing their own map of dominion over the continent's entire midsection. By the late 1770s, Spain faced an ominous situation in the far north: rather than bases for a great imperial extension beyond the Río Grande, New Mexico and Texas had become peripheries in a new imperial order that pivoted around Comanchería.

The Comanche-centric order was the product of two sweeping, interlocked sequences of political and economic innovation. The first sequence saw Comanches turning the southern plains from a geopolitical backwater into a major hub of commerce and diplomacy. By doing so, Comanches not only won access to food, horses, and guns but also enveloped Comanchería with the kind of political and economic ties that give invading powers staying power. The second sequence, an outgrowth of the first, saw Comanches adopting more aggressive policies toward Spanish colonies. As the eastern Comanches gradually supplanted the Wichitas as the trade gateway to the lower Mississippi valley and Spanish Louisiana, they simultaneously turned a large section of Spanish Texas into a raiding hinterland that fueled their trade with stolen stock and captives. Western Comanches treated New Mexico as an imperial holding where they plundered virtually at will while also using it as an outlet for stolen Spanish goods and as a source of food and European technology.

The rise of this new geopolitical order in the Southwest, like the Comanche conquest of the southern plains during the first part of the century, was ultimately a matter of numbers—and food. The Comanche population had grown explosively during the first part of the eighteenth century, and it continued to do so through the 1760s and 1770s, sustained by a healthy, vigorous economy. In the 1760s, after having ousted the Utes, Tonkawas, and Hasinais from the southern plains, the Comanches had nearly exclusive access to some seven million bison, a seemingly bottomless reservoir of meat, fat, and hides. This animal wealth, sustained by Comanchería's prolific patchwork of buffalo, blue grama, and bluestem grasses, supported a highly specialized hunting economy that yielded enough food and hides for domestic use and for trade. By exchanging animal products for maize, fruit, and vegetables, moreover, Comanches were able to create a dietary safety net, which allowed them to diversify their resource base and offset the dangers that accompanied the intense specialization in bison hunting—one-sided diet, overexploitation of bison herds, and the unpredictability of bison population dynamics.[67]

The availability of more and better food translated into an explosive population growth. Numbering between ten and fifteen thousand at midcentury, the Comanches may have tripled their population during the next three decades. In 1773, Gaignard learned, either from Taovayas or from Comanches themselves, that the Comanches "comprise fully four thousand warriors." Assuming that warriors made up half of the total male population and that the Comanches had more or less balanced gender ratio, Gaignard's account suggests a total Comanche population of sixteen thousand. Other sources support this notion of rapid growth. In the mid-1780s, according to Spanish observers, the western Comanches alone numbered between sixteen and eighteen thousand, while a 1785 account states that the eastern Comanches had two thousand fighting men, which translates into a total eastern Comanche population of some eight thousand. But that same account also notes that the eastern Comanches had lost a few years earlier two-thirds of their members to smallpox, which suggests that the pre-epidemic population approached twenty-four thousand people. This would mean that the *total* Comanche population in the early 1780s reached or exceeded forty thousand people—more than the Spanish colonies in New Mexico and Texas had combined.[68]

Comanches needed a large population base to balance their swelling foreign political ambitions, which in the late 1770s seemed almost overwhelming. In the space of a single year, they may have fought the Utes deep in the Great Basin, attacked the Apaches near El Paso, and raided the Taovaya villages on the eastern fringe of the Texas plains. They may have pillaged horses and slaves across New Mexico and Texas, sent raiding expeditions to the lower Río Grande, and blocked the Osage hunters in the east and the New Mexican hunters in the west from entering Comanchería's bison range. They may have sponsored a series of trade fairs on the upper Arkansas valley, bartered with British peddlers on the Red and Brazos rivers, and visited the Taos markets. The Comanche foreign policy, in short, was a dynamic, constantly changing balancing act that only a demographically powerful nation could carry out without overstretching itself.

If a large population formed one underpinning of Comanche power, political organization formed another. To Spanish officials, however, Comanches were savages who were incapable of planning or organization. Puzzled and put off by their constant shifting between raiding and trading and violence and mediation, they labeled Comanche maneuvers as prepolitical acts springing from "bizarre discipline" or such inborn impulses as "cruelty" or "propensity to steal." They saw little or no planning behind Comanche actions. Modern scholarship often echoes these assessments, depicting the Comanches as a collection of autonomous bands that spontaneously responded to local conditions rather than to centralized leadership and planning. A closer look reveals, however, that underneath the localism and individualism that permeated Comanche political culture, there were compelling centralizing elements that instilled coherence and coordination to Comanche foreign policy.[69]

In 1767, just as the western Comanches launched their extended raiding spree in New Mexico, Governor Mendinueta learned from a Comanche captive that "a barbarian has raised himself up among that nation with the appearance and accouterments of those of a little king." This man, Cuerno Verde (Green Horn), was said to have "near his person a guard of armed men, pages who serve him when he mounts and dismounts from his horse, holding a canopy or shade of buffalo skins for him in which he takes his seat." "All obey him" and two "confidants execute his orders," concludes Mendinueta's report. Twelve years later, when the Comanche raids had nearly destroyed New Mexico, Cuerno Verde reentered historical record. In 1779 Juan Bautista de Anza, Mendinueta's successor, depicted him as "the cruel scourge of this kingdom" and "the leader of the barbarians" who had "exterminated many pueblos, killing hundreds and making as many prisoners whom he afterwards sacrificed in cold blood." Together, Mendinueta's and Anza's accounts portray Cuerno Verde as a man of considerable authority, whose name and vision marked western Comanche foreign policy during the crucial period between the late 1760s and late 1770s.[70]

But Mendinueta and Anza probably missed the subtleties that defined the scope and substance of Cuerno Verde's authority. It is unlikely that Cuerno Verde was an autocratic "little king," for the very idea would have been alien to the consensus-bound Comanches. Instead, Cuerno Verde was probably a Jupe war chief, *mahimiana paraibo,* who also established himself as a *paraibo,* civil leader, and rose to lead western Comanches' burgeoning raiding industry in New Mexico. He may have appeared to Spanish observers as a warlord operating in a milieu of political anarchy, but there is no reason to believe that his actions were not sanctioned and structured by Comanche conventions. Cuerno Verde's authority probably stemmed from traditional Comanche leadership qualities—personal charisma, courage, and generosity—which made it possible for him to forge a large network of *tʉbitsinahaitsInʉʉs* (true friends) and *haits* (formal friends), who themselves may have been leaders of local rancherías. Such a network would have allowed Cuerno Verde to influence—and perhaps even dominate—decision making at the periodically convening grand councils, which had defined the western Comanche political culture at least since midcentury. As was shown in the previous chapter, the complex treaty negotiations with New Mexico in 1752 and 1762 had revealed a sophisticated western Comanche political organization, complete with institutionalized leadership positions, a hierarchy of "superior" and "secondary" chiefs, and massive divisional meetings.[71]

It was within the confines and possibilities of such a political culture that Cuerno Verde maneuvered his way into a position of authority. He may have been able to manipulate western Comanche politics to his own advantage, but that does not mean that the western Comanche political system lacked organization or order. In fact, rather than promoting political anarchy, Cuerno Verde's rise seems to have fostered political centralization. "His own nation accuse[s] him, ever since he took command," Anza's 1779 report notes, "of forcing them to take up arms and volunteer against the Spaniards, a hatred of whom has dominated him because his father who also held the same command and power met death at our hands." Anza's Cuerno Verde may have been the son of the Cuerno Verde Mendinueta had mentioned twelve years earlier, a possibility that only reinforces the notion of consolidated political authority among the western Comanches: chiefs not only possessed considerable power but could pass their offices on to their descendants.[72]

A similar political culture existed in eastern Comanchería, as Spaniards discovered in the mid-1780s when two of their emissaries toured the region. Instead of the anticipated political chaos, the emissaries found in eastern Comanchería a structured and centralized polity. The estimated eight thousand eastern Comanches were divided into twelve local rancherías led by *capitanes* (captains) or *capitanes chiquitos* (little captains). The rancherías did not have a fixed number of people, which suggests that the local chiefs competed among one another for followers. As in most nomadic societies, band membership was fluid, and each *capitane* competed with the others for the critical mass of adherents needed to form a functioning ranchería. This kind of fluidity was crucial in the Southwestern borderlands where communities had to adjust to constantly changing political, economic, and ecological circumstances. Since families and individuals could move freely among the rancherías, they could also move swiftly to exploit emerging opportunities for raiding, trading, and diplomacy on Comanchería's expansive borders.

But these diffuse elements of the eastern Comanche politics were balanced by strong centralizing institutions. The local chiefs, the visitors observed, considered themselves "subjects" to two head chiefs whom they listened to with "much respect." The Spaniards also mention "principal or general councils" where important political matters were introduced and, if consensus was reached, decided. Those general councils also served as a forum where the head chiefs were selected in formal elections in which all eastern Comanche chiefs and warriors were entitled to participate. Reflecting the importance of raiding to eastern Comanche economy in the late 1770s and early 1780s, war exploits were the main criteria for head chieftainship: an impressive war record attracted followers who hoped to benefit from the association with a prominent warrior, who in turn could capitalize on the support of his many followers in the elections.[73] The eastern Comanche political organization thus appears a near replica of the western Comanche system. Both were at once diffuse and centralized, both featured large-scale formal councils, and both placed great value on leaders' personal military skills.

The commonalities between the western and eastern Comanches call attention to the last factor behind Comanche ascendancy: macroscale political cooperation. At first sight, the late eighteenth-century Comanche nation with its distinct western and eastern branches appears deeply fractured; in fact, the nation seemed to be dissolving in its new, vastly expanded geopolitical setting. Until the mid-eighteenth century, the three original Comanche divisions—Yamparikas, Jupes, and Kotsotekas—shared a relatively small land base on the western plains between the Arkansas and Red rivers. Because of territorial proximity, political identities were fluid and the three divisions often appeared indistinguishable from one another.[74] This politicogeographical compactness exploded in the 1750s and 1760s, however, when several Kotsoteka bands—the eastern Comanches—broke away from the main Kotsoteka body and pushed deep into the Texas plains. From then on, divergent foreign political ambitions began to pull the two branches in opposite directions and even farther apart. Western Comanches fashioned a raiding and trading economy that spanned New Mexico and the northern plains, and they were drawn, both politically and physically, to the west and north. Eastern Comanches focused on raiding Texas and trading toward the Mississippi valley, gravitating to the south and east.

The apparent dissolution of the Comanche community was, ironically, accompanied by a concurrent process of national unification. If political and economic specialization was pulling western and eastern Comanches away from one another, it also helped draw them back together. By the late 1770s, the two branches were engaged in an active trade that was fueled by their contrasting—and complementing—resource domains. With their secure access to European goods through the Mandan and Hidatsa villages, western Comanches provided guns, powder, ammunition, cloth, and metal utensils to their eastern relatives, who had a more tenuous access to European markets but, thanks to their proximity to Texas ranches, possessed vast surpluses of horses and mules. Eastern Comanches sold a part of their surplus to the western Comanches, who then funneled the animals to the central and northern plains through the upper Arkansas trade center, the paramount redistribution point of livestock across the midcontinent.[75]

The interdivisional trade was a means for material sharing, but, less obviously, it also doubled as a social and political adhesive. The regular trade fairs that convened around Comanchería served as an arena where Comanches nourished their sense of common identity. When western and eastern Comanches met for trade, they exchanged not only commodities but customs, ideas, and political views as well. They intermarried and forged crucial personal and kinship ties that bound their fractured nation back together. The unity of the larger Comanche community made a deep impression on foreign visitors. "Cumanches Occidentales," one wrote, "are differentiated from the Orientales only by the haircut. They speak the same language and see each other as brothers, and companions, and assist each other in their wars when necessary." The same year, Estevan Rodriguez Miró, the governor of Louisiana, sent a similar account from Louisiana. Comanches, he wrote, "dominate all the neighboring tribes, and although divided into several war parties, or *parcerías* [rancherías], they all live in perfect friendship."[76]

Those commonalities and connections, always essential culturally but perhaps less so strategically during the 1760s and 1770s, became critically important after the 1780s, when the reinvigorated Spanish empire moved to contest Comanches' hegemony in the Southwest. Building on their enduring tradition of mutual support and solidarity, Comanches fashioned in the late eighteenth century a new agency of political unity, the Comanche confederacy, which enabled them to repulse and eventually overturn the last expansionist effort of New Spain.

3

The Embrace

On February 25, 1786, Juan Bautista de Anza, lieutenant colonel in the Spanish Army and the governor of New Mexico, stood in front of his palace, preparing himself for the ceremony. He had waited for this moment too long, ever since the glorious day on the llanos seven years ago when he held the green-horned headdress in his hands. The memory of his triumph was already growing faint, making his gubernatorial tenure seem like a failure, but now there was hope again. He examined his subjects—*hispanos, indios, genízaros,* men, women, children—who swarmed in the dirt plaza, filling it with nervous expectation. Then the crowd shivered, erupting into shrieks and yells, and Anza saw him. Ecueracapa, the *capitan general* of the western Comanches, emerged at the end of a corridor of shouting people. The Indian rode slowly toward him, flanked by three adjutants and escorted by a column of Spanish soldiers and Santa Fe's most prominent citizens. He calmly crossed the square, dismounted in front of Anza, and gently embraced him. It was there, in the arms of the man he could think of only as a savage, that Anza knew there would be peace.[1]

The embrace brought together two men and two nations, and it saved New Mexico. The meeting of Anza and Ecueracapa put an end to a century of on-and-off warfare, which in the 1770s had nearly broken the kingdom of New Mexico. For the remaining Spanish tenure in the Americas, the western Comanches maintained an uninterrupted peace with the Spaniards, allowing New Mexico to heal and even prosper. A similar and simultaneous development took place in Texas, where the eastern Comanches and Spaniards forged a separate peace treaty, ending thirty years of nearly constant bloodshed.

But if Anza and Ecueracapa's encounter is one of the cardinal moments of the colonial Southwest, it is also one of the most enigmatic. What made the

Comanches give up their lucrative raiding-and-trading policy which brought them unforeseen prosperity and gave them such power over New Mexico? And why did the Spaniards, who had fought, feared, and despised the Comanches for generations, suddenly welcome their embrace?

When Spaniards later chronicled the dramatic transformative events of the mid-1780s, they thought they could explain them clearly and exhaustively: they stemmed from Spain's rediscovered imperial resolve. During the 1760s and 1770s, even as New Mexico and Texas were disintegrating under the Comanche pressure, the core of Spain's New World empire had experienced a gradual but sustained revival. Building on sweeping domestic reforms in Spain during the early eighteenth century, Carlos III, the most American-oriented of Spain's Bourbon monarchs, had implemented a series of reforms that modernized New Spain in the spirit of the Enlightenment. Carlos and his officials sought to rationalize administration, curb the power of the church, increase the flow of revenues to the mother country, foment economic growth in the lagging parts of the empire, and domesticate the wild, unruly frontiers. Collectively known as the Bourbon Reforms, these initiatives seemed to have given New Mexico and Texas the power to stop the Comanche tide.

The Bourbon Reforms in northern New Spain bore the distinctive mark of José de Gálvez, who served between 1765 and 1772 as visitor general to New Spain and then, from 1776 to 1787, as minister general of the Indies. Possessing almost unrestricted power to modernize the empire's administrative structures, Gálvez implemented and supervised an astounding array of reforms. He reorganized the tribunals of justice, reformed taxation, and was a central force behind the ordinance that expelled the Jesuits—potentially the strongest opponents to Carlos III's secular reforms—from New Spain in 1767. He devised plans to boost the circulation of currency in the northern provinces and subsidized the region's silver production at the expense of Peru. He streamlined the top-heavy mercantilist bureaucracy, dismantled the suffocating monopoly of the merchant guild of Cádiz on the imports and exports to American colonies, and established royal monopolies on the manufacture and sale of tobacco and gunpowder. He founded a colony in the valley of Sonora and initiated the colonization of Alta California.

The creation of the Commandancy General of the Interior Provinces of the North in 1776—in many ways an emergency measure to repel the seemingly uncontainable expansion of Comanches and Apaches across northern New Spain—brought unparalleled top-level administrative attention to the empire's northern territories. Under the new strategic layout, New Mexico and Texas were assigned crucial roles as buffers for the silver mining districts of Sonora, Nueva Vizcaya, and Coahuila. More funds, livestock, and high-caliber administrators poured to the beleaguered far north and particularly to New Mexico, whose large population and economic potential earned it special treatment. Commerce between northern Mexico and the frontier provinces—an activity that had suffered greatly in the late 1770s under Comanche and Apache attacks—was revived, and from the 1780s on unprecedented amounts of commodities moved between New Mexico and Chihuahua City along the Chihuahua Trail. In the closing years of the eighteenth century, New Mexicans shipped annually fifteen to twenty thousand sheep and several tons of wool, cotton, textiles, and foodstuffs southward to Chihuahua markets, while huge northbound caravans carried various manufactured goods to New Mexico. After nearly two centuries of relative isolation, the far north finally became an integral part of the empire's economic fabric.

Thanks to their strategic importance as barriers against Comanche expansion, New Mexico and Texas also fared well in the wholesale reorganization of frontier defenses that was finally brought to a conclusion in the late 1770s—years after marqués de Rubí had submitted his recommendations. The new layout rested on a cordon of fifteen presidios that connected the gulfs of Mexico and California roughly along the thirtieth parallel, the true frontier line in Rubí's mind. Seven garrisons north of that line were abandoned. Texas lost the presidio of Los Adaes (which now lost its status as the province's capital to San Antonio), but both Santa Fe and San Antonio retained their garrisons, even though they sat far to the north of Rubí's cordon. The two northern presidios also received extensive backing from the royal treasury and in the early 1780s had more soldiers than any other presidio in the Interior Provinces.[2]

The restored force of Bourbon Spain caught up with the Comanches in 1779, when Anza, New Mexico's governor for two years, moved to make war on the western Comanches in their own territory. A third generation army officer, a veteran Indian fighter, the pioneer of the Sonora-California overland trail, and one of New Spain's ablest servants, Anza had been handpicked by Commanding General Teodoro de Croix to pacify the Comanches and restore order in the troubled, ailing far north. Anza mustered almost six hundred presidial soldiers, militias, and Indian auxiliaries and equipped each man with a good horse. He set out in mid-August from Santa Fe. As the expedition made its way toward Comanche camping grounds northeast of Taos, some two hundred Utes and Jicarillas joined it, making Anza's party the biggest military expedition Spain would ever send on the plains.

Anza's eight hundred fighting men marched northward from Santa Fe, carefully avoiding the open plains, and surprised a Comanche ranchería of 120 lodges on present-day Fountain Creek. They killed eighteen warriors and thirty women and children, "the latter running where their fathers were," and captured thirty-four women and children. The prisoners divulged startling information: Anza's troops had stumbled upon the ranchería of Cuerno Verde, the legendary "little king" of the western Comanches. The captives also told that Cuerno Verde had left with some fifty warriors to attack Taos. Anza saw here an opportunity to strike at the heart of western Comanche military organization and decided to follow the raiders' path back toward New Mexico. Two days later, Anza encountered the returning Comanches "who gave themselves up to a blind and headlong fight." The Comanches repulsed the first attack, but the next day Anza's troops cut their forces in two and trapped Cuerno Verde and his closest followers in a gully. Cuerno Verde, along with "his first-born son, the heir to his command, four of his most famous captains, a medicine man who preached he was immortal, and ten more," perished. Anza returned to Santa Fe with more than thirty captives, displaying to the citizens the green headgear of the fallen Comanche chief. He reported a major victory to his superiors and sent the headdresses of Cuerno Verde and his "second in command" to Commanding General Croix as the "first trophies which I pay in tribute to you from this province." Comanche raids to New Mexico stopped immediately, and some Comanche leaders began to make peace overtures to Anza. While the previous twelve years had witnessed almost constant attacks, there were only occasional forays after 1780. With a single strike, the Spaniards believed, Anza had brought the raids to a bloody halt and reduced the fearsome Comanches to submission.[3]

A closer look suggests, however, that Anza's victory was more temporally convenient than it was militarily decisive: it occurred just as the Comanches faced a series of crises, whose combined impact forced them to reevaluate their policies toward Spaniards. For years Comanches had enjoyed relative tranquility on their borders, but in the late 1770s wars flared out again. The Kiowas, with whom western Comanches had traded peacefully since midcentury, pushed from the central plains toward Comanchería. Drawn by the warm weather and vast herds of feral horses of the southern plains, and pressured by the westward migrating Cheyennes, Kiowas marched into the Arkansas River basin, where they clashed violently with Yamparikas and Jupes. Hostilities also broke out between the Comanches and Pawnees, destroying the alliance that had existed since 1750. The causes of the rift are not clear, but it is possible that the two nations collided over hunting privileges in the upper Arkansas basin, where bison herds had become depleted during the drought years of the mid-1770s. By the early 1780s, Comanchería's entire northern border had become a battle zone. And while new wars erupted in the north, old ones smoldered on other fronts. Osage hunting and war parties continued to test the hold of Comanchería's eastern border, and Apaches fought bitterly to keep Comanches out of their raiding sphere in southern Texas. The early 1780s also saw the Comanches' seemingly unstoppable expansion into the Ute territory west of the Rockies turn into a retreat.[4]

Engulfed in war, Comanches were also struck by severe economic and commercial reversals. Not only did western Comanches see their long-standing trade links with Kiowas and Pawnees disintegrate into bloodshed, but they also lost their connections with Kansas and Iowas, whose trading power was undercut by overhunting and Osage attempts to monopolize Spanish fur trade from St. Louis. Eastern Comanches faced a similar commercial crisis. In the late 1770s, after a protracted rivalry, they had finally replaced Wichitas as the trade gateway to the lower Mississippi valley—only to see how changing imperial geopolitics smothered the eastern markets. The first blow came in 1779, when Spain joined the thirteen rebelling colonies against Great Britain and seized the eastern bank of the lower Mississippi valley, thus preventing British traders from slipping into Comanchería. Then Franco-Spanish traders of Louisiana withdrew from the plains in order to reap profits from the war that raged up and down the Mississippi and along the Gulf Coast. By the early 1780s the westbound trade from the lower Mississippi valley had all but dried up, rendering eastern Comanches' victory over Wichitas meaningless: they were a trade gateway without trade.[5]

But such military and economic setbacks pale in significance to the demographic disaster that fell upon the Comanches. In 1780 or 1781 a sprawling continent-wide smallpox epidemic descended into Comanchería, causing unforeseen destruction among its nomadic population that had not yet been exposed to the disease and thus formed a virgin soil for the virus to spread and kill. The epidemic, raging from Mexico City to Hudson Bay and the war-ravaged East to the Northwest Coast, struck New Orleans in the winter of 1779–80. It then moved up the Red River to a cluster of newly established Wichita villages north of the Red River and leaped into Comanchería. The devastation was unfathomable. Eastern Comanches stated that they lost two-thirds of their population, perhaps as many as sixteen thousand people. The epidemic also hit New Mexico, but it failed to spread among the nearby western Comanches, who had shunned the province after Anza's shock victory over Cuerno Verde. But even with half of the Comanche nation spared, waves of horror and despair reverberated across Comanchería.[6]

It was in the aftermath of this catastrophe that Comanches finally began to reassess their policies toward the Spaniards. With Native enemies edging into their domain, with their trade network in shambles, and with the eastern rancherías decimated by alien microbes, they found it practical and perhaps necessary to seek closer diplomatic and commercial ties with Spanish colonies. Eastern Comanches cut back their raiding into Texas in the winter of 1781–82, and in 1783 western Comanches opened peace talks in Santa Fe.[7]

Fortunately for Comanches, their desire for peace coincided with a parallel process of political reevaluation on the Spanish side. That reassessment was brought about by the mixed consequences of the American Revolution for Spain. In the treaty accords signed in Paris in 1783, Britain returned the Floridas to Spain, but it also granted the new United States a generous southern boundary on the thirty-first parallel. This outraged Spanish officials who insisted that their West Florida province extended in the north all the way to the Tennessee valley and the confluence of the Ohio and Mississippi rivers. Eager to secure access to the Mississippi frontage and southeastern fur trade, Americans refused to negotiate for a compromise, and so the Spaniards found themselves embroiled in a bitter border dispute with a republic of "a new and vigorous people, hostile to all subjection, advancing and multiplying."[8] The Treaty of Paris thus created an unexpected predicament for the Spaniards. The acquisition of the Floridas fulfilled their long-standing dream of a continuous transcontinental empire in North America, and yet their position felt more threatened than ever.

Spain's simultaneously strong and susceptible position spawned several drastic foreign political schemes. Spanish officials closed the lower Mississippi to American shipping in order to isolate the settler-farmers in Kentucky and Tennessee from transportation and market outlets, but opened Louisiana and the Floridas for American emigrants who promised to become Catholics and the king's vassals. But this policy of confining and co-opting the Americans was a mere emergency measure: Spain's chief tactic in checking the expansionist United States was a new secularized Indian policy.[9]

Lacking the demographic and military power to restrain the Americans, Spanish officials set out to build extensive barriers of loyal Indians on both sides of the Mississippi valley to block the seemingly imminent American expansion to the Great Plains and northern Mexico. Instead of conversion and coercion, the traditional cornerstones of Spain's Indian policy, the agents were now instructed to rely on treaties, trade, and gifts to win Indians' allegiance. East of the Mississippi, the officials negotiated by 1784 agreements with Creeks, Alabamas, Choctaws, Chickasaws, and Seminoles, creating an extensive Indian-alliance network that covered much of the area under dispute with the United States. Carlos III then appointed Bernardo de Gálvez, Louisiana's celebrated governor during the American Revolution and nephew of José de Gálvez, as the viceroy of New Spain. Gálvez's jurisdiction was extended over the Interior Provinces, Louisiana, the Floridas, and Cuba in the hope that the energetic young officer could organize those wide-ranging dominions into a unified front against the United States.[10]

In May 1785, Gálvez sent a letter to Texas Governor Domingo Cabello, demanding that he match Spain's recent diplomatic successes with southeastern Indians on the western side of the Mississippi. All that Cabello had to show for his efforts at that point were a series of aborted treaty talks with the Taovayas and Tawakonis. He immediately began to plan a diplomatic mission to Comanchería and chose two emissaries: Pedro Vial, a French-born blacksmith and Indian trader who had lived for several years among the Taovayas before his recent return to Texas, and Francisco Xavier Chaves, a *vecino* (non-Indian citizen) from New Mexico who had been captured by Comanches at the age of eight and traded to the Taovayas after his adoptive Comanche mother died sixteen years later. Vial possessed intimate knowledge of the political and economic milieu of the southern plains, while Chaves was fluent in the Taovaya and Comanche languages. Cabello equipped Vial and Chaves with two servants, six horses, four mules, four hundred pesos worth of gifts, and a daunting commission: to negotiate a treaty of peace with the eastern Comanches, who had raided and ravaged Texas for decades.[11]

Guided by a delegation of Taovayas who were visiting Nacogdoches, Vial and Chaves arrived in late August at a large Comanche ranchería stretching across a broad plain along the Red River. As the emissaries approached the Comanche village, they were immersed in an intricately orchestrated indigenous diplomacy in which gestures, touches, utterances, and rituals carried deep significance. Some two hundred Comanches, moving in two lines, rode out from the ranchería with their weapons on display. Vial and Chaves unfurled a Spanish flag, the Comanches discharged gun volleys and then embraced the visitors. Vial, Chaves, and the Taovaya guides were escorted to the lodge of the ranchería's *capitan*, who placed their animals and goods under his protection and feasted the visitors with various meats and *papas* (potato-like tubers). When Vial and Chaves announced the purpose of their visit, the Comanche village began to transform into a massive council ground. Arrows were sent to all directions to call the scattered eastern Comanche rancherías together, and within a week ten rancherías had arrived. Among the arrivals were "the two great *capitanes* of the nation"—Camisa de Hierro (Iron Shirt), so named for wearing a coat of mail he had taken from a fallen Apache chief, and Cabeza Rapada (Shaved Head) who shaved half of his head and kept the hair on the other half very long. Vial called the leaders of the eight other rancherías *jefes* (chiefs) or *capitanes chiquitos* (little captains), and remarked that each of them "brought some elder Indian *principales* and many young men."[12]

With the majority of their members present, the eastern Comanches sponsored several successive meetings. These, as recorded by Vial, open an illuminating window into the Comanche statecraft. The first meeting included Vial, Chaves, the two Taovaya chiefs, Guersec and Eschas, and a delegation of Comanche leaders and elders. Vial and Chaves distributed gifts of tobacco, cloth, knives, vermilion, and beads and declared Spain's desire for peace. Comanches appeared wary, however, demanding to know whether the Spaniards "had brought some illness that would bring death to their nation." Once convinced that the visitors were healthy and that it would be safe to assemble a large meeting, the chiefs "gave the order to their criers so that they would carry the word to all of those of their respective groups, with the instruction that they gather at night at the designated place to hold their own councils." "Thereafter," Vial reported, "one could hear a confusion of shouting that would burst out during the day, and murmuring throughout the night." By dawn the Comanches decided to hold a general council "so that all might hear from our own mouths the reason for our coming."[13]

The grand council made a deep impression on Vial with its meticulous ceremonialism, open yet hierarchical composition, and sheer size. "Carrying the Spanish flag hoisted on a very tall pole," he reported, "we presented it in a very large circle which all of the Indians had formed, seated on the ground as many as four deep, seeming in our opinion about 700." The concentric rows of the grand circle were occupied by the two head chiefs, the leaders of individual rancherías, and senior and junior warriors, and they were surrounded by "an infinity of young men, women, and children, who were standing." The council was presided over by Camisa de Hierro and Cabeza Rapada, who introduced the emissaries "with great civility and courtesy" and made them "sit beside them in the first row of the center of the circle." After the "indispensable" prelude of ritual smoking, Vial delivered his message in the "Taovayaz language, which all of the Cumanches understand and speak very well."[14]

Vial began by drawing attention to Chaves, who as a former captive and adopted Comanche personified the possibility of forging kinship-based political relations between the Comanches and Spaniards. He then warned the Comanches that they were about to be excluded from the circle of trade, gifts, and friendship Texas was presently building with other Indian nations. He related how he and Chaves had wept in front of "Capitán Grande" (Governor Cabello), pledging him to extend the alliance to the Comanches, who they insisted "were good people, very generous and very good friends to . . . [their] friends." Finally, Vial presented Cabello's personal peace offer, which rested on four pillars: general war against the Apaches, cessation of all other hostilities, mutualistic trade, and political gifts. "I want them not only to be my friends, but also of the nations who are my friends, and that if they want to enjoy the pleasure of fighting, they should make war against the Apaches and Lipanes who steal many horses and mules from me. . . . I shall give my hand and I shall try to give them whatever I can. And finally, if they be my good friends, I shall order that traders go to their camps to provide all of the traffic that they need, in exchange of skins and whatever goods the said traders may sell. And besides that, every year at the time that I set for them, I shall try to have the *capitanes* and *principales* of the Cumanche Nation come to this Presidio of San Antonio, where I will give them a little present to assure them how highly I regard them."[15]

When Vial concluded, Guersec took the floor to corroborate Vial's assertion that a genuine change had occurred in Spanish Indian policy. Cabello, the Taovaya assured, had committed to offer gifts and liberal trade that included guns, powder, and ammunition. Like Vial, Guersec issued a warning: "I let you know that it is more important for us to maintain friendship with the Spaniards than with you . . . if you continue to be foolish, we will turn our backs to you and we will join with the Spaniards who, after all, succor our needs." Guersec's words must have struck a chord among the Comanches, who had already lost most of their trading links and were now in danger of being excluded from the Taovaya-Spanish coalition.[16]

After Guersec's speech, "commotion erupted among all the Cumanches in the circle," and the meeting adjourned. To Vial it seemed that the ten gathered rancherías dissolved into a single consensus-seeking organism. "The criers spent the remainder of the . . . day talking with their respective groups so that they might understand everything we had related. The same happened at night. All of the passageways of that *ranchería* were so full of bonfires that we thought that none of them might be able to sleep." The two Taovaya chiefs, too, were involved in the talks, conferring in a private council with Camisa de Hierro, Cabeza Rapada, and the headmen of individual rancherías. By morning "all of the Cumanche *capitanes* and *principales* had agreed to make peace."[17] The grand council reconvened, each Comanche occupying the same spot as before, and the ceremonies from the previous day were repeated. Camisa de Hierro then delivered a formal reply to Spain's offer. He emphasized Comanche understanding of what constituted an acceptable peace, framing the accord in kinship terms.

> With great joy we have heard the good words that our Father, the Capitán Grande of San Antonio, has sent us, which we all have embraced in our heart. And thus mollified, we note that in all of the times that you have spoken to us, you have not disquieted us. . . . Therefore, forgetting the killings that the Spaniards have committed against our fathers, sons, and brothers, we are all very content, particularly knowing that our Father, the Capitán Grande of San Antonio, does not like the Apaches nor Lipanes, against whom we make war wherever we may find them. And thus, from now on, the war with our brothers the Spaniards has ended. They will not see our footprints around San Antonio, for we will not subject them to any injuries or thefts. And thus, three *capitanes chiquitos* from our nation are already chosen, so that they may go with you to see what reception our Father, the Capitán Grande, accords us, and what he says to them about the way that we are to commence the peace that we have agreed to make with him, to prove the affection that we have for the Spaniards.[18]

Camisa de Hierro made Spanish noninterference in Comanche-Apache relations a condition for peace: "we shall remain ready to make a solid peace, once our Father, the Capitán Grande of San Antonio, accepts its wholeheartedly, making for our part only the condition that he give us passage [through Texas] and that he not oppose our making war against the Lipanes, our ancient enemies." When the chief concluded his statement, "he began to twirl the length of cloth that we had given him and he had on, and with that, such a shouting and whooping burst out from all those in the circle and from those who were behind it, that they left us deafened for a long time." That demonstration, Vial understood, was "a sign by all of the nation of accepting and agreeing to the said peace." Two days later, Vial and Chaves set out on a return trip to San Antonio with three Comanche *capitanes*.[19]

The three Comanche ambassadors received a cordial welcome in San Antonio. They were paraded around the main streets and welcomed by Cabello at the governor's house. A few days later, a formal treaty, an elaborated version of the preliminary accord made in Comanchería, was concluded. Cabello, apparently having taken to heart Vial's notion that Comanches would remain peaceful only "if they are given what is equivalent to the pillaging . . . they make when they are at war," promised annual gifts to Comanche chiefs "as a manifestation of our good friendship." He also pledged to send in licensed traders "who provide them with merchandise in exchange for hides." The Comanche emissaries in turn promised that their nation would cease all hostilities against Texas, return Spanish captives to Texas, and refrain from interactions with the enemies of Spain. War against the Apaches, as Camisa de Hierro had insisted, was explicitly discussed in the treaty, which stipulated that Comanches and Spaniards would act as brothers against the Apaches, their common enemy. Comanches were given a free reign to make war on the Apaches in Texas, for the treaty only specified that they should seek a permit from Texas governor if they intended to pursue Lipans and Mescaleros into Coahuila.[20]

After three weeks of talks, the Comanche delegates left, clad in Spanish military uniforms, carrying canes of office and a white flag with a Burgundian cross, and escorted by forty-two Spanish soldiers. During the fall and winter several other Comanche chiefs visited San Antonio to broaden the peace. Their travois were loaded with hides, peltries, and meat they intended to trade, and they often brought their families with them. They also offered Spanish officials Apache slaves who had been captured in Sonora, anticipating the wide-ranging geopolitical changes that the Comanche-Spanish alliance would soon engender across New Spain's northern borderlands. Cabello, having discovered that it was "necessary to treat them [Comanches] with great love and consistency because they are very sensitive and will not tolerate any rudeness," opened the capital to the people who a few years ago had nearly obliterated the colony. He feasted Comanche chiefs at his residence, lavished them with gifts, and built their families a 144-foot-long wattle-and-daub house on the banks of the San Antonio River, where the Indians could enjoy their daily baths.[21]

While Comanche-Spanish relations steered a new course in the east, Governor Anza in New Mexico struggled to open conclusive peace talks with the western Comanches. The shock effect of his victory over Cuerno Verde had evaporated long ago, and although Comanches were again trading in Taos in large numbers, the peace process had stalled. In October 1785 a Comanche trading party revealed the reason for the deadlock: unable to agree over a common policy toward the Spaniards, the western Comanches had split into two opposing blocks. Most Kotsoteka chiefs and rancherías favored general peace with New Mexico, but they were resisted by the chiefs who had risen to power through their ability to lead successful raids into New Mexico. Some of the resistance had melted away with Cuerno Verde's demise, but another powerful chief, Toroblanco (White Bull), had risen to lead the war faction. Toroblanco enjoyed wide support among the Yamparikas and Jupes, and the peace faction was losing ground. Anza sent word that he would not begin negotiations unless the western Comanches united behind one chief who could speak for all of them. To keep the avenues for dialogue open, the Comanche party returned two New Mexican captives and voluntarily left two of their own members among the Spaniards as hostages.[22]

In late fall 1785, however, the Kotsoteka-centered peace faction received a boost when the news of the eastern Comanches' treaty with Texas reached western Comanchería. It is possible that the news was brought by Camisa de Hierro, who had conferred with Vial and Chaves in September and promised to report of the talks "to the Yambericas, our comrades and brothers." In November six hundred western Comanche households, some six thousand people, gathered at the Big Timbers of the Arkansas to prepare for peace talks with Anza. A Kotsoteka chief called Ecueracapa was elected as western Comanches' delegate to New Mexico. As Pedro Garrido, a Spanish official who summarized New Mexican reports to the commanding general of the Interior Provinces, understood the events, Ecueracapa was chosen "to seek a new adjustment and establishment of their commerce in New Mexico" by conferring "directly with the governor to remove the deterring obstacles."[23]

Ecueracapa was uniquely equipped for an intermediary role between the western Comanches and Spaniards. Indeed, it is possible that the Ecueracapa of the western Comanches and Camisa de Hierro of the eastern Comanches were the same person: the Spaniards in New Mexico knew Ecueracapa also as Cota de Malla (Coat of Mail), and several Spanish officials stated that Ecueracapa/Cota de Malla was the same person as Camisa de Hierro—"Ecueracapa" may have been a derivative of Spanish words *cuera*, "leather jacket," and *capa*, "cape" or "cloak." Ecueracapa may have thus been an eastern Comanche envoy turned into a western Comanche representative who traveled across Comanchería with his accumulated experience in dealings with Spanish colonial agents. According to Garrido, Ecueracapa was known as "one without equal in military achievements" and, more important, distinguished "by his adroitness and intelligence in political matters." Perhaps because he was a newcomer to western Comanche politics, he took decisive measures to consolidate his authority. He reportedly warned the council that elected him that if the other western Comanche chiefs were to abandon him, "he would attach himself to the Spanish party." Soon after, Kotsoteka agents assassinated Toroblanco, demolishing the war faction. After this, Garrido wrote, Toroblanco's followers "adhered to the dominant party of the Cuchanecs [Kotsotekas], except some belonging to the . . . [ranchería] of the dead captain who separated into a little band to commit hostilities."[24]

In December an unanticipated opening to start peace talks with the Spaniards appeared to Ecueracapa. An Indian member of a plains-bound Spanish hunting party became separated from the main group and "was made prisoner by the spies of Ecueracapa, who took him for a pagan whose costume he was wearing." Upon learning that the man, José Chiquito, spoke the Comanche language, Ecueracapa decided to use him as an intermediary. He called together four consecutive councils to discuss the details of peace talks and, having reached an agreement with the other chiefs, sent Chiquito and two Comanche envoys to inform Anza that he would be arriving shortly in Santa Fe.[25]

The announcement electrified the Southwest, where news traveled quickly through the networks of commerce and kinship. Settlers along the New Mexican border were ecstatic over the prospect of peace that would put an end to their long suffering under Comanche onslaughts. "The news of these events ran rapidly through the pueblos of the province," Garrido wrote, "because of its circumstance of which there was no previous example, and spread among the inhabitants the belief that this time peace with the Comanche nation would be attained." In January 1786 a group of western Comanches attacked Pecos in what proved the last gush of the war faction. Kotsotekas tracked down the perpetrators, and Ecueracapa personally executed their leader. He then sent a delegation to Santa Fe to apologize for the transgression and to offer the news of the execution as a ritual compensation.[26]

Word of the forthcoming Comanche-Spanish negotiations also reached the Utes, who were outraged by the new Spanish policy. Having nurtured a stable and mutually beneficial alliance with New Mexico since midcentury—an alliance that had been sustained by common dread of the Comanches—they now feared that Comanche-Spanish rapprochement would leave them marginalized and exposed to Comanche violence. In January 1786 Moara and Pinto, "two of their most authoritative chiefs," arrived in Santa Fe. They met with Anza and "heatedly declared against the attempted peace, advancing the most vindictive and even insulting and barbarous arguments to destroy it, even stating to that chief, Anza, that he preferred frequent, unfaithful rebels to friends always obedient and faithful." "They were so inflamed," Garrido stated, "that for more than four hours while they repeated their arguments, they did not wish to smoke or accept any presents." Anza listened to the chiefs' grievances, insisting that the king "could not avoid extending this grace to whoever implored it," and finally "promised to interpose all his meditation with the Comanches in proof of the appreciation which he had of their faithful and ancient friendship." He invited the Ute delegates to stay in Santa Fe for the forthcoming negotiations with Ecueracapa.[27]

When Ecueracapa arrived in Santa Fe on February 25, 1786, the town stirred with expectant tension. Anza extended the chief a stately welcome, and Ecueracapa responded in kind, maintaining the elaborate social performance that culminated in the momentous embrace at the doorway of the Governor's Palace. The negotiations inside the palace, however, were more pragmatic than ceremonial. Ecueracapa came armed with a detailed agenda that had been approved in large western Comanche assemblies. (It also appears that Comanche emissaries had discussed possible treaty stipulations in Taos and other border villages with close ties to Comanchería.) That agenda, presented "in the name of all his people," stemmed from the outstanding problem the western Comanches faced in the mid-1780s: the acute lack of goods resulting from the disruption of trade. Having lost their exchange links in the north and east, Comanches now sought to dominate the exchange networks and resources of the Southwest borderlands.[28]

Ecueracapa wanted a "new and better established peace" with New Mexico, and to that end, demanded a number of concessions from the Spaniards: the right to "settle and subsist a short distance from the settlements," "the establishment of fairs and free trade with Pecos," and "free and safe passage through Pecos to Santa Fe" for the purpose of cultivating "reciprocal friendship and commerce." Finally, Ecueracapa proposed a joint war against "the common enemies, the Apaches." Collectively, these stipulations would have given the Comanches a virtual monopoly over New Mexico's eastern markets: they already possessed a secure access to the Taos fairs, and now Pecos and Santa Fe would fall within their commercial sphere. Unhindered exchange was thus the basic tenet of the peace, and the idea of an anti-Apache military alliance, too, sprang from this concern. Although most Apache groups had fled the plains, a few Jicarilla bands still resided near Pecos and Santa Fe, compromising Comanches' access to New Mexico's border villages. These Jicarilla rancherías also prevented Comanches from entering the prime hunting range west of the Pecos River where bison herds congregated in winters. By demanding the right to "settle and subsist a short distance" from Spanish settlements, Ecueracapa in effect pressured Anza to recognize Comanche control over those key border zones and hunting ranges. Spaniards, he demanded, should make an unequivocal commitment to the Comanches, cut off all support to the Apaches, and, if necessary, help Comanches eliminate the remaining Apaches from Pecos's and Santa Fe's vicinity by force.[29]

After laying out the framework for peace, Ecueracapa moved to the specifics. He asked Anza to deliver a formal reply to his offer in the more eastern village of Pecos, where other Comanche chiefs were already gathering. He also asked the governor to assign "him at that same moment a token or credential" of his standing among the Spaniards so that "he would be able to prove to his scattered rancherías that all their nation was admitted to peace." Here, it seems, Ecueracapa's political agenda blended with a personal one: he wanted to expose the treaty stipulations to public display and public censure by his followers while by the same token using the public space to boost his own power base among the western Comanches.[30]

These talks had been carried out in the presence of seven Ute delegates, and the summit ended with Ecueracapa and the Ute representatives forming a peace agreement. The agreement was cemented "according to their manner": the two sides exchanged clothes to cleanse the relationship of ill-feeling and rekindle their frayed kinship bond. The accord, which ended more than thirty years of on-and-off Comanches-Ute warfare, becomes understandable in the context of Ecueracapa's treaty conditions to Anza. If Comanches were to gain unrestricted access to Pecos and Santa Fe fairs in central New Mexico, there would be less need to keep the Utes out of northern New Mexican markets. The focus of Comanche commerce was about to shift to the south, which gave the Utes on New Mexico's northern borderlands more breathing space. Comanche chiefs declared later during the peace process that "the advantages they had secured [from the Spaniards] would serve to stimulate them to carry on . . . trade with greater zeal, transferring, if not all, the greater part of their fairs to the pueblo of Pecos."[31]

Anza, the celebrated slayer of Cuerno Verde, found himself upstaged by the assertive diplomacy of Ecueracapa who had faced the governor as an equal, if not in fact as a superior. Confounded, the governor improvised. He broke off formal council and invited Ecueracapa to a private tête-à-tête. Deeply impressed by the "talent, judiciousness, and remarkable genius of this captain," Garrido later explained, "the politic idea [had] occurred to Anza—suggested before but never given effect in similar cases—namely that by means of his person, elevating him above the rest of his class, he would be able, perhaps, to submit subtly all his nation to the dominion of the king without using violent means contrary to his sovereign intentions." Out of the public eye, Anza urged Ecueracapa to "take charge of the government and absolute direction of its national interests." Appealing to what he understood as Indians' penchant for personalized politics, he promised to decorate Ecueracapa "with the medal of his royal bust" on the condition that the chief give the governor "token of his submission and fidelity to the king." Ecueracapa's response was polite but noncommittal. He accepted the medal but insisted that he would have worked "for the execution of as much as Anza had suggested to him . . . even if Anza had not interposed to aid him toward the general command." Ecueracapa, in other words, accepted the bestowal of the medal as an honorific gesture symbolizing his social standing and Anza's respect for his authority, but subtly rejected the governor's meddling with Comanche politics. Through affirming his own agency, he erected strict boundaries for the alliance.[32]

In keeping with Ecueracapa's request, the conference then moved to Pecos, where hundreds of Kotsotekas had gathered to hear the outcome of the talks.

When Anza arrived, the settlement resembled less a Pueblo Indian village than a Comanche ranchería. The governor was guided into a massive Comanche camp at the town's center where some two hundred Kotsoteka men lined up to embrace him "with excessive expressions of affection and respect to which," an appalled Garrido noted, "they were hardly entitled by their rank and standing." The embraces Garrido saw as improper, uncivil exhibitions of intimacy and emotion in fact constituted an essential bonding ritual intended to translate physical touch into personal ties on which diplomatic relations could rest.[33] Thus, after the ceremony, eleven Kotsoteka chiefs and thirty-one headmen received Anza in a large hide lodge, the site of the summit. Surrounded by the headmen, the chiefs "seated themselves according to order . . . in the first place, Ecueracapa, followed successively by Tosacondata, Tosapoy, Hichapat, Parraginanchi, Cuetaninaveni, Quihuaneantime, Sohuacat, Canaguaipe, Pisimampat, Toyamancare and Tichinalla." Tosapoy, who acted as *tekwawapi̲*, designated speaker for the Kotsotekas, reiterated the main Comanche concern, requesting Comanches and Spaniards to "conduct themselves with the demonstrations and affections of children, and with equity and justice in the particular matter of commerce." To invoke such unconditional affinity, Tosapoy ruefully admitted his personal "quarrel with a Spaniard who was present." He then "delivered (on his knees) a native of Santa Fe whom they had [held] . . . prisoner among them for eleven years."

With a proper ritual social space thus created, Anza gave his formal reply to Ecueracapa's treaty terms. He accepted them one by one, but he did so "in the name of the king whose great power he was shortly imposing upon them." He presented Ecueracapa with his personal staff of office (rather than the proposed medal with a bust of the king of Spain) and expressed a wish that the chief would display the cane at "the absent rancherías" as "the most certain token of their having been admitted to peace." Ecueracapa, however, in a symbolically momentous act, asked that the cane "be transferred to Tosacondata, second in authority, whom from that moment he was commissioning to conduct and exhibit the emblem where he would advise him." Comanches concluded the talks by making "in the soil a hole which they refilled with various attendant ceremonies. In this (as they say, and is the custom among them) they also buried the war on their part."[34]

The next day, at Comanches' request, Anza sponsored a trade fair. In line with the treaty terms, the governor ordered the Pecoseños to refrain from "excesses experienced in similar events." He also adjusted a previous tariff from 1754 in Comanches' advantage, specifying that they should receive not one but two *belduques* (butchering knives) for a buffalo robe and thirteen *belduques* for an average horse. To institute order, Anza "marked off two lines so that the contracting parties, placed on the outside of both, could exhibit and deliver to each other in the intermediate space the effects which they had to exchange." Visibly "gratified" by the arrangement, Comanches bartered more than six hundred bison robes, fifteen horses, three guns, and "many loads of meat and tallow" for hard bread and iron tools.[35]

That fair sealed the outcome of the negotiations, for its meaning was more than material. By regulating the prices and by pledging to establish "just rule" at the fairs, Anza had, at least superficially, embraced the Comanche idea that trade was more than a means of profit-making; it was an avenue for sharing. By trying to satisfy Comanche needs through exchange, moreover, Anza unknowingly secured the political alliance itself, for in Comanche culture economic ties could not be divorced from political ones. Sustained exchange was a precondition for sustained peace, and an alliance could endure only between people who took care of each other's needs, political and material alike. It is telling that when the bartering was concluded and the fair closed, Comanche chiefs told Anza "that they understood now more than ever the assurance of our peace, and by virtue of the justice and sympathy employed with them, were bound to be faithful forever."[36] As they had done with Governor Tomás Vélez de Cachupín a generation before, Comanches guided Anza through the proper process of building an enduring peace. And like Cachupín before him, Anza did his best to advance Spain's imperial ambitions within the parameters of Comanche cultural logic—however imperfectly he may have understood those parameters.

The Comanche treaty was a momentous coup for Anza and it gave him leverage to enter into negotiations with the powerful Navajos who dominated a vast territory west of New Mexico. In March 1786, only weeks after the conclusion of Comanche talks, Anza invited Navajo leaders to a peace conference. His objective was to pacify the Navajos by forcing them to resign their alliance with the Gileño Apaches, and he had laid the ground for this move a year before when he banned all trade between the Navajos and the inhabitants of New Mexico. Now eighty Navajos came to meet with him in Santa Fe where, significantly, a small Comanche delegation was also present. When the talks between Anza and Navajo leaders began in the Governor's Palace, two Comanches, at Anza's request, made a surprise entrance "so that the Navajos, having seen them, might be moved by the fear and respect they have for this warlike nation." According to Garrido's report, one of the Comanches demanded that the Navajos become Spain's allies, lest "the forces of the Comanches as good allies and friends of the Spaniards would come and exterminate them. He menaced and terrorized them so much that with the same submission which the governor [received] they replied to the Comanches that they would fail in nothing agreed upon." The Navajos agreed to a treaty in which they pledged to sever ties with the Gileños, form a military alliance with Spain, and enter a nonaggression pact with the Comanches. The resulting borderlands détente, midwifed by Comanches, served Comanche interests as much as it served Spanish ones: if Comanches were to develop closer commercial relations with New Mexico, they needed the colony to be safe and prosperous.[37]

The Spanish-Navajo-Comanche treaty completed a burst of cross-cultural diplomacy that, in the space of two years, reconfigured the cultural and geopolitical landscape of the Southwest. Whereas earlier contestation and violence had defined intergroup relations, now the region's four major nations—the Spaniards, Comanches, Navajos, and Utes—came together in diplomacy and trade. The new multipolar coalition was made possible by the Comanche-Spanish alliance, but it was hitched in place by common animosity against the Apaches, the great losers of the geopolitical reordering. Segregated from the tightening circle of commerce, conciliation, and kinship, the Apaches were shut out as enemies of all. Only the ever-adaptable Jicarillas managed to maneuver into the alliance network and maintain a narrow foothold in the ravines of the Sangre de Cristo Range near Picurís. But they were marginal members of the network, living far from New Mexico's political and commercial centers, and their political and economic relations with the Spaniards were made subordinate to Comanche needs and demands.[38]

With New Mexico and Texas seemingly protected through Comanche treaties, Spanish officials refocused the empire's vacillating Apache policy around the exterminationist agenda marqués de Rubí had advocated two decades earlier. Viceroy Bernardo de Gálvez announced in 1786 that he was "very much in favor of the special ruination of the Apaches" and authorized a genocidal war against all Apaches who refused to submit to Spanish domination. "In the voluntary or forced submission of the Apaches, or in their total extermination," he explained, "lies the happiness of the Provincias Internas." Spaniards launched coordinated campaigns with their Pima and Opata Indian allies against various Apache groups in Sonora and Nueva Vizcaya and increased military pressure on the Gileños and Mescaleros in southern New Mexico. Spanish officials began offering bounties for pairs of Apache ears across the northern provinces and promised Comanches a bridled horse and two *belduques* for each Apache captive they delivered to Santa Fe.[39]

After the conclusion of the treaties in 1785 and 1786, Comanches and Spaniards worked diligently to cultivate and expand the peace that had stabilized the

Southwest. In early May of 1786, when the Comanche–New Mexico accord had been in effect for two months, Tosacondata, Ecueracapa's lieutenant, reported in Santa Fe that he had traveled across western Comanchería, visiting Kotsoteka, Jupe, and Yamparika rancherías. "In all he had announced peace, exhibiting to them the cane in testimony of it and of his trust," and all had accepted the cane "as a sure sign" of their approval of peace. Anza, now using language that blended Comanche ideas of metaphorical kinship with Spanish notions of patriarchal order, responded that he "was watching with the tenderness of a father the rapidity with which they were moving toward their own happiness."[40]

During the late spring and early summer, several Jupe and Yamparika embassies came to Pecos and Santa Fe to meet with Anza in person and declare their support for the peace that had begun as a narrow Kotsoteka-Spanish pact. As had happened during Governor Cachupín's tenure a generation ago, a nascent common ground of mutual compromise and tolerance began to emerge out of these meetings. The Comanche visitors, Spanish officials rejoiced, "showed a great desire to understand our language, to accommodate themselves to our customs in whatever they could imitate, even in matters of religion." For their part, the Spaniards spent more than six hundred pesos in feeding and housing the Comanches and "for presents voluntarily divided among them and for demonstrations of our affection."[41]

The frequent visits to New Mexico reflected the Comanche principle that relationships between societies should be forged and cemented through intimate, face-to-face interactions. Comanches had begun to mold the Spaniards into metaphorical kin whose actions would be guided more by familial obligations than political contracts. This personalization of Comanche-Spanish relations through fictive kinship culminated in late May 1786, when Paraginanchi, a Kotsoteka captain, brought Ecueracapa's third and youngest son, twenty-year-old Tahuchimpia, to Santa Fe, stating that Ecueracapa "charged Anza strongly to instruct his son in the language and customs of the Spaniards as if he were his own child." By now conversant in Comanche diplomacy, Anza accepted Ecueracapa's offer and pledged to treat the young man "as his very own."[42]

With Ecueracapa's and Anza's close personal bond now at its core, the western Comanche–New Mexican alliance won widespread acceptance on both sides. In July, Ecueracapa traveled to Santa Fe where he told Anza that the western Comanches would soon formally recognize his status as "Superior Chief." On the Spanish side, Jacobo Ugarte y Loyola, the newly elected commanding general of the Interior Provinces, approved Anza's settlement with Ecueracapa. But Ugarte also made several additions to the treaty stipulations, which he seems to have found too lenient. He ordered Anza to find ways to induce the Comanches to settle in permanent farming villages near New Mexico so "they might forget hunting." He commanded the governor to bestow Ecueracapa with an annual salary of two hundred pesos, and in keeping with Spanish expectations of hierarchical government, he wanted Anza to persuade the Kotsotekas, Jupes, and Yamparikas to each elect a lieutenant general who would be subordinate to Ecueracapa and receive one hundred pesos per annum from the Spaniards. Finally, Ugarte addressed the politically and culturally charged question of captives and slaves. He demanded that Comanches return all their Christian captives without compensation but authorized Anza to ransom from them all Apache captives under the age of fourteen. This "useful and Christian thought," Ugarte explained, would encourage Comanches to "conserve [the] life of those of the above-mentioned age," but unmentioned in his humanitarian reasoning was the fact that Indian children were highly desired commodities across northern New Spain. Intentionally or not, Ugarte's oblique decree sanctioned the continuation of the age-old *rescate* institution in Spanish-Comanche borderlands.[43]

The peace process culminated in the winter of 1786–87. In November Anza traveled to Comanchería where he witnessed a large western Comanche council appointing Ecueracapa as "captain general" with Tosacondata as his lieutenant. Comanches ratified a modified treaty that included Ugarte's revisions. A few weeks later Oxamaguea, Ecueracapa's son, and Tosacondata led a delegation of nine Comanche men and two women to Ugarte's headquarters in Chihuahua City, where the commanding general ratified the peace treaty and bestowed each Comanche man with a medal and a musket in recognition of his status. Finally in April 1787, Anza journeyed for the last time to Comanchería to observe how Ecueracapa and Tosacondata were formally recognized as general and lieutenant general of the Kotsotekas and witness Paruanarimuca (Bear Harness) appointed as lieutenant general for the Jupes and Yamparikas.[44]

Then, in July 1787, Chief Paruanarimuca came to Santa Fe with a startling proposal: he wanted the Spaniards to build an *establecimiento fijado* for his people on the upper Arkansas River near the Rocky Mountains. The idea of a fixed settlement probably stemmed from yet another dry spell that spread starvation in Comanchería: Paruanarimuca, it appears, hoped to create a secure supply depot inside Comanchería to help his followers through the hard times. Anza, however, saw in Paruanarimuca's anguish an opportunity to realize Ugarte's vision of cultural engineering that would mold Comanches into sedentary farmers. He dispatched a master builder and thirty laborers to construct adobe houses and sheep and ox corrals on the upper Arkansas River, the chosen cradle for Comanche urbanization. When Anza was reassigned to Sonora in the fall, Ugarte ordered his successor, Fernando de la Concha, to make certain that the Jupes participated in the construction work so they "develop an affection for their possession." The construction was slow and expensive, costing New Mexico nearly seven hundred pesos, more than 10 percent of its annual budget for Indian affairs. By early winter, numerous Jupe households had settled in the half-finished village, prompting Concha to exult how "the disposition of the Comanche nation is such that it will embrace any proposal made to them with gentleness, affection, and a few gifts." This settlement may well have grown into an important link between New Mexico and Comanchería had Paruanarimuca's favorite wife not died suddenly in January 1788. The chief and his followers immediately deserted the village, which they now considered uninhabitable, possibly infested with a deadly disease. Spanish officials pleaded them to return but to no avail.[45]

As dramatic a demonstration as the settlement experiment was of the nascent Comanche-Spanish rapprochement, border fairs formed the heart and the sinews of the union. Spanish officials opened New Mexico's border villages to Comanches who embarked on a vigorous exchange to satisfy their pent-up demand for European imports. Jupes and Yamparikas traded in Taos, where, at the standing orders of Viceroy Gálvez, they "never should be denied whatever they request." Kotsotekas concentrated their business in Picurís and especially in Pecos, which soon began to compete with Taos as New Mexico's main gateway to Comanchería. Most Comanche convoys came to the border fairs in late summer and early fall, after the great summer hunts in Comanchería and the fall harvest in New Mexico. In addition to bulk provisions, Comanches obtained from the fairs a wide variety of luxuries and manufactured goods—raw sugar, cigarettes, scissors, soap, mirrors, saddlebags, hatchets, war axes, lances, knives, scarlet cloth, serapes, woolens, cloaks, indigo, and vermilion—which flowed into New Mexico from Chihuahua via the Chihuahua Trail. In exchange, Comanches traded "Indian captives of both sexes, mules, moccasins, colts, mustangs, all kinds of hides and buffalo meat" and so many horses that Taos and Pecos were soon reported having "a considerable number." Comanches and Spaniards also shared resources outside the market. Between 1787 and 1789, for example, New Mexico donated almost three hundred bushels of corn to the drought-ravaged Comanches who were struggling to keep hunger out of their camps.[46]

Just as Spaniards opened New Mexico to Comanches, Comanches unlocked the plains to New Mexicans. They allowed New Mexican bison hunters, ciboleros, to enter Comanchería's hunting ranges, and soon large caravans of two-wheeled *carretas* journeyed annually eastward from New Mexico's various border towns. During their long travels, ciboleros engaged in trade with Comanches, supplying them with bread, flour, sugar, and beads in exchange for the right to hunt bison. Governor Concha gave a formal endorsement to such a commerce in 1789 by authorizing New Mexican traders to travel to Comanchería under the pretext that their activities helped accumulate "a complete knowledge of the waterholes and lands in which [the Comanches] are situated, in order to wage war with this advantage in case they suffer some alteration in the established peace." The itinerant New Mexican traders were initially called *llaneros* (plainsmen) or *viageros* (travelers), but would later become known simply as comancheros.[47]

While expanding political and economic ties, Comanches and Spaniards also launched a joint war against the Apaches. Spanish officials equipped Comanche war parties with horses and guns and informed them of the locations of distant Apaches camps. Between 1786 and 1788, Comanches and Spaniards combined their forces for at least fiver major campaigns against the Apaches, razing Gileño and Mimbreño villages across New Mexico. All the while Comanches also raided the Apaches on their own, seizing captives whom they absorbed into their ranks or sold to Spanish authorities in New Mexico and Texas, who in turn shipped shackled Apache slaves to labor camps in central Mexico and sugar plantations in the Caribbean. By decade's end, Gileños and Mimbreños were fleeing in droves to Sonora and Nueva Vizcaya—only to run into the anti-Apache coalition the Spaniards had forged with the Pimas and Opatas. Caught between two aggressive fronts, many Apache groups sought peace with the Spaniards, allowing New Spain to enjoy at long last a measure of tranquility on its northern borderlands. As for Comanches, the Apache capitulation marked the realization of Ecueracapa's vision. They had eliminated the Apache presence from their borders and hunting ranges and won a monopoly over New Mexico's eastern markets.[48]

On the Comanche-Texas borderlands, meanwhile, a similar, albeit less intense, process of cross-cultural conciliation and cooperation was unfolding. The political alliance between the eastern Comanches and Spaniards never reached the depth of the western Comanche–New Mexico union, in part because Commanding General Ugarte had assigned New Mexico the lead role in Comanche diplomacy, and in part because Cabeza Rapada, the powerful eastern Comanche head chief, died in 1786, leaving behind a temporary power vacuum and political confusion in eastern Comanchería. Unlike in New Mexico, therefore, Spanish officials in Texas had only sporadic interactions with and limited knowledge of the top-level Comanche leadership. Between eastern Comanchería and Spanish Texas there was no parallel to the unifying Ecueracapa-Anza bond.[49]

Trade, however, flourished on the Comanche-Texas border. Spanish traders frequented Comanche rancherías, and Comanche trade convoys visited the Texas border towns. In 1806 alone more than two thousand Comanches visited

San Antonio and Nacogdoches to barter bison products and Apache captives for horses, *belduques*, clothing, and iron tools. As in New Mexico, Spanish officials regulated the prices at the fairs and distributed abundant presents—medals, canes, uniforms, flags, tobacco, and guns—to Comanche chiefs, who in turn pledged to honor the peace with the province. Comanches even invited Spaniards to reactivate the San Sabá mission as a trading depot for eastern Comanchería.[50]

Much as their western relatives did with New Mexico, eastern Comanches commenced close militarily cooperation with Texas. This collaboration was given particular urgency by the revival of the Lipan Apaches, who had gradually rebuilt their economy and military power in the early 1780s, at a time when smallpox devastated the Comanches and the American Revolutionary War preoccupied the Spaniards. With their enemies temporarily weakened or distracted, Lipans raided horses and mules in Coahuila, Nuevo León, and Nuevo Santander; bartered stolen livestock for food and manufactures at the Spanish towns along the lower Río Grande; and obtained guns from the lower Mississippi valley through Native middlemen. Thus reinforced, Lipans made yet another bid to reenter the buffalo plains in the north. So forceful was their thrust that the Comanches persuaded the Taovayas to relocate from the Red River south to the Pedernales River, where their reconstructed villages served as a bulwark for eastern Comanchería.[51]

The revived Lipan power pushed the eastern Comanches, the Wichitas, and Spanish Texas into a firm anti-Apache alliance. Beginning in 1786, Comanches and Wichitas staged several individual and joint attacks against the Lipans and their Mescalero allies, all of them strongly endorsed by Spanish officials who supplied provisions, horses, and guns as well as information on the whereabouts of Lipan rancherías. In 1789 and 1790 the Spaniards briefly entered the war on the ground by joining the Comanches and Wichitas in raiding Lipan rancherías near San Antonio. A subsequent series of Comanche attacks broke Lipan power. In a repeat of the 1750s, the Lipans retreated to the Río Grande, and like the Gileños and Mimbreños farther west, many of them sued for peace and solicited Spanish protection.[52]

By the early 1790s, then, northern New Spain had entered a new era. The Apaches who had kept vast expanses of the Spanish empire in chaos since mid-century appeared pacified. From Sonora to southern Texas, different Apache groups accepted subordinate positions under Spanish rule and settled in *establecimientos de paz*, peace establishments, where they were to live in towns near presidios and missions and learn the civilized arts of farming, ranching, and self-government under Spanish tutelage and control. By 1793, there were eight *establecimientos* in Sonora, Nueva Vizcaya, Coahuila, and New Mexico, housing some two thousand Apaches. Farther north, the formidable Navajos lived in peace with New Mexico, having severed their ties to the Gileños with whom they had raided the colony for decades. The Utes, Jicarillas, and Wichitas, too, had made treaties with the Spaniards, who in turn had modified their paternalistic and aggressive policies in favor of diplomacy and trade.[53]

But the most dramatic changes took place on the plains borderlands where the Spanish empire brushed against Comanchería. Whereas in the 1760s and 1770s Comanches had treated New Mexico and Texas almost as colonial possessions and nearly destroyed both, coexistence and cooperation now seemed to define Comanche-Spanish relations. Things that only a few years before would have been unthinkable suddenly appeared almost commonplace. Spanish officials supplied guns, uniforms, and staffs of office to Comanche chiefs, who in turn pledged loyalty to their "father," the king of Spain. Sons of Comanche elite lived among the Spaniards to learn their customs and language, and several Comanches accepted baptism in New Mexico. Spanish officials fed their Comanche allies during times of hardship and New Mexicans hunted bison on Comanche lands. Pedro Vial and other Spanish explorers blazed trails across Comanchería to connect the hitherto separated San Antonio and Santa Fe, and Comanches camped freely within the borders of Texas and New Mexico. Spanish-Comanche-Navajo war parties ranged from Texas to Nueva Vizcaya, turning Apachería's expansion into contraction, and Nueva Vizcaya officials believed that the time was ripe to start missionizing the Comanches.[54]

If looked at quickly, Comanchería, New Mexico, and Texas seemed to blur into a single political and economic entity within which peoples, commodities, customs, and ideas moved fluidly across borders that connected, rather than separated, the two nations. As one Spanish visitor to Comanchería reported in 1786, Comanches "say that now the Comanches are Spaniards, and Spaniards, Comanches."[55]

But that image of the Comanche-Spanish borderlands as a middle ground in the making was a façade, an elaborate artifice. Beneath the surface of amity and mutual adaptation and respect, a different kind of development was unfolding. Spanish officials were working methodically to reduce the Comanches to dependence and vassalage, using the very acts and institutions—gifts, trade, and political-military collaboration—that seemingly were creating a common ground between the nations. The embrace the Spaniards offered to Comanches was fatherly and supportive, but it was also cynical, calculated, restraining, and potentially suffocating. When Bourbon officials cast themselves as fathers for

Comanche children, they meant to command, not compromise. They intended to be less benevolent parental figures than authoritarian patriarchs.

Such plans of controlling Indians through commerce and personal diplomacy were not new to Spanish policymakers. Progressive officials had debated the merits of war and commerce as the best instrument for controlling Indians since midcentury when an anonymous manuscript, *Nuevo sistema de gobierno económico para la Ameríca,* began to circulate in the colonies, and frontier officials like Cachupín, Cabello, and Anza had improvised and experimented with new strategies as they dealt with powerful independent Indians who refused to submit to Spanish arms. But the new policies were not codified in northern New Spain until 1786 when Viceroy Bernardo de Gálvez issued his famous *Instructions for Governing the Interior Provinces of New Spain.*[56]

The *Instructions* of 1786 built on and refined José de Gálvez's temporary guidelines from 1772, but Bernardo de Gálvez added a distinctively cynical and exploitative streak to his uncle's orders. As acting governor of Louisiana from 1777 to 1783, Gálvez had observed firsthand how the colony's French agents used gifts and trade to induce dependence among Indians and had become convinced that the French model would allow Spain too to achieve what he called "peace by deceit." His *Instructions* advocated unrestricted trade with Indians as the means to control them. Reiterating the widely held belief that Indians raided Spanish colonies because they were foraging nomads and therefore chronically poor, Gálvez noted that hunting and warfare "are not enough to supply the prime necessities of existence. And so, if they do not rob, they perish of hunger and misery." But the primitiveness and poverty, Gálvez argued, also exposed the Indians to external manipulation: "The interest in commerce binds and narrows the desires of man; and it is my wish to establish trade with the Indians." He elaborated: "We shall benefit by satisfying their desires. It will cost the king less than what is now spent in considerable and useless reinforcements of troops. The Indians cannot live without our aid. They will go to war against one another in our behalf and from their own warlike inclinations, or they may possibly improve their customs by following our good example, voluntarily embracing our religion and vassalage. And by these means they will keep faith in their truces."[57]

Gálvez also authorized the sale of firearms to Indians, arguing that the use of guns would weaken Indians' fighting ability, because the muzzle-loading rifle was less effective than the bow, which "is always ready to use." As detailed as they were sweeping, Gálvez's *Instructions* specified that guns should have "weak bolts without the best temper" and long barrels, which would "make them awkward for long rides on horseback, resulting in continual damages and repeated need for mending or replacement." This, he explained, would make the Natives dependent on the Spaniards for repairs and replacements. When Indians "begin to lose their skill in handling the bow," he predicted, they would not only lose their military edge; to keep themselves continually supplied with guns, powder, and shot, "they would be forced to seek our friendship and aid." And if hostilities erupted, Spaniards could simply withhold powder and lead from Indians.[58]

Prompted by Gálvez's *Instructions*, Spaniards also adopted a strategy of remolding Native polities in ways that would render them susceptible to external manipulation. Rather than trying to incorporate or contain indigenous societies, the new objective was to transform them into an entity that Spanish agents could understand, manage, and control. In New Mexico and Texas, where Spaniards were virtually engulfed by ostensibly unorganized nomadic Comanches, the strategy of imposed political reform became the cornerstone of frontier diplomacy. Bourbon officials had initially thought that more authoritative Comanche leaders were needed to unite unruly Indians behind peace treaties, but once the treaties were formalized, the officials reconceived political centralization as a means to subdue their new allies. Inspired by pragmatic visions of a consolidated New Spain, the Bourbon officials had concluded that they could never bring the empire to Comanchería. Instead, they resolved to bring the Comanches into the empire.

Bourbon officials applied the centralizing pressure most systematically on the western Comanches, whose continuing loyalty they considered critical for the survival of New Mexico and, by extension, the silver provinces of northern New Spain. The policy was first articulated by Anza in 1786 when he argued that by elevating Ecueracapa "above the rest of his class" Spaniards could reduce the entire Comanche nation to vassalage. The idea was to create a well-defined hierarchical structure extending from principal chiefs to the bottom of Comanche society though strategic distributions of political gifts. Accordingly, Spanish officials in New Mexico and Texas funneled vast amounts of gifts among the Comanches through Ecueracapa and other head chiefs, hoping to originate a downward flow of presents from Spanish authorities to principal chiefs, local band leaders, and commoners and, conversely, an upward-converging dependency network on top of which stood the king of Spain. The institution of principal chieftainship, as Pedro Garrido explained, was "the most appropriate instrument that we could desire for the new arrangement of peace, not only to assure the continuance of the peace celebrated, but also to subject the warlike Comanche nation to the dominion of the king."[59]

To further induce centralization among the Comanches, Spanish officials also arranged informal gift distributions to trading envoys in a hierarchical manner. Gálvez specified that band leaders, *paraibos*, should receive fifteen or twenty pesos in "goods, tobacco, provisions, etc." when visiting New Mexico, while the heads of individual households should receive only one or two pesos worth of presents. Invoices from the late eighteenth century reveal an even more finely grained scale by which the recipients were divided into five classes—generals, captains, little captains (*capitancillos*), warriors, and women and children. Although Spaniards distributed gifts to several Indian nations after 1786, Comanches, thanks to their numerical and military strength, received special treatment. Writing in 1794, New Mexico Governor Concha reported that "it is customary to regale them [Indian visitors] with some clothing, hats, mirrors, orange paint, indigo, knives, cigars, sugarloaves, and so forth. In these gifts the Comanches must be preferred provided they are not in attendance with the other tribes, for in this case the distribution must be equal in order that no preference may be noticed and result in jealousies among them." The allocation of gifts, Concha further specified, "should be made by the hand of the governor himself, in order that they [Native leaders] may be more grateful." To monitor that the gifts had the desired political effect, Spaniards dispatched special emissaries—"interpreters"—to Comanchería. It was necessary, Concha argued, to have one agent in Comanchería at all times "to observe them and to give an account of their movements."[60]

The policy seemed to succeed in western Comanchería even beyond Spanish hopes. As Spanish officials saw it, their gifts and guidance cleansed the western Comanche political system of chaos and instability by turning a previously unorganized people into a centralized and orderly polity that was more amenable to control. From 1786 on, the Spaniards believed, the western Comanches were under the command of Ecueracapa, whose status in turn depended on Spanish gifts and backing. It also seemed that the office of head chieftainship had become a permanent institution in western Comanchería. When Ecueracapa died on a raiding expedition against the Pawnees in 1793, a western Comanche congress elected Encanaguané (Red Fox) as head chief "by universal approbation." Encanaguané was succeeded in 1797 by Canaguaipe, who in turn was followed by Quegüe around 1805. Like Ecueracapa, Encanaguané, Canaguaipe, and Quegüe were all Kotsotekas. In 1812 Tahuchimpia, Ecueracapa's son who had returned from New Mexico after seven years, was reported to be holding the office, although Spanish sources identified Quegüe as a Kotsoteka general until his death in 1818. Tahuchimpia was succeeded by Cordero, who had represented eastern Comanches as Sargento-Cordero. Except for Cordero, all these principal chiefs asked Spanish authorities to formally recognize their status and pledged loyalty to Spain. And during their tenure, the western Comanches kept an unbroken peace with New Mexico.[61]

All this convinced Bourbon officials of the success of the Indian new policy. In their minds, political reform and peace were inherently linked: Comanches observed treaties because they were controlled by powerful leaders, who in turn were personally attached to the Spanish imperial system. Gifts and careful micromanaging seemed to have domesticated the fierce and formidable Comanches, reducing them to obedient, pliable subjects. As Concha boasted in 1794: "All the other chiefs and all of the members of this tribe, recognize them [Encanaguané and his Jupe lieutenant, Paruanaranimuco] as such [head chiefs] and obey them in their fashion, (that is to say, expressing myself as they do), they listen to their councel [*sic*] and follow it in good faith." Writing five years later, José María Cortés, lieutenant in the Royal Corps of Engineers, reported that the Comanches "are led by a general and lieutenant chosen by a plurality of votes among their countrymen. . . . They listen to the general's advice with the same subordination and follow it in the same good faith that these Indians keep their treaties." Taking such self-promoting reports at face value, many historians have concurred.[62]

But outside appearance of political actions and their internal meaning were not necessarily one and the same. The office of single supreme chief and the accompanying chain of command of principal and secondary chiefs were novel ideas, Spanish imports, in Comanche politics, but that does not mean that Comanche political organization had lost its autonomy or become a mere appendix of the Spanish empire. In fact, the reordering of the western Comanche political system is best seen as a pragmatic response to a drastically shifted strategic situation.

The late Bourbon-era New Spain was experiencing a dramatic revival, which manifested itself in New Mexico in burgeoning long-distance trade with Chihuahua, rapid economic and population growth, and increasingly forceful foreign policies. Facing a suddenly reinvigorated imperial power on their borders, western Comanches responded by creating a pronouncedly hierarchical political system that featured authoritative leaders who could deal as equals with assertive Spanish colonial agents. Boosted by the Bourbon Reforms, New Mexico was transformed in the late eighteenth century from a wasteland into a dynamic regional economy, and the Comanches needed to find ways to channel that vitality to their own advantage. To do so, they did what nonsedentary politically flexible pastoral societies have done throughout history: they modified their internal organization to reflect (though not necessarily to copy) the developments of a neighboring state society.[63]

Moreover, the notion of Comanche subjugation through external manipulation ignores culture, the meanings Comanches attached to their political actions and institutions. When Comanche head chiefs pledged to be loyal vassals of their "father," the king of Spain, they were not talking about subordination but rather the familial bonds of mutual care that were to be at the core of any sustained relationship. Despite Spanish assertions, Comanches considered the principal chieftainship not as a real political office but rather as an instrument to derive economic and political favors from Spaniards. Far from being Spanish puppets, western Comanche head chiefs played a double role. They catered to Spanish expectations by maintaining an illusion of a rigid centralized hierarchy in order to guarantee access to Spanish markets and to streamline the distribution of Spanish gifts, but they made no effort to interfere with the internal politics of the numerous local rancherías. Rather than implementing Spain's imperial objectives, they subverted them.

When dealing with Spanish authorities in New Mexico's colonial centers, Ecueracapa and other principal chiefs projected an impression of uncompromised authority; they carried staffs of office, wore Spanish uniforms and medals, and invariably promised to control their followers. In internal matters, beyond direct Spanish gaze, however, they behaved in a manner expected of typical Comanche headmen who were more arbitrators than autocrats. Indeed, Ecueracapa seems to have been uneasy with his new role from the outset, as is suggested by his insistence during the Pecos talks that Anza's staff of office be passed on to Tosacondata. That act must be understood in the context of Comanche political tradition of collective and diffuse leadership: it was an attempt to share power with other Comanche chiefs. Ecueracapa continued to honor Comanche political conventions even after he was formally elected "captain general." He represented the Comanche nation in high-level diplomatic negotiations with Spanish officials, but there is no evidence that he played any part in the internal Jupe and Yamparika politics. When conferring with Spanish colonists, Ecueracapa was a commanding supreme chief; inside Comanchería, he remained a typical Kotsoteka headman with limited, clearly defined authority.[64]

The dual role of western Comanche principal chiefs became even more apparent after Ecueracapa's death in 1793. Unlike Ecueracapa, none of his followers appear to have sent envoys touring around Comanchería to endorse their status among all divisions. This alone was enough to reduce the office to honorific title, because power without physical presence was meaningless among Comanches, who believed that authority could be exercised and validated only in direct face-to-face interaction. Ecueracapa's successors also ignored the Spanish design of a fixed hierarchy in which Jupe and Yamparika lieutenant generals would be subordinate to Kotsoteka supreme chiefs. All Kotsoteka principal chiefs—Ecueracapa, Encanaguané, Canaguaipe, Quegüe, Tahuchimpia, and Cordero—adhered to the diffuse tradition of Comanche politics and refrained from interfering with the internal affairs of other divisions. Indeed, Commanding General Ugarte had predicted in 1787 that the Yamparikas and Jupes would not accept subordination to Kotsoteka head chiefs.[65]

Rejecting Spanish demands of political centralization, the Jupes and Yamparikas dealt directly with Spanish officials. They even pressured the officials to recognize their own head chiefs. In 1805, for example, three Yamparika captains came to Santa Fe and asked Governor Joaquin Real Alencaster to recognize Chief Somiquaso as the "general" of the Yamparikas "like Guegue [is] for the Cuchanticas [Kotsotekas]." The Yamparikas, in other words, insisted on separate head chiefs for the Kotsotekas and themselves, and when Alencaster granted their request, there was no mention of Somiquaso being subordinate to Quegüe. It is also telling that the Yamparikas accompanied their request for Somiquaso's appointment with a long list of demands: they wanted Alencaster to "clothe them and present them gifts," "set free certain prisoners and criminals," and "build them houses of wood forming a plaza" on the Colorado River. The last request, like the San Carlos experiment two decades before, seems to have been spurred by a dry spell and the need to secure additional Spanish aid. The governor furnished the visitors with gifts, promised to send constructors, and, finally, offered unrestricted trade with favorable terms: "On giving the staff of office (*bastón*) to the [Comanche] general, I had him give his word that they would come every year to trade and I promised him justice in exchange of [their] goods for [those of our] goods which were desired, saying that this was a good way to avoid unpleasantness."[66]

Ultimately, the Spanish attempts at political manipulation crushed against the persisting traditions of Comanche political culture. Bourbon officials insisted on labeling the supreme chiefs as marionettes whose very existence was dependent on Spanish support, but in reality all western Comanches head chiefs entered the foreign political arena as established leaders who already enjoyed wide support in Comanchería. Spanish officials always learned of their appointments after the fact, and Comanches only asked them to recognize the chiefs' authority with appropriate gifts. Spanish endorsement was not a requirement for Comanche leadership positions.[67] Western Comanche head chiefs maneuvered the diplomatic space between the Spanish empire and Comanchería, but they were not Spanish creations.

And even if Spanish officials did manage to exert limited influence on some western Comanche chiefs through gifts and titles, the Comanche political culture contained several built-in mechanisms that made the nation relatively immune to such external manipulation. The maxim that important decisions were to be reached through consensus functioned as an effective screen against external interference. Such charismatic and powerful chiefs like Ecueracapa could wield considerable influence over divisional and interdivisional politics, but even they could not dictate policies because the Comanche political culture demanded that all crucial decisions had to be unanimous. Comanches made a considerable effort to press this point on Spanish officials by allowing them to witness grand councils that made final decisions on such paramount issues as the 1786 New Mexico–Comanche treaty. The tradition of fluid band membership reinforced the filtering effect of consensus politics, for if a chief tried to enforce decisions that seemed corrupt, he risked losing his social face, and with that, his political support. If Comanches sensed corruption in their leaders, they simply walked away from them.[68] Beneath the surface, then, the diffuse nature of the western Comanche political system endured.

Comanches modified their political structures to accommodate the pressures exerted by the reinforced Spanish empire, but they did so within the parameters of their traditional culture. As they had done at least since the mid-eighteenth century—and possibly since they had first moved to the southern plains—they dispersed into multiple rancherías, which periodically congregated into divisional meetings to deliberate important community-wide issues. The head chiefs with access to Spanish authorities introduced Spanish initiatives to these councils, but it was the attending mass that decided how the community responded to those initiatives.[69]

The Bourbon strategy of political manipulation failed even more glaringly in Texas, where Spanish officials operated in a more complicated and delicate geopolitical setting and with fewer funds than their counterparts in New Mexico. While New Mexico was surrounded by three big Native nations, the Comanches, Navajos, and Utes, Texas balanced among two major Native powers, the Comanches and Wichitas, as well as a multitude of smaller groups, such as the Akokisas, Tejas, Tonkawas, and Karankawas. It placed overwhelming demands on Texas's limited imperial resources; in 1795, for example, thirty-three nations solicited Spanish friendship, commerce, and gifts in San Antonio, which had access to only a fraction of Santa Fe's wealth. New Mexico spent each year four to six thousand pesos in Indian diplomacy or "peace expenditures," but Texas often had less than half of that sum available for supplying its numerous Indian allies. Trade fairs, too, were more modest in Texas, which lacked its western counterpart's access to the prosperous Chihuahua markets and consequently suffered from a chronic shortage of guns, iron tools, and other valuable commodities.

Because Texas could offer only few material incentives, eastern Comanches felt little need to conciliate the Spaniards with an appearance of a centralized government. Texas officials made desperate efforts to gain an access to eastern Comanchería's political elite, but their attempts were destined to fail: throughout Spain's tenure in the Southwest, their maneuverings were limited to supporting a small number of local Comanche chiefs.[70]

Comanches' success in neutralizing Spanish interference meant that the cross-cultural space between the two nations would become a setting for a battle of wills over the meaning of the alliance. Bourbon authorities sought to attach the Comanches to the Spanish empire as political vassals, but to status-conscious Spaniards the idea of treating illiterate, nomadic Natives as social equals was unthinkable. Comanches, by contrast, regarded the alliance as a pact between equals and sought merger in the social realm and autonomy in the political. The language that the two sides used to explain their relationship to one another captures the discord. Spanish officials employed patriarchal father-children metaphors and used the diminutive designation "children" for Comanches, whereas Comanche chiefs spoke of Comanches and Spaniards as brothers bound together by affinial ties and obligations. Casting themselves as fathers, Spanish officials meant to command, but Comanches expected them to act like siblings who would care for their needs. These debates over words and meanings remained largely hidden, emerging only when Spanish officials, acting on their belief that they could dictate to Indian children, pressured Comanches to adopt courses of action that did not correspond with Comanche interests.[71]

A series of events and episodes during the last decade and a half of the eighteenth century revealed to Spanish officials just how tenuous their influence over the Comanches was. The first episode occurred in the late 1780s when the officials tried to resolve the question of captives and captive trade. Treaty stipulations obliged Comanches to return all Hispanic captives, but when Spanish officials pressed the issue, Comanches understood—or purposefully misunderstood—the demand as an offer to ransom the captives. They did return Hispanic women and children to Texas and New Mexico, but the Spaniards had to pay exorbitant sums for them, which ran as high as eight horses per captive. Comanches also conducted sporadic raids into the Coahuilan missions and Spanish-protected Apache *establecimientos de paz*, possibly to obtain female captives for the illicit slave traffic that continued unabated in Spanish Louisiana. In 1790, after repeated peace overtures from Faraone, Gileño, Natagé, and Mimbreño Apaches, Governor Concha brought several bands from all four groups back to New Mexico, hoping that they could be turned into settled farmers at El Sabinal, a small Spanish community forty miles south of Albuquerque. Comanches, however, seem to have viewed the reservation experiment as a threat to their commercial interests, which since 1786 had hinged on their exclusive control over New Mexico's markets. Ignoring Spanish objections, they raided El Sabinal for four years until the settlement was nearly abandoned.[72]

The joint military campaigns against the Apaches formed another arena where Spanish authorities found their influence over the Comanches seriously compromised. In 1790 Concha requested western Comanche chiefs to supply men for yet another collaborative military campaign, this time against Apache settlements near the Big Bend of the Río Grande. By that time, however, most Apaches had retreated far from Comanches' sphere and no longer posed a threat to their interests. The chiefs rejected Concha's appeal and instead asked him to provide troops for an incursion against the Pawnees on the central plains. The proposal was at odds with New Spain's Indian policy, which targeted Spanish military muscle against the Apaches and avoided conflicts with other Native nations, but Concha accepted it nonetheless, explaining later that "if we had not granted their requests they would have developed a grudge which might have had regrettable results." The expedition itself was a failure. Operating under Comanche leadership in unfamiliar conditions, the Spanish auxiliaries (20 *vecinos* and presidial troops) disrupted the routines of the 340-lodge-strong Comanche outfit that doubled as an army and a movable village. Eventually, after repeated quarrels, Ecueracapa and Paruanarimuca sent the Spanish troops back to New Mexico. This marked the effective end of Comanche-Spanish military collaboration. In 1797 Governor Chacón made one last bid to draft military aid from Comanchería when he asked Chief Canaguaipe for men against Mescalero raiders around El Paso. The governor offered guns and abundant rations but was flatly refused by the Kotsoteka captain, who declared that his warriors were preparing for military campaigns of their own.[73]

Even more alarming to Spanish officials was the unauthorized war Comanches declared in the early 1790s on the Utes and the Navajos. The Comanche-Ute-Navajo peace had unraveled soon after its inception in 1786, evidently because Utes and Navajos feared that the Comanche-Spanish union would marginalize them and shut them out of New Mexico's markets: Concha noted tersely a few years later that the Utes "hate the Comanches because of their present friendship with us." The severe drought in the late 1780s also fueled rivalry over local resources and induced Utes and Navajos to send raiding campaigns into Comanchería. Spanish officials tried to placate Comanches by retrieving stolen horses and captives, but in 1792 Comanches went to war, ignoring Spanish pleas for pacification. This independent maneuvering not only revealed the fallacy of Comanche submission to Spanish control but threatened to turn New Mexico once again into a war zone. "Regrettable are the consequences," Concha lamented in 1793, "which the Province may suffer if the Comanches are not restrained in their just anger which they feel toward the Navajos, because to search out and attack them in their haunts, [the Comanches] will be forced to pass through the center of New Mexico, thus disrupting the tranquil state that has been maintained up to this time."[74]

Behind such lamentations lay a deeper truth that would become increasingly clear during the early nineteenth century: Comanches, not Spaniards, would dictate the limits of the alliance and determine its character. Comanches would continue to formulate their relationship with Spanish colonists through their own interests and on their own terms, and the Southwest would remain an open field of power where relations among nations were determined on the ground, not in distant colonial centers. And out of this configuration would emerge an imperial order the Spaniards could not have imagined: the Comanche empire.

4

The Empire of the Plains

The first half of the nineteenth century was the era of American imperial expansion in the Southwest. Powered by burgeoning industrial, technological, and demographic growth and roused by the chauvinistic nationalism of Manifest Destiny, the United States purchased, fought, and annexed its way from the Mississippi valley to the Río Grande, infringing Spain's imperial claims, sweeping aside the Mexican Republic, and dispossessing dozens of indigenous societies. This expansion was set in motion in 1803 by the Louisiana Purchase, which roughly doubled the size of the nation, and was followed, in rapid succession, by the founding of the Anglo-dominated Republic of Texas in 1836, the annexation of that republic nine years later, and the market incorporation of Mexican New Mexico. The expansion culminated in the Mexican-American War in 1846–48, in the aftermath of which the United States bought New Mexico and California for fifteen million dollars and extended its territory to the Río Grande by assuming responsibility for the three million dollars its citizens claimed against Mexico. Finally, in 1853, the United States purchased a strip of land south of the Gila River from Mexico, thereby stretching its border to what today are southern Arizona and southwestern New Mexico.

But growing American power alone does not define this era, for it also saw Comanches resuming their expansionist thrust. Intensifying and elaborating the foreign political strategies that had fueled their expansion before the hiatus of the mid-1780s, Comanches built in the early nineteenth century a loose but imposing empire on the southern plains and in the Southwest, in conjunction with the emerging American empire. In the late 1840s, just as the United States prepared to oust Mexico from the Southwest by war, Comanches reached the zenith of their power. They had revived their defunct trade and alliance network and expanded it into a vast commercial empire, which allowed them to integrate foreign economies into their market circuits and control the flow of crucial commodities on the lower midcontinent. They had halted the expansionist Texas in its tracks and carved out a vast raiding domain in northern Mexico. They held several nearby peoples in a state of virtual servitude and their market-oriented and slavery-driven economy was booming. Comanchería itself had transformed into a dynamic, multiethnic imperial core that absorbed large numbers of voluntary immigrants from the weaker societies and radiated cultural influences across the midcontinent. Like the imperial Americans, Comanches were powerful actors who had the capacity to remake societies and reshape histories.

That may sound implausible. How could one region, even one as broad as the Southwest, accommodate two simultaneous and successful imperial projects? Would not the expansion of one power inevitably impinge upon, and eventually cancel out, the expansion of the other? But such traditional zero-sum logic does not necessarily apply to the early nineteenth-century Southwest, because the Comanche and U.S. expansions stemmed from disparate impulses and advanced on divergent levels. Comanche power politics were aimed at expanding the nation's access to hunting grounds, trading outlets, tributary gifts, and slaves, whereas U.S. expansion, shaped by a bitter sectional dispute over slavery, focused on securing formal territorial claims and extending the nation's boundary to the Pacific. Comanches desired the resources of the land, Americans wanted legal titles to it. Distinct in their objectives and strategies, Comanche and U.S. expansions posed a fatal threat to neither. In fact, as I argue in the next two chapters, the parallel expansions did not so much clash as *co-evolve,* feeding on one another's successes.

In this and the following chapter I flesh out the form and function of the Comanche empire, here examining Comanches' political, economic, and cultural power on the Great Plains, and in chapter 5 exploring their foreign policies in the Southwest. The chapters are based on the notion that U.S. expansion into the Southwest was built on a Comanche antecedent. Comanches are at the center of the story and the westward-pushing Americans remain in the sidelines, stepping in, often unknowingly, to seize territories that had already been subjugated and weakened by Comanches. The narrative does not ignore the vast imperial ambitions and resources of the United States, but it shows that the stunning success of American imperialism in the Southwest can be understood only if placed in the context of the indigenous imperialism that preceded it.

But in the beginning, at the turn of the eighteenth century, it seemed that the Southwest's imperial future belonged to neither the Comanches nor the

United States. New Spain, revitalized by the Bourbon Reforms and bolstered by a dynamic Indian policy, was determined to control the region and its peoples. Spanish officials envisioned a great imperial extension to the interior, and they pinned their hopes on the Comanche nation. Like the Iroquois to the British, the Comanches were to Bourbon Spain the Indian proxy through which a vast continental empire could be claimed and commanded.

In 1800 Spanish authorities in New Mexico and Texas thought they had a firm hold over the Comanche nation. Border fairs thrived across the frontier from Taos to Natchitoches, and Comanche delegations often stayed for weeks in Santa Fe and San Antonio, interacting freely with the Hispanic and Indian residents. As they collected the annual treaty presents, Comanche chiefs routinely renewed their allegiance to New Spain, projecting the image of devoted allies. "In this tribe," New Mexico Governor Fernando de la Concha wrote in 1794, "one finds faith in the treaties that it acknowledges, true constancy, and hospitality, and modest customs. . . . The need for which we make them liberal grants of arms and ammunition makes them dependent upon us." Deplored as "inconstant and mistrustful" savages only a few years earlier, the Comanches were recast by early nineteenth-century Spanish officials into ideal allies, almost archetypal noble savages. Pedro Bautista Pino, New Mexico's representative in the Spanish Cortes, wrote a brief treatise on the "idea of the Comanche" in which he marveled at the "magnificent size," "graceful appearance," and "frank martial air" of a typical Comanche. After condemning the cruelty and obnoxiousness of the Apaches—the necessary dialectic counterpoint—Pino confidently declared that "the Comanche nation . . . would, with little effort on our part, unite with the Spaniards."[1]

For Spanish Texas, such a union was quite literally a matter of life and death, for it shielded the colony against Comanche raids, which had wreaked unimaginable havoc in the 1770s and early 1780s and nearly destroyed the all-important ranching industry. Ranching began to revive in the late eighteenth century under the Comanche peace, but the colonists lived in constant fear of renewed attacks. At a broader geostrategic level, the alliance with the Comanches shielded entire northern New Spain against a possible invasion from the young and expanding United States. In theory, the role of a buffer territory belonged to Louisiana, but that overextended, disjointed colony was utterly incapable of meeting the challenge. In fact, Louisiana had become more a magnet than a barrier for footloose Americans in the late eighteenth century when Spanish officials, after having failed to people the province with immigrants from other Spanish colonies, opened its borders to American settlers. By 1795 Madrid had concluded that attempts to defend Louisiana from American takeover were futile and started the preparations for selling the money-draining colony to France. While Bourbon officials played the imperial board game with Louisiana, the role of buffer fell once again to Texas. To fulfill its lofty mission, the relatively sparsely populated colony needed to keep a critical mass of Indians under its influence in order to create a barrier of pro-Spanish Natives that would help offset growing American power. The alliance with the eastern Comanches, by far the most powerful Native group on the Texas borderlands, was the focal point of that barrier.[2]

But the Comanche alliance was more precarious than Spanish officials believed. Eastern Comanches—like their relatives in western Comanchería—had never given Spain the kind of loyalty Bourbon administrators expected from them. They offered the Spaniards their amity but not their compliance. They traded with the Spaniards and accepted their treaty presents, but they jealously guarded their political autonomy. This had begun to dawn on Spanish officials almost immediately after the 1785–86 treaties. Comanches refused to return Hispanic captives without ransom, turned down requests to participate in joint military campaigns that did not advance their interests, and made unauthorized raids into Apache reservations, jeopardizing the delicate peace process between Apaches and Spaniards. Such actions tested the consistency and limits of the alliance, but Spanish officials, careful not to alienate their vital allies, routinely ignored or forgave the transgressions. Indeed, Jacobo Ugarte, the commanding general of the Interior Provinces, had specifically advised the governor of New Mexico that "a case can occur in which it may be convenient to use clemency even when the crime has been committed against ourselves . . . when inflexibility on the part of your lordship could cause some important altercation. Prudence requires then that indulgence be preferred to satisfaction for the injury."[3]

A more subtle but ultimately more serious challenge to the Comanche-Spanish alliance emerged in the late 1790s, when American merchants and agents operating out of Spanish Louisiana began to push into the southern plains. Evading Louisiana's Spanish officials—and sometimes cooperating with them—itinerant American traders infiltrated the contested borderland space between Spanish Texas and the United States and then proceeded toward eastern Comanchería. Americans' arrival constituted a litmus test for the pact between eastern Comanches and Texas, for the treaty of 1785 had anticipated the United States' westward thrust and explicitly prohibited Comanches from dealing with American agents. Spanish officials expected eastern Comanches to honor the treaty, remain loyal to Texas, and banish the intruders. They expected that not only because Comanches had signed a political contract but also because Spanish gifts and generosity obliged them to do so.

The Americans, however, did not come as conquerors carrying guns and banners but as merchants carrying goods and gifts, and eastern Comanches eagerly embraced them as potential trading partners. Comanches simply viewed the linkage between presents and politics differently from Spaniards. Gifts, Bourbon administrators insisted, were contractual objects that created a political bond, an exclusive bilateral union, whereas for Comanches the meaning of gifts was primarily of a social nature. Bourbon officials insisted that Spanish gifts should forbid Comanches from trading with foreign nations, but this was a narrow interpretation of loyalty and friendship that did not easily translate into the Comanche worldview. If foreigners—American, French, or any other kind—who entered Comanchería were willing to adhere to Comanche customs and expectations, Comanches had no reason to reject them. Indeed, as the pages that follow will show, by demanding eastern Comanches to choose between devotion to Spain and hospitality to Americans, Texas officials eventually wrecked their alliance with the Comanche nation.

And so, by simply letting American newcomers in, eastern Comanches began to turn away from their fledgling, uneasy alliance with Spain and toward American markets and wealth. It was a momentous shift that changed the history of the Southwest. By establishing exchange ties with Americans, and by linking their pastoral horse-bison economy to the emerging capitalist economy of the United States, eastern Comanches set off a sustained commercial expansion that eventually swept across Comanchería. Spanish officials were slow to recognize this change and even slower to react to it. When José Cortés applauded Comanches' loyalty to Spain in 1799, eastern Comanches were already engaged in an active trade with the westering Americans, and when Pino echoed Cortés's praise thirteen years later, eastern Comanches had already turned their rancherías into a thriving gateway between the Southwest and the U.S. markets. By the time the Spanish colonial era came to an end in 1821, the entire Comanche nation had moved out of the Spanish orbit. They commanded a vast commercial empire that encompassed the Great Plains from the Río Grande valley to the Mississippi and Missouri river valleys, and they looked to the north and east for markets, wealth, allies, and power.

The first known American to test Comanchería's commercial waters was Philip Nolan, an aspiring Kentucky entrepreneur who had immigrated to New Orleans in the late 1780s, only to realize that greater economic opportunities loomed on the Great Pains to the west. He secured in 1791 a passport from Louisiana's governor to catch wild horses in Texas and during the next ten years led five major forays to the west, often setting out from Nacogdoches, a Texas-

Louisiana border town that developed into a major hub of contraband trade soon after its founding in 1779. Nolan carried large numbers of horses to Louisiana's markets and militia troops, but he also traded extensively with the Indians of the southern plains. In 1799 he returned with twelve hundred wild and Indian horses, infecting Natchez and other frontier settlements with a trading fever that sent large numbers of American merchants to the plains. But Nolan's activities also had political underpinnings. He was the protégé of General James Wilkinson, onetime Spanish spy and from 1798 on the commander of the U.S. Army's Southern Department. Although still conspiring with Spanish agents, Wilkinson keenly promoted U.S. exploration and filibustering in the Southwest under the sponsorship of Vice President Thomas Jefferson.[4]

Realizing the mistake they had made by admitting Nolan, Spanish officials stopped issuing passports by 1799, but neither that nor Nolan's death at the hands of Spanish troops in 1801 deterred the westward-pushing Americans who received strong support from Wilkinson and Washington, D.C. This support only intensified after the Louisiana Purchase, which left the boundary between Spanish Texas and U.S. Louisiana undetermined and, as Americans saw it, up for grabs. The 1806 Neutral Ground Agreement, in which Wilkinson and Lieutenant Colonel Simón de Herrera declared a demilitarized neutral zone between the Sabine River and the Arroyo Hondo near Natchitoches, only added to the confusion and contestation. Quietly urged on by Wilkinson—from 1805 the governor of the newly organized Louisiana Territory—and other U.S. agents, several American trading parties and individual merchants pushed into the disputed Red and Brazos river countries in the early years of the nineteenth century.[5]

Viewed from the Mississippi valley, the westward thrust of American traders gave rise to the "Texas Trading Frontier," a zone of bustling commercial activity stretching from the Arkansas River to the Gulf Coast. For eastern Comanches, however, the U.S. commercial expansion did not constitute anything as dramatic as a new frontier. Rather, it caused their old rivalry with the Wichitas over trading privileges to flare up. Earlier, in the late 1770s, eastern Comanches had been on the verge of replacing the Wichita confederacy as trade gateway to the Texas plains, but they had eased their pressure in the 1780s when smallpox devastated their rancherías and when the revolutionary convulsions in the East disrupted westbound trade from the Mississippi valley. By the late 1780s, Comanches were again interacting and trading peacefully with the Wichitas. The cessation of Comanche aggression allowed Wichitas to regain their former strength, and when American traders arrived, they were once more in the position to dominate the east-west commerce. From the late 1790s on, U.S. traders visited the Wichita villages along the Red River on an annual basis, bringing in guns, metal weapons, and clothing; exchanging gifts; and creating strong political and kinship bonds.[6]

As in the 1770s, Wichitas locked the Comanches out of eastern markets, and as before, they demanded what Comanches considered excessive prices for serving as middleman traders. Unlike in the 1770s, however, Comanches were reluctant to rely on force, largely because an ominous military situation had developed on their northeastern border: the Osages had embarked on yet another expansionist round. This time, however, Osages' aggression in the west was triggered by their dispossession in the east. In the 1790s the expansion of Anglo-American settler frontiers in the Southeast exiled large numbers of Choctaws, Cherokees, Delawares, and Shawnees west of the Mississippi, where they clashed violently with Osages, forcing several villages to relocate closer to Comanchería. At the same time, Spain's liberal immigration policy in Louisiana lured thousands of Kentuckians and Tennesseans to the lower Missouri valley, where they established farmsteads on traditional Osage hunting grounds, compelling many Osages to withdraw toward Comanche and Wichita lands. Restraining these Osage encroachments remained a strategic priority for eastern Comanches through the 1830s and they needed Wichitas' military and material assistance to manage the task.[7]

Rather than trying to break the Wichita trade barrier with force, therefore, Comanches attempted to circumvent it through diplomacy. They rebuilt their alliance with the Wichitas during the 1790s and peacefully visited their villages for trade. Then, in 1807, they dispatched a large delegation to Natchitoches, the westernmost U.S. settlement within the Louisiana Purchase, hoping to persuade the agents to send traders among them. The delegation was enthusiastically welcomed by Doctor John Sibley, the Indian agent of "Orleans Territory and the region South of the Arkansas River," who had been commissioned by Congress to sweep the southern plains Indians from the Spanish orbit into the American one. Armed with a lavish budget of three thousand dollars to win over the Natives, Sibley staged a series of ritual performances to display the wealth, munificence, and attentiveness of the Americans. He gratified the Comanche visitors with guns, powder, lead, vermilion, blankets, metal gear, and officers' uniforms. Then, in the presence of Comanche, Wichita, Caddo, and Tonkawa headmen and with the "Calumet & Council fire lighted," he delivered a remarkable speech in which, through expedient historical amnesia, he claimed nativeness for Americans. "It is now so long since our Ancestors came from beyond the great Water that we have no remembrance of it," he asserted. "We ourselves are Natives of the Same land that you are, in other words white Indians, we therefore Should feel & live together like brothers & Good Neighbours." He also addressed the larger geopolitical context: "we are not at war with Spain, we therefore do not wish, or Ask you to be less their friends for being Ours, the World is wide enough for us all, and we Ought all of us to live in it like brothers."[8]

By proclaiming his readiness to treat Comanches as kin, by refraining from interfering with the relations between Comanches and Spaniards, and by exhibiting exceptional largesse, Sibley demonstrated the Americans' willingness to conform to the Comanche cultural order. One of the Comanche chiefs responded to him, declaring that he was "highly pleas'd" to see the Americans, "our New Neighbours." The practical matter of trade, however, was foremost in the Comanche agenda, and the chief promptly moved to explain how Comanches' desire for European technology created ready markets for American goods: "we are in want of Merchandize and Shall be Always Glad to trade with you on friendly terms. . . . You have every thing we want."[9]

Those wants were stimulated not only by the guns and powder that helped Comanches cordon off the Osages and other enemies. Having used European technology for generations, they had come to rely on its availability and consumption in countless everyday activities; from cutting meat to cooking it, and from keeping their bodies warm to beautifying them, they had grown dependent on imported products. Spanish Texas had failed to meet their expansive and complicated needs, and eastern Comanches now put their trust in the United States. To press the point to Sibley, Comanches let him understand that Spaniards had "imposed" their trade on the Comanches. Two months later, another Comanche party visited Natchitoches, hoping to jumpstart commerce. The head of the delegation (whose name went unrecorded) promised Sibley that American traders would "be well treated" and find the longer journeys to Comanche rancherías well worth the effort, because "Horses & Mules were to them like grass they had them in Such plenty," and because "they had likewise dress'd Buffalo Skins & knew where there was Silver Ore plenty."[10]

Eastern Comanches thus aggressively sought market relations with the United States and appeared to be willing to sacrifice their alliance with Spain to achieve their goal. One of their chiefs, Sibley exulted, had laid a Spanish flag at his feet, declaring that Comanches "were very desirous of having Our Flag and it was the Same to them whether Spain was pleas'd or displeas'd and if I would give him One it Should wave through all the Hietan Nation, and they would all die in defence of it before they would part with it." This, Sibley argued, was no small feat, for the Comanches dominated all lands from the vicinity of San Antonio to the Missouri River and, along the east-west axis, from the Wichita villages far beyond the Rocky Mountains. But Sibley's euphoria over his coup conceals a more somber reality. He had been assigned to persuade the Indians to shift their loyalties from New Spain to the United States, but it was starting to seem that it was the Comanches who were calling the shots: they were pulling the United States westward into their vast sphere of power, which the Americans could barely comprehend let alone manipulate. Indeed, Wilkinson himself had argued two years earlier that if the United States hoped to win a foothold in the Southwest, it could happen only by forming a treaty with the Comanches, "the most powerfull Nation of Savages on this Continent [who] have in their power to facilitate or impede our march to New Mexico, should such movement ever become Necessary."[11]

In summer 1808, accordingly, Sibley outfitted and licensed Anthony Glass, a prominent Louisiana merchant, to lead an expedition of eleven men to the Red River country. Glass spent two months in the Wichita trading villages on the Red River, but in the late fall he decided to proceed farther west among the Comanches. Clinging to their privileged position, Wichitas first begged Americans not to proceed and then tried to misdirect their reconnaissance party away from Comanche rancherías. Glass and his men pushed forward, however, and had a profitable trading season in Comanchería. Moving from one ranchería to another, the Glass party was transformed into a movable fair that increased steadily in size as more Comanches joined the assembly. In the space of a month, Glass's mobile marketplace hosted several hundred Comanches who purchased all the goods the Americans had to offer. Glass's success lured in other American trader-agents, who were eager to tap into Comanchería's vast commercial potential. In 1810 Americans were reported to be operating a trading settlement on the Colorado River and interacting with several prominent eastern Comanche leaders.[12]

American merchants had thus already begun to bypass Wichita villages and move their operations into Comanchería when, in 1811, the Wichita confederacy suffered a paralyzing blow. Awahakei, longtime principal chief of the confederacy, died in a battle against the Osages. Unable to agree on Awahakei's successor and suffering under Osage pressure from the north, Wichitas abandoned their Red River villages and scattered across the southern prairies. Some moved westward and sought refuge among the Comanches, initiating a process of gradual merger of Comanche and Wichita communities. Other bands congregated into nine small villages along the Brazos, Navasota, and Trinity rivers and encircled themselves with large defensive dugouts and earthworks.[13]

As the Wichita blockade dissolved, Comanche commerce boomed. From the early 1810s on, American trading parties from the newly established state of Louisiana frequented eastern Comanche rancherías along the middle Red and Brazos rivers, now the focal point of U.S. commerce on the southern plains. In 1818, W. A. Trimble, commander of the western section of the 8th District of the

U.S. Army, reported that eastern Comanches "carry on, with traders from Red River, an extensive traffic, in horses and mules, which they catch in the plains or capture from the Spaniards." Another observer noted that eastern Comanches "are becoming quite expert in fire-arms within a few years, having been furnished by traders from the United States, by way of exchange, for horses and mules, which the Indians would, from time to time, plunder the Spanish settlements of." Governor Antonio Martínez of Texas, monitoring the developments from a different angle, reported in helpless frustration that "the traffic between the Comanches and the traders from the interior continues without interruption, and that arms, munitions, and other war supplies are being brought in."[14]

Comanches also established commercial ties with the Spanish-American filibusters and revolutionaries who, after a briefly successful revolt in Texas in 1812 and 1813, took refuge in Natchitoches, turning the frontier outpost into a quasi-autonomous political entity on the Comanche-Texas borderlands. Still determined to fight the Spanish regime, the refugee rebels began operating as middlemen between the Comanches and the American merchants, carrying guns, munitions, and powder to the west and horses and mules to the east. Nemesio Salcedo, commanding general of the Interior Provinces, lamented in 1813 that this contraband trade utterly undermined Spain's "national commerce" in Texas. By 1818, the traffic had created "a well worn road through the unsettled region towards Natchitoches."[15]

Then, in 1821, Spain's American empire collapsed, and the resulting confusion in the Southwest opened the floodgates for Comanche–U.S. commerce. Only a year later Stephen F. Austin reported that eastern Comanche rancherías had become the nexus point of three well-established trade routes that connected them to U.S. markets along the Mississippi valley. The northernmost route linked eastern Comanchería to St. Louis via a chain of Native middlemen traders. Below was the Red River channel, which funneled traders from Vicksburg, Natchez, Baton Rouge, and New Orleans into the heart of eastern Comanchería. The busiest of the trade routes was the southernmost one, leading from eastern Comanchería to Nacogdoches, which had nearly expired during the 1812–13 revolt in Texas and then, like Natchitoches, became a haven for American merchants and filibusters. With close ties to Natchitoches and New Orleans, Nacogdoches grew into a major trading community, boasting an annual trade of ninety thousand dollars in the early 1820s.[16]

The newly established Mexican government tried to keep American peddlers out of the land it considered Mexican soil, but controlling the porous Texas-Louisiana frontier was beyond its capacity. In 1823 two special investigators advised Mexico City to immediately deploy two hundred troops to Nacogdoches to repel the burgeoning American contraband trade with Indians. The troops never came, and Anglo immigrants and merchants continued to pour into Nacogdoches and Comanchería. So lucrative was this illicit commerce that it attracted a large number of Yamparikas to relocate eastward. By the 1820s, those Comanche immigrants had assumed a new identity as Tenewas (Those Who Stay Downstream) and established a distinct political organization on the middle Red River, where they joined the eastern Kotsotekas in trading with the Americans.[17]

Eastern Comanche rancherías along the Red and Brazos rivers were now the gateway to and from the southern plains, a busy central place where the American homesteader frontier's seemingly inexhaustible demand for livestock met an equally boundless supply, the massive horse herds of the Southwest. Facing east, Comanche rancherías anchored an extensive, triangle-shaped hinterland that stretched across the southern prairies toward St. Louis and New Orleans and into the farms and plantations of Missouri, Kentucky, Tennessee, Louisiana, and Mississippi. Facing west, they were the tip of a wide-mouthed trade funnel that moved livestock toward eastern demand and wealth. As gateway traders, Comanches no longer had to travel to trade; they could simply wait in their rancherías for American trade convoys to arrive. This made a strong impression on the French scientist Jean Louis Berlandier, who visited Comanchería in the late 1820s, reporting how American traders "bring their merchandise right into the [Comanche] rancherías and . . . get from them not only the furs they have to sell, but also the mules and horses they have stolen from the townspeople [of Texas]."[18]

The eastern Comanche gateway also drew Native nations into its sphere. One such nation was the Panismahas, a three-thousand-member offshoot of the Pawnees that in the late eighteenth century had escaped Lakota expansion in the lower Missouri valley and fled to the middle Red River. Once relocated to the south, the Panismahas sought an alliance with the Wichitas, their linguistic and cultural relatives, but they soon gravitated toward the more powerful Comanches. They reportedly sent "600 well-armed men" to a peace ceremony in 1822, after which they began conducting regular trade journeys up the Red, Brazos, and Colorado rivers. Panismahas were a crucial addition to the Comanche trade network. While American traders furnished Comanches with guns, powder, shot, and clothing, Panismahas offered maize, squash, and other staple foods. Most important, Panismahas traded high-quality smoothbore British rifles, which they obtained from their Pawnee relatives, who in turn received the guns from British fur traders on the Missouri. Assessing eastern Comanches' commercial arrangements in the late 1820s, one visitor was struck by the complementary nature of their trade links and the drawing power of their markets: "The Aguaje . . . sell guns made in Great Britain which are preferred by the Comanches. The Anglo-Americans supply the Comanches with ammunition. The Aguaje Indians come all the way to the Brazos River to deal with the Comanches. The latter do not visit the Aguaje settlements." According to another observer, the volume of this gun trade was enough to keep the Comanches "abundantly supplied with firearms" and make them "equally at home with the gun, the bow, and the lance."[19]

The eastern Comanche trade system operated steadily through the 1820s, but the next decade brought dramatic changes. With the passing of the Indian Removal Act in 1830, the United States government began a wholesale relocation of eastern Indians across the Mississippi valley—the proclaimed permanent Indian frontier—into Indian Territory in what today are Oklahoma and Kansas. The removal policy brought thousands of Indians into present-day Oklahoma and Kansas, creating a new and deeply volatile geopolitical entity on Comanchería's borders. The most populous of the transplanted peoples—the Cherokees, Creeks, Chickasaws, and Choctaws—were placed in the southern and western sections of Indian Territory where, around the Wichita Mountains, their lands overlapped with Comanchería's eastern fringe. Hundreds of removed Cherokees, Delawares, Shawnees, and Kickapoos also moved across the Red River into Texas, where Mexican officials offered them legal land grants if they served as border sentinels to protect the province from Comanche raiders and to keep illegal American traders from entering Comanchería.[20]

A clash was immediate and, it seems, inevitable. Dismayed by the agricultural prospects in subhumid Oklahoma, many immigrant groups began to experiment with bison hunting. The westernmost bands of the Delawares, Kickapoos, and Shawnees developed a typical prairie economy of farming and foraging and started making regular hunting excursions to the plains, tapping into Comanchería's bison reserves. Comanches responded to these transgressions by attacking the intruders and by raiding deep into Indian Territory to exact revenge and to plunder maize, cattle, and captives. The death toll climbed on both sides. The fighting also disrupted the Comanche-American trade that had flourished for two decades on the southern plains. Unable to penetrate the wall of immigrant Indians and put off by the escalating violence, American traders gave up their ventures from the Mississippi valley into Comanchería.[21]

In moving across the Mississippi valley, the immigrant nations had encroached upon the Comanche realm but, more important, they had entered an ancient borderland where commercial gravity tended to pull peoples together. Their position between the livestock-rich Comanchería and the livestock-hungry Missouri and Arkansas territories invited the removed Indians to become middlemen who facilitated the movement of goods among the centers of wealth around them. Like the Wichitas, French, and Americans before them, several of the immigrant nations responded. A propitious diplomatic opportunity to attach themselves to the Comanche trade network opened to them in 1834 and 1835 when the U.S. government sponsored two large-scale political meetings among the Comanches, their allies, and the immigrant Indians, hoping to quell the violence that threatened to abort the entire Indian removal policy. In August 1835 some seven thousand Comanches and their Wichita allies gathered at Camp Holmes near the Canadian River, where nineteen Comanche chiefs signed a treaty and agreed to open their lands "west of the Cross Timber" to the immigrant tribes. In return, they expected trade.[22]

The immigrant Indians did not disappoint, and within a few years the border region between Comanchería and Indian Territory had become a site for thriving trade. Although uprooted and dislodged, the removed Indians could still generate impressive surpluses of manufactured and agricultural products, which they were keen to exchange for the plains products they needed to survive in their new homelands.[23] Comanches sponsored massive intertribal gatherings along the Red and Brazos rivers and on the Salt Plains of north-central Oklahoma, often sending messengers to Indian Territory to announce a forthcoming fair. Cherokee, Choctaw, Chickasaw, Creek, and Seminole trading convoys frequented Comanche rancherías, bringing in maize, wheat, potatoes, tobacco, vermilion, wampum, beads, powder, lead, and government-issued rifles. In exchange, they received robes, skins, meat, salt, horses, and mules, a part of which they traded again to American settlers in Missouri, Arkansas, and Louisiana. Sometimes the seminomadic and more mobile Delawares, Kickapoos, and Shawnees served as intermediaries, moving commodities between Indian Territory and Comanchería. The thriving commerce also pulled more marginal groups to the Comanche orbit. Quapaws, who had found a refuge among the Cherokees, frequently attended the fairs, and in 1843 Omahas sent a trading delegation to eastern Comanchería from their villages in present-day Nebraska. Omahas were reported to have traded all their guns and bullets for Comanche horses, which they needed to defend themselves against the expanding Lakotas.

The dynamics of this exchange mirrored the direct Comanche-American trade it had supplanted, but there was an important new element: slave trade. The removed Cherokees, Choctaws, Chickasaws, Creeks, and Seminoles had brought with them approximately five thousand black slaves, and the bondage institution persisted in Indian Territory as the planter-slaveholder elite set out to rebuild its exchange-oriented cotton and tobacco economy. This created secure markets for Comanche slavers who now commanded extensive raiding domains in Texas and northern Mexico. More improvised than organized, the slave traffic offered multiple opportunities for its practitioners. Removed Indians purchased kidnapped Mexicans, Anglo-Americans, and black slaves from Comanches either to augment their own labor force or to resell them to American Indian agents, who generally ransomed the offered captives, especially if they had fair skin. At times Comanches bypassed the middlemen and took their captives directly to U.S. officials at Fort Gibson and other frontier posts, and sometimes they relied on comanchero intermediaries who then delivered the captives to American agents. Occasionally, Comanches even kidnapped black slaves from Cherokees, Chickasaws, Choctaws, and Creeks and then sold them to Delawares, Kickapoos, and Shawnees. They also captured black runaway slaves from Indian Territory and incorporated them into their ranks.[24]

Alongside the pacification of Comanche–eastern Indian relations, another critical peace process unfolded: eastern Comanches formed an alliance with the Osages with whom they had been at war since the early eighteenth century. The conciliation stemmed from Osages' suddenly plummeted fortunes. In the 1820s and early 1830s, after years of brutal fighting against the Cherokees, Osages surrendered most of their old homelands in present-day Missouri, Kansas, and Oklahoma and relocated their villages west, closer to Comanchería. Hemmed between two aggressive and expanding geopolitical entities—Comanchería and Indian Territory—Osages clustered in a narrow belt between the Verdigris and Arkansas rivers in northwestern Oklahoma. According to one observer, their diminished power was such an acute source of "anxiety" for Osages "that very often when they knew the Patoka [Comanches] were in the field around the Arkansas they changed the usual direction of their hunts in order not to cross this river, for on the other side they would be in a continuous state of warfare." Cornered and collapsing, Osages began to seek accommodation with the Comanches and found a diplomatic avenue in the peace talks the United States sponsored between the Comanches and the immigrant Indians. Comanche and Osage representatives met at Fort Gibson in 1834 and concluded a formal peace at Camp Holmes in 1835. "Half of my body belongs to the Osages and half to the Comanches," Comanche Chief Ishacoly declared at the council, evoking a sense of kinship between the long-standing enemies, "and the rest I will hold close to my heart."[25]

With peace came commerce. Eastern Comanches opened their eastern hunting ranges to Osages who in turn kept their access to the bison herds open by supplying their new allies with American goods. Although disease organisms and pressures from removed eastern Indians had eroded Osages' hegemony on the southern prairies, forcing them to abandon their old homelands near the Arkansas River, they still controlled trade at several American posts in Missouri. Like the immigrant Indians, Osages now became middlemen between U.S. and Comanche markets. In 1838 Victor Tixier, a French traveler, reported a flourishing exchange. Comanches, "no longer able to obtain any of the things manufactured by the whites . . . sought the friendship of the Osage, who had such frequent and easy dealings with the civilized people and obtained without difficulty what the Patoka needed. Trading was started after the war; every year the day of the full moon in July is the meeting time for the two nations. The Osage bring red paint, kitchen utensils, blankets, cloth, iron, and the Patoka give in return horses which they breed, mules stolen from Texans, all kinds of pelts, etc."[26]

Annual rendezvous were held at the junction of the Arkansas and Cimarron rivers and on the Big Salt River, a tributary of the Brazos, where in 1843 "the whole body" of the Comanches was reported to be waiting for Osage traders. The amount of goods exchanged at these meetings could be astounding. In 1845 the *Arkansas Intelligencer* reported that Osages had purchased twenty white captive children from Comanches, a transaction that would earn Osages several thousand dollars' worth of goods if they ransomed the children to American agents. Two years later Osages reportedly purchased fifteen hundred mules from eastern Comanches with a selection of guns, powder, ammunition, blankets, blue cloth, and strouding. The value of the transaction was estimated at sixty thousand dollars, several hundreds of thousands in modern equivalents. And as gateway traders, Comanches had yet another possibility for increasing profit margins; according to a U.S. Indian agent, they could resell Osage guns to their Mexican and Indian trading partners for three times the value. To put these transactions into perspective, the average annual volume of the Santa Fe trade, the largest single economic enterprise in the early nineteenth-century American West, was estimated in the 1840s at approximately two hundred thousand dollars.[27]

The stabilization of relations among Comanches, immigrant tribes, and Osages also made possible a restoration of direct commercial ties between eastern Comanches and Americans. As Comanchería's eastern border transformed from a contested into a commercial zone, American merchants returned. Among them were familiar itinerant traders like Josiah Gregg, but, unlike before, Americans now built permanent trading posts, hoping to tap into the booming commerce that was developing between the Comanches and their Native allies. Holland Coffee, an Anglo-Texan merchant, established a fortified trading house on the Red River just east of Comanchería and by the late 1830s traded regularly with Comanches, Cherokees, Choctaws, Delawares, and Shawnees. He was reported to be handing munitions to Comanches on a daily basis and encouraging them to raid Mexican settlements for horses and mules. Auguste Chouteau, of the eminent St. Louis fur-trading family, built a post on the middle South Canadian River on Comanchería's eastern edge, and Abel Warren erected a trading house on Cache Creek within Comanchería's borders.[28]

The advent of these trading posts along and within Comanchería's borders opened a new chapter in the economic history of Comanches, the beginning of mass-scale market production of bison robes. The posts provided a secure outlet for hides, which found ready markets in Texas and the United States east of the Mississippi and were moved to those locations by regular supply trains. Comanches had traded bison meat and robes for generations, but that exchange had largely been limited to local subsistence bartering. Now Comanchería's bison became an animal of enterprise, slaughtered for its commodified hides and robes for distant industrial markets. It was not long before the herds started to show signs of overexploitation.[29]

If peace and commerce had undesired ecological ramifications, they also had unexpected and far-reaching geopolitical repercussions. Seen from the vantage point of Washington, D.C., the transformation of Comanchería's eastern front from a battlefield into a thriving trading zone meant that the removal of indigenous nations from the east into Indian Territory could continue. And with that, so too could continue the unrelenting westward march of the cotton kingdom and its settlement frontier.

In western Comanchería, meanwhile, a parallel commercial expansion was taking place, and as in eastern Comanchería, it was set off by the westward thrust of American merchants and markets. Trade between western Comanches and Americans probably began as an offshoot of eastern Comanche-American commerce: some of the Louisiana-based American traders who visited eastern Comanchería from the 1790s on continued farther west to open new markets for their products. But the upper western Comanche divisions, the Yamparikas and Jupes in the upper Arkansas basin, also attracted itinerant American traders directly from St. Louis and other settlements along the middle Mississippi and lower Missouri valleys. In 1796 a rumor reached Spanish officials in Natchitoches that a group of American traders had built a blockhouse among the Yamparikas, sparking fear that the United States was about to invade New Spain by way of Comanchería.[30]

The acquisition of Louisiana, which by Washington's sweeping interpretation extended all the way to the Río Grande and the Rockies, stirred up the incipient American interest in the commercial possibilities of the Southwest. Scores of plains-bound American traders and Rockies-bound American trappers ascended the Arkansas, Canadian, and Red rivers into western Comanchería where their presence and products, especially guns and powder, were eagerly welcomed. Conducted under the watchful eye of Spanish officials, the burgeoning western Comanche–American trade became one of worst-kept secrets in the early nineteenth-century Southwest borderlands. In 1804, for example, Manuel Merino y Moreno, secretary of the Commandancy General of the Interior Provinces, reported that western Comanches bore guns with "markings that leave no doubt that they were manufactured in London"—a revealing sign of their connections to U.S. market circuits.[31]

Such reports alarmed the Spanish officials in Santa Fe who once again found themselves in the familiar quandary: a rival colonial power threatened Spanish interests by extending its commercial operations deep into Comanchería. Although American trade openly violated the 1786 treaty, Bourbon officials were reluctant to pressure the Comanches, fearing that force would push them closer to the United States. Instead, the officials kept the border fairs open and continued to offer favorable exchange rates and abundant gifts, hoping to retain whatever hold they could on the Comanches. Between 1790 and 1815 an average of some one hundred Comanches visited Santa Fe each year, collecting thousands of pesos worth of gifts. Comanche chiefs were provided with special guest quarters, and governors entertained Comanche elite at their table, serving them wine and sharing ritual food with them. The town maintained a general store where Comanches could purchase cloth, vermilion, and other luxuries, and the chiefs even received guns, which remained in short supply in New Mexico, as gifts.[32]

The presents, fairs, and favorable terms of exchange helped preserve diplomatic bonds between New Mexico and Comanchería, but on a more abstract level, they turned Spain's Indian policy into a caricature of its original intention. The gifts now had almost none of the meaning Spanish policymakers attributed to them. Rather than a political adhesive affixing Comanches to Spain as faithful allies, they became payments for loyalty Comanches were not willing to give. Yet, even against the mounting evidence, many Spanish officials refused to relinquish the idea of Comanche obedience. Writing in 1812, Pino insisted that "a continued state of peace and friendship of the greatest importance in checking other tribes has been the result of the small number of presents given them. At first the Comanches thought they had to reciprocate. They brought all the fine pelts they could collect in order to exceed the munificence of our presents.

When they were informed that favors given them in the name of our king should not be returned, they were greatly astonished. Thus they were placed under obligation to us."[33]

Pino's account underlines the unrealistic rationale of Spain's Indian policy, which had created a substantial one-way stream of gifts from New Mexico among the Comanches, who accepted the material goods but rejected their political implications. Two Spanish reports from 1818 reveal just how badly Spain's Comanche policy had fallen short of its objectives. In the first, New Mexico Governor Facundo Melgares complained bitterly how his hosting of a party of one thousand Comanches had required so many gifts that he did not have goods to gratify other Indian nations. But the gifts did little to bring the Comanches to Spain's exclusive embrace, as the second report illustrates. The Indians "who live to the east of the mountains on the waters of the Arkansas," an anonymous observer wrote, undoubtedly referring to Comanches, "have frequent communication with the English [i.e., Canadian traders] and Americans" and "are doing everything possible to allure the traders of these two nations to themselves." Spanish policymakers, he concluded, were caught in a delicate play-off situation and should commit themselves to searching "for means to furnishing" the Comanches: "For there is no doubt that in the hands of the one or the other governments, these savages would become either important means of defense or an important means of attack."[34]

Spanish authorities may have felt pressured to mete out more gifts to Comanchería in order to counterbalance American influence, but it is likely that no amount of presents would have persuaded Comanches to cut off their ties to those Americans who were willing to operate within Comanche cultural parameters and hand out gifts. The experiences of Thomas James, one of the pioneers of the Santa Fe Trail, is an illuminating case in point. James led his first commercial expedition to western Comanchería in 1821, traveling from St. Louis to the Texas Panhandle, where he encountered an assemblage of Comanche rancherías. James, at the request of Comanche chiefs, made several rounds of gift distributions, dispensing thousands of dollars' worth of merchandise. Oblivious to the intricacies of Comanche protocol, however, he tried to save the bulk of his goods for New Mexican markets and disregarded the chiefs' demands for further gifts. When James insisted on continuing to Santa Fe with his remaining goods, Comanches arrested him and his men and threatened to kill them. Yet despite repeated errors of judgment, the gifts had won James the trust of key Comanche leaders. He visited Comanchería again the next year, was ritually adopted by a powerful chief, and purchased more than three hundred high-quality animals, a transaction worth several thousand dollars in St. Louis.

James himself depicted his travels into Comanchería as a high adventure with repeated near brushes with death, but the real story is his submersion into a new cultural logic. Comanche chiefs were not so much extorting or abusing James as keenly—although not always patiently—teaching the newcomer how to negotiate the Comanche ritual forms and cultural etiquette.[35]

Despite Spanish protests, then, the trade between Comanches and Americans continued unabated, but the collapse of the Spanish empire in 1821 turned the trickle of American traders into a stream. Mexican authorities immediately lifted the restrictive trade laws of the Spanish empire and opened New Mexico to U.S. merchants and markets. The result was the Santa Fe trade, a burgeoning commercial enterprise that revolved around regular trading caravans between Missouri and New Mexico. The main artery of the trade, the Santa Fe Trail, ran across western Comanchería, along the Arkansas River to its headwaters before turning southwest toward New Mexico. In the 1820s, 1830s, and 1840s, tens of thousands of dollars' worth of merchandise traveled through Comanchería each year, but a substantial part of it stayed there. Comanches demanded compensation for granting right-of-ways through their territory, and the overlanders routinely engaged in trade with them. Some, like Thomas James, found the horses and hides of Comanchería more enticing than the mules and furs of New Mexico and traveled to the west to trade specifically with the Comanches. James was back in western Comanchería in 1822 and this time capably maneuvered the Native protocol. The exchange, as he recounted, followed a rigorous structure, which made a clear distinction between gift giving and actual trade:

> I prepared for trading by making presents, according to custom, of knives, tobacco, cloths for breech garments, &c., which, though a large heap when together, made a small appearance when divided among all this band. The trade then began. They claimed twelve articles for a horse. I made four yards of British strouding at $5.50 per yard and two yards of calico at 62½ cents to count three, and a knife, flint, tobacco, looking-glass, and other small articles made up the compliment. They brought to me some horses for which I refused the stipulated price. They then produced others which were really fine animals, worth at least $100 each in St. Louis. I bought seventeen of these, but would not take any more at the same price, the rest being inferior. The refusal enraged the Chief, who said I must buy them, and on my persisting in my course, drove away the Indians from around me and left me alone. After a short time he returned with a request that I should buy some buffalo and beaver skins, to which I acceded. He went away and the women soon returned with the fur and skins, of which I bought a much larger quantity than I wished then to have on my hands.

James spent several days with the Comanches, participating in a series of similar fairs. He smoked the calumet with his hosts, was adopted as brother by one of the chiefs, and eventually returned to St. Louis with more than two thousand dollars' worth of horses, skins, and furs, a feat few, if any, New Mexico-bound American trading convoys could duplicate. James's commercial success was remarkable but not unique in the middle space between Mexican and American markets. In 1838, sixteen years after the opening of the Santa Fe trade, a Texas newspaper reported that several American merchants from Arkansas and Missouri were active in western Comanchería, tapping deeply into the "immense" horse wealth of Comanches. Far more than a thoroughfare, western Comanchería was an integral part of a flourishing multinational commercial institution that linked the economies of the United States, northern Mexico, and Comanchería.[36]

Yet despite the enduring links, New Mexico was becoming increasingly peripheral to Comanches. Just as American trade and markets had drawn the eastern Comanches away from Texas's sphere of influence, so too did American commerce cause western Comanches to turn away from New Mexico. And just as in eastern Comanchería, the political and economic reorientation of the western Comanches was accelerated by the emergence of new trading relations with other Plains Indian nations. In the early nineteenth century, at the same time as they forged ties with U.S. merchants, western Comanches also began restoring trade links with their Native neighbors, links that had become badly frayed during the intertribal wars of the 1780s. The first step to this end was the termination of the Pawnee wars, which had raged on for more than a decade and taken the lives of such prominent Comanche leaders as Ecueracapa and Hachaxas. The peace process began in 1793, when Encanguané, Ecueracapa's successor as western Comanche head chief, persuaded New Mexico Governor Fernando de la Concha to send Pedro Vial to the north to mediate a truce between the Comanches and the Pawnees. An experienced borderland ambassador, Vial traveled to the Pawnee villages on the Kansas River, where, according to Zenon Trudeau, lieutenant governor of Upper Louisiana, he "delivered a medal, a complete suit of clothes and other things to the [Pawnee] Chief." The gesture helped "cover" the deaths inflicted by Comanches and "caused peace to be made as . . . desired." Commerce apparently played a key role in the proceedings, and after the peace talks were concluded, Vial conducted a trade convoy from Pawnee country to Comanchería. Regular Pawnee trade journeys to the south commenced soon after, opening for western Comanches an access to the manufactured goods Pawnees obtained from Spanish and American traders who operated—and competed over Native customers—along the lower Missouri

River. Although often interrupted by bouts of violence that required careful mediation, the Comanche-Pawnee connection endured into the 1840s.[37]

Meanwhile, western Comanches had already initiated peace talks with Kiowas and Naishan Apaches (also known as Kiowa Apaches or Plains Apaches), a small group of Athapascan speakers who, unlike most Apaches of the plains, fled Comanche expansion north to the Missouri valley, where they attached themselves to the Kiowa nation. Comanches and Kiowas had been trading partners in the 1760s and 1770s, but the alliance had unraveled during the tumultuous 1780s. Kiowa traditions relate that the restoration of peaceful relations began in 1790, but a broader peace process did not get under way until 1806, when Yamparika and Kiowa parties unexpectedly met at the New Mexican border town of San Miguel del Vado, where a Spanish settler brokered a meeting. According to Kiowa traditions, Guik'áte (Wolf Lying Down), the second highest ranking Kiowa chief, proclaimed his desire for peace. Päréiyä (Afraid of Water), the Yamparika leader, replied that the matter "would have to be considered by the whole tribe" and invited Guik'áte to visit the main Yamparika village on the Brazos River. Accompanied by a Comanche captive who had been with the Kiowa party, Guik'áte followed Päréiyä to the Yamparika ranchería, where he spent the summer hunting and feasting with his hosts. A Yamparika council guided by the village chief Tutsayatuhovit ratified the treaty. In the fall, a large Kiowa delegation arrived in the Yamparika ranchería, and the two parties made peace, which was sanctioned with elaborate gift exchanges and a three-day feast. Again, kinship secured the peace: Guik'áte married the daughter of Somiquaso, the newly elected Yamparika head chief, and moved his tipi among the Yamparikas. The peace process then shifted among other Comanche and Kiowa bands, each of which ratified the treaty.[38]

The alliance that resulted was the firmest and most durable in Comanche history. After the peace had been consolidated, Kiowas and Naishans moved from the central plains into north-central Comanchería, thereby gaining access to the milder climates and fertile horse pastures of the southern plains. For the Naishans, moreover, the alliance signified a return to the ancestral homelands of the southern plains, which they had abandoned almost a century before in the face of Comanche expansion. For Comanches the alliance offered obvious political advantages. Collaboration with the relatively small Kiowa and Naishan nations—approximately twelve and three hundred people, respectively—augmented their military and political weight without putting excessive pressure on Comanchería's resources. Comanches incorporated both groups in their protective border campaigns against the Utes in the west and the Osages in the east. Commerce, however, was the heart of the union. The three groups embarked on an active exchange, which involved a distinct division of labor: Kiowas and Naishans acted as middlemen between the upper Arkansas-based Comanches and the Mandan-Hidatsa villages on the middle Missouri valley, carrying horses and mules to the north and metal goods and high-quality short-barreled British muskets back to Comanche rancherías. It was a lucrative arrangement for Comanches, whose livestock was in high demand in the horse-poor northern plains. In the early years of the nineteenth century the standard price of a stolen Spanish horse in the middle Missouri villages was "a gun, a hundred charges of powder and balls, a knife and other trifles."[39]

Western Comanches' northbound exchange channel soon became a main axis of the Plains Indian trade system, a central conduit that siphoned crucial commodities back and forth across the interior. But the thriving commerce also attracted competitors, most notably the allied Cheyennes and Arapahoes from the northern plains. Pushed out from their homelands near the Black Hills by the expanding Lakotas around 1800, several Cheyenne and Arapaho bands moved southward to the central plains, where they gradually ousted the Kiowas and Naishans from the middleman trading niche and entered the Comanches' expanding of alliance network of trade and peace. In 1820 a U.S. exploring expedition led by Stephen H. Long learned about a mixed western Comanche, Kiowa, Naishan, Cheyenne, and Arapaho camp on the upper Arkansas, and a year later, on the Big Timbers of the Arkansas, another American expedition led by Jacob Fowler came across a massive western Comanche-sponsored trade assembly that hosted some five thousand Kiowas, Naishans, Cheyennes, and Arapahoes as well as many Spanish traders from Taos. If anything, the shift in middlemen was favorable for western Comanches. Cheyennes emerged in the early nineteenth century as highly specialized middleman traders who carried Comanche horses not only to the upper Missouri villagers but among the powerful Blackfeet as well.[40]

Already bustling with activity, western Comanches' trade system received a further boost when they established commercial ties with their Shoshone relatives. Once a single people, Shoshones and Comanches had split in the late seventeenth century, when the former left the central plains and headed north and the latter moved toward the south. By 1800, however, Shoshones had pulled back from the northern plains under the pressure from well-armed Blackfeet and Crows and crossed the Continental Divide to the mountain ranges of Montana and Wyoming. Cut off from the Canadian fur trade and the northern plains buffalo country by their enemies, Shoshones turned to the south and sought to restore their ties with the Comanches. Both the Long and Fowler expeditions encountered Shoshones among the many groups who attended western

4. *Yamparika Comanche.* Watercolor by Lino Sánchez y Tapia, ca. 1836. A Comanche man displays his trade gun, gunpowder pouch, metal ax, and metal-tipped lance. Comanches' far-reaching trading empire gave them access to numerous market outlets and varied European manufactures, making them attractive commercial partners for near and distant Native groups. Courtesy of Gilcrease Museum, Tulsa, Oklahoma.

Comanche trade fairs in the upper Arkansas valley in the early 1820s. The chief attraction for Shoshones must have been Comanches' gun supply: in 1802 one traveler had found them hiding "in caverns from their enemies," unable to fight back the armed forces of Blackfeet with their small bows and stone war clubs. In exchange for the much-needed weapons, Shoshones were able to offer large numbers of horses, for they maintained vast herds in the deep, protective valleys of their Rocky Mountain homelands. Shoshones were not the only far northern group drawn into Comanchería's commercial sphere. As the Mandan and Hidatsa trading villages on the middle Missouri River began to decline in the early nineteenth century, Crows, too, began to send trading convoys among the Comanches from their homelands on the northwestern plains.[41]

In the early nineteenth century, then, western Comanches once again ran a flourishing commercial center in the upper Arkansas basin, with exchange links fanning out over a vast area, connecting them to New Mexico, American market entrepôts along the Mississippi valley, the Mandan and Hidatsa trade citadels in the Missouri valley, and the rich horse reservoir of the Rocky Mountains. Pawnee, Kiowa, Naishan, Cheyenne, Arapaho, Shoshone, Crow, American, and New Mexican trading convoys frequented western Comanche rancherías, which seasonally morphed into vibrant cosmopolitan marketplaces where Yamparikas, Jupes, and Kotsotekas could transmute their horses for guns, skins for fabrics, and meat for corn. Winter months, when Plains Indians gravitated to the south and west in search of warmth and the bison, were the main trading season, and in December, January, and February one could find massive trading villages spreading out for miles along the deep protective valley of the Arkansas River. Sites of intensely concentrated commercial activity, those trading villages were also symbols of an increasingly Comanche-centric economic configuration of the Great Plains.

But then, just as eastern Comanches faced an economic crisis in the aftermath of the Indian Removal, western Comanches too faced a sudden reversal of fortunes. In the late 1820s, Cheyennes and Arapahoes abruptly cut off diplomatic and commercial ties with western Comanches and forced their way into the upper Arkansas basin. They did so in part because their existing economic arrangements on the central plains could no longer sustain them. Repeated waves of disease epidemics and Lakota raids had pushed the Mandan and Hidatsa trading villages into a steep decline, which in turn cut into the profits the Cheyennes and Arapahoes could make operating as middlemen between the middle Missouri and Comanchería. Forced to search for new economic strategies, Cheyennes and Arapahoes began to push toward Comanche territory, lured by its powerful economic inducements: hospitable climate, lush horse pastures, and proximity to New Mexico's border markets. Cheyennes and Arapahoes were not alone in this bid to march into Comanchería. In around 1830 they forged an alliance with two prominent St. Louis merchants, Charles and William Bent, who ran a small fur-trading post near Pike's Peak. Yellow Wolf, a Cheyenne chief, approached the Bents and asked them to move their post near the Big Timbers of the Arkansas River. Fully aware of the region's history as a commercial hub, and persuaded by Yellow Wolf's promises to provide protection, the Bents joined the invasion into Comanchería as gun dealers for the Cheyennes and Arapahoes.[42]

Fighting lasted for several years, during which the Bents built an imposing two-story adobe fort on the north bank of the Arkansas River, a few miles upriver of the Big Timbers, just off the northwestern corner of Comanchería. But as on the Comanchería–Indian Territory border, mutual economic interests gradually steered the rival coalitions toward conciliation. In spring 1839, with death tolls mounting on both sides, the Cheyennes sued for peace, sending messengers among the Comanches and Kiowas, who in turn dispatched a Naishan delegation to establish an armistice. Preliminary talks were held the next year near the mouth of Two Butte Creek on the Arkansas, where the chiefs of the five nations smoked the calumet and buried the war. The final peace was concluded a few months later in a massive council near Bent's Fort. Trade, which before the outbreak of the hostilities had bound the five nations together, was the key discussion point. The negotiations lasted for two days and featured several rounds of elaborate gift giving during which Comanches and Kiowas gave away hundreds of horses and mules. The gifts placated mourners and covered the casualties of the war, but they also framed the future relations among the nations. With the gift exchanges completed, one of the Cheyenne chiefs announced: "Now, we have made peace, and we have finished making presents to one another; tomorrow we will begin to trade with each other. Your people can come here and try to trade for the things that you like, and my people will go to your camp to trade."[43]

The "Great Peace" of 1840 was a momentous diplomatic feat that spawned an enduring alliance among the Comanches, Kiowas, Naishans, Cheyennes, and Arapahoes, reconfiguring the geopolitics of the southern and central Great Plains. As a territorial agreement, the accord established a joint occupancy of the Big Timbers of the Arkansas valley. The Cheyennes and Arapahoes retreated on the northern side of the Arkansas, keeping their home ranges on the central plains, but they retained a right to winter in the Big Timbers. As a political pact, the accord created a loose but lasting political coalition among the five nations, who in the mid and late nineteenth century would often fight together encroaching Texan settlers and the U.S. Army. As an economic agreement, the accord launched a thriving commercial partnership that eventually came to include the Bents as well.[44]

Under the new commercial arrangement, Comanches, Kiowas, and Naishans bartered horses and mules for the manufactured goods that Cheyennes and Arapahoes obtained from Fort Laramie, Fort Lupton, and other American

5. Bent's Fort. From Message from the president of the United States: in compliance with a resolution of the Senate, communicating a report of an expedition led by Lieutenant Abert, on the upper Arkansas and through the country of the Camanche Indians, in the fall of the year 1845, 29th Cong, 1st sess., S. Ex. Doc. 438. Courtesy of Yale Collection of Western Americana, Beinecke Rare Book and Manuscript Library.

trading posts that emerged on the central plains in the 1830 and 1840s after the collapse of the Rocky Mountain–based beaver trade. The peace also made possible direct trade between the Comanches and the Bents. The Bents had begun to shift to livestock trade since the economic panic of 1837 in the United States, and they were eager to expand their supply area into the horse-rich Comanchería. They maintained a moderately successful log post on the south fork of the Canadian River between 1842 and 1845 and a larger post, the "Adobe Walls," just north of the Canadian during the winter of 1845–46. Comanches, however, centered their activities on Bent's Fort, drawn by its abundant wares, standardized exchange rates, and multicultural social milieu. By 1841 the Bents expected fifteen hundred Comanches would visit their post.[45]

In America's historical memory, Bent's Fort stands as a vanguard of the westward expansion. It was the pioneering frontier post that introduced modern capitalist institutions and ideology to the Plains Indians and into Mexican New Mexico, preparing the ground for the U.S. takeover of the Southwest. For Comanches, however, Bent's Fort represented simply another commercial outlet, a conduit that facilitated the movement of goods between Comanchería and distant markets. Through Bent's Fort, the western Comanches gained a secure access to the vast American markets, and like their relatives in eastern Comanchería, they became the chief suppliers of an extended trade chain that channeled horses and mules to the expanding settler-farmer frontiers in Missouri, Arkansans, Illinois, Kentucky, and Tennessee. Comanches also traded Mexican captives, whom the Bents used as herders and laborers at the fort, as well as large volumes of buffalo robes, which found ready markets in eastern urban centers. That outpouring of livestock, robes, and captives was matched by a sizeable inflow of various staple products, craft items, and manufactured goods. Fed by regular supply trains from New Mexico and Missouri, Bent's Fort siphoned into Comanchería commodities from several distinct markets—Pueblo maize and Spanish shawls from New Mexico; blankets from Navajo country; beads from Iroquois villages; molasses from New Orleans; and coffee, flour, knives, kettles, pans, and hoop iron from all across the United States. Most important, Bent's Fort provided quantities of lead, powder, pistols, and high-quality British muskets—enough for Comanches to keep hundreds of warriors well armed and enough for them to extend their military hegemony from the Southwest deep into Mexico.[46]

The twin commercial networks of the eastern and western Comanches—the eastward-facing gateway of the former and the multibranched trade center of the latter—together formed an imposing trading empire. Featuring a thick web of short, midrange, and long-distance exchange routes that arched across the midcontinent from the upper Río Grande valley toward the northern plains, the Mississippi valley, and Texas, the trading empire connected Comanchería to several different ecosystems, economies, and resource domains. And while the trade network reached outward to affix Comanchería to surrounding regions, it also opened inward, connecting Comanche groups to one another. Rancherías met regularly for exchange and social recreation, and summers saw thousands of Comanches gravitating toward Comanchería's center for massive community-wide political councils, which doubled as trade fairs. As a result, the imports that entered Comanchería at its various exchange points also circulated within Comanchería, ensuring that the tools and sources of power—guns, metal, and corn—were accessible across the realm.[47]

Commercial dominance brought prosperity and, predictably, security. Like other Native trade systems in the Americas, the Comanche trade network was embedded in a social nexus. Comanches feasted, smoked the calumet, and exchanged gifts with foreigners whom they considered more than trading partners: they were fictive kinspeople who were socially obliged to supply for each other's needs through material sharing. Affinity was the medium through which Comanches organized exchange across boundaries, and their trading empire can be seen as a vast kinship circle where ritual exchanges of words, food, gifts, and spouses stabilized intersocial spaces, creating a high threshold for intergroup violence. Comanches fought the removed eastern Indians as well as the Cheyenne-Arapaho coalition in the early 1830s, but the carnage of those years was exceptional: by standards of the age, early nineteenth-century Comanchería was a safe place to live. Like the Iroquois in the Northeast, the Comanches attached on their sphere numerous Native and non-Native groups as exchange partners, political allies, and metaphorical kin, enveloping themselves in a protective human web. This process had its most dramatic manifestation in the massive intergroup gatherings along the upper Arkansas valley, where thousands of Comanches, Kiowas, Naishans, Cheyennes, Arapahoes, Shoshones, Americans, and New Mexican comancheros regularly gathered to trade, socialize, and mediate political issues, creating vast ephemeral multiethnic worlds on Comanchería's northern edge.[48]

Commerce and kinship helped build and maintain peace, but so too did power, coercion, and dependence. Comanches nurtured peace on their borders through active diplomacy, but they maintained stability also through their capacity to influence other societies and govern the relations among them. By dominating the major east-west and south-north trading arteries on the southern plains and in the Southwest, Comanches were able to regulate the flow of cru-

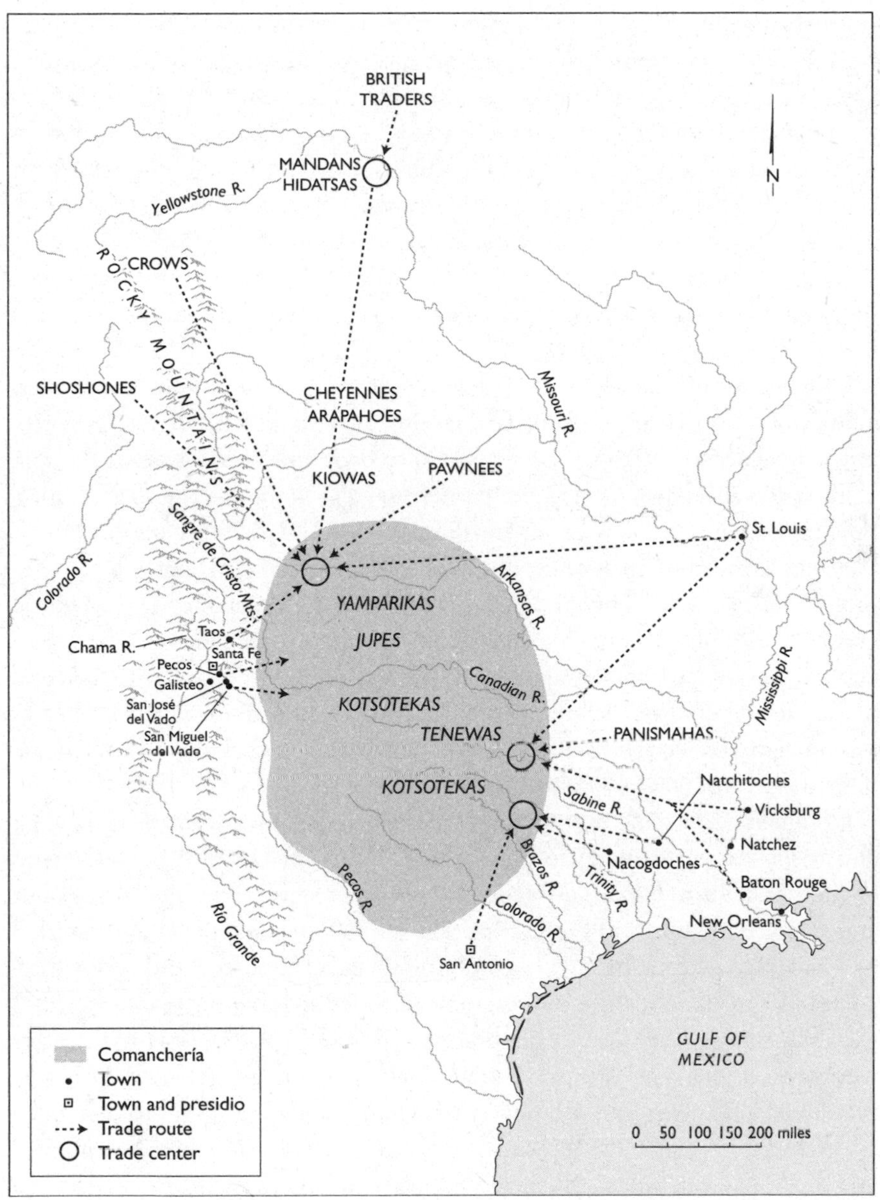

6. Comanche trading empire in the early nineteenth century. Map by Bill Nelson.

cial commodities over vast areas and extend their sphere of influence far beyond their borders. Numerous Native groups around Comanchería—Cheyennes, Pawnees, Mandans, and Hidatsas on the central and northern plains; Wichitas and Caddos on the southern prairies; and the immigrant nations in Indian Territory—needed a constant inflow of domesticated horses and mules for their economic survival, and they all looked toward Comanchería to meet that need. This put the Comanches in an extraordinarily powerful position: by controlling the diffusion of animals from the livestock-rich Southwest to the north and east, they could literally control the technological, economic, and military evolution in the North American interior.

Comanches' privileged position undoubtedly caused resentment among their allies, but it also fostered peaceful relations. In a stark contrast to the northern plains, which collapsed into long and bloody intertribal wars in the late eighteenth century when rival groups attempted to dominate the region's multiple trade chains, the southern plains remained relatively calm: except for the Cheyenne-Arapaho intrusion in the 1830s, Comanchería was not subjected to prolonged trade wars. The difference, it seems, was Comanches' monopolistic grip on horse trade. As much as their trading partners may have detested their dependence on Comanche suppliers, few were willing to jeopardize their access to Comanchería's livestock reserves by starting an uncertain trade war. Just as multipolarity fueled instability on the northern plains, apolarity promoted stability in and around Comanchería.[49]

Commercial hegemony shielded Comanchería against external aggression, and it allowed Comanches to project their influence outward from Comanchería, for hard political and economic power readily translated into softer and more subtle forms of cultural power. At once dependent on and dazzled by Comanchería's wealth, many bordering societies emulated and adopted aspects of Comanche culture. For example, Cheyenne traditions speak of extensive mimicking of the Comanches that ranged from equestrian lore to the basic techniques of nomadic culture. One story relates a meeting between the horse-mounted Comanches and still pedestrian Cheyennes. Cheyennes were at once astonished and hesitant at this singular moment: "We never heard of horses," said one Cheyenne priest. "Perhaps Maheo [All-Father Creator] wouldn't like for us to have them." Comanches, eager to open trade relations, assumed the role of a proponent: "'Why don't you ask him?' a Comanche said. 'We'll trade with you, if you're too afraid to go and get them [from New Mexico].'" Cheyennes did so and received Maheo's blessing for their decision, after which "Comanches stayed with the Cheyennes another four days, and their women showed the Cheyenne women what kind of wood to use for tipi poles, and how to cut and sew a tipi, and how to tie the poles to their horses, and load them with the tipis and the other things they needed."[50]

Such stories may not always have been literally accurate, but their significance lies elsewhere: more than of conventional facts, they speak of Indians' understanding of defining historical trends. Groups like the Cheyennes or the Poncas probably acquired their first horses from the nomadic middleman traders of the northern plains, but their stories emphasize the example and guidance of Comanches, whose spectacularly successful pastoral culture represented the ideal for the indigenous societies across the Great Plains.[51] Horses spread to the Great Plains from several sources—Texas, New Mexico, the Rocky Mountains, the Mississippi valley, even Canada—but the people tended to look south toward Comanchería for how to best put them in use.

Comanches' cultural influence was not limited to equestrian knowledge but affected things as diverse as religious ceremonies, military societies, clothing accessories, hairstyles, and weaponry. To contemporary Euro-Americans the most illuminating sign of Comanches' cultural power was the spread of their language across the Southwest and the Great Plains. By the turn of the eighteenth century, Comanches were able to conduct most of their business at New Mexico's border fairs in their own language, and many of the comancheros and ciboleros who visited Comanchería to trade and hunt were fluent in the Comanche language. The diffusion of the Comanche language accelerated in the early nineteenth century when Comanches extended their commercial reach across the midcontinent, connecting with a growing number of people. Several Euro-American observers noted matter-of-factly that the Indians of the southern and central Great Plains used the Comanche language in commercial and diplomatic interactions, and Native oral traditions attest that Comanche challenged sign language as the universal language of exchange. Comanche was thus to a large section of the middle North America what the Chinook Jargon was to the Northwest or Mobilian to the Mississippi valley: a trade lingua franca. When people and societies meet and intermingle on frontiers, their choice of language is often an accurate gauge of relative power dynamics between them: economically and politically weaker groups tend to adopt the words, phrases, and even syntaxes of stronger ones. So too does the ascendancy of the Comanche language denote a larger truth: having wielded unparalleled economic, political, and cultural influence, the Comanches were re-creating the midcontinent in their own image.[52]

Encircling Comanchería there thus lay an extensive sphere of cultural penetration that bore an unmistakable imprint of Comanche influence. The people inhabiting that zone were tied to the Comanche nation as allies, dependents, and exchange partners and more or less willingly embraced elements of Comanche culture. But cultural diffusion was only one facet of a much more inclusive and intensive process of Comanchenization: a large portion of the foreign ethnicities attached to the Comanche orbit would eventually immigrate into Comanchería, seduced by its prosperity and security. The immigrants took many different roads into Comanchería, but all paths merged into a single process. Whether the newcomers blended into the Comanche society, becoming in effect naturalized Comanches, adopted a subordinate status as junior allies, or retained a larger measure of political and cultural autonomy, the net effect of their arrival was Comanchería's transformation from an ethnically homogenous national domain into a multicultural and politically stratified imperial realm.

Large-scale incorporation of foreign ethnicities into Comanchería began with the Kiowas and Naishans. The closely allied Kiowas and Naishans migrated into Comanchería during the first and second decades of the nineteenth century, after having lost their middleman trading niche on the central plains to Cheyennes and Arapahoes. They established residence on the upper Canadian and Red rivers where, at the very heart of Comanchería, they slowly began to blend in with the Comanches. The three groups camped and hunted together, intermarried extensively, and joined their forces in frequent raiding expeditions and defensive military campaigns. According to one observer, some Naishans "settled in Comanche villages" and the Kiowas were often mistaken for Comanches, "since they sometimes share their encampments." The three groups worshipped together and exchanged customs, rituals, and beliefs; Comanches, who apparently did not practice the Sun Dance before 1800, participated in the Kiowa ceremony and in time developed their own version of the Kiowa ritual.

A dearth of sources on the early nineteenth-century Kiowas and Naishans prevents determining how deeply the two nations were incorporated into the Comanche political system, but that dearth is also suggestive: Kiowas and Naishans, even while maintaining a separate political organization with tribal councils and chiefs, largely conformed to Comanches' political designs. While Comanches became increasingly involved in interimperial rivalries and power politics, Kiowas and Naishans remained more local actors who rarely figure in colonial powers' diplomatic considerations, especially during the first third of the nineteenth century. Kiowas sometimes played a central role in Indian-Indian diplomacy—they negotiated the great peace of 1840 side by side with Comanches—but Comanches often represented both the Naishans and Kiowas in high-level political meetings with colonial powers. Some Euro-American sources listed Kiowas and Naishans as simply one of the "tribes" or "peoples" of the Comanche nation or confederacy. As contemporary Euro-Americans understood it, Kiowas and Naishans resided on the southern plains under the auspices and partial domination of the Comanches. On an outward-extending gradient of privilege and participation, the Kiowas and Naishans were closest to the empire's core.[53]

Sometime after 1800 Comanches also accepted the Chariticas, an Arapaho group from the central plains, into its fold. As with many other groups that gravitated toward Comanchería, the immediate attraction for the Chariticas was the region's horse wealth and hospitable climate for animal husbandry. Before moving to the southern plains, the Chariticas had possessed few horses and used castrated dogs to pull their belongings, but they emerged in Comanchería "as good horsemen as their allies." In the course of the 1810s and 1820s, the Chariticas severed ties to the main Arapaho body, crossed the Arkansas River into Comanchería, and amalgamated into the Comanche nation. In 1828 General Manuel de Mier y Terán, then the leader of a scientific and boundary expedition into Texas, wrote that Chariticas had relocated some fifteen years earlier from the north, and "Comanches have admitted them. Today they are identical and live in mixed camps." Berlandier reported that Chariticas "often live among the Comanches . . . with whom they are very good friends," and that they "resemble the Comanche in their clothing and war ornaments but differ from them in their customs and their language, which is much harsher and without harmony." Ruíz emphasized the hierarchical nature of the relationship. "The Chariticas steal horses habitually; they are, in my opinion, the most barbarian of all people. Even their best friends are in danger when they visit a Charitica encampment if there are no Comanches present at that time. The Comanches exert certain influence over the Chariticas, and the latter do not dare do some things in their presence." By midcentury, the Chariticas were considered part of the Comanche nation.[54]

The Wichitas followed yet another path into Comanchería. Initially close commercial and military allies, Wichitas and Comanches clashed violently in the late eighteenth century over trading rights. But as Wichitas' power faded in the early 1810s, Comanches reversed their policy and sought cooperative relations. The Taovayas, Tawakonis, and Wacos gradually drew closer to Comanchería and entered a partnership that became increasingly unequal. Comanches traded with the three groups, supplying them with horses and bison products in exchange for farming produce, while at the same time curtailing their autonomy. They prevented the Wichitas from trading directly with Americans and represented them in political meetings with Spain, Mexico, and the Republic of Texas. By the 1840s, Wichita foreign policy had become subordinate to Comanche leadership. When Texas officials approached the Tawakonis in 1844 with the intention of negotiating a peace accord, their chief immediately recoiled: "I can't say that I will make peace . . . until I see the Comanche, else I may tell a lie. My people will do as they do." Comanches also used Taovaya, Tawakoni, and Waco villages as supply depots, replenishing their food storages and recruiting warriors before launching raids into Texas, and some Mexican officials believed that Comanches pressured Tawakonis to raid for them. Taovaya, Tawakoni, and Waco villages also served Comanchería as buffers that cushioned the blows of colonial reprisals. Wichitas were widely deemed as irredeemable thieves and the "worst" Indians in Texas, a notion some Comanche leaders deliberately fostered. "The Wichita are like Dogs," Chief Pahayuko stated in 1845. "They will steal. You may feed a dog well at night and he will steal all your meat before morning. This is the way with the Wichitas." Although not nearly as effective raiders as the Comanches, the Wichitas suffered some of the bloodiest reprisals at the hands of Mexican troops and Anglo-Texas militia.[55]

Over time, Comanches absorbed entire Wichita bands into their realm, which served two immediate purposes: it removed the last remnants of the Wichita trading barrier to eastern markets and allowed Comanches to recruit warriors against the Osages, their principal enemy. In 1811, after the collapse of the great Taovaya-Tawakoni villages on the Red River, John Sibley reported that a portion of Taovaya refugees "joined a wandering band" of Comanches. As the Wichitas' power declined in the ensuing years, nearly all their bands sought protection within Comanchería's expanding borders, conforming to Comanche leadership as junior allies and partially blending into the Comanche body politic. Berlandier listed three of the four Wichita tribes—the Taovayas, Tawakonis, and Wacos—as Comanches' subordinates, "lesser peoples whom poverty or fear has driven to seek their protection," and Mexican officials noted that the Comanche nation "is made very strong by the nine nations that are subordinate to it" (several of those nine nations undoubtedly were Wichita groups). Writing in the 1830s, Josiah Gregg noted that Comanches "generally remain on friendly terms with the petty tribes of the south, whom, indeed, they seem to hold as vassals," and the traveler Thomas J. Farnham reported that Comanches "stand in the relation of conquerors among the tribes in the south." Although Comanches themselves never explicitly called the Taovayas, Tawakonis, and Wacos "subordinates" or "vassals," the three groups had fallen under heavy Comanche influence. With their autonomy curtailed, geopolitical space narrowed, and economic opportunities compromised, they had become dependents of the Comanche empire.[56]

In addition to the wholesale incorporation of ethnic groups, there seems to have been a nearly constant stream of immigrants, refugees, renegades, and exiles from adjoining societies into Comanchería. Untold numbers of Wichitas, Caddos, Apaches, Pawnees, Shoshones, Cherokees, Chickasaws, Choctaws,

Delawares, Shawnees, Seminoles, Quapaws, and black slaves from Indian Territory voluntarily left their communities to join the increasingly multiethnic Comanche nation, evidently lured by its growing prosperity and security. Not even the Spanish colonies were immune to Comanchería's pull. Native subjects and *genízaros* escaped exploitation, harsh conditions, and curtailed opportunities in New Mexico and Texas by fleeing to Comanchería, as did a number of socially marginalized and impoverished Spanish citizens.

Little is known about the actual incorporation processes; unlike captives who sometimes were ransomed back to their relatives, voluntary immigrants tend to vanish from the historical record after entering Comanchería. It seems, however, that most of them married into Comanche families, adopted Comanche customs and language, relinquished outward signs of their former identity, and were eventually Comancheanized. Sometimes only physical traits remained, as Sibley realized in 1807, when he noticed among visiting Comanche rancherías several people of "light Brown or Auburn Hair & Blue or light Grey Eyes." A half century later voluntary immigration and ethnic incorporation had transformed the very fabric of Comanche society, prompting Texas Indian agent Robert S. Neighbors to write that "there are at the present time very few pure-blooded Comanches."[57]

In crudely materialist terms, the flow of immigrants into Comanchería is easy to explain. Whether one was looking in from the central Great Plains in the north, Wichita country or Indian Territory in the east, Spanish or Mexican Texas in the south, or New Mexico in the west, Comanchería appeared safe, dynamic, and prosperous. People from nearby societies, Post Oak Jim told an ethnographer in 1933, "frequently snuck into [Comanche rancherías] to give themselves up—they came from poor tribes where there was not enough food." Spaniards, Mexicans, and Pueblo Indians from New Mexico and Texas variously sought in Comanchería asylum from political persecution, religious oppression, poverty, and enslavement. People, in other words, exchanged themselves—their bodies and their labor—for the protection and wealth that kinship bonds with Comanches made available. But while grounded in material impulses, immigration was also a social and psychological process. That process is largely inaccessible to us for the sources fall silent—Spanish officials, for example, simply brushed off the problem of outward immigration by labeling the renegades who abandoned them to live with *salvajes* as "perverse"—but it is possible to delineate its approximate contours.[58]

A passage to Comanchería was not necessarily a trek to the unknown. Living within Comanchería's seductive cultural sphere, the Wichitas, Chariticas, Mexicans, and others who embarked into Comanchería were often preacclimatized

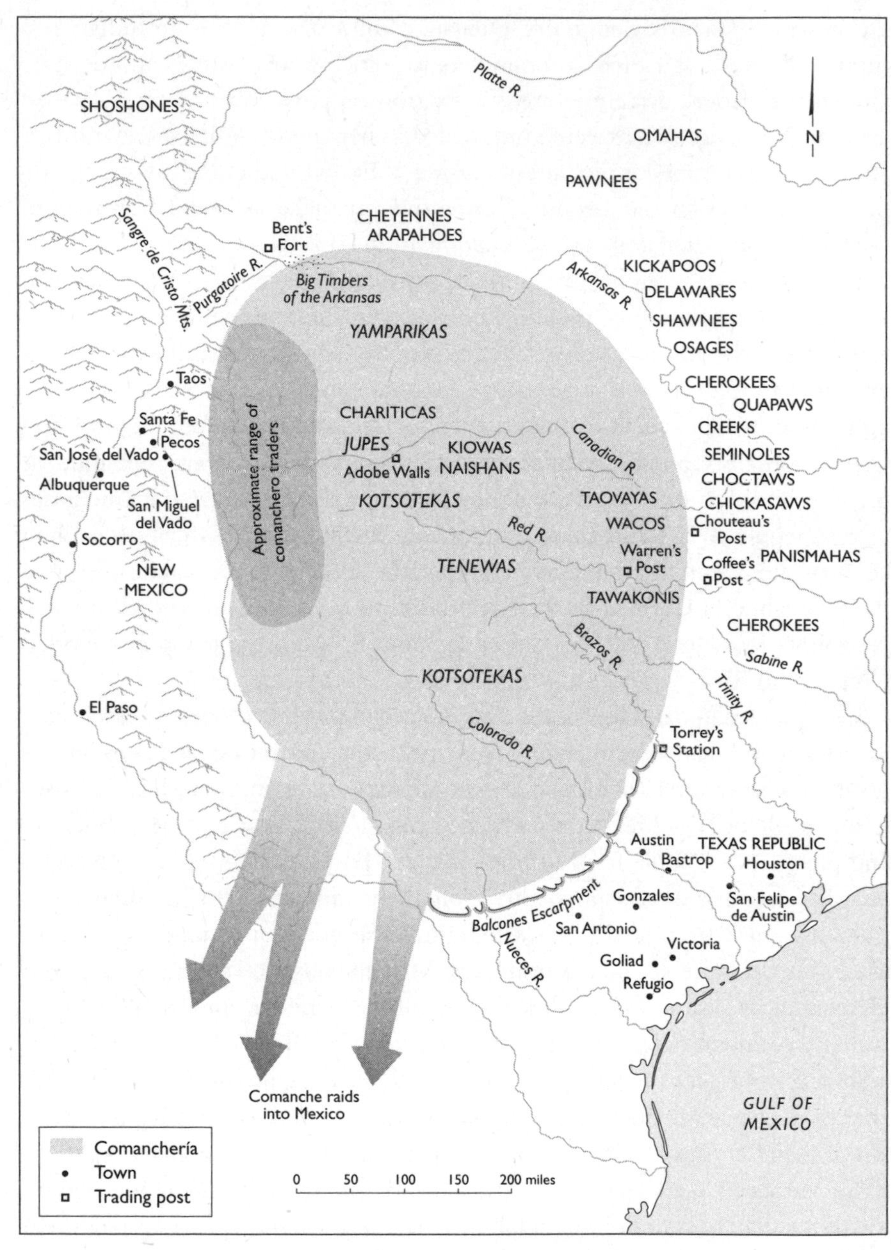

7. Imperial Comanchería and its alliance network in the 1830s and 1840s.
Map by Bill Nelson.

to Comanche way of life, customs, traditions, and language. Nor did a move into Comanchería necessarily involve negotiating racial barriers, for Comanches did not define the world in terms of color lines. Race for early nineteenth-century Comanches was essentially a political conception. They talked about their mistrust and hatred toward the whites (*taibooʔs*), but it was always in a specific geopolitical context and generally directed toward the encroaching Anglo-Texan settlers. Behavior and beliefs, not blood lineages, determined who would be accepted into Comanchería and could become Comanche. If a newcomer of Hispanic, Anglo, Caddoan, or any other ethnic descent was willing and able to adopt the proper code of behavior, he or she would be accepted as a member of the community. Acting like a Comanche—honoring kinship obligations, respecting camp rules, obeying taboos, yielding to consensus rule, adhering to accepted gender roles, and contributing to communal affairs—was more important than looking like one. "When at war with us if Mexicans are in their camps," one Mexican observer wrote in 1828, "the Comanches will not harm them, showing that he who lives with them is their friend, regardless of his nationality."[59]

If Comanche society welcomed newcomers, it also sustained them after their entrance. Naturalized Comanche carried no visible stigma of their background and apparently faced few obstacles for social fulfillment and elevation. They could marry into Comanche families, enter kinship networks, and achieve positions of power. In 1834 the traveling American artist George Catlin visited Comanchería with a U.S. peace commission and painted a portrait of His-oo-san-ches, "one of the leading warriors of the tribe." It was only after finishing the painting that Catlin realized that his model was actually Jesús Sánchez, a progeny of a Comanche-Spanish union.[60] As stories like Jesús Sánchez's show, outsiders embraced Comanche identity precisely because that identity was at once distinctive, accommodating, and negotiable. Comanches may have used language that had nationalistic overtones and felt strong ethnic pride, but they were permissive in determining who could claim membership in their community. Later in the nineteenth century, when the U.S. expansion threatened their very existence, Comanches tried to build an anti-American pan-Indian alliance by appealing to race—a more exclusive concept than tribe or nation—but in the early part of the century they still believed that almost anyone could become Comanche.

Why, then, did Comanches open their borders for such a massive influx of new peoples and foreign practices, beliefs, and languages? Just as the many peoples who crossed the border into Comanchería displayed a multitude of motives for doing so, so too did Comanches accept them for a wide variety of reasons. The newcomers provided Comanches with information about distant

8. *His-oo-san-ches (Commanche Warrior).* Oil on canvas by George Catlin, 1834. Courtesy of Yale Collection of Western Americana, Beinecke Rare Book and Manuscript Library.

lands and markets, defense systems on colonial frontiers, and raiding opportunities within them. They introduced novel ideas about animal husbandry, explained the workings of exotic diseases and perhaps provided new cures, and offered new skills that could repair guns or heal the wounds inflicted by them. Some groups came to operate as middlemen traders, shuffling goods between Comanchería and faraway markets, while others produced maize and other necessities that were not available in Comanchería. Some, by simply moving into Comanchería, afforded Comanches a more direct access to surrounding markets and resources.

In the end, however, large-scale ethnic absorption was a necessity born less of strategic calculations than of shifting demographics. Comanches' far-reaching trading network opened their communities to new markets, but it also opened them to deadly microbes traveling with the traders who flocked in from all directions. After the first devastating outbreak of smallpox in 1780–81, the Comanches were hit by repeated waves of disease. Smallpox erupted into major epidemics in 1799, 1808, 1816, 1839, 1848, and 1851, and a potent cholera virus washed over Comanchería in 1849. The epidemics claimed thousands of lives, grinding deep dents into Comanchería's demographic base. Comanche population may have peaked around forty thousand in the late 1770s, but most estimates in the 1820s and 1830s put it between twenty and thirty thousand. This drop, moreover, occurred when the communities around Comanchería experienced steady and at times explosive growth. Natural increase and immigration from the United States boosted New Mexico's population from thirty-one thousand in 1790 to forty-two thousand in 1821 and to some sixty-five thousand in 1846. In Texas, a deluge of American immigrants and their slaves swelled the province's population from approximately two thousand in the early 1820s to some forty thousand in 1836. Indian Territory, fed by constant removals, was home to some twenty thousand Indians by 1832.[61]

Under such conditions, incorporation of people, groups, and even entire nations into Comanchería became a matter of preserving political and economic power. On one hand, the newcomers were essential workers who sustained Comanchería's burgeoning pastoral economy as spouses who produced children for the community. Comanches themselves believed, one mid-nineteenth-century observer wrote, that "they have increased greatly in numbers . . . by the connexion with other small prairie bands." On the other hand, the new nations residing within Comanchería acted as allies in wars and buffers when those wars swept back into Comanchería. Wichita villages cushioned Comanchería's eastern border against Osage raids and its southern border against Anglo-Texan soldier-settlers, while the Kiowas bore a disproportionate brunt of the Cheyenne and Arapaho attacks during the struggles over the Arkansas basin. More abstractly, the sheer mass of peoples under their auspices gave Comanches substantial esteem and leverage in their diplomatic dealings with Euro-Americans—a point not lost on colonial agents, Comanches themselves, and the people caught between them. As many Euro-Americans saw it, negotiating with Comanches often meant yielding to their demands or risking a clash with a broad Comanche-led intertribal coalition.[62]

The willingness of other peoples to become Comanche is a striking manifestation of Comanches' international power and prestige. It made a deep impression on American visitors like Josiah Gregg, who claimed that Comanches "acknowledge no boundaries, but call themselves the lords of the entire prairies—all others are but 'tenants at will.'" For the resident Spaniards and Mexicans, however, Comanchería's gravitational pull was a source of fear and envy. In 1828, following the signing of a boundary treaty with the United States earlier that year, the Mexican government dispatched a Comisión de Límites (Boundary Commission) under General Manuel de Mier y Terán to determine the northern and eastern borders of Texas. The commission was also assigned to survey the attitudes of Texas tribes and explore the possibilities of incorporating the Plains Indians into "the Mexican family" and, if they settled down and embraced Catholicism, as citizens of the republic.

The situation in Texas shocked the commission. American immigrants were flooding in from the east, blurring the boundary line between Texas and Louisiana, and Comanches were incorporating Mexico's prospective Indian allies across the entire province. "The weaker tribes that cause the Comanches no concern are added through alliance," Terán noted. "By allowing them to live independently distributed into camps of two or three hundred persons, the Comanches teach them their own martial habits and help to improve their condition." Lieutenant José María Sánchez found Mexican presence in Texas weak and reported in disbelief how the Comanches systematically absorbed and assimilated other Native societies into their ranks. To him, the Comanches appeared an expanding hegemonic people who imposed their identity on other groups whom they kept under paternalistic rule. The "desire to increase their tribe," he wrote, "makes the Comanches very considerate of the small tribes with which they have friendly relations, protecting them, teaching them their habits and customs, and finally amalgamating them into their nation. For this reason the Comanches are the most numerous of those [indigenous nations] found in Texas."[63]

5

Greater Comanchería

Like most empires, the Comanche empire had many faces. Viewed from the north and east, it was an empire of commerce and diplomacy, an expanding transnational nexus that radiated prestige and power, absorbed foreign ethnicities into its multicultural fold, and brought neighboring societies into its sphere as allies and dependents. Viewed from the Southwest and Mexico, however, the Comanches showed a different kind of face. Here their empire brushed directly against Euro-colonial frontiers, and its tactics were often grounded in violence and exploitation. This was an empire that marginalized, isolated, and divided Spanish and Mexican colonies, demoting them, in a sense, from imperial to peripheral status. But while distinctive, the opposite faces of the Comanche empire were connected, parts of an integrated whole. Comanches knitted the deep sinews of their power by looking north and east toward the vast political and economic resources of the Great Plains and the cis-Mississippi east. It was there, in landscapes far removed from the opportunities and dangers of the colonial Southwest, that they found the allies, subordinates, and markets on which they built their imperial ascendancy in the Southwest and northern Mexico.

In this chapter I explore how Comanches' plains hegemony shaped their policies toward the colonial regimes. Sustained more by mediation and cultural sway than force and coercion, Comanches' far-flung trading and alliance network pacified their northern and eastern borders, liberating resources to confront the expansionist Bourbon Spain in the west and south. They subjected Texas to systematic stock-and-slave raiding and tribute extortion, bringing the colony on the verge of collapse, but they traded peacefully in New Mexico, using the colony as a source of political gifts and an outlet for surplus stock. These policies aborted the promising developments of the Bourbon era and ultimately dissolved Spain's imperial system in the far north. Isolated from the interior and its resources by the Comanches, New Mexico gravitated economically, politically, and even culturally toward Comanchería even as Texas nearly expired under Comanche pressure.

Independent Mexico inherited in 1821 a badly fragmented frontier in its far north, and the fledgling nation failed to put it back together. New Mexico continued its drift toward Comanchería, distancing itself from the rest of Mexico, while Texas, in a doomed attempt at self-preservation, opened its borders to U.S. immigration. The founding of the Republic of Texas posed a grave threat to Comanches, but ironically, it also spurred one of the most dramatic extensions of their regime. While struggling to secure their border with the Lone Star Republic through war and diplomacy, Comanches shifted their market-driven raiding operations south of the Río Grande, turning much of northern Mexico into a vast hinterland of extractive raiding. That subjugated hinterland was what the United States Army invaded and conquered in 1846–48.

This chapter, then, is about how Comanches harnessed and exercised power but it is also about how they imagined, managed, and produced space. Comanches refused to recognize national and international boundaries as Euro-Americans defined them. They treated New Spain and Mexico not as undivided imperial realms but as collections of discrete entities, devising distinct policies toward New Mexico, Texas, and other colonial states. By doing so, they imposed an alternative spatial geometry on what historians have called the Spanish and Mexican borderlands. Spanish and Mexican mapmakers invariably depicted the far north as intact and cohesive, an inseparable part of New Spain or Mexico, but it is also possible to view New Mexico and Texas as a part of an expanding Comanche dominion, or the Greater Comanchería. Whether through violent exploitation, coercive diplomacy, economic dependence, or intimate cultural ties, New Mexico and Texas were irrevocably bound to Comanchería, whose effective sphere of influence, if not actual political boundaries, extended far to the south and west of its southern plains core area. The composition of this chapter is designed to highlight this hidden geographic reality. Rather than following the orthodox temporal organization of dividing the early nineteenth-century Southwest into Spanish, Mexican, and American periods, I adopt a spatial approach in order to make visible the geopolitical structures, divides, and continuities enforced by Comanches. Doing so reveals the blueprint of the Comanche empire.

In spring 1803, when the Louisiana Purchase raised the specter of a U. S. invasion into Spain's North American empire, the frontier province of Texas was already gripped by fear. Eastern Comanches, who had entered into a formal alliance with the colony in 1785 and honored the peace for a decade, were raiding again. Attacks had continued for eight years, spreading terror across the province. Comanche chiefs frequented San Antonio to apologize for the raids and to return an occasional stolen horse, but they seemed either unwilling or unable to stop the violence.

Part of the problem was that the violence had become personal. In 1801 Spaniards had killed the son of Chief Blanco, a local Yamparika leader, near San Antonio, and Blanco had been carrying out a private vendetta against Texans ever since. The situation had spiraled out of control in spring 1802, when Blanco's followers attacked a Spanish hunting party on the plains. The fleeing hunters exacted arbitrary vengeance on a lone Comanche they accidentally met and brought his scalp to Governor Juan Bautista Elguézabal in San Antonio. In March 1803 Elguézabal tried to diffuse tension by inviting Comanche leaders to a council in San Antonio, but the meeting ended uneasily. The shipment of goods from the south was late that year, and the governor was able to offer the chiefs only few gifts.[1]

A month later the United States purchased Louisiana from France, which sparked off a bitter quarrel over the boundaries of the purchased area. Spain insisted that Louisiana comprised no more than the west bank of the Mississippi and the cities of New Orleans and St. Louis, while the United States asserted that it extended to the crest of the Rockies and to the Río Grande, encompassing half of New Mexico and all of Texas. Spanish authorities had feared for some time that Philip Nolan and other American trader-agents operating on the southern plains had fomented anti-Spanish sentiments, and the Louisiana dispute elevated the anxiety to a fever pitch. With the United States disputing Spanish imperial claims north of the Río Grande and with Comanches raiding again along the frontier, Texas suddenly became the most valuable and vulnerable of Spain's American colonies.[2]

The escalating violence in an uncertain geopolitical situation caused deep anxiety in Texas, where the carnage of the previous outbreak of Comanche raiding was still fresh in memory. The officials seemed powerless. They not only lacked the military muscle to repel the raids but knew that hard-line policies ran the risk of alienating the Comanches and pushing them toward Americans. In the end, Spanish administrators had only one feasible option: to channel a large portion of the much-needed funds that the Bourbon Reforms had made available into Comanche gifting in the hope of generating enough goodwill to avoid bloodshed. Fueled by fear, the volume of Indian gifting in Texas escalated to the point that in 1810 the colony invested almost four thousand pesos in Indian diplomacy, handing out presents—weapons, metal utensils, cloth, tobacco, food, vermilion—to more than thirteen hundred Comanche visitors. Such liberal distributions, which nearly bankrupted San Antonio's treasury, prompting one governor to accuse Comanches of an insatiable "lust for lucre," did help curb raids for short periods. But they also locked Texas into a tricky dynamic: for the next half century, Comanches would step up and cut back raiding in the province in line with the availability of gifts. Under the ever-present possibility of violence, offerings of diplomatic presents became fixed tribute payments to protect the exposed colony.[3]

Most Spanish officials refused to acknowledge this unsettling reversal of power relations and insisted on calling the payments presents or charity, and the Comanches, who thought that gifts symbolized social bonds, never explicitly articulated the connection between peace and gifting. Yet, resting on the knife-edge of violence, the relationship was unmistakably tributary in nature. In summer 1803, after two years of fear-inducing attacks across Texas, more than eleven hundred Comanches visited San Antonio to trade and collect presents. Generous gifting continued through the next two years, and in 1806 Spaniards gratified more than two thousand Comanches in San Antonio. In 1808 Texas ordered seven thousand pesos worth of Indian gifts from Mexico City. In return for liberal presents, Comanche chiefs pressured their followers to curtail raiding and even offered assistance to Spain in a possible border conflict with the United States. One powerful leader, Sargento, attached the name of the Texas governor to his own and as Sargento-Cordero traveled around Comanchería endorsing peace and retrieving stolen horses. What the Comanches did not do was to reciprocate Spain's generosity. Their recompense was the absence of violence. Holding a pronounced power advantage over Texas, they seem to have placed the Spaniards in an ambiguous social space where they were not quite friends nor outright enemies.[4]

The peace lasted only as long as gift distributions did. The outbreak of the Hidalgo Revolt in Mexico in the fall of 1810 disrupted the flow of funds to the northern provinces, undermining Texas's policy of buying peace. As the gift distributions dwindled, Comanches resumed attacks, raiding and extorting tribute across the colony from the San Sabá River to the Río Grande. Spanish officials made desperate efforts to amass enough gifts to restore good relations, and in the summer and fall of 1811 Comanche chiefs Sargento-Cordero, Chihuahua, Paruaquita, and Yzazat visited San Antonio, sustaining Spanish beliefs that peace would be possible. Then, however, the officials committed a diplomatic gaffe that alienated the entire Comanche nation. El Sordo (The Deaf One), a renowned Tenewa war leader with close ties to Tawakonis and Taovayas, went to

San Antonio to report on the raiding activities of his rival Wichita leaders. El Sordo arrived unarmed with his family and under a banner of truce, but Spanish officials, betraying a deepening panic, arrested and jailed him. The diplomatic breach killed the artificial peace. Even Sargento-Cordero abandoned his pro-Spanish stance and joined the other Comanche rancherías in attacking Texas. He reentered the historical record—simply as Cordero—in 1817 at Natchitoches where he tried to open diplomatic and commercial relations with the Americans.[5]

The collapse of Comanche-Spanish peace occurred just as the livestock trade between the Comanches and Americans was becoming big business, and the consequences were disastrous for Texas. American traders had a seemingly insatiable demand for horses and mules, and the collapse of the Spanish alliance allowed the Comanches to pillage Texas with impunity to meet that demand. Systematic pillaging began in winter 1811–12 when Comanches "collected a great number of animals both horses and mules, leaving horror and devastation in this industry in the Province of Texas and on the frontiers of the other Provinces." Although Nemesio Salcedo, the commanding general of the Interior Provinces, had managed to recruit several hundred militiamen, the presidial forces of Texas failed to the seal the frontier. In early August, after the Comanches had carried off more than two hundred horses from San Marcos, Texas Governor Manuel María de Salcedo proposed a series of campaigns against them—only to be denied by his uncle the commanding general who insisted that "war against the Comanches had always been considered the greatest evil that could befall the province."[6]

The elder Salcedo managed to deflect the evil of full-blown Comanche war, but he could not foresee another evil that was about to fall on Texas. In August 1812, as the Salcedos debated the Comanche situation, a detachment of Mexican and American revolutionaries and filibusterers invaded Nacogdoches to launch a popular revolt against the Spanish regime. Suddenly Texans found themselves caught in a two-front conflict. The revolt that would eventually fail lasted for a year, and its aftermath left Texas vulnerable and exposed to Comanche raiders. The victorious royal army carried out violent purges in San Antonio and Nacogdoches, reducing the colony's manpower by hundreds, and the Spanish crown prohibited settlers from carrying arms, inadvertently compromising their ability to defend the province against Indian assaults. And then, disastrously, the money ran out. The repercussions of the 1808 Napoleonic invasion of Iberia and the subsequent rebellions throughout New Spain had tied up resources, forcing the officials in Texas to scale down Comanche gifting. With the Comanche-American livestock trade now booming, this condemned Texas to ruination.

Soon Comanches were raiding from San Antonio all the way down to the Río Grande, attacking supply convoys, razing ranches, killing farmers in the field, and slaughtering entire herds of cattle. By 1814, Texas was expiring. Having lost tens of thousands of animals to Comanchería, it was nearly destitute of livestock, and the governor ordered the ranches around San Antonio to be abandoned. Food was scarce, soldiers were left without supplies and pay, and settlers began to flee the colony.[7]

The year 1816 brought more alarming news: Comanches had made a truce with the Lipan Apache group led by El Cojo, ending more than sixty years of on-and-off warfare. Spanish officials had worked since the 1770s to weaken the Lipans by isolating them from the other Native groups in southern Texas and northern Coahuila. They had feared that an alliance with a powerful Native group could turn the strategically located Lipan villages on both sides of the Río Grande into an invasion point into the soft underbelly of Texas, and the accord with the Comanches realized their worst fears. The Comanche-Lipan alliance would not survive beyond the early 1820s, but the few years of its existence allowed Comanches to subject almost all of Texas to wholesale pillaging.[8]

With the truce, El Cojo's Lipans won hunting privileges in southern Comanchería and in return opened their territories to Comanches, who swiftly extended their stock and slave raids to the lower Río Grande valley and its many villages and haciendas. Lipans, one observer noted, also "served as guides to the Comanche, since they knew the roads, the villages, and the arms, to the great detriment of all the populations along the Rio Bravo del Norte." Texas was struck with constant attacks in the summer, and in the following year a massive raiding party of more than one thousand warriors—probably a joint Comanche-Lipan effort—ran over the town of Refugio near the Gulf Coast, stealing some ten thousand horses and mules, slaughtering cattle, sheep, and goats, and killing several settlers. In 1818 Texas Governor Antonio Martínez despaired that "not a single day passes without their [Comanches] making some depredation or attack."

Spanish militia and presidial troops were powerless against Comanche guerrilla tactics. Capitalizing on their superior mobility and knowledge of the terrain, Comanches concentrated overwhelming force against a target and escaped before a counteroffensive was organized, sometimes setting the grass on fire to thwart pursuing presidial troops. They regrouped at a safe distance and then attacked another target. Since they hunted while moving about, they could repeat the cycle several times before retreating into the immensity of Comanchería. The only way to contain them would have been to bring the war to their home range, but Spain's northern army, debilitated by lack of resources, had consigned itself to a wholly defensive stance: no Spanish military expedition had penetrated Comanchería since Juan Bautista de Anza's 1779 offensive. The council of San Antonio pleaded in vain with the provincial officials to organize a large punitive campaign against the Comanches.[9]

Texas spent its last years under Spanish rule as a raiding hinterland of the Comanches, who used it as a stockroom for their export-oriented livestock production system. The province, for all practical purposes, had ceased to function as a Spanish colony. Its connections to the rest of New Spain were frequently cut off, as traders and travelers refused to use the roads in the fear of running into Comanche war parties. Its once-flourishing ranching and farming economies lay in waste, and the colonists were reduced to operating at subsistence level. Cattle were left unbranded and abandoned because the settlers lacked horses for roundups and because animal concentrations attracted Comanche raiders. Leather, textile, and sugar industries disappeared altogether. The number of Hispanic settlers dropped from approximately four thousand in 1803 to roughly two thousand in 1821. Nacogdoches was hanging in by a thread, and San Antonio, the economic heart of the colony, was besieged by the Comanche-Lipan coalition.[10]

Comanches had a virtual monopoly on violence in their dealings with Texas. Spanish troops were demoralized by constant "attacks of the savages who each time become more daring," and they were kept in "continuous movement" along the frontier, which left their horses in "deplorable condition," "so weak and exhausted that they cannot even be saddled." Without massive reinforcements from Mexico City, Governor Martínez warned in 1819, "this province will be destroyed unwittingly by lack of inhabitants . . . because no one wishes to live in the province for fear and danger and because the few inhabitants now existing are being killed gradually by the savages." The destruction left a lingering legacy in Texas, as one Mexican officer noted in the mid 1830s: "early in 1810 there was a terrible invasion of wild Indians that destroyed the greater part of the cattle and even property, razing to the ground many of the establishments located at a distance from the centers of population. The decline of Bexar, Bahia del Espíritu Santo [Goliad], and Nacogdoches, the only Mexican settlements that have been able to subsist amidst the calamities that beset them, dates from that time and unless their misfortunes are remedied they will disappear entirely."[11]

Destruction of such magnitude requires explanation. Why did Comanches adopt such a relentlessly aggressive policy toward Texas and why did they nearly destroy a colony that posed virtually no military or political threat to them? They did not consider Texans racially or culturally inferior people and had in fact once considered them allies and kin, so why were they so willing to divest them of all possessions? The prevailing contemporary explanation was both perceptive and mechanistic: Comanche violence was fueled by the gifts, goods, and guns that flowed into Comanchería from the United States. Spanish officials came to believe that it was American markets and American machinations that alienated Comanches from Spaniards and fomented the violence in Texas. The idea that the near-destruction of Texas was ultimately the work of American borderland agents who provided Comanches with the motive (the market for livestock) and the means (guns) to raid became in time etched in the common Texas consciousness. Empresario Stephen F. Austin, casting himself as a victim of Anglo rapaciousness, condemned Comanche–U.S. trade as a "species of land Piracy" whereby "traders from the United States fit out expeditions to the Comanches . . . who are at war with this nation [Texas], and not only furnish them with arms and ammunition to carry on the war, but hire them to pillage the frontiers by purchasing the fruits of that pillage." Seeing American intent behind every Comanche action, the contemporaries thus relegated Comanche dominance in Texas to a mere by-product of the United States capitalist expansion.[12]

Although Comanches did gravitate actively and at times aggressively toward American markets—thereby inadvertently abetting the United States' southwestern encroachment—the link between markets and raids was not as straightforward as contemporary accounts suggest. Where colonists saw American goods and gifts as methods of a proxy war that sent Comanche warriors into Texas, Comanches understood those items as symbols of social bonds. If American wealth did persuade them to attack Texas, the cause and effect was articulated through the cultural politics of kinship, cooperation, and violence. Liberal trade and lavish gifts drew Comanches toward Americans, who acted like genuine kinspeople—and away from Spaniards, who failed to match Americans' generosity. In comparison to the American traders who offered high-quality guns, powder, and ammunition, Spaniards appeared stingy, disrespectful, uncommitted, and unloving.

In 1808, a year after the U.S. agent John Sibley had courted Comanches in Natchitoches and Comanches had replaced their Spanish flag with an American one, Spanish officials in San Antonio sensed that their ties to the Comanche nation were in jeopardy. Governor Manuel Antonio Cordero y Bustamente dispatched Captain Francisco Amangual, a sixty-nine-year-old veteran officer, to resuscitate the alliance. Amangual met with Sofais, a prominent eastern Comanche chief, on the Colorado River, and delivered a passionate speech. He reaffirmed "the love of our king and father" toward the Comanches and urged them to retain their "loyalty and fidelity" to the king. He advised that the Comanches "not trade with any other nation that may come to induce them, for their object is none other than that of afterward turning them from their loyalty to us." The Comanches responded that "they considered themselves Spaniards," and Amangual, whatever reservations he may have had about its sincerity, carried the message to San Antonio. But such a sentiment of affinity had to be constantly nourished with acts of generosity, which gave tangible meaning to abstractions like loyalty and love, and Comanches found Spanish acts increasingly wanting.[13]

Comanches were particularly offended by the Spaniards' failure to provide guns, which not only had enormous military value but were treasured as important prestige items and symbols of chiefly authority. Gun shipments from Mexico City to Texas were often unreliable. In 1806, for example, the rifles intended for Indian allies were of larger caliber than usual and Comanches refused to accept them because they were difficult to handle on horseback. To offset such problems, the Spanish government licensed much of Nacogdoches' Indian trade to the trading house of William Barr and Samuel Davenport, two former U.S. citizens who acquired the bulk of their gun supply from Natchitoches. But in 1808, as the rivalry between Spain and the United States intensified, Natchitoches's American agents cut off Barr's and Davenport's supply line, leaving them unable to provide guns to Spain's Indian allies. When visiting San Antonio two years later, two eastern Comanche chiefs, Chihuahua and El Sordo, bluntly told Governor Salcedo that they were disappointed in the Spaniards because they did not "give them rifles" and because they did not "let them trade with the Americans." They warned the governor that people who displayed such indifference to their needs were not "friends." By failing to act the role of generous kinspeople, Spanish officials had unknowingly alienated the Comanches, and when they tried to prevent the Comanches from trading with the Americans who did offer liberal gifts and goods, the already thinned attachment snapped.[14]

But the American success among the Comanches is open to a second, more mundane interpretation. Americans did not necessarily read Comanche culture any better than Spaniards did. Instead, their fuller adherence to Comanche conventions may have been—at least in part—a fortuitous accident made possible by the ways in which their commerce with the Comanches was structured. The trade between the Comanches and Spanish Texas took place mainly in San Antonio and Nacogdoches, where Comanches visited fairs and trading houses that, until the troubled 1810s, abounded with merchandise. When Comanche visitors departed, Spanish merchants were likely to still have plenty of goods left. Comanche-American trade, by contrast, rested on itinerant American traders who ventured into Comanchería from distant frontier outposts and spent long periods of time in Comanche rancherías, hoping to sell all their goods before returning home. Thus, the basic logistics of their business directed the Americans to behave like true kin. Unlike Spanish officials, they lived, traveled, ate, and slept with Comanches, and unlike Spanish merchants, they shared without restraint.[15]

Comanche violence in Texas, then, had a distinctive sociocultural component that was articulated through kinship politics. And yet contemporary observers were right in that the raids were materially motivated. Comanches may have been provoked to punish the Texans for being bad relatives, for failing to respect their sense of cultural order, but their principal reason to raid Texas was commercial: they needed a steady access to horses and mules in order to maintain their privileged access to the United States markets, the only reliable source of manufactured imports in the early nineteenth-century Southwest.

But yet again things were not so simple. Why raid Texas when Comanchería itself swarmed with massive herds of feral horses and offered one of the best conditions in North America for horse breeding? Comanches did take advantage of this ecological potential and built massive domestic horse herds, but they still preferred to fuel much of their trade with plundered animals. There were compelling economic, ecological, and cultural reasons for this. Feral horses could be turned into superior hunting mounts, but their taming was a difficult and time-consuming process, whereas raiding supplied domesticated, ready-to-sell horses that commanded high prices in eastern markets. Raiding also yielded mules which, thanks to their endurance and resilience to heat, were the preferred draft animal in the Deep South, where a large portion of Comanche livestock was eventually sold.[16]

So close, in fact, was the association between livestock raiding and trading that Comanches kept two separate sets of animals that served different economic and cultural needs. They channeled the stolen horses and mules swiftly into trading routes, but rarely sold processed mustangs or domestically raised animals, which had been specifically trained for various tasks from pulling travois to bison hunting and war. Such animals were treated almost like family members, as one American official found out in the early 1850s. Sanaco, an eastern Comanche chief, refused to sell his favorite horse to the American, explaining that trading the animal "would prove a calamity to his whole band, as it often required the speed of this animal to insure success in the buffalo chase. . . . Moreover, he said (patting his favorite on the neck), 'I love him very much.'"[17]

When Mexico won its independence from Spain in 1821, it inherited in Texas a bankrupt province whose ruinous state endangered the very existence of the infant nation. As the buffer province of Texas teetered toward collapse under

Comanche pressure, northern Mexico lay exposed to an invasion from the United States, whose citizens had already infringed on the border areas along the Sabine and Red rivers. Although preoccupied with the nation's turbulent center, Mexico City realized the urgency of rebuilding of Texas and ordered frontier officials to seek appeasement with the Comanches.[18]

And so, in September 1821 at a Wichita village on the Brazos River, a delegation of Mexican officials met with Comanche chiefs Barbaquista, Pisinampe, and Quenoc. The chiefs listened as the emissaries explained the shift of power in Mexico City but, unimpressed with their gifts, refused to a sign a treaty. Mexican authorities tried again two months later when José Francisco Ruíz, now as an officer of the Mexican Army, journeyed to eastern Comanchería and presented a peace offer to a grand council presided over by principal chiefs and attended by some five thousand Comanches. The council reached consensus after three days' deliberation, and in summer 1822 the "ancient" Pisinampe, the "father" of the eastern Comanches, led a delegation of chiefs to San Antonio to formalize a truce. Later that year Ojos Colorados, "a general of the Comanche nation," signed a treaty with Nuevo Vizcaya Governor Mariano Urrea and recognized Mexico's new government. Mexico's diplomatic cajoling culminated in fall 1822, when its troops escorted a Comanche delegation led by Chief Guonique to Mexico City. Guonique attended Agustín Iturbide's coronation as emperor and later signed a formal treaty between "the Mexican Empire and the Comanche Nation."[19]

The grandiose title notwithstanding, the treaty bespoke Mexico City's desperate need to reach a settlement with the Comanches, who controlled the balance of power in Mexico's far northern borderlands. The government offered Comanches duty-free trade in "silk, wool, cotton, hardware, food supplies, hides, tools for various crafts, all types of hand work, horses, mules, bulls, sheep, and goats" in San Antonio and, in reference to the Americans, asked them to notify Mexican officials about "people who come into their territory to explore it." Comanches were asked to return Mexican prisoners, "excepting those who wish to stay," and they were invited to send "twelve youths every four years, so that they may be educated at this Court in sciences and arts to which they are most suited." The treaty granted Comanches a right to round up wild horses near the Mexican settlements and even promised them a standing reward for "any iron-shod horses" they might end up capturing in the process. Finally, the Comanche nation was assigned an emissary-interpreter who would be in permanent residence in San Antonio and have direct access to the Mexican secretary of state. Pleased with the generous terms, Chief Guonique promised that if Spain would attempt to recapture Mexico—a threat that remained acute throughout the 1820s—Comanches would squash the attempt with "the rifle, the lance, and the arrow." To make clear to the Mexicans who held sway over the Southwest, he boasted that the eastern Comanches could mobilize "within six months . . . a body of twenty-seven thousand man" to protect Mexico against its enemies.[20]

The treaty spawned one of the recurring but fleeting attempts at accommodation on the Comanche-colonial borders. Comanche chiefs collected gifts and even accepted honorary ranks in the Mexican militia, Mexican officials such as Ruíz visited Comanchería to nourish the all-important personal ties between the two nations, and border trade thrived in San Antonio and Nacogdoches. The French scientist-traveler Jean Louis Berlandier reported how eastern Comanches visited the Nacogdoches presidio "in caravans of several hundred, provided they are at peace with the garrison, to sell their buffalo hides (covered with painting), bear grease, smoked and dried meat, and, above all, furs. . . . It is like a little fair to see a town square covered with the tents of a tribe, with all the hustle and bustle of a bazaar going on among them."[21]

But as Berlandier's report suggests, raiding continued. Mexicans assumed that the treaty covered all their communities; Comanches did not. Replicating their policies toward Spanish New Mexico in the 1760s and 1770s and Spanish Texas in the 1800s and 1810s, Comanches alternated raiding and trading with Mexican Texas. They plundered farms and ranches for livestock and captives, but traded peacefully in San Antonio and Nacogdoches. Seeing little contradiction in their actions, they expected Mexicans to follow the Comanche protocol in its intricate details whenever they visited the province for trade. To Berlandier, it seemed that they expected to be treated with the honors and courtesies due to a supreme power:

> As many as two or three hundred of these natives arrived at a time, bringing their wives and very young children. Whenever they came like this, bringing their offspring, the visit was a proof of peace, of friendship, and of trust; whereas, when they had only a few women with them, it was because they were at war. . . . When such a band of natives approaches a presidio, they make a camp a league away and send a courier with notice of their arrival and a request for permission to enter. Sometimes the garrison troops mount and go out to escort them. The formal entry then is something quite singular. As the bugles sound, you can see all the natives, holding themselves very proudly, riding in between the ranks of cavalry drawn up with sabers flashing in salute. I have seen one such group of Comanches take umbrage because no escort went to meet them. This slight was enough to make them decide not to enter the presidio at all.[22]

In the course of the 1820s the balance between accommodation and antagonism tipped toward the latter. This was in part due to Mexico's inconsistent Indian policy. Despite the lavish outlays of gifts and extensive promises of further presents during treaty talks, Mexico City procrastinated in sending the necessary moneys to the north, moving the governor of the recently unified states of Texas and Coahuila, Rafael González, to warn in 1824 that the lack of gifts and goods in the province was about to bring "a total collapse of the peace." Soon Comanches and their allies were raiding all across Texas and Coahuila, turning the lower Río Grande settlements into a dreadful world "where widows and orphans weep for dear ones slain" and "for sons and daughters carried into captivity." More funds became available for northern provinces in the late 1820s, but the politically unstable and economically impoverished Mexican republic struggled to keep the subsidies steady and sufficient. As the gift flow fluctuated, so too did the frontier relations; Comanches intensified and cut back their raiding activities in proportion to the availability of presents.[23]

But as during the Spanish era, the raids were also stimulated by the Comanches' need to supply their trading economy, which in the 1820s became increasingly enmeshed with the United States markets and grew rapidly. In 1826 the *Natchitoches Courier* reported matter-of-factly that the Americans were engaged in "an extensive and often very lucrative trade" with Comanches, who "are supported with goods, in return for the horses and mules, of which they rob the inhabitants of the province [of Texas]." Itinerant American peddlers provided Comanches with nearly bottomless markets for stolen stock while supplying them with weapons that made raiding more effective. Acutely aware of the linkage between American trade and Comanche raids in Texas, Mexico's secretary of state in 1826 asked the United States minister in Mexico to suppress the livestock trade, calling the westering Americans "traders of blood who put instruments of death in the hands of those barbarians."[24]

Like their Spanish predecessors, Mexican officials simplified Comanche violence and reduced it to mere subset of American imperialism. It was a misconception that led to a massive miscalculation. As the authorities in San Antonio, Saltillo, and Mexico City saw it, the relentless Comanche attacks in Texas threatened to turn the province into an easy catch for the United States, which clamored for western lands to accommodate its growing population and its seemingly bottomless demand for raw materials. Faced with what it saw as an entangled threat of Comanche aggression and American expansion, the Mexican Congress adopted in the fall of 1824 a desperate measure: it opened the northern provinces to foreign immigration, hoping to solve both outstanding frontier threats at once.

Behind the new policy was the calculation that generous land grants and tax exemptions would turn the encroaching *norteamericanos* into loyal Mexican subjects. Mexico tried, in other words, to counter American colonization by absorbing the colonizers themselves into its national body. In March 1825 the legislature of Coahuila y Texas implemented the new law, opening its borders to all foreigners willing to accept Mexican rule and worship the Christian god. In short order, the state signed some two dozen contracts with *empresarios*, immigration agents who were responsible for selecting and bringing in the colonists, allocating lands, and enforcing Mexican laws. The other objective of the immigration law was to use the American colonies as shields against Comanches. The designated empresario grants covered almost all of Texas to the west, north, and east of San Antonio, sheltering—at least in theory—the state's vital parts from Comanche invasions. The largest of the empresario colonies, Stephen F. Austin's cluster of five adjacent grants, would eventually extend from the Gulf Coast to some two hundred miles northeast of San Antonio.[25]

Far from imposing frontier buffers, the new Anglo colonies were in their early years weak and exposed. Established on sprawling grants, they were scattered, isolated, and an easy prey for the mobile Comanche war parties. Rather than shields against Comanche raids, they became targets for them. Discouraged by the prospects of his settlement plans—and fully aware of the geopolitical dynamics of the Comanche trading-and-raiding economy—Austin in 1830 complained to the Mexican government that peace with the Comanches would be impossible as long as there was a market in the United States for horses stolen from Texas. By purchasing Comanche livestock, he bristled, American traders had effectively "hired" Comanches "to prosecute a pillaging war against the frontiers of Texas, Quahuila, and Nuevo Sentender, robbing those Provinces of Horses and Mules." But even Austin himself was not aware just how vulnerable his colony was: Texas officials suspected that some of Austin's own settlers were engaged in contraband livestock and arms trade with Indians.[26]

The wealthy and well-connected Austin eventually managed to organize effective militia or "ranger" units, which provided a measure of protection against Comanche attacks, and in the mid-1830s his colony boasted more than eight thousand settlers, extensive cotton plantations, regular mail service, and a dynamic capital, San Felipe de Austin, with three thousand residents and four schools. The vast majority of American immigrants, however, quickly learned to shun the violent interior of Texas and instead established themselves near the Nacogdoches region and along the Gulf Coast. This left the Mexican-controlled Tejano Texas around San Antonio wide open to Comanche raiders, whose mili-

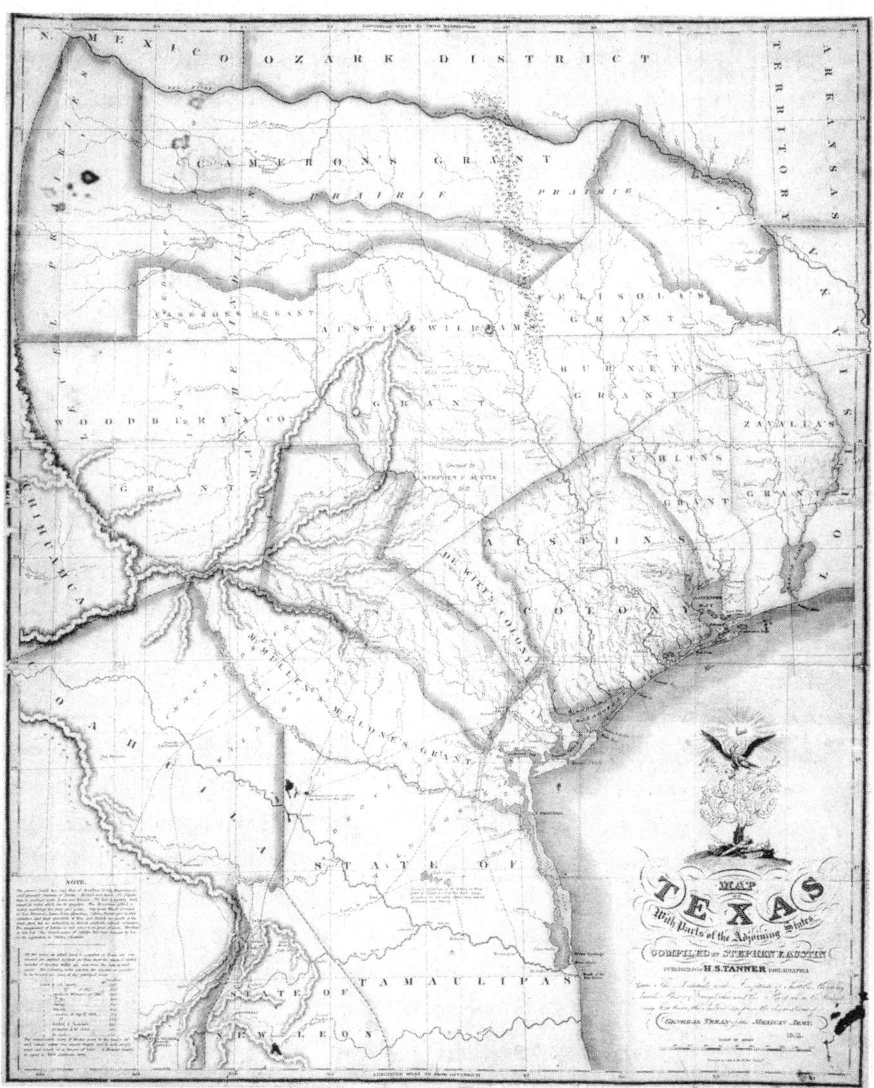

9. Map of Texas by Stephen F. Austin, 1835. Published by H. S. Tanner. This map captures the process of "cartographic dispossession." Euro-Americans diminished and delegitimized the power and territorial claims of indigenous inhabitants through map making. Although Comanches dominated much of the territory shown on Austin's map, they are depicted as almost landless: Comanchería has dissolved into Anglo-Texan empresario grants and Comanches seem to float above the southern plains, unattached to land and the political landscape. Courtesy of the Center for American History, University of Texas at Austin.

tary complex now had an international reach. They fought with American and British guns and enlisted auxiliaries among the Kiowas, Naishans, Apaches, Wichitas, and removed Indians. They used the Wichitas' Brazos River villages as staging areas for long-distance plundering forays, and their numerous Mexican captives provided crucial intelligence about those unfamiliar lands.[27]

From the mid-1820s on Comanches held much of Mexican Texas as a colonial appendage. In 1824 and 1825 several multiethnic war bands from Comanchería raided across Texas and into Coahuila, seeking horses and captives and killing resisting settlers. Many bands were reported to be using captured Mexican peasants as guides. San Antonio descended from helplessness to humiliation: in June 1825 a party of 330 Comanche men, women, and children rode into the capital and leisurely looted the town for six days. Attacks continued through the following year, but in 1827, in San Antonio, Comanche leaders buried the war with General Anastasio Bustamante, the military commander of the Eastern Interior Provinces. Mexican officials worked frantically to secure enough gifts to expand the truce into a peace, and when Tenewa Chief Paruakevitsi (Little Bear) visited San Antonio the next year to "renew the bonds of amity," the officials "showered [him] with gifts." Comanches embarked on an active border trade, visiting settlements from Nacogdoches to Aguaverde, and their chiefs frequented San Antonio to collect gifts and profess peace.[28]

But mirroring the developments during the late Spanish era, gift distributions soon morphed into tribute payments, for Comanches kept the peace only as long as presents were available. Mirabeau Buonaparte Lamar, the future president of the Republic of Texas, remarked how the Mexicans "used to have to purchase peace from the Comanchees, who came to Bexar [San Antonio] regularly every year to get their annual tribute." The arrangement reached a nadir for San Antonio in 1832, when a party of five hundred Comanches entered the capital and extorted and tormented its citizens for several days, undisturbed by the Mexican troops in the nearby garrison who failed to intervene. Upon leaving, moreover, Comanches forced the disgraced soldiers to escort them back to Comanchería, for a Shawnee war party was in the neighborhood. This incident exhausted San Antonio's funds for gifting, and Comanches responded with a prolonged raiding spree that lasted until 1834, when presents again became available, producing a brief interlude of tranquility. Gift payments, in short, had become the condition for peace, turning Texans into tributaries of the imperial Comanches. Tadeo Ortiz, a Mexican reformer-colonizer, considered the arrangement intolerable, "an insult and degradation to the honor of the nation." "Millions of *pesos* are being spent on . . . impossible truces," he bristled, "which under the name of peace, are ignominiously formed. . . . [Indians'] good will is

10. *Military Plaza—San Antonio, Texas.* Steel engraving by James D. Smillie from drawing by Arthur Schott. Before the U.S. annexation of Texas in 1845, San Antonio lingered for decades in virtual tributary vassalage under the Comanche empire. From U.S. Department of the Interior, *Report on the United States and Mexican Boundary Survey, Made under the Direction of the Secretary of the Interior, by* William H. Emory, *Major First Cavalry and the United States Commissioner,* 3 vols. (Washington, D.C.: Cornelius Wendell, 1857–59), vol. 1. Courtesy of Yale Collection of Western Americana, Beinecke Rare Book and Manuscript Library.

won with numerous presents at the expense of the people whom they continually insult, murder, and despoil of their property."[29]

Although it yielded only imperfect protection, the policy of paying for peace gave the vital Tejano regions of Texas much-needed if tenuous respites from violence. Settlers who had sought protection in urban centers began to move back into the countryside, revitalizing the province's ranching industry, which had nearly expired under Comanche raids between 1811 and 1821. The number of active ranches along the San Antonio–Goliad corridor rose from eleven in 1825 to eighty in 1833, and several Tejano oligarchs built large estates with multiple buildings and elaborate fortifications. But the policy also had the unintended effect of redirecting Comanche raids into other northern Mexican departments.

In 1830, with Comanches trading peacefully in San Antonio, municipalities along the lower Río Grande reported intense Comanche attacks. In 1833, Berlandier reported, Comanches "launched a dreadful war against the peaceable inhabitants of the state of Chihuahua." They "overran several haciendas in Nuevo Leon, in the immediate vicinity of the capital. Around Matamoros they have pushed as far as the banks of the Rio Bravo, where they perpetrated a number of atrocities." Comanche leaders routinely disassociated themselves from the raids in the south to keep their access to the gifts open, but sometimes their stratagems were exposed. In 1834 Berlandier met in San Antonio a Comanche chief who blamed "a few hotheads" for the raids in Chihuahua, but he soon discovered that the chief too had been raiding in Chihuahua, "for every one of his horses had been stolen from the haciendas of the region he just had warned me away from."[30]

By the mid-1830s, it was clear that the Indian policy of Texas was a complete failure. The decision to open the province to American immigrants had backfired. Rather than moving to the interior to shield the province's core areas around San Antonio from Comanche attacks, most Americans stayed east of the Colorado River, beyond the Comanche range and within an easy reach of Louisiana, their main commercial outlet. The result was a splintering of Texas into two distinct and increasingly detached halves. The Anglo-dominated eastern half experienced steady growth, developing a flourishing export-oriented cotton industry and spawning nearly twenty new urban centers by 1835. This half was part of Mexico only in name. Its main economic and political ties extended eastward to the powerful mercantile houses of New Orleans, and its settlers often spoke no Spanish, held slaves in spite of a widespread aversion toward the institution in Mexico, and harbored separatist sentiments.[31]

The Tejano-dominated western half, meanwhile, descended into underdevelopment. As raids and violence engulfed vast portions of western and southern Texas during the early 1830s, basic economic functions began to shut down. Villages and farms were stripped of livestock and the reviving ranching industry faltered once again. Agriculture deteriorated as farmers refused to work on fields where they were exposed to attacks. Laredo on the lower Río Grande lost one-sixth of its population between 1828 and 1831 to Comanche attacks and smallpox, and Goliad, already weakened by Comanche raids, nearly expired during a cholera outbreak in 1834. Settlers lived in perpetual fear and near-starvation even in San Antonio, where, in the words of one observer, "nothing can be planted on account of the Comanches and Tahuacanos [Tawakonis] who frequently harass the city even in time of peace." Villages curled inward and grew isolated, for settlers "seldom venture more than a mile from town on account of the Indians." Major roads leading to San Antonio were frequently cut off, and Berlandier traveled on deserted roads lined with crosses marking places "where the Comanches had massacred travellers or herdsmen." The road from Coahuila to Texas crossed "an uninhabited country" where Indian raiders ruled, and commercial and political links between Texas and New Mexico existed only on paper. When assessing the long-term impact of Comanche raids on western and southern Texas, Berlandier depicted a decaying, psychologically disfigured captive territory: "Their war against the Creoles in Mexico, when they were allied with the Lipans, spread terror among the settlers up and down the border. . . . Their raids then became almost continuous and the garrisons were always besieged. The fields were left to run wild, and often even the solitary farmers were massacred in the midst of their households. The Comanche so thoroughly devastated most of the eastern interior states that many families there are still poverty stricken."[32]

It was this divided Texas that in 1835 rebelled against the central government and in 1836 became an independent republic with close ties to the United States. The Texas Revolution was the product of several long-simmering problems, which came to a head in 1834 and 1835 when the military strongman Antonio López de Santa Anna assumed dictatorial powers in Mexico City and imposed a conservative national charter known as Las Siete Leyes. Las Siete Leyes ended the federalist era in Mexico and ushered in a centralist regime bent on curtailing states' rights and sovereignty. The momentous shift galvanized Texas, turning the smoldering tensions over slavery, tariff exemptions, and immigration (further immigration from the United States had been banned in 1830) acute and then violent. When centralist forces marched into Texas in fall 1835 to rein in the renegade province, they faced unified resistance that included the vast majority of Anglo colonists and many prominent members of the Tejano elite. In November, delegations from twelve Texas communities met at San Felipe de Austin, declared allegiance to the federalist constitution of 1824, and cut off ties to the centralist regime.

Texan independence may have been predetermined by geography—Texas was simply too far from Mexico City and too close to the United States—but the event can be fully understood only in a larger context that takes into account the overwhelming power and presence of the Comanches in the province in the years leading to the revolt. The need to protect northern Mexico against Comanche attacks had been a central factor behind the 1824 and 1825 colonization laws, which opened the floodgates for American immigration into Texas, and the Comanche threat remained a burning concern into the 1830s, when Texas severed its ties to Mexico. In 1832, when delegates from Texas communities met at San Felipe de Austin and petitioned Mexico City for the separation of Texas and Coahuila—a move that bordered on treason—they complained bitterly about the utter inability of the distant state capital in Saltillo to deal with the Comanche question: "These communities [Jáen, San Marcos, Trinidad, and San Sabá Presidio] have disappeared entirely; in some of them the residents dying to the last man. . . . Many early settlers and their descendants have been sacrificed to the barbarians. . . . Every last one of us is probably threatened with total extermination by the new Comanche uprising."[33]

Many Tejano oligarchs shared those concerns, for their economic well-being had become dependent on the Anglo-Texas cotton industry and unrestricted access to U.S. markets. They were deeply incensed with the federal government's failure to provide the funds and soldiers with which Texas could have protected itself against Indian raids. Santa Anna's centralist government not only disregarded these sentiments but moved ahead with its plan to dissolve state militias, the safeguard of state sovereignty. That plan, if successful, would have left much of Texas wide open to Comanche attacks, and the federal government's resolve with the issue alienated many Tejano leaders and pushed them to support the revolt. Separation from Mexico remained an alien, even unpalatable idea to most Tejanos, who had no illusions about their political position in an independent Texas, but the centralist government's policy forced them to revolt to save themselves.[34]

Comanches represented a potentially fatal threat to American colonists, but more abstractly, they also constituted a useful political foil for American newcomers to justify their revolt against Mexican authority and the subsequent takeover of Texas. Like the Anglo-Texan conviction that Tejanos passively submitted to Santa Anna's dictatorial policies, Mexico's failure to fend off the Comanches were for Anglo-Texans signs of degradation of the Mexican character—its supposed stupidity, docility, lethargy, and lack of masculine vitality. Anglo-Texans denounced Mexican men guilty of numerous irredeemable defects: they had failed to protect property against Comanche raiders, they had paid tribute to heathen savages to save themselves, they had lost women and children to Indian captivity, and they had left Texas soil in the hands of primitives and thus in the state of wilderness. These failures, the Anglo-Texans argued, conveyed a moral and manifest path for history: Mexico neither could nor deserved to keep Texas. And predictably, the list of Mexican failures read as an inverse list of Anglo virtues. William H. Wharton, a leading Anglo-Texan politician, wrote in the early days of the revolt a pamphlet subtitled "Exposition of the Causes which have induced the Existing War with Mexico." In it he rationalized the revolt by explaining that Anglo immigrants had not so much received land grants from Mexico as conquered an underused wilderness from the Indians. Where the "lazy" and fearful Mexicans "could not be induced to venture into the wilderness of Texas," the robust Anglo pioneers had pushed ahead. And so, "under the smiles of a benignant heaven," the Anglo colonists "triumphed over all natural obstacles, expelled the savages by whom the country was infested, reduced the forest into cultivation, and made the desert smile. From this it must appear that the lands of Texas, although nominally given, were in fact really and clearly bought."[35]

In the emergent national mythology of the Texas Republic, Anglo immigrants *earned* Texas because they alone possessed the masculine and martial vigor to wrestle the land away from the Comanches and savagery. (This view conveniently neglected the fact that Anglo colonies had by and large steered clear of Comanche range; it also neglected the fact that after the catastrophe at the Alamo, Sam Houston had frantically tried to win over the Comanches and persuade them to block Santa Anna's advance.) When the uprising led to independence, the conviction that Mexicans had lost claim to Texas through their failure to defend it against Indians solidified into a dogma. "Mexico can never conquer Texas!" wrote Mary Austin Holley, cousin of Stephen Austin and the author of the first known English-language history of Texas in 1836. "The wilderness of Texas has been redeemed by American blood and enterprise. . . . I repeat it again and again. Mexico can never conquer Texas."[36]

On the borderlands of New Mexico, meanwhile, the relations between Comanches and colonial powers followed a different trajectory. While violence and exploitation came to define eastern Comanches' policies toward Spanish and Mexican Texas, western Comanches kept an unbroken peace with New Mexico from 1786 until the end of the Spanish colonial era. But this does not mean that the relations between Spanish New Mexico and western Comanches had become cleansed of contention, for beneath a thin veneer of tranquility the Comanches and colonists were engaged in an intense rivalry. That rivalry was only incidentally a typical Indian-white struggle for subjugation, survival, and territorial control; it was instead a multilayered, essentially imperial rivalry over political sway, the control of labor and resources, and spheres of cultural influence. The result was widespread economic, political, and cultural amalgamation across ethnic lines, amalgamation that was actively embraced by the Comanches and the great New Mexican masses but abhorred by the Spanish and, later, Mexican elites.

After the landmark treaty of 1786 between Chief Ecueracapa and Governor Juan Bautista de Anza, Spanish officials believed that the complete subjugation of the western Comanches was but a matter time. The architects of New

Mexico's Indian policy had a specific plan for the western Comanches who were to be made dependent on Spanish gifts and goods, isolated from the United States, and, eventually, Hispanized. Once this was achieved, even grander imperial schemes would become attainable. Bourbon officials meant to use the Comanche alliance to extend Spain's reach deep into the North American interior to prevent the United States from expanding its realm westward. They envisioned North America's heartland as the setting for a human web that was firmly anchored in New Mexico through the powerful yet obedient Comanches.[37]

In the course of the early nineteenth century, however, an almost diametric dynamic would emerge: it was New Mexico that would became dependent, isolated, and culturally transformed under rising Comanche power. Rather than becoming an instrument for Spain's imperial extension, the western Comanches became a hindrance to it. They detached themselves from Spain's restrictive embrace, refused to accept the role of a subordinate ally, and continued to maneuver independently and on their own terms. They forged ties with American merchants and built an imposing trade and alliance system that gradually mantled the midcontinent. By 1810, the real nerve center of the Southwest was not Santa Fe but the western Comanche rancherías along the upper Arkansas, Red, and Brazos valleys, where peoples from numerous nations congregated to exchange goods, forge and maintain political alliances, and organize large-scale multiethnic military campaigns. New Mexico's economic and political ties to Comanchería endured, but they had come to reflect its dependence on, not control over, the Comanche nation.

Comanches' ascendancy over New Mexico was in many ways a straightforward matter of economic size and reach. Comanchería dwarfed the densely populated but spatially unimposing colony, and Comanches' thick and far-reaching exchange network isolated New Mexico almost completely from North America's interior. Standing next to Comanchería, New Mexico appeared diminished and detached. Its political and economic reach extended no farther to the continental plains than Comanchería's edge, and it was shallow even there. Spain's weak control over the North American interior was betrayed by its officials' hazy geographic knowledge of the Great Plains. In 1804, when the Louisiana Purchase and the Lewis and Clark expedition fomented fears of Anglo expansion, Spanish officials anguished that U.S. agents prepared to invade northern New Spain through the Missouri River, which they believed provided an easy access to New Mexico. As the American threat forced Spanish geopolitical imaginings into a sharper focus, the notion of a Spanish-controlled interior suddenly appeared a mere fallacy, as Charles Dehault Delassus reported from St. Louis, now a U.S.

city: "perhaps it will result that those Indians who are the friends of the Spaniards [now], will become enemies, incited by the Americans."[38]

Moreover, in a reversal of Spanish designs, New Mexico grew increasingly dependent on Comanchería for basic resources. A vigorous border trade bound the New Mexican and Comanche economies together: both relied on each other's products and both experienced steady growth. Comanche exports—horses, mules, meat, hides, slaves, and salt—revived New Mexico's subsistence economy, and the many improvements that the Bourbon Reforms spawned in New Mexico opened new commercial prospects for Comanches. A booming trade with Chihuahua brought unforeseen quantities of Spanish products to New Mexico, allowing its inhabitants to supply Comanches with high-quality manufactured goods. New Mexicans also built a dynamic craft industry that produced woolen stockings, blankets, and textiles for both Chihuahua and Comanche markets. Perhaps most important, Comanche peace allowed New Mexicans to reclaim and rebuild villages, farms, and pasturelands that had been destroyed or abandoned during the prolonged raiding onslaught in the 1760s and 1770s. Pecos experienced a phoenix-like revival, and other vibrant population centers emerged in the Mora valley and around Taos, Abiquiu, and Albuquerque. Genuine borderland creations, these communities produced large quantities of maize, beans, and horses for domestic use as well as for Comanche trade.[39]

But the mutualism of the Comanche–New Mexican relations faltered after 1800. Western Comanches' commercial expansion on the plains simultaneously lessened their reliance on New Mexican markets and isolated the colony from the grasslands and its resources. The carefully laid out Spanish plans to induce dependence among the Comanches through the sale of inferior technology crumbled when Comanches extended their trade networks across the plains and gained access to high-quality British guns. And the trade links that attached Comanchería to distant markets in the east and north also worked to isolate New Mexico from the interior. In the early nineteenth century, Comanches had a virtual monopoly over New Mexico's eastbound trade, for the only Plains Indian groups trading in New Mexico were the Kiowas and Naishans, and even they did so only sporadically and likely under Comanche control. This put New Mexico's Spaniards in a bind: they needed Comanches' trade more than Comanches needed theirs. Spanish New Mexico, like the Pueblo communities that it subsumed, had always relied heavily on the products of the plains, but now the colony depended almost entirely on the Comanches for its access to those exports. Across the eastern frontier, from Taos to Albuquerque, the border towns looked to Comanchería for the necessities that kept them alive.

Perhaps the most tangible sign of Comanches' growing economic sway was the changing commercial geography on the Comanche–New Mexico border. At first Comanche trade convoys frequented New Mexico's border towns, but in time the trade began to shift from Taos, Pecos, and Picurís toward Comanchería. The declining commercial pull of the Río Grande valley became apparent during the first decade of the nineteenth century when the number of Comanche visits to Pecos and Santa Fe dropped sharply. Comanches shifted their commercial activities farther east and closer to their own rancherías, dividing their trade among new border villages that rose on the eastern side of the Sangre de Cristo Mountains. In 1803 Governor Fernando Chacón described these border villages as sites of bustling exchange: "The products traded by the Spaniards to said nomad Indians are horses, saddlebags, *anqueras* (leather skirt covering the horse's rump), bits, hatchets, war axes, lances, knives, scissors, scarlet cloth, serapes, cloaks, woolens, indigo, vermilion, mirrors . . . loaf sugar, native tobacco, corn in flour and on the ear, bread, and green or dried fruit. In exchange, the nomads give captives of both sexes, mules, moccasins, colts, mustangs, all kinds of hides and buffalo meat."[40]

By 1810, San Miguel del Vado and San José del Vado along the Pecos and Mora valleys had replaced Taos and Pecos as New Mexico's main gateways to Comanchería. Besides their easy accessibility, Comanches were drawn to these eastern villages by their distinctive ethnic makeup. Many of their inhabitants were *genízaros,* who had lived in captivity among the Comanches before being ransomed by New Mexicans. Although nominally Spanish subjects, *genízaros* often maintained attachments to their former masters. Seized as children and raised in captivity by Comanches, they saw Comanches as lost relatives, and that sentiment led many to form new kinship ties: marriages between *genízaras* and Comanche men were common and several Comanches moved to live in San Miguel del Vado in the early nineteenth century. Wedded to Comanchería by deep historical, familial, and economic ties, San Miguel del Vado, San José del Vado, La Cuesta, and other eastern settlements were only superficially part of colonial New Mexico. When authorizing their grants, Spanish officials had envisioned them as vanguards that would shield the province against the Comanches and project Spanish power to the interior, but such designs soon dissipated. The rise of *genízaro* settlements did not signify New Mexico's expansion into the Comanche realm but rather the colony's persisting gravitation toward the economic and cultural power of Comanchería.[41]

Indeed, as the relations between the new villages and Comanches solidified, the trails that carried Comanches westward to New Mexico transformed into avenues for eastbound trading expeditions from New Mexico to Comanchería. In 1789 Governor Fernando de la Concha had authorized New Mexicans to visit

Comanches for trade, hoping that such interactions would allow Spanish officials to better monitor developments inside Comanchería, but it was not until the early nineteenth century that the comanchero commerce emerged as a distinct economic enterprise. The early comanchero trade was a fluid, often improvised affair that saw small New Mexican parties roaming the trackless Llano Estacado with their *carretas*, hoping to find some of the migratory Comanche bands, but the exchange could be brisk nevertheless. In 1814, for example, two comancheros traveled two months around the Llano Estacado, bartering forty-six serapes, five hundred pounds of provisions, and large quantities of tobacco for twenty horses and mules and six to eight hundred pounds of meat and lard. Most comancheros headed to the Canadian and Red rivers, which were easily accessible from San Miguel del Vado and other eastern villages, but they also frequented the western Comanche trade center in the upper Arkansas. In 1810, for example, more than two hundred New Mexicans traveled to the Arkansas, and ten years later the Stephen H. Long expedition found a well-marked trail leading from the upper Arkansas toward Taos along the Purgatoire valley.[42]

The comanchero trade was a borderland institution that rose to meet the needs of two societies across a narrowing cultural gulf. For Comanches, the trade offered several advantages. It shortened the distance they had to travel for trade and allowed them to avoid the microbe pools that prospered in New Mexico's urban centers. By concentrating trade in their own rancherías, Comanches could also exert greater control over the terms, mechanics, and forms of exchange. As for New Mexicans, trading in Comanchería opened a more direct access to the enormous wealth that circulated within the Comanches' commercial network. By taking their trade to the plains, New Mexicans could also shun government control, avoid taxes, and engage in illicit forms of exchange, such as smuggling branded livestock Comanches had stolen from Texas and Nueva Vizcaya. This kind of underground trade rarely shows up in the New Mexican records, but one American observer noted in the late 1810s that Comanches "carry on a small traffic with the Spaniards of Santa Fe, from whom they receive blankets, knives, and tobacco, in exchange for mules and horses which they capture from the Spaniards of the adjacent Provinces" of Texas and Nueva Vizcaya.[43]

The deepening linkages between eastern New Mexico and western Comanchería evoked panic among Spanish administrators, who feared that the border trade to Comanchería had the potential of disfiguring the entire economic structure of the colony. When Governor Chacón conducted an inspection of New Mexico's economic conditions in 1803, he was appalled to learn that the strongest economic ties of many local settlements extended eastward to Comanchería. This was a disturbing development to the Spanish elites who hoped to build an ordered surplus-producing economy in New Mexico and then plug that economy to the market centers in Chihuahua and Mexico City. But as Chacón found out, much of New Mexico's wealth did not flow southward along the Chihuahua Trail but leaked eastward into Comanchería. Disgusted, he contrasted the chaos of the official provincial commerce with the orderliness of the Comanche trade: "The internal commerce [of New Mexico] is in the hands of twelve to fourteen [local] merchants who are neither properly licensed nor well versed in business matters. . . . The rest of the citizenry are so many petty merchants who are continuously dealing and bartering with whatever products they have at hand. Territorial magistrates are forced to mediate these exchanges [which are attended by] malicious and deceitful behavior and bad faith. Only does formality prevail in the trading carried on with the nomad Indians (*Naciones gentiles*), that being a give-and-take business conducted in sign language."[44]

Spanish officials, however, fretted more over the Comanches' social and cultural influence over New Mexico than their economic sway. At the same time that some administrators still entertained plans for the Hispanization of the Comanches, eastern New Mexico was rapidly blending into Comanchería. By the early nineteenth century, Comanche was widely spoken in New Mexico's eastern frontier, and in such border towns as Taos and San Miguel del Vado one often heard Comanche phrases mixed with Spanish. Also, the subsistence patterns in eastern New Mexico bore a strong Comanche imprint. When Spanish administrators bestowed land grants to new settlements in eastern New Mexico in the early and mid-eighteenth century, they conceived them as nuclei for what would become urban, Spanish-style agricultural centers with straight streets and central plazas. But the 1803 survey of the province's economy startled the officials; except for the Pueblo Indians, New Mexicans were "little dedicated to farming." In eastern New Mexico, bison hunting was taking over. By the early 1810s, the eastern villagers were harvesting between ten and twelve thousand bison a year from the Llano Estacado—enough to meet the subsistence needs of several thousand people—and the bison hunter, cibolero, was emerging as the cultural embodiment of frontier New Mexico. Mostly commoners with no access to raised meats, ciboleros made two annual hunting excursions to the plains. The first one in June was a relatively quick effort, but the fall hunt after the corn harvest was a large-scale operation that often included entire families and could take several months.[45]

The long trading and hunting trips into Comanchería inevitably promoted intimate ties with the Comanches, leading to extensive cultural borrowing. The ciboleros lived essentially like nomadic Indians, following the bison in massive caravans. The American trader Josiah Gregg described how they hunted, "like wild Indians, chiefly on horseback, and with bow and arrow, or lance, with which they soon load their carts and mules. They find no difficulty in curing their meat even in mid-summer, by slicing it thin and spreading or suspending it in the sun; or, if in haste, it is slightly barbequed. During the curing operation they often follow the Indian practice of beating or kneading the slices with their feet, which they contend contributes to its preservation." Comancheros, too, fell under Comanche influence. When visiting the western Comanches trade fair on the upper Arkansas in 1821, Jacob Fowler encountered a "Spanish" comanchero party whose members "were painted like the Indians the day they traded." Many nineteenth-century observers found it impossible to differentiate ciboleros, comancheros, and Comanches from one another.[46]

In the minds of the Spanish officials, the extensive material and cultural borrowing was but the first step in a deeper corruption of New Mexico. Governor Concha had little but scorn for the colony's eastern villagers whom he saw as unreliable aliens impregnated by Comanche culture. "Under a simulated appearance of ignorance or rusticity they conceal the most refined malice. He is a rare one in whom the vices of robbing and lying do not occur together." As the governor saw it, this character degeneration was caused by "the dispersion of their settlements, the bad upbringing resulting from this, [and] the proximity and trade of the barbarous tribes in which they are involved."[47]

Most disturbingly, Concha believed that the villagers harbored separatist sentiments. When authorizing new villages in Comanchería's proximity, Spanish officials had expected the settlers to organize militias to defend the frontier against possible Comanche raids. Concha's investigation revealed a different reality. He noted that as many as two thousand eastern villagers defied royal authority and attributed this to their "desire to live without subjection and in a complete liberty, *in imitation of the wild tribes which they see nearby.*" "They love distance which makes them independent," he continued, "and if they recognize the advantages of union [with Spanish New Mexico], they pretend not to understand them, in order to adapt the liberty and slovenliness which they see and note in their neighbors the wild Indians." Looking east from Santa Fe, Concha found it difficult to say where New Mexico ended and Comanchería began. Betraying his anxiety, he recommended an extreme remedy: "the removal of more than two thousand laborers to another area would be very useful to society and the state." In early nineteenth-century New Mexico, the fundamental Spanish fear of being culturally consumed by the *bárbaros* seemed on the verge of becoming reality.[48]

Just how tight the economic and cultural bonds between eastern New Mexico and the Comanches were—and, conversely, how thin the links between the frontier settlements and Santa Fe had become—dawned on Spanish administrators in 1805, when the newly appointed governor Joachín del Real Alencaster tried to both control and tap into the Comanche–New Mexican commerce by implementing a new license and taxation system. Furious over this meddling with their livelihood, the settlers of San Miguel del Vado and San José del Vado contrived to challenge the governor, mount a trading expedition into Comanchería as an act of defiance, and, if necessary, unite with other border villages against Santa Fe. Some reportedly even traveled to Comanchería to incite Comanches to rise up against Spanish authorities. The conspirators were captured before they could take further action, but their arrest only aroused more uproar. A mob of angry settlers from several villages moved to Santa Fe and threatened to start a rebellion, forcing the humiliated Alencaster to cancel his policy. Alencaster's successor, Alberto Maynez, further loosened the regulations and issued a slack passport system that allowed New Mexican traders to venture into Comanchería virtually unhindered.[49]

New Mexico's final decade as a Spanish colony was marked by mounting Comanche influence within its borders. As revolutionary spasms gripped the empire's core areas after 1810, compromising Mexico City's ability to support the frontier provinces, New Mexico grew increasingly dependent on the Comanches for resources and protection. Its settlers traded in Comanchería with such fervor that their long absences from home exposed the border to Ute and Apache attacks, and its officials gratified Comanche delegations with lavish gifts the colony really could not afford, fearing that a cessation of payments would prompt the Comanches to resume raiding and perhaps join the Americans for a feared invasion into Mexico.[50]

This unflinching pro-Comanche stance set New Mexico apart from the other Spanish colonies. While New Mexican communities clung to Comanchería, replicating its culture and economy like a double helix, Comanche raiders exploited and devastated large tracts of Texas, northern Coahuila, and northern Nuevo Santander. Gradually, Comanches divided the vast span of northern New Spain from the Nueces River to the upper Río Grande into distinct zones: they raided in one region, drew tribute in another, traded in the third, and peddled stolen Spanish goods in the fourth. Spanish administrators never managed to develop a uniform response to this onslaught, a failure that both denoted New Spain's helplessness in the face of Comanche power and exposed it to further exploitation. By the late 1810s, one observer noted, Comanche politics had fragmented New Spain's northern frontier almost to the point of nonexistence: "The Comanches have made themselves so redoubtable to the Spaniards that the governors of the different provinces of the frontiers have found it necessary to treat separately with them. Often they are at war with one province and at peace with another; and returning, loaded with spoil, from massacring and pillaging the frontiers of one province, driving before them the horses and frequently even prisoners whom they have made, they come into another to receive presents, taking only the precaution of leaving a part of the spoil, above all the prisoners, at some distance from the establishments."[51]

Liberal gifts and a clandestine trade that did not exclude stolen Spanish property allowed New Mexicans to maintain stable relations with the Comanches until the end of the Spanish period, but the transfer to Mexican rule brought about a dramatic change. After having maintained an uninterrupted peace with New Mexico for thirty-five years, Comanches began raiding in the province again. The first flash of violence occurred in August 1821, only months after Mexico's independence, and its causes are revealing. Mexican authorities in Santa Fe denied a visiting Comanche delegation the customary annual gifts—which Comanches apparently had become to view as a perpetual privilege—and the disgruntled Comanche party took revenge on nearby settlements, pillaging several houses, killing sheep and cows, and raping two women. Governor Facundo Melgares pressed other districts to make donations for Indian gifting lest "desolation and death" follow, but such emergency measures did little to remove the larger structural problem. Lacking movable funds, the new Mexican nation failed to keep up the gift distributions that had helped maintain the peace during the Spanish era. Acutely aware of the connection between presents and peace, Mexican officials struggled to scrape together enough money for gifting, but their efforts were undermined by the meager support they received from the central government, which was preoccupied with the internal power struggles among the self-designated Emperor Iturbide, the congress, and the insurrectionists led by Generals Santa Anna and Guadalupe Victoria. By 1822, officials in Santa Fe had been forced to borrow more than six thousand pesos from the private sector for Indian gifts but received no compensatory funds from Mexico City.[52]

As gift flow from New Mexico to Comanchería ebbed and flowed in the following years, so too did the tempo and intensity of Comanche attacks in the province. The relations continued to deteriorate through the early 1820s, and by mid-decade the situation became so bad that the federal government had a reason to fear that New Mexicans might revolt if they did not receive better protection against the Indians. Santa Fe received in 1826 less than seven hundred pesos for gifts—not nearly enough to gratify New Mexico's many Indian neighbors—and the next year Comanches raided the border from Taos to Abiquiu.

But in 1827, in the aftermath of the failed Fredonian Rebellion in Texas, General Anastasio Bustamante extended a proclamation of truce to the Comanches. In August 1828 New Mexican ambassadors met with some six hundred western Comanches on the Gallians River and witnessed how they elected Toro Echicero (Sorcerer Bull) as head chief and ratified a formal treaty. Comanches promised to refrain from raiding on the condition that gifts would be made available in New Mexico, and in 1829 Paruakevitsi, the prominent Tenewa chief, met with Mexican officials near Bosque Redondo, endorsed Bustamante's peace declaration, and received generous gifts. But in 1830 funds were once again scarce, forcing Governor José Antonio Cháves to plead with Comanche chiefs to accept inferior gifts and honor the peace, but to no avail. A wave of violence of such force swept over New Mexico and the neighboring Chihuahua that the Mexican authorities cut all commercial ties to Comanchería and declared a general war on the Comanches.[53]

It was at this juncture of escalating Comanche violence that New Mexico began to cut loose from Mexico City. The colony had began to turn from central Mexico toward the power and wealth of Comanchería during the late Spanish era, and the rise of the American-dominated Santa Fe trade after 1822 had accelerated that eastern reorientation. But it was not until after 1830 that New Mexico began to disentangle itself politically from the rest of Mexico. Terrified by the prospect of a full-scale raiding war, New Mexicans put self-interest first and continued to bestow gifts on and trade with Comanches, ignoring the fact that their actions fueled violence elsewhere in Mexico. Comanches took this as a license to raid Chihuahua and Coahuila for horses and mules and then trade the animals to New Mexicans, who seemed determined to keep their commercial lines to Comanchería open. In 1831, after a violent episode at a trade rendezvous on the Comanche border, Mexican officials in Santa Fe banned the comanchero trade as "detrimental to order," but the embargo did little to suppress the institution that had become an integral part of New Mexico's economic and social world. Indeed, only a year later Captain José María Ronquillo insisted that the purchase of horses from Comanchería should be made an official policy on the grounds that New Mexico needed more horses to defend itself against Navajo raiders on the province's northwestern frontier. Ronquillo was fully aware that Comanches were engaged in livestock raiding in Chihuahua and that buying horses from them might further encourage those raids, but he promoted the commerce regardless. New Mexicans had resigned themselves to purchasing peace from the Comanches, even if it meant inflicting death and suffering for the rest of northern Mexico.[54]

This independent maneuvering ran up against Mexico City's ambitious nation-building project, which gathered momentum after 1830. In 1835 political power in Mexico City moved from liberal federalists to conservative centralists, a momentous shift that immediately sparked a secessionist revolt in Texas and a federalist revolt in California. New Mexico followed suit in August 1837 when an armed rebellion erupted in Río Arriba. Sparked in part by class inequalities, the Chimayó Rebellion was a full-fledged popular revolt against the centralists' plans to impose direct national taxation and introduce nationwide religious reforms. There was also a borderlands element to the revolt, for direct taxation would have interfered with the eastern villagers' lifeblood, the Comanche trade. The rebels, mostly poor *vecinos*, *mestizos*, Creoles, and Pueblo Indians, captured and beheaded Governor Albino Pérez and named José Gonzalez, a cibolero hunter from Taos, as governor. They managed to take over most of northern New Mexico before being crushed by a "Liberating Army" led by Manuel Armijo. The repression of the Chimayó movement, together with Mexico's loss of Texas a year before, resulted in an outpouring of patriotic rhetoric in New Mexico and launched a nationalist campaign to preserve Catholicism and the Mexican culture.[55] But that campaign did not draw the province any closer to the rest of Mexico politically or economically.

If anything, in fact, the chasm only widened, for the 1830s also saw the escalation of the comanchero trade into a major economic institution that wedded New Mexico's economy firmly to that of Comanchería and inexorably pulled the province further apart from the rest of Mexico. This expansion of the comanchero trade stemmed from changing geopolitics in Comanchería: western Comanches had temporarily lost their control of the lucrative upper Arkansas trade center to the invading Cheyenne-Arapaho-American bloc and turned to New Mexico as an alternative source of crucial imports. New Mexicans seized the opportunity, and the 1830s and early 1840s saw comancheros making regular annual trips into Comanchería, traveling along well-marked trails, and bringing in guns, powder, serapes, brown sugar, corn, wheat tortillas, and specially baked hard bread. In return for the all-important weapons and foodstuffs, Comanches offered bison robes, bear skins, and, above all, horses and mules, which were in high demand among the New Mexicans who had embarked on a large-scale overland trade with the United States. Comancheros, many of them *genízaros* with strong cultural ties to Comanchería, had few qualms with doing business in stolen animals with Mexican brands. By decade's end, Comanches routinely used New Mexico as an outlet for war spoils taken elsewhere in northern Mexico. "Though at continual war with the south of the republic," Josiah Gregg wrote, "for many years the Comanches have cultivated peace with the New Mexicans . . . because it is desirable . . . to retain some friendly point with which to keep amicable intercourse and traffic. Parties of them have therefore sometimes entered the settlements of New Mexico for trading purposes; while every season numerous bands of New Mexicans, known as *Comancheros,* supplied with arms, ammunitions, trinkets, provisions and other necessities, launch upon the Prairies to barter for mules, and the different fruits of their ravages upon the South."[56]

It was as if New Mexico had developed a certain immunity to Mexico City's designs and decrees, a condition that in 1840 took on concrete political shape at the highest level. In that year federal officials ordered New Mexico Governor Manuel Armijo to cancel the livestock trade with the province's bordering Indians, including the Comanches. Armijo summarily refused the order, condemning it as unreasonable. If trade was banned, he argued, Comanches would lose their interest in maintaining peace with New Mexico and launch open war, something the province could not endure. Moreover, he warned, the livestock trade was New Mexico's prime outlet for cash crops and so crucial for the Pueblo Indians that canceling it would risk igniting a general revolt. The ban was quietly forgotten, but a year later General Mariano Arista ordered Armijo to join Tamaulipas, Nuevo León, and Coahuila in a united—and unprecedented—campaign against the Comanches. The ambitious plan involved taking the war into Comanchería with two thousand troops while concurrently soliciting an armistice with Texas rebels. Again Armijo refused, insisting that New Mexico would not survive an all-out war against the Comanches, and once more the federal authorities capitulated.[57]

By now New Mexico had distanced itself from Mexico City to a point where its political ties to Comanchería began to seem tighter. In 1844 a Comanche delegation visited Santa Fe and told Mariano Martínez, now governor of New Mexico, that three hundred Comanche warriors were about to invade Chihuahua. Instead of trying to pressure the chiefs to call off the raid, Martínez sent them away with presents and dispatched a letter warning his counterpart in Chihuahua of the imminent assault. A year later New Mexico's administrators refused yet another call for a general campaign against the Comanches, making their disassociation from Mexico City and its Indian policy complete. In their efforts to protect the vulnerable province—and their own positions within it—New Mexican elites had been forced to choose between appeasing one of two imperial cores and, in more cases than not, they chose Comanchería.[58]

Viewed in context, the story of Mexican New Mexico becomes a dramatic counterpoint to that of Mexican Texas. Whereas Texas violently dismembered itself from Mexico starting in 1835, New Mexico remained within the Mexican fold until the end of the Mexican-American War in 1848. The Chimayó Rebellion tested the federal government's mettle in New Mexico, and the Anglo-dominated Santa Fe trade served as a vanguard for "the unconscious process of economic conquest," yet neither development spawned a strong secessionist movement. The divergent trajectories of Texas and New Mexico as Mexican provinces owed much to geography and demographics: New Mexico was shielded from the expansionist embrace of the United States by its relative isolation, which made it less attractive a destination for American immigrants, and by its larger Hispanic population, which ensured that the Americans who did immigrate remained a minority. Indeed, even if American entrepreneurs did serve as agents of capitalist expansion, anticipating the U.S. absorption of New Mexico, many of them married into the local gentry, integrating themselves into Mexican kinship networks and becoming something quite different from the color-conscious and isolationist "Texians," who casually labeled Mexicans "a mongrel race, inferior even to negroes." More broadly, New Mexico's relative immunity against American influence reflected the enduring power of the Catholic Church, which maintained a strong position in the territory and emerged as a potent national agent that regulated foreign-born residents' access to marriage, citizenship, and land.[59]

But while compelling, the dichotomy of wavering Texas and steadfast New Mexico is a simplification, for it neglects the penetrating, if often unspoken, influence of Comanches over New Mexicans. Intimate, violent, exploitative, and mutualistic all at once, New Mexicans' ties with Comanches both forced and seduced them to act and organize themselves in ways that were often deplorable and at times disastrous to the rest of Mexico. Indeed, it seems justifiable to ask to what extent the New Mexicans who paid tribute to a Comanche nation at war with the rest of northern Mexico, who made profit by trafficking in goods Comanches had stolen from other Mexican departments, who openly defied federal orders to sever unsanctioned ties to Comanchería, and whose way of life was permeated by Comanche influences were still Mexican subjects?

On March 2, 1836, at Washington-on-the-Brazos, delegates from more than forty Texas communities voted to separate from Mexico. Mexican officials had anticipated the rebellion, as official forces and Texas revolutionaries had clashed violently several times during the previous nine months, and at the time the declaration of independence occurred, General Antonio López de Santa Anna was besieging the San Antonio garrison with more than two thousand troops. A series of battles ensued—at the Alamo, Goliad, and San Jacinto—but the Texan forces prevailed, and on May 14, Santa Anna signed the Treaty of Velasco, in which he recognized the independence of Texas and promised to withdraw Mexican troops below the Río Grande. The government of Mexico refused to ratify the treaty and continued the war for nine more years, but Texas considered itself an independent republic. The future of the Southwest suddenly lay wide open. Could Mexico recapture Texas and restore its national unity? Could it hold on to New Mexico and fend off the Texans who claimed that their republic's western border extended to the Río Grande? Would Texas be annexed by the United States or would there be two Anglo nations west of the Mississippi? And how would the new republic solve what was perhaps its most pressing problem—the war against the Comanches that it had inherited from Mexico?

The Republic of Texas was a political anomaly, an independent nation that did not expect—or much want—to remain as such. Anticipating fast annexation by the United States, it kept its eastern border open and took in thousands of American immigrants each year. Its government, modeled after that of the United States, was strong only on paper and soon proved incapable of accommodating the prodigious demographic and material growth. There was no treasury to speak of, no functioning taxation system, and no money economy. Geographically, the republic was a patchwork of disparate and in many ways incompatible parts. Its division into a flourishing Anglo cotton kingdom and a poor Tejano Texas clustered around San Antonio and Goliad prevailed, but in the late 1830s, as the immigrant flow from the United States swelled, yet another distinctive subsection emerged: a restless northern frontier of poor, land-hungry subsistence farmers. Texas, in short, was disjointed, expansionist, volatile, and potentially self-destructive. Those were also the attributes of its Indian policy.[60]

The relations between the Lone Star Republic and Comanches were erratic from the outset. Sam Houston, the first regularly elected president, believed that the republic's fate hinged on the Indian question. He first tried to foment a general Indian war to bring the U.S. Army into Texas and to expedite annexation, but when that scheme fell through, he worked passionately to formalize the relations with Indians. Unlike most prominent Texan officials, Houston, who had married a mixed-blood Cherokee woman and lived for years in Indian Territory, believed that Texas could have peace only if the republic made concessions to Indian nations. He signed treaties with the Cherokees and Shawnees in fall 1836 and in December of that year sent messengers into Comanchería. Well versed in Indian diplomacy, he promised Comanches the three perquisites of peaceful relations: gifts, trade, and face-to-face diplomacy. "You can let us have horses, mules and buffalo robes in change for our paints, tobacco, blankets and other things which will make you happy" his message promised. "When the grass rises in the Spring, you must come with your Chiefs to see me and I will make you and them presents."[61]

But as Houston was trying to win over the Comanches through diplomacy, the Texas Congress opened all Indian lands to white settlement, overriding the president's veto. The settler frontier leaped up the Brazos, Colorado, and Guadalupe rivers toward Comanche hunting ranges, and the relations between Texas and Comanches degenerated into violence. Comanches raided the new farms, killing settlers and taking horses, mules, and captives, and Texas militia units patrolled the frontier, killing Comanches. Attempting to restore peace, Houston dispatched commissioners into Comanchería in March 1838. Alarmed by the republic's palpable zeal and capacity for expansion, Comanches now deviated from their traditional notion of fluid borders and demanded that the territories of the two nations should be separated by a fixed boundary line guaranteed by a treaty. "They claim," the commissioners reported, "all the territory North and West of the Guadalupe mountains, extending from Red river to the Rio Grande, the area of which is nearly equal to one fourth of the domain of Texas." Forbidden by Texas law to yield any lands claimed by the republic, the commissioners evaded the issue and the talks remained inconclusive. Yet trading parties from Texas visited Comanchería during the spring, and in May Comanches signed a "Treaty of Peace and Amity" in the newly established town of Houston.[62]

In late 1838, however, Houston lost the election for president to Mirabeau B. Lamar who summarily renounced his predecessor's conciliatory Indian policy. Envisioning an independent empire that would eventually expand to the Pacific Ocean, he authorized the Texan Santa Fe Expedition to divert a portion of the U.S. overland trade from Santa Fe to Texas and, if possible, to occupy the eastern half of New Mexico. To solve the Indian problem, Lamar recruited nine companies of mounted volunteers and rangers, which routed the Cherokees, Shawnees, Delawares, and Kickapoos north of the Red River. On the northwestern front, Lamar sent surveyors into Indian lands and moved the capital to Waterloo (soon to be renamed Austin) at the fringes of Comanche territory. Driven in part by land-hunger and in part by virulent fears and hatred of all things Mexican and Indian, Texas launched a genocidal war against the Comanches. The first non-Indians to bring the war to Comanchería since Juan Bautista de Anza's invasion in 1779, Lamar's soldiers hunted down Comanche bands, often indiscriminately killing men, women, and children. Comanches retaliated by razing farms, slaughtering cattle, seizing captives, and killing settlers and mutilating their bodies. They raided deep into Texas and put San Antonio under siege. A wave of toxic racism washed over the Texas frontier, where Indians became branded as "red niggers" or "wild cannibals of the woods."[63]

In January 1840, after a destructive smallpox epidemic swept Comanchería, Comanches sued for peace and sent representatives to San Antonio. To evoke sympathy, they returned a white boy and explained that their nation had "rejected the offers of the [Mexican] Centralists, who have emissaries among them, striving to stir up a general revolt." Texas officials pressured Comanches to return all white captives and invited their principal chiefs to visit. Meanwhile, Texas Secretary of War Albert Sidney Johnston instructed the officials in San Antonio to impress on Comanches that they were to avoid all Texas settlements and allow Texas officials to "dictate the conditions" of their residence. He ordered the officials to take the Comanche delegates as hostages if they failed to deliver captives. In March, Muguara, a powerful eastern Comanche chief, led sixty-five men, women, and children to San Antonio, but they brought only one captive, a sixteen-year-old white girl. The chiefs and captains were taken to the local jail that had a council room. When Chief Muguara refused to deliver more captives on the grounds that they were held in the rancherías of other chiefs, soldiers opened fire at point-blank range and killed twelve. Twenty-three more Comanches were shot on the streets of San Antonio and thirty were taken captive.[64]

In the following weeks Comanches exchanged Anglo and Mexican captives for their own in San Antonio, but the massacre had left them distraught and enraged. Midsummer brought retaliation. Some five to seven hundred warriors, led by Potsanaquahip (Buffalo Hump) and possibly armed with guns obtained from Bent's Fort, swept down the Guadalupe River, killing, plundering, and burning their way down to the shores of the Gulf of Mexico, where they sacked and looted the towns of Victoria and Linnville. On their way back, the party was intercepted at Plum Creek by Texas Rangers and their Indian auxiliaries. Armed with Colt revolvers, the rangers gunned down several warriors. In October, Texas volunteers ambushed a Comanche ranchería north of the Colorado River, killed 140 men, women, and children, and seized 500 horses. By the winter, most Comanches had retreated north, leaving thousands of square miles open for settlers from Texas.[65]

But then the pendulum of Texas Indian policy swung again. The war had exhausted Texans as much as it had Comanches. Lamar's three-year campaign had taken countless lives, drained the republic's treasury, and ruined its credit. There were rumors that Mexican agents had instigated the Comanche march to the Gulf Coast and were trying to join forces with the Plains Indians to invade Texas. And although the Texas frontier had penetrated Comanchería, it was clear that the frontier would not be safe without a solid peace with the Comanches, who could tear through Texas and siege and sack its largest cities. Lamar, whose popularity had plummeted among the proannexation section as well as the planter-merchant elite who carried the financial burden of Indian wars, lost the 1841 election to Houston. Houston embarked on restoring diplomatic ties with Comanches. He sent peace feelers into Comanchería and established several government-sponsored trading houses in Austin, San Antonio, and New Braunfels, and near present-day Waco, where Comanches could obtain manufactured goods, ransom Anglo captives for handsome profits, and collect gifts that helped cover the dead and maintain peace. He moved the capital from Austin to Houston, farther away from Comanchería, and dismantled most ranger companies, which put the plans for frontier expansion on hold, allowing Comanches to reclaim lost territories. Out of the bloodshed, horror, and hate of the Lamar years a fragile compromise emerged, which saw both sides, for their particular strategic purposes, reaching toward accommodation.[66]

Forging a formal treaty proved more difficult, however, because the Council House massacre had left the Comanches guarded and cynical. They declined in early 1843 an invitation to talks by declaring that "the bones of their brothers that had been massacred at San Antonio had appeared on the Road and obstructed their passage," and they were now adamant that a defined boundary line should separate Texas from Comanchería. But in the late fall Chief Mopechucope (Old Owl) dispatched a message detailing that any treaty would have to include a boundary line running from the Cross Timbers to the confluence of the Colorado and the San Sabá rivers and "from thence in a direct line to the Río Grande." It was a demand that no Texas official could concede, for Texas law did not recognize land titles to Indians, but Houston, skirting the law, responded that he was willing to discuss the proposed line. In fall 1844 Comanches finally met Houston and his representatives at Tehuacana Creek near the Torreys' trading post. In attendance were also representatives from the Cherokees, Delawares, Shawnees, Caddos, Wacos, and Lipans, whom Houston wanted to include in treaty relations.[67]

When the talks began, Comanches set the course and tone. Potsanaquahip, the principal Comanche delegate, proclaimed his desire for peace, but, to Houston's shock, he also wanted a new border line: the boundary Mopechucope had proposed earlier was "too far up the country." Potsanaquahip demanded a new line that started at the southern tip of the Cross Timbers, a "good days ride" above Austin, then ran southwestward skirting San Antonio, and finally followed the San Antonio Road to the Río Grande. The chief, in other words, claimed all of Texas except for a 125-mile belt along the Gulf Coast, insisting that his people needed the land for their bison and wild horses. But Potsanaquahip also had a more imperial agenda. "I want my friends," he stated, "these other Indians, to settle on the line and raise corn and I can often come down among them"—an apparent attempt to create buffer villages that would shield Comanchería from Texas while simultaneously serving it as supply depots.[68]

Potsanaquahip's expansive demands outraged Houston, forcing him to leave out the border clause from the final treaty, which mentions the border line only in the future tense: it was "to be marked and run." But Potsanaquahip's maximalist approach may have been a premeditated negotiating tactic aimed at securing what Comanches had for a long time considered theirs. The Treaty of Tehuacana Creek did not specify an exact boundary, but it implicitly states that the string of Indian trading houses at the Comanche Peak and on the middle Brazos and lower San Sabá rivers were to be considered a demarcation line separating the two nations. That line was farther north and west than Potsanaquahip's proposed boundary, but it followed closely the historical southern border of Comanchería, securing Comanches their traditional plains core territory.[69]

The Treaty of Tehuacana Creek ushered in a delicate imperial détente between the Comanche empire and Texas. Texas continued to sponsor licensed trading houses where Comanches could sell their surplus stock; purchase ironware, fabrics, and flour; and have their guns repaired by blacksmiths. The Texas government invested vast sums in gifting and obliged its merchants to obey Comanche protocols, and Comanches largely refrained from raiding in Texas. With Delawares serving as messengers, Comanches and Texans met in frequent councils to forge new geopolitical arrangements that would meet the needs of their nascent alliance. Mopechucope promised to exert his power to prevent the Wichitas from raiding in Texas and suggested a new policy toward the Lipans, whose presence around San Antonio drew Comanche war bands below the boundary line: all Lipans should be removed north into Comanchería, where they would live under Comanche control. Texas officials, in turn, issued passports that allowed Comanche war parties to travel undisturbed through Texas into Mexico. When the United States and Texas moved toward annexation in winter 1844–45, the Comanche question loomed large in the process: the western counties of the republic voted for annexation largely out of hope that the U.S. Army would neutralize the Comanches and expell them from the state. Yet in May 1846, three months after a formal transfer of authority from the republic to the newly founded state, U.S. delegates signed a treaty with the Comanches, pledging to continue gift distributions in Texas. In June a Comanche commission led by Chief Santa Anna visited Washington, and the next year Texas Governor James Pinckney Henderson ratified the boundary by establishing a neutral zone thirty miles above the state's northernmost settlements.[70]

In 1847, then, Comanchería's southern border stood almost exactly where it had been ten years before. By enforcing a formal boundary line, Comanches had drawn a major concession from the far richer and far more populous Texas: although official maps failed to show it, Texans had signed away nearly half of their claimed territory to the Comanche nation. But Comanches, too, had compromised. When they imposed a fixed border, they in effect gave up their arrogated privilege to raid Texas for livestock and slaves and extort it for tribute, privileges that had sustained their economic growth for nearly a century. Texas transformed, even if briefly, from a fluid tributary and raiding frontier into bordered land of international coexistence with well-demarcated lines. It was a concession from Comanches but one they could well afford to make, for they had already built a new and much larger raiding hinterland below the Río Grande.

After their conquest of the southern plains in the eighteenth century, Comanches expanded their domain slowly and in small increments. Their systematic stock-and-captive raiding in Texas and New Mexico could be seen as a kind of territorial expansion, as it allowed them to control a good deal of the revenue-generating assets of the colonial Southwest, but the attacks never transformed into permanent occupation. Comanches did experiment in other fronts with extending their range beyond the grasslands, most notably in the 1770s when they pushed deep into Ute territory beyond the Rockies, but such campaigns did not have lasting success and were invariably abandoned. The Comanches, it seems, had reached the natural limits of expansion. All the things they had grown to need—hunting ranges, pasturelands, market outlets, raiding domains—were close at hand, making further expansion unnecessary and potentially counterproductive.

But then, in the late eighteenth and early nineteenth centuries, Comanchería burst out of its plains confines. Through remote operations and measured mass violence, Comanches created a new raiding economy in northern Mexico below the Río Grande. They escalated the range and scope of their plundering operations until vast expanses of Mexico's Far North had been turned into an extractive raiding domain: their war bands harnessed the region's transportable resources—horses, mules, cattle, and captives—so thoroughly and suppressed local resistance so completely that, in economic and military terms, much of northern Mexico became an extension of Greater Comanchería. By the 1830s contemporaries started to speak of northern Mexico as a Comanche colonial possession. "Comanches," the Indian officials of the Republic of Texas concluded in 1837, "[are] the natural enemies of the Mexicans whom they contemptuously discriminate their *stockkeepers* and out which nation they procure slaves." "They declare," another observer wrote, "that they only spare the whole nation [of Mexicans] from destruction because they answer to supply them with horses. The assertion seems to be fully carried out in practice, for it is no uncommon occurrence for a party of Comanches to cross the Rio Grande and after spreading terror wherever they go to drive off large numbers of animals."[71]

Comanche war parties first pushed south of the Río Grande in the late 1770s and for the next four decades raided the region intermittently. Various motives drew them this far south. Some raids seem to have been destroy-and-kill operations aimed at weakening the Apache villages in southern New Mexico and Texas and preventing Lipan and Mescalero hunting and war parties from entering the contested raiding and trading grounds around San Antonio. Comanches also seized Apache captives, who fetched high prices in San Antonio, Santa Fe, and Nacogdoches, and whose enslavement underwrote the Comanche-Spanish alliance. Some Comanche war parties targeted Spanish outposts and extracted gifts from the Spanish presidios along the Río Grande, thereby extending their tributary hinterland far to the south of their borders. For western Comanches, who had kept an uninterrupted peace with New Mexico between 1786 and 1821, the forays opened the possibility of forging a new raiding economy in the south.[72]

The raids increased markedly in 1816, when Comanches and Lipans formed a short-lived alliance. The truce gave Comanches virtually unrestricted access to the lower Río Grande valley and the Spanish settlements along and beyond it. For several years, Comanches and Lipans raided Laredo, Revilla, and other villages along the Río Grande for horses and captives, sometimes plunging south of the valley to attack the wealthy haciendas in Tamaulipas, Nuevo León, and Coahuila. Texas became a thoroughfare for Comanche war parties. "The Comanches are obliged to cross this country to go to pillage the frontiers of the Provincias Internas," one observer wrote in 1818, noting the established nature of the operations: "They have there some regular camping grounds at places where they find water and some pasturage for their horses. This trail is known under the name of *Chemin de Guerre des Comanches.* The war parties, which are rarely less than two hundred to three hundred men, leave it but little." Then, however, the raids into Mexico slowed down. In 1822 Comanches signed a national treaty in Mexico City and a provincial treaty in San Antonio and for a while refrained from raiding Mexican settlements. The Comanche-Lipan alliance unraveled the same year when Lipans, for unknown reasons, killed several Comanche men who had married into Lipan villages. For the next few years Comanches were preoccupied with a "bitter warfare" against the Lipans.[73]

Large-scale raiding resumed in 1825 and 1826. Accompanied by Kiowas and apparently guided by Mexican captives, western and eastern Comanches sent several war parties to the south, lashing the Río Grande frontier from El Paso to Coahuila. From there on, the raids escalated steadily, eventually engulfing much of northern Mexico. In 1828 Comanches razed the recently built military town of Palafox on the lower Río Grande, killing most of its inhabitants. A few years later, "emboldened by the slack defensive system of the Mexicans," their war parties crossed the Río Grande in several places. They seized control of Apache war trails from Matamoros to northern Chihuahua, forcing the Lipans and Mescaleros to shift their raiding operations west, south, and north.

By the late 1830s, Comanches were making "continual inroads upon the whole eastern frontier of Mexico, from Chihuahua to the coast; driving off immense numbers of horses and mules, and killing the citizens they may encounter, or making them prisoners." Moving through Texas at will, they claimed its entire western part down to the Rio Grande—"the most healthy, fertile, and desirable portion of the republic," as one Anglo-Texan put it—as their own. There was still another upsurge of raiding activity in 1840 and 1841 when large-scale war parties struck deep into Mexico, and soon the Comanche raiding network covered much of Chihuahua, Coahuila, Nuevo León, Tamaulipas, Durango, Zacatecas, and San Luis Potosí. When the Mexican-American War broke out in 1846, Comanche war bands ranged into the Mexican tropics. They were active in Jalisco and attacked at least once the city of Querétaro, which lies 135 miles north of Mexico City, and their war trails extended 1,000 miles—almost fifteen degrees of latitude—south of Comanchería's center.[74]

It is not difficult to read strategic intention into such a dramatic expansion. Like most imperial powers, Comanches strove to separate the zones of conflict from the zones of peace within their realm. By shifting the geographic focus of their raiding operations far to the south—and far from their borders—they were able to decrease the possibility of punitive campaigns into Comanchería. In this sense, the expansion could be seen as a defensive measure, an attempt to render violence remote. The deeper into Mexico the Comanches pushed, the safer they could feel at home.[75]

Seen from a different angle, Comanches' thrust into northern Mexico stemmed from the simultaneous vitality and vulnerability of their power complex. Early nineteenth-century Comanchería was a dense and dynamic marketplace, the center of a far-flung trading empire that covered much of North America's heartland. The Comanche trade pump sent massive amounts of horses and mules to the north and east—enough to support the numerous equestrian societies on the central, northern, and eastern Great Plains and enough to contribute to the westward expansion of the American settlement frontier. In return for their extensive commercial services, Comanches imported enough horticultural produce to sustain a population of twenty to thirty thousand and enough guns,

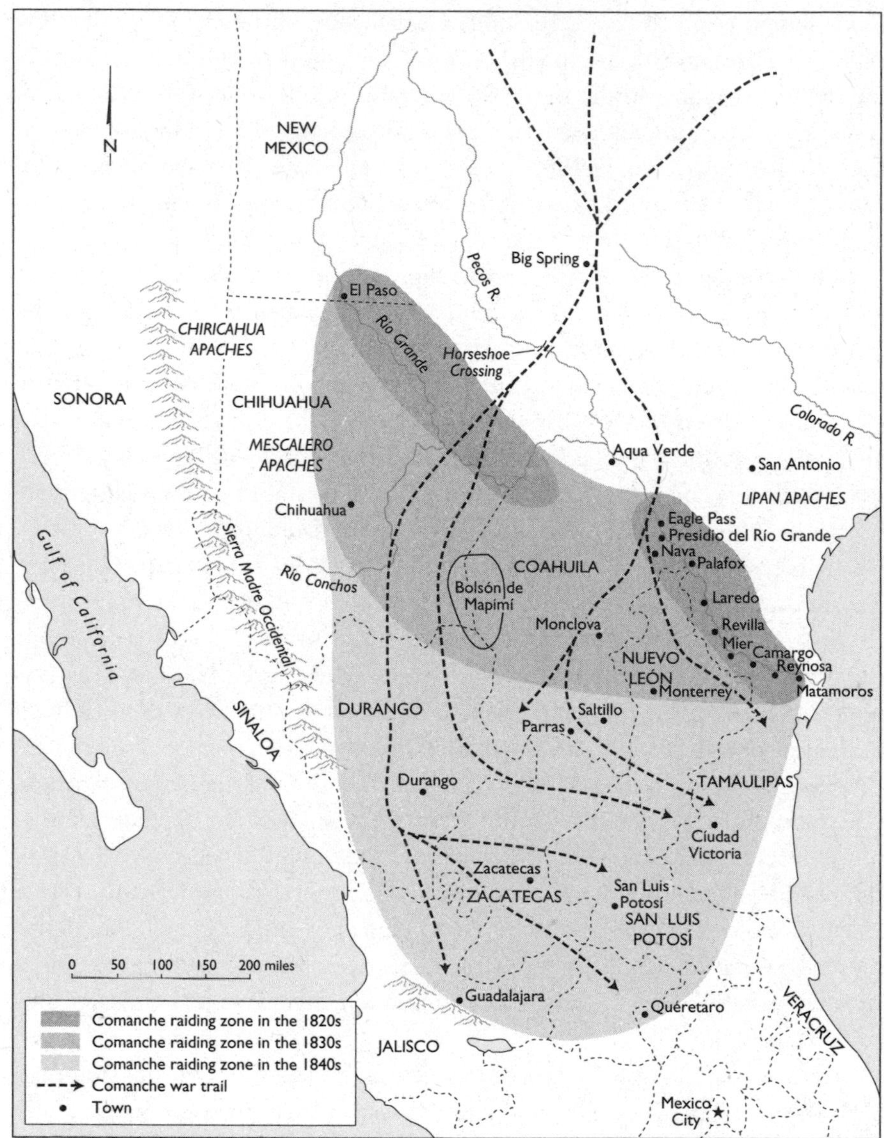

11. Comanche raiding hinterland in northern Mexico. Map by Bill Nelson.

lead, and powder to defend a vast territory against Native enemies as well as the growing, expansionist Republic of Texas.

But that thriving exchange system was rapidly approaching the limits of its productive foundation. Since Comanches reserved the bulk of domestically raised horses for their own use, the viability of their trading network depended on continuous livestock raiding. But by the 1820s, the traditional raiding domains had become either exhausted or unavailable. Decades of on-and-off pillaging had wrecked the pastoral economy of Texas, whereas New Mexico, the site of intense raiding in the 1760s and 1770s, had attached itself to Comanchería through a tribute relationship. Comanches continued sporadic raiding in Texas through the 1820s and 1830s, but the returns failed to meet their expansive livestock demand, which skyrocketed in the late 1830s and early 1840s when they opened trade with the populous nations of Indian Territory. To keep their commercial system running, Comanches needed new, unexhausted raiding fields, and they found them in northern Mexico. U.S. Army Captain Randolph B. Marcy saw a direct link between the trade with removed Indians and the raids into Mexico. "A number of Delawares, Shawnees, and Kickapoos," he noted in 1849, "have for several years past been engaged in a traffic with the prairie Indians, which has a tendency to defeat the efforts of the military authorities in checking their depredations upon the citizens of the northern provinces of Mexico."[76]

In addition to livestock, Comanches pushed south of the Río Grande in search of Apache and Mexican slaves. The old eastbound slave traffic had all but collapsed with the U.S. takeover of Louisiana and the subsequent advent of large-scale black chattel slavery in the province, but Comanches could still find profitable markets for captive women and children in New Mexico and Texas. Moreover, devastated by three successive smallpox epidemics in 1799, 1808, and 1816, Comanches needed to supplement their workforce with systematic coerced labor drafts. They transformed themselves into large-scale slaveholders, and they did so by combing northern Mexico for captives (see chapter 6). According to Miguel Ramos Arizpe, a well-informed priest and diplomat, Mexico's northern provinces lost more than two thousand men, women, and children to Indian captivity between 1816 and 1821. Comanches, another observer noted, "are exceedingly fond of stealing the objects of their enemies' affection. Female children are sought with greatest avidity, and adopted or married."[77]

Comanche raiding thus generated a massive northward flow of property from Mexico into Comanchería and its trade channels, a development promoted by many interest groups in North America. The Bent brothers encouraged Comanches to raid Mexican settlements, as did Holland Coffee, who "advised them to go to the interior and kill Mexicans and bring their horses and mules to him." By the late 1830s it had become a common belief that "enterprising [American] capitalists" had established trading posts on the Comanche-Texas border in order to tap the "immense booty" that the Comanches, "the most wealthy as well as the most powerful of the most savage nations of North America," were hauling from northern Mexico. Texas officials provided Comanche war parties free access through their state, hoping to direct the raids to Mexico, and even supplied southbound war bands with beef and other provisions. By the mid-1840s, the arrangement had solidified to the point that Chief Pahayuko (Amorous Man) could ask Texas Rangers to go with his band "to war agenst [*sic*] the Mexicans." New Mexico's officials routinely turned a blind eye to the fact that their subjects traded in horses and mules taken from other Mexican provinces, and some New Mexicans were even rumored to be joining Comanche war parties south of the Río Grande. From the vantage point of Chihuahua, Coahuila, Nuevo León, or Tamaulipas, it easily seemed that a depraved North American coalition of Indians, Americans, and New Mexicans had emerged to exploit and enfeeble northern Mexico.[78]

Comanche raiding in northern Mexico was a veritable industry. By the 1830s, the single path across Texas had evolved into a grid of well-trodden war trails. The trails started at the present-day Big Spring, a pool of artesian water near the headwaters of the Colorado River, which served as a staging area where Comanche and Kiowa parties from all across Comanchería gathered in spring to rest and water their horses before heading south. From the Big Spring two trunk lines carried raiders south. The two lines forked into four near the Río Grande and then plunged deep into Mexico, skirting major cities and military forts. Leading from the main prongs there were numerous lateral lines, which webbed across much of northern Mexico, allowing Comanches to adjust to variations in weather, availability of game, and Apache competitors. Along and around the trails, Comanches knew numerous waterholes, lookout points, way stations, and prime campsites with winter pasturage.[79]

Once south of the Río Grande, Comanche war parties often camped and rendezvoused at the Bolsón de Mapimí, a lightly populated desert plateau nestled amidst the jagged mountain ranges and sierra forests of southeastern Chihuahua, western Coahuila, and northern Durango. The Bolsón was easily accessible from the western and central trails and offered Comanches and their herds a sanctuary of mild weather, natural springs, clear streams, seasonal lakes, and protective rock entrenchments for camping. From the 1830s on, the raids into Mexico began to take the shape of seasonal migrations. Comanche war bands started to bring entire families with them and extend their sojourns over several seasons, turning the previously desolate Bolsón into a permanent, self-sustaining settlement colony. As in Comanchería proper, Comanches spent their days hunting local game for subsistence, collecting wild foods, and bearing and rearing children, and like the southern plains, the Bolsón was dotted with large, slowly migrating Comanche rancherías that lined streams and river valleys with massive horse herds. Comanches walled their favorite campsites like Laguna de

Jaco with parapets, and their large horse and mule herds cut wide roads into the terrain. For the occasional American or Mexican visitors, the region had an eerie feel of a colonized landscape. "In the fall and winter season," one observer wrote, "their home is . . . in the *Bolson de Mapimi*, a vast basin shut in by high mountains at the west. Here they enjoy uninterrupted possession of a wide extent of country, whence they make their sallies into the heart of Mexico."[80]

Part settlement colony and part staging area, the Bolsón plateau was the nest from which Comanche war parties fanned out westward, eastward, and southward, launching wide-ranging campaigns across northern Mexico. Sometimes in small parties, sometimes in big war bands, they moved from one target to another, living off the land while sacking ranches, haciendas, villages, towns, and mining communities. They drove off entire horse and mule herds; captured women and children; and butchered cattle, pigs, sheep, and goats for food. To suppress resistance, they killed Mexican men, burned houses, destroyed food storages, and slaughtered animals they could not take or did not need. Once the parties had accumulated booty, they returned to winter in the Bolsón, waiting for grass to grow along the trails to sustain their massive herds.

The excursions were carefully planned and organized. In 1847 Chief Potsanaquahip stunned a U.S. Indian official by explaining how he was going to take his band to Parras, Chihuahua, and by identifying in detail the villages he would raid on the return journey. Several Mexican observers remarked that the Comanche war parties that moved in seemingly random patterns were in fact highly disciplined units, organized under "generals" and "captains" who exercised complete authority over their followers during the campaign. "When the march is in war formation," Berlandier wrote, "the scouts and spies ride ahead, then the chief of the tribe at the front of his people, with the women staying behind. If the enemy makes a surprise attack on a trail camp the women protect their offspring, if necessary with bows and knives, fighting to the death if they cannot take flight. Warhorses are never ridden on the trail, except at the approach of the enemy. Each Comanche fighting man has three or four horses for the trail." After an attack, Comanche war bands often dispersed to confuse pursuing parties. Disappearing into the countless canyons of the Sierra Madres, they later reunited in the Bolsón de Mapimí. If they faced superior forces and could not escape, the war parties used captives to negotiate safe return into Comanchería.[81]

The operations could be extraordinarily profitable. Although Apaches had pillaged northern Mexico for decades, many areas had been spared and now offered largely untapped targets for Comanche raiders. In a nine-day stretch in January 1835, for example, Comanches pilfered two thousand horses from Chihuahua City and its hinterland, and in June, after repeated attacks throughout the spring, several hundred Comanche warriors "laid waste" Rancho de las Animas near Parral, burning several buildings, destroying food bins, and taking thirty-nine captives. In all, eastern Chihuahua lost several thousand horses and hundreds of captives in the space of five months. Chihuahua's governor raised one thousand volunteers for a pursuit but failed to capture the culprits. A similar sequence unfolded in northern Nuevo León and Tamaulipas in the aftermath of the Texas Revolution. With Mexican troops preoccupied with the Texas rebels, Comanches orchestrated a flurry of raids. They depleted the horse and mule herds of Laredo and Matamoros; seized numerous captives; burned houses and fields; and slaughtered entire herds of cattle, sheep, and goats. They drove off the residents of newly built Mexican ranches from the strategically sensitive strip between the Río Grande and Nueces River, which both Mexico and the Texas Republic claimed. The attacks continued through the late 1830s, reducing the lower Río Grande villages to a "sad and disgraceful condition" by 1841.[82]

By the late 1830s, raiding had become big business across northern Mexico. One report stated that Coahuila alone lost nearly four hundred captives and some thirty-five thousand head of livestock to Indian raiders between 1835 and 1845, while almost twelve hundred died defending their lives and livelihood. Another report, from 1841, asserted that a Comanche war party of two to three hundred had made it to north of the Río Grande with eighteen thousand head of Mexican livestock, leaving behind three hundred casualties. This report may have been hyperbolic, but other evidence suggests that Comanches frequently returned from Mexico with oversized herds that were all but unmanageable. The Horseshoe Crossing on the Pecos River, the favorite camping site of the returning Comanche parties, was littered with horse and mule skeletons. Exhausted by the long travel and unguarded by the outnumbered herders, the animals overdrank and died by the hundreds.[83]

Far from passive victims, Mexican *fronterizos* (borderlanders) fought relentlessly—both with weapons and words—to protect their lives, lands, and property. Northern officials rejected national policymakers' wildly unrealistic aspirations of incorporating the Comanches into the "Mexican family" and instead recast them as alien others, animalistic barbarians who had to be erased in the name of civilization, religion, and national honor. Wealthy northerners turned their haciendas into veritable fortresses and organized private mini-armies, local militias patrolled roads and town limits, and provincial troops staged ambushes along Comanche trails, sometimes inflicting heavy losses on the enemy; in 1844 alone, Comanches lost some 150 men in four separate engagements with Mexican troops. And while individual departments labored with local defenses, the federal government tried to formulate broader strategic solutions. Mexico City appointed three commanding generals to coordinate the defenses in northern Mexico and sent a military detachment to Nacogdoches to expel American peddlers whose goods fomented Comanche raids in Mexico. It offered small land grants and tax exemptions for citizen soldiers who showed bravery in battle, and it tried to recruit Lipans to fight the Comanches. In 1843 Santa Anna even invited Jesuits back to Mexico so that they would rebuild missions across the northern frontier and exert a civilizing influence over the marauding Indians.[84]

Yet in the end, the Comanches' avalanche-like expansion below the Río Grande mirrored Mexico's weakness. For all their creative countermeasures, the Mexicans were often powerless against Comanche guerrilla tactics. Most farms, ranches, and villages in northern Mexico were small, isolated, and poorly manned—sitting ducks for highly mobile, well-organized mounted raiders. The large haciendas, too, were vulnerable, their sheer size making them difficult to defend against fast hit-and-run assaults. The Hacienda de la Encarnación in southern Coahuila lost six hundred horses and mules between 1840 and 1845, and the heavily fortified La Zarca rancho in northern Durango lost six hundred horses in March 1844 alone. Frontier defenses across northern Mexico were in pitiable condition. Volunteer militia units were ill-fed, ill-trained, and often undisciplined, and provincial troops suffered from chronic shortages of quality horses, guns, and munitions. The antiquated presidio system, a leftover from the Spanish era, was decaying, undermined by Mexico City's preference to reinforce the nation's core at the expense of its perimeters. The popularity of army service collapsed in the far north, forcing the presidios to fill their ranks with convicts and vagabonds. Local officials pleaded with Mexico City to revive the presidial system and send more soldiers, horses, and weapons to the north, but the chronically bankrupt federal government was slow to react. The result of this federal neglect was pitiful scenes of *fronterizos* going against heavily armed Comanche war bands with bows and arrows and slings and stones.[85]

From a military standpoint, then, much of the Mexican Far North remained an open field for the Comanches. Josiah Gregg, who had a cuttingly low opinion of the Mexicans' military prowess, remarked that Mexican troops were hesitant to engage with the more mobile and better-armed Comanches and that pursuits were sometimes made only for appearances. "It has been credibly asserted," he wrote, "that, during one of these 'bold pursuits,' a band of Comanches stopped in the suburbs of a village on Rio Conchos, turned their horses into the wheat-fields, and took a comfortable *siesta*—desirous, it seemed, to behold their pursuers face to face; yet, after remaining most of the day, they departed without enjoying that pleasure." Contemporaries believed that Comanches spared northern Mexico from utter destruction only because it supplied them with horses.[86]

It was out of desperation, therefore, when Sonora, Chihuahua, and Durango passed bills offering bounty prices for Indian scalps. The bills provided scaled bounty payments with prices ranging between twenty-five and one hundred pesos, depending on the victim's sex and age, and stated that the booty from slain Indians would be awarded to the vanquishers. State officials contracted foreigners residing in Mexican territory to kill Indian raiders with such frequency that by the late 1830s virtual bounty wars raged across northern Mexico. Mexico City condemned the scalp bounties as an excessive, unsavory measure but was powerless—or perhaps unwilling—to the stop the practice. The scalp wars devastated the Apaches who, unlike the Comanches, could not evade mercenary scalping squads by escaping far to the north. James Kirker, the most notorious of the soldiers of fortune, focused his business-style operations almost solely on Apaches, delivering almost five hundred Apache scalps to Chihuahuan authorities by 1847, but he largely avoided the more mobile and better-armed Comanches. In fact, as scalp payments became an established practice in Chihuahua in the late 1830s, Comanches, too, began to hunt Apaches for the standard bounty prize, a crown with an ear on each end.[87]

The only viable way to fend off the Comanches, whose operations in northern Mexico amounted to an imperial extension, would have been coordinated interstate campaigns targeting Comanche rancherías in Mexico as well as in Comanchería proper. But national policymakers, though swamped with bitter, desperate reports from the north, refused to consider the Comanche invasion a threat to the regime. Fearing that both the United States and Great Britain entertained plans of invading and capturing Mexico, they saw Indian attacks as a local problem that required local solutions. Mexico City urged the *fronterizos* to provide their own defenses and made only sporadic attempts to confront Comanches with a more unified front. The most ambitious of these efforts, General Arista's 1841 plan of a grand invasion into Comanchería, was also one of the most illuminating in its futility. The campaign never got off ground largely because New Mexico Governor Manuel Armijo, fearing Comanche retribution, refused to take part in the campaign. Mexico City neither reprimanded nor removed Armijo.[88]

In fact, the federal government not only relegated the escalating Indian problem to the local level but also obstructed, even if inadvertently, local attempts to organize effective defense. Many *fronterizo* communities tried to pool their meager resources by organizing joint defensive and punitive operations only to have federal policies undermine their efforts. The northern villages of Tamaulipas experimented with collective campaigns in the early 1830s, but such efforts became increasingly difficult after the Texas Revolution. In the late 1830s, for example, the officials of Matamoros complained bitterly that the town had supplied so many horses, steers, carts, and servants to the campaigns against the Texas rebels that its residents had difficulties in carrying out basic subsistence tasks, not to mention mounting effective defense against Indians. Such disputes over military priorities sometimes occurred within states. In 1841 the northern villages of Tamaulipas petitioned the state legislature for an exemption from military service on the grounds that they formed the front line against Comanche attacks. The state government denied their appeal and also refused all aid in fighting the Indians, causing deep resentment in the hard-pressed frontier communities.[89]

As it became clear that the federal government could not or would not offer a comprehensive solution to the Indian problem, the northern departments began to follow independent policies. They tried to fend off Comanche aggression any way they could, which often meant adopting strategies that merely deflected the violence. New Mexico set the precedent for this in the early 1820s, when it began to purchase peace from Comanches with commerce and gifts, and other departments soon followed suit. In 1824 the Presidio del Río Grande in Coahuila began collecting foodstuffs from the surrounding settlements to placate the Comanche war parties that were just starting to invade northern Mexico. This policy bought northern Coahuila a measure of protection, but it redirected Comanche raids into the neighboring Chihuahua, triggering a destructive chain reaction that eventually nearly obliterated that province.[90]

By 1826, raiding had taken a hard toll in northern Chihuahua, prompting Commanding General Gaspar Ochoa to invite Comanche chiefs Paruaquita and Cordero to peace talks in Chihuahua City. Ochoa proposed an accord "to end the horrors of war within the great expanse of our borders," and Paruaquita and Cordero accepted it. Desperate to protect the tormented province, Ochoa promised Comanches annual gifts in Santa Fe and San Antonio and asked them to obtain passports before entering Chihuahua. But Ochoa's efforts were undermined by Coahuila and Texas, whose citizens continued to traffic in stolen Chihuahuan goods. Texas officials tried to smother the contraband trade by forbidding their subjects from purchasing branded livestock from Comanches; at times, however, they engaged in the illegal traffic themselves. To spin their actions, the officials asserted that Comanches did not sell but "returned" Chihuahuan booty and deserved to be rewarded with gifts for their "good faith." Coahuila's move to Comanche orbit became complete in 1830, when Saltillo began supplying Comanche war bands with money, food, clothes, and tobacco. Like Santa Fe and San Antonio before it, Saltillo acceded to pay tribute to Comanches to escape violence. In 1834, Chihuahua finally joined New Mexico, Texas, and Coahuila in tributary collaboration. Its officials signed a treaty with the Comanches in El Paso and promised them military aid against the Apaches in the hope of diverting the violence. The attempt met with only partial success. Comanches launched a raiding war against the Mescalero and Coyotero Apaches in northwestern Chihuahua, giving the region's Mexican settlers a respite, but they also moved to raid the Mexican settlements in central and southern Chihuahua.[91]

The independence of Texas in 1836 changed the geostrategic context in which northern Mexicans operated, but it did not change their Comanche policies, which remained embedded in self-interest. In the aftermath of the Texas Revolution, Coahuilan officials signed two more treaties with the Comanches, hoping to harness their military might against the rebel republic. The first treaty, in 1838, designated the village of Nava as a trading outlet, and the second one, five years later, opened Aguaverde in Coahuila and Laredo in northern Tamaulipas to Comanche traders. Comanches also gained extensive hunting privileges in Coahuila. Contrary to Mexican designs, however, the treaties and concessions did not redirect Comanche warfare northward into Texas but southward into central Mexico. Comanches extended their raids into southern Coahuila, Durango, and Zacatecas and then disposed the plundered stock at Nava, Aguaverde, and Laredo. By fall 1844, the raids had become so severe that General Arista decreed trading with the Comanches a capital offense. Some *fronterizo* communities obeyed the law, thus exposing themselves to Comanche reprisals: in late 1845 Chief Santa Anna explained to Texas officials "that the cause of the [recent] war with Mexico was the Spaniards breaking a treaty that was made some years since."[92]

Comanches raided northern Mexico for nearly a century, but the early and mid-1840s saw the climax. Not coincidentally, those years also marked the pinnacle of their plains-based trading empire. Eastern Comanches absorbed several removed nations of Indian Territory into their trade network, launched a lucrative commercial partnership with the Osages, and accepted Anglo-American trading posts on their borders. Western Comanches made peace and opened trade with Cheyennes and Arapahoes, embarked on large-scale exchange at Bent's Fort, and turned the comanchero trade into a major commercial institution. All these exchange circuits centered on horses and mules, creating an almost insatiable demand for stolen Mexican stock. "Nearly all these [traded] animals are pilfered from the Mexicans," Captain Marcy observed, "and as the number they traffic away must be replaced by new levies upon their victims, of course all that the traders obtain causes a corresponding increase in the amount of depredations." The trading boom on the plains, moreover, coincided with the appeasement of Comanche-Texas relations, which prevented Comanches from rustling in the Lone Star Republic and liberated men and resources for long-distance raiding south of the Río Grande.[93]

The result was an "incessant and destructive war" in northern Mexico. Starting in 1840 Comanches, together with their Kiowa allies, each year dispatched several major expeditions below the Río Grande. These campaigns were noticeably larger than in the previous years, typically involving between two hundred and one thousand fighting men. Massive war bands ranged wider than ever before, hitting Corpus Christi some 150 miles north of the Río Grande, then penetrating deep into southern Durango, Zacatecas, San Luis Potosí, and Jalisco, where they entered a new world of jungles and high sierras. Perhaps to debilitate local defenses, the first excursions to the far south were unusually destructive; the fall of 1840 saw some three hundred Mexican deaths. After such spectacular demonstrations of power, a grinding routine set in. With their lines greatly elongated, Comanches lived off the enemy, slaughtering cattle and sheep and attacking pack and merchant trains loaded with supplies and ore. Their deep, looping maneuvers cut off vital lines of communication and commerce; imperiled the mining towns in Durango, Zacatecas, and San Luis Potosí; and ravaged the countryside to the extent that tending fields became difficult. Communities from northern Nuevo León to southern Durango were reduced to operate near or below subsistence level.[94]

Comanches now treated northern Mexico and its fabulously wealthy ranches as virtual warehouses. In 1846 James Josiah Webb, a Missouri trader, witnessed how they rounded up twenty-five thousand head of livestock in the city of Durango, "threatening and attacking the soldiers who remained behind their barricades on the defensive." George Ruxton, an English explorer and travel writer who got much of his information from the Mexicans, reported that Comanche war bands moved across seven Mexican states virtually unopposed. Having traveled unused roads "overgrown with grass" and flanked by endless "deserts of the frontier," regions that were "annually laid waste by the Comanches," he stopped to wonder: "It appears incredible that no steps are taken to protect the country from this invasion, which does not take its inhabitants on a sudden or unawares, but at certain and regular seasons and from known points. Troops are certainly employed *nominally* to check the Indians, but very rarely attack them, although the Comanches give every opportunity."[95]

If Ruxton lacked answers, it was because he could not see the big picture: Comanches had turned a large section of Mexico into a semicolonized landscape of extraction from which they could mine resources with little cost. "Beyond the immediate purlieus of the towns," Gregg reported, "the whole country from New Mexico to the borders of Durango is almost entirely depopulated.

The haciendas and ranchos have been mostly abandoned, and the people chiefly confined to the towns and cities." Another report stated that Comanche war parties had invaded Durango "in all of its extremities," reducing its citizens to a "most grave and deplorable condition." Saltillo and its environs lost 1,149 horses, 1,062 head of cattle, and 46 people in 1841, and the Chihuahua legislature lamented that "we travel along the roads . . . at their whim; we cultivate the land where they wish and in amount that they wish, we use sparingly things that they have left to us until the moment that it strikes their appetite to take them for themselves, and we occupy the land while the savages permit us." The all-important Chihuahua road had become an Indian plunder trail, commerce was paralyzed, and mines languished unused. Writing in 1846, Ruxton reported that the Comanches "are now . . . overrunning the whole department of Durango and Chihuahua, have cut off all communication, and defeated in two pitched battles the regular troops sent against them. Upwards of ten thousand head of horses and mules have already been carried off [between fall 1845 and fall 1846], and scarcely has a hacienda or rancho on the frontier been unvisited, and everywhere the people have been killed or captured. The roads are impassable, all traffic is stopped, the ranchos barricaded, and the inhabitants afraid to venture out of their doors. The posts and expresses travel at night, avoiding the roads, and the intelligence is brought in daily of massacres and harryings."[96]

When Comanche war parties finally returned home with trains of captives, horses, and mules, the war trails that had carried them south served them as commercial highways. They could stop in Mexican towns, ranches, and presidios in northern Coahuila, Chihuahua, and New Mexico and peacefully trade fresh Mexican booty for food, guns, and manufactured goods. All across Chihuahua, southern New Mexico, and southern Texas, they could also sell stolen livestock to American contraband traders and gunrunners, who pushed south from Santa Fe, El Paso, San Antonio, and Goliad, hoping to tap into the enormous northbound current of wealth from Mexico.[97]

The decades of Comanche raiding in Texas and northern Mexico—which from the late 1820s on coincided with increasing Apache pillaging in Sonora, Chihuahua, and Durango—had a lasting hemispheric legacy. The escalating violence left Mexico dangerously weakened during critical years in its history, for it overlapped with mounting U.S. pressure on Mexico's borders. The consequences were disastrous to the fledgling republic: between 1835 and 1848, Mexico lost more than half of its territory to the United States. Historians have customarily attributed Mexico's capitulation to the overt material and military superiority of the United States, but they have missed a crucial element: the

Native American expansion that paved the way for the Anglo-American one. The U.S. takeover of the Southwest was significantly assisted by the fact that Comanches and Apaches had already destabilized Mexico's Far North. Apaches had devastated vast stretches of northwestern Mexico, but Comanches left the deepest imprint. In each major stage of its expansion, the United States absorbed lands that had been made ripe for conquest by Comanches, who themselves were not interested in direct political control over foreign territories.[98]

After the Texas Revolution, Mexico City refused to accept the loss of Texas and considered it a Mexican department under the temporary rule of a rebel government. But just as the Comanche threat had propelled Texas to allow immigration from the United States, ushering it into Anglo-dominated independence, Comanche violence now blocked Mexico's attempts to recover its lost dominion. Mexico made several attempts at reconquest, but the turmoil of Comanche raiding in the bordering states—Coahuila, Nuevo León, and Tamaulipas—and particularly in the disputed Nueces Strip prevented the Mexican Army from organizing sustained campaigns. The officials of the Texas Republic, fully aware of these dynamics, offered Comanche war parties unrestricted travel through their lands. Comanche violence also thwarted Mexico's hopes of recapturing Texas from within. The citizens in the Río Grande villages had grown alienated from the central government that had failed to protect them from Comanche incursions and repeatedly refused to provide men, horses, and food for federal operations. In late 1839, moreover, just as Mexico attempted to launch a campaign into Texas, Antonio Canales, the commander of the federalist forces in Tamaulipas, instigated an anticentralist revolt to create an independent border republic out of Tamaulipas, Nuevo León, Coahuila, and southern Texas. The scheme won wide support among the embittered *fronterizos*, and the centralist troops did not manage to crush it until the spring of 1840. The Mexican Army, then, was forced to wage a war of reconquest from a decimated and rebellious war zone, an attempt that was doomed from the outset.[99]

The linkages between Comanche power politics and U.S. expansion culminated in the Mexican-American War, a war so one-sided that Ulysses S. Grant called it "one of the most unjust ever waged by a stronger against a weaker nation." Grant's candid statement meant to acknowledge the staggering power imbalance between the two republics—the war pitted a rapidly industrializing nation of some 18 million people against a young agrarian nation riddled by chronic political instability and fragile local economies—but it missed the underlying fact that the Comanches had exacerbated nearly all of Mexico's weaknesses through their power policies along and below the Río Grande. When U.S. troops marched south of that river in 1846, they did so alongside Comanche warriors who had raided there for decades, sabotaging Mexico's nation-building project in the far north and unintentionally preparing the ground for the American invasion. This is a point often missing from modern accounts of the war but not lost to the contemporaries. In 1848, for example, the Chihuahua legislature explained Mexico's defeat by noting that its northern half had been ravaged for years by Indian war bands. This wasteland of plunder, it derided, was a "worthy stage" indeed for the United States to display its might.[100]

As much as Americans despised the Mexicans for yielding to savage rule, their own self-styled civilizing campaign into Mexico was closely intertwined with Comanche power politics. At the outbreak of the war in spring 1846, Mexico's principal military initiative was not building defenses against the impending U.S. assault but rather a failed attempt to build a line of forts from Matamoros to El Paso to contain Comanche incursions. In the fall of 1845, moreover, Comanches staged a series of destructive raids deep into Durango and Zacatecas, tying up Mexican forces toward the nation's center at a time they were needed at its borders. The United States' and Mexico's lopsided capacities to wage war came into sharp relief in March 1846, when General Zachary Taylor led U.S. troops from Corpus Christi to the north bank of the Río Grande and asserted American sovereignty over the disputed Nueces Strip. Mexico protested fiercely, insisting that Taylor's Army of Occupation had entered Mexican soil the moment it crossed the Nueces, but there was no meaningful Mexican presence above the Río Grande to bolster that claim. Taylor had stepped into a power vacuum created by the Comanches, and Mexico would have to face the invading army not on the Nueces but amidst vulnerable civil settlements on the Río Grande.[101]

When U.S. troops pushed deeper into northern Mexico in the summer and fall of 1846, they entered the shatterbelt of Native American power. The U.S. Army marched south on abandoned roads littered with corpses, moving through a ghost landscape of ruined villages, decaying fields, horseless corrals, and deserted cattle herds. It faced Mexican cavalries mounted on "miserable little half-starved horses" and Mexican troops who lacked horses and mules to set up supply trains and move artillery. The few presidios dotting this wasteland were all but defunct. Their failure to curb Indian depredations had further diminished Mexico City's interest in supporting them, and the morale of the troops was dreadful, corrupted by wretched living conditions, food shortages, poor salaries, and mortal terror of Comanche attacks. The two hundred soldiers of the Presidio del Río Grande withdrew to Monclova without resistance, letting U.S. troops cross the Río Grande undisturbed near Eagle Pass, a key Comanche entryway into Mexico. It was as if northern Mexico had already been vanquished when the U.S. invasion got underway. If Mexico's collapse in 1847 was quick and complete, it was because the nation had to fight two invading powers at once.[102]

If Comanche power politics made northern Mexico militarily and materially vulnerable to the U.S. invasion, they also rendered it politically and psychologically susceptible for the U.S. occupation. Decades of unremitting exploitation and manipulation by Comanches had critically weakened the northern departments as well as Mexico City's hold on them. On the eve of the U.S. invasion, the Mexican North was destabilized, drained, and, it seems, unresponsive to the orders of federal officials, who had refused to treat Comanche raids as a national crisis that required a national response. War-torn northern Mexico was also deeply divided, so much so that it can be asked whether Mexico itself had become a mere collection of semiautonomous provinces. Most northern provinces put little value in the policies emanating from the distant, neglectful Mexico City and harbored deep-seated antipathies toward one another. This antagonism had crystallized during the long decades of Comanche violence when most provinces adopted self-interested policies, which often brought destruction to neighboring communities. (Comanches themselves seem to have been well aware of these developments: an Anglo captive held in Comanchería reported how Comanches, when planning a large-scale invasion into Mexico in the late 1830s, "expected to be joined by a large number of Mexicans who are disaffected by the government.") All this ate away at the already fragile sense of common identity, to the point that it was not unusual for high-ranking officers to openly rejoice when Comanche war parties left their departments for the neighboring ones. By 1846, northern Mexico was a compilation of disconnected communities with ambivalent identities and loyalties.[103]

It is not surprising, then, that U.S. troops faced little local resistance on their march south. Building on a long tradition forged under Comanche violence, many northern Mexican communities put self-preservation first and cooperated with the invaders. They sold U.S. troops supplies, rented out lands for camping, and served as guides. The Mexican Army fought fiercely at Resaca de la Palma and Buena Vista, but Matamoros, Monclova, Parras, Mier, Camargo, and Santa Fe all surrendered without a fight. In occupied Matamoros, U.S. Army officials dined at the homes of middle-class Mexicans and soldiers took Spanish lessons from the townspeople. In the lower Río Grande villas of Reynosa and Mier, Mexican officials requested General Taylor to send American troops to protect the settlements against Comanche raiders, and in Chihuahua, General William Worth dispatched dragoons to protect villages from Comanche depredations. In

Tamaulipas, U.S. troops ran into Antonio Canales who was still trying to carve out an independent republic of northeastern Mexico, thereby encumbering Mexico's war effort.

Behind northern Mexicans' rebellious fraternizing with invaders was a virulent bitterness toward the federal government, which had been unable and, as it seemed in the north, unwilling to invest resources to solidify the frontier against Indian incursions. They perceived the unchecked growth of Comanche power as a sign of Mexico City's indifference, which it was. The centralist regime that assumed power in 1835 had never taken the Indian threat seriously and had actually reduced the armaments and manpower of local militias to weaken state power, effectively abandoning the north to the mercy of Indian raiders. So when the distressed Mexico City appealed to the northerners in 1846 and 1847, many refused to join the fight against the Americans.[104]

Realizing this, U.S. policymakers and commanders proclaimed themselves as liberators from Comanche oppression. The war department assigned General Taylor to read in conquered cities a proclamation—simultaneously translated into Spanish—whose key passages evoked Mexicans' long suffering under Comanche terror and Mexico City's failure to alleviate their misery: "Your army and rulers extort from the people, by grievous taxation, by forced loans, and military seizures, the very money that sustains the usurpers in power. Being disarmed, you are left defenceless, an easy prey to the savage Cumanches, who not only destroy your lives and property, but drive into captivity, more horrible than death itself, your wives and children. It is your military rulers who have reduced you to this deplorable condition. . . . It is our wish to see you liberated from despots, to drive back the savage Cumanches, to prevent the renewal of their assaults, and to compel them to restore to you from captivity your long lost wives and children." Laced with allusions to female debasement and injured masculine honor, Taylor's proclamation echoed the rhetoric of beleaguered *norteño* elites, who felt abandoned and victimized by Mexico City. In June 1846, unaware that President James K. Polk had already declared war on Mexico, Donaciano Vigil addressed the New Mexico assembly, detailing the horrors that Mexico City's neglect had produced in the northern provinces: "I have heard reports regarding the barbaric tribes: of the number of Mexican captives, and especially of young Mexican women who serve the bestial pleasures of the barbaric Indians; of the brutal treatment they receive. . . . Those reports make me tremble with horror. . . . The more so when I contemplate what the fate will be of many people whom I esteem, if timely measures are not taken to guard against such degrading misfortunes."[105]

Whatever the real impact of the U.S. Army's proclamations, widespread popular insurgencies against *norteamericanos* broke out in northern Mexico only after the occupation had become a fact, and they were almost invariably inspired by the excesses and meddling of U.S. officials. But the liberation rhetoric was not aimed at the Mexicans alone. Its real audience, in a sense, was the Americans themselves, who were being steered to see the war through a morally tilted racial lens. The United States, its top officials insisted, was justified and indeed obliged to usurp territory from the mongrelized and inept Mexicans who not only had failed to civilize the land but lost much of it to savage Comanches. The conquest of Mexico, as scripted and sold by U.S. policymakers, morphed into an ideological crusade to stop the advance of savagery, to extend the dominions of peace, and to purify a racially defiled landscape.[106]

The signature event of the United States–Mexican War was not the Battle of Buena Vista or the Battle of Mexico City, but the bloodless takeover of New Mexico. By the time General Stephen W. Kearny's Army of the West marched into Santa Fe in August 1846—unopposed by Governor Armijo, who fled to Chihuahua, and four thousand New Mexican volunteers, who disbanded immediately after Armijo's escape—New Mexico was in many ways a Mexican province in name only. Its postmortem revealed an orphaned province, abandoned by Spain and neglected by the Mexican government, "a very mean step-mother to us," as one of the residents put it. Ignored and isolated, New Mexico had, as it were, turned its back on central Mexico and embraced foreign wealth and foreign influences, entering the path that eventually led to Santa Fe's peaceful surrender in 1846.[107]

But contrary to the conventional view, New Mexico's separation from the rest of Mexico did not begin in 1821, when it opened its borders to American merchandise and markets; it had begun three and a half decades earlier, in 1786, when New Spain formed a broad diplomatic and commercial alliance with the Comanches. That alliance wedded New Mexico to Comanchería through intimate political, economic, and cultural ties and increasingly set it apart from other Spanish colonies. While Texas languished during the late Spanish period as a virtual tributary state of the Comanche empire, New Mexico's border communities drew closer and closer to Comanchería. They plugged their lagging economy to Comanchería's expansive market circuits, adopted Comanche cultural influences, did business in stolen Texas and Coahuilan livestock, and fiercely defended their ties with the Comanches against Mexico City's or Santa Fe's interference.

In 1821 New Mexico was by far the most populous and prosperous of Spain's North American colonies, and it owed much of its privileged position to its special bond with the Comanches. Already partly disconnected from the rest of

Mexico in 1821, New Mexico accelerated its drift from Mexico City's orbit during the Mexican era, when it was subjected to the pressures and pull of *both* Comanchería and the United States. Once Comanches began systematic raiding in northern Mexico in the mid-1820s, and as New Mexicans adopted the policy of purchasing peace to protect themselves, the province began a gradual but irrevocable parting from the Mexican body politic. During the quarter-century of Mexican rule, New Mexicans went to great lengths to protect their alliance with the Comanches and in doing so alienated themselves from other northern Mexican provinces that were at war with the Comanches.

That erosion of political ties went hand in hand with a sweeping economic realignment that saw New Mexico shifting its commercial system from south to east. Comanche raiding south of the Río Grande dissolved old economic lifelines between Mexico City and the northern frontier, pushing New Mexico to intensify its reliance on the markets and goods of Comanchería and the United States. Mexico City fought this development, trying to infuse the northern frontier with national institutions, rules, and rituals, but it was powerless to offset the combined gravitational power of Comanchería and the United States. By the mid-1840s, just prior to the Mexican-American War, New Mexicans across the social strata had grown openly defiant toward Mexico City's centralist government, whose nation-building project they thought was at odds with their economic and political interests, which had long ago become affixed to the power and wealth flowing in from the east.

6

Children of the Sun

Behind the spectacular acts and institutions that made the Comanches an imperial power were untold everyday deeds. These mundane activities—elders debating in protracted councils, women running multilodge households, slaves tanning hides, teenage boys tending horses, young men jostling for recognition—may have lacked the immediacy of long-distance raids or international treaties and trade fairs as imperial acts but they were no less essential: they formed the foundation of the Comanche empire. This quotidian substratum is my focus in this chapter, which looks at the Comanche power complex from within, exploring the internal adjustments that made Comanches so domineering externally. Here I ask two interrelated questions: how did Comanches organize themselves to augment their external power, and, conversely, how did their external expansion compel them to adjust existing economic, political, and social arrangements?

The Comanches were a nation that was in a state of constant and at times uncontrolled change, a society that creatively reinvented itself while scrambling to absorb outside pressures, and an imperial people who both savored and struggled with their newly found might. Comanches' external dominance rested on a series of internal compromises, which kept them balancing between hunting and pastoralism, market production and subsistence production, localism and centralization, egalitarianism and inequality, individual ambition and group solidarity, slavery and assimilation. This internal balancing and compromising sustained the Comanche hegemony, but it was also precarious and dangerous: the Comanche society was a high-strung organism that was constantly threatened by political disarray, economic overheating, and intersocietal conflict. Such hazards would come to haunt the Comanches later in the nineteenth century, but for some 150 years balancing and compromising served them well, supporting their continued expansion and dominance.

The horse was to Comanches what ships, guns, and gold were to European imperial powers—a transportation device that compressed spatial units into conquerable size, an instrument of war that allowed them to wield much more power than their numbers would have suggested, and a coveted commodity around which a trading empire could be built. During their imperial ascendancy and dominance in the late eighteenth and early nineteenth centuries, the Comanches owned nearly four horses per capita, a number that attests to a flourishing herding economy. Basic hunting and transportation needs on the grasslands of the Great Plains required an average of one horse per person: a Comanche household of ten needed two running horses for hunting, raiding, and warfare; three or four pack horses (or mules) to transport the tipi and household belongings; and four to six animals for the women and children. Although most plains societies faced constant difficulties in meeting the minimum requirement of one horse per capita, the Comanches possessed an average of nearly three extra animals per person, or some thirty surplus animals per family. In absolute numbers, this meant huge reservoirs of surplus livestock. Numbering between 30,000 and 40,000 in the late eighteenth and early nineteenth centuries, the Comanches may have possessed between 90,000 and 120,000 excess animals.[1]

Comanches needed these enormous numbers in part because horses were such an uncertain form of wealth. They always lost animals during cold seasons, and the damages were especially severe if a harsh winter was followed by a dry spring, which prolonged the deficiency of water and vital nutrients over several months. Enemy raiders, wolves, and parasites preyed on their herds, and when hunting failed, Comanches routinely subsisted on horseflesh, making inroads into their own herds.[2] But the principal purpose of large animal surpluses was commercial. For more than a century, Comanchería operated as a trade pump that moved thousands of horses and mules each year to the central, northern, and eastern Great Plains and across the Mississippi valley into Louisiana, Missouri, and beyond. A large section of the midcontinent relied on Comanchería for animal imports, and the Comanches needed vast surpluses to satisfy that demand.

The Comanches were almost perfectly positioned to generate such surpluses. Their proximity and privileged access to the horse-raising districts in Texas, New Mexico, and northern Mexico allowed them to procure animals with relative ease. There were also some two million feral horses roaming within and near Comanchería's borders, forming a nearly bottomless pool of exploitable animal wealth. Even more vitally, Comanchería's southerly location and temperate climates permitted Comanches to maintain their herds with less effort and far greater success than the more northern Plains Indian societies. It was not an accident that the Comanches built their empire on the southern plains below the Arkansas valley, for that river marked an ecological and institutional fault line, north of which climatic conditions turned increasingly unfavorable for animal herding and equestrian cultures. With a long growing season, abundant grasses, and relatively mild winters, the southern plains formed an ideal setting for a trading culture that drew horses from the south and sent them north, and Comanches turned that ecological advantage into a spectacular commercial success.

Yet Comanches' commercial hegemony was not a simple matter of harvesting nature's gifts for economic gain. To build and maintain their prodigious animal wealth, Comanches had to implement far-reaching economic and social changes that sometimes were drastically at odds with existing practices. Paradoxically, horses' greatest advantage for human utilization—the fact that they are herbivores—was also their greatest disadvantage. By digesting grasses, horses transformed solar energy into easily exploitable muscle power, but this conversion took place only if Comanches met their horses' extensive foraging needs. Moreover, large horse herds represented something of an anomaly for hunters, who were used to arranging their movements, labor patterns, and annual cycle around the habits of the bison. Horses enhanced Comanches' ability to exploit the buffalo herds, but their tending demanded adaptations that conflicted with the requirements of the hunt. All this amounted to a daunting challenge: to keep their horse herds healthy and growing, Comanches had to transform their specialized foraging economy into a mixed economy of hunting and pastoralism.[3]

The shift toward pastoralism became perceptible in the mid-eighteenth century. In 1750, Felipe de Sandoval, a French explorer-trader, noted how the Comanche rancherías along the Arkansas valley had embraced the essential element of pastoralism: they orchestrated the timing and destinations of their movements to accommodate their horses' foraging and watering needs. "There were many rancherias in different places," he wrote, "which, according to the seasons, are moved from time to time in search of pasturage, wood, water, and buffaloes." Writing twenty-five years later, Pedro Vial explicitly linked Comanche nomadism with horse herding: "The Cumanche nation does not have fixed *rancherías* because they have many horses, for which it is necessary to find pasture." The need to protect the herds against enemy raiders further complicated the incessant search of pasture, as Anthony Glass noted in 1807. Comanches, he wrote, tied most of their horses with "Ropes made of Buffalo skins" within the camp circle, which made it "impossible to remain at the same place but a short time on account of the Grass being soon Eaten up." Comanche rancherías seem to have shifted campsites every two to five days, frequently leaving behind exhausted pastures where "ground in every direction is cut up & the grass eaten close." Perhaps to lessen the harmful effects of overgrazing, they began to experiment with transhumance and move their herds cyclically between cool mountain pastures in summer and the warmer lowland valleys of the plains in winter. In 1776 one Spanish observer learned that during the warm season the western Comanches regularly brought "a thousand or more animals" to the uplands of the Sangre de Cristo Range and pastured them in a large swampy area near Taos where "there is no lack of fodder."[4]

Intensive animal herding, with its never-ending search for pasture and its nervous balancing between herd maximization and overgrazing, forced the Comanches to modify their basic social organization. An average horse requires twenty pounds of grass a day in a normal year, which means that a Comanche ranchería with one thousand horses would have exhausted an area of roughly seven acres each day. In reality, the required area was even larger, because horses are selective grazers and tend to move to ungrazed areas rather than to eat less preferred grasses; it has been estimated that on the plains horses consumed less than half of the available grass before moving to an ungrazed area. And these estimates apply only in normal years. During droughts the average-acre yields collapsed, forcing the animals to graze over a wider radius. When precipitation fell from the annual average of twenty inches to ten, grass yield dropped to 15 percent of normal.[5]

Such ecological realities brought about a profound change in Comanche social structure. As the pastoral side of their economy continued to expand, Comanches had to carefully control the size of their rancherías, for large human-animal concentrations would quickly exhaust fodder and water around campsites. This led to an accelerating process of social fission, since the total Comanche population was growing rapidly. There were between 30,000 and 40,000 Comanches in the late eighteenth and early nineteenth centuries, and a typical ranchería probably included around 250 people—or, more to the point, approximately one thousand horses and mules.[6] As the Comanche population grew, the number of Comanche rancherías multiplied. Athanase de Mézières noticed this development in 1772. The Comanches, he wrote, "divide themselves into an infinite number of little bands for the purpose of seeking better pastures for their horses, and cattle [bison] for their own food."[7] During the height of its power in the early nineteenth century, the Comanche nation consisted of roughly one hundred rancherías scattered widely throughout Comanchería to permit optimal use of the available forage.

While readjusting their nomadic traditions and social organization to accommodate the pastoral shift, the Comanches also reconfigured their labor patterns to meet the new economic demands. The replacement of the pedestrian hunting methods with the mounted chase in the early eighteenth century had transformed bison hunting from a time-consuming and labor-intensive activity into a highly efficient, low-cost activity, freeing vast amounts of labor. Most of that liberated labor force was absorbed by horse herding, which, in terms of labor investments, became the Comanches' principal economic activity by 1800. If pastoralists are defined as people who consume a great share of their time and energy in such activities as protecting, pasturing, and training domestic herds, the nineteenth-century Comanches were typical pastoralists. In this respect, they did not differ much from such renowned pastoral people as the Huns or Mongols.

Like many pastoral societies, the Comanches developed a strict gender- and age-based division of labor. Adult men, usually headmen of extended families, made the strategic decisions concerning camp movements and grazing areas, but the arduous daily herding was entrusted to teenage boys. These boys worked with the animals every day and formed the true pastoral core of the Comanche community. In 1849 Captain Randolph B. Marcy noted this labor division in a ranchería of some 300 people and nearly 2,500 horses and mules. Family headmen assigned 150 animals to each boy who performed the duty "with the strictest vigilance and attention." Such diligence was in order since herding involved a demanding round of duties. Horses had to be protected from animal predators, moved between different pastures, and watered two or three times a day. They had to be treated for dehydration, wounds, sore feet, and saddle sores. The daily round usually ended with driving the most valuable horses into the camp area where they were placed under night watch. The romantic ethnographic view of Comanche boys spending their days in joyful play and learning the skills and arts of a warrior had very little to do with the social realities of the market-oriented imperial Comanchería.[8]

Daily herding became even more burdensome during winters, when low temperatures, freezing winds, and declining resources depleted horses' strength. Winter care was relatively easy as long as dormant grasses were available, but when this resource was exhausted considerable effort was needed to save the herds from starvation. Each day the boys took the animals farther from the camp for fresh grass until the ranchería itself was moved. During harsher winters, when low temperatures and thick snow cover prevented horses from grazing, herders had to secure supplemental forage. Comanche herders cleared large patches for grazing and gathered cottonwood bark, the chief emergency food, feeding their horses with peeled limbs or pieces of trunk. When exploring the Red River valley in 1852, Marcy noted the extensive use of cottonwood by the Comanche and Kiowa herders: "We found the stumps of the trees that they had cut from year to year in various stages of decay—some entirely rotten, and others that had been cut during the past winter. The fine mezquite and grama grass furnishes pasturage for their animals during a great part of the winter; and the cotton-wood is a never-failing resort when the grass is gone."[9]

In tending the herds boys often received help from women, who added this laborious task to their already extensive list of chores. In accordance with the extant gender roles, women were responsible for child rearing, meat processing, and a variety of household duties ranging from constructing the tipi to cooking. They also dressed the thousands of buffalo skins that the Comanches brought each year to the market. Yet, as the horse herds continued to grow, women became deeply involved in various pastoral activities as well. Domestic and pastoral chores, as John Sibley noted, consumed the days of Comanche women: "They Appear to be Constantly and Laboriously employ'd In dressing Buffalo Skins . . . Collecting feuel, Attending & guarding their Horses & Mules, in Cooking, Making Leather Halters & Ropes, Making & repairing their Tents, & making their riding & Pack Saddles &c. &c."[10]

The combined labor input of boys and women allowed men to avoid daily herding and concentrate on more specialized pastoral activities. They were responsible for the key nomadic task of orchestrating camp movements and selecting grazing sites. Jean Louis Berlandier, who in 1828 traveled with an eastern Comanche ranchería for a week, noted how the chief, "performing the role of orator, began at least one hour before daybreak to address the entire tribe in a loud voice," giving "orders about what was to be done, the hour of departure, and the place where we are going to camp." Men also captured and tamed feral horses—an arduous, high-skill task that took weeks—and tended to special war and hunting horses, devoting vast amounts of time in brushing, grooming, rubbing, and training these valuable animals whose qualities largely determined a household's economic viability and a man's success as a provider. Their most time-consuming responsibility, however, was livestock raiding. Preparations were meticulous and involved strategic planning, the recruitment of participants, and performing the proper rituals. After reaching their targets, raiding parties often spent several days assessing the situation to ensure the greatest results with the fewest losses. The act of theft was usually a swift surprise attack, preferably carried out at midnight in moonlight, but the homeward journey could take days, even weeks, for successful parties might return with hundreds of animals, driving the unruly herd for hundreds of miles, often night and day to shake off pursuers.[11]

Comanches developed a distinctively businesslike approach to raiding: they saw it primarily as an act of production, a means to fuel their market-oriented pastoral economy with horses, mules, and donkeys. They controlled the intensity of their pillaging operations to ensure sustained yield and refrained from clearing entire areas in New Mexico and Texas of horses and mules, leaving the ranches and farms enough animals to continue viable livestock production. This strategy was apparent in Texas, where they conducted lucrative raids from the 1760s to the early 1830s, when declining returns forced them to shift their operations south of the Río Grande. Comanches, in short, saw the Spanish and Mexicans ranches, missions, and settlements as an economic resource that was to be exploited rather than destroyed. As ironic as it may have seemed to the contemporary Spaniards and Mexicans, Texas spent three-quarters of a century as a carefully managed livestock repository for Comanchería.

But emphasizing Comanches' proficiency and prudence in raiding can obscure a central facet of their pastoral economy: domestic production. Comanches relied almost solely on raiding during the early stages of their horse acquisition, but in time they became skillful horse breeders who could generate a sustained domestic increase in herd sizes and manipulate the endurance, speed, size, and color of their animals. They produced animals with distinct qualities for warfare, hunting, and hauling and recognized at least seventeen different types of horses based on color alone. De Mézières observed in 1778 that the Comanches had become "skillful in the management of the horse, to the raising of which they devote themselves," and by the early nineteenth century Comanche horses and mules were generally considered to be of better quality than Spanish or Mexican stock. "Their wealth consisted of horses and mules; those raised by themselves are generally of superior order," one observer wrote, noting that whereas Comanches willingly sold their stolen Mexican stock, their "fine horses they could scarcely be induced to sell." Theodore Ayrault Dodge, a U.S. Army officer who traveled widely in the West and visited Comanchería in the mid-nineteenth century, wrote: "In one particular the Comanche is noteworthy. He knows more about a horse and horse-breeding than any other Indian. He is particularly wedded to and apt to ride a pinto ('painted' or piebald) horse, and never keeps any but a pinto stallion. He chooses his ponies well, and shows more good sense in breeding than one would give him credit for. The corollary to this is that the Comanche is far less cruel to his beasts, and though he begins to use them as yearlings, the ponies often last through many years."[12]

Comanche breeders employed a wide variety of techniques. They gelded the best riding horses to improve their stamina and tractability and weeded out weaker animals by letting them perish during winters or simply by eating them. They manipulated genetic changes through systematic breeding selection: they typically allowed only select stallions to mate with mares and castrated others. The product of these techniques was the well-proportioned, even-tempered, and agile Comanche horse, which excelled in bison hunting and warfare. During their wars with the Spaniards and the U.S. Army, the Comanches routinely evaded the cavalry columns, outpacing the bulkier Euro-American horses with their swift-footed mounts.[13]

In the early nineteenth century, Comanches expanded their pastoral economy from horses to mules. When visiting a large eastern Comanche camp in 1834, George Catlin estimated that one-third of that group's substantial herd consisted of mules, which suggests that Comanches not only raided the hybrids from colonial settlements but had acquired enough male donkeys to breed their own. Strong-backed, short-legged, and sure-footed even in rugged terrain, mules were better suited to hauling and carrying than the more delicate horses. Mules fetched high prices on the plains markets—the standard exchange rate was two horses for one mule—and Comanches reaped handsome profits in trading them. But the acquisition of mules can also be seen as a herding strategy that allowed Comanches to adapt to Comanchería's drought-prone weather. Mules withstand dehydration better, adjust to browsing more readily, and survive with fewer nutrients than horses, qualities that made them a desirable alternative for Comanche pastoralists, who wanted to minimize the effects of weather fluctuations on their livestock production. Through systematic herd diversification, they were able to reduce their overall losses and turn Comanchería into a pastoral success.[14]

The conversion to pastoralism turned Comanchería into a booming center of production, but the shift was difficult, demanding, and risky. By gearing their movements and labor patterns around the grazing needs of domestic herds, Comanches seemed to have seriously compromised their ability to follow and harvest the bison, the mainstay of their subsistence economy. There was an inbuilt tension between horse pastoralism and bison hunting, which required contrasting nomadic behavior: pastoralism rested on frequent, at times nearly constant movements, whereas hunting demanded more sweeping migrations punctuated with relatively long periods of immobility. Horses and bison also competed for the same resources and microenvironments—grass, water, and river valleys—which rendered any economic system that depended on both animals ecologically precarious.[15]

But rather than binding themselves in an economic deadlock, Comanches managed—undoubtedly through trial and error—to weave intensive herding and full-time hunting into a smoothly running dual economy. By the time they committed to pastoralism, Comanches had perfected horse-mounted hunting to such a level that it was reasonably easy for them to combine it with pastoral pursuits. Mobility was the key. The bison has a relatively small migratory radius, and the well-mounted Comanche hunters could quite easily reach the herds even if they did not follow them as closely as specialized hunters would have done. Horses also allowed Comanches to transport large quantities of dried meat and pemmican, lengthening the breaks they could take between hunts and lessening the need to stay within striking distance of the bison herds. An advantageous climate helped. Their location on the southern tip of the Great Plains provided Comanches with an exceptionally long hunting season, allowing them to spread their subsistence activities over several months. Their increased hunting efficiency combined with a favorable climate allowed Comanches to concentrate their hunting operations on frequent but swift sprees that yielded enough food to last for most of the year. Not so much hunters who used horses as herders who also hunted, they lived most of the year by the terms of their horses.[16]

Comanches had turned their economy and society inside out to accommodate animal herding, but it was not enough. Intensive pastoralism allowed them to raise more livestock to fuel their expanding exchange networks, but it also absorbed vast amounts of time and energy, divesting labor from other sectors of the economy. As households continued to enlarge their herds, they inevitably faced labor shortages and risked compromising their capacity to produce food, robes, and other necessities. Some households failed or chose not to acquire more horses and mules than they could comfortably maintain, but others sought ways to increase their labor force, market production, and wealth. They found a solution in polygyny and slavery.

Polygyny, a marriage system in which men have several wives, was traditional among the Comanches, but the practice expanded dramatically under the pressures of escalating market production, which put a premium on women's work. Hunting, raiding, and horse breeding, the main production activities of men, stressed daring and risk-taking, whereas the female activities of robe dressing, meat processing, and horse herding emphasized manual labor. Since a man could procure horses and robes faster and with less effort than a woman could feed, tend, and process them, men began to seek multiple wives to enlarge their labor pool. Polygyny became widespread by the turn of the eighteenth century and expanded steadily thereafter. Texas Governor Domingo Cabello y Robles wrote in 1786 that Comanche men sometimes had four wives, Pedro Bautista Pino remarked in 1812 that "men of rank often have as many as seven wives," and Juan Antonio Padilla reported eight years later that some Comanche men had eight wives. Josiah Gregg noted that prominent men in the 1830s and 1840s could have eight to ten wives, and Robert Neighbors wrote at midcentury that some wealthy men had more than ten wives.[17]

Polygyny was the primary means for mobilizing the female labor force for expanding market and domestic production. Writing around 1804, Manuel Merino y Moreno, the Spanish official, explicitly linked polygyny to the increased labor demands: "The practice of polygamy, or multiple wives, is common among the Comanches. . . . [Extra wives] are employed . . . in the work of curing skins, herding horses, and loading the animals with their tents and possessions when they move their *rancherías* from one territory to another." A few years later, David G. Burnet made a similar remark. Women in polygynous marriages, he wrote, "are literally 'hewers of wood and drawers of water,' to their dominate and supercilious husbands. Every description of domestic labour is imposed upon them to a degree not usual, even among savages." Berlandier wrote that women were even employed as laborers during long-distance raiding expeditions: "the few women that they take with them are expected to accommodate their husbands' relations and friends, not to mention guarding the horses and helping to carry off whatever the men have stolen."[18]

By relegating women to horse herding, robe dressing, and meat curing, polygyny seems to have produced a marked decline in their overall social status. Comanche women worked exceedingly hard, but they received few material or social rewards. José María Sánchez, the Mexican official, wrote in the late 1820s that Comanche women "are real slaves to the men, who occupy themselves with war and hunting only. The wives bring in the animals that are killed, they cut and cure the meat, tan the hides, make the clothes and arms of the men, and care for the horses." According to Burnet, the exploitation of female labor resulted in a broader social debasement: "Held in small estimation, [Comanche women] pay much less attention to personal adornment than the men, and appear, in the degradation of their social condition, to have retained but little self-respect. They are disgustingly filthy in their persons, and seemingly as debased in their moral as in their physical constitution." This social degradation resulted from the dynamic that has undermined women's status in many strictly gendered nonagricultural societies where men dominate the public sphere and women the domestic one. In such societies, women often carry the burden of market production, but the final products belong to men who can garner the prestige that flows from the control and redistribution of the critical wealth-generating goods.[19]

As polygynous marriages became more common, Comanche men began to see their wives less as companions and more as laborers. The extra wives were responsible for the most onerous household chores, such as hide tanning, meat curing, and winter care of horses, and they often toiled under the supervision of first wives, the respected matrons of households. The expansion of polygyny also enhanced men's control over the marriage institution itself. In the early nineteenth century, many marriages were arranged by the father or brother of the bride, who often could not refuse the selected husband. Berlandier may have exaggerated the contractual nature of marriages, but he captured the essence of the change: "Marriage among the Comanches is a purchase which the man makes, rather than a contract between two individuals. Polygamy is the rule, and a man marries only in order to increase the number of his servants." Besides altering marriage from an emotional bond more toward an economic investment, polygyny had several adverse practical effects on the female population. As the demand for female labor increased, girls were married younger, frequently before they reached puberty. Many Comanche parents tried to marry several of their daughters to the same man, thereby hoping to pressure the son-in-law to treat them better, but the downside of the practice was that marriage contracts were often made when the girls were still in their early teens.[20]

In writing about Native American women, Euro-American observers often projected their own cultural expectations on societies that operated by vastly different principles, and their conclusions were often distorted by the Western ideal that women were to be cloistered and protected. Moreover, since they typically recorded only what was visible to the naked eye, white observers rarely wrote about the more veiled domestic sphere where women exerted considerable moral authority. In the lodge, beyond Euro-American gaze, women were the principal decision makers. *Paraiboo?s*, senior first wives, controlled the distribution of food and commanded secondary wives and slaves, enjoying the privileges of wealth. "It is perhaps this alleviation of their labor by slaves," Gregg wrote, "that has contributed to elevate the Comanche women above those of many of the northern tribes." Women directed child rearing, owned packhorses, and could trade a small portion of the robes and meat they produced for the market. Women in sororal polygynous marriages found emotional support among their sisters, and women who were married to abusive or underachieving husbands frequently ran off with lovers or neglected household duties until their husbands divorced them.[21] And yet the overarching theme of contemporary observations—that the escalation of polygyny had a negative effect on women's status—is unquestionably true. The countless secondary wives of polygynous marriages formed a new exploited underclass of servile laborers in the Comanche society that was gearing its very foundation around market-driven surplus production.

The escalation of polygyny went hand in hand with the escalation of slavery. The two institutions had a common genesis—both developed to offset chronic labor shortages arising from market production—and they were functionally linked: many female slaves were eventually incorporated into Comanche families as wife-laborers. Most elementally, polygyny and slavery sprang from common cultural and ideological foundations: both reflected a larger patriarchal system that rested on male control and subordination of women and children and tended to reduce women and children to the objects of male honor, rivalry, and militarism.[22]

Comanches had raided other Native societies for captives long before European contact, and they became in the early eighteenth century the dominant slave traffickers of the lower midcontinent. It was not until after 1800, however, that human bondage became a large-scale institution in Comanchería itself. Comanches conducted frequent slave raids into Texas and northern Mexico during the second and third decades of the new century and soon emerged as the paramount slaveholders in the Southwest.

José Francisco Ruíz, who spent several years in asylum in eastern Comanchería in the 1810s, reported that his hosts possessed more than nine hundred "prisoners of both sexes." A Mexican report from 1823 states that eastern Comanches "held as captives in their power" more than "two thousand, five hundred of all classes, sexes, and ages," and Berlandier, writing in the early 1830s, noted that they held "five to six hundred" Creole captives, a figure that did not include the hundreds of slaves seized from the Osages and other enemy Indian nations. The estimates thus vary wildly, but they do indicate that eastern Comanchería's slave population had grown rapidly. Since the total eastern Comanche population in the early nineteenth century was around ten thousand, the slave component seems to have ranged between 10 and 25 percent. Information on western Comanchería is scantier, but the existing sources suggest that slavery was widespread there as well. In 1850, for example, a New Mexican from San Miguel del Vado reported of his visit to a western Comanche ranchería where "there were almost as many Mexican slaves, women and children, as Indians." That report was echoed by George Bent, who knew Plains Indian cultures intimately and who recalled that "nearly every family" among the Comanches "had one or two Mexican captives." Bent's conjecture would put the entire nation's slave population at several thousand, which is what Waddy Thompson, a Texas envoy to

Mexico in the early 1840s, believed to be the case: "there are not less than five thousand Mexicans at this moment slaves of the Comanches."[23]

Several forces converged to produce this escalation of captivity and slavery. One was the traditional but still-potent notion of captives as ritual conduits or symbolic currency. Comanches ritually tortured and killed some captives to avenge the deaths of slain members of their community, seeking consolation for grieving relatives and reassurance of their superiority over enemies. Ruíz reported how old women asked "the warrior for the slain enemy's hair (the scalp of the victim is exhibited in a high place in the warrior's home)." The women then "parade[d] the scalp through the village" while men, mounted on horses, sang, shouted, and fired their guns. Women cried for "those who have died recently, particularly the mothers who [had] lost a son." But captives were not only symbolic vehicles for revenge; they could also become symbolic conduits for peace. Exchanges of captives often marked diplomatic negotiations between the Comanches and colonial powers, helping resolve grievances and heal emotional wounds.[24]

Another persisting motive behind Comanche slavery was the captives' value as marketable human capital or investments for *rescate*. The vast slave markets in New Mexico and French Louisiana had declined or disappeared with the collapse of the old empires, but Comanches continued to seize captives in Texas, New Mexico, and interior Mexico with the intention of selling them back to their natal societies or, alternatively, to U.S. government agents in Indian Territory. Most ransomed captives were Spanish and Mexican women—the control of women still loomed large in the honor-laden masculine social milieu of the Southwest—but Comanches also ransomed Spanish and Mexican men "of certain age who have somehow escaped the fury of their masters." When Comanches took such captives to border villages for *rescate*, one contemporary noted, "the settlers hasten[ed] to contribute to the ransom and help free one of their kind, offering some trinket, or perhaps a mule or a gun, or whatever other object the owner thinks worth the trifling value of a Christian prisoner among the savages." As prospective high-value commodities, Spanish and Mexican captives were treated especially well. "Creole prisoners taken by the Indians in war against the villages and garrisons of the frontier receive fair treatment, as compared with that meted out to members of enemy peoples."[25]

Although traditional commercial and cultural motives continued to shape and stimulate slavery in Comanchería, the institution underwent a fundamental change in the early nineteenth century when the Comanches experienced a rapid economic and commercial growth. Their new exchange-oriented dual economy of hunting and pastoralism had an immense need for labor, which could be satisfied only through slavery and which fostered a new conception of bondage: Comanches began to see captives less as instruments of exchange and retribution and more as laborers who could be employed to produce livestock and robes for the market. Under mounting market pressures, then, Comanches gave the indigenous slave systems of the Southwest a new face: they practiced slavery for distinctively economic purposes.

The disease epidemics that ravaged Comanchería in the early nineteenth century gave the shift toward economically driven slavery particular urgency by creating an acute need to replace dead members and replenish devastated kinship networks with captured peoples. Comanches put special value on female captives, who could be employed, alongside with the Comanche women of polygynous marriages, in tending horses, tanning hides, curing meat, cooking meals, and packing possessions when moving camp. Comanches put women to work almost immediately after capture and used various methods, from physical abuse to monthly quotas of finished robes, to increase their productivity. Captive women were also forced to provide domestic and sexual services, and female captives of European ancestry added to Comanches' reproductive power as potential mothers of children who may have carried greater resistance to European microbes. Adolescent males, too, were highly valued because, as one observer put it, they could be made to "perform such menial service as usually pertains to squaws." "They have several Mexicans (slaves) among them," another contemporary remarked, and "make use of the boys to herd their animals." Mostly Mexican, captive women and boys became a central element of the Comanche labor system, performing tasks that the economically expanding but demographically stagnating nation could not shoulder alone.[26]

Comanches deemed adult male captives less adaptable to a new life as slaves and were less likely to try to turn them into laborers. In their slave raids in Mexico, one observer believed, "men were usually massacred on the spot, while women and small children were carried off into slavery." But if the captured men possessed special talents, Comanches readily employed them in such industries as saddle-making, gun repairing, preparation of weapons and utensils from scrap metal, and taming of feral horses. They put a special value on literate captives, who could translate intercepted dispatches and serve as interpreters in diplomatic encounters with colonial agents. They also used Mexican captives to guide raiding expeditions into colonial settlements, exploiting their intimate knowledge of geographic features and settlement patterns. George Bent believed that many captive boys, after serving as herders for several years, became "regular warriors" and as such an important addition of the Comanche raiding economy. Comanches even allowed Mexican captives to lead war parties, exploiting the enduring ties of such "peon" war leaders to Mexican peasants, whose loyalties often lay closer to Comanches than to the colonial elite: "Some of these peon war leaders had friends among the peons in Mexico, and they learned from these friends where the finest herds of horses and mules were to be found, and the movements of the Mexican troops. By making use of this information the peons often led their war parties into the heart of the Mexican settlements and made big hauls of plunder."[27]

The presence of thousands of enslaved people in Comanchería posed a daunting challenge to a noncoercive society that lacked institutionalized mechanisms to control a large unfree population. Comanches never drew a hard line between masters and slaves, and they possessed neither the necessary means to enforce unconditional submission nor a racist ideology to mentally suppress the slave population. Yet the Comanche slave system endured and expanded, largely escaping the potential hindrances of growth—social discord, escapes, and the rise of a discontented underclass. Paradoxically, Comanches were able to negotiate the pitfalls of large-scale slavery because they did not relinquish their traditional ideas of the slavery institution itself. Instead of attempting to restrain the alien people with rigid systems of control and punishment, Comanches clung to tradition and kept the slavery institution malleable. Despite its scale, vast economic importance, and emphasis on labor, Comanche slavery remained quite distinct from chattel-oriented slave systems.

While partly shading into the older, softer systems of kinship and captivity, Comanche slavery was in its essence a coercive, economically driven system of exploitation—an extension of imperial power. Most enslaved people toiled and often were overworked in horse herding, hide processing, and other labor-intensive tasks that reduced their lives to a tedious and tiring routine. "Their condition is always harder to bear than of the Patoka [Comanche] women," Victor Tixier, the French traveler, observed of captive women: "they have to perform the most disagreeable duties in the lodge." Rachel Plummer, an Anglo woman captured in Texas, remembered how robe tanning kept her "employed all the time in day-light": "Often I would have to take my buffalo skin with me, to finish it whilst I was minding the horses." Unskilled male slaves, if they escaped death upon capture, faced abuse and exploitation that amounted to symbolic emasculation. "The men prisoners are terribly maltreated," Tixier wrote. "They are made to attend the work which women alone are supposed to do. This in itself is a mark of contempt; besides, they are forced to train the horses, which are reputed untamable."[28]

All captives also went through an often brutal indoctrination phase during which they shed their former identity and, in a sense, became a socially blank slate. Comanches stripped new captives off all visible vestiges of their former life by renaming them and dressing them in Comanche clothes. They forced men to follow the Comanche practice of plucking out facial hair and made non-Native boys go naked so that their skin would turn brown. They sometimes tattooed the faces of younger captives. For most captives the first days in Comanchería were filled with horror and humiliation inflicted by beatings, whippings, mutilations, and starvation. "The lot of the [captured] women is dreadful," Berlandier wrote, "if only because the natives of their own sex amuse themselves by tormenting them, striking them at every turn for no reason at all." What to Berlandier appeared an act of wanton cruelty was in fact an elaborate transition ritual, a process of "natal alienation," which rendered the captives utterly powerless and emotionally dependent on their new masters, thereby separating them from their natal societies. To Comanches, the tortured captives were socially dead people who could be reborn as Comanches.[29]

Delivering this kind of social death could take extremely violent forms, especially if the captive was an adult male taken in a battle that had resulted in Comanche casualties. Burnet wrote how such a captive "is hurled to the [village] centre, while the shouting throng gather around in tumultuous circles, and assail him with clubs, and thongs, and knives, and javelins, and firebrands, in unmeasured and reckless fury, compelling him the while, to unite his voice with the hellish choir, to dance and sing, and wave the standard, reeking with the gory scalps of his kindred, until he sinks to the ground." But Burnet's account continues: "If haply, he survives this severe initiation, he is afterwards exempt from corporal punishment, is considered a member, *sub conditionis*, of their society, and is attached as a slave to the family of the warrior who captured him, where he is generally treated with humanity." This paradoxical statement—social membership coexisting and intertwined with slave status—encapsulates a central characteristic of the Comanche slave system. Human bondage in Comanchería was not a rigid, nonnegotiable institution, but a fluid, spacious, and inherently ambiguous social continuum that offered captives numerous roles and spaces with different degrees of freedom, privilege, and servitude.[30]

Comanches considered some slaves as alienable property, treating and trading them as commodities that could be sold, bought, or handed over as gifts. But Comanches also recognized personal slaves, blood bondsmen, who were attached to individual Comanche men through a patrimonial blood covenant. Whenever such a slave was sold, a ceremony in which blood was let from the slave's hand or arm was repeated in order to affirm the quasi-filial and patriarchal bond between the slave and his owner. As Burnet noted, Comanches had a reputation of treating their slaves with compassion, and many slaves found a measure of emotional comfort and social acceptance amidst the pain and horror of captivity. Captive women, one observer wrote, may have been "abject slaves" but they enjoyed a measure of protection against abuse. Male slaves could market their talents to secure fair treatment, and many captive women found physical and psychological shelter among Comanche women, whose affinial embrace protected them against sexual assaults through an incest taboo. Sarah Ann Horn, an Anglo-Texan captured in 1834, later described how she was informally adopted by an old widow woman who worked her hard as hide dresser but also protected her against sexual abuse. It was, Horn said, "an exception to the general character of these merciless beings, and greatly did she contribute, by her acts of kindness and soothing manners, to reconcile me to my fate." Chief Is-sa-keep (Wolf's Shoulder), spoke in 1849 of deep attachments when U.S. agents pressured him to give up his Mexican captives. The demand, the chief said, "gave him much pain."[31] Most important, slavery was not necessarily a permanent condition in Comanchería. A large portion of slaves were eventually adopted into Comanche families, which had lost members to disease, war, or other calamities. Such integrated individuals became *kwʉhʉpʉ̲s*, literally "my captive." There are no exact figures, but it is possible that only a minority of slaves remained true slaves, *tiriʔaiwapIs*.[32]

For adult women the principal avenue to adoption was marriage, which turned them into wives, mothers, and full-fledged tribal members. "Of their female captives they often make wives," Gregg noted, and a large number of secondary wives living in polygynous Comanche households in the early nineteenth century were former slaves. These wives, whether of Native or Euro-American heritage, were considered pure Comanches. Captive children were adopted into families as sons and daughters, apparently without ceremonial flourish but also "without distinction of color or nation." For girls, the line separating adoption from marriage was not always clear, because some of them were kept in households in anticipatory wifehood. When Wahawma bought Hekiyan'i, a Mexican captive, from another Comanche man, he told her, "When you grow up, you'll be my wife." For boys, age was crucial in determining their fate, as one Comanche elder, Tasúra, told ethnographers in 1933: "[we] adopted young captives into the family, [but] we made slaves of the older boys." This principle may have been determined by practicalities—the younger the boy, the easier he was to assimilate—but Euro-Americans saw deeper symbolic significance in it. Berlandier, with palpable anguish, wrote how male children captured in Texas and other frontier settlements were "raised with great care." His notions are those of a person whose expectations about Indians, Europeans, identity, and power have been violently overturned. White captive boys, he lamented, "grow up with such

12. *The Spanish Girl (A Prisoner)*. Watercolor by James Abert. This teenage girl was captured in 1841 by a young Comanche man, Little Mountain, who made her a gift to his father. From Message from the president of the United States: in compliance with a resolution of the Senate, communicating a report of an expedition led by Lieutenant Abert, on the upper Arkansas and through the country of the Camanche Indians, in the fall of the year 1845, 29th Cong, 1st sess., S. Ex. Doc. 438. Courtesy of Yale Collection of Western Americana, Beinecke Rare Book and Manuscript Library.

good [Comanche] tutors that they become so active and so evil the garrison people fear the prisoners more than the natives. . . . So thoroughly are the principles of the vagabond life inculcated in these children that, when they reach a certain age, they are the greatest enemies of the peoples of their forebears."[33]

The odds of incorporation were slim for adult males, but some were assimilated through the traditional replacement ceremony in which the captive inherited the vacant social space of a diseased Comanche. If a candidate for replacement endured and survived the kind of "severe initiation" described by Burnet, he assumed the responsibilities and obligations of the lost family member and became kin. Such replacements had both biological and emotional meaning: they restored fractured lineages and consoled bereaved relatives by assuring them of social continuity. "The prisoner adopted into the tribe recognizes as his father the man who kidnapped him and takes him as his family," Berlandier wrote. "At that moment they change their names and are treated with tenderness, as if they actually were the man who died in combat." Those grown men who were not assimilated through the replacement ritual were fated to live out their days as *tiri?aiwapIs*, common slaves and manual workers, and yet even they could find ways to enhance their cultural value. Several *tiri?aiwapIs* won social acceptance through war deeds or years of loyal service, and some eventually gained the right to marry, become Comanche, and continue their lineages. "The captives are allowed rights and privileges after they join in a battle with the tribe," Ruíz observed, "and particularly if they distinguish themselves in the campaign." He also noted that Indian captives were more likely to win social privileges than white captives, probably because they were culturally better equipped to meet Comanche expectations.[34]

Yet adoption did not remove alien status completely, and it did not lead to unconditional social acceptance. Comanches made a clear distinction between *nʉmʉ rʉboraṟʉ*, those "born of Comanche parents," and *nʉmʉnaitʉ*, those who "live as Comanche," and most adopted captives lived out their lives in a kind of social limbo where they were at once members of the society and servile laborers. Comanches used the derogatory "chore wife" for those captive women who were brought into polygynous households as wife-laborers, and they were said to have kept adopted captive children "in a kind of filial servitude." According to Tixier, "young boys are generally taken in or adopted in a fashion by a brave, whom they serve in the quality of a squire or a slave. When they grow up, they are allowed some freedom, for they cannot miss the family which they have hardly known." But even if assimilation did not erase the social stigma associated with former slave status, it did open access to such elemental social privileges as the right to marry and own property. What attached adopted slaves "most to these wandering hordes," one contemporary observed, "is the fact that they may win the right to marry. When they manage that, they lose no time in taking several wives and settling down as if they had been born to the life."[35]

This kind of soft slavery, where the line between the master and slave was mutable, had an obvious downside: since many or most slaves were eventually adopted and assimilated, Comanches had to constantly raid to acquire new captives to perform menial work and demeaning services. Slaves were a continuously evaporating resource in Comanchería, and Comanches had to invest vast amounts of time and energy in renewing that resource.

Then again, the malleability of Comanche slavery made it remarkably stable as a social institution. The fact that Comanches granted their slaves extensive privileges—including freedom—prevented slavery from becoming a socially disruptive force. There were only occasional runaways, and most slaves became productive and at least superficially content members of the society. "Spanish boys from 10 to 15 years old," Burnet wrote, "will become so reconciled to their captivity . . . as to be distinguishable only by the slight variations of nature, from their savage companions." Contemporary Euro-Americans also believed that Comanches' Creole captives "are so happy in this life that many of them have forgotten their mother tongue, have no wish to return to civilization, and loathe the villages of their families and friends." Creole captives, who undoubtedly came from the lowest rungs of colonial societies, had discovered unexpected spaces of opportunity among the Comanches and seem to have found their bondage almost liberating: "These prisoners do not return to their homes," one observer noted, "because the nomadic life and the marriages they have contracted afford them an independence they prize, not because their masters watch them so closely they cannot escape." Comanches, another observer wrote, "wisely judge" that the privilege to marry "is a powerful incentive to keep them [captives] with the tribe and thus increase its number." Although Comanches captured most of their slaves in Texas and northern Mexico, there never emerged a substratum of Spanish-Mexican discontents who could have rebelled against the regime. On the contrary, George Bent argued, the familial and emotional bonds between the Comanches and their captives ran so deep that ransomed captives often escaped and returned to Comanchería.[36]

Yet all epithets one might attach to Comanche slavery—soft, pliable, voluntary—fail to capture the full human dimensions and costs of the institution. While ascending the Canadian River to Santa Fe in 1839, Gregg encountered in a Comanche ranchería a captive Mexican boy who was "ten or twelve years old, [and] whose nationality could scarcely be detected under his Indian guise." When he learned from the boy, who still spoke Spanish, that he was from Parral,

Gregg offered to ransom him and take him back to his relatives. But the boy, hesitating a little, said "in an affecting tone" that he had become too much of a brute to live among Christians. Gregg also related the story of a Mexican woman from Matamoros who had refused to be ransomed although one thousand dollars had been offered for her freedom. "She sent word to her father, that they had disfigured her by tattooing; that she was married and perhaps *enceinte* [pregnant]; and that she would be more unhappy by returning to her father under these circumstances than by remaining where she was."[37]

Theirs was a recurring story. There must have been countless others like this boy and this woman, captive-citizens who had resolved to live their lives among the Comanches in quiet, self-imposed exile, serving people who were not their masters but not quite kin either, toiling, propagating, and dying for an empire that bred destruction in the homelands they would never see again.

Chief A Big Fat Fall by Tripping, it is told, owned fifteen hundred horses, but he was so fat that he could not ride any of them and had to be moved around on a travois. That a man so obese rose to a leadership position in a society known for its martial skills may be unexpected, but it was far from exceptional. In 1834 George Catlin encountered the Tenewa principal chief Tabequana (Sun Eagle) on the north fork of the Red River during treaty talks with the United States. He painted the chief's portrait and, fascinated, described his physical appearance in its fleshy detail: "there was a huge mass of flesh, Ta-wah-que-nah [Tabequana] . . . , who was put forward as head chief of the tribe. . . . This enormous man, whose flesh would undoubtedly weigh three hundred pounds or more, took the most wonderful strides in the exercise of his temporary authority." In 1843 representatives of the Texas government negotiated with another powerful Tenewa head chief, Pahayuko, a "large and portly" man "weighing . . . upwards of two hundred pounds with a pleasing expression of countenance, full of good humor and joviality," and six years later Captain Marcy was entertained by an unnamed Comanche chief, "a very corpulent old man," along the Red River. Tutsayatuhovit (Black Prairie Dog), the Yamparika chief who played a central role in peace talks with Kiowas in 1806, is remembered by Comanches as a man not only of "gigantic stature but also of great breadth."[38]

Rich, powerful, flamboyant, and physically striking, A Big Fat Fall by Tripping, Tabequana, Pahayuko, and Tutsayatuhovit represented the new elite men who led the Comanche society in the early nineteenth century. They were too massive to distinguish themselves in war, the traditional avenue to status and power among Plains Indian societies, but that did not prevent them from reaching the top of Comanche hierarchy. For contemporary observers like Catlin, they were

13. *Mountain of Rocks, Second Chief of the Tribe (Comanche)*. Oil on canvas by George Catlin, 1834. Courtesy of Smithsonian American Art Museum, Washington, D.C. / Art Resource, N.Y.

mere curiosities, overweight men leading a nation of physically superb warriors, but the voluminous men have more than anecdotal meaning. They embody the essence of complex changes that transformed the Comanche society during the zenith of Comanche power. Their ascendancy captures a new social reality in which material wealth and political power had become intricately intertwined and in which passivity and relaxed benevolence could bring more prestige than overt ambition and industry.

Just as the rise of Comanche hegemony was made possible by horses, so too did the new elite base its privileged position on horse wealth. An average early nineteenth-century Comanche family owned twenty to thirty horses and mules, but wealthy families—almost by rule the largest households capable of mobilizing the most labor—could possess two, three, or even ten times that number. Burnet, who gathered his knowledge about the Comanches mainly in the 1810s, wrote, "industrious and enterprising individuals will sometimes own from one to three hundred head of mules and horses, the spoils of war," and Marcy noted in the late 1840s that the "most successful horse-thieves among them own from fifty to two hundred animals." There are reports of Comanche men owning colossal herds of thousands.[39]

Comanches always considered their horses private property—their name for the animal was *puku* or *puc*, "one's personal horse"—and massive herds of horses represented a source of immense economic, political, and social capital to their owners. Horses were tools that allowed men to raid for more livestock and slaves, and they were means of production that multiplied a family's productive capacity. Men with large herds could support large extended families (*nʉmʉnahkahnis*) and several slaves, who provided supplemental labor for hunting, herding, and other household chores. Horses also provided the social currency that gave men access to women. The Comanches were a bridewealth society in which grooms were expected to compensate brides' parents with gifts. Although most men could eventually afford the favored bride-price, one or two high-quality horses, only the wealthiest men could pay the price several times over and amass a substantial labor pool of extra wives. Rich horse owners could thus invest their assets to acquire several slaves and wives to prepare robes, meat, and other tradable goods, which in turn enabled them to dominate the wealth-generating export-and-import trade. Although almost all Comanche men participated in trade, high-volume commerce was the privilege of wealthy horse owners with multiple slaves and wives.[40]

Few men became superrich, the elite of the elite. Typically senior men in their fifties, sixties, and seventies, they accumulated enough wealth to turn their *nʉmʉnahkahnis* into veritable manufactories. They had the means to purchase and adopt numerous personal slaves and *kwʉhʉpʉ̱s*, and they had several wives who not only labored themselves but could feed and care for a multitude of captive children. While most Comanche *nʉmʉnahkahnis* had one or two slaves, the wealthiest ones had several dozen. Preeminent polygynous elders also had several marriageable daughters, who attracted courting bachelors and their lavish gifts, and several sons, who hunted and raided for them. In 1849 Marcy met with an old eastern Comanche chief Is-sa-keep who explained to the captain the ingredients of his status: "He was the father of four sons, who he said were as fine young men as could be found; that they were a great source of comfort to him in his old age, and could steal more horses than any other young men in his band."[41]

Belonging to the new aristocracy meant being able to maintain large and diverse *nʉmʉnahkahnis* that included several wives, children, slaves, bondsmen, and adoptees, but it also meant being able to claim other Comanche men as social dependents. Prosperous elite men lent running mounts to horseless young men in return for a share in the bounty, in effect employing the junior men as hired hands. They also might marry their daughters to less accomplished men who paid the bride-price through labor, serving their fathers-in-law as debt bondmen, sometimes for years. If a man had several married daughters, he might have been able to stop hunting himself, because custom obliged his sons-in-law to provide him with meat even after the marriage was concluded. Blood relatives, too, were sometimes turned into quasi laborers. Wealthy, polygynous elite men were known to give one of their wives to their younger, less established brothers in return for serving the household as hunters and horse raiders.[42]

The most successful elite men could retire almost completely from physical labor, becoming something of an anomaly in what was still, in essence, a labor-intensive foraging economy. They were protocapitalists in what was essentially a noncapitalist society, spectacularly wealthy "big men" whose extensive networks of social dependents and privileged access to the means of production enabled them to have other people performing servile work for them. They could mobilize the labor of several slaves, secondary wives, and social marginals, who hunted, herded, raided, and prepared food and robes for them under coercion or in the hope of improving their prospects through the association. Indeed, they could generate more wealth by simply controlling wealth, a position of privileged leisure where physical prowess was no longer a requisite for economic success. They could leave the life of a warrior-hunter, grow fat, and carry their bulk as a marker of masculine honor and privilege. They abandoned the standard warrior costume of plain buckskin shirts and pants and publicized their rank through extravagant displays of status goods and ostentatious clothing that included colorful coats, military uniforms, trousers, neckties, and fur sashes. To manifest their control over women and labor, they cut the hair of female captives and attached it to their own. "Some of the Chiefs . . . wear in that manner the Hair of Twelve or fourteen Wives at the Same time," one observer wrote, "[their hair] hanging almost to the ground, and so thick a top smear'd over with grease & a redish Coloured Clay as a Substitute for Vermilion, that they Could Scarsely wear a Hat of Double the Ordinary Size."[43]

When men reached the status of prosperous leisure, they were in a position to amass considerable political power. Since they no longer had to prove their worth in aggressive competition with other men, they could appear indifferent about their personal status and more concerned about group welfare, a quality the Comanches thought essential for leaders. Excess wealth also allowed elite men to display another fundamental leadership virtue: generosity. Possessing several daughters and secondary wives, they could cede their claims to women to bachelors and unmarried brothers and thus help other men acquire wives. And if they were among the select few with dozens of extra horses, they could hand out animals to poorer men in exchange for political support and loyalty. Such acts of munificence can be seen as conspicuous generosity—an inverse parallel to conspicuous consumption—through which individuals publicized their social worth and superiority. At the same time, however, generous acts also promoted group solidarity and stability, earning the givers the moral authority to tell others what they ought to do.[44]

A man who gave lavishly and consistently could eventually become a *paraibo* and set up his own ranchería, which in effect was a collection of families attached to a single big man and his *nʉmʉnahkahni* through overlapping ties of generosity, dependency, loyalty, and patronage. Comanche men measured their political power not by the number of people they could command but by the extent of welfare networks they could support. Comanche rancherías were generally identified by the names of their leading men, who held the communities together through their welfare practices. The most powerful *paraibos* could persuade others to attach their rancherías to theirs and accept subordinate roles as secondary leaders—or, as Spaniards called them, *capitanes chiquitos.* For example, the celebrated Ecueracapa led a band of 157 lodges, probably some 1,500 people, which was a composite village of several rancherías, and the powerful Tenewa chief Paruakevitsi had three secondary chiefs in his ranchería.[45]

If the leaders of large rancherías formed the upper echelon of the Comanche society, the bottom end consisted of young men with few or no horses. The building of a substantial herd was a slow and grueling process, and most men spent several years in this lowly position. Like most foraging societies, Comanches put high value on individual self-reliance and expected young men to make their own fortunes; even the sons of elite men had to devote years to livestock raiding, because it was considered inappropriate for young men to ask their fathers to provide them with horses. And raiding did not offer junior men such a fast track to wealth and status as one might assume. Communal norms dictated that the senior men who led war parties had the first pick of the booty; younger men were fortunate to score a few low-quality horses. Moreover, young men frequently gave away all or most of their captured horses to the parents of a potential bride in the hope of earning the right to begin courtship. Successful raiders were pressured to give a portion of their plunder to unmarried women in the Shakedown Dance, and some young men repeatedly gave away all their captured horses to publicize their prowess and self-confidence as raiders.[46]

The lack of horses excluded young men from key activities that brought men wealth, respect, and status. They had to borrow animals from senior men and pay them with a portion of the kill or plunder, which in turn prevented them from accruing surplus animals and robes for exchange purposes. High-quality guns, metal tools, blankets, and other imported goods were all but inaccessible to them. Marriage, too, was but a distant prospect. Not only had the escalation of polygyny diminished the pool of potential wives, but junior men lacked the horses with which to pay the bride-price. Poor and prospectless, they were undesirable to adolescent unmarried girls and their fathers, who were acutely aware of the burdens of wifehood and carefully weighed their options before agreeing to a marriage. Negotiating the delicate balance between emotions and interests, many unattached Comanche women viewed marriage as a vehicle for social mobility and shunned less established suitors.[47]

Excluded from marriage, horseless and horse-poor young men found their route to full social enfranchisement severely compromised. Comanches saw marriage as both the symbol of and the path to masculine honor, the confirmation of a man's ability to claim women and defend his claim against other men, and unmarried men, *tuibihtsiʔs*, fell outside that circle of respect. Spaniards called them *gandules* (loafers) since they lived in all-male gangs on the outskirts of rancherías, sleeping in makeshift shelters, subsisting on small animals, and serving wealthy senior men as hunters and raiders. Many Comanche men spent more than a decade in this kind of intermediate social place, struggling to accumulate enough horses to acquire a wife and support a family: while most women married in their midteens, men typically did not do so until their late twenties. Underprivileged, needy, and ambitious, the *tuibihtsiʔs* formed a pool of readily available laborers whose exploitation allowed the elite to expand its herds and wealth.[48]

Between these two extremes was a large segment of middling sorts, the families of early middle-aged men who had acquired enough horses to be considered secure if not quite rich. These men owned enough running horses for hunting and raiding and enough pack animals to put a large family on horseback. A small reserve of surplus animals enabled them to participate in the wealth-generating export-import trade and announce themselves as potential heads of large polygynous households. Enjoying the prestige of full manhood that came with marriage, they distanced themselves from the unmarried men and emulated the lifestyle of the elite. Although they could not retire entirely from active labor, their wives' labor allowed them to specialize in hunting and raiding. It was such men Captain Marcy described when he wrote about a "prairie warrior [who] performs no menial labor; his only occupation is in war and the chase. His wives, who are but little dearer to him than his horse, perform all the drudgery. He follows the chase, he smokes his pipe, he eats and sleeps; and thus he passes his time, and in his own estimation he is the most lordly and independent sovereign in the universe." But the social clout of these men had its limits. While enjoying the prestige and personal autonomy that came with marriage, the men of the middle layer were outranked and outpowered by the senior elite men who possessed several wives and dependents, dominated the marriage market as wife-givers, and monopolized leadership positions.[49]

By the beginning of the nineteenth century, the injection of privately owned horse and human wealth had turned the Comanches into a stratified society with pronounced distinctions in prestige and privilege among individuals and families. Wealth, status, and power had become conflated, giving rise to widening inequalities organized around age, marriage, and uneven access to women and labor. Yet those social cleavages never coagulated into a rigid class society with formalized ranks. The Comanche society had become more hierarchical, but it retained its traditional flexibility, which reduced the social distance between the elite and commoners and militated against a fully developed class system. This was the result of several factors, the chief one being a persisting, age-old individualistic mentality, the belief that each man and woman had to prove his or her moral worth through personal achievement. Although there were instances of sons following fathers as *paraibos*—the two Cuerno Verdes in the late eighteenth century being the most famous example of this—the general attitude was that positions of privilege had to be earned, not inherited. Comanche big men were self-made men who were not born into wealth and power but gradually emerged from the masses. As one observer concluded, "Each man endeavors to obtain as high a position as their merits allow."[50]

These meritocratic elements went hand in hand with the belief that a man's status was not fixed but forever contestable. A Comanche man had to reaffirm his standing and manhood again and again in relation to other men, which made social standing a matter of unending negotiation. The social ladder on which men moved up or down as their personal fortunes and reputations ebbed and flowed was not fixed, keeping the avenues for upward mobility open. Those avenues were available even to former slaves: there was no glass ceiling for *nʉmʉnaitʉs*. The adopted slaves may have carried the social stigma of not being born Comanche, but there were no institutional hindrances to prevent them from engaging in horse raiding, accumulating property, and obtaining several wives and even slaves of their own.[51]

This dual nature of the Comanche society, its deepening segmentation and its persistent plasticity, fueled fierce social competition. The opportunities for dramatic social ascent together with the ever-present danger of social descent pitted men of different age and status groups against each other. Comanche men, especially unmarried junior men who had not yet distinguished themselves in battle, were extremely sensitive about their standing and eager to improve their position over other men, whom they by necessity viewed as rivals. The society could support only so many privileged positions, and there was a large pool of marginalized individuals, men who did not enjoy full social acceptance. Operating within the open parameters of fulfillment and failure, young Comanche men were culturally conditioned to be ambitious, aggressive, and competitive.

The competition took many forms. An upwardly aspiring lower-status man might steal or wound the horse of a senior man or seduce one of his wives. Although technically illicit, such actions were common enough: later ethnographers learned that Comanches had developed a standardized procedure for resolving disputes involving cuckolding, horse theft, and horse wounding. Since Comanches expected senior men to be dignified, composed, and willing to overlook insults, an aggrieved individual could not rely on overt violence without losing face. He could punish his adulterous wife by mutilating or killing her without suffering personal shame, but he was expected to prosecute the male offender and demand *nanʉwokʉ*, material compensation that was usually paid in horses, mules, or guns. In most cases, the offender agreed to pay and the matter was settled. All this was structured and predictable, which suggests that Comanches tolerated face challenging as a pressure-releasing mechanism that offered lower-status men an alternative way to distinguish themselves. The act of challenging was a social performance, a dramatization of status concerns that allowed the less privileged members of the Comanche society to manage their emotions and social lives. Face challenging temporarily reversed the prevailing social hierarchy, relieving the tensions and psychological stress resulting from growing inequality, while the *nanʉwokʉ* symbolically reaffirmed the social order based on clearly defined roles for senior and junior men.[52]

The main arena for social competition, however, was the battlefield. Senior elite men could effectively withdraw from war, but a military career remained the most effective vehicle for social ascent for young men. By distinguishing themselves in combat—by earning recognition as *tekwʉ̱niwapi̱s* (braves)—junior men gained symbolic capital that brought them honor, and by seizing horses and slaves they gathered tangible capital that gave them access to women and moved them closer to full social enfranchisement. For young men, Marcy noted, a military career was a prerequisite for any kind of social recognition: "a young man who has not made one or more of these [raiding] expeditions into Mexico is held in but little repute."[53]

Comanches actively encouraged young men to be competitive in war. They valued selflessness in their elders but expected junior men to be preoccupied with proving themselves as warriors. Like most Plains Indian societies, Comanches had an institutionalized procedure for recognizing and ranking war honors: the counting of coup, which endorsed such daring military acts as hand-to-hand combat and killing at close range. Coup points accelerated a man's social rise by serving as a public announcement of his military prowess and of his potential value as a husband and provider, and they constituted a strong incentive for young men to prove themselves in battle. Military feats could even serve as a shortcut to marriage. Fathers, one contemporary reported, sometimes gave one of their daughters to a distinguished warrior, apparently without asking the bride-price.[54]

The preparations for war culminated in elaborate dancing and singing rituals in which older men formed a firm, unified front to exploit younger men's social insecurities and competitive instincts. "The ones on foot walk in two single files forming a long street," Ruíz reported. "The chiefs march down the middle with their best warriors and children in their finest attire. . . . Old men who have been brave warriors in their youth ride on the outside of the single line formation and relate their past deeds in a loud voice, advising the younger men to die rather than commit an act of cowardice." Rights to women, the ultimate measure of masculine honor, figured prominently in these rituals of war. Older men, Ruíz wrote, "urge young women to marry only those who are brave and courageous in battle and to spurn the cowardly warrior. Thus the elders continue haranguing the assembly and to wander through the camp."[55]

The ambition and insecurity of young men in the face of these social pressures help explain one of the most spectacular manifestations of the Comanche military culture—the Lobos. The Lobos was an elite society consisting of prominent warriors who had designated military duties and distinctive regalia and ceremonies and who were willing to take extreme risks in battle. The members, in Ruíz's words, marched separately, wearing "profuse adornments which only they can use, including wolf-skin belts which reach to the ground. . . . The Lobos are not allowed to retreat from the scene of the battle, not even when they are vastly outnumbered. It is their duty to die rather than surrender their ground, although the other warriors may be in full retreat." A successful member of the society enjoyed great respect as well as privileged access to women. "When they return victorious from a campaign," one observer noted, "impromptu dances are begun to which only the unmarried girls are invited, with orders to comply with every desire of the victorious warriors."[56]

Comanche cultural norms, then, supported a highly structured and competitive warrior cult, which drove young men to take extreme risks in order to achieve social acceptance. It is always tricky to read deliberate planning into

14. *Western Comanches in War Dress.* Watercolor by Lino Sánchez y Tapia, ca. 1836. The Comanche military complex was fueled by a fierce competition among young men for horses, women, status, and masculine honor. Many warriors wore headdresses plaited together from the hair of their wives and captives. Courtesy of Gilcrease Museum, Tulsa, Oklahoma.

cultural traditions and social rituals, but in the case of the Comanche warrior cult, strategic intention seems plausible. By stressing fighting prowess as a measure of a man's social worth, the warrior cult deemphasized the significance of status challenging as an avenue for social ascent and helped direct the disruptive effects of male rivalry outside the Comanche community and against enemy groups. If Captain Marcy was correct in noting that young Comanche men's "only ambition consists in being able to cope successfully with . . . [their] enemy in war,"[57] it was not because they were inherently violent but because they were desperate to cross the social fault lines from bachelorship to marriage, poverty to prosperity, and drudgery to leisure. They were fixated on war so that some day, perhaps, they no longer would have to fight.

Reconstructing this competitive social dynamic illuminates the conditions and pressures under which the nineteenth-century Comanches matured, married, had children, and sought personal fulfillment, but the social dynamic has broader implications as well: within it can be found a fundamental cause of the rise and continued expansion of the Comanche empire. If there was an all-embracing internal force behind the rise of the Comanche empire, it was the relentless competition for social prestige among Comanche men. Violent seizure of livestock and captives through pillage represented for men the main path to social acceptance: it gave them access to wealth and women and lifted them toward full manhood. For Comanche men, raiding was a matter of social life and death, and it was that mixture of anxiety and raw ambition that pushed them to repeatedly risk life for loot, devote much of their lives in arduous raiding, and travel hundreds of miles into Mexico to find fresh opportunities for plundering. Comanches embraced battle and built vast hinterlands for raiding because their nation needed pasturelands, buffer zones, slaves, commodities, and commerce, but they did so also because their young men needed to prove their worth as providers and husbands.

Individual status competition and large-scale raiding were closely interwoven in the Comanche society, but that does not mean that the Comanche raiding industry was a mere reflection of raw individual ambition, a blind social impulse. Status competition among men served as a potent engine for violent external action, but its thrust was checked and controlled by overarching political institutions that gave direction to Comanche foreign policy. Comanches never developed a unitary, statelike decision-making system, but their evolving political structures were powerful enough to harness young men's competitive urges for the greater national good and cohesive enough to incorporate the raiding economy into a coordinated diplomatic and military policy. This was as much a psychological process as it was a political one, involving a creative and sometimes uneasy dialogue between individual self-interest and group solidarity, and it takes us to the very core of the polity that built the most enduring empire in the colonial Southwest.

The basic political unit among the Comanches was the ranchería, a network of related and allied extended families. A product of compelling economic, ecological, and political forces, the ranchería was agile enough to pursue the migratory bison herds, small enough not to exhaust local pastures with its domestic herds, and large enough to organize local defenses. Rancherías operated in many ways as independent political units, making autonomous decisions about camp movements, residence patterns, and small-scale trading and raiding. The ranchería was the primary social group with which people identified, although individuals and families moved between local bands. Most marriages took place within rancherías, and the married couple usually lived in the husband's lodge near his parents.[58]

Rancherías were held together by interlaced affinial ties and led jointly by *paraibos* and councils of adult men. Rancherías did not choose their *paraibos* in formal elections but instead gradually acknowledged the person who exhibited the ideal attributes of a leader. Comanches placed great value on social face and determined a person's moral worth by his or her ability to adhere to common codes of conduct. Ideally, a *paraibo* had demonstrated his diplomatic skills in action, had amassed a personal fortune, and had given chunks of that fortune away. Wealth, if managed in a socially acceptable way, formed an effective path to leadership, and a successful *paraibo* gave more than other men. He cultivated patriarchal relationships with his followers, pooling resources at times of need, and his generosity attached other family headmen to his household as socially indebted *haits* (formal friends) or *tʉbitsinahaitsInʉʉs* (true friends). A successful *paraibo*, in short, understood the social arithmetic of wealth: when hoarded, it divided people; when given away, it drew them together. "From the liberality with which they dispose of their effects on all occasions of the kind," Indian Agent Robert S. Neighbors wrote of Comanche big men, "it would induce the belief that they acquire property merely for the purpose of giving it to others."[59]

Comanche rancherías were close-knit communities bound by intimate and intertwined kinship linkages, but their leadership patterns were strikingly fluid and diffuse. "The authority of their chiefs is rather nominal than positive, more advisory than compulsive," Burnet concluded in the early nineteenth century. *Paraibos* certainly appeared powerful. Most of them had personal heralds, who announced their decisions to the camp, and some kept a staff of young men as aides and bodyguards. Yet their formal power was always limited. *Paraibos* mediated rather than disciplined, and they led more by example than by giving orders. They held the ranchería together by arbitrating disputes, but they did not have the right to judge or hand out verdicts. They used their dense ecological knowledge to decide when and where the camp was moved, thus safeguarding the group's ecological viability, and their *puha*, medicine power, shielded the ranchería against disease, hunger, and strife. Yet they could not force their followers to stay in the ranchería: any man unhappy with his *paraibo* simply moved to another band. And if the number of malcontents exceeded a critical level, the *paraibo* himself was removed. Should a chief "disgrace himself by any act of cowardice or mal-administration," Marcy wrote, "[his followers] do not hesitate to depose him and place a more competent man in his stead." To the commissioner of Indian affairs of the Republic of Texas, the Comanches were "the most perfect democracy on the face of the globe; everything is managed by primary assemblies, and the people have a right to displace a chief and elect a successor at pleasure."[60]

But *paraibos* were not leaders without authority. One setting where they exercised considerable power was the band council, which dealt with matters like bandwide military campaigns, disposition of spoils derived from large-scale operations, the time and place of summer hunts, and community religious services. All grown men were allowed to participate and speak in councils, but the meetings were dominated by *paraibos*, who typically sponsored the councils in their tipis and cautiously choreographed the proceedings. As Ruíz noted: "The Chief takes the principal seat, and sends the crier to give notice [to] all the warriours to come to the council of the pipe. . . . A Sentinel is placed at the door and they come to the door one at a time one and say 'here I am, what seat shall I occupy?' The answer is given by the Chief, on the right or left, as the case may be and he enters and seats himself accordingly[,] each one as he enters divesting himself of the ornaments and clothing he wears and depositing them in enclosure in the back part of the tent."[61]

By having personal ornaments removed, the councils downplayed self-aggrandizement and stressed social harmony. They always sought consensus, gearing their decisions as close to prevailing public sentiments as possible. Yet in practice the consensuses were often narrow, involving only *paraibos* and few senior men whose families and interests were closely linked. The majority of men had little influence on policy making. "After the elders had stated their views," ethnological accounts relate, "middle-aged men expressed theirs, and even younger men might speak a few words." Generational tensions were palpable. Marcy wrote that elders used the councils as a mechanism to "curb the impetuosity of ambitious young warriors," and the representatives of the Texas Republic noted in 1845 tangible frustration among young Comanche warriors. Chief Mopechucope, one official reported, counseled the young men toward reconciliation, asking "each and singly if they were for peace. Some of them replied that it was a matter of very little consequence whether they were or not as they should abide by the advice of the old men." And yet, as oral histories assert, junior men regarded council decisions as "sacrosanct." They may have obeyed the councils "more from fear of arousing the anger of their chiefs and the displeasure of the supernatural powers" than from abstract notions of political obedience, but the effect was the same: *paraibos* and their supporters dominated rancherías and their diplomatic and military affairs.[62]

Paraibos also dominated the economically essential but socially sensitive arena of foreign trade. Like the leaders of other firmly structured Native societies of the plains, they possessed a culturally sanctioned power to determine when, where, and how trading took place and what was exchanged and at what prices. When a foreign trading party arrived in a Comanche ranchería, the leader was taken to the *paraibo's* lodge where, according to M. C. Fisher, the chief "receives him as his guest, and commands his squaws to unpack his ponies, and convey all his goods, blankets, and cooking kit to the lodge set apart for his reception." This practice allowed *paraibos* to examine the visitors' wares and place them under their personal protection. The next phase involved feasting, smoking, and gift exchanges, which helped transform the visitors into metaphorical kin. *Paraibos* typically accepted pretrade presents and then redistributed them among their followers, a privilege that earned them great prestige. Finally, *paraibos* agreed on the list of tradable goods and negotiated prices. They then announced the visitors to the camp, thereby authorizing the trade. If things followed the proper protocol, the exchange itself was a mere formality. "In Comanche trade," Gregg wrote, "the main trouble consists in fixing the price of the first animal. This being settled by the chiefs, it often happens that mule after mule is led up and the price received without further cavil."[63]

Paraibos thus acted as brokers and buffers between their followers and foreigners, regulating the social space in which goods exchanged hands. By personally supervising pretrade negotiations, they were able to eliminate attempts by Euro-American traders to push up prices and preserve their rancherías' bargaining power. *Paraibos* also managed to block the introduction of alcohol into their rancherías through the simple measure of confining pretrade talks to their lodges, where they invariably banished the liquor from lists of authorized goods. Since foreign traders had little or no contact with their Comanche clientele until the actual barter commenced, they were unable to incorporate that dependency-inducing commodity to the exchange. The Comanches, like the Pawnees whose chiefs exercised similar control over foreign trade, remained an exceptionally temperate people well into the late nineteenth century.[64]

In a similar manner, *paraibos* controlled their own followers during fairs to provide a safe environment for foreign traders. If necessary, they relied on violence, whipping and intimidating dissidents into obedience. Thomas James's experiences are again revealing. When young Comanche men stole some of his horses, James informed the *paraibo* who had adopted him as brother. The chief immediately "mounted his horse, with whip in hand, and in about two hours returned with two of the stolen horses. In the afternoon he brought back a third, and at night came up with the fourth." His leadership challenged, the chief reasserted his authority with fury: "His whip was bloody, and his face distorted with rage. He was in a mood to make men tremble before him." "After he had left the last horse with me," the relieved James recalled, "I heard his voice in every part of the camp, proclaiming what the interpreter told me was a warning for the protection of my property. 'Your horses are yours,' said he, 'to sell or keep as you please.'"[65]

If trading was a structured, top-down-controlled activity among the Comanches, so too was raiding. Ambitious underprivileged young men might launch unsanctioned forays, defying *paraibos* and elders, and powerful senior warriors who felt confined by consensus policies sometimes struck out on their own and set up raiding-oriented rancherías with discontented junior men. But such incidents were exceptional. Comanche raiding resembled an industry in terms of scale, and it resembled an industry also in terms of organization: it was an institution run by many and managed by few. Although in theory any man with a reputable war record could lead a war party, in practice only a few senior men possessed sufficient personal clout to launch a major expedition. Some *paraibos* acted as war leaders themselves, but most relinquished large-scale raiding operations to specialized war chiefs, *mahimiana paraibos*, usually early middle-aged men whose renowned military records enabled them to recruit numerous followers. War chiefs had nearly absolute authority over the campaigns they led. They determined the objectives of the raid, assigned roles to the members of the party, planned the attack, and decided how the plunder was distributed. Under their leadership, raiding parties—which often included hundreds of men and women—operated as autonomous political entities, following their own agendas during their temporary existence.[66]

All this was profoundly puzzling to the colonial agents cowering near Comanchería's borders. The same *paraibos* who acted as virtual autocrats in diplomatic and exchange settings seemed curiously weak in, or even excluded from, warfare and raiding. Colonial officials took this as a sign of political disorder, deriding the "impotent authority" and worthlessness of Comanche leaders, but it is possible that Comanches deliberately cultivated the power dichotomy for political purposes. Comanches' principal foreign political challenge in the late eighteenth and early nineteenth centuries was not steering all their compatriots behind unified policies of peace and war but rather finding ways to organize composite policies of raiding, trading, and tribute extraction. The dual leadership of civil and war chiefs facilitated that effort.

Comanches founded their raiding-trading-tribute policy on raw military power and the threat of violence, but the policy also had a more abstract political dimension. The arrangement by which *paraibos* controlled trade and diplomacy but seldom interfered with raiding gave Comanches tremendous maneuvering space, allowing them to keep their strategic options open. When colonial officials confronted *paraibos* about raids and pressured them to honor existing peace agreements, the chiefs routinely excused themselves by claiming an inability to restrain the warriors and their leaders. Colonial authorities pressured, pleaded, and scolded the *paraibos* but rarely blamed them for outright treachery or cancelled their trading and gifting privileges because, as the *paraibos* themselves were ready to point out, their inability to curb the raids stemmed from institutional restrictions, not from personal choice.

Governor Tomás Vélez de Cachupín despaired over this kind of maneuvering in 1750, when, in the midst of one of the first Comanche raiding sprees in New Mexico, he chastised the supposedly peaceful *paraibos* over their followers' raiding activities. The chiefs evaded the accusations "by blaming others of their nation, saying that among them are warlike captains who commit these outrages and those who are well disposed are unable to prevent them." Cachupín, in a fateful precedent, grudgingly accepted the explanation and allowed trading and gifting to continue even as raiding raged on. Almost a century later, David G. Burnet, the former president of the Republic of Texas, shared Cachupín's frustration with the dual leadership: "One captain will lead his willing followers to robbery and carnage, while another, and perhaps the big chief of all, will eschew the foray, and profess friendship for the victims of the assault." Other observers remarked how Comanche chiefs excused themselves from responsibility by insisting that their followers moved freely between rancherías and were therefore beyond their authority, and still others openly blamed the chiefs for deceit. G. W. Bonnell, the commissioner of Indian affairs of the Republic of Texas, wrote how Comanche chiefs entered into endless little treaties with Mexico only to "*get presents*, and throw their enemies off their guard, and give them a better opportunity of committing acts of rapine and plunder." U.S. Army officer H. G. Catlett reported likewise in 1849: Comanche *paraibos* sometimes returned stolen horses to Texas "but evidently as a mere blind to hide their duplicity." As these disillusioned officers saw it, *paraibos*' image of powerlessness was a subterfuge aimed at confusing colonial agents and keeping the avenues of exchange open in the midst of pillaging and violence.[67]

Bonnell's and Catlett's helpless exasperation was familiar to countless colonial officials in the Southwest, who failed to comprehend and contain the Comanches. Comanches deflected the controlling gaze of colonial agents through their traditional political culture in which power was dichotomized, leaders could be both strong and weak, and group membership was flexible. A vast collection of relatively autonomous bands organized for multipolarity and fluidity, the Comanche nation appeared formidable and fragmented, structured and shapeless, incomprehensible and impregnable all at once. Seen from the outside, the Comanche nation was an amorphous entity that lacked a clear center to negotiate with—or obliterate—and an explicit internal structure that would have rendered its external actions predictable. The Comanches, it seems, were so domineering not in spite of their informal, almost atomistic social organization but because of it.

The diffuse social structure, so crucial for Comanches' composite foreign policy, could also be a liability. The deepening social fission, the fact that Comanches lived in and identified with numerous local rancherías, inevitably eroded the sense of common identity, threatening to dissolve their nation into a collage of isolated, self-contained fragments. This danger became acute in the early nineteenth century, when Comanches consolidated their hegemony over the lower midcontinent. The key components of their power complex—the multifaceted trade and alliance network, the expanding hinterlands of pillage and piracy, the maintenance of tributary client states—demanded centralized planning and governing. To both realize and survive their rise to imperial dominance, it therefore became necessary for Comanches to find ways to bind the scattered pieces of their nation into a more coherent political entity. This necessity spawned the Comanche confederacy.

The Comanche confederacy was not a corporate polity—it had no charter, no standing army, and no supreme ruler—but rather a cyclic arrangement that periodically brought together the many units of the Comanche community. It can be visualized as a recurring political process whereby local and divisional headmen came together in interdivisional councils to discuss common concerns, to offset the perils of social fragmentation, and to express and reinforce their sense of national unity. Such macrolevel councils had been part of the Comanche political organization at least since the mid-eighteenth century, but they seem to have gained new meaning and importance during the Comanches' post-1800 ascendancy. Although sporadic, the divisional and interdivisional meetings provided an arena for national cooperation and a mechanism for the numerous rancherías to share the burdens and fruits of expansion.[68]

The macrolevel meetings sprang from the inherent mobility of the Comanche nation. In their constant search for pasture, water, shelter, and game, Comanche rancherías tended to gravitate from Comanchería's outer reaches toward its center, where winters were relatively mild and manageable for horses and where the bison congregated to mate in late summer. Although rancherías and divisions had distinct geographical identities, Comanches regarded Comanchería as a common domain available to all. "The utmost harmony subsists between these several bands," Burnet observed. "They have no distinct limits assigned them, neither does one party claim, in relation to another, any exclusive sovereignty over the particular section of country which custom seems to have appropriated to its more special use and occupancy." He noted how the Yamparikas "frequently intermingle with, and are found among the Comanchees [eastern Comanches]," and how the Tenewas "often mingle with the Yamparacks when traversing the southern extreme of their range."[69]

Most multidivisional assemblies took place within and around a small zone bounded by three elevations—the Medicine Mounds, a line of four conical hills in northwestern Texas; the Wichita Mountains, a sixty-mile-long mountain range two days' ride northeast from the Medicine Mounds; and the Caprock Escarpment, a steep, rugged canyon face that separates the Llano Estacado uplands from the Texas plains below. This sphere was a sacred space where Comanches from all rancherías and divisions met and melded. (Sometimes the allies of the Comanche nation also participated.) Designated police societies—apparently a post-1800 innovation—maintained order in the massive camps where thousands of people hunted, feasted, danced, and sought medicine powers together for weeks. They exchanged goods and information, reinforcing the idea of Comanchería as a single economic area, and they married across divisional lines, forging kinship networks that flowed from the upper Arkansas valley to the south Texas plains. Tracing their lineage to two or more divisions, many prominent Comanche leaders were living proofs of such crosscutting alliances.[70]

The gatherings culminated in large political councils, where vital domestic, diplomatic, and military matters could be introduced to a central forum. The assembled rancherías decided on treaties, trading privileges, and major offensive and defensive campaigns and elected principal chiefs to represent them in diplomatic dealings with outsiders. And while delegating power, the councils also controlled its use. They were occasions of social regulation where the policies of local and divisional leaders were exposed to public sanction: any *paraibo* or principal chief whose actions did not meet collective approval was bound to lose social face, followers, and influence.[71]

The grand councils were massive, ordered, hierarchical, and democratic all at once. They could have hundreds of participants organized into several concentric circles, women and unmarried junior men occupying the far perimeter, the prominent elders sitting next to the center stage, and principal chiefs guiding the proceedings, ensuring that rituals and protocols were honored. "In order to transact an important business or receive any important communication from an other tribe," one observer reported in 1836, "the principal chief always convokes the lesser ones in his tribe to meet in general councel when each occupies the seat corresponding to his grade, and after many Ceremonies peculiar to themselves on such occasions, the tobacco pipe is introduced into the assembly, and after passing around, & each taking a 'Whiff' the object for calling the convention is made known by the principal chief. . . . The results of the counsel are proclaimed to all the tribe by order of the princip[al] chief through the medium of a person called 'Talolero,' (orator) appointed then for the purpose."[72]

In the end, however, the role of principal chiefs was more ceremonial than authoritative. Vested with little formal (or nonconsensual) power, they were spokespeople who articulated common interests in diplomacy, defense, exchange, and war. Once the agenda of a meeting was identified, the grand council began deliberations to build consensus. If consensus proved elusive, the council sometimes split into numerous informal councils where the *paraibos* and elders of assembled rancherías met and mingled to find a compromise. When an agreement was reached, the principal chief introduced it to the council, exposing it to public criticism and formal approval or rejection. In this sense, the grand councils were open political arenas that helped legitimize policies in the eyes of the masses. Principal chiefs had little room to maneuver outside such publicly sanctioned policies. In 1843, for example, the representatives of the Texas Republic lavished Tenewa head chief Pahayuko with presents in the hope of persuading him to sign a treaty of nonaggression, but Pahayuko declared that no such treaty was possible without consulting the other leaders of his division. All Tenewa *paraibos* had to be heard, he told the frustrated officials, so "that there may be no lies spoken on my side."[73]

Multidivisional political cooperation both promoted and was made possible by a common culture and worldview. Regardless of divisional background, all Comanches shared certain core ideals about proper social and political organization; they all knew, for example, that wealth had social meaning only when given away, that power meant giving advice rather than orders, and that individual social existence was defined by an ever-widening range of kinship obligations. The Comanches also shared a collective legal culture, an informal system of private law that recognized universal wrongs and sanctions and allowed individuals to seek retribution across band and divisional lines. There was, in short, a proper way of being a Comanche, a set of beliefs and behaviors through which Comanches ordered their knowledge of the world and themselves. "Notwithstanding the extreme laxity of their whole economy of government, and their entire exemption from [formal] legal restraint," Burnet wrote, "they live together with a degree of harmony that would do credit to the most refined and best organized societies."[74]

Along with shared social, political, and legal practices and sensibilities, the Comanches found a common cultural ground in religion. Early ethnographers described Comanche beliefs and religious practices as "vaguely defined and almost wholly devoid of ceremonial structure" and portrayed Comanches as a people "with little interest in building a coherent corpus of belief." But more recent studies have shown that underneath the varied local ritualism there was a structured religious core. The Comanche life cycle was punctuated with rituals common to all rancherías and divisions. The reliance on *puha* cut through the community, and members of all rancherías sought visions, trained their extrasensory skills, and visited graves of powerful individuals in order to become *puhakatʉs*, "possessors of power." There were recognized dance, medicine, and military societies—some of which had been "captured" from other nations in war—which shared *puha* and drew members, both men and women, from several divisions. The bonds that such societies generated among their members rivaled biological bonds in depth and durability.[75]

In the end, regardless of their band or divisional affiliation, all Comanches were children of the sun. During his prolonged exile among the Comanches, Ruíz wrote extensively of their uniform, sun-centered religion: "The whole Comanche nation believes in the existence of a supreme being which is the sun. They call it the 'father of the universe.' All their religious rites center around the worship of the sun. The doors of their homes or tents face east so that the rising sun can shine upon them and they can adore it. . . . The earth is considered by them the mother of all living beings and the sustained force aided by the sun, which in turn keeps them warm. It is believed that the sun can see everything 'from the outside.' If a Comanche wants to be believed by his peers, he calls the sun and the earth as witness in an oath." Multidivisional meetings often climaxed in the Sun Dance ceremony, which reflected the inclusive, integrated nature of the Comanche society: Comanches had borrowed many songs and dances for their ceremony from other nations. Such collective beliefs and religious institutions were both the prerequisite for and the product of a sustained communitywide interaction. Every time the Comanches congregated at the Medicine Mounds and other sacred sites, they realized their nation anew, reaffirming their sense of themselves as one people, the Numunu, who shared similar views on cosmology, human responsibilities, and good society.[76]

This sense of unity and belonging made an impression on Euro-American observers like Manuel Merino, who in 1804 remarked that the Comanche divisions "form a close union" and "share a common destiny." Burnet, writing more than forty years later, noted that the Comanches fell into several divisions but were "essentially one people: [they] speak the same language, and have the same peculiar habits, and the same tribal interests." Conflict with one Comanche division, he warned U.S. policymakers, "would involve a conflict with all; for the Comanche, the lower party, if pressed, would retire to, and coalesce with, their kindred, who would adopt the quarrel without an inquiry into its justice or expediency." Mirroring Burnet, Agent Neighbors wrote that the Comanches "appear to have a strong connecting link in the similarity of habits and language, and frequently they unite in war or council." Neighbors's brief remark makes an essential distinction. More than symbolic venues to act out a collective identity, joint councils formed a political mechanism that steered the many components of the Comanche nation into a common orbit, interlocking them into a political confederacy capable of projecting a unified front to rivals and allies.[77]

That unity was realized most tangibly in war. The ubiquity of Comanches' hit-and-run stock and slave raiding on colonial frontiers has obscured the fact that they waged many national wars that typically stemmed from territorial disputes over hunting and grazing privileges and frequently involved wholesale killing and destruction. Kinship responsibilities, the obligation to avenge slain relatives and protect live ones, activated such wars and sometimes propagated them for generations. "Their fathers inculcate the ideal of vengeance in them from their tenderest infancy," Berlandier noted. "They are so thoroughly accustomed to the violence of this passion that they constantly invoke it to incite their compatriots to arms." When outsiders killed their members, Comanches' response was decisive, ritualized, and collective. As Ruíz realized, organizing a large multiband military campaign was essentially a matter of invoking the pity of the maximum number of local leaders and then mustering their respective kinship networks for war: "The Comanches are ready to avenge the death of one of their warriors. They [the relatives of slain warrior] ride into Indian camps . . . crying, and urge the dwellers to follow them. . . . Each chief who agrees to participate in the raid invites all his relatives to go along with him."[78]

If private revenge campaigns of kinship groups kept escalating through repeated cycles of retribution, violence could reach a tip-off point and become a full-scale war involving entire Comanche divisions and their non-Comanche allies. When this happened, Berlandier wrote, the war became the matter of the confederacy and its coordinating mechanisms: "When the war is a general one, with the entire people gathered in tribes to go on the warpath, public authority intervenes. The chiefs assemble in council, and the old men are admitted to provide the lessons they have learned in their long experience. There the whole matter is discussed with sagacity and prudence, and the advantages and disadvantages of each course of action carefully weighed. If the decision is for war, the rallying points are first established, then the strategy and tactics to be used against the enemy in all foreseeable circumstances." In such national campaigns—which often included several thousand warriors—Comanches employed a rigid if temporary command structure: "On these great expeditions involving whole peoples," Berlandier wrote, "the most experienced captains from each tribe are put in command. . . . Despite the fact that tribal chieftains may and do take part in such excursions, they must obey the temporary chief in all matters pertaining to the war for the entire duration of the campaign." Such centrally orchestrated and commanded campaigns were the military backbone of the Comanche empire and ranged from Pawnee country on the central plains and the Osage border on the southern prairies deep into Mexico.[79]

Large-scale campaigns were bracketed by elaborate ceremonies that fostered collective ethos and turned the assembled bands into a temporary army. Pan-Comanche campaigns began with war councils where participating rancherías selected leaders and scouts, agreed on goals and strategy, and exchanged pledges of mutual help. The Lobos and other warrior societies played a central role in these councils, maintaining order, evoking martial ethos through war dances, and providing a sense of cohesion though membership that transcended divisional boundaries. Each step was shrouded in rituals of kinship, honor, and retribution. "When another rancheria arrives" at a designated rallying point, one contemporary wrote, "the captain and the warriors of the tribe, bedecked with feathers and covered with their war ornaments, mount their horses and form two lines, in which formation they make a tour of the camps of those who have already arrived, singing as they go. . . . The host tribe replies to this visit with a ceremony of the same sort, and this scene is repeated at the camp of each tribe that has come to join. . . . These meetings sometimes take place some one or two hundred leagues distant from the enemy. They are sometimes major events, lasting two or three months, so as to give everyone a chance to get there, and meanwhile the most complete harmony prevails among all the tribes." A successful campaign ended with celebrations in which the victors nurtured their communal identity through ritualized violence: "The Comanches have a custom of helping the neighboring rancherias share in the victory just won by one of their tribes. They send the neighbors an arm or a leg of the victim so that they may celebrate their own festival. A man who has killed an enemy may also give the scalp to another, who then receives all the honors and makes all the gifts." The exhibition of enemy body parts around Comanchería was more than a gory victory ceremony; it was a symbolic performance of solidarity that dramatized the power and unity of the Numunu in the face of common, vanquished enemies.[80]

The Comanches operated in unison in war, and they did so also in diplomacy. Before 1850, the Comanche nation entered into several major treaties with colonial powers, and each of those treaties was preceded by multidivisional councils that agreed on terms and delegates under the guidance of elders. An example of these inclusive diplomatic processes is the 1822 treaty with Mexico, which was endorsed by both Kotsotekas and Tenewas. According to a Mexican report, Comanches, "persuaded by the advice of ancient Pitsinampa [Pisinampe], whom they venerate as a father," decided to pursue peace with Mexico. "To that end, toward the latter part of the March of the past year of twenty-two, they held a council of principal chiefs, captains, and elders, which was attended by five thousand persons." The grand council was opened by "paternal speeches of Pitsinampa," after which the question of peace was discussed for three days. The council finally "resolved, by unanimous vote, that . . . one of their principal chiefs should go forward to negotiate for peace under the terms he might find most appropriate and useful for the Comanche Nation." That chief, Guonique, traveled to Mexico City, where, armed with "the plenipotentiary power conferred upon him by his nation," he negotiated a detailed fourteen-point treaty that was highly favorable to the Comanches. Oral traditions suggest that the Comanches also had a specific society, the Big Horses, which was responsible for completing peace treaties with other Native nations.[81]

Like any complex society, Comanches did not always speak with one voice. In fact, they sometimes appeared outright cacophonic: dissident chiefs opposed majority agreements, and leaders sometimes vied fiercely for political sway within divisions. Yet the Comanche leadership managed time and again to either neutralize or accommodate such conflicts and forge long-lasting consensuses behind foreign policies. The crowning examples of such unified diplomacy are the many long periods of peace in the late eighteenth and early nineteenth centuries. Peace, one scholar has perceptively argued, was to Native Americans primarily a matter of mind, a mental state nurtured by words, rituals, and good thoughts,[82] but to the numerous and wide-ranging Comanches peace was also—if not indeed primarily—a political process involving constant consultation, coordination, and mediation. The Comanche nation, through its integrated multilevel political structure, kept a long-standing peace with the Kiowas and Naishans dating from 1806 and the Osages from 1838. They lived in general harmony with the Wichitas from the 1810s until the reservation era and honored decades-long truces with the Pawnees. In the early nineteenth century, they maintained a seven-year-long peace with the Apaches, with whom they had been at war more than a century. And for thirty-five years after the monumental treaty between Chief Ecueracapa and Governor Anza in 1786, no Comanche band violated the peace with New Mexico.

These were remarkable diplomatic achievements in an erratic colonial world where alliances, enmities, and balances of power tended to shift frequently and abruptly, and they testify to the sophistication of pan-Comanche statecraft. Information and initiatives flowed constantly from rancherías to divisional and multidivisional councils, where the actions of local leaders were censured and the broad outlines of Comanche foreign policy were formulated. This was not easy, for the formation of national policies of peace and war required more than bringing large numbers of people to a certain place at a certain time. An entire political culture had to be reconfigured. *Paraibos* had to commit themselves to obeying and executing policies they did not necessarily advocate. Bands had to forfeit a degree of their treasured autonomy to the confederacy and its administrative machinery. People known for their ferocious individuality and egalitarian ethos had to subordinate themselves to orders and rules emanating from the top.

The new centralized political culture generated broad agreements on fundamental issues, but it did not eradicate the traditional local autonomy, and it did not turn the Comanches into a monolith. The grand councils decided only on general war and general peace, in the absence of which rancherías were free to determine their relations with outsiders as they saw best. The core ideals of personal autonomy and freedom of association endured, permeating the entire community: just as individuals could move between bands without restraint, so too could entire rancherías shift between divisions. The early nineteenth-century Comanchería was a human kaleidoscope whose particles—bands, families, and individuals—moved around constantly, seeking new political and economic opportunities in the distant parts of the realm, often shifting their affiliations in the process. Sometimes, as when El Sordo's Yamparikas relocated to eastern Comanchería and reinvented themselves as Tenewas, entirely new divisions developed and sometimes old ones dissolved. The Jupes vanished from the historical record in the early nineteenth century, probably as a result of the amalgamation of Comanche divisions.[83]

This enduring social flexibility was as essential to Comanche hegemony as were the new centralized political institutions. Fluid group membership gave the Comanche nation extraordinary resilience by allowing its component parts to coalesce, dissolve, and unite again into various configurations as external exigencies demanded. The freedom of association also served as a political safety valve: individuals and bands that found it difficult to conform to the policies of their division could simply move to another. Macrolevel political unification and local fluidity, moreover, were not necessarily contradictory developments. The constant shifting of people and bands turned rancherías and divisions into rather loose entities, but such mobility also helped stitch the larger community together: each relocation outside one's own ranchería or division created a new kinship bond that transcended existing social and political boundaries. This creative balancing between flexibility and unity did not escape the attention of colonial officials, whose imperial projects were often wrought with stifling bureaucracies and defiant subject peoples. It must have been with perplexing resentment that Fernando de la Concha, the late eighteenth-century New Mexico governor who tried in vain to bring order to his unruly colony, described the political organization of New Mexico's ostensibly savage neighbors: "They agree among themselves perfectly, and the internal quarrels never exceed the limits of the petty disputes which arise between individuals. All four of the divisions live in a close union, and it frequently happens that those of one go to live among the others, so that their interests are common, and they share a common destiny."[84]

Nomads, the historical record shows, can evade, resist, stop, sustain, exploit, destabilize, and destroy empires. They can also build enduring empires of their own, but only if they modify the essence of their being and become less nomadic. Nomadism appears fundamentally incompatible with empire-building. Empires thrive on structure and stability, whereas nomads—at least the nomads one finds in most scholarly studies—are shifting and factional. Their institutions, like their very way of life, tend to be fluid and ephemeral, and they lack such classic elements of empires as state structure and surplus-generating agriculture. Indeed, to preserve their might, nearly all nomadic empires developed over time more fixed institutions of governance and production that required at least seasonal sedentarism.[85]

So too did the Comanches, although this may seem implausible at first sight. We have been taught to see Comanches as quintessential nomads, the ever-roaming lords of the southern plains, but they lived almost half of each year in large, nearly stationary villages. These villages were a response to the seasonal ecological riddles posed by the Great Plains environment, and they existed primarily to facilitate hunting and herding. But they had another function as well: they were seats of power and centers of production that sustained an empire. To understand how Comanches incorporated extended village sojourns into a predominantly nomadic way of life—to understand, in other words, how they combined nomadic plasticity with imperial rigidity—it is necessary to reexamine their annual cycle, its seasonal pattern of convergence and dispersal, its intricate slotting of various domestic and foreign political activities, and its creative blending of mobility and sedentarism.

The annual cycle of the Comanches began and ended at the junction of fall and winter, which marked a shift from a season dominated by foreign political activities to a season dominated by domestic activities. In late November, after the great fall hunt, Comanche rancherías left the open plains and took to the wooded river valleys for winter camps. This migration mirrored the habits of the bison, which retreated into the riverine forests during cold months, but it was also motivated by the exigencies of the new pastoral economy: Comanches needed the shelter, water, grass, and cottonwood bark of the river bottoms to support their vast horse and mule herds through the cold season.

Essentially extensions of the eastern woodland environment in a semiarid climate, the river valleys invited the Comanches to lead an existence that had little to do with the stereotyped image of horse-mounted nomads. Having settled along the streams by early or mid-December, Comanche rancherías stayed virtually immobile for several months, moving only when grasses or cottonwoods gave out or when feces and camp refuse became a health hazard. Men divided their time between tool manufacturing and brief but frequent hunts—the congregation of the bison in river valleys saved them long excursions. One visitor noted how a camp of nine hundred lodges on the upper Arkansas consumed roughly one hundred bison a day, which suggests that each household killed an animal every nine days or so. Since the camps were more or less stationary, women focused on processing the thick and sumptuous winter robes for the market. Raiding and warfare did not stop, but they now revolved around small-scale campaigns. Southern rancherías, whose horses were taxed less by the cold season than those of their more northern relatives, often launched minor raiding excursions into Texas during the winters. On Comanchería's eastern front, rancherías conducted sporadic defensive campaigns against Osage war and hunting parties through November, December, and January.[86]

For most Plains Indian societies, winters were a time of social dispersal: tribes splinted into bands, and bands scattered across the land, trying to expand their resource base at a time when nature yielded little. For Comanches, however, the opposite was often true. Comanchería's river valleys were long and fertile and could sustain massive human-animal congregations. Stretches of the Arkansas, North Canadian, Canadian, Red, Brazos, and Colorado rivers transformed in most winters into some of the most crowded places in the early American West. Hosting thousands of people and animals for months at end, Comanche winter camps resembled cities more than makeshift nomadic camps. A large village extended for several miles along a streambed, flanked by lookout points, usually high natural peaks, and it contained various structures for political councils, religious ceremonies, household chores, and lodging. In places like Paint Rock along the Concho River, dramatic pictographs adorned bluffs and canyon walls, and there is even a report of a village that was fortified with a circular moat, picket palisades, and a "small bastion in the center." Comanches returned to favorite sites year after year, profoundly altering local ecosystems in the process. These villages' voracious need for firewood left long stretches of riverine valleys treeless, and their many horses and mules often cropped grass to the ground and depleted cottonwood growths beyond repair.[87]

Winter villages were an ecological innovation that helped Comanches exploit the bison and support their horses through the cold season, but the villages also served as venues for two crucial imperial institutions: macrolevel political councils and large-volume foreign trade. Most divisional and interdivisional meetings took place in winter camps, which provided auspicious conditions for broadly based decision making and consensus building: numerous relatively immobile rancherías clustered together for months constituted a unique administrative opportunity for a nation of nomads. Seen from another angle, Comanchería's winter camps were massive concentrations of wealth—horses, mules, robes, meat, slaves—which attracted foreign traders. The principal wintering grounds along the upper Arkansas and Red River valleys routinely transformed into large, multiethnic trade fairs, where large quantities of commodities exchanged hands. Many neighboring societies arranged their own seasonal migrations around these annual winter fairs.

Comanches did not emerge from river valleys until early or mid-April, when they entered the migratory half of their yearly round. Their main concern now was to fatten their thinned horses and mules on the sprouting short grasses, for which purpose the winter villages split into numerous small rancherías to maximize foraging area. The rancherías moved frequently, seeking fresh pastures, watering places, and salt, and carefully coordinated their movements in relation to one another to avoid overlapping grazing ranges. They often burned large patches of grassland to encourage early grass growth. These pastoral activities were punctuated by brief hunts aimed at restocking exhausted food supplies and occasional livestock raids to replace winter losses. In June, after horses had regained their strength and when the bison began to assemble for the rut, Comanches conducted the summer hunt. For a few busy weeks they focused almost solely on hunting, butchering, skinning, tanning, and meat curing. Unlike in winters, skin processing was now largely a subsistence activity as the summer hides had little exchange value but could be turned into tipi covers, leggings, and moccasins.[88]

After the summer hunt, foreign policy took precedence. Through June, July, and early August, Comanches alternated small-scale border raids with tribute-extracting and trading visits to New Mexico and Texas, which, after the winter's respite, suddenly became almost a Comanche possession. Early and midsummer was also the time when the dispersed rancherías came together in huge camps to launch mass-scale campaigns against common enemies. These annual operations were aimed at preserving neutral zones around Comanchería, but as some perceptive observers noted, extended summer campaigns into Osage and Pawnee countries doubled as hunting excursions, which temporarily expanded Comanches' bison domain to the central and eastern Great Plains. Late summer saw another such temporary extension of Comanchería when Comanche raiders swept into Mexico. Late August and September were the rainiest period in northern Mexico, which allowed Comanche war bands to support their massive herds of stolen stock during the extended forays. Comanche forays were so punctual that September became known across the Southwest as the Comanche or Mexico Moon. During that violent season, Mexicans knew to establish chains of sentinels on hilltops to warn their villages of approaching war bands.[89]

Although Comanches seemed to be all over the map during the summer months, Comanchería itself did not lay dormant. Women, boys, and slaves ran the subsistence and herding economies, and enough men stayed behind to organize defense, diplomacy, and exchange. Foreign trading convoys came in regularly, drawn by the thriving trade fairs Comanches sponsored across their realm and the fresh supplies of captives and stolen colonial stock.[90] As in winter, there were big, bustling villages, temporary urban constructions that lined Comanchería's main riverine arteries. Finding such urban scenes in a seemingly desolate steppe landscape was often a disorienting experience to Euro-American visitors. The 1835 U.S. dragoon expedition under Colonel Henry Dodge was designed to impress the Plains Indians with its military muscle and organizational flourish, but when the troops arrived in mid-June at a large Comanche settlement along the Cache Creek near the Wichita Mountains, it was the Americans who were left in awe. One of their members, George Catlin, left a description of the Comanche welcoming ceremony, which began as an intimidating display of martial prowess but, seen up close, softened into a public demonstration of friendship:

15. *Comanche Warriors, with White Flag, Receiving the Dragoons.* Oil on canvas by George Catlin, 1834–35. Courtesy of Smithsonian American Art Museum, Washington, D.C. / Art Resource, N.Y.

> Several hundreds of their braves and warriors came out at full speed to welcome us. . . . As they wheeled their horses, they very rapidly formed a line, and "dressed" like well-disciplined cavalry. . . . Two lines were thus drawn up, face to face, within twenty or thirty yards of each other, as inveterate foes that never had met; and, to the everlasting credit of the Camanchees, whom the world had always looked upon as murderous and hostile, they had all come out in this manner, with their heads uncovered, and without a weapon of any kind, to meet a war-party bristling with arms, and trespassing to the middle of their country. . . . They galloped out and looked us in our faces, without an expression of fear or dismay, and evidently with expressions of joy and impatient pleasure, to shake us by the hand, on the bare assertion of Colonel Dodge, which had been made to the chiefs, that "we came to see them on a friendly visit."[91]

The Americans had won entrance to the inner sanctum of Comanchería: the encampment they had come upon was the principal eastern Comanche

16. *Comanche Village, Women Dressing Robes and Drying Meat.* Oil on canvas by George Catlin, 1834–35. Courtesy of Smithsonian American Art Museum, Washington, D.C. / Art Resource, N.Y.

village, where rancherías from several divisions had congregated. Its sheer size left Catlin confounded. There were between six and eight hundred ornamented tipis organized into long parallel lines, which gave the settlement a gridlike appearance of streets and rowhouses. A nearby streambed, "speckled with horses and mules," had been converted into an immense grazing area. The entire complex "with its thousands of wild inmates, with horses and dogs, and wild sports and domestic occupations" hummed with action. Boys and slaves moved back and forth between the village and the stream, taking shifts in guarding, tending, and watering the herds, while women and slaves hauled wood, gathered seeds, picked fruit, dug roots, cured meat, and processed robes. Racks of drying meat and tanned robes ran parallel with the tipi rows, attesting to thriving domestic and market production. Some men participated in and gambled on horse races and other communal games; others honed their fighting skills in endless drills, reenacting the military prowess that had help expand Comanches' imperial realm to the Tropic of Cancer and beyond. Young warriors left Catlin "completely puzzled" by riding horizontally behind their horses' bodies in full speed, "effectually screened from [their] enemies' weapons," firing arrows under the horse's neck. But there were also things that evaded Catlin's scrutiny. He was

17. *Comanche Feats of Horsemanship.* Oil on canvas by George Catlin, 1834–35. Courtesy of Smithsonian American Art Museum, Washington, D.C. / Art Resource, N.Y.

not invited to religious ceremonies that complemented large village gatherings, and he could not witness the political activities that took place behind closed tipi doors: the nightly pipe rituals where the everyday matters of the village were discussed and the more formal councils where important political issues were resolved. Here, in short, was one of those temporary administrative and economic nerve centers that shaped and sustained the Comanche empire.[92]

The annual cycle of the Comanches ended with a great fall hunt, which took place in late November and early December, just before the vast bison concentrations splintered into riverine fragments and bears went into hibernation. Along with winter and midsummer, this was the third time in a year that Comanches gathered into large villages. Rancherías congregated at designated places for multiband councils, where the time and location of the hunt was agreed. The fall hunt was the nutritional pivot of the yearly cycle, the last chance to stock up on protein and fat before the lean season, and the villages took extensive measures to ensure success. A group of distinguished warriors served as marshals who made sure that no one alarmed the prey prematurely, and a chief hunter led mounted hunters in coordinated collective chases. Women and slaves butchered the carcasses at the site of the kill and hauled the slabs of flesh to the villages, which for a few weeks looked like meat-processing manufactories. When enough buffalo meat, buffalo tallow, and bear oil had been processed and stored, the rancherías headed toward the river valleys and their communal duties and challenges.[93]

Comanchería in the early nineteenth century was not the place it had been a century or even half a century before. There were elemental continuities in how Comanches related to the world and to one another, but the tempo and texture of their lives had changed irrevocably. An early eighteenth-century Comanche would have found the early nineteenth-century Comanchería both familiar and eerily disorienting. The two worlds had many things in common—horses, slaves, rich, poor, *paraibos*, war chiefs—but the later world was vastly magnified. Horse herds were colossal and slaves or incorporated former slaves were everywhere. The old subsistence-oriented foraging economy had been transplanted by a market-oriented dual economy of hunting and herding that featured such embryonic capitalist features as concentrated ownership of the means of production, a complex labor division geared toward market production, and a cadre of privileged individuals who used their wealth to create more wealth. The relatively egalitarian society had yielded to a configuration in which there was room for strictly gendered and ethnically segmented production groups and vast gradations in possession and privilege. Political power had become both concentrated and curiously divided between civil and war chiefs, and the multidivisional councils now held together both a nation and an empire.

Collectively, these changes amounted to a classic process of internal intensification that most rapidly expanding societies go through: economies are recalibrated, inequalities exacerbated, social cleavages accentuated, and levers of political power realigned.[94] Such readjustments helped Comanches meet the countless challenges of empire-building, but they came at a cost. The new economy threatened Comanchería's ecological stability, and institutionalized slavery shook its social foundations. The yawning gap between the poor and the prosperous undermined communal solidarity and fueled a fierce male rivalry over women and horses. Gender relations deteriorated when men began to marry their daughters into massive polygynous households as quasi laborers. Yet the Comanche society retained its flexible cohesiveness, its capacity to absorb change without losing its core principles. Slavery remained embedded in kinship relations and never evolved into a socially divisive chattel system. A persisting vision of generosity as a paramount social virtue helped alleviate disintegrative effects of individual aggrandizement and communitywide social hierarchization. An ingrained warrior cult channeled aggressive male competition outside of Comanchería. As the nineteenth century inched toward its midpoint, it seemed that Comanches could survive their expansion. They had no way of knowing that the grass under their feet was about to die.

7

Hunger

The Mexican-American War marked the culmination of Comanche power, the hinge on which 150 years of expansion turned toward retreat. Although few Americans acknowledged it, the war of 1846 was a display of both United States and Comanche power. Washington argued that the takeover of Mexican soil was simply a matter of fulfilling America's manifest destiny, but on the ground, where military power meant more than political rhetoric, the conquest seemed more propitious than predestined: the Americans who marched into Mexico in the name of destiny and democracy did so in the footsteps of Comanches, whose expansion had paved the way for theirs. And yet, when the dust settled and treaties were signed, the Comanches discovered that they were considered a conquered people.

The Treaty of Guadalupe Hidalgo ushered in a new order in the Southwest. The United States secured its hold on Texas and absorbed New Mexico, extending its possessions from the Nueces River to the Río Grande. In Article Eleven of the treaty, the United States agreed to police the border to prevent Indian raiders from crossing the Río Grande into Mexico. For the Comanches, this was unfathomable: their home territory had fallen squarely within the borders of a vastly more powerful nation that meant to box them in and tie them down. That pressure, meted out by the U.S. military, federal agents, and soldier-settlers, began immediately after the Mexican-American War and increased steadily until the Civil War and its aftermath brought a short respite. But when the Americans resumed their expansionist thrust in the late 1860s, the Comanches, along with more than twenty other Plains Indian nations, were swiftly swept aside. Abruptly and almost effortlessly, the United States overthrew the formidable Comanches.

This reading of Comanche decline has certain chronological and causal symmetry to it, but the impression of American expansion and Comanche collapse as connected developments is deceiving. The United States would eventually obliterate the Comanches' way of life and confine them to a reservation, but the American expansion did not trigger their decline. When the United States fought its way into the Southwest after 1846, the Comanches were both at the peak of their power and on the verge of collapse. For decades, and almost imperceptibly, several in-built economic and ecological problems had been brewing, erupting into a full-blown crisis in the closing years of the 1840s. That crisis sent the Comanches into a spiraling decline; by the time they came into critical contact with the United States in the 1850s, they had ceased to be an imperial power.

In 1849, when U.S. Army Captain Randolph B. Marcy extended his exploratory tour of the southern plains into Comanchería, he was struck by the Comanches' uncompromised sense of power. They believed themselves "to be the most powerful nation in existence," the baffled officer wrote, "and the relation of facts which conflict with this notion . . . only subjects the narrator to ridicule." Marcy considered the Comanches fools, ignorant of such wonders as the steam engine or the telegraph, but they had every reason to be confident. They were prosperous and powerful. Although epidemics had cut into their numbers, their population hovered near the twenty-thousand level, making them by far the most populous Native nation of the southern and central plains. There were still an estimated six to eight hundred Mexican slaves and countless Native captives in Comanchería. The various Comanche bands owned collectively well over one hundred thousand horses and mules, more than all the other plains nomads combined, and the Comanche alliance network comprised more than twenty different ethnic groups, who sent regular trading envoys into Comanchería, bringing in firearms, metal, food, and luxuries. Several groups were attached to the Comanches as trading partners, junior allies, and political satellites. Such facts and figures denote impressive power, but, less perceptibly, they also carry a bleaker significance. They speak of the costs of the empire, and they suggest that the Comanche economy had surpassed the limits of ecologically sustainable growth.[1]

Comanchería was a land of great riches and enormous bison herds, which provided the Comanches a seemingly bottomless reservoir of hides, protein, and fat, but that abundance rested on a shaky ecological foundation: Comanchería was a hunter's paradise but only for a limited number of people. Calculations based on the range-use efficiency of livestock in the early twentieth-century southern plains suggest that the nineteenth-century Comanchería could support approximately seven million bison. These vast herds thrived on Comanchería's dense and nourishing shortgrasses, but they also faced severe hazards: wolves killed huge numbers of calves, grass fires annihilated entire herds, and droves of buffalo drowned attempting to cross frozen rivers in winter. The critical gap, the difference between mortality and the bison's ability to reproduce, was therefore rather narrow. Modern bison reproduce at an average annual rate of 18 to 20 percent, while the nineteenth-century bison's annual losses to nonhuman causes—natural mortality, accidents, and predation—can be estimated at 15 percent. Based on these figures, the Comanches and their allies could kill approximately 280,000 bison a year without depleting the herds.[2]

Although substantial on first glance, this number suggests a startling possibility: the Comanches were off balance with the bison herds for much of the early nineteenth century, gradually eroding the ecological foundation of their way of life. It has been estimated that full-time plains hunters needed a yearly average of 6.5 bison per person for food, shelter, and clothing, which means that the Comanches and their allies were killing approximately 175,000 buffalos a year for subsistence alone. Moreover, although first and foremost horse traders, Comanches also produced bison robes, meat, and tallow for the market. In the early nineteenth century, their commercial harvest probably rarely exceeded 25,000 animals, but their hunting practices seriously aggravated the damage. Like most Plains Indians, Comanches did their market hunting in winter, when the robes were the thickest and most valuable, and they preferred killing two- to five-year-old cows for their thin, easily processed skins. Since bison cows produce their first calves at the age of three or four and their gestation period usually extends from mid-July to early April, Comanches slaughtered disproportionate numbers of pregnant cows, thus impairing the herds' reproductive capacity.[3]

Making matters worse, Comanches' commercial ambitions induced them to open their hunting grounds to outsiders. For much of the eighteenth century, Comanches had restricted outsiders' access to their hunting ranges, but that environmental policy became increasingly difficult to maintain as their trading links multiplied. One by one, they disposed of the neutral buffer zones skirting Comanchería, inadvertently depriving the bison of their crucial sanctuaries. Particularly inauspicious in this respect was the 1835 Treaty of Camp Holmes, in which Comanches granted the Osages and the populous immigrant tribes of Indian Territory access to their lands in exchange for trading privileges. Discouraged by the poor lands of Indian Territory, Cherokees, Chickasaws, Choctaws, and Creeks—all numerous groups—embarked on active bison hunting, and many Delaware, Shawnee, and Kickapoo bands became specialized hunters.

Together with Osages, the removed Indians did most of their hunting in the prime bison range between the upper Canadian and Red rivers, in the heart of eastern Comanchería. By 1841 the region's bison populations were thinning rapidly.[4]

At the same time on Comanchería's western edge, ciboleros, the New Mexican bison hunters who had won hunting privileges in Comanchería in the aftermath of the 1786 Spanish-Comanche treaty, made annual hunting expeditions to the Llano Estacado, harvesting an estimated 25,000 animals per season. Even more pressure fell on the bison herds with the peace of 1840 among Comanches, Kiowas, Naishans, Cheyennes, and Arapahoes, which unlocked northern Comanchería for Cheyenne and Arapaho hunters, who embarked on a large-scale robe trade at Bent's Fort on the Arkansas. Cheyennes and Arapahoes delivered tens of thousands of robes to Bent's Fort and probably harvested a large portion of them in Comanchería. In all, in the early 1840s tens of thousands of Comanchería's bison died every year in the hands of people not living in the region.[5]

The combined toll of Comanches' and their allies' subsistence and market hunting probably neared, and in some years exceeded, the sustainable yearly rate of killing of 280,000, placing Comanchería's bison herds on a precarious balance. This balance was rendered even shakier by the Comanches' burgeoning horse herding economy. Horses and bison have an 80 percent dietary overlap and very similar water requirements, which makes them ecologically incompatible species. Even more critically, both animals could survive the harsh winters of the plains only by retreating into river valleys, which provided reliable water, shelter against the cold, and cottonwood for emergency food. But suitable riverine habitats were becoming increasingly scarce. To meet the expansive grazing needs of their growing domestic herds, Comanches had turned more and more bottomland niches into herding range, gradually congesting Comanchería's river valleys. By the mid-nineteenth century, huge winter camps and horse herds could be seen stretching for dozens of miles along key wintering sites, covering the prime foraging and watering spots, and forcing the bison to retreat to poorer areas.[6]

Most such areas were at the headwaters of major rivers and far from Comanches' principal hunting and wintering grounds, but when the bison gravitated toward these peripheral habitats, they were blocked there as well. Southern Comanchería near the Texas frontier was the home for massive herds of wild horses, which had virtually taken over the region's river valleys and resources. On the western portion of the Llano Estacado, at the headwaters of the Canadian, Red, and Brazos rivers and their tributaries, the bison had to compete for grass, water, and shelter with thousands of sheep driven there each winter by New Mexican herders, *pastores*. Perhaps most disastrously, freighting along the Santa Fe Trail grew into a large-scale industry in the early 1840s. A typical trade caravan consisted of some two dozen freight wagons and several hundred oxen and mules, and each year hundreds of such caravans trekked back and forth along the Arkansas corridor, destroying vegetation, polluting springs, accelerating erosion, and driving out the bison from their last ecological niches in the valley. It is also possible that the traders' livestock introduced anthrax, brucellosis, and other bovine diseases to the bison herds.[7]

Struggling under multiple pressures, Comanchería's bison population lost the ability to maintain its numbers. The herds may have declined all through the early nineteenth century, first slowly and intermittently, then faster and more steadily. By the 1840s the herds had thinned perceptibly across the region. In 1843 one Mexican official in Taos warned that the bison would soon become extinct as a species, and a few years later another observer noted, "It is a singular fact that within the last two years the prairies, extending from the mountains to a hundred miles or more down the Arkansa, have been entirely abandoned by the buffalo."[8] Comanchería's core bison population was under severe pressure, but that pressure was somewhat alleviated by the fact that the 1830s and early 1840s were unusually wet on the southern plains. The above-average rainfall sustained prolific grass growth, which mitigated the bison's problems. But then, suddenly, the rains stopped and a full-blown crisis set in.

In 1845 a long and intense dry spell struck Comanchería. The rains resumed briefly around 1850, but the drought returned and lasted in varying degrees until the mid-1860s. As the rains failed or came only as drizzles, springs, ponds, and creeks dried up and rivers shrank to trickles. Shortgrasses stored nutrients in their extensive root systems, producing stunted above-ground growth, and vast swathes of Comanchería's lush grass cover turned into brownish, lifeless matter. It was a difficult time for the Comanches and a disastrous one for the bison. To protect their horses and themselves against dehydration and starvation, Comanches headed for the few spots where forage and water were available, thus blocking the bison's access to their drought refuges. Already strained by grazing competition and human predation and now left to endure the drought without the vital resources of the river valleys, Comanchería's bison herds collapsed. Staggering numbers of animals died, and entire herds drifted out of Comanchería, seeking relief in the moister and cooler conditions in the north and east. In 1847, reporting on the situation on the western plains of Texas, Indian agent Robert Neighbors wrote, "The buffalo and other game have almost entirely disappeared." Two years later Captain Marcy reported that buffalo "seldom go south of Red river, and their range upon east and west has also very much contracted. . . . They are at present confined to a narrow belt of country between the outer settlements and the base of the Rocky mountains." It is impossible to know exactly how many animals perished, but it is not infeasible that the total population was reduced to 3.5 million by 1860.[9]

Although an unexpected climatic swing brought on the bison crisis, the Comanches' actions had contributed to the damage. By monopolizing the river basins for their horses, by slaughtering vast numbers of bison for subsistence and for trade, and by opening their hunting grounds to outsiders, Comanches had critically undercut the viability of the bison population, rendering it vulnerable to ecological reversals. Given the inherently unpredictable nature of the plains environment and bison ecology—the herds were always declining and bouncing back—it would have been very difficult to tell one of the recurring fluctuations apart from a more permanent drop. Indeed, Comanches' actions remained ecologically inconsistent even after the herds had begun to shrink rapidly in the late 1840s. They adopted steps to preserve the herds, insisting, for example, that the ciboleros take fewer pack animals on their hunting sojourns and curb the amount of robes and meat they carried back to New Mexico. At the same time, however, Comanches continued to kill large numbers of bison for commercial purposes. In 1855 John W. Whitfield, the Indian agent of the upper Arkansas, reported that the thirty-two hundred Comanches living in the river basin were killing 30,000 bison annually despite the fact that they were "confined to a district of country from which the buffalo has almost entirely disappeared." That slaughter translates to an average of 9.3 bison per capita, nearly three more animals per person than subsistence hunting alone would have required. The extra animals, Whitfield noted, were killed for their robes, which were sold to American traders.[10]

Perhaps Comanches simply misread the ecological warning signs. The deterioration of Comanchería's bison ecology to near the breaking point was the result of so many factors and happened so gradually that the inevitability of the catastrophe is perceivable only in hindsight. Moreover, even when the bison numbers had become visibly depressed in the 1850s, Comanches may well have thought that they were facing one of the cyclic drought-induced fluctuations that were an inherent part of the plains bison ecology and usually passed automatically when wetter conditions returned. In the mid-nineteenth century, the Comanche community had already survived several severe dry spells on the southern plains, and each time, even after the repeated droughts of the 1770s and 1780s, the bison herds had rebounded, sustained by their exceptional fertility. It appears, in fact, that the bison is such a prolific species that it was chronically liable to increase beyond the plains' carrying capacity and that human predation functioned as a crucial preventive against unsustainable growth. In terms of game management, therefore, the main challenge for buffalo hunters had not necessarily been the scarcity but the overabundance of their prey. This might also explain why Plains Indian societies developed relatively few social taboos against overhunting and why the hunters, whose very way of life rested on the buffalo, routinely indulged in wasteful acts, such as taking only the choicest parts of the fattest cows.[11]

This does not mean that Comanches sacrificed the bison for shortsighted economic gain. Comanches' failure to implement a systematic conservation policy also stemmed from a complex conflict of motives involving ecological, economic, and religious interests. When the herds began to dwindle in the 1840s, Comanches could not simply halt their commercial hunts to give the depleted herds a respite. They had traded products of the hunt for products of the farm for generations and had grown utterly dependent on the arrangement. They needed the imported maize, beans, and squash as much as they needed the buffalo, and to get them they had to keep dipping into the shrinking herds. Another hypothetically possible solution for Comanches would have been to reduce the size of their horse herds to allow more room for bison, but that option was rendered impossible by more pressing economic and military imperatives. Like bison, horses were crucial commodities that opened an access to a different but equally vital set of imports—guns, ammunition, powder, and metal. Around midcentury, external pressures on Comanchería's borders were mounting rapidly. Settlers and ranchers from Texas, immigrant tribes from Indian Territory, and overland traders and settlers from the eastern United States were all gravitating toward the southern plains, compelling the Comanches to keep their horse herds large and their commercial system running—even if it meant depleting their resource base. Comanches needed the bison's meat and robes for long-term survival, but in the short run it was more critical for them to have as many well-mounted and well-armed warriors as possible.

Finally, Comanches' spiritual worldview may have prevented them from working out an ecological equilibrium. Most Plains Indians believed that the bison's well-being was less a matter of human utilization than a sort of ritualistic herd management. Social checks against overhunting were an important part of their environmental policy, but they mattered less than the ceremonies, which alone could ensure that the bison would return and the herds would be renewed. An integral part of this belief was a conviction that buffalos were supernatural in origin and therefore infinite in numbers. Colonel Richard Irving Dodge wrote that Plains Indians "firmly believed that the buffalo were produced in countless numbers in a country under the ground; that every spring the surplus swarmed, like bees from a hive, out of great cave-like openings to this country, which were situated somewhere in the great 'Llano Estacado,' or Staked Plain of Texas." Comanches believed that hunters' success was dependent on prayers and ceremonial smoking, and their oral histories relate how bison could take human form, appear among starving Comanches, and lead them to large buffalo herds and great kills.[12]

Faith in the supernatural origin and qualities of the buffalo may have had far-reaching consequences for how Comanches responded to the bison's decline. Although Comanches undoubtedly intimately understood the dynamics of wildlife populations and the environmental and human-induced causes of bison mortality, they could also believe that the bison's abundance was ultimately a matter of the supernatural realm. These two sets of beliefs were at odds only superficially, for conservation meant maintaining a total relationship with the animals through ceremonies and rituals rather than by tracking actual numbers or densities of the species. The root of the disaster, then, was that Comanches may have realized that the bison herds were dwindling yet remained convinced that there would always be bison as long as the proper rituals were observed. Unable to envision the bison's extinction, Comanches were also unable to envision a policy to conserve them.[13]

The collapse of the bison population was an ecological and economic catastrophe for the Comanches. In 1852 Horace Capron, special Indian agent in Texas, found seven hundred Comanches on the upper Concho River "suffering with extreme hunger, bordering upon starvation." The chiefs said: "The game our main dependence is killed and driven off, and we are forced into the most sterile and barren portions of it [the plains] to starve. We see nothing but extermination left for us, and we await the result with stolid indifference. Give us a country we can call our own, where we might bury our people in quiet." Three years later, agent Whitfield reported that the disappearance of bison from the "sterile wilds" of the upper Arkansas basin had forced the starving Comanches to eat so many horses and mules that their herds were shrinking at an alarming rate. The Comanche economy was losing its most basic function: the people who had enjoyed a century of almost continuous economic growth suddenly could not feed themselves.[14]

The subsistence crisis fueled—and was in turn fueled by—an escalating commercial crisis. Comanches struggled to hold on to their trading network, but its exchange links dissolved one by one. Discouraged by shrinking profits, American hide traders closed all posts along the Texas frontier by the mid-1850s. To the north, the Bents burned their Canadian River post in 1846, and after the 1849 cholera epidemic devastated their Native clients, they blew up the great Arkansas fort. Clinging to his dream of a lasting plains emporium, William Bent built in 1853 yet another post in the Arkansas valley, thirty-eight miles downstream of the Old Fort, but the new post never reached the prosperity of its predecessor. Bison populations had also declined dramatically on the central plains north of the Arkansas (and largely for the same reasons as in Comanchería), which enveloped the post in a massive animal graveyard. Moreover, escalating overland traffic and migration along the Arkansas corridor scared off game and destroyed plant life, enraging the resident Indians and undermining the commercial and diplomatic middle ground on which the Bents had thrived. With tensions between American traders and Indians mounting, William Bent closed his post in 1860 and with that ended almost 150 years of organized Comanche trade in the Arkansas valley.[15]

Comanches' trading relations with their Native allies crumbled as well. During the late 1850s the Cheyennes and Arapahoes gradually deserted the desolate Arkansas valley and moved northward to the Platte and Smoky Hill river valleys, where they tried to scrape a living by stealing livestock and extorting food from overland travelers. They stopped trading with the Comanches. Several Kiowa and Naishan bands also abandoned the southern plains for the central plains, where they sought protection from an alliance with the Cheyennes, Arapahoes, and Lakotas. The Wichitas, too, gradually disentangled themselves from the Comanche orbit. No longer able to subsist by the hunt, they settled by the mid-1850s on a reservation on the Brazos River, where they set up houses, cleared fields, and began raising hogs and cattle. Their trade with the Comanches was restricted to clandestine food and hide exchanges on the reservation's fringes where the agents' control could not reach them. But occasionally the impoverished Comanches also raided the reservation for maize, cattle, and horses, prompting many Wichitas to join the U.S. Army's Comanche expeditions as scouts and auxiliaries.[16]

Comanche relations with the removed tribes degenerated more rapidly and violently. As the bison herds dwindled, Comanches and their allies grew increasingly intolerant of the westbound hunting parties from Indian Territory. Then, in June 1854, the United States Office of Indian Affairs and immigrant Indians concluded a series of treaties, which opened the Kansas Territory for white settlement and removed thousands of Indians to the central and western Indian Territory, at the very edge of Comanchería. Full-scale conflict erupted soon after when fifteen hundred Comanches, Kiowas, Naishans, Wichitas, and Osages joined their forces "to '*wipe out*' all frontier Indians they could find on the plains." The massive force descended the Smoky Hill River toward Indian

Territory but suffered a crushing defeat against a much smaller group of Sauks and Foxes, who killed more than one hundred warriors with their American rifles. From thereon, both the removed tribes and Comanches claimed the remaining buffalo as their own, and the border zone between them—essentially the entire western part of present-day Oklahoma between the 98th and 100th meridians—became a bloody ground. By 1855, only months after their failed joint effort to vanquish immigrant Indians, relations between Comanches and Osages degenerated into violence over hunting privileges.[17]

By the late 1850s, the great Comanche trading empire had dissolved. The comanchero trade was the only remaining facet of the once-imposing exchange system, and even that thread was unraveling. The Treaty of Guadalupe Hidalgo obligated the United States to prevent Indian forays into Mexico, to suppress cross-border contraband trade, and to reclaim and repatriate Mexican captives held by Indians. But policing the long border proved militarily impossible—or simply too expensive—and federal officials instead moved to remove the economic impetus behind Comanche raids by eliminating the markets for spoils. In 1850 James S. Calhoun, the Indian agent and future governor of New Mexico, instituted a strict license system for the comancheros, making them pay expensive fees for trade permits and prohibiting them from trafficking in munitions. Also, to both fulfill the United States' treaty obligations to Mexico and cut into comanchero profits, Calhoun sent emissaries into Comanchería to buy all Mexican captives they could find. By 1851 the agents had redeemed some twenty Mexican captives, making a dent in comanchero business.[18]

In this context of mounting uncertainty, disconcerting news reached Santa Fe: one of the head chiefs of the Comanche rancherías residing in northern Mexico had concluded a pact with the Mexican government and "appeared to be very solicitous of forming a League with the other wild tribes of Texas & New Mexico for the alleged purpose of uniting them with the Mexicans, to expel, or exterminate, the Americans now in this Country." That Comanche chief, U.S. officials feared, was recruiting Pueblo Indians to join the coalition. The grand alliance dissolved before any action was taken, but its possibility alarmed American officials in New Mexico, who lived in constant fear of a general borderlands rebellion. Rather than a sign of broad intercultural anti-American stance, however, the aborted Comanche–New Mexican–Mexican alliance may have been an attempt to mend what was already crumbling.[19]

In 1853 Comanches and Kiowas clashed violently with their longtime New Mexican allies over hunting rights on the Llano Estacado. The Indians had tolerated the hunting operations of the New Mexican ciboleros on their territory for generations, but the decline of the bison herds changed their attitude.

Comanches and Kiowas began to demand the ciboleros cut back the numbers of pack animals they took on their massive expeditions, which could include as many as 50 wagons; 150 men, women, and children; and 500 horses and mules. Considering the hunts as an ancient, undeniable privilege, the ciboleros refused to comply, and overt hostilities erupted. Several ciboleros were killed, and violence crept into comanchero trade. Tensions ran high along the Comanche–New Mexican border for the rest of the 1850s, nearly stifling the trade that for three generations had fastened eastern New Mexico to Comanchería.[20]

The decline of comanchero commerce left the Comanches weakened and impoverished. Their access to guns, shot, and powder was severely compromised, but even more troubling, they had lost their only reliable source of maize and other garden produce. It was a disaster for a people already suffering from serious deficiencies of protein and fat, and by the late 1850s the Comanches were vulnerable to several types of malnutrition, including kwashiorkor (protein deficiency, especially in infants), marasmus (combined protein and calorie deficiency), and ketoacidosis (severe carbohydrate deficiency, especially in pregnant women). Serious malnutrition alone would have pushed the Comanche population into a decline, but a combination of starvation and disease turned the decline into a veritable demographic collapse. In 1848, three years into a dry spell, smallpox ravaged Comanchería, and in 1849 a virulent cholera epidemic introduced by California-bound overlanders carried away uncounted numbers, including many prominent leaders. And finally in 1862, the seventeenth year of famine, smallpox struck again. In previous decades, the Comanche population had repeatedly rebounded from epidemic losses, but malnutrition and the consequent lowering of fertility now made such recoveries impossible.[21]

Comanches fought desperately to avert catastrophe. They cut back their traffic in captives and instead incorporated them into their families. Slave raids into Mexico, one observer wrote in 1853, "tend to keep up the numbers of the tribe," because most captives were now made "husbands of their daughters and mothers of their children." Comanches also raided outlying frontier settlements for corn, sheep, pigs, and cattle or, alternatively, promised to refrain from plundering if New Mexicans stopped hunting buffalo on the plains. Whereas earlier the appearance of Comanche war parties on colonial frontiers had invariably meant livestock and captive raids, the parties now left the settlers in peace if given beef, fruit, or clothing. Comanches tried to fend off hunger by hunting large numbers of deer, elks, and bear, and some bands even began to keep sheep and goats. Horseflesh, previously strictly an emergency food, became a staple, and cultural norms were relaxed to broaden the subsistence base. Fish and fowl were originally considered taboo, but from midcentury on Comanches routinely ate both, especially during the dietary nadir in February and March, the season "when babies cry for food." Such efforts may have slowed the population decline, but they did not prevent it. In the late 1840s there may have been as many as twenty thousand Comanches, but by the mid-1850s only a half or less of that number remained.[22]

The 1850s, a decade defined by starvation and decline in Comanchería, was a period of explosive growth in the United States. Railroads, factories, mechanized agriculture, and soaring immigration ushered the nation into an era of capitalist industrialism that both demanded and supported continued expansion. The United States in 1850 was a continental empire stretching from the Atlantic to the Pacific, but its vast midsection, the Great Plains and the Intermountain West, was largely beyond reach and exploitation—a seemingly disordered, uncontainable world of grasslands, deserts, buffalos, and Indians. The federal government was undecided as to what to do with this newly claimed inland empire, for expansion had by now become inseparable from the far more volatile problems of slavery, sectionalism, and states' rights. But while their leaders wavered, Americans pressed ahead, pouring across the Mississippi valley in the search of new lands and riches.

And so, in an hour of profound crisis, the Comanches faced an invasion they could neither stop nor escape. The new American wealth and power generated in the East seeped into the Southwest with the hundreds of thousands of settlers, ranchers, miners, merchants, traders, freighters, soldiers, and federal officials who streamed into Kansas, Colorado, New Mexico, and Texas after the conclusion of the Mexican-American War. This human surge marked a dreadful turn for the Comanches, who were already struggling with too many problems. Starving and weakened, they were besieged by the encroaching frontiers of an expanding empire that wielded unforeseen military and economic power. In the space of just a few years, their hegemony over the southern plains collapsed.

The invasion of Comanchería began with the first stage in America's westward expansion: overland migration. In 1849 some three thousand hopefuls rushing to the California goldfields blazed an overland route along the Canadian River, where they found more grass, timber, and fresh water than along its heavily trafficked northern counterpart, the Santa Fe Trail. Weakened by a cholera epidemic, Comanches were powerless to stop the encroachment, which left in its wake a swathe of trodden vegetation and polluted water holes in the heart of northern Comanchería. The situation was becoming even worse in the Arkansas valley, where overland freighting along the Santa Fe Trail matured into a big business. In 1853, when some six hundred wagons were expected to move between Missouri and New Mexico, the U.S. government dispatched Thomas Fitzpatrick, the famous fur trapper, guide, and Indian agent, to meet with the Comanches and their allies to secure the crucial artery with treaties.[23]

Six Yamparika and Kotsoteka rancherías were present at Fort Atkinson in southwestern Kansas when agent Fitzpatrick laid down demands: the Indians were asked to allow free travel through their territories and permit the army to mark out roads and establish military and other posts on their lands. In line with the United States' treaty obligations to Mexico, Fitzpatrick also demanded that Comanches stop raids into Mexico and release all Mexican captives. Palpably appalled, the Indians retorted that forts and roads destroy timber, drive off game, and impede their mobility, and Comanches "positively and distinctly" refused to surrender any captives, insisting that they had been absorbed into their kinship networks and had "become a part of their tribe . . . identical with them in all their modes of life." Yet, eventually, all chiefs signed the 1853 treaty, evidently to get access to the guns and other treaty inducements that brought immediate relief to their misery.[24]

For several years after the treaty, Comanches collected flour, rice, bread, blankets, flintlock guns, and other federal supplies along the Arkansas and traded robes and skins for food and utensils with licensed American traders. They extorted a toll, usually in bread, sugar, and coffee, from overlanders along the river valley, but generally refrained from attacking the immigrant trains. But in 1858, when gold was discovered in Colorado, the arrangement fell apart. In spring 1859 tens of thousands of migrants poured through the Arkansas valley to the gold fields around Denver. Unlike the Santa Fe traders, who mostly took the Cimarron Cutoff to New Mexico, the goldseekers followed the Arkansas all the way to the Front Range, devastating the last ecologically viable section of the valley. The gold rush was largely over by 1860, but the upper Arkansas valley, once a haven for Comanches and their horses, had become a barren dust highway.[25]

Meanwhile on northern Comanchería's eastern front, tribes from Indian Territory continued their hunting excursions up the Canadian, Washita, Red, and Pease rivers, pushing through the thinned Comanche-Kiowa-Naishan cordon. Ravaged by hunger, both sides needed the bison so desperately that the rivalry failed to create a neutral ground between them and northwestern Comanchería became a vast killing zone. "If the hunters of these tribes [Comanches, Kiowas, and Naishans] venture into the region of the buffalo," U.S. Indian agent Whitfield wrote in 1855, "they are liable at any moment to come into contact with the border Indians, the Osages, Delawares, and others, who claim as their own hunting grounds all the lands over which the buffalo now roams." Unable to hold back their more numerous and better-armed enemies, Comanches retreated eastward, surrendering much of what today is western Oklahoma and the Texas Panhandle. In 1855 some Comanche bands from Texas arrived in Santa Fe, where they asked the governor for a refuge on the New Mexico border, for "they had been driven from their own Country by the Osages."[26]

But pressure was increasing along the Comanche–New Mexico border as well. In the mid-1850s American newcomers established several sheep and cattle ranches along the upper Canadian and Pecos valleys, regions that Comanches regarded as theirs. In 1858 Comanches burned a ranch on the Canadian and sent a warning to Santa Fe that no settlements would be allowed east of the Gallinas River, the traditional eastern limit of New Mexico's *genízaro* settlements. The following year, however, U.S. officials dispatched a surveying party to chart the upper Canadian valley for settlement. Comanches captured the surveyors and, after an aborted meeting with U.S. agents, launched a series of attacks along the Santa Fe Trail and across New Mexico's eastern front. Unlike before, they struck indiscriminately, attacking American, Hispanic, and Pueblo ranches in New Mexico. The U.S. Army in turn sent several expeditions into northern Comanchería to chase and destroy Comanche camps. In May 1861 Comanches made a treaty with federal agents in New Mexico, but the armistice was only days old when Comanches attacked the settlements in Chaperito on the Gallinas River.[27]

While Comanchería's borders in the north, east, and west were becoming increasingly porous, its southern border with Texas burst wide open. In midcentury, Texas was experiencing dramatic growth, which in many ways was an extension of the cotton-driven economic boom in the American South. Settlers from Alabama, Tennessee, Kentucky, Georgia, Mississippi, and Missouri flooded into Texas, whose population swelled from 140,000 in 1847 to 210,000 in 1850 and more than 600,000 in 1860. A new slavery-based cotton plantation system flourished along the broad, muddy rivers of the coastal plains, and corn farming thrived in the rich soil of blackland prairies. The cattle industry expanded from south Texas toward the northern frontier, fueled by livestock markets in New Orleans, the West Indies, and California. This vibrant growth, most Anglo-Texans believed, was restrained only by the fact that a half of the state was still under Comanche control, beyond reach and use. A collision was inevitable. Texas launched a forceful northward expansion, and the boundary line Comanches and Texans had so carefully constructed in the mid-1840s to separate the two powers became a dead letter.[28]

The first phase of Texas expansion was led by newly arrived German immigrants. In 1842 a private immigration company run by a group of Prussian entrepreneurs secured from the Republic of Texas a three-million-acre grant between the Llano and Colorado rivers, all of it on Comanche range, and launched a vigorous recruitment campaign. By 1845 several thousand Germans had arrived on the Gulf Coast, only to find that the immigration company had gone bankrupt. Ravaged by hunger and typhus on the humid coast, the would-be colonists began an arduous migration to the north and in 1846 built Fredericksburg within Comanchería's southern border. Southern Comanches, whom Anglo-Americans knew as Penatekas (Honey Eaters), killed the first German surveyors, but in 1847 the colonists managed to negotiate a treaty with Penateka leaders, who opened their southern lands for settlement in exchange for three thousand dollars' worth of presents. In the late 1840s and 1850s, as impoverished Penatekas frequented Fredericksburg to barter their meager goods for food and merchandise, thousands of Germans settled on Comanche territory. By 1860, a large segment of southern Comanchería had become Texas-German farming and grazing range.[29]

To the east, the Penatekas faced a more disorganized—and more threatening—invasion from central Texas. Since the annexation, Americans had streamed into Texas in thousands, seeking lands that the "giant arms of the United States" would soon vacate of Indians. Settlers began to infringe upon Comanche lands across a wide zone between the San Antonio and Trinity rivers, advancing under the protection of Texas Rangers who brought the weapons, experience, and hardiness they had acquired during the Mexican-American War to the Comanche frontier. To control the disorderly immigration and to shield Texas from Comanches and other plains nations, the U.S. Army built seven garrisons between the Trinity River and the Río Grande. Rather than keeping the Texans and the Indians apart, however, the protective presence of the forts encouraged settlers to press on farther to the west and north. By 1850 the frontier had pushed beyond the military cordon to the arched perimeter of the Balcones Escarpment, impinging on Penateka range.[30] The result was the first full-blown territorial war between Comanches and Euro-Americans.

Comanches entered that war starved, weakened, and fanatical. The urgency to protect homes and kin combined with the need to patch a collapsing economy with stolen stock, igniting a deadly raiding war. Comanches attacked settlers across the encroaching Texas frontier while also raiding deep into northern Mexico. Denying having "consented not to war on Mexicans," they made mockery of the Treaty of Guadalupe Hidalgo by crossing the Río Grande in such numbers that the border region seemed "infested" with war parties. They struck Mexican villages all the way to Durango and seized livestock and captives from the newly established Kickapoo, Seminole, and maroon settlements in northern Coahuila. Nuevo León alone suffered more than eight hundred Indian raids between 1848 and 1870. The one potentially positive outcome of the Mexican-American War for Mexico—a hard, policed international boundary that would have thwarted Comanche incursions below the Río Grande—evaporated into violence.[31]

As before, the Mexican-bound raids were often large-scale efforts that drew members from several Comanche divisions. Comanche rancherías, agent Neighbors reported, "keep up continual intercourse with each other, and are equally engaged in their depredations and war parties. Whenever a chief from one of the upper bands starts for Mexico or to any point on our frontier, they send runners to the lower bands, and all their warriors join him, so they are in fact but one people." Hunger, Neighbors wrote, fueled the raids: "they cannot subsist by any other means." In fact, several Comanche bands now lived permanently in northern Mexico, eking out a living by plundering livestock and hunting Apache scalps, which brought two hundred pesos in Chihuahua and Durango. In 1851 the Comanche leadership, an old woman named Tave Peté, the "generaless and prophetess" of the Comanches, and her grandsons Bajo el Sol and Magüe, signed a peace treaty in Chihuahua. They promised to stop raiding in the province and agreed to deliver Apache scalps. In Nuevo León and Coahuila, meanwhile, Comanche raids contributed to the outbreak of a widespread separatist revolt against the central government that still seemed inattentive to northern needs.[32]

Comanches had mounted a forceful military response that resembled their imperial actions of old, but Texas, too, organized itself for war. The state created new ranger companies and dispatched them against the Penatekas, while the federal government continued its efforts to pacify Texas. With several top officials now demanding that the Comanches be either isolated or exterminated, the army constructed by 1852 seven new frontier garrisons to keep the Comanches out of Texas. The new cordon lay roughly one hundred miles northwestward from the previous garrison line, and five of the forts—Belknap, Chadbourne, McKavett, Phantom Hill, and Mason—were well within Comanchería's borders, situated at key watering places where infantry troops could intercept raiding parties heading to Texas and Mexico. By fall 1853, the Texas frontier had engulfed Comanchería all the way to the Comanche Peak, and Comanche raiding in Texas dwindled to sporadic actions along the Río Grande.[33]

The Penatekas' strength was also undermined by growing factionalism within their ranks. Starvation fueled competition over shrinking resources, corroding internal solidarity and fracturing existing political arrangements. Penateka politics, one observer noted, became an opportunistic competition for resources and followers: "Ketumsee is an ambitious and astute leader, pursuing a discreet and complacent policy in the government of his followers calculated to enhance his popularity, and he has already alienated several of Sanaco's band, who have transferred their allegiance to him. This has engendered a feeling of ill will and jealousy between them which causes each to be suspicious of the motives of the other." Gradually, the Penatekas broke into three factions that settled in opposing parts of southern Comanchería. Sanaco took his followers to the middle Colorado River, while Potsanaquahip settled farther north of the Brazos River, where his bands blended with Pahayuko's Tenewas. Only Ketumsee, who had risen to power after the 1849 cholera epidemic carried away chiefs Mopechucope and Santa Anna, stayed in the south, trying to negotiate food and resources from Texas for his dwindling ranchería.[34]

Overt dispute among the Penatekas had broken out in 1851 when Ketumsee met with Texas Indian agents on the San Sabá River and asked the United States to "*set apart* a Section or peice [*sic*] of Country" for his people "*to settle* on and cultivate." The next year Ketumsee received rations at Fort Graham, met again with federal agents, released twenty-seven Mexican captives, and renewed his request for a reservation. These actions shocked and infuriated the other chiefs, who took them as an admission that the United States had the right to hand over Comanche lands and prevent their traditional stock-and-slave raids into Mexico, and they pledged to kill Ketumsee "for having given up the Mexican prisoners." By year's end, the southern Comanche political organization had disintegrated. "There is evidently a great want of a proper governmental organization amongst these bands of Comanches," Texas Indian agent Horace Capron remarked: "although originally from the same tribe (the Honey Eaters) they are now divided into small parties under different leaders, each one considering himself entitled to equal respect, and requiring a separate audience."[35]

Ketumsee's request for a sanctuary received little interest among Texas policymakers, who had resisted the federal government's repeated demands to set aside lands for Indian reservations. Texas had retained full control of its public domain under the exceptional terms of its admission into the United States, and its politicians intended to preserve these lands for their own constituents, who were each entitled to 640 acres for free. In 1853, however, Secretary of War Jefferson Davis used his considerable political clout in Texas to convince the state to adopt a reservation policy, and in the following year the legislature allotted some 53,000 acres for the three largest Indian tribes residing within the state's claimed borders. The Wichitas and Caddos were allocated a 30,000-acre reservation on the upper Brazos River, and 23,000 acres on the Clear Fork of the Brazos were reserved for the Penatekas.[36]

Robert Neighbors, the supervising Texas Indian agent, and Captain Marcy were sent to coax the three groups to move to these areas. In a meeting with Penateka chiefs, Marcy exploited the Comanches' economic distress, warning that the bison were disappearing so rapidly that "in a few years they and their children would have to resort to some other means than the chase for subsistence. . . . They must learn to cultivate the soil." Both Sanaco and Ketumsee agreed to move to the Clear Fork, where the latter settled in a wooden house and received a monthly salary so he would not have to hunt. Sanaco soon left the reservation, but hunger drove other bands in, and within a year more than five hundred Comanches were collecting annuities of beef, flour, and corn meal on the Clear Fork. By 1856, two hundred acres of the reservation had been plowed and fenced for cultivation, although much of the tilling had been done by the Comanches' Mexican captives.[37]

The reservations marked a turning point in Texas Indian policy, but they failed to resolve the larger issues. There were still thousands of Comanches on the plains, who were growing increasingly desperate. When large-scale raiding began anew in 1854, all seemed chaos. Some Comanche rancherías fragmented into small parties that struck settlements across Texas, while others raided into Mexico, skirting Fort Clark on the Nueces. War parties sometimes moved on foot, hoping to return with stolen horses, and sometimes overran newly established farmsteads and ranches with mounted hit-and-run assaults. Comanches raided the Delawares, Choctaws, and Cherokees in Indian Territory and were in turn raided by them. They dispatched war parties into Navajo country and attacked the Wichitas and Caddos in the Brazos reservation at harvest time. They were said to have "declared War upon all people south of Red River, White and Red," and yet they traded with itinerant Texas traders, such as the famed Jesse Chisholm, for guns. They raided the Kickapoos and Seminoles but at times also teamed up with them to form multiethnic raiding gangs. They plundered Apache rancherías along the Río Grande but used Mescalero rancherías as way stations to Mexico. They sometimes allowed a small number of Lipans to reside on the plains and join their war parties. Some of the attacks that Texans blamed on Comanches were probably the work of Wacos, Tawakonis, Mexicans, or whites dressed as Indians.[38]

Lacking a clear target amidst the chaos, Texans and the U.S. Army struck randomly. Ranger companies and spontaneously organized Texas militias killed all Indians they could find, and U.S. troops were ordered to "*search out and attack all parties or bands* . . . whether these [depredations] be notoriously attributable to the whole band, or only chargeable apparently to a few individuals." Only gradually did Texans begin to see what they thought was a pattern. Accumulating evidence suggested that most Indian raids originated in northern Comanchería, which served as a haven for such renowned southern Comanche war chiefs as Potsanaquahip. "The strangest feature of this state of affairs," agent Neighbors wrote in 1857, "is the fact that, at the same time that those bands of Camanches . . . are depredating on our citizens, waylaying our roads, destroying our mails to El Paso, &c., an agent of your department is distributing to them a large annuity of goods, arms, and ammunition on the Arkansas river." That, Neighbors seethed, "is arming them, and giving them the means more effectually to carry on their hostile forays."[39]

The objective of those forays, Neighbors learned from northern Comanche chiefs, was nothing less than the extermination of white settlements in Texas. But Neighbors's own reservation bands were also implicated in those forays. War bands from the north were reported to be using the Clear Fork reservation as a way station, a place where they recruited additional warriors, ate, and rested before striking into Texas or Mexico. Neighbors himself admitted that he could not "resist the influence of the outside band of Camanches, or to prevent the young men from quitting the reserve to join in the continued forays made by them both upon our frontier and that of Mexico." Comanche raiding, then, appeared to be a seasonally organized enterprise that revolved around Anglo-American sanctuaries on the upper Arkansas and Clear Fork. By 1858, the raids had taken a heavy toll on Texas. Numerous ranches and farms were abandoned in the western part of the state, and, as one observer put it, fear and uncertainty "paralyzed business almost entirely."[40]

For U.S. and Texas officials, a discernable pattern meant targets. Indian agents cancelled annuity distributions along the Arkansas, hoping to pressure Comanches to acknowledge that Texas was part of the United States and that war with one meant war with both. Meanwhile, the U.S. Army and Texas Rangers began to act offensively. Until 1858 neither had ventured far from the line of settlements, but now they carried war deep into the heart of Comanchería, turning it into a battleground for the first time since the late eighteenth century. In May an outfit of 100 Texas Rangers and 113 Caddo, Wichita, and Tonkawa scouts surprised a Kotsoteka camp of seventy lodges on Little Robe Creek, a few miles to the north of the Canadian River. Using the Indian auxiliaries as skirmishers, the rangers charged into the village. Comanches fled and scattered, and the rangers killed seventy-four warriors and two principal chiefs and took eighteen captives, "mostly women and children." Among those killed was a renowned Tenewa chief, Pooheve Quasoo, also known as Iron Jacket for the coat of mail he wore in battle. The rangers cut up the dead chief's armor for souvenirs and later sent a piece to the newly elected Texas Governor Hardin R. Runnels, who had pledged to pacify the frontier.[41]

In late September 1858 the Second Cavalry, which had been policing the Texas frontier for three years, duplicated the rangers' maneuver by riding into northern Comanchería with 135 Tawakoni, Waco, Caddo, Tonkawa, and Delaware scouts. After a long night march, the troops made contact with a large Comanche camp spread along the bottom of Horse Creek in western Oklahoma. Feeling secure deep in their home territory, Comanches had assigned no sentinels and left their horse herd unguarded. When they awoke to gunshots, their horses were already gone, stampeded by the charging cavalry. Immobilized, the men dug behind rocks and trees, fighting bullets and sabers with bows and arrows and knives as the women and children crawled up the riverbank. Brevet Major Earl Van Dorn reported that his troops killed fifty-six men and two women and burned 120 lodges with their contents. It was later learned that the Comanches—mainly Kotsotekas together with a band of Potsanaquahip's Penatekas—had been on their way to a peace council with federal agents in Indian Territory. Van Dorn denied any knowledge of the planned council and next spring led the Second Cavalry to another attack on Potsanaquahip's camp, now near the Arkansas River, killing forty-nine and capturing thirty-seven people.[42]

Demoralized by repeated defeats deep in their home territory, the Comanches withdrew from the open plains and retreated north and westward to the high plains and canyonlands of southwestern Kansas and the Oklahoma and Texas panhandles. By late fall 1859, nearly all Comanches and Kiowas, some ten thousand people, had clustered on a strip between the Arkansas and Canadian rivers, where they faced new, grim realities. The retreat deprived them of prime wintering grounds in the south, which had sustained a flourishing pastoral economy, and confined them to the colder northern latitudes, where life with horses was more precarious. The spatial compression, coupled with the deaths of several prominent *paraibos*, undercut existing social and political systems. Living in close proximity, the Yamparikas, Kotsotekas, Tenewas, and Penatekas began to reorganize themselves around new leaders whose authority stemmed primarily from military prowess and who drew followers across the fraying divisional lines. The old configuration of cohesive, geographically distinct divisions began to fade, giving way to more transient, hybrid formations.[43]

In Texas, meanwhile, the Penatekas' position in the Clear Fork reservation had become insufferable. Popular opinion tagged the reservation as a launch station for Comanche raids in Texas and demanded that it be removed from the state. Roused by frenzied newspaper articles—many of them penned by John R. Baylor, a dismissed Comanche agent turned Indian fighter turned political agitator—frontier Texans organized vigilante gangs that camped around the Clear Fork and Brazos reservations, launching night raids into Indian settlements. The gangs declared Cedar Creek, a tributary of the Brazos, a "dead line" and threatened to shoot all Indians south of it. By spring 1859, Baylor and his followers were demanding that the reservation Indians be exterminated rather than removed, insisting that the Indians would never stop raiding Texas. Army officers, many of whom privately shared Baylor's views, refused to restrain the rampant violence, thus paving the way for the Texas racial order in which there was no place for landed Indians. In late July 1859, amidst indiscriminate killings, agent Neighbors hastily led nearly four hundred Comanches from the Clear Fork reservation and more than a thousand Wichitas and Caddos from the Brazos reservation across the Red River to the southwestern Indian Territory. They were resettled in the Leased District, which had been secured from the Choctaws a few years earlier.[44]

By late 1859, Comanches had all but vanished from Texas. Their departure left a vacuum that was rapidly filled by settlers, who flocked into a wide zone between the Colorado and Trinity rivers. The farmer-settler frontier was trailed by the ranching frontier, which soon emerged as the primary dynamo of Texas expansion. In the course of the 1850s, sustained by a growing domestic demand for beef and ignoring the drought conditions, Texas ranchers had gradually extended their operations northward from the overcrowded and overgrazed early nucleus on the coastal plains. Skirting the steep cliffs of the Balcones Escarpment, the ranching frontier inched its way northward, reaching the northern tip of the Balcones by the end of the decade. There the expansion turned westward to the open plains of central Texas, where the removal of Comanche and Wichita reservations had opened thousands of square miles of prime grazing land for cattle ranching. By 1860, Palo Pinto, Erath, and Comanche counties, all within the historical Comanche range, had emerged as the core area of Texas ranching.[45]

The Comanches in 1860 were in desperate straits. Almost four hundred Penatekas were confined to a reservation in Indian Territory, cut off from their kinspeople and living as refugees, and Comanchería itself had been torn asunder. New Mexican ranchers had engulfed wide stretches of its western flank, and tribes from Indian Territory had colonized the bison hunting grounds of eastern Comanchería. Overland immigration was turning the Arkansas valley and northern Comanchería into a wasteland, and the Texas settler-ranching economy had swallowed up much of southern Comanchería. The Comanches had suffered a sickening collapse from hegemonic dominance to poverty and starvation in a mere decade. The two great foundations of their international power—long-distance raiding into Mexico and long-distance trading across the Great Plains—had crumbled, and their empire lay in ruins. The future seemed even bleaker. In 1860 the dry spell was in its fifteenth year, and the grass burned brown and dead in what was left of Comanchería. The bison herds were evaporating, as were Comanches' hopes of survival on the plains.

The outbreak of the Civil War eased the pressure on Comanchería's borders, but it did not halt the decline. Caught between Union New Mexico and Confederate Texas and Indian Territory, Comanches played the two sides off against each other, trying to draw concessions from both. During the four years of war, they negotiated with Confederate and Union agents but maintained an appearance of neutrality that allowed them to collect provisions at the Confederate Fort Cobb as well as the Union Fort Wise. The year 1863 seemed to bring new hope to the Comanches. They raided the exposed Texas frontier for large quantities of horses and cattle, which they sold to Union beef contractors in New Mexico. Two of their chiefs, Prick in the Forehead and Paruasemena (Ten Bears), visited Washington to sign a treaty. But these were small solaces in a deepening crisis. Smallpox had carried away uncounted numbers in the previous year, and the dry spell continued unabated. And when the Senate failed to ratify the treaty, a vicious war broke out on the Comanche–New Mexico border. As many as four thousand Comanches may have perished during the early 1860s, leaving a total population of only five thousand in 1865.[46]

But then two things happened. First, in the mid-1860s, the rains returned. The catastrophic, generation-long drought passed, rainfall bounced back to the normal level, and the grasses began to heal. The precipitous decline of the bison populations slowed down, giving Comanches a new lease on survival. Second, in 1865, the Confederacy collapsed, and Comanches' struggle for survival turned into military expansion and economic growth. The North treated the vanquished South essentially as an imperial holding that was to be demilitarized, transformed, and harnessed for profit. The inadvertent consequence of this was that west Texas became once more a setting for Comanche power politics.[47]

This development was set in motion in mid-October 1865—six months after Appomattox—when eleven Comanche chiefs met with a U.S. peace commission on the Little Arkansas River in present-day southern Kansas. The commissioners came with a dramatic proposal: if the Comanches agreed to live in peace, return all captives, and allow military forts on their lands, the United States would recognize their claim to a territory that included western Oklahoma, the panhandles of Oklahoma and Texas, and a triangle-shaped slice of northwestern Texas below the panhandle. Although the proposal obliged the Comanches to stay within that reservation, Chief Eagle Drinking urged other chiefs to accept it. But he also refused to cede any lands. "I am fond of the land I was born on," he told the commissioners. "The white man has land enough. I don't want to divide."

The final treaty, known as the Treaty of Little Arkansas, reflected this vision of undivided Comanchería. Of the eleven chiefs who signed the treaty, nine were Yamparikas, Kotsotekas, Tenewas, or Nokonis (Wanderers, a small new division with close ties to the Tenewas), whose territory fell within the limits of the proposed reservation. The supposedly ceded lands that fell outside of the reservation belonged to an emerging faction called Kwahadas (Antelope Eaters), who resided far in the south on the Llano Estacado and were not present at the Little Arkansas talks. The treaty was contested on the American side as well, for a large portion of the reservation fell within the claimed borders of the state of Texas, which had never explicitly recognized Indian claims on its lands. Yet, on October 18, the two sides signed a final treaty, in which the United States reaffirmed Comanches' claim on some forty thousand square miles of Texas territory.[48]

Texas was the great loser in the Comanche–U.S. rapprochement. The federal government not only had used its lands to buy peace from the Comanches, but reconstruction politics left the state utterly vulnerable to Comanche exploitation. Considering Texas a conquered territory, Washington sent thousands of troops to the state but assigned most of them to the eastern population centers to reassert federal authority and to the Mexican border to contain possible ramifications of the French invasion of Mexico. The frontier posts of the interior plains were not regarrisoned until the late 1860s. The government also kept large numbers of Texans imprisoned after the Civil War, depriving farms and ranches of a workforce. The upshot was that in 1865 there were several million head of unprotected cattle wandering in Texas, free of fences and free for the taking. In 1866 the army assigned two cavalry regiments to the Comanche border, a pitiful deterrent in a situation that was structurally primed for violence.[49]

That was the setting for an extended Comanche raiding spree that lasted into the early 1870s, devastating not only Texas but large parts of New Mexico, Indian Territory, and the central plains. These raids represented a departure for Comanches. Consummate horse raiders, they now focused increasingly on cattle, which earlier they had either ignored or killed on the spot for food or revenge. By 1867, after two years of raiding, Texas had lost almost four thousand horses and more than thirty thousand head of cattle. Human casualties mounted as well: 162 people were killed and 43 carried into captivity during the same period. And once again Comanche war bands began crossing the Río Grande into Mexico. Comanches also pushed northward to the Smoky Hill River and eastward deep into Indian Territory, where the Civil War had left the Indian nations divided and weakened. They marched to eastern New Mexico to raid and attack the eight thousand Navajos whom the U.S. Army had forcibly removed to Bosque Redondo, which Comanches considered part of Comanchería. Pillaging horses, mules, cattle, and captives, Comanche war bands covered a range that extended more than eight hundred miles from north to south and five hundred miles east to west.[50]

Comanche herds burgeoned. Most early nineteenth-century estimates placed the horse-to-person ratio at between three and four animals per person, but after midcentury many bands possessed from five to ten animals per capita. The numbers signaled a momentous change: Comanches were becoming full-fledged pastoralists who relied on domesticated animals for their material well-being. This transformation was most visible among the Kwahadas, the new cross-divisional faction that emerged from the political turmoil of the 1850s. When Lorenzo Labadi, an Indian agent from New Mexico, inspected the eastern Llano Estacado in 1867, he found there a mixed Kwahada-Kotsoteka camp of seven hundred lodges with some fifteen thousand horses and three to four hundred mules. They raised "much of their own stock" and had more than one thousand cows. "They also have Texas cattle without number," Labadi reported, "and almost every day bring in more." Eighteen war parties were in Texas plundering for horses, mules, and cattle, and a large party led by the head chiefs had left to attack Bosque Redondo.[51]

The growing domestic herds served a double function. Most immediately, they helped patch up the drought-ravaged subsistence economy. The decline of the bison herds slowed after 1865, but the herds had settled at such a low plateau that Comanches were forced to search for alternative sources of subsistence. They slaughtered cattle on the homebound legs of long raiding expeditions and, as Labadi noted, raised cows for food and hides. Horses, too, were turned into sources of food and hides. George Bent recalled how Comanches used "horse hides in the way other plains tribes used buffalo hides, in making clothing, lodge covers, etc." and even argued that they grew to prefer horseflesh to buffalo meat.[52]

The other purpose of the massive Comanche herds was commercial. The animals that were not eaten were channeled into the comanchero trade, which experienced a dramatic revival, recovering fully from its midcentury hiatus. Texas longhorns, the result of random mixing of Spanish *retinto* (criollo) and English cattle, were an ideal commodity for the comanchero trade. The very qualities that would make them so suitable for the great cattle drives of the late 1860s, 1870s, and 1880s made them easy to move from Texas to the comanchero rendezvous on the Llano Estacado. The longhorns were efficient browsers, reason-

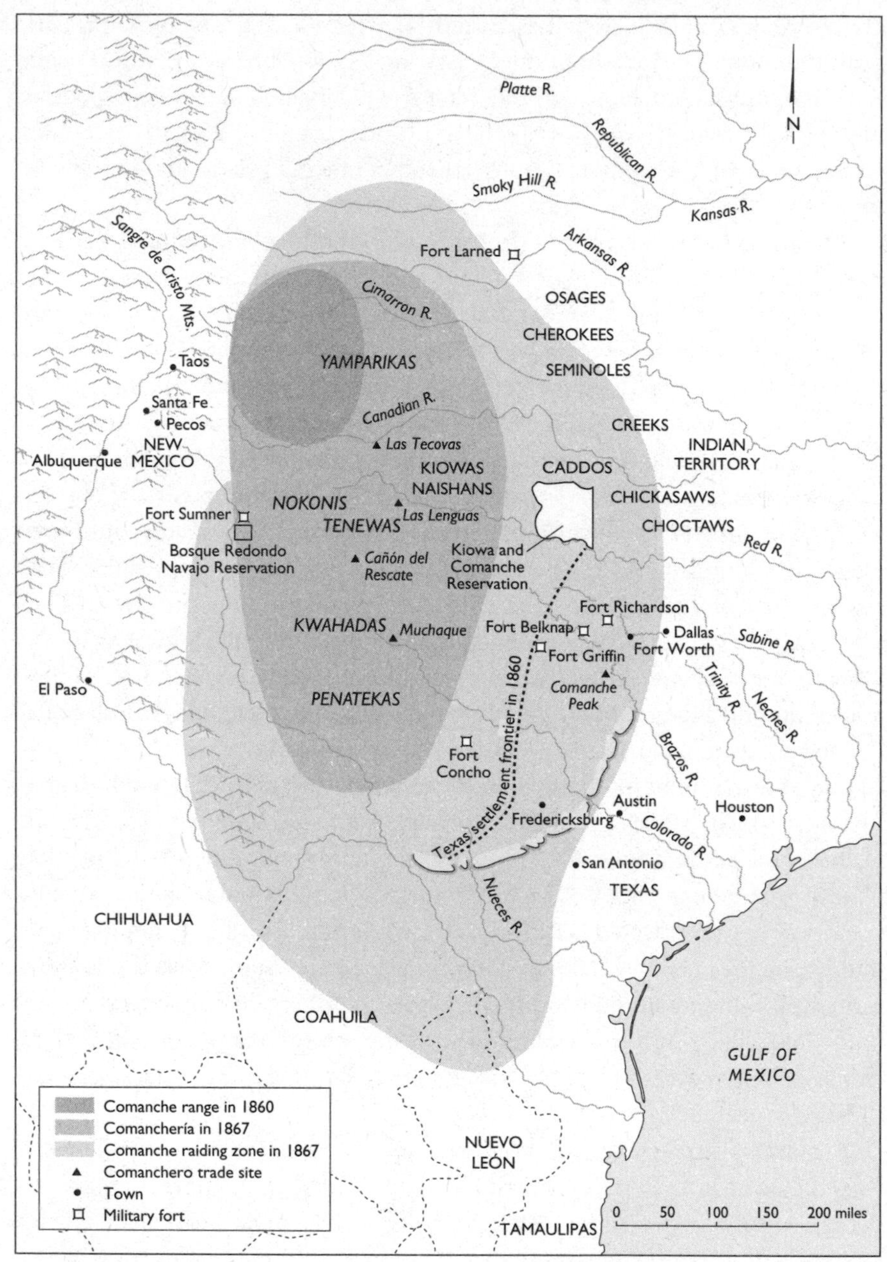

18. Revival of Comanche power in the late 1860s. Map by Bill Nelson.

ably simple to handle, and, with long legs and hard hoofs, could move enormous distances on little water without losing weight—all important considerations for Comanches, who had been horse herders for generations but had had no experience with domesticated bovines.[53]

The easily transportable longhorns found ready markets in New Mexico, where U.S. Army officers quietly invested their own funds in the comanchero commerce, carrying on the shadowy practice that had began during the Civil War. In 1866 and 1867, in fact, a cartel of army officers and cattle barons assumed control over a large section of the comanchero business. For a share of the profits, they furnished comanchero parties with supplies and merchandise and protected them against government intervention. But the increasing profits also drew *ricos*, wealthy New Mexican elites, who began sponsoring comanchero parties with horses, goods, and laborers, both peons and slaves. For a while, Americans and *ricos* competed and coexisted as the patrons of the comanchero trade, which had become a nexus of a covert transnational scheme where New Mexicans, American merchants, U.S. officials, and the Comanches came together to profit from exploiting the Anglo-Texas cattle industry.[54]

Shielded from federal control and backed by wealthy patrons, the comancheros flocked onto the Llano Estacado in unforeseen numbers. In 1866 they were reported to be "constantly" among the Kwahadas, their main suppliers, "furnishing them goods, arms . . . in fact anything . . . they want." "This trade," another observer reported, "has been immense of late. I know of one man here in Santa Fe who took about one hundred and fifty dollars' worth of goods there [the Llano Estacado], and came back with one hundred head of Texas cattle for his goods."[55]

The eighty-year-old trade transformed into a structured enterprise with fixed centers, an elaborate transportation system, and a secure financial base. The chance meetings of the old were replaced by fixed rendezvous points, where irrigation ditches and semi-subterranean adobe shelters provided the infrastructure for seasonal occupation. The canyonlands in the central and eastern Llano Estacado were dotted with such sites, three of which served as the nerve centers for the entire system: Las Tecovas by perennial springs near present-day Amarillo; Las Lenguas on the upper Pease River; and Cañón del Rescate (Ransom Canyon) near present-day Lubbock. Linked to New Mexico by a web of well-established cart roads and smaller pack trails, those sites could attract hundreds of comancheros. An estimated seven hundred New Mexicans left for the plains during the 1867 season, which culminated in a massive rendezvous where four hundred comancheros sold twenty thousand dollars' worth of merchandise to

Comanches; one official reported that New Mexico was full of Texas cattle by the season's end.

Such mass gatherings lasted for several days, during which huge amounts of commodities exchanged hands. The involvement of wealthy Americans and *ricos* had expanded the depth and range of comanchero wares, which now included traditional goods—salt, hard bread, flour, sugar, tobacco, blankets, and knives—and such novelties as whisky, tea, candy, army caps, Colt revolvers, and ten-shot, lever-action rifles. Comanches paid for the goods mostly with stolen Texas cattle and horses, but they also offered Mexican and Indian captives, who remained "very much in demand among the 'ricos' and prospective bride-grooms" in New Mexico even though the territory had prohibited all forms of involuntary servitude and slavery in accordance with the Thirteenth Amendment of the United States Constitution.[56]

The silent investors, fixed rendezvous, varied merchandise, and sheer volume of the exchange point to a fundamental change in the comanchero commerce: the ancient borderland institution of face-to-face transactions was becoming integrated into a capitalist system of formal market relations. Yet despite the new elements, the comanchero commerce remained embedded in tradition. As they had done for generations, Comanches and comancheros enveloped the mundane exchange of material goods in social rituals, which renewed and elaborated the sense of solidarity and kinship between their communities. The actual trading was preceded by wrestling and archery matches, horse races, gambling, and feasts, practices that brought participants into closer personal contact and alleviated the tensions of the bartering that followed. Although some contemporaries claimed that the introduction of alcohol and the involvement of American and *rico* financers inflated prices to the Comanches' disadvantage, the traditional norms of reciprocity and interdependence persisted; one captive later recalled how Comanches especially valued Pueblo Indian comancheros who "would pay good price for cattle" and "were faithful to their promises." The comanchero middlemen, through their commitment to customary forms, thus functioned as a buffer that shielded the Comanches from the corrupting and alienating influences of the market. And finally, while one end of the comanchero trade was now anchored to the expanding capitalist economy of regularized market exchanges, the other end remained firmly planted in the borderland tradition of violent economic action and redistribution. It was an open secret that the livestock and laborers that fueled New Mexico's economic growth during and after the Civil War years were looted from Texas and northern Mexico.[57]

The contraband cattle and captive trade and the violence it fueled in Texas were a stinging embarrassment for the federal agents in New Mexico, Kansas, and Indian Territory. They had failed to restrain the Comanches, who ignored the reservation boundaries as defined in the Treaty of Little Arkansas, refused to relinquish slave traffic, and yet frequented Fort Larned, their assigned agency near the Big Bend of the Arkansas, to collect government supplies. Shameful reports of "lives taken and property stolen by Indians . . . fed and clothed and armed by the representatives of the U.S. Gov" poured out of Texas, putting enormous pressure on the Indian Office and its agents. Determined to extend emancipation from the South to the Southwest, federal agents repeatedly demanded that the Comanches and Kiowas relinquish their captives. But instead of eradicating slavery and captive trade, such interventions ended up supporting them. Comanches and Kiowas did turn numerous captives over to U.S. agents, but only if they received handsome ransoms in cash or goods. As one agent despaired: "every prisoner purchased from the Indians amounts to the same as granting them a license to go and commit the same overt act. They boastfully say that stealing white women is more of a lucrative business than stealing horses." The United States' emancipation efforts had created a new outlet for slave trafficking for Comanches, and its punitive reconstruction policies in Texas opened a deep supply base: the demilitarized western part of the state lay wide open for Comanche slaving parties.[58]

The struggle over the captives epitomized the collision between the Comanches and the United States and precipitated its progression to open war. The persistence of slavery and captive traffic convinced U.S. policymakers that the Southwest was not big enough for both traditional borderland cultural economies and the new American system of state-sponsored, free-labor capitalism. Perplexed and put off by their own involvement in the captive business, U.S. authorities, most of them Civil War veterans, started to call for tougher policies and, if necessary, the extermination of the slave-trafficking Indians. In 1867, when presented with the case of a captured thirteen-year-old Texas boy for whom Comanches demanded "remuneration," General William Tecumseh Sherman, the commander of the U.S. Army, responded that the officials should no longer "Submit to this practice of paying for Stolen children. It is better the Indian race be obliterated."[59]

The young Texan captive may have brought it to the surface, but Sherman's racial wrath had other, deeper causes. The Comanches, supposedly subjugated reservation dwellers, still raided all across the American Southwest, frustrating the United States' modernizing plans for the region. Near collapse in 1865, the Comanches had experienced a dramatic revival after the Civil War. Shedding what had become a burden and keeping and modifying what was still usable, they pieced together a dynamic new economy from the fragments of the old one. They repaired the crippled subsistence system by shifting to intensive pastoralism, by diversifying their bison-centered hunting economy, and by accepting U.S. annuities. Exploiting the general chaos around them—especially in the disarmed and disordered post–Civil War Texas—they forged a thriving transnational raiding-and-trading network that plugged them to the larger continental economy. They had lost too many people to re-create their early nineteenth-century hegemony, but the Comanches were expanding once more. That this ascent could not continue is obvious only in hindsight.

The full extent of the devastation the Comanches were sowing did not become clear until the spring and summer of 1867, when Texas Governor John W. Throckmorton solicited data on Indian depredations across the state. As reports arrived in the governor's office in Austin, an alarming picture emerged: the frontier was caving in across a three-hundred-mile stretch from the Red River to San Antonio, exposing the very center of Texas to destruction. Clay, Montague, Cooke, Jack, Erath, Comanche, Coleman, Comal, and Medina counties reported severe losses of population as settlers fled the Comanche attacks from the north and Lipan assaults from the south. Towns were crumbling, farms lay abandoned, and killings were becoming commonplace. "The murders that have been Committed on our frontier," one official despaired, "are so frequent that they are only noticed by their friends and acquainted as they would notice ones dying a natural death." The cattle ranching industry whose prospects in 1860 had seemed so promising was nearly paralyzed: "nearly every drove of Cattle that attempt to cross the plains are captured by the Indians which will cut off the Stock raisers of the frontiers from a market for their beef Cattle." As a half century earlier, in the late Spanish and Mexican eras, Texas was disintegrating under Comanche pressure.[60]

8

COLLAPSE

When the Civil War ended, the Great Plains emerged as the most violent place in North America. With peace, Americans once again became mobile, swarming across the Mississippi and onto the Great Plains in the thousands. For most of these westbound migrants, the plains were merely a barrier, a distance to cross on the way to greater riches beyond, and that was the problem. The federal government made only token efforts to negotiate with the powerful nomadic Indian nations of the western plains for right-of-ways across their lands. Overlanders became trespassers and killings became routine. In some instances Americans triggered the bloodshed; in others they stepped into pockets of long-existing violence.

The Comanche-Texas frontier was only one of many crisis points on the post-bellum Great Plains. Friction between Indians and whites in eastern Colorado increased throughout the fall of 1864, erupting in November when Colonel John Chivington led seven hundred Colorado militia troops to attack a non-combatant group of Cheyennes and Arapahoes at Sand Creek, slaying some 130 men, women, and children. Enraged by the unprovoked massacre, Cheyennes and Arapahoes approached their Lakota allies and declared war on the United States. They attacked wagon trains, stage stations, military posts, and ranches across the Platte River valley and burned the town of Julesburg. Cheyenne, Arapaho, and Lakota Dog Soldiers, a militant multitribal faction, shunned peace talks, and by winter 1866 the central plains were the scene of unrestrained violence. Lakotas, meanwhile, waged a war of their own against the U.S. Army, which had begun constructing unauthorized forts to secure the Bozeman Trail that led from southeastern Wyoming to the gold camps of Montana, bisecting the Lakotas' best hunting grounds in the Bighorn country. The escalating conflict of raids, reprisals, and futile attempts of treaty-making erupted into full-scale war in fall 1866, and in December Lakotas ambushed and killed Captain William Fetterman and eighty soldiers near Fort Phil Kearny.[1]

The sensational defeat, the army's worst disaster in the West to date, propelled the Indian question into America's national consciousness, forcing Washington to take cognizance of the turmoil on the plains. With the trauma of the Civil War still fresh, the American public demanded humanitarian rather than military solutions, and Congress created an Indian Peace Commission to negotiate treaties with the Plains Indians. The commission, led by Commissioner of Indian Affairs Nathaniel Taylor, investigated the outstanding issues across the plains but soon focused on the middle section between the Platte and Arkansas rivers. The construction of the transcontinental railroad was well under way, and the Platte and Kansas river valleys were the projected settings for Union Pacific and Kansas Pacific trunk lines.

To clear this crucial belt for development, the commissioners set out to relocate Indian nations in two out-of-the-way reservations. The Lakotas, Northern Cheyennes, Northern Arapahoes, and Crows would share a reservation in the Black Hills country of Dakota Territory, and the Comanches, Kiowas, Naishans, Southern Cheyennes, and Southern Arapahoes would be collected and confined in western Indian Territory. Once this segregation of the plains into Indian and non-Indian sectors was realized, the commission envisioned, a program of civilization and assimilation could commence. Protected from the unsavory Western influences in their isolated reservation crucibles, the Indians could be taught to live in fixed houses; till the soil on individual farms; and speak, read, and write English. As wards of the government, they could shed the trappings of their tribal identity and the burdens of their race and start their long individual journeys into the American mainstream.[2]

The rampant Comanche raiding in Texas and Indian Territory in 1867 and the Cheyenne and Arapaho terror on the central plains made the southern reservation a priority. In October 1867, after weeks of aggressive promotion by government messengers, more than five thousand Comanches, Kiowas, Naishans, Cheyennes, and Arapahoes congregated at Medicine Lodge Creek, sixty miles south of Fort Larned, to meet with a U.S. peace commission. The Kwahadas stayed out, but all other Comanche divisions were represented.

The council opened with mutual exchanges of pleasantries and promises of goodwill, but when the talks began, the Americans' determination to dismantle Indian nations as sovereign polities became immediately clear. The commissioners extended to the Comanches and Kiowas the familiar provisions of perpetual peace but then pressured them to accept a 5,500-square-mile reservation in the Leased District of Indian Territory. Here the two groups would have access to physicians, blacksmiths, millers, engineers, teachers, and schools, all parts of an intensive civilization program aimed at transforming them into literate yeoman farmers within a generation. They could hunt within the bounds of their territory as long as the bison remained, but the nominal ownership of the off-reservation lands would shift to the United States. In exchange for surrendering their claim to more than 140,000 square miles, the commission offered the Comanches and Kiowas twenty-five thousand dollars per year for three decades. The Cheyennes, Arapahoes, and Naishans received similar offers.[3]

The proposals outraged the Indian delegates, provoking several chiefs to deliver angry speeches. Yet within a week, all five nations had signed treaties. Standard explanations to this change of heart assert that the Indians failed to understand the treaty-making process and were overwhelmed by the government's inducements: the commissioners handed out $120,000 worth of presents, a sum so large that it supposedly clouded the chiefs' judgment. That political naiveté, it would seem, was personified in Paruasemena, the prominent Penateka leader who had visited Washington in 1863. Seventy-five-years old and spectacled now, the chief addressed the peace commission in a long and passionate speech, which has entered American mythology as an archetype of Indian oratory, an eloquent enunciation of a vanquished people's grief over a doomed world. But underneath its esthetic splendor, the speech had a sophisticated political agenda that affected the final treaty to a degree that has not yet been realized.[4]

Paruasemena began his address by listing past grievances and bluntly turned down the commission's proposal: "There are things which you have said to me which I did not like." He reminded the commissioners of his powerful bargaining position, buttressed by the Comanche expansion into Texas after the Civil War, and emphasized his people's military strength: "The Comanches are not weak and blind, like pups of a dog when seven sleeps old. They are strong and far-sighted, like grown horses. We took their road [war with Texas] and we went on it. The white women cried and our women laughed." He accepted government annuities but rejected the idea that they were compensation for relinquished lands. Instead, he invoked the Comanche ideal of mutual affection: "When I get goods and presents I and my people feel glad, since it shows that he [the president of the United States] holds us in his eye." Paruasemena explicitly rebuffed the reservation policy on which the land transfers rested: "You said that you wanted to put us upon a reservation, to build us houses and make us medicine lodges. I do not want them. . . . I want to die there [on the plains] and not within walls." To underpin his stance, he reminded the commission of the earlier agreements that secured Comanche claims to all of the Great Plains below the Arkansas River and emphasized his people's long tenure in the region: "I know every stream and every wood between the Rio Grande and the Arkansas. I have lived and hunted over that country. I live like my fathers before me, and, like them, I have lived happily. When I was in Washington the Great Father told me that all the Comanche land was ours and that no one should hinder us living upon it. So, why do you ask us to leave the rivers and the sun and the wind and live in houses."[5]

Having rejected territorial transfers, Paruasemena made a counterproposal. As in previous treaties, Comanches would permit limited right-of-ways across their lands in exchange for annuities: "I want no more blood upon my land to stain the grass. I want it all clear and pure, and I wish it so that all who go through among my people may find peace when they come in and leave it when they go out." Paruasemena's proposal, in short, stemmed from the position that had guided Comanche policies with the United States since the early 1850s: he was willing to make minor concessions to secure annuities but categorically rejected demands that could have jeopardized the traditional Comanche way of life.

Marred by obscure meanings, mutual misconstructions, and uneasy compromises, the final agreement was a typical U.S.–Indian treaty. Some of the stipulations were familiar and unambiguous. Comanches pledged to refrain from slave raiding and attacking U.S. travelers, allow the construction of military posts, and permit the building of railroads along the Platte and Smoky Hill rivers. The question of the use and ownership of land, however, remained deeply problematic. The way the commissioners intended and interpreted the treaty, Comanches, by accepting a reservation, had given up all claims to the lands that had been determined as their reservation in the 1865 Little Arkansas Treaty. On those lands they retained only a temporary hunting privilege, which would remain in effect "so long as the buffalo may range thereon in such numbers as to justify the chase." But for Comanches, that hunting privilege *was* ownership. Whereas Americans made a clear distinction between the use and ownership of land, Comanches regarded them as inexorably linked; they saw themselves as custodians, looking after the land for their future generations simply by living on it. As long as there were Comanches residing on a piece of land, the generational cycle would continue, and the land would remain theirs.[6]

By guaranteeing Comanches' right to hunt and dwell on the open plains below the Arkansas valley, the treaty seemed to sanction rather than alter the existing territorial status quo. Moreover, the treaty explicitly prohibited all white settlements "on the lands contained in the old [1865] reservation," and Indian signatories later maintained that the commissioners had made oral promises to keep American hunters from entering the southern plains below the Arkansas River; from Comanches' viewpoint, this must have further strengthened the notion that the treaty secured their territorial rights. Indeed, except for Chief Tosawa (White Knife), who had lived in Indian Territory since 1859, all Comanche chiefs refused to accept houses in the reservation, which suggests that they expected the reservation to be not a place of residence but a seasonal supply base. Eager to conclude the talks and move to the north to deal with the Lakotas, Northern Cheyennes, and Northern Arapahoes, the commissioners did not press the issue. The treaty articles mentioned only a "dwelling-house" for Tosawa; the other chiefs were merely expected to make the "reservation their permanent home and . . . make no permanent settlement elsewhere."[7]

Whatever hopes U.S. agents had entertained about Comanche submission, they vanished almost immediately. In winter 1867–68 several thousand Comanches and Kiowas visited a temporary agency in the Eureka valley near Fort Cobb in western Indian Territory to collect annuities, but only a fraction of the Indians stayed to start new lives in the reservation. The majority of the Comanches and Kiowas set out to the plains, where they spent the summer and fall raiding cattle and horses from Texas, Bosque Redondo, and Indian Territory and trading with comancheros. Losses in Texas were described as "almost incredible." Meanwhile, Cheyenne Dog Soldiers continued their raiding war against the Americans in Colorado and Kansas, threatening railway construction along the Platte and Kansas valleys. With the peace process in tatters, the Senate appointed General William Tecumseh Sherman to administer Indian policy and suppress the violence. In fall 1868 Sherman authorized General Philip H. Sheridan to launch a winter campaign to drive all Cheyennes south of the Kansas line. In late December, a month after George Custer's Seventh Cavalry destroyed a Cheyenne village on the Washita River, the Third Cavalry attacked a Comanche camp at the Soldier Spring, killing twenty-five people. Sherman ordered the Comanche and Kiowa agency moved from Fort Cobb thirty-five miles south to Cache Creek, where the army built a new soldier town, Fort Sill, to oversee the Indians.[8]

Then, the U.S. Indian policy shifted unexpectedly. In 1869 newly elected President Ulysses S. Grant introduced his Peace Policy, which advocated Christian education over coercion and brought Protestant missionaries to oversee the reservation programs. Lawrie Tatum, a stanch Iowa Quaker, was put in charge of the Comanche and Kiowa agency, and the army was removed from the reservation. Troops continued to police the southern plains, but they were authorized to attack and make arrests only if the Indians had been positively identified as hostile. No arrests were allowed inside reservations without Indian agents' express consent. In practice, the army patrols could detain Indian raiders only if they managed to catch one of the highly mobile trading parties with stolen livestock before the animals were sold to the comancheros, eaten, or rebranded and absorbed into the vast Comanche herds.[9]

Comanches took the new approach as a mandate to continue their traditional ways and policies. They hunted, raided, and traded on the plains and in Texas for most of the year, but in winters they moved in large numbers near the agency to live on rations. In a sense, Comanches incorporated the reservation into their traditional yearly cycle as a different kind of river valley: like river bottoms, the reservation provided food and shelter during the cold months, and like the river valleys, it never held the appeal of the open grasslands. Essentially a new resource domain, the reservation helped Comanches preserve their nomadic way of life on the plains rather than easing them into sedentary existence.

To facilitate this maneuvering between the reservation and the open plains, the Comanches splintered into two geographically distinct but politically linked factions. Most Penatekas and some Tenewas had settled permanently in the reservation, where they cultivated close ties with the agency officials, but the majority of Kwahadas, Yamparikas, and Kotsotekas lived on the Llano Estacado and Texas plains, visiting the reservation only seasonally. Although the reservation and nonreservation chiefs occasionally clashed over the frequency and legitimacy of raiding, individual bands and families could move fluidly between the agency and the plains, exploiting the resources of both.[10]

Kiowas, Naishans, Cheyennes, and Arapahoes adopted a similar strategy, and many of their nonreservation bands joined, and partially blended into, the Kwahadas, Yamparikas, and Kotsotekas in northern Comanchería. By doing so, they both carried on and intensified the long tradition of ethnic mixing in Comanchería. By the late 1860s, the Llano Estacado had become a hub for numerous intertribal rancherías whose driving force was their members' shared antagonism toward the restrictive modernizing policies of the United States. These new units were led by men like Satanta, Pacer, Quanah Parker, Mowway (Shaking Hand), Paruacoom (He-Bear), and Tebenanaka (Sound of the Sun), men who have entered the frontier mythology as iconic, unyielding tribal leaders who fervently protected their people against the rising American tide. But the primary role of these chiefs may well have been their shared role as co-leaders of new multitribal communities of interests that both transcended and obscured ethnic boundaries.[11]

The Comanche strategy of using the reservation as a seasonal supply base put enormous strain on Agent Tatum and the Quaker experiment. Tatum pressured the Indian Bureau to increase the annuities to make the reservation more appeal-

19. Quanah Parker, chief of the Comanche Indians. Quanah Parker was one of the most powerful Comanche leaders of the early reservation period and arguably the most famous Comanche. He was also the embodiment of the dynamics of ethnic incorporation that defined the Comanches' imperial experience. Son of Peta Nocona, a Comanche chief, and Ann Cynthia Parker, an Anglo-Texan captive woman, Quanah Parker became a prominent leader in the early 1870s. His rise to power illustrates the opportunities the multiethnic Comanche society offered to people who were not full-blood Comanches. From J. E. Irwin, *Photographs of Kiowa and Comanche Indians* (Chickasha, I.T.: Irwin, ca. 1898), folder 19. Courtesy of Yale Collection of Western Americana, Beinecke Rare Book and Manuscript Library.

ing, and he struggled to identify the raiders in order to withhold their rations. Comanches, however, annulled such controlling attempts by the simple measure of insisting that all rations be issued through their chiefs. After receiving the rations at the Fort Sill agency, the chiefs redistributed them among the women, who then took the food and other items to their camps, which were often located at the reservation outskirts, as far from the agency as possible. The effect was that Tatum dealt with only a few headmen; the rest of the Comanches appeared to him as one undifferentiated mass. Shielded by anonymity, individual warriors remained beyond the official gaze and could enter and leave the reservation untracked and unopposed. Instead of the Comanches becoming immersed into reservation life, the reservation became immersed into the Comanche political economy. In fall 1870, for example, as Tosawa, Paruasemena, and other reservation chiefs came to listen a conciliatory message from Commissioner of Indian Affairs Ely S. Parker, Comanche and Kiowa war parties brought a large number of captives, mostly women and children, to the agency for ransoming. Although scandalized, Tatum felt morally obliged to rescue the captives from what he deemed as savagery and abject Comanche womanhood. He redeemed fourteen Americans and twelve Mexicans, paying as much as a hundred dollars per person.[12]

The U.S. military elite observed such incidents with growing frustration, which triggered an impassioned verbal exchange between the army and the Indian Bureau. General Sheridan, now the commander of the Department of the Missouri, ridiculed the Peace Policy: "If a white man commits murder or robs, we hang him or send him to the penitentiary; if an Indian does the same, we have been in the habit of giving him more blankets." Exacerbating the army's frustration, many Comanche and Kiowa raiders used the reservation not only as a supply depot but as an asylum. The Peace Policy stipulated that reservations were demilitarized zones under the Indian Office's exclusive control and that army patrols could not pursue Indian raiders into reservations. Comanches and Kiowas exploited that loophole systematically, turning Fort Sill into a protective enclave for their raiding parties. The army's impotence reached a symbolic nadir in 1870 when Comanches stole seventy-three mules from Fort Sill's quartermaster corral. When the fort commander reported the incident to Commissioner Parker, he was ordered to take no action.[13]

Agent Tatum received intense criticism for his actions, but unwilling to concede the failure of Quaker policies, he put the blame on the shortcomings of the annuity system—corrupt contractors, delayed shipments, and substandard goods. His argument was not groundless. The Indian Office used a large part of the annuity funds to settle depredation claims filed against the Comanches, creating serious shortages of supplies at Fort Sill. But the biggest problem was rampant corruption, which led to numerous distortions: funds disappeared, flour was infested with worms, bacon sacks contained stones, and annuity goods ended up with agency traders who made Indians pay for the goods they were supposed to get for free. "What are we to do for food?" Tatum asked in summer 1869. "Their rations are not sufficient. They are licked up like the morning dew. Seven days rations are gone in four."[14] Yet blaming the annuity system missed the fundamental point: most Comanches refused to stay on the reservation simply because they could still support their families out of it. Although federal agents repeatedly proclaimed it obsolete, Comanches' off-reservation economy remained viable, generating a strong pull to the plains.

By the turn of the 1860s and 1870s, the bison ecology had stabilized, thanks to steady rains and Comanches' systematic search for alternative sources of sustenance. Indeed, there is tantalizing evidence suggesting that Comanches had found a way to regulate the ebb and flow of bison numbers through cattle raiding and beef consumption. In 1872 federal agents brought a Cherokee, Creek, and Seminole delegation to Fort Sill to meet with the Comanches, Kiowas, Naishans, Cheyennes, and Arapahos in an attempt to convince the nomads to become farmers. When told that the bison would soon die off, a Yamparika speaker retorted that "there were yet millions of Buffalo, and there was no danger on that hand." But if the herds "might fail," he continued, "the Comanches had determined to hunt buffalo only next winter, then they would allow them to breed a year or two without molestation, and they would rely on Texas cattle for subsistence meantime." Confident in the viability and validity of their way of life, Yamparikas labeled the Cherokees, Creeks, and Seminoles as "an old dirty inefficient looking set, hardly capable of managing their own affairs." "We don't take much stock in them," they concluded.[15]

If hunting remained viable, raiding thrived. In the late 1860s, the Texas cattle industry entered its first boom phase, creating new opportunities for Comanche poachers. Texas ranches became bigger, but their size made them harder to defend against Comanche raiders, who could enter and exit the open range pastures undetected. The first northbound cattle drives from 1867 on provided another target for Comanches. Managed by a small number of cowboys and vaqueros, the early trail trains were vulnerable to guerrilla attacks, and Comanche raiders drove off whole herds along the Goodnight-Loving Trail, which skirted Comanchería along the Pecos valley. According to one report, Texas lost 6,255 horses and 11,395 head of cattle to Indian pillaging between 1866 and 1873, but these data were incomplete and the real losses may have been several times higher. In 1869 the citizens of Jack County in central Texas claimed a loss of fifty thousand dollars' worth of horses to pillaging in the month of April alone, and in 1871, in the space of three months, Comanches brought more than thirty thousand head of Texas cattle to New Mexico. Comanches also raided in southwestern Indian Territory, whose western portion lay on their main war trail into Texas. Most attacks fell on immigrant Indians—the Chickasaws filed 123 separate depredation claims to agent Tatum between 1869 and 1873—but not even Fort Sill agency was safe from Comanche raiders.[16]

As before, the Comanche cattle raiding remained closely linked to New Mexican markets through the comanchero commerce, although the United States had begun to take more resolute steps to curb the trade. In 1869, realizing that the comanchero commerce was one of the key resources supporting the off-reservation Comanche rancherías, General Sheridan ordered all New Mexicans found on the plains with cattle to be seized and their stock killed. Within two years, the army had established a patrol line on New Mexico's eastern flank, arrested several trading convoys, and recovered more than one thousand head of livestock. But although the pressure strained the Comanche-comanchero trade, it did not suppress it. Comanches and comancheros pooled their resources in new ways and began to transform their enterprise into a paramilitary underground activity in which the division between producers and buyers became increasingly blurred. Avoiding army patrols along the large cart trails, comancheros, sometimes disguised as bison hunters, took smaller unmarked paths to the hidden trading canyons of the Llano Estacado, where they often accompanied Comanches on raids into Texas. Herman Lehmann, a Texan who was captured and adopted by Comanches, remembered how 60 New Mexicans joined 140 Comanches to stampede and seize "a big herd being driven to Kansas." Comanches, in turn, provided military escorts for comanchero caravans returning to New Mexico with packs of cattle. Thus, even as their space to maneuver was shrinking, Comanches and comancheros preserved their age-old relationship. One arrested comanchero described the commerce in the early 1870s as a "regular business." The key sites, Muchoque and Quitaque, were still operative, drawing hundreds of Comanches to trade in "arms, ammunition, cloth, flour, bread, sugar, coffee, etc."[17]

Few of the American dignitaries at the Medicine Lodge treaty talks in 1867 expected the Comanches to last on the plains for long. American representatives believed that the Plains Indian way of life was already disintegrating and that the United States could therefore afford to be generous. The U.S. government granted the Comanches the right to reside on their former lands as long as there were enough bison for successful hunts, but the concession stemmed from the conviction that both the buffalo and the Comanche culture were mere years away from extinction. In fact, even Paruasemena, who so fiercely defied the commissioners' demands, seemed to have abandoned hopes for long-term survival on the plains. He had visited Washington four years earlier and witnessed the immense infrastructure—the cities, factories, railroads, telegrams, infinite farms—that was propelling so many settlers and soldiers to the West. "It is too late," he said. "The white man has the country which we loved, and we only wish to wander on the prairie until we die."[18]

Yet as the new decade dawned, there were no signs of capitulation. Comanchería, in American minds a defunct political unit since 1867, still existed in fact. Most Comanches continued to live on the open plains, chasing and hunting the bison, stealing and trading horses and cattle, raiding and ransoming captives. The U.S. government insisted that those Comanches were reservation Indians who visited the plains seasonally, but in reality Comanches visited the reservation seasonally and then only to seek annuities and asylum. The imperfectly agreed-on stipulations of the Medicine Lodge Treaty stated that Comanches should limit their off-reservation activities to hunting and stay within the confines of the bison range, but Comanches were militarily and commercially active from Indian Territory to New Mexico and from Kansas to central Texas. Although they now numbered less than five thousand, they had buttressed their political and military strength by forming close bonds with New Mexicans, Kiowas, Naishans, Cheyennes, and Arapahoes. Some Comanches believed that they had established a new equilibrium between their needs and those of the environment, and given their extraordinary haul of stolen livestock from Texas in 1871, they may well have believed they would be hunting, raiding, and trading in the Southwest forever.[19]

The continued existence of Comanches and their allies on the southern plains collided with the United States' desire to make the Great Plains and the Southwest safe for agrarianism, industrialism, and free-labor capitalism. Americans dreamt of a new empire of rails, ranches, farms, and firm borders, which was diametrically at odds with the Comanche political economy of hunting, raiding, ransoming, and fluid borders. American boosters proclaimed the rise of the cattle kingdom in Texas, and sheepherding was on the verge of becoming big business in New Mexico, but both enterprises were circumscribed by an inability to expand onto the rangelands of the Llano Estacado and the Texas Panhandle. In Texas, moreover, long stretches of the settlement frontier were again collapsing under Comanche pressure, and in Kansas tens of thousands of homesteaders were crammed in the eastern part of the state, demanding that the upper Arkansas valley and its environs be cleared of all Indians.[20]

For federal Indian officials, the Comanche situation was a stinging embarrassment: half a decade after the Civil War had eradicated institutionalized slavery, Comanches were trafficking in human merchandise on U.S. soil and with U.S. agents. The distressed settlers, sheep and cattle magnates, and government officials directed their frustration at the Peace Policy, which in their view had weakened rather than strengthened the United States' hold on the Indians. They found a powerful ally in the military elite, who had opposed the Peace Policy from the beginning for strategic and personal reasons: the end of the Civil War and the subsequent reduction of the army had closed avenues for promotion, which only another war could reopen.[21]

The opponents of the Peace Policy found their opportunity in May 1871, when a Comanche and Kiowa raiding party attacked a supply train near Fort Richardson, killing and mutilating seven teamsters. The raiders narrowly missed General Sherman, who was on an inspection tour in Texas. Hearing of the attack, Sherman improvised a policy change, ordering four cavalry companies to pursue the raiders and, if necessary, to continue the chase into the Fort Sill reservation. He then stormed to Fort Sill to confront agent Tatum. The flustered agent conceded that the Quaker experiment was failing. On the next ration day, Tatum authorized the soldiers to arrest three Kiowa chiefs—Satanta, Satank, and Big Tree—and send them to Texas for civil trial. His Quaker ideology crumbling, Tatum asked the army to pursue the Kwahadas and Kotsotekas into Texas, confiscate their stolen stock, and force them to enter the reservation "as kindly as the circumstances will admit." Although the Peace Policy remained the official policy, by fall 1871 it had become a dead letter on the southern plains. Tatum was replaced in early 1873 by an agent more committed to Quaker principles, but by that time hard action had become the norm.[22]

When planning Comanche campaigns, the U.S. Army was able to draw on its rapidly accumulating experience in fighting the Plains Indians. The Lakota wars had revealed that regular soldiers, although armed with Colt revolvers and Winchester repeating rifles, were a poor match for the highly motivated and mobile Indian warriors, convincing the military leadership that the army needed a decisive numerical advantage to defeat Plains Indians on the battlefield. But numbers were exactly what the army lacked. The eastern public, weary of war and eager for normalcy, was unwilling to finance Indian wars in the West. Young men were equally unenthused: the prospect of fighting Indians for meager pay and under vigorous discipline on the distant Great Plains drew few volunteers. The army's main instrument in Indian wars was therefore the light cavalry, composed of ten regiments, approximately five thousand men in total.

Short of troops and wary of open battles, the army set out to deprive the

Comanches of shelter and sustenance by destroying their winter camps, food supplies, and horse herds. By the early 1870s this kind of total warfare against entire populations was an established practice in the U.S. Army. Sherman had pioneered it against the Confederacy in his "March to the Sea," and Sheridan had introduced a stripped-down version of it to the plains in his 1868–69 winter campaign against the Cheyennes. Culminating on the Washita River where the Seventh Cavalry killed nearly a hundred noncombatants and eight hundred horses and mules, Sheridan's campaign broke Cheyenne resistance on the central plains. This success convinced the army that targeting civilians and economic resources was the most efficient—and since it shortened the conflict, the most humane—way to subdue the Indians. But the army could not simply duplicate Sheridan's straightforward offensive against the Comanches, who ranged over a vast territory and had a more diverse subsistence base than the Cheyennes. To subdue the Comanches, the army was forced to launch the largest and most concentrated campaign of total war in the West.[23]

It was only now, twenty-three years after the Treaty of Guadalupe Hidalgo, that Comanches came to feel the depth of the United States' expansionist power. They had been exposed to that power before—most tangibly through Texas, whose territorial expansion into Comanchería was a corollary of the South's economic expansion into Texas—but its full force had been curbed by several factors: relative American disinterest toward the Great Plains, the Civil War, and finally the Peace Policy. It was therefore all the more shocking when the United States unleashed its military might on Comanchería in 1871. Whatever difficulties the army may have faced in mobilizing soldiers for Indian wars, the troops that were mustered could draw on their nation's enormous resources—superior technology; bottomless supply lines; an elaborate communication system; and a strong, tested central state apparatus. More important perhaps, the troops formed the vanguard of an ascending nation-state driven by a civilizing mission and bent on expanding its frontiers through conquest and exclusionary borders. The U.S. Army that moved into Comanchería was an adversary unlike any Comanches had encountered.[24]

The invasion began from Texas, the state with the longest list of grievances against the Comanches. Comanche raids had taken a heavy toll in Texan lives and livestock since the late 1850s, stunting the state's projected economic growth. Blocked by a wall of Comanche violence, the expanding Texas cattle kingdom had bypassed the Great Plains, extending instead toward less desired regions in New Mexico and the Rocky Mountains. By 1871, Texans considered the situation intolerable. Thriving postwar northern cities like Chicago and New York had a seemingly unquenchable hunger for western beef, Texas bustled with some five million head of readily marketable cattle, and the Kansas Pacific railhead at Abilene linked the northern demand to Texas supply. The only element missing from a true cattle boom in Texas was unhindered access to the prime pasturelands and the natural highways of the southern plains, much of which still lay under Comanche control.

But if Texans felt victimized by the Comanches, they also possessed the power and the determination to subdue them. There were several U.S. Army detachments in the state, urged into action by ambitious and aggressive entrepreneurs and thousands of frontier settlers who were eager to see the Comanches defeated. In fall 1871, under intense pressure from Texas officials, General Sherman ordered the Fourth Cavalry and two companies of the Eleventh Infantry, a total of some six hundred troops, to rein in the Comanches. Colonel Ranald Mackenzie took his troops through the Blanco Canyon into the eastern Llano Estacado, where his Tonkawa scouts located a large Kwahada band led by Quanah Parker. Brushing occasionally with small Indian squads, the cavalry pushed the Kwahadas deep into the llano until cold weather forced them to pull back. The next spring Mackenzie tried again. He first instituted an effective border patrol system that was anchored in newly established Forts Richardson, Griffin, and Concho and then embarked on another long-range expedition on the Llano Estacado, this time with some three hundred soldiers and Tonkawa scouts. Supported with heavy supply columns, the troops spent several months tracking Comanche rancherías, charting war trails, and mapping comanchero sites. Avoiding direct engagements, Mackenzie wore down the Comanches by disrupting their seasonal cycle of activities. Constantly on the move, Comanches did not have the time to pasture and tend their horses, hunt buffalo, dry the meat, and prepare hides for winter lodges.

In September 1872 the Fourth Cavalry ambushed a Kwahada-Kotsoteka camp of 262 lodges on the North Fork of the Red River and attacked. In a brief and brutal engagement, the soldiers killed twenty-four warriors, captured more than one hundred women and children, seized "a very large number of horses and mules," and burned all the lodges, robes, and food. Pursuing Comanche parties managed to recapture most of the animals in night raids, but the battle had left the Comanches destitute. They had lost all their winter supplies, and the capture of women prevented the families from performing the necessary winter preparations. Mackenzie took the captives to Fort Concho in Texas and sent out word that they would not be returned unless Comanches stopped raiding. Most of the Comanches complied and, unable to alleviate their hunger with stolen stock, moved onto the reservation. Among the arrivals were Tebenanaka, Paruacoom, and other prominent Comanche chiefs who had visited the agency only fleetingly before.[25]

As Mackenzie closed in on the Comanches on the southern and central Llano Estacado, the army opened a second front on the western Llano Estacado. Here the objective was to demolish the comanchero trade and cut off Comanches from their source of weapons and imported food. Mirroring Mackenzie's actions, Colonel Gordon Granger, the commander of New Mexico District, kept his troops in the field through 1872. Ranging across the llano from the Canadian to the Río Hondo, the troops arrested comancheros, broke up trading camps, and slaughtered stolen livestock. Short of men, Granger ordered surplus arms to be distributed to a group of more than ninety Texas cattlemen who set out in the summer of 1872 to recover stolen stock; the Texans spent three months on the Llano Estacado and in eastern New Mexico intimidating livestock buyers and terrorizing ranches and villages that owned comanchero cattle. These actions all but destroyed the comanchero trade. In 1873 only a few comancheros headed out to the plains, where they unsuccessfully tried to find the Comanches, who had either withdrawn to the reservation or scattered across the Llano Estacado to evade Mackenzie's troops.[26]

The year 1873 saw the Comanches and Americans moving simultaneously toward both a tenuous accommodation and a massive, violent clash. With unprecedented numbers of Comanches wintering at Fort Sill, the level of violence dropped sharply along the Texas frontier. The Comanche bands in the reservation showed increased interest in farming, and the agents spoke about a new spirit of compliance. By spring, Comanches had erected fifty houses near Fort Sill. They released several Anglo-American and Mexican captives, hoping to retrieve their relatives held at Fort Concho, and in April the army released all the detained Comanches. When the captives arrived at Fort Sill in June, American agents were able to observe firsthand the power of captivity to induce both conflict and conciliation. In a meeting with the officer who had brought the captives in, Comanche men, their families and honor now restored, "came forward, and took him by the hand. Some of them, embracing him, expressed their gratitude and thankfulness for his care, attention, and uniform kindness to their women and children. . . . One of them told him that he should always respect a white soldier for his sake."[27]

That goodwill was put to a severe test in the fall of 1873. Earlier that year, at the request of the secretary of the interior, Texas Governor Edmund Davis agreed to release the Kiowa chiefs Satanta and Big Tree (Satank had died in an escape attempt), and in October the governor brought the two men to Fort Sill.

Meeting with Kiowa and Comanche chiefs in a grand council at the fort, Davis demanded complete submission from both nations. They were to take up full-time farming, give up their weapons and horses, and withdraw from the Texas plains at once. This ultimatum, which in effect would have annulled the Medicine Lodge Treaty, outraged the Indians, who insisted that the transition into reservation life was to be gradual. Federal Indian agents dissociated themselves from Davis's demands and sided with Comanches and Kiowas, defending the Medicine Lodge agreement, which granted the Indians the right to dwell on the southern plains as long as the bison herds yielded sufficient subsistence.[28]

But even before Comanches and federal agents joined together to defy Governor Davis at Fort Sill, an American onslaught on the southern plains bison had begun. Rooted in the industrial East, this assault had been set in motion three years earlier. In 1870 tanners in Philadelphia perfected a chemical process for turning bison hides into elastic industrial leather suitable for making machine belts, an innovation that unlocked the plains bison for industrial exploitation. The price of bison hides skyrocketed, and in 1871 hundreds of hide hunters swarmed onto the Great Plains to cash in on the latest western boom. Calling themselves buffalo runners, these professional hunters centered their operations on the central plains, which had been recently cleared of Cheyennes and were connected to the eastern markets by the Kansas Pacific Railroad. The slaughter was immense and wasteful, and by the end of 1872 the central plains were almost devoid of buffalo. By spring 1873, the hide hunters were eager to open new killing fields on the southern plains, even if it meant violating the Medicine Lodge Treaty, which reserved the bison herds below the Arkansas valley for Comanches' and Kiowas' exclusive use.[29]

The U.S. Army, which occupied three forts along the Arkansas valley, now stood to protect the Comanches and the bison from industrial absorption and annihilation. But when buffalo hunters began pouring south of the river in spring 1873, the army units at Forts Lyon, Dodge, and Larned took no action to enforce the treaty line. By the summer, hundreds of runners roamed the high plains of southern Kansas and the Oklahoma Panhandle, operating out of base camps on the Cimarron and North Canadian rivers. By now the army had adopted a proactive role in the bison's destruction, providing protection for hunting squads and supplying them with equipment and ammunition—"all you could use, all you wanted, more than you needed," as one runner marveled.

By year's end, the hunters had reached the Canadian River, one of the key winter habitats of the bison. In March 1874 a coalition of merchants built a settlement complex called Adobe Walls near the ruins of the Bents' upper Canadian River fort to serve as base for the hunting outfits. Other outfits operated westward out of Fort Griffin, which was transformed almost overnight into a thriving shipping town. Comanches, short of guns and ammunition and spread across the canyons and river bottoms of the Llano Estacado in their winter camps, mounted only sporadic resistance. When they returned to the open plains in late spring, they entered an alien landscape, an industrial wasteland. Where the ground was not littered with skinned, rotting carcasses, the buffalo runners were annihilating the last isolated herds. The spring hunts, performed amidst American hunting squads, failed. Already weak from the winter's hardships, Comanches collapsed into starvation.[30]

The devastation the Comanches faced that spring was more than material. The buffalo was the foundation of their economy and the centerpiece of their cosmology, and the wholesale slaughter shook their existence at its core. Facing immediate economic, societal, and cultural collapse, Comanches looked both backward and outward. Paralleling a dynamic that had already played itself out numerous times in the course of the United States' westward expansion, they embraced eschatological visions and pan-Indian resistance to keep their world from dying.

The catalyst was Isatai, a young Kwahada medicine man. His message, delivered to him through a powerful vision, was at once symbolic and pragmatic, blending a religious prophecy with a political agenda, and it bore a striking resemblance to the Ghost Dance movement that would sweep the Great Plains fifteen years later. Isatai sought to beget the restoration of Comanche power through ritual invocation. If Comanches came together to share his *puha* (medicine power) and performed the Sun Dance, he preached, they could liquidate the whites and pave the way for the buffalo's return. He said he could raise the dead, stop bullets in midflight, and vomit all the cartridges the Comanches would need. Like the Ghost Dance religion, Isatai's message was at its core nativistic. Nations like the Wichitas, he said, had grown weaker on the reservation, suffering from disease, poverty, and cultural declension. Preservation of old ways and unified resistance were the only ways to survival.[31]

Isatai's apocalyptic prophecy found a fertile ground among the anguished Comanches. As word of his message spread across the southern plains, bands began to gravitate toward a designated meeting place on Elk Creek near the North Fork of the Red River, the center of what was left of Comanchería. Isatai's preaching also drew Comanche bands from the reservation, where things had gone from bad to worse during the winter of 1873–74. The troubles began when the superintendent of the Indian Office, pressured by Texas Governor Davis, decided to withhold annuity distributions until Comanches turned over individuals who had raided Texas settlements. The chiefs considered this a declaration of war, and although the embargo was soon revoked, the incident left relations strained. Worse still, when the agents resumed distributions, the rations proved utterly inadequate. In May, with famine spreading in the reservation, the majority of Comanches and some Kiowas moved to Elk Creek. In early June the Indians performed the Sun Dance, and within days, the revival movement reached the Cheyennes and Arapahoes at the Darlington agency. By mid-June, some seven hundred warriors and their families had gathered on Elk Creek to eradicate the whites and reclaim their lives.[32]

The Elk Creek medicine camp was the closest the southern plains Indians came to forming a collective front against the United States, but like most eighteenth- and nineteenth-century attempts of pan-Indian resistance, it was undermined by internal disputes and divisions. Although Comanches, Kiowas, Cheyennes, and Arapahoes had hunted, raided, and lived in multiethnic communities since the 1860s, tribal lines were still visible. Those lines, moreover, were becoming harder rather than softer under the desperate circumstances, and the incipient coalition nearly foundered in its Elk Creek cradle. The various factions, each facing its own set of ordeals, struggled to find a common course of action. Some, including Quanah Parker, demanded that the coalition attack the Tonkawa villages at Fort Griffin to punish the Tonkawas for serving the U.S. Army as scouts. Others, most likely Yamparikas, Cheyennes, and Arapahoes, wanted to strike the Anglo hunters in the Texas Panhandle. Still others, most of them probably Kwahadas, insisted on launching a concerted attack against Texans to avenge the relatives who had been slain by Mackenzie's troops. A few Penateka, Yamparika, and Nokoni chiefs refused to commit to any violence and returned to the agency to alert the agents.[33]

The coalition that finally moved against the buffalo hunters was severely fractured. At dawn on June 27, 1874, Isatai and Quanah Parker led a massive frontal charge at the Adobe Walls. Although facing only twenty-eight hunters and one woman, the Indians soon lost their momentum against the complex's thick log-and-sod walls and the hunters' long-range, rapid-fire buffalo rifles. Several warriors died, and when Isatai's horse was killed by a stray shot, the medicine man's support evaporated. The Indians maintained a desultory siege for several days and then split up.[34]

If the battle itself was inconclusive, its aftermath was a disaster for the allied Indians. Immediately after the battle, Kwahadas launched a raid into Texas, while Cheyennes, together with some Comanches, attacked the farmers, overlanders, and army detachments across southern Kansas and Colorado. This dispersal of the coalition relived the pressure on the buffalo hunters, allowing them to continue their slaughter for another season. Fort Griffin on the Clear Fork of the

Brazos River emerged as a major hide depot from which buffalo runners opened new killing ranges on the Texas plains. The military fort was soon supplemented with a thriving "Buffalo Town," which served as a supply base for west- and north-bound hunting squads and a shipping center to eastern markets. The southern plains bison were now under assault from both the north and the south. Aggravating the damage, 1874 was a drought year, which further narrowed the bison's chances of survival.[35]

The battle of Adobe Walls hardened the federal government's resolution to break Indian resistance. President Grant and the Interior Department abolished the last remnants of the Peace Policy on the southern plains and assigned hundreds of troops for a massive field operation. All Comanches and Kiowas were ordered to return to the agency by August 3 or they would be denounced as hostiles and hunted down. When the deadline passed, some two thousand Comanches and Kiowas were still on the plains. Generals Sheridan and Sherman sent in five columns, some fourteen hundred soldiers from Kansas, Indian Territory, Texas, and New Mexico, coordinating them to converge at Comanche and Kiowa sanctuaries in the canyons along the Caprock of the Texas Panhandle. The advancing troops engaged the Comanches only once, but their looming presence prevented fleeing Comanche bands from searching for the few remaining bison and making preparations for the winter.[36]

On September 28, 1874, Tonkawa scouts led Mackenzie's Fourth Cavalry to the upper end of the Palo Duro Canyon, a wide, forty-five-mile-long crevasse at the north end of Comanches' panhandle refuge. At the bottom of the canyon Mackenzie saw a serpentine village of several hundred Kwahadas, Kiowas, and Cheyennes, apparently unaware of his approach. He ordered a surprise attack. Scattered across the canyon floor, the Indians failed to organize a united defense. They fled onto the open plains, leaving their possessions behind. Mackenzie called off a chase and had the camp and the supplies destroyed. The soldiers piled the covers and poles of more than two hundred tipis, hundreds of robes and blankets, and thousands of pounds of dried meat, flour, and sugar in a huge mound and set it on fire. They rounded up more than 1,400 horses. Mackenzie gave 350 animals to the Tonkawas and ordered the rest shot.[37]

The body count after the battle of the Palo Duro Canyon revealed only three dead Comanches. But it is precisely that paucity of killing that makes the battle such a poignant symbol of Comanches' collapse, for it underscores the fact that their defeat was not a military but an economic one. In their battles with the U.S. Army in the early 1870s, the Comanches suffered only a few hundred casualties, yet their population plummeted from four or five thousand in 1870 to around

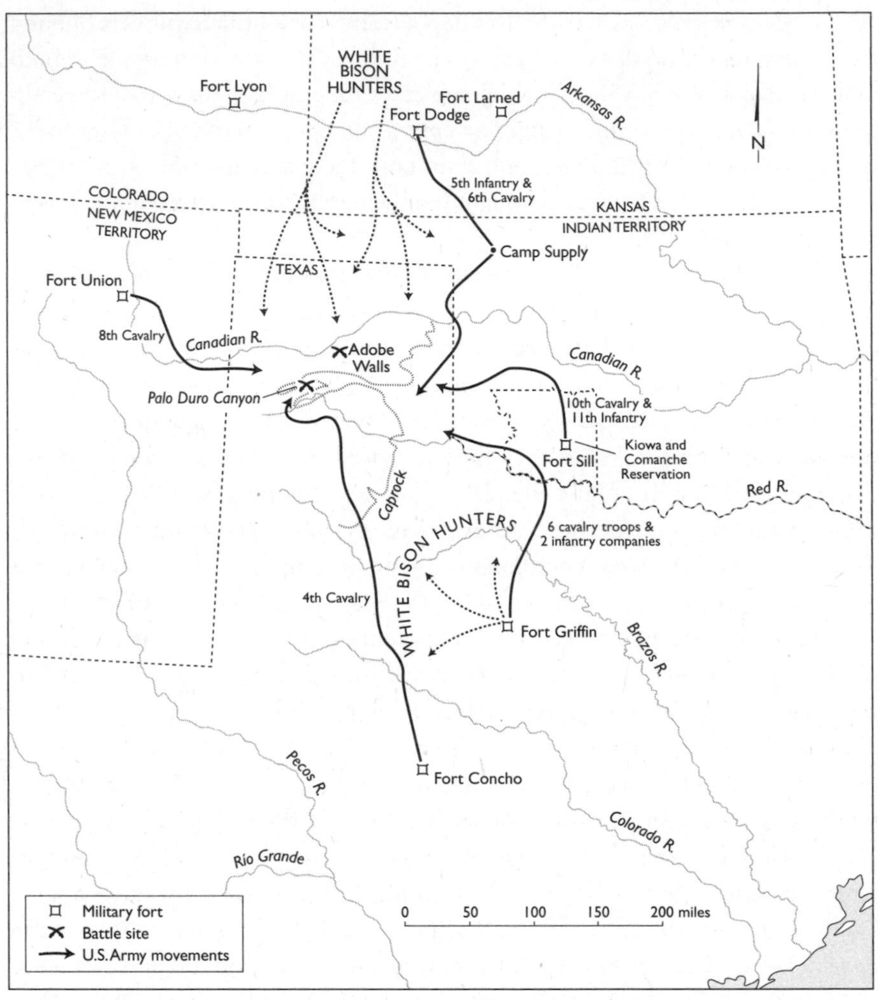

20. Invasion of Comanchería, 1874. Map by Bill Nelson.

fifteen hundred in 1875.[38] The cause was a systematic assault on the Comanches' economy, which after the midcentury drought crisis had become untenable. The Comanches trapped on the floor of the Palo Duro Canyon had not suffered decisive defeats in the hands of U.S. troops, but they were a society fatally crippled by poverty, malnutrition, and a loss of cultural order. With their raiding-trading economy extinguished and the bison herds vanishing, their subsistence was reduced to the few supplies they had carried with them. As they fled the Palo Duro for the plains, they could see a thick smoke rising from the canyon, and with it their last tie to independence dissolving in the air.

After Palo Duro, most Comanche bands headed toward the reservation, this time to stay. A few small bands refused to surrender, and they scattered across the canyonlands of the Texas Panhandle, where they lived through the winter on roots and rodents. Facing starvation, they yielded. During the winter and spring, small groups of Comanches trudged to Fort Sill, where they were processed for a new life. They were stripped of their horses, weapons, and remaining possessions. Women and children were removed from their husbands and fathers and placed in separate camps. Men accused of particular crimes were put in irons to await trial and expulsion to Florida. The rest of the warriors, many of whom had never been in the reservation, were locked in a roofless and windowless icehouse. They slept on a stone floor, huddled in U.S. army blankets. In the morning, they received their first rations when the soldiers threw chunks of raw meat over the wall.[39]

CONCLUSION

The Shape of Power

The icehouse at the Fort Sill agency was not a burial place of a people—the Comanche nation would endure and, in time, flourish again—but it was a burial place of an era. Past and present fell abruptly apart as new peoples, new economic regimes, and new ways of life descended onto the Great Plains, now eerily devoid of any material or geopolitical marks of Comanche presence. Comanches had ruled the Southwest for well over a century, but they left behind no marks of their dominance. There were no deserted fortresses or decaying monuments to remind the newcomers of the complex imperial history they were displacing. Envisioning a new kind of empire, one of cities, railroads, agricultural hinterlands, and real estate, Americans set out to tame, commodify, and carve up the land. Buffalo runners all but eradicated the southern plains bison in the space of a few years, and Texas ranchers laid down a maze of cattle trails that crisscrossed the region. Settlers turned the open steppes into irrigated fields and fenced farms, and boosters conjured towns, highways, and railroad tracks on old Comanche camping sites. With each new layer of American progress, the memory of the Comanches and their former power grew dimmer.[1]

For Americans in the East, the Comanche nation faded even more quickly. In summer 1875, as the last Comanche bands drifted to Fort Sill to surrender, the United States was preparing elaborate centennial celebrations to display its industrial might, continental reach, and hard-won national unity. But a few days before the July Fourth grand finale, disquieting news arrived from the northern Great Plains: the Lakotas and their Cheyenne and Arapahoe allies had annihilated Custer's Seventh Cavalry, more than two hundred soldiers, in the Little Bighorn valley in Montana. From then on, America's attention was absorbed by the campaigns against the Lakotas, which did not end until 1890 at the horror of

Wounded Knee. By that time, Lakotas were fixed in the national consciousness as the "noble and doomed savages" of Buffalo Bill's hugely successful Wild West Show. They became multipurpose icons, immensely useful and marketable as the sounding board of America's shifting feelings of awe, terror, and remorse toward Native Americans and their fate. Fictionalized beyond recognition, Sitting Bull's ever-malleable stage Lakotas came to symbolize all Indians of the Great Plains, then of the West, and then of all North America, while the other Indian nations were pushed to the margins of collective memory. Already deprived of their traditional lands and lifestyle, Comanches were now deprived of their place in history.

The waning popular interest stifled potential scholarly interest. During the sixty years that followed their confinement to reservation, the Comanches drew little scholarly attention and inspired few academic studies. Scholars did not rediscover them until the 1930s, when two prominent Texas historians, Walter Prescott Webb and Rupert Norval Richardson, gave them a key role in their renowned studies of the Great Plains. The Comanches presented by Webb and Richardson were, however, startlingly different from the Comanches European colonists had known in the eighteenth and early nineteenth centuries. Where the Spaniards and French had viewed Comanches variously as diplomats, raiders, allies, foes, traders, spouses, and kinspeople, Webb and Richardson, drawing heavily on the records of mid-nineteenth-century American settlers and soldiers, portrayed them simply as warriors. And whereas Spanish and Mexican sources spoke of the overwhelming economic, political, and cultural power of Comanches, Webb and Richardson depicted them as a military obstacle to America's preordained expansion across the continent.[2]

Thus emerged the idea of the Comanche barrier to the westward-expanding American frontier, a metaphor that recast Comanches as savages who resisted conquest with raw military prowess but were devoid of other qualities that make human societies strong and resilient. Reconceived in the minds of early twentieth-century Americans, Comanches were equated with other natural obstacles—aridity, deserts, and distance—that encumbered the colonization of the American West. Aggressive and impulsive, powerful yet passive, they blended into the natural environment to form a potent, essentially nonhuman impediment to the U.S. empire.

This tendency to simultaneously naturalize and demonize the Comanches—and, arguably, to rationalize their subjugation—is apparent in Webb's 1958 presidential address to the American Historical Association, in which he nostalgically contemplated the forces that shaped his writing in his Texas home. "In the hard-packed yard and on the encircling red-stone hills was the geology, in the pasture the desert botany and all the wild animals of the plains save the buffalo," he mused. "The Indians, the fierce Comanches, had so recently departed, leaving memories so vivid and tales so harrowing that their red ghosts, lurking in every mott and hollow, drove me home all prickly with fear when I ventured too far." A generation later, novelist Cormac McCarthy offered in *Blood Meridian* what was perhaps the most troubling reenvisioning of the Comanches. He describes the destruction of a crew of Anglo-American filibusters at the hands of beastlike Comanches who, without provocation or hesitation, abandon themselves on the other side of humanity, "ripping off limbs, heads, gutting the strange white torsos and holding up great handfuls of viscera, genitals, some of the savages so slathered up with gore they might have rolled in it like dogs and some who fell upon the dying and sodomized them with loud cries to their fellows."[3]

The unanthropocentric barrier metaphor trivialized the Comanches as a society and, by extension, abridged their role as historical actors. By reducing them to a primal warrior society, Webb, Richardson, and the scores of historians and nonhistorians influenced by them created a caricature of Comanches' culture and their place in history. The Comanches who appeared in historical studies from the 1930s on terrorized the Spanish and Mexican frontier with relentless raids, but beyond that they merely occupied space. Weak in organization and warlike by nature, they lacked the complex diplomatic, economic, and cultural arrangements that fasten peoples to their environments and instead relied on brutal, almost pathological raiding to defend their homelands. The narratives that spoke of different kinds of Comanches were marginalized. "Los Comanches," the New Mexican conquest romance that captures Comanches' penetrating influence on the political, economic, and cultural milieu of the early Southwest, was dismissed as local folklore and ignored by mainstream historians.

Thus, bit by bit, the nature and scope of Comanche power became distorted. Memories of Comanches stirred horror and awe in twentieth-century Americans like Webb—not because they conjured up impressions of imperial-scale power but because they evoked images of nativistic resistance and mindless, primitive violence. In 1974, a century after the battle of the Palo Duro Canyon, T. R. Fehrenbach, another renowned Texas historian, depicted Comanches as "scattered bands of wanderers, never a nation," and their system of power as a "barrier [that] had stopped European penetration of these plains for almost two centuries. It did not show on maps; it had no shape or form. The Comanche barrier was a wisp of smoke on the horizon, riders appearing suddenly on the ridges, shots and screams at sunset, horror under the summer moons." Comanches, he concluded, "remained proud, savage, and aloof, determined to deal with Europeans on their own terms. . . . Whether the stance was conscious or instinctive, the People had become a powerful barrier to all future movement across the plains."[4] Fehrenbach's portrayal of a phantasmal Comanche barrier was a product of its time, and it represented how historians understood colonialism and Indian-white relations into the closing years of the twentieth century: European imperialism moves history; Native resistance is raw, violent savagery; and frontiers, if indigenous peoples have a hand in their making, are confusing, unsophisticated places.

My task in this book has been to recover Comanches as full-fledged humans and undiminished historical actors underneath the distorting layers of historical memory and, in doing so, to provide a new vision of a key chapter of early American history. In these pages I have traced the evolution of a Comanche power complex that was neither shapeless nor formless, a Comanche foreign policy that involved much more than plundering and killing, and Comanche people who were neither savage nor nationless. Instead of merely defying white expansion through aggressive resistance, I have argued, Comanches inverted the projected colonial trajectory through multifaceted power politics that brought much of the colonial Southwest under their political, economic, and cultural sway.

How did this happen? How did a group of nomadic hunter-gatherers that numbered only a few thousand in the early eighteenth century manage to challenge and eventually eclipse the ambitions of some of the world's greatest empires? What gave Comanches their edge in the collision of cultures? And conversely, why was it that only the Comanches—among the hundreds of Native American nations—managed to build an empire that eclipsed and subsumed Euro-American colonial realms? In the preceding chapters I have emphasized various mental and cultural traits, ranging from Comanches' strategic flexibility to their willingness to embrace new ideas and innovations, but those are traits shared by most Native American societies. What was it that made Comanches exceptional?

The historian's instinct suggests that the Comanches' extraordinary ascendancy must have intersected with parallel Euro-American weakness and disinterest, but in reality Comanches operated in one of the most fiercely contested imperial arenas in North America. The period from the early eighteenth century to the middle of the nineteenth century was a time of intense struggle among Spain, France, Britain, the United States, and Mexico over the control of the southern Great Plains and the Southwest. In the minds of metropolitan strategists, the territory west of the lower Mississippi valley, north of the Río Grande, and east of the Rocky Mountains was an imperial borderland where the empires and emerging nation-states of North America were bound to collide and where their fates would be determined. Euro-American interest in that borderland was particularly intense from the late eighteenth century to the mid-nineteenth century, the period that also witnessed the zenith of Comanche power.

Rather than a reflection of Euro-American indifference, Comanches' rise to dominance stemmed from their own adaptive culture, their ability to harness Euro-American resources—both material and nonmaterial—to their own advantage. Like the powerful Iroquois in the Northeast, Comanches were geographically fortunate: their homeland was both centrally and peripherally situated. Lying deep in the continental grasslands, Comanchería was distant from the major seaboard colonies and away from the main disease corridors along the heavily trafficked waterways. The inland location also meant that Comanches were always situated between two rival colonial spheres: Spanish and Mexican settlements in New Mexico and Texas lay to the west and south, and French and American outposts on the lower Mississippi valley extended their spheres toward Comanchería from the east. This geopolitical setting permitted Comanches to use one imperial regime as a counterweight when negotiating with another to enforce political and commercial agreements or to compel Euro-Americans to modify their aggressive policies. Their central location also gave them an access to multiple colonial and indigenous markets, each of which offered a distinctive combination of commodities and services.[5]

But favorable geography is just potential, a historical opportunity that could be transformed into tangible power by human initiative. Among the Indians of the Great Plains, Apaches, Caddos, Wichitas, and Osages enjoyed roughly the same geopolitical advantages as Comanches, but they never turned those advantages into sustained, all-pervading dominance. The main difference was cultural. As newcomers to the southern plains and immigrants used to modifying their lifestyles, Comanches were able to integrate innovations with less difficulty than the semi-sedentary Apache, Caddo, Wichita, and Osage agriculturists. The long migration from the central plains to the southern Rockies forced Comanches to reshape their economic strategies and social traditions, and they entered the southern plains with an elastic cultural system to which new elements could be added with relative ease.

The most important of those elements was the horse. Spanish-introduced Barb horses found a nearly ideal habitat on the shortgrass southern plains—a circumstance that was not repeated anywhere else on the continental grasslands—and Comanches took full advantage of that singular fact. They colonized the entire region, expelling the Apaches to the west and south, and turned themselves into the richest horse owners of the Great Plains. That animal wealth was the foundation of Comanches' imperial ascendancy. Horses enhanced their ability to move about and wage war, enabling them to eliminate Spain's military edge and turn the tables on colonial expansion. Serving as both transport vehicles and valuable commodities, horses allowed the Comanches to dominate long-distance trade networks and extend their raiding sphere hundreds of miles south of the Río Grande, far beyond the grasslands, which were the natural core area of North America's hunting-pastoral societies. With horses, Comanches could transfer information more effectively, spread out more widely, and come together more frequently. The equine revolution, in short, compressed time and distance, reducing the daunting expanses of the Great Plains, the Southwest, and northern Mexico to a size a single polity could manage and dominate.

Economic ramifications were equally profound. An innovation with unforeseen and unpredictable transformative power, the horse both simplified and diversified the Comanche economy. Inspired by the efficiency and sheer drama of mounted hunting, and encouraged by a favorable climate of mild winters and a long growing season, Comanches scaled down their gathering system and switched to specialized bison hunting and systematic horse herding. The resulting dual economy of hunting and pastoralism was the most energy-intensive production system the Great Plains had ever seen. On the simplest level, Comanches used horses as hunting tools to harness the enormous biomass stored in the bison herds; on a more profound level, they used the horses' ability to convert plant life into muscle power to tap more directly into the seemingly inexhaustible pool of thermodynamic energy stored in grasses. The horse-bison-grass economy also supported a flourishing exchange economy, which gave access to two other crucial forms of energy: human-digestible plant energy (vegetables and cereal grains) and the products of the Europe's mineral and chemical economy (guns, gunpowder, and metal).

By realigning the streams of energy around them, Comanches redefined the realm of the possible, and the repercussions went broad and deep. The economic bottleneck of nomadism, the need to concentrate on a few subsistence activities, burst wide open. Comanches instituted a nuanced labor division that saw women specializing in food and hide production; boys in animal herding; and adult men in raiding, trading, and hunting. They became large-scale slave owners, who relied on forced labor to support a burgeoning market economy, and they reallocated labor resources in the Southwest. Horses set in motion a cycle of sustained growth, which in the end manifested itself in an exceptional demographic development. Comanche population multiplied tenfold in the early eighteenth century, reaching forty thousand before the first smallpox epidemic in the early 1780s, after which it hovered between twenty and thirty thousand for more than sixty years. The repeated waves of epidemics did not cut severely into Comanche numbers until the late nineteenth century, decades later than among the other Native nations of the southern plains.

A large population denotes a potential for both expansive and staying power, but it could also become a liability, pushing the polity's subunits farther apart from one another and toward independent action. Such a propensity toward fissure was in fact the critical weakness of many powerful Native American nations, which in the end failed to unite their many subgroups and factions against Euro-American invaders. Examples range from the late seventeenth-century Iroquois to the early nineteenth-century Cherokees, to the late nineteenth-century Cheyennes and Lakotas, to the early twentieth-century Navajos.[6]

Comanches, too, struggled with strong centrifugal forces. The ecological constraints of nomadic pastoralism and bison hunting compelled them to live in relatively small bands, and the strategic challenge of defending a vast territory forced the bands to spread out across the southern plains; by the late eighteenth century, there must have been some one hundred rancherías dispersed around Comanchería. Yet, linked into wider associations by kinship, sodalities, and common culture, Comanches never lost their ability to operate as a community. Following a carefully synchronized yearly cycle, the scattered rancherías gathered each year for inclusive political meetings, which inserted cohesiveness into Comanche foreign policy. Local bands came together to form regional divisions, and Kotsoteka, Jupe, Yamparika, and Tenewa headmen met periodically in multidivisional gatherings to make strategic decisions on issues concerning the whole nation. Development toward centralized government may have remained embryonic, but Comanche leadership managed time and again to coordinate trade and diplomacy, build broad consensuses behind treaties, mobilize large interdivisional military operations, and neutralize the manipulative interferences of Euro-American state powers. Comanche chiefs were local and regional actors first, but periodically they also ran a larger political entity, the Comanche confederacy.

That hybrid political organization may well have been the elemental factor that set the Comanches apart. Blending centralizing impulses with local pluralism, the Comanche political system was both formal and loose. It allowed coordinated decision making at the national level without compromising social and strategic plasticity on the local level. The numerous Comanche rancherías could react rapidly and creatively to the constantly changing circumstances around the expanding Comanchería, for the only internal check on their policies was that they could be defended at the divisional and interdivisional councils. And even those grand councils, the seat of the confederacy, were lithely adaptable. They always strove toward consensus—and not through coercion but through careful (and often lengthy) mediation. Allowing for centralization without bureaucratization, local freedom without national fragmentation, and disagreement without dissolution, the Comanches' political system largely escaped the internal disputes that disrupted or paralyzed many of the more rigidly organized Native American powers.[7]

Taken together, Comanches possessed several of those crucial assets that gave Europeans competitive advantage and allowed them to conquer and colonize much of the globe after 1400. Indeed, during the eighteenth and early nineteenth centuries, Comanches routinely held a strategic, tactical, technological, economic, demographic, and organizational edge over their main colonial rival, New Spain. Their flexible unity, vast horse herds, cavalry skills, abundant firepower, and ability to muster thousands of warriors were sources of dread and envy to Spanish administrators whose options were curtailed by stifling mercantilist regulations, grueling bureaucracies, an acute lack of high-quality weapons and soldiers, and uncooperative subject peoples.

But even though Comanches managed to reverse Europe's material, technological, and organizational superiority, they did not try to use that advantage to create a mirror image of European imperialism. Rather than single-minded conquerors, they were strategic pluralists who achieved widespread dominance with policies that defy easy categorization. They relied on strategies and operations that can be easily recognized as expansionist and exploitative, but the geopolitical order they created was at once distinctly imperialistic and distinctly indigenous in nature. But what exactly was imperial and what was not about the Comanche power complex? And what accounts for the differences?

The parallels between the Comanches and other imperial powers are compelling. The Comanche empire was built on conquest—its rise marked the obliteration of the centuries-old Apache civilization from the Great Plains—and at its peak it was a prodigious creation with an enormous, at times hemispheric reach. Comanches operated a trade and alliance network that spanned and integrated several ecological, economic, and political spheres, and they reduced many of their bordering societies and regions to tributary client states, captive markets, and extractive raiding domains. They transformed Comanchería into an ethnic melting pot that had spaces for a diverse array of incorporated peoples—junior allies, slaves, adopted kinfolk, and naturalized Comanches—and they projected penetrating cultural power out of their home range. Distant peoples spoke their language and emulated their economic innovations and lifestyle, and their norms of war, peace, violence, exchange, and retribution largely governed the negotiation of the intersocietal space on what historians have called the *Spanish* borderlands. A bird's-eye view of the early nineteenth-century Southwest would have revealed an expanding Comanchería that was bustling with economic activity and diverse peoples, a wasting Spanish Texas that was seeping vital resources to the north through tribute payments and plunder, and a Spanish New Mexico whose eastern front was slowly dissolving into Comanchería. It would have revealed a sprawling continental economic network anchored to Comanchería; a constant flow of animals, slaves, and technology from Spanish colonies to Comanche rancherías and trade channels; and an immense, diverging plains hinterland where Comanches' power, prosperity, and products functioned as a gravitational cultural force.

Staggering geographical range, core-periphery hierarchies, vast hinterlands of extraction, systematic incorporation of foreign ethnicities, dynamic multiculturalism, and penetrating cultural influence—these are the traits of an imperial power. But the Comanche power complex differed from full-blown empires in several important respects. Those differences were a matter of both capacity and choice, and eventually they can be traced to the very impulses that set off Comanche expansion in the first place.

The southern plains the Comanches entered in the early eighteenth century was a world already destabilized by colonial intrusions. Locked into a bitter rivalry over the grasslands that separated them, the French in Louisiana and the Spaniards in New Mexico and Texas vied to chain the region's Indians into their respective orbits through force and strategic alliances. They provided new technologies of violence—guns, iron weapons, and horses—and new stimuli for aggression—trade and slave markets—which turned the southern plains into a volatile, militarized place where violent social action was often a necessity. In this atmosphere of chronic conflict, Comanche newcomers struggled to carve out an existence, and their survival and eventual rise to power grew out of a series of adaptations to external pressures and perils.

Indeed, their first imperial act, the conquest of the southern plains, was a two-front war against both the Apaches and the Spaniards, who formed a series of alliances to curb Comanche expansion and at times posed grave threats to Comanche interests. Comanches' raiding industry was fueled by the failure of colonial powers to make livestock, guns, and necessities readily available through trade, and the very heart of their empire, the great trade and alliance network, allowed Comanches to neutralize Spain's attempts to induce dependence through monopolistic trade policies and helped them stabilize their borders at a time when the ripple effects of U.S. expansion—tribal removals, political chaos, disease—were beginning to destabilize the Southwest. Finally, Comanches' explosive thrust into northern Mexico in the 1830s and 1840s was in part propelled by the relocation of eastern tribes across the Mississippi, the establishment of the expansionist Republic of Texas, and the need to offset disease-induced population losses with captive raiding. It often seemed that Comanches could protect their borders only by extending them.

But the Comanche empire was more than a sum total of creative adaptations to external forces: it also originated from powerful internal dynamics, the most important of which was a new and thriving pastoral economy. Indeed, had Comanches remained specialized bison hunters, it is unlikely that they would have developed the expansionist foreign political agenda they did. The kind of intense pastoralism practiced by Comanches hinged on the availability of three resources—forage, carbohydrates, and labor—and their imperial policies were to a large extent an exercise in guaranteeing secure access to each of those resources. Because domestic horse and mule herds required extensive grazing areas, the growing pastoral economy created a voracious need for territorial expansion, which ultimately drove Comanches to colonize all the shortgrass plains below the Arkansas River, the ecological fault line north of which horse herding became increasingly difficult. Pastoralism also entangled Comanches in antagonistic relations with bordering agricultural societies. As specialized hunter-pastoralists, they needed to have a steady access to imported carbohydrate products from Spanish, Mexican, and Wichita villages, an access that often had to be secured through violent action or the threat of such action.

But the resource Comanche pastoralists desired most was labor. They needed a constant supply of herders and other pastoral laborers to maintain their herds, which eventually spurred them to create several successive slaving frontiers: Apachería, New Mexico, Texas, Chihuahua, Coahuila, Nuevo León, Tamaulipas, Durango, Zacatecas, and San Luis Potosí were all at one point or another subjected to systematic Comanche slaving. Beyond overt enslavement, moreover, Comanches acquired coerced labor indirectly. By pillaging Spanish and Mexican settlements for domesticated, ready-to-sell horses and mules, they enforced a new, macrolevel division of labor: they specialized in the high-profit, low-labor investment activities of livestock raiding and trading and reassigned the menial task of raising the animals to other peoples. In this sense, Comanche imperialism was pronouncedly an economic enterprise. It was fueled by large-scale market production of livestock and aimed at exploiting the labor force of the surrounding urban-based societies.

Pastoralism also gave rise to internal social dynamics that fueled external expansion. Like many other powerful pastoral societies, Comanches developed into a rank society in which men amassed material possessions, especially horses and slaves, to increase their family wealth and to enhance their personal prestige and political influence through gifting and advantageous marriages. Since pillage provided the fastest and broadest avenue to horses and slaves, status competition generated a forceful incentive for external aggression; in this respect, the livestock-and-slave raiding economy, a key component of the Comanche power complex, was a social institution. It would be an exaggeration to say that Comanches became an imperial power because of internal social pressures, but it would also be impossible to understand their expansion without acknowledging the motivational thrust of those pressures.

But while stimulating Comanches' expansion, pastoralism also posed limitations on their power. As hunters and pastoralists reliant on a mobile and diffuse social organization, Comanches lacked both the capacity and the desire to subject other societies to direct political rule. Having built an equestrian culture that was beautifully adapted to the plains environment, they could not effectively control lands beyond the grasslands without abandoning their way of life. Thus, like the Mongols and other nonsedentary imperial powers, Comanches did not seek to absorb other polities into a single imperial framework. On the contrary, to flourish as hunters and pastoralists, they needed viable agricultural societies on their borders to guarantee a secure access to carbohydrates, livestock, and other imports through trade, theft, or tribute. That structural dependence is the key to the history of the colonial Southwest, for it explains why Comanches, even at the height of their power, preferred parasitical exploitation over replacement and incorporation.[8]

Comanches were not, therefore, self-conscious imperialists, following a premeditated expansionist agenda, nor were they all-conquering militarists bent on subjugating other societies. They established their preeminence in stages, responding often in an ad hoc fashion to circumstances that on first inspection seem to have little to do with imperial power politics. Their actions were shaped by the political maelstrom released by European colonialism, as well as by such ostensibly nonpolitical matters as pastures, water, and social prestige. The resultant imperial system reflected that eclecticism. It was based on loose domination and articulated through an intersecting set of coercive and cooperative intersocietal networks aimed at keeping Comanchería protected, prosperous, and powerful. Comanches exercised power on an imperial scale, but they did so without adopting an imperial ideology and without building a rigid, European-style empire.[9]

Yet the Comanche empire was not merely a notional entity, a latter-day concept imposed on people who did not know or identify with it. Although Comanches did not think of themselves as an imperial power (at least not in the sense the term is understood today), it does not mean that we should not recognize them as one. Like the Atlantic world, ecological imperialism, or the French-Algonquian middle ground on the Great Lakes, the Comanche empire was a historical phenomenon so complex and abstract in nature and so vast in scope that contemporaries were able to grasp, at best, only fragments of it. All at once, however, Comanche imperialism was a tangible social fact with distinct genesis, demonstrable inner logic, and far-reaching influence. For the people living in the eighteenth- and early nineteenth-century Southwest it would have been as impossible to perceive the depth and expanse of Comanche imperialism as it would have been to escape its embrace and effects.

As it is traditionally told, the history of colonial North America is a story of European metropolitan expansion. Jamestown, Boston, Quebec, New Orleans, and Santa Fe, themselves products of European metropolitan visions, are the engines of history, the seats of imperial imposition that dispatch agents of change—soldiers, traders, technology, germs, weeds—from the fringes of the continent to its interior, repeatedly entangling new regions and new peoples into an expanding transatlantic web. Recent studies have corrected that picture by emphasizing the role of Native peoples in the making of the continent's manifold frontiers, but they have not yet reenvisioned the basic story line itself: power flows in only one direction, from the imperial edges toward the indigenous interior, which merely responds to these outside forces. How does the story of the Comanche empire fit into that model? To what extent it is it possible to create a counternarrative of colonial America in which governing historical forces emanate from the continent's center, Comanchería, and spread toward its margins?

Components for such a narrative are most visible on Comanchería's southern and western fringes, where the Comanches scraped and pounded against the Spanish empire. Historians generally consider Spain's colonial enterprise in the far north as an economic and religious failure that nevertheless became a geopolitical success. According to this view, New Mexico and Texas failed to deliver the minerals and neophytes that Spanish administrators expected from them, but they did achieve their strategic objectives of shielding northern Mexican mining districts from foreign assault and supplying the empire's more vital areas with foodstuffs and livestock.[10]

This interpretation is patently Eurocentric and incomplete. Northern New Spain may have escaped European invasion, but Comanches held New Mexico and Texas in a state of siege for decades, reducing the colonies to financial pits that drained, rather than replenished, the economic veins of the Spanish empire. Worse still, New Mexico and Texas failed utterly in their mission of protecting Mexico's mining districts from foreign encroachments. France, Britain,

Russia, and the United States never looted northern New Spain, but Apaches, aggressively removed from the plains by Comanches, pillaged the silver districts of Nueva Vizcaya and Coahuila virtually at will. Gran Apachería, which in the late eighteenth century covered an enormous segment of the interior provinces, was essentially a spin-off of Comanche expansion. Then, in the early nineteenth century, Comanches themselves extended their raiding economy south of the Río Grande, inflicting severe damage on the silver districts of San Luis Potosí, Parral, and Zacatecas. In the arena of Euro-American imperial rivalry, Texas and New Mexico were moderate strategic successes; outside of it, they were dismal failures.

The economic structure of the Spanish Far North, too, was heavily shaped by Comanche policies. The arrested economic development of Texas and New Mexico is often seen as an outcome of their status as peripheral provinces in the Spanish imperial system, but a more exact explanation is that Texas and New Mexico were peripheries of *two* core regions. One, central Mexico, furnished them with men and money—but not enough to lift them to the imperial heights of, say, the Río de la Plata region. The other, Comanchería, drained them through theft and tribute, but only to the extent that their survival was not jeopardized. It was this position as dual peripheries that gave Texas and New Mexico their distinctive mixed character of underdevelopment and resilience. Similarly, any hopes of prosperity in the Spanish Far North were contingent on attaining the support of both the central Mexican and the Comanche cores. The most dramatic example of this is late Bourbon-era New Mexico. A vigorous crown program of economic and administrative reforms revitalized the damaged province by easing its tax load and by promoting transprovincial commerce, but New Mexico's recovery had another, equally important, source: the colonists established a peace with Comanches, which, after decades of paralyzing violence, allowed New Mexicans to channel their energy into state-building, long-distance trade, craft production, and animal herding.[11]

Comanche influence was more than macroscale economic abstractions; the people of northern New Spain felt it in their everyday lives, for the very fabric of their societies bore an indelible stamp of Comanche power. Texas, with its access to arable lands circumscribed by Comanche raiders, did not develop a broad-based agricultural economy until the mid-nineteenth century, evolving instead into a socially stratified ranching economy dominated by a handful of elite families. New Mexico, both dependent on and exploited by Comanches, found itself on a trajectory that was in many ways unique among Spain's North American colonies. Its social composition grew increasingly volatile in the eighteenth century as people shifted around the province, struggling to find respite from Comanche raids or, alternatively, to secure access to Comanche markets. The feudal tradition of New Spain, embodied by powerful local landlords, dissolved in the war-ridden kingdom, where the access to arable land was restricted by the fear of Comanche raids, where haciendas remained relatively small, and where officials continuously issued new village grants to resettle lands vacated by war.

The overwhelming presence of Comanches also promoted widespread ethnic mixing and social democratization in New Mexico. Pulled together by shared anxieties over Comanche power politics, Spanish colonists and Pueblo Indians embraced in the eighteenth century a mode of coexistence that manifested itself in an increasing number of intermarriages and (officially forbidden) mixed settlements. That incipient ethnic accommodation crumbled during the security and prosperity of the late Bourbon era, when Spanish settlers distanced themselves from Pueblo Indians, and yet efforts to Hispanize all of New Mexico were destined to fail: the peace with the Comanches spawned numerous *genízaro* villages on New Mexico's eastern perimeter, and these communities began to gravitate away from Santa Fe's orbit and toward Comanchería. Struggling under Comanchería's shadow, the Spaniards failed in their endeavors to build a *new* Mexico, a centralized Spanish-controlled colonial society, in New Mexico.[12]

If looked at closely, Comanche influence extended far beyond the confines of New Mexico. In the late seventeenth century, before the arrival of the Comanches, it seemed that the Utes were poised to be the dominant Native people in the Southwest as they had obtained horses early and gained a military edge over neighboring communities. Utes' prospects rose further after 1700 when they allied with Comanche newcomers and expanded onto the southern plains, but that arrangement backfired at midcentury when the increasingly powerful Comanches turned against their allies, banished them from the plains, and drove them back into the mountains. Dislodged and vulnerable, Utes courted another group threatened by Comanche expansion, the Spaniards, and drew them into a tight union that lasted through the Spanish colonial era. A century after Iroquois expansion had forced Algonquin Indians and the French to enter a middle ground in the Great Lakes region, Comanche expansion spawned an embryonic common ground between the Utes and northwestern New Mexico. Pushed together by common fear of the Comanches, who had rendered them in a state of roughly equal weakness, Utes and Spaniards fashioned a consensual alliance based on ritualistic diplomacy, active trade, and mutual accommodations. The alliance became the cornerstone of New Mexico's stability in the northwest and boosted Ute fortunes, but it had a darker side. Denied access to the plains and its marketable resources by the emergent Comanche empire, Utes embarked on vigorous slave raiding across the Great Basin, capturing and commodifying countless Paiute and Shoshone women and children whose labor, souls, and flesh were in high demand in New Mexico. This slave raiding-and-trading system, which endured well into the nineteenth century, is one of the most traumatic corollaries of Comanche imperialism.[13]

If the histories of northern New Spain or the Intermountain West cannot be properly understood without Comanches at their center, neither can that of North America's continental grasslands. If Comanches changed the history of the Southwest, northern Mexico, or the Great Basin by rocking the foundations of Spain's colonial project, they altered the history of the Great Plains through their cultural ingenuity and drawing power. Facing northward, Comanchería was the cradle of the Plains Indian horse culture, the rise of which marked a watershed event in the history of the early West. The three-thousand-mile northward spread of horses and horse use from central Mexico to the Canadian Shield has often been cited as the prime example of Spanish colonialism's deep transforming influence in the Americas.[14] What has been less clearly understood is how profoundly the spread of equestrianism was altered and amplified by Comanches, who, by virtue of their location near Spanish livestock depots, pioneered a horse-centered way of life that swept the North American grasslands in the eighteenth century.

The horse's spread across the Native American Great Plains was not simply a story of people eagerly embracing an innovation of exhilarating possibilities; it was also a process of conscious imitation under duress. When Comanches reinvented themselves as mounted hunters and nomadic pastoralists in the early years of the eighteenth century, they set a new standard for military strength and material wealth on the plains, triggering an extended sequence of cultural replication and reinvention. As horses and the knowledge of their use spread northward from Comanchería, each plains tribe in its turn was forced to become mounted to avoid military and economic marginalization. Equestrianism exploded across the grasslands, revolutionizing existing economic, social, political, and ecological patterns and deflecting the region's history onto a new path. By 1800, the western shortgrass plains had become a stage for a new and wide-ranging civilization, a spectrum of variously successful equestrian societies that were all replicas of the model established by the Comanches. The most powerful and enduring of those societies, the Lakotas, repressed many Native groups of the northern plains under their rule and resisted the United States' conquest of the northern plains until the 1880s.[15]

In the north, south, and west, then, the Comanche sphere of influence extended, with varying degrees, from the Canadian plains to New Mexico, Texas, and northern Mexico. On the eastern front, in contrast, the impact would seem to have been much shallower. Comanches' raiding sphere did not extend east of Nacogdoches, and they did not visit Louisiana for commerce or diplomacy. For the eighteenth-century French and Spanish colonists along the Mississippi valley, Comanches were a rather abstract source of livestock, slaves, and bison robes; their goods may have moved eastward, but their historical influence did not. This is consistent with our tendency to view American history as a westward-flowing process, which makes anything coming *from* the west—people, commodities, historical influences—seem irrelevant or misguided at best. Early American history moves latitudinally and in only one direction: from eastern power and dynamism toward western weakness and passivity.

Seen from Comanchería, such a view appears wildly skewed. Before 1800 Comanches formed a daunting barrier against westward expansion—not of European colonial powers but of Osages, the most dominant Native people of the eastern Great Plains. Empowered by their privileged access to the French markets along the Mississippi valley, Osages launched in the early eighteenth century a vigorous conquering campaign to expand their territory and hunting grounds beyond a core region between the lower Missouri and Arkansas rivers. In the west, however, that campaign crashed against the rising Comanche empire, which stopped Osages in their tracks and forced them to redirect their territorial ambitions from the west to the south and north. This compression and reorientation of Osage expansion turned the southeastern prairies, the long but narrow belt between the Mississippi valley and the ninety-seventh meridian, into a congested and contested ground, where Osage policies often determined the form and content of relations and where European colonists found little maneuvering space.[16]

By confining the expansionist Osages to the east, the Comanche empire profoundly shaped the history of European colonialism along the Mississippi valley. Yet all of this would seem to lose significance in 1803, when the Louisiana Purchase launched the United States' expansion into the Southwest. From then on, we assume, the history of the Southwest is defined by the overpowering westward thrust of the United States and the futile resistance and gradual retreat of Spain and Mexico. But again, the first impression is deceptive. The United States did not push into a power vacuum in the Southwest but rather into the expanding imperial realm of the Comanches. In fact, United States and Comanche expansions intersected in complex and unexpected ways. New Mexico's reorientation toward the United States economy after 1821 was accelerated by the simultaneous deterioration of north-south economic lifelines under Comanche attacks in northern Mexico; cut off from the south by Indian aggression, New Mexico turned its back on Mexico City and looked to the east for profits and protection. This sweeping reorientation was not a new development but the intensification of a much older one. New Mexico had gravitated toward the east, toward the dynamic economic and political power of Comanchería, since the late eighteenth century when Bourbon officials opened the province for Comanches' commerce and, as it turned out, their political and cultural influence. By the time the United States began to exert its economic influence over New Mexico in the early 1820s, its inhabitants had already began to question their loyalties to Mexico.

If Mexico City was losing its hold on New Mexico by the time of Mexico's independence, to all intents and purposes it lost Texas in 1825, when the state of Coahuila y Texas opened its borders to American immigrants. That momentous decision was influenced by several factors, but key among them was an acute need to recolonize the border regions of Texas that had become almost vacant under Comanche raiding during the early nineteenth century. It was a desperate act aimed at turning the westering Americans from imperial forerunners into Mexican subjects and shielding the decaying frontier against Comanche violence, and it failed on both accounts. Texas was flooded by Anglo-Americans who stayed clear of Comanche raiding routes but used Mexico's failure to suppress the raids as a political pretext for declaring the department an independent republic.

Mexico City's failure to restrain Comanches also thwarted its hopes to reconquer Texas. During the years following the Texas revolt, Comanches extended their stock-and-slave raiding operations deep into northern Mexico, wreaking havoc in seven departments. Not only did the recapture of Texas become impossible, but the entire northern part of the nation began to slip out of Mexico City's grip. Citizens across all the north were perturbed by the federal government's inability—and apparent unwillingness—to curb Comanche raids, and they grew increasingly alienated from Mexico City and its nation-building project. The linkages between American and Comanche expansions climaxed in the Mexican-American War. When the U.S. Army marched south of the Río Grande in 1846, Comanches had already turned vast segments of Mexico's heartland into an economically underdeveloped, politically fragmented, and psychologically shattered world that was ripe for conquest by Americans, who, in a sense, came to occupy what was a vanquished hinterland of Greater Comanchería. In northern Mexico, U.S. imperialism was the direct heir to Comanche imperialism.[17]

The notion that Comanche imperialism paved the way for the United States' takeover of the Southwest forces us not only to rethink the process of American expansion but also to reconsider what that expansion meant and how it should be understood. Recent debates over the roots and realities of the American empire have revealed a disconcerting tendency in the national historiography. Resuscitating once more the enduring fallacy of American exceptionalism, many prominent historians have insisted that the nineteenth-century United States was not an imperial power. The arguments for the position are many, but they all rest on the dogged belief that the United States expanded across a continent so sparsely populated that the land was essentially free for the taking. Westering Americans, the argument goes, did not face densely populated and highly organized indigenous societies, which in turn meant that their expansion was not a case of imperialism; it was an occupation of a semi-virgin land. America's westward expansion was punctuated by instances of overt imperialism—the Mexican-American War being the most blatant one—but those instances did not involve Native Americans.[18] This mainstream interpretation is diametrically at odds with the vision of this book. When Americans invaded the Mexican North with such brutal efficiency in 1846, they did not just clash with the Mexican nation: they plunged into an old, complex, and still evolving history of indigenous imperialism.

The legacy of the Comanche empire is imprinted on the modern-day political map of North America, but it has also left its mark on North America's ethnic landscape. The Comanche slave complex—the capture, assimilation, commodification, and ransoming of thousands of northern Mexicans in the nineteenth century—profoundly shaped the process of *mestizaje*, the mixing and reconfiguration of racial identities, in what now is the U.S. Southwest. Comanche captivity, it has been argued, had a decisive impact on the articulations of race, nation, and citizenship in the Southwest by generating transnational networks of adoption and affiliation, by moving captives between supposedly fixed racial categories, and by creating fragmented and conflicting ethnic identifications. Comanches' cross-border captive traffic, which continued into the 1870s, framed official *norteamericano* discourses about the place that Mexicans would occupy in the U.S. Southwest, promoting the idea of a distinctive transborder Mexican identity. In the minds of U.S. policymakers who came in direct contact with the human products of Comanche captivity—Mexicans who appeared indistinguishable from Comanches, Mexicans who were neither white nor Indian, Mexicans who refused to leave their Indian masters and seemed to conspire with Comanches against U.S. authority—Mexicanness became entwined with Indianness and thus incompatible with Anglo-Americanness and U.S. citizenship. Comanchería and its slave system, in other words, formed a crucible which forged Anglo-American understandings of Mexicans as a mixed, stigmatized, and subordinated class.

To subvert such Anglo-American constructions of racial mixing and impurity, many Chicanas and Chicanos in the U.S. Southwest have attempted to reclaim for themselves a Spanish identity, but some, mostly working-class New Mexican mestizos, have actively embraced Comanchería-derived models of identity. They have memorialized their historical connections to Comanchería in artwork, clothing, and oral traditions, and they reenact those linkages in popular local performances of "Los Comanches." In doing so, they disassociate themselves from the privileged coalition of Anglo- and Spanish Americans, undermine the hegemonic pretensions of that coalition, and promote a distinct brand Chicana/o consciousness that traces its roots to the ethnic melting pot that was Comanchería.[19] Their struggle for identity evokes the multilayered, often painful history of the North American Southwest and northern Mexico, a history that hangs suspended between the Comanche empire of the past and the Anglo-American empire of the present.

Beyond illuminating colonial dynamics and Indian-white relations in a particular place, in this book I have attempted to expand our understanding of the role of indigenous peoples in the making, and unmaking, of colonial worlds. As such it is fundamentally a study of indigenous agency—its character, contours, and capacity to influence large-scale historical processes. But human agency works in two directions, for the very achievements that make societies wealthy and powerful often lead or contribute to their downfall. Accordingly, while I set out to show in this book how the interplay between the Comanches' actions and external conditions made them the dominant people in the colonial Southwest, in the end it had to become an examination of how that interplay contributed to the collapse of the Comanche empire. To acknowledge that Comanches were complicit in their own demise is not to downplay the destructiveness of the United States' political, economic, and military expansion into the Southwest after 1850, but rather to recognize the full potential of indigenous agency, its positive, negative, predictable, and unpredictable dimensions. To paraphrase one prominent historian, recognizing human fallibility in the actions of Native peoples is the basis for writing compassionate Indian history.[20]

Comanches spent their tenure on the southern plains and in the Southwest as an imperial power, and they also fell like one. Like most empires, the Comanche empire carried within itself the seeds of its destruction; its collapse, at least at the beginning, came from within. In their drive to maintain a large population base and control commerce in the midcontinent, Comanches fashioned a prodigious production system that eventually collapsed under its own bloated size. What had begun as a self-sustaining, ecologically stable economy evolved into a surplus-generating market economy that was chronically off balance with its ecological base. The prolonged dry spell between 1845 and 1865 brought on a full-scale crisis, but that crisis was rooted in a classic Malthusian squeeze. There had simply been too many Comanches (and their allies) raising too many horses and hunting too many bison on too small a land base.

In the 1850s, with the bison herds declining sharply, the center caved in. In the space of a few years Comanches lost the bases of their power. Their population plummeted, their trading empire collapsed, and they stopped collecting tribute. They surrendered large tracts of Comanchería to Texas and splintered into local factions that no longer operated as a cohesive confederacy. The decline was remarkably rapid, and it tells a great deal about the nature of the power system the Comanches had built. The Comanche empire was not a tightly structured, self-sustaining entity but rather a continually transmuting set of intersecting networks of power, and when those networks began to crumble, so did the system itself. There was no imperial substructure or ideology to support a slow, gradual decline whereby subjugated peripheries uphold a decaying center. There could be no imperial afterlife.

The outbreak of the Civil War and the onset of a wetter climatic cycle in the mid-1860s allowed Comanches to experience a brief but intense regeneration, which saw them reclaiming parts of their territory and building a new economy on large-scale cattle raiding and full-blown horse pastoralism. But this revival only made the final, inevitable defeat all the more shocking and harrowing. The end of the Civil War heralded the extinction of all sovereign and separatist political systems in the regions the United States claimed as its own—whether those systems existed in the South or in the West. The years between 1865 and 1877 were a period of massive national consolidation, which saw the reduction of the South to a conquered captive territory, the wholesale dispossession of some twenty indigenous nations on the Great Plains, an explosive takeoff of free-labor corporate capitalism, and the introduction of new racial policies that went far beyond the old black-and-white dichotomy.[21] The final subjugation of the Comanches was but a small chapter in this sweeping imperial reorganization. Unleashing its overwhelming economic and technological might, the United States pushed the remains of Comanche power aside with a brief, concentrated scorched-earth campaign. Less an elimination of a military threat than an eradication of a way of life, it was hardly the stuff of which national myths are made. The campaign, along with the Comanche civilization it demolished, was widely ignored and easily forgotten.

ABBREVIATIONS

AC Alfred Barnaby Thomas, ed. and trans., *After Coronado: Spanish Exploration Northeast of New Mexico, 1696–1727* (Norman: University of Oklahoma Press, 1935)

ADM Herbert Eugene Bolton, ed., *Athanase de Mézières and the Louisiana-Texas Frontier, 1768–1780*, 2 vols. (Cleveland: Arthur H. Clark, 1914)

AGN:CA Archivo General de la Nación, Mexico City, Ramo de Californias, Photostatic copy, Zimmerman Library, University of New Mexico, Albuquerque

AGN:HI Archivo General de la Nación, Mexico City, Ramo de Historias, Photostatic copy, Zimmerman Library, University of New Mexico, Albuquerque

AGN:PI Archivo General de la Nación, Mexico City, Ramo de Provincias Internas, Photostatic copy, Zimmerman Library, University of New Mexico, Albuquerque

ARCIA U.S. Office of Indian Affairs, *Annual Report of the Commissioner of Indian Affairs*

BA Béxar Archives, General Manuscript Series, 1717–1836, University of Texas at Austin, Microfilm copy, Zimmerman Library, University of New Mexico, Albuquerque

CO *Chronicles of Oklahoma*

FF Alfred Barnaby Thomas, ed. and trans., *Forgotten Frontiers: A Study of the Spanish Indian Policy of Don Juan Bautista de Anza, Governor of New Mexico, 1777–1787* (Norman: University of Oklahoma Press, 1942)

GPO	Government Printing Office
HD	Charles Wilson Hackett, ed., *Historical Documents Relating to New Mexico, Nueva Vizcaya, and Approaches Thereto, to 1773*, 3 vols. (Washington: Carnegie Institution, 1923–37)
IPTS	Dorman H. Winfrey and James M. Day, eds., *The Indian Papers of Texas and the Southwest, 1825–1916*, 5 vols. (Austin: Pemberton, 1966)
JAH	*Journal of American History*
LR	Letters Received
LR:OIA	Letters Received by the Office of Indian Affairs, Record Group 75, Records of the Bureau of Indian Affairs, M234, National Archives Microfilm Publication
MANM	Mexican Archives of New Mexico, New Mexico State Records Center and Archives, Santa Fe
NAMP	National Archives Microfilm Publication
NMA	New Mexico State Archives, Center for Southwest Research, University of New Mexico, Albuquerque
NMHR	*New Mexico Historical Review*
PINM	Alfred Barnaby Thomas, ed., *The Plains Indians and New Mexico, 1751–1778: A Collection of Documents Illustrative of the History of the Eastern Frontier of New Mexico* (Albuquerque: University of New Mexico Press, 1940)
PT	Charles Wilson Hackett, ed., *Pichardo's Treatise on the Limits of Texas and Louisiana*, 4 vols. (Austin: University of Texas Press, 1931–46)
PV	Noel M. Loomis and Abraham P. Nasatir, *Pedro Vial and the Roads to Santa Fe* (Norman: University of Oklahoma Press, 1967)
RCS	Records of the Central Superintendency, Record Group 75, Records of the Bureau of Indian Affairs, M856, National Archives Microfilm Publication
SANM I	Spanish Archives of New Mexico, New Mexico State Records Center and Archives, Santa Fe, series I, land grant records
SANM II	Spanish Archives of New Mexico, New Mexico State Records Center and Archives, Santa Fe, series II, provincial records
SHQ	*Southwestern Historical Quarterly*
TSA:RR	Texas State Archives, Austin, Texas Governor Hardin Richard Runnels Records

NOTES

INTRODUCTION. REVERSED COLONIALISM

1. The term *Lords of the South Plains* was coined by Ernest Wallace and E. Adamson Hoebel in their classic ethnography *The Comanches: Lords of the South Plains* (Norman: University of Oklahoma Press, 1954).
2. For the genesis and persistence of this view, see Rupert Norval Richardson, *The Comanche Barrier to South Plains Settlement: A Century and a Half of Savage Resistance to the Advancing Frontier* (Glendale, Calif.: Arthur H. Clark, 1933); Wallace and Hoebel, *Comanches;* W. W. Newcomb, Jr., *The Indians of Texas: From Prehistoric to Modern Times* (Austin: University of Texas Press, 1961), 155–56; T. R. Fehrenbach, *Comanches: The Destruction of a People* (New York: Da Capo, 1974); and Martha McCollough, *Three Nations, One Place: A Comparative Ethnohistory of Social Change among the Comanches and Hasinais during Spain's Colonial Era, 1689–1821* (New York: Routledge, 2004). Despite their differing approaches and emphases, all of these works depict Comanche actions as reactive, defensive strategies of containment, attempts to resist European expansion and establish some measure of control over the process of colonial incorporation.
3. For Powhatans, see James Axtell, *The Rise and Fall of the Powhatan Empire: Indians in the Seventeenth-Century Virginia* (Williamsburg: Colonial Williamsburg Foundation, 1995). The idea of the Iroquois as empire-builders was replaced in the 1980s by the idea of a "Phantom Iroquois Empire," a deliberate fiction aimed at advancing Britain's imperial ambitions. By exaggerating Iroquois' sway over other indigenous groups while also insisting that the Iroquois be subordinate to the British empire, British officials claimed control over vast stretches of the American interior. See Richard Aquila, *The Iroquois Restoration: Iroquois Diplomacy, 1701–1754* (1983; reprint, Lincoln: University of Nebraska Press, 1997); and Francis Jennings, *The Ambiguous Iroquois Empire: The Covenant Chain Confederation of Indian Tribes with English Colonies* (New York: W. W. Norton, 1984). More recently, historians have recast the Iroquois as a nation of diplomats, traders, and warriors struggling to survive in a world dislocated by European colonialism. See Daniel K. Richter, *The Ordeal of the Longhouse: The Peoples of the Iroquois League in the Era of European Colonization* (Chapel Hill: University of North Carolina Press for the Omohundro Institute of Early American History and Culture, 1992); and Matthew Dennis, *Cultivating a*

Landscape of Peace: Iroquois-European Encounters in Seventeenth-Century America (Ithaca: Cornell University Press, 1993). The Osages, too, should be mentioned here. Willard H. Rollings has used the term *hegemony* to describe the Osages' relationships with their Native neighbors on the southern prairies along and around the lower Arkansas valley in the eighteenth century. More recently, Kathleen DuVal has used the metaphor of empire to describe these regional relationships. See Willard H. Rollings, *The Osage: An Ethnohistorical Study of Hegemony on the Prairie-Plains* (Columbia: University of Missouri Press, 1992); and Kathleen DuVal, *The Native Ground: Indians and Colonists in the Heart of the Continent* (Philadelphia: University of Pennsylvania Press, 2006). For Lakotas as expansionist, imperial people, see Richard White, "The Winning of the West: The Expansion of the Western Sioux in the Eighteenth and Nineteenth Centuries," *JAH* 65 (Sep. 1978): 319–43; James O. Gump, *The Dust Rose Like Smoke: The Subjugation of the Zulu and the Sioux* (Lincoln: University of Nebraska Press, 1994); and Pekka Hämäläinen, "The Rise and Fall of Plains Indian Horse Cultures," *JAH* 90 (Dec. 2003): 859–62.

4. Several recent works have shown how Native cultural forms and social controls—the ways in which cross-cultural matters were negotiated and agreed on—prevailed in Indian-white contact zones outside European colonies. Faced with overwhelming multitudes of Native peoples on their frontiers, European newcomers were able to protect their territorial holdings and imperial interests only if they respected and adapted to indigenous cultural conventions. In this book, in contrast, I show how a single Native American power, the Comanches, achieved broad-spectrum dominance—military, political, economic, commercial, social, as well as cultural—within its expanding sphere of influence that came to include several European colonial outposts. Rather than being sites of European imperial presence in the midst of indigenous domains, I argue, colonial New Mexico, Texas, and northern Mexico were incorporated into the Comanche empire as tributary client states; exploited raiding hinterlands; and sources of trade, military allies, technology, and slaves. For significant works emphasizing the persistence of Native cultural forms and mores in the face of European colonizing efforts, see Richard White, *The Middle Ground: Indians, Empires, and Republics in the Great Lakes Region, 1650–1815* (New York: Cambridge University Press, 1991); Jill Lepore, *The Name of War: King Philip's War and the Origins of American Identity* (New York: Vintage, 1998); Juliana Barr, "Beyond Their Control: Spaniards in Native Texas," in *Choice, Persuasion, and Coercion: Social Control on Spain's North American Frontiers,* ed. Jesús F. de la Teja and Ross Frank (Albuquerque: University of New Mexico Press, 2005), 149–77; and DuVal, *Native Ground.*

5. The Comanche case bears resemblance to many other historical cases across the world in which nomadic societies have dominated and exploited sedentary urban societies. For an argument of Mongols as a parasitical "shadow empire" presiding over China, see Thomas J. Barfield, "The Shadow Empires: Imperial State Formation along the Chinese-Nomad Frontier," in *Empires: Perspectives from Archaeology and History,* ed. Susan E. Alcock, Terence N. D'Altroy, Kathleen D. Morrison, and Carla M. Sinopoli (Cambridge: Cambridge University Press, 2001), 10–41. For an instructive comparative overview focusing on Central Asia, Siberia, and Africa, see Anatoly M. Khazanov, *Nomads and the Outside World* (1983; reprint, Madison: University of Wisconsin Press, 1994), esp. 222–27.

6. Here I draw less on Immanuel Wallerstein's classic model of the modern capitalist world economy than on his followers and critics who argue that nonstate precapitalist societies—agrarian empires, confederations, and chiefdoms—can unify large regions and create hierarchical inter-

ethnic power structures. World-systems are not necessarily global. Instead, "world" means an integrated, organic, and hierarchical interaction network that has definite boundaries and an internal logic of its own that drives it. For modified world-system models, see Christopher Dunn-Chase and Thomas D. Hall, *Rise and Demise: Comparing World-Systems* (Boulder: Westview, 1997); Janet L. Abu-Lughod, *Before European Hegemony: The World System, A.D. 1250–1350* (New York: Oxford University Press, 1989); Andre Gunder Frank and Barry K. Gillis, eds., *The World System: Five Hundred Years or Five Thousand?* (London: Routledge, 1994); and Peter N. Peregrine and Gary M. Feinman, eds., *Pre-Columbian World-Systems* (Madison, Wis.: Prehistory, 1996).

7. This shift in paradigm can be traced through the following works, which, while focusing on different places, periods, and themes, demonstrate that early American history can be understood only in concert with American Indian history: Francis Jennings, *The Invasion of America: Indians, Colonialism, and the Cant of Conquest* (Chapel Hill: University of North Carolina Press for the Institute of Early American History and Culture at Williamsburg, 1975); Neil Salisbury, *Manitou and Providence: Indians, Europeans, and the Making of New England, 1500–1643* (New York: Oxford University Press, 1982); James Axtell, *After Columbus: Essays in the Ethnohistory of Colonial North America* (New York: Oxford University Press, 1988); James H. Merrell, *The Indians' New World: Catawbas and Their Neighbors from European Contact to the Era of Removal* (Chapel Hill: University of North Carolina Press, 1989); White, *Middle Ground*; Daniel H. Usner, Jr., *Indians, Settlers, and Slaves in a Frontier Exchange Economy: The Lower Mississippi Valley before 1783* (Chapel Hill: University of North Carolina Press, 1992); David J. Weber, *The Spanish Frontier in North America* (New Haven: Yale University Press, 1992); Colin G. Calloway, *New Worlds for All: Indians, Europeans, and the Remaking of Early America* (Baltimore: Johns Hopkins University Press, 1997); Eric Hinderaker, *Elusive Empires: Constructing Colonialism in the Ohio Valley, 1673–1800* (New York: Cambridge University Press, 1997); Andrew R. L. Cayton and Fredrika J. Teute, eds., *Contact Points: American Frontiers from the Mohawk Valley to the Mississippi, 1750–1830* (Chapel Hill: University of North Carolina Press for the Omohundro Institute of Early American History and Culture, 1998); Elliott West, *The Contested Plains: Indians, Goldseekers, and the Rush to Colorado* (Lawrence: University of Kansas Press, 1998); Daniel K. Richter, *Facing East from Indian Country: A Native History of Early America* (Cambridge: Harvard University Press, 2001); Alan Gallay, *The Indian Slave Trade: The Rise of the English Empire in the American South, 1670–1717* (New Haven: Yale University Press, 2002); Jane T. Merritt, *At the Crossroads: Indians and Empires on a Mid-Atlantic Frontier, 1700–1763* (Chapel Hill: University of North Carolina Press for the Omohundro Institute of Early American History and Culture, 2003); David J. Weber, *Bárbaros: Spaniards and Their Savages in the Age of Enlightenment* (New Haven: Yale University Press, 2005); Alan Taylor, *The Divided Ground: Indians, Settlers, and the Northern Borderlands of the American Revolution* (New York: Vintage, 2006); Ned Blackhawk, *Violence over the Land: Indians and Empires in the Early American West* (Cambridge: Harvard University Press, 2006); and DuVal, *Native Ground*. Two compelling, continent-wide syntheses show just how profoundly the incorporation of Native Americans into our stories has changed the master narrative of North America: Alan Taylor, *American Colonies* (New York: Viking, 2001); and Colin G. Calloway, *One Vast Winter Count: The Native American West before Lewis and Clark* (Lincoln: University of Nebraska Press, 2003).

8. Quote is from Vine Deloria, Jr., *We Talk, You Listen: New Tribes, New Turf* (New York: Macmillan, 1970), 39. See, too, Frederick Hoxie, "The Problem of Indian History," *Social Science Journal* 25

(1988): 389–99; Daniel Richter, "Whose Indian History?" *William and Mary Quarterly* 50 (Apr. 1993): 381–82; James A. Hijiya, "Why the West Is Lost," *William and Mary Quarterly* 51 (Apr. 1994): 285–87; and Neil Salisbury, "The Indians' New World: Native Americans and the Coming of Europeans," *William and Mary Quarterly* 53 (July 1996): 435–37. Traditionally, the most common formulation of the extent of Native agency in the making of colonial North America has been that Indians often controlled the balance of power among European imperial powers—a notion that may hold true for the continent's eastern half during the times of war (especially the Seven Years' War) but does not necessarily capture the magnitude of indigenous agency in other places and periods.

9. For critiques and reconstructions of the frontier concept, see, e.g., Leonard Thompson and Howard Lamar, "Comparative Frontier History," in *The Frontier in History: North America and South America Compared*, ed. Howard Lamar and Leonard Thompson (New Haven: Yale University Press, 1981), 3–13; Patricia Nelson Limerick, *The Legacy of Conquest: The Unbroken Past of the American West* (New York: W. W. Norton, 1987); William Cronon, George Miles, and Jay Gitlin, "Becoming West: Toward a New Meaning for Western History," in *Under an Open Sky: Rethinking America's Western Past*, ed. William Cronon, George Miles, and Jay Gitlin (New York: W. W. Norton, 1992), 3–27; Robert V. Hine and John Mack Faragher, *The American West: A New Interpretive History* (New Haven: Yale University Press, 2000); Jeremy Adelman and Stephen Aron, "From Borderlands to Borders: Empires, Nation-States, and the Peoples in Between in North American History," *American Historical Review* 104 (June 1999): 814–41; and J. Parker Bradley and Lars Rodseth, eds., *Untaming the Frontier in Anthropology, Archaeology, and History* (Tucson: University of Arizona Press, 2005). For the impact of borderlands history on frontier studies, see, e.g., the various essays in Cayton and Teute, eds., *Contact Points*. In contrast, Weber's *Spanish Frontier* employs a modified frontier construct to retell the history of the original borderlands, Spain's North American empire: he frames Spain's North American colonies not as a fixed spatial entity but as one side of a shifting, multisided frontier.

10. Usner, *Indians, Settlers, and Slaves*; White, *Middle Ground*; and Adelman and Aron, "From Borderlands to Borders."

11. For a parallel dynamic on the mid-eighteenth-century Cherokee-British borderlands, see Gregory Evans Dowd, "'Insidious Friends': Gift Giving and the Cherokee-British Alliance in the Seven Years' War," in *Contact Points*, 114–50.

12. Similar views of the Southwest can also be traced in scholarly studies. See, e.g., Ray Allen Billington, *Westward Expansion: A History of the American Frontier*, 4th ed. (New York: Macmillan, 1974), 364–66, 370–71, 490; D. W. Meinig, *The Shaping of America: A Geographic Perspective on 500 Years of History*, vol. 1, *Atlantic America, 1492–1800* (New Haven: Yale University Press, 1986), 193–202; Felipe Fernández-Armesto, *The Americas: The History of the Hemisphere* (London: Phoenix, 2004), 84, 105–6; James Pritchard, *In Search of Empire: The French in the Americas, 1670–1730* (New York: Cambridge University Press, 2004), 41–43, 420–22; and Niall Ferguson, *Colossus: The Rise and Fall of the American Empire* (London: Penguin, 2004), 35–39. The notion that the American Southwest stood low in Spain's imperial priorities also informs J. H. Elliott's masterful *Empires of the Atlantic World: Britain and Spain in America, 1492–1830* (New Haven: Yale University Press, 2006). For a profoundly important study that modifies the world-system theory by emphasizing local initiatives but also promulgates the view of Euro-American colonial weakness in the Southwest, see Thomas D. Hall, *Social Change in the Southwest, 1350–1880*

(Lawrence: University Press of Kansas, 1989). For a sweeping assessment of the historiography of the Southwest in general and Texas in particular, see Gerald E. Poyo and Gilberto M. Hinojosa, "Spanish Texas and Borderlands Historiography in Transition: Implications for United States History," *JAH* 75 (Sep. 1988): 393–402.

13. Weber, *Spanish Frontier;* David J. Weber, *The Mexican Frontier, 1821–1846: The American Southwest under Mexico* (Albuquerque: University of New Mexico Press, 1982); Weber, *Bárbaros;* Ross Frank, *From Settler to Citizen: New Mexican Economic Development and the Creation of Vecino Society, 1750–1820* (Berkeley: University of California Press, 2000); Andrés Reséndez, *Changing National Identities at the Frontier: Texas and New Mexico, 1800–1850* (New York: Cambridge University Press, 2005); Blackhawk, *Violence;* Morris W. Foster, *Being Comanche: A Social History of an American Indian Community* (Tucson: University of Arizona Press, 1991); Thomas W. Kavanagh, *Comanche Political History: An Ethnohistorical Perspective* (Lincoln: University of Nebraska Press, 1996); and Pekka Hämäläinen, "The Western Comanche Trade Center: Rethinking the Plains Indian Trade System," *Western Historical Quarterly* 29 (Winter 1998): 485–513.

14. Gary Clayton Anderson, *The Indian Southwest, 1580–1830: Ethnogenesis and Reinvention* (Norman: University of Oklahoma Press, 1999); and James F. Brooks, *Captives and Cousins: Slavery, Kinship, and Community in the Southwest Borderlands* (Chapel Hill: University of North Carolina Press for the Omohundro Institute of Early American History and Culture, 2002).

15. Brooks, *Captives and Cousins*, esp. 30–35. Also see James F. Brooks, "'This Evil Extends . . . Especially to the Feminine Sex': Negotiating Captivity on the New Mexico Borderlands," *Feminist Studies* 22 (Summer 1996): 280. Brooks's work focuses on New Mexico borderlands. As for Texas, Juliana Barr has concluded that although "Native modes of social control, broadly defined and distinctive within each group, prevailed" in Texas, "no one group controlled the entire region. . . . All groups, be they Spaniard or Indian, stood on relatively equal footing in their continued struggles to hold territory and to survive." See Barr, "Beyond Their Control," 152–53, 169.

16. See, e.g., Nancy P. Hickerson, "Ethnogenesis in the South Plains: Jumano to Kiowa?" in *History, Power, and Identity: Ethnogenesis in the Americas, 1492–1992*, ed. Jonathan D. Hill (Iowa City: University of Iowa Press, 1996), 70–89; Patricia C. Albers, "Symbiosis, Merger, and War: Contrasting Forms of Intertribal Relationship among Historical Plains Indians," in *Political Economy of North American Indians*, ed. John H. Moore (Norman: University of Oklahoma Press, 1993), 93–132; Anderson, *Indian Southwest;* and Brooks, *Captives and Cousins.*

17. Like James Merrell's interpretation of the colonial Northeast, this study argues that the recent historiographical focus on cross-cultural crossings and collaborations threatens to obscure a fundamental fact about the history of colonial America—that it is in its essentials a story of conflict, hatred, violence, and virtually insurmountable racial, ethnic, and cultural barriers. See James Merrell, *Into the American Woods: Negotiators on the Pennsylvania Frontier* (New York: W. W. Norton, 1999); and James Merrell, "Shamokin, 'the very seat of the Prince of Darkness': Unsettling the Early American Frontier," in *Contact Points*, esp. 21.

18. For an illuminating discussion on the development, methodology, and limitations of ethnohistory, see James Axtell, *Natives and Newcomers: The Cultural Origins of North America* (New York: Oxford University Press, 2001), 1–12. The term *side-streaming* comes from Richter, *Ordeal*, 5.

19. Frederick E. Hoxie, "Ethnohistory for a Tribal World," *Ethnohistory* 44 (Fall 1997): 603–12. See, too, Richard White, "Creative Misunderstandings and New Understandings," *William and Mary Quarterly* 63 (Jan. 2006): 13–14.

20. Bruce Trigger, "Early Native North American Responses to European Contact: Romantic versus Rationalistic Interpretations," *JAH* 77 (Mar. 1991): 1195–1215. The shift from local, tradition-bound behavioral models toward practices that were based on more "universal" economic laws is also at heart of Richard White's masterful chapter on the fur trade in *Middle Ground* (pp. 94–141). For White, however, the real story is not so much the change itself but the lasting, only partially resolved contention between the two models of thought and behavior. The literature on subtantivist-formalist (or relativist-rationalist or idealist-materialist) debates is far too extensive to be discussed here at any length. Besides the above-cited works by Trigger and White, the most relevant discussions in the context of Native North America include Arthur J. Ray and Donald Freeman, *Give Us Good Measure: An Economic Analysis of Relations between the Indians and the Hudson's Bay Company before 1763* (Toronto: University of Toronto Press, 1978); Calvin Martin, ed., *The American Indian and the Problem of History* (New York: Oxford University Press, 1987); George R. Hamell, "Strawberries, Floating Islands, and Rabbit Captains: Mythical Realities and European Contact in the Northeast during the Sixteenth and Seventeenth Centuries," *Journal of Canadian Studies* 21 (Winter 1987): 72–94; and Shepard Krech III, *The Ecological Indian: Myth and History* (New York: W. W. Norton, 1999).
21. It should be emphasized that such cultural categories and meanings were not static. Although difficult to verify from the thin and fragmented historical record, it is important to keep in mind the possibility that even the most deep-seated practices and conventions—such as the gift giving—acquired new meanings as Comanches expanded their sphere of influence, came in contact with other peoples, and were exposed to different ways of thinking. Accordingly, I have, whenever possible, tried to adhere to Marshal Sahlins's maxim of the dialectical relation between history and structure and show how "in action meanings are always at risk." See Sahlins, *Islands of History* (Chicago: University of Chicago Press, 1985), ix.

CHAPTER 1. CONQUEST

1. This Spanish-Franco rivalry in North America's southern fringes had, of course, a broader geopolitical dimension: French Louisiana was established to challenge Spain's claim to exclusive control of the North American Gulf Coast and break its monopoly over the strategic sea-lines of the Gulf of Mexico.
2. "Diary of Juan de Ulibarrí to El Cuartelejo, 1706," and Pedro de Rivera to Juan de Acuña, marqués de Casa Fuerte, Sep. 26, 1727, AC, 61, 211. Quotes are from Pedro de Rivera, *Diario y derrotero de lo caminado, visto y observado en la visita que hizo a los presidios de la Nueva España Septentrional el Brigadier Pedro de Rivera*, ed. Vito Alessio Robles (Mexico City: Secretaría de la Defensa Nacional, 1946), 78.
3. David Rhode and David B. Madsen, "Where Are We?" in *Across the West: Human Population Movement and the Expansion of the Numa*, ed. David B. Madsen and David Rhode (Salt Lake City: University of Utah Press, 1994), 213–19; and Alice Beck Kehoe, *America before European Invasions* (London: Longman, 2002), 125–27, 131.
4. Shoshonean-related archaeological material east of the Rocky Mountains becomes increasingly prevalent in the sixteenth century, which points to at least more frequent seasonal migrations and perhaps permanent relocation across the Rockies. See Demitri B. Shimkin, "Shoshone-Comanche Origins and Migrations," in *Proceedings of the Sixth Pacific Science Congress of the*

Pacific Science Association, 6 vols. (Berkeley: University of California Press, 1940), 4:20–21; and Sally T. Greiser, "Late Prehistoric Cultures on the Montana Plains," in *Plains Indians, A.D. 150–1550: The Archaeological Past of Historic Groups*, ed. Karl H. Schlesier (Norman: University of Oklahoma Press, 1994), 49–52. For the mountains-plains ecotone and its historical importance, see Elliott West, *The Contested Plains: Indians, Goldseekers, and the Rush to Colorado* (Lawrence: University of Kansas Press, 1998), 22–24. For the drought and its effects, see David A. Baerreis and Reid A. Bryson, "Historical Climatology of the Southern Plains: A Preliminary Survey," *Oklahoma Anthropological Bulletin* 13 (Mar. 1963): 70–75; and Waldo R. Wedel, *Central Plains Prehistory: Holocene Environments and Culture Change in the Republican River Basin* (Lincoln: University of Nebraska Press, 1986), 42–48.

5. For migrations, see Charles A. Reher, "Adaptive Process on the Shortgrass Plains," in *For Theory Building in Archaeology*, ed. Lewis R. Binford (New York: Academic, 1977), 13–40; and Karl H. Schlesier, "Commentary: A History of Ethnic Groups in the Great Plains, A.D. 150–1550," in *Plains Indians*, ed. Schlesier, 308–81.
6. For Shoshone migration, see Colin G. Calloway, "Snake Frontiers: The Eastern Shoshones in the Eighteenth Century," *Annals of Wyoming* 63 (Summer 1991): 84–85; and Dan Flores, "Bison Ecology and Bison Diplomacy: The Southern Plains from 1800 to 1850," *JAH* 78 (Sep. 1991): 468. For pedestrian plains hunters, see Theodore Binnema, *Common and Contested Ground: A Human and Environmental History of the Northwestern Plains* (Norman: University of Oklahoma Press, 2001), 37–54; and Charles A. Reher and George C. Frison, "The Vore Site, 48CK302, A Stratified Buffalo Jump in the Wyoming Black Hills," *Plains Anthropologist* 25, Memoir 16 (1980): 136–43.
7. For Shoshone expansion into the northern plains, see Binnema, *Common and Contested Ground*, 88–94.
8. For the Apaches on the central plains, see Wedel, *Central Plains Prehistory*, 135–51. For Comanche and Shoshone traditions, see Ernest Wallace and E. Adamson Hoebel, *The Comanches: Lords of the South Plains* (Norman: University of Oklahoma Press, 1954), 9–10. At least some late nineteenth-century Comanches maintained that it was the Shoshones who were an offshoot of their nation rather than the other way around. See W. P. Clark, *The Indian Sign Language* (Philadelphia: L. R. Hamersley, 1885), 120.
9. For the diffusion of horses, see Pekka Hämäläinen, "The Rise and Fall of Plains Indian Horse Cultures," *JAH* 90 (Dec. 2003): 835–37. Quote is from Clark, *Indian Sign Language*, 120.
10. For various interpretations of *kumantsi*, see Marvin K. Opler, "The Origins of Comanche and Ute," *American Anthropologist* 45 (Jan.–Mar. 1943): 155–58; Wallace and Hoebel, *Comanches*, 4; Thomas W. Kavanagh, "Comanche," in *Handbook of North American Indians*, vol. 13, *The Plains*, ed. Raymond J. DeMallie, 2 parts (Washington, D.C.: Smithsonian Institution, 2001), 2:902; and James A. Goss, "The Yamparika—Shoshones, Comanches, or Utes—or Does It Matter?" in *Julian Stewart and the Great Basin: The Making of an Anthropologist*, ed. Richard O. Clemmer, L. Daniel Myers, and Mary Elizabeth Rudden (Salt Lake City: University of Utah Press, 1999), 79–80.
11. For early Ute history on New Mexico's borderlands, see Ned Blackhawk, *Violence over the Land: Indians and Empires in the Early American West* (Cambridge: Harvard University Press, 2006), 27–35.
12. According to the conventional view, the Comanches moved from the central plains directly to the

southern plains. See, e.g., T. R. Fehrenbach, *Comanches: The Destruction of a People* (New York: Da Capo, 1974), 129–32; and Thomas W. Kavanagh, *Comanche Political History: An Ethnohistorical Perspective* (Lincoln: University of Nebraska Press, 1996), 58–62. But Comanches themselves maintain that they came to the southern plains from the Rocky Mountains. See Robert S. Neighbors, "The Na-Ü-Ni, or Comanches of Texas; Their Traits and Beliefs, and Divisions and Intertribal Relations," *IPTS*, 3:348; and Clark, *Indian Sign Language*, 118. In 1706, furthermore, New Mexico Governor Francisco Cuervo y Valdez listed the Comanches and Utes as immediate neighbors of the Navajos, whose eastern border ran along Cañon Largo and the Jémez Mountains, deep in the Great Basin. See "Report of Francisco Cuervo y Valdez," Aug. 18, 1706, *HD*, 3:381.

13. For the annual cycle of activities, see Marvin K. Opler, "The Southern Ute of Colorado," in *Acculturation in Seven American Indian Tribes*, ed. Ralph Linton (New York: D. Appleton-Century, 1940), 124–27. For Ute and Comanche trade in New Mexico, see Carl I. Wheat, ed., *Mapping the Trans-Mississippi West, 1540–1861*, 6 vols. (San Francisco: Institute of Historical Cartography, 1957–63), 1: facing 108; and "Opinion of Cristobal de la Serna," Aug. 19, 1719, *AC*, 105. For Ute-Comanche raids into Navajo country, see Rick Hendricks and John P. Wilson, eds. and trans., *The Navajos in 1705: Roque Madrid's Campaign Journal* (Albuquerque: University of New Mexico Press, 1996), 6, 100. For the emergence of Comanche divisions, see Andrew C. Isenberg, *The Destruction of the Bison: An Environmental History, 1750–1920* (Cambridge: Cambridge University Press, 2000), 34; and Kavanagh, "Comanche," 904. For divisional names, see Lila Wistrand Robinson and James Armagost, *Comanche Dictionary and Grammar* (Arlington: University of Texas at Arlington, 1990), 30, 157.

14. For Ute adoption of the horse, see Demitri B. Shimkin, "Introduction of the Horse," in *Handbook of North American Indians*, vol. 11, *Great Basin*, ed. Warren L. d'Azevedo (Washington, D.C.: Smithsonian Institution, 1986), 517–24. For Comanches needing assistance in the first stages of horse adoption, see Alice Marriott and Carol K. Rachlin, *Plains Indian Mythology* (New York: Thomas Y. Crowell, 1975), 91. For raids, see Cristóbal Torres to Juan Páez Hurtado, Aug. 22 and Sep. 7 and 9, 1716, and Diego Marquez to Hurtado, Sep. 8, 1716, SANM II 5:626–28 (T-279) (this designation is the Twitchell number, the numerical designation Ralph Emerson Twitchell assigned to particular document sets of the Spanish Archives of New Mexico); and "Opinion of Ensign Xptobal de Torres, "Opinion of Ensign Bernardo Casillas," and "Opinion of Cristobal de la Serna," Aug. 19, 1719, *AC*, 104–5. See, too, Blackhawk, *Violence*, 35–40, 48. For a comparison of horses and dogs as beasts of burden, see John C. Ewers, *The Horse in Blackfoot Indian Culture: With Comparative Material from Other Western Tribes*, Bureau of American Ethnology Bulletin 159 (Washington, D.C.: Smithsonian Institution, 1955), 306–7.

15. For intriguing studies of connections between exploitation of horse use and energy, see West, *Contested Plains*, 34–54; and Dan Flores, *Caprock Canyons: Journeys into the Heart of the Southern Plains* (Austin: University of Texas Press, 1990), 82–83 (quote is from p. 82).

16. For Native views of firearms, see West, *Contested Plains*, 49.

17. For the origins of Indian slavery in New Mexico, see Ramón A. Gutiérrez, *When Jesus Came, the Corn Mothers Went Away: Marriage, Sexuality, and Power in New Mexico, 1500–1846* (Stanford: Stanford University Press, 1991), 101–27, 155–56; David J. Weber, *The Spanish Frontier in North America* (New Haven: Yale University Press, 1992), 127–29; and Elizabeth A. H. John, *Storms Brewed in Other Men's Worlds: The Confrontation of Indians, Spanish, and French in the South-*

west, 1640–1795 (Norman: University of Oklahoma Press, 1975), 62–85. For deep roots of *rescate* in Spain's New World colonialism, see John E. Kicza, "Patterns in Early Spanish Overseas Expansion," *William and Mary Quarterly* 49 (Apr. 1992): 230–31.

18. For Utes in New Mexico's slave trade, see Blackhawk, *Violence*, 32–35; and James F. Brooks, *Captives and Cousins: Slavery, Kinship, and Community in the Southwest Borderlands* (Chapel Hill: University of North Carolina Press for the Omohundro Institute of Early American History and Culture, 2002), 50, 108, 148–50. For Comanche and Ute trade in Apache slaves in New Mexico, see Antonio de Valverde y Cosío to Baltasar de Zúñiga y Guzmán, marqués de Valero, Nov. 30, 1719, *AC*, 141. For Apache and Pawnee slaves in New Mexico, see Gutiérrez, *When Jesus Came*, 147; Brooks, *Captives and Cousins*, 49–51; L. R. Bailey, *Indian Slave Trade in the Southwest* (Los Angeles: Westernlore, 1966), 23–24; and Russell M. Magnaghi, "The Indian Slave Trade in the Southwest: The Comanche, a Test Case" (Ph.D. diss., University of Nebraska–Lincoln, 1979), 153–54. Quote is from "Decree," Sep. 26, 1714, cited in David M. Brugge, *Navajos in the Catholic Church Records of New Mexico, 1694–1875* (Tsaile, Ariz.: Navajo Community College Press, 1985), xix.

19. For Navajos, see Frank McNitt, *Navajo Wars: Military Campaigns, Slave Raids, and Reprisals* (Albuquerque: University of New Mexico Press, 1972), 23. For intermarriage, see Neighbors, "Na-Ü-Ni," 348. For Comanche-Ute trading and raiding policy, see "Opinion of Ensign Bernardo Casillas," "Opinion of Captain Miguel Thenorio," "Opinion of Cristobal de la Serna," and "Opinion of Juan de Archibèque," Aug. 19, 1719, *AC*, 104–7. Quote is from "Opinion of Capt. Joseph Truxillas," Aug. 19, 1719, *AC*, 102.

20. "Opinion of Ensign Bernardo Casillas," Aug. 19, 1719, *AC*, 104.

21. "Diary of Ulibarrí," and Valverde to Valero, Nov. 30, 1719, *AC*, 61–76, 141–45 (quotes are on pp. 65, 142).

22. Comanche traditions support the notion that the eastward migration to the plains took place around the turn of the seventeenth and eighteenth centuries. See Clark, *Indian Sign Language*, 118. For the suitability of the southern plains environment for Spanish horses, see Dan Flores, *Horizontal Yellow: Nature and History in the Near Southwest* (Albuquerque: University of New Mexico Press, 1999), 82–100; and Hämäläinen, "Rise and Fall," 4.

23. For a detailed analysis of the advantages of mounted hunting over pedestrian hunting, see Ewers, *Horse*, 148–70.

24. For the patterns of early southern plains trade, see Katherine A. Spielmann, *Interdependence in the Prehistoric Southwest: An Ecological Analysis of Plains-Pueblo Interaction* (New York: Garland, 1991), 239–43; and Susan C. Vehik and Timothy G. Baugh, "Prehistoric Plains Trade," in *Prehistoric Exchange Systems in North America*, ed. Timothy G. Baugh and Jonathon E. Ericson (New York: Plenum, 1994), 249–74. For early French trade along the Arkansas and with Apaches, see "Diary of Ulibarrí," 73. Apaches soon assumed a central role in France's commercial schemes on the southern plains. See Bénard de La Harpe, "La Harpe's First Expedition in Oklahoma," trans. Anna Lewis, *CO* 2 (Dec. 1924): 347.

25. For early eighteenth-century Spanish accounts of Apache farming on the southern plains, see "Diary of Ulibarrí," and Antonio de Valverde y Cosío, "Diary of the Campaign . . . against the Ute and Comanche Indians, 1719," *AC*, 64, 68, 73, 112. For key studies on the Apache way of life on the southern and central plains, see Wedel, *Central Plains Prehistory*, 135–51; and James H. Gunnerson, "Plains Village Tradition: Western Periphery," in *Handbook of North American Indians*, vol.

13, *The Plains*, ed. Raymond J. DeMallie, 2 parts (Washington, D.C.: Smithsonian Institution, 2001), 2:239–43. For the late seventeenth-century droughts, see David W. Stahle and Malcolm K. Cleaveland, "Texas Drought History Reconstructed and Analyzed from 1698 to 1980," *Journal of Climate* 1 (Jan. 1988): 65.

26. Richard White, *The Roots of Dependency: Subsistence, Environment, and Social Change among the Choctaws, Pawnees, and Navajos* (Lincoln: University of Nebraska Press, 1983), 152; F. Todd Smith, *The Wichita Indians: The Traders of Texas and the Southern Plains, 1540–1845* (College Station: Texas A&M University Press, 2000), 16–17; Gary Clayton Anderson, *The Indian Southwest, 1580–1830: Ethnogenesis and Reinvention* (Norman: University of Oklahoma Press, 1999), 55–66, 105–27; Nancy Parrott Hickerson, *The Jumanos: Hunters and Traders of the South Plains* (Austin: University of Texas Press, 1994), 160–230; and Charles L. Kenner, *The Comanchero Frontier: A History of New Mexican–Plains Indian Relations* (1969; reprint, Norman: University of Oklahoma Press, 1994), 16–19.

27. It has been estimated that horticulturists needed as much as three acres per family to sustain themselves on the arid western plains, which suggests a compelling explanation to Comanche-Apache wars: there simply was not enough room for both Apache farmers and Comanche herders. For Apache farming, see Wedel, *Central Plains Prehistory*, 135–51; and Susan C. Vehik, "Cultural Continuity and Discontinuity in the Southern Prairies and Cross Timbers," in *Plains Indians*, ed. Schlesier, 246–63. For the importance of microenvironments in understanding the ecological adaptations and history of Plains Indians, see Elliott West, *The Way to the West: Essays on the Central Plains* (Albuquerque: University of New Mexico Press, 1995), chs. 1 and 2.

28. For Comanche plant lore and gathering on the plains, see Flores, "Bison Ecology," 471; Wallace and Hoebel, *Comanches*, 73–74; and Domingo Cabello y Robles, Responses Given by the Governor of the Province of Texas to Questions Put to Him by the Lord Commanding General of the Interior [Provinces] in an Official Letter of the 27th of January Concerning Various Conditions of the Eastern Comanches, Apr. 30, 1786, BA 17:418. For the lack of reliable sources of carbohydrates among plains hunters and its possible adverse effects, see John D. Speth and Katherine A. Spielmann, "Energy Source, Protein Metabolism, and Hunter-Gatherer Subsistence Strategies," *Journal of Anthropological Archaeology* 2:1 (1983): 1–31. For the effects of excess protein consumption (more than 35–40 percent of total energy intake) among hunter-gatherers in other regions, see Loren Cordain et al., "Plant-Animal Subsistence Ratios and Macronutrient Energy Estimations in Worldwide Hunter Gatherer Diets," *American Journal of Clinical Nutrition* 71 (Mar. 2000): 682–92.

29. For Faraones, see "Testimony of Don Gerónimo," July 20, 1715, "Testimony of Don Lorenzo," July 22, 1715, and "Order of Council of War," Nov. 9, 1723, *AC*, 80–82, 194. For Comanche-Ute cohesion, see "Opinion of Ensign Bernardo Casillas," and "Opinion of Captain Miguel de Coca," Aug. 19, 1719, *AC*, 104–5. For Comanche-Ute tactics, see Valverde, "Diary," 112–15. Quote is from Rivera to Casa Fuerte, Sep. 26, 1727, *AC*, 211.

30. For Indian attempts to monopolize French trade, see Claude Charles Du Tisné to Jean Baptiste Le Moyne, Sieur de Bienville, Nov. 22, 1719, in *Découvertes et établissements des français dans l'ouest et dans le sud de L'Amérique Septentrionale, 1614–1754: Mémoires et documents originaux*, ed. Pierre Margry, 6 vols. (Paris: D. Jouaust, 1879–88), 6:313–15; and Willard H. Rollings, *The Osage: An Ethnohistorical Study of Hegemony on the Prairie-Plains* (Columbia: University of Missouri Press, 1992), 117–18. For Pawnee-French trade and Pawnee-Apache wars, see Valverde, "Diary,"

132; and Wedel, *Central Plains Prehistory*, 173. For Wichita-French trade in Apache slaves, see "Diary of Ulibarrí," 74; and Bénard de La Harpe, "Account of the Journey of Bénard de La Harpe: Discovery Made by Him of Several Nations Situated in the West," trans. and ed. Ralph A. Smith, *SHQ* 62 (Apr. 1959): 529. For Wichita-Apache conflict, see "Relation du voyage de Bénard de La Harpe," Dec. 12, 1719, in *Découvertes*, 6:290–92. Quote is from "Opinion of Captain Miguel de Coca," 105.

31. Quotes are from Juan de la Cruz to Valero, 1719, and "Order of Valero," Aug. 1, 1719, AC, 138–39. For Spanish deliberations on the Apache request, see "Council of War," Aug. 19, 1719, and Valverde to Valero, Nov. 30, 1719, AC, 100–10, 138, 141–45.
32. Valverde, "Diary," 110–19 (quotes are from pp. 110, 112–13, 115).
33. Ibid., Valverde to Valero, Nov. 30, 1719, and Manuel San Juan de Santa Cruz to Valero, Dec. 11, 1719, AC, 119–33, 142, 147 (quotes are from pp. 132, 142). For El Cuartelejo, see "Diary of Ulibarrí," 60–77.
34. For the Villasur expedition, see Weber, *Spanish Frontier*, 170–71. For Spain's vacillating attitudes toward assisting the Apaches and building a presidio on the plains, see, e.g., Valverde to Valero, May 27, 1720, "Council of War," June 2, 1720, and Juan de Olivan Revolledo to Valero, Dec. 9, 1720, AC, 154–60, 175–77.
35. "Council of War," Nov. 9, 1723, and Revolledo to Casa Fuerte, July 12, 1724, AC, 195–97. Quotes are from "Decree for Council of War," Nov. 8, 1723, Juan Domingo de Bustamante to Casa Fuerte, Jan. 10, 1724, and Revolledo to Casa Fuerte, July 12, 1724, AC, 194, 196, 201, 206.
36. For the events in 1723 and 1724, see Council of War, Juan Mirabel to Bustamante, Jan. 29, 1724, SANM II 6:105–6 (T-324); Bustamante to Casa Fuerte, Jan. 10, 1724, *PT*, 3:226; and Bustamante to Casa Fuerte, May 30, 1724, AC, 208. For the debate over La Jicarilla, see Bustamante to Casa Fuerte, May 30, 1724, "Reply of the Fiscal," Dec. 14, 1726, Revolledo to Casa Fuerte, Mar. 31, 1727, and "Council of War Ordering Presidio at La Jicarilla," Sep. 26, 1720, AC, 208–9, 217–19, 234–39. For the battle of El Gran Sierra del Fierro, see William Edward Dunn, "Apache Relations in Texas, 1718–1750," *SHQ* 14 (Jan. 1911): 220.
37. This sequence of retreat, relocation, ethnogenesis, and alliance-making by the Apache refugees has been pieced together from the following sources: Council of War, Opinion of Lt. Gen. Juan Páez Hurtado, Feb. 6, 1724, SANM II 6:129 (T-324); Juan Agustín de Morfí, "Geographical Description of New Mexico," *FF*, 96–97; Bustamante to Casa Fuerte, May 30, 1724, and Apr. 30, 1727, AC, 208, 256–58; and Bustamante to Casa Fuerte, Aug. 26, 1727, *PT*, 3:246. Quotes are from Morfí, "Geographical Description," 97; and Bustamante to Casa Fuerte, Apr. 30, 1727, AC, 257–58.
38. See Rivera to Casa Fuerte, Sep. 26, 1727, AC, 209–17 (quotes are from pp. 213 and 214).
39. Traditionally, the Comanche-Apache wars on the southern plains have been seen as a primal struggle for living space or, as one historian put it, "for cultural life and death." Most historians have reduced the clash to a one-dimensional territorial contest driven by greed, hatred, and the Indians' inherent passion for war. See, e.g., Fehrenbach, *Comanches*, 132–33 (the phrase "cultural life and death" is on p. 132). I argue here that the wars are best understood as a multifaceted strategic struggle over specific natural resources, river valleys, and trade privileges, a view that is corroborated by the cessation of fighting in the late 1720s for nearly a decade: driven by strategic considerations rather than territorial greed or ethnic hate, the Comanches stopped fighting when they had temporarily met their needs.

40. The few existing sources suggest that during the late 1720s and 1730s, Comanches gradually extended their control several hundred miles to the east of the Rocky Mountain Front Range. See Bustamante to Casa Fuerte, Apr. 30, 1727, *AC*, 256; and "Declaration of Fray Miguel de Menchero," May 10, 1744, *HD*, 3:401. For the Big Timbers, see Jacob Fowler, *Journal of Jacob Fowler*, ed. Elliott Coues (Lincoln: University of Nebraska Press, 1970), 41–44; and Edwin James, *Account of an Expedition from Pittsburgh to the Rocky Mountains, Performed in the Years 1819, 1820*, vols. 14–17 of *Early Western Travels, 1748–1846*, ed. Reuben Gold Thwaites (Cleveland: Arthur H. Clark, 1906), 16:20, 31, 61. For cottonwood as emergency food, see Randolph B. Marcy, *Adventure on Red River: Report on the Exploration of the Headwaters of the Red River by Captain Randolph B. Marcy and Captain G. B. McClellan*, ed. Grant Foreman (Norman: University of Oklahoma Press, 1937), 60–61, 141–42. For plains winters and horse ecology, see Hämäläinen, "Rise and Fall," 14–15.
41. For the link between horse pasturing and social division, see Athanase de Mézières to Juan Maria Vicencio, barón de Ripperdá, July 4, 1772, *ADM*, 1:297.
42. For Comanche horse wealth and seasonal migrations, see "Declaration of Felipe de Sandoval," Mar. 1, 1750, and "Declaration of an Unnamed Frenchman," June 26, 1751, *PT*, 3:323–24, 348. For mounted chase, see Isenberg, *Destruction*, 88.
43. Benito Crespo to the viceroy, Sep. 25, 1730, in Benito Crespo, "Documents Concerning Bishop Crespo's Visitation, 1730," *NMHR* 28 (July 1953): 230; Proceedings in the Case of Juan García de la Mora vs. Diego de Torres, Apr. 13–May 16, 1735, and Henrique de Olavide y Michelena, Bando, Jan. 7, 1737, SANM II 7:365, 552 (T-402, 414); "Declaration of Fray Miguel de Menchero," 401–2; and Marc Simmons, *Coronado's Land: Essays on Daily Life in Colonial New Mexico* (Albuquerque: University of New Mexico Press, 1991), 42–43. Owing to its illicit nature, gun trade between Spanish subjects and Indians is rarely mentioned in sources. It must have been quite widespread, however, because New Mexican authorities saw it necessary to issue specific *bandos* to prohibit it. See, e.g., Gervasio Cruzat y Góngora, Bando, May 2, 1735, SANM II 7:398 (T-403). Indicating growing Comanche trade in Apache captives, the number of Apache baptisms in New Mexico jumped from 97 in the 1720s to 153 in the 1730s. See Brooks, *Captives and Cousins*, 146.
44. For attacks, see John L. Kessell, *Kiva, Cross, and Crown: The Pecos Indians and New Mexico, 1540–1840* (Washington, D.C.: National Park Service, 1979), 371. For Comanche camps in the Arkansas valley, see "Declaration of an Unnamed Frenchman," 348. A typical Comanche camp in this period probably contained between 100 and 300 people, but camp sizes could vary considerably. In 1749 a visitor from French Louisiana reported that he had seen one Comanche camp of "eighty-four tents, containing 800 persons," as well as two others, containing 23 and 40 tipis, or approximately 230 and 400 people, respectively. In 1750 another Frenchman reported that he had lived for four months in a massive Comanche camp that consisted of 400 tipis. See "Declaration of Luis del Fierro," Apr. 13, 1749, and "Declaration of Felipe de Sandoval," Mar. 1, 1750, *PT*, 3:303, 323.
45. The Comanche military society had become fully mature by the late eighteenth century, when historical sources begin to shed more light on Comanches' internal affairs. For an early remark on connections between war record and social status, see Francisco Marin del Valle, Description of the Province of New Mexico, 1758, AGN:CA 39:1, 21V. For nineteenth-century society, see Wallace and Hoebel, *Comanches*, 216, 245.
46. For renewed Comanche attacks on Apaches, see Kessell, *Kiva, Cross, and Crown*, 371–72. For the

Comanche war machine, see Frank Raymond Secoy, *Changing Military Patterns on the Great Plains*, Monographs of the American Ethnological Society 21 (New York: J. J. Augustin, 1952), 30–31.

47. For Apache baptisms, see Brugge, *Navajos*, 21–22. For Apaches seeking shelter from New Mexico's border towns, see Kessell, *Kiva, Cross, and Crown*, 371–72. For contention over trading privileges, see Anderson, *Indian Southwest*, 206–7.
48. For an insightful contemporary account of Comanche views of gifts, see Marcy, *Adventure*, 159, 174.
49. Tension and conflicts between Comanches and New Mexicans at trade fairs is a consistent theme in the eighteenth-century Spanish sources. For a revealing account, see "Instruction of Don Tomás Vélez Cachupín, 1754," *PINM*, 133.
50. Gaspar Domingo Mendoza, Order to alcaldes mayores, Feb. 2, 1742, and Joachín Codallos y Rabál, Bando, Feb. 4, 1746, SANM II 8:108, 213–15 (T-443, 495); and Kavanagh, *Comanche Political History*, 69–70. For the quote on Abiquiu, see Tomás Vélez de Cachupín to Juan Francisco de Güemes y Horcasitas, conde de Revillagigedo I, Nov. 27, 1751, *PINM*, 79. For the events in 1747, see "An Account of Lamentable Happenings in New Mexico and of Losses Experienced in Daily Affairs Spiritual and Temporal; Written by Reverend Father Fray Juan Sanz de Lazaún, in the Year 1760," *HD*, 3:477; and Hubert Howe Bancroft, *History of Arizona and New Mexico, 1530–1888* (San Francisco: History Company, 1889), 249. Records provide conflicting information about the ethnic composition of the raiding party that struck Abiquiu and about the Indian camp that Governor Codallos's troops demolished in 1747; it is likely, however, that both were mixed Comanche-Ute units.
51. For the Comanche-Pawnee conflict, see Opinion of Lt. Gen. Juan Páez Hurtado, SANM II 6:129; "Declaration of Luis del Fierro," 304; and White, *Roots of Dependency*, 152, 179. Fierro speaks of hostilities between Comanches and "A nation," which probably refers to the Arapahoes. See Douglas R. Parks, "Enigmatic Groups," in *Handbook of North American Indians*, vol. 13, *The Plains*, ed. Raymond J. DeMallie, 2 parts (Washington, D.C.: Smithsonian Institution, 2001), 2:971–72. For Osages, see Stephen Aron, *American Confluence: The Missouri Frontier from Borderland to Border State* (Bloomington: Indiana University Press, 2006), 24–26, 48–49; and Kathleen DuVal, *The Native Ground: Indians and Colonists in the Heart of the Continent* (Philadelphia: University of Pennsylvania Press, 2006), 103–10.
52. For Comanche-Wichita relations, see "Declaration of Luis del Fierro," "Declaration of Joseph Miguel Raballo," Apr. 13, 1749, and "Declaration of Felipe de Sandoval," *PT*, 3:303, 307–8, 323; and Valle, Description, AGN:CA 39:1, 22R. Not all Apache captives were sold. While visiting Comanchería, Sandoval noted that Comanches "keep for themselves whatever [women] they seize from their enemies in war."
53. For French traders among the Comanches in 1748, see Antonio Duran de Armijo to Joachín Codallos y Rabál, Feb. 27, 1748, in Ralph Emerson Twitchell, *The Spanish Archives of New Mexico*, 2 vols. (New York: Arno, 1976), 1:148. Quote is from Tomás Vélez de Cachupín, Brief Description of the Province and Territory of New Mexico in the Kingdom of New Spain, in "New Mexico in the Mid-Eighteenth Century: A Report Based on Governor Vélez Cachupín's Inspection," trans. and ed. Robert Ryal Miller, *SHQ* (Oct. 1975): 173. For the remark of Apache slaves in Louisiana, see Juliana Barr, "From Captives to Slaves: Commodifying Indian Women in the Borderlands," *JAH* 92 (June 2005): 28.

54. For Comanche and Ute raids against Pecos and Galisteo, see Cachupín to Revillagigedo I, Mar. 8, 1750, *PT,* 3:328; Kessell, *Kiva, Cross, and Crown,* 379n24, 380; and Frances Levine and Anna LaBauve, "Examining the Complexity of Historical Population Decline: A Case Study of Pecos Pueblo, New Mexico," *Ethnohistory* 44 (Winter 1997): 96. For Abiquiu, Ojo Caliente, and Quemado, see Petition by Vecinos of Ojo Caliente, Abiquiu, and Pueblo Quemado to Abandon Their Settlements Due to Indian Hostilities, 1748, SANM I 1:263–66 (T-28); and "Account of Lamentable Happenings," 477. For the execution of Comanche-Ute raids and the fortification of Pecos and Galisteo, see marqués de Altamira, "Opinion," Jan. 15, 1753, *PINM,* 127; and Cachupín to Revillagigedo I, Mar. 8, 1750, *PT,* 3:328. For Taos fairs, see Codallos to the viceroy, 1748, in Twitchell, *Spanish Archives,* 2:227.
55. Quotes are from Cachupín, Brief Description, 173; and Cachupín to Revillagigedo I, Mar. 8, 1750, *PT,* 3:328. For Cachupín's policies, see John, *Storms,* 314–15.
56. For Spanish reactions to the French threat, see Cachupín to Revillagigedo I, Mar. 8, 1750, and "Report of Doctor Andreu," June 7, 1751, *PT,* 3:326, 343; and Altamira, "Opinion," Apr., 26, 1752, *PINM,* 79. Quotes are from Cachupín, Brief Description, 173; and Cachupín to Revillagigedo I, Nov. 27, 1751, and "Instruction of Cachupín," *PINM,* 75, 135.
57. Varo's account is cited in "Report of the Reverend Father Provincial, Fray Pedro Serrano, to the Most Excellent Señor Viceroy, the Marquis of Cruillas, in regard to the *Custodia* of New Mexico. In the year 1761," *HD,* 3:486–87.
58. "Report of Serrano," *HD,* 3:487; and Altamira to the viceroy, Jan. 9, 1751, *HD,* 3:332.
59. Tomás Vélez de Cachupín, Account of Campaign against Comanches in the Fall of 1751, SANM II 8:1049–54 (T-518); and Cachupín to Revillagigedo I, Nov. 27, 1751, *PINM,* 68–76 (quotes are from pp. 71–73).
60. See, e.g., "Declaration of Felipe de Sandoval," 323.
61. Juan Joseph Lobato to Cachupín, Aug. 28, 1752, and Cachupín to Revillagigedo I, Sep. 29, 1752, *PINM,* 114–17, 118–25 (quotes are from pp. 115–16, 120). Lobato's report was based on a testimony given by a captive Indian woman who had lived among the Comanches at the time of the negotiations and was later sold to New Mexico by Utes. Her testimony was translated into Spanish by an Indian servant whose "sincerity" allowed Lobato to "understand the essential facts of the account."
62. Cachupín to Revillagigedo I, Sep. 29, 1752, *PINM,* 119–21 (quotes are from pp. 120 and 121).
63. "Instruction of Cachupín," 132–35 (quotes are from pp. 134–35).
64. Cachupín to Revillagigedo I, Sep. 29, 1752, and "Instruction of Cachupín," *PINM,* 124, 135–36. For the Miera y Pacheco map, see Wheat, *Mapping the Trans-Mississippi West,* 1: facing 108.
65. "Declaration of Luis Fuesi," and Cachupín to Revillagigedo I, Sep. 18, 1752, *PINM,* 107, 110. Little is known about Comanche–Skidi Pawnee relations, except that their alliance was often marred by hostilities. See, e.g., Pedro Tamarón y Romeral, *Bishop Tamarón's Visitation of New Mexico, 1760,* ed. Eleanor B. Adams (Albuquerque: University of New Mexico Press, 1954), 62. For the 1751 battle, see Jacques-Pierre de Taffanel de la Jonquière, marquis de la Jonquière to the French minister, Sep. 25, 1751, in *The French Regime in Wisconsin,* ed. Reuben Gold Thwaites (Madison: Wisconsin Historical Society, 1908), 87–88.
66. For Taovayas, see Smith, *Wichita Indians,* 27–28; and Anderson, *Indian Southwest,* 152. For Comanche-Osage border, see Henry Dodge, Journal of the March of a Detachment of Dragoons, 24th Cong., 1st sess., H. Doc. 181, 18.

67. See Cachupín to Revillagigedo I, Mar. 8, 1750, *PT*, 3:327; and Lobato to Cachupín, Aug. 28, 1752, and "Instruction of Cachupín," *PINM*, 114–15, 130–32.
68. "Instruction of Cachupín," 136. The significance of a common enemy for the stability of the Comanche-Ute alliance is further illustrated by the fact that the coalition had suffered a brief rupture in the mid-1730s, when the wars against Apaches had been temporarily halted. See Proceedings in the Case of Juan García de la Mora vs. Diego de Torres, SANM II 7:365 (T-402).
69. For a study looking at the collapse of the Comanche-Ute alliance from Ute perspective, see Blackhawk, *Violence*, 52–54, 61–62.
70. Quote is from Cachupín to Joaquín de Montserrat, marqués de Cruillas, June 27, 1762, *PINM*, 149–50. For Valle's trade restrictions, see Francisco Marín del Valle, Bando, Nov. 26, 1754, SANM II 8:1191–96 (T-530).
71. Revillagigedo I to marqués de Ensenada, June 28, 1753, *PINM*, 111–12; Tamarón, *Visitation*, 45, 54, 57–58 (quotes are from p. 58); and Bernardo de Miera y Pacheco, "Miera's Report," ed. Herbert S. Auerbach, *Utah Historical Quarterly* 11 (1943): 121.
72. Juan Candelaria, "Noticias que da Juan Candelaria vecino de esta villa de San Francisco Xauier de Alburquerque de edad de 84 años," ed. Isidro Armijo, *NMHR* 4 (July 1929): 291–94; Tamarón, *Visitation*, 58–59 (the quote on Comanche intentions is from p. 58); and Francisco Atanasio Domínguez, *The Missions of New Mexico, 1776: A Description by Fray Francisco Atanasio Domínguez*, trans. and ed. Eleanor B. Adams and Angelico Chavez (Albuquerque: University of New Mexico Press, 1956), 251, 257–58 (the quote on ruins is from p. 251).
73. Candelaria, "Noticias," 291; and Tamarón, *Visitation*, 59–61 (quotes are from p. 61).
74. Tamarón, *Visitation*, 61–62.
75. Ibid., 62. For Comanche social code and masculine honor, see Jane Fishburne Collier, *Marriage and Inequality in Classless Societies* (Stanford: Stanford University Press, 1988), 47–63.
76. Cachupín to Cruillas, June 27, 1762, *PINM*, 148–49.
77. Ibid., 150–51. Also see James F. Brooks, "'This Evil Extends Especially . . . to the Feminine Sex': Negotiating Captivity on the New Mexico Borderlands," *Feminist Studies* 22 (Summer 1996): 299.
78. Cachupín to Cruillas, June 27, 1762, *PINM*, 152–53.
79. For Cachupín's motives, see Cachupín to Cruillas, June 27, 1762, *PINM*, 153–54.
80. Quote is from Cachupín to Cruillas, June 27, 1762, *PINM*, 150. For Cachupín's attempts to put an end to the Comanches' raiding-and-trading policy, see ibid., 151. It should be emphasized that the 1762 negotiations, together with peace talks a decade before, formed only the beginning for a development that eventually could have led to a full-blown middle ground. As Richard White has shown, the creation of a middle ground was an arduous and delicate process that took generations and, moreover, was never complete. See Richard White, *The Middle Ground: Indians, Empires, and Republics in the Great Lakes Region, 1650–1815* (New York: Cambridge University Press, 1991), esp. chs. 2, 7, and 8. For a study that casts the Southwest as a middle-ground failure, see Jeremy Adelman and Stephen Aron, "From Borderlands to Borders: Empires, Nation-States, and the Peoples in Between in North American History," *American Historical Review* 104 (June 1999): esp. 823–29.
81. For the resettlement of Abiquiu and Ojo Caliente, see Proceeding Regarding the Resettlement of Ojo Caliente, 1751–53, and Tomás Vélez de Cachupín, Order to Resettle the Paraje de Abiquiu, 1750, SANM I 4:265–78, 5:1561–64 (T-650, 1100). For Ute trade at Abiquiu and Ojo Caliente, see

Domínguez, *Missions*, 252–53. The Utes emerged by the 1770s as fully fledged mountain people, who based their economy on small game hunting, wild plant gathering, and captive raiding in the Great Basin. They still traveled occasionally onto the plains to hunt bison, but these expeditions now had more ritual than economic meaning. See Fernando de la Concha to Juan Vicente de Güemes Padilla Horcasitas y Aguayo, conde de Revillagigedo II, May 6, 1793, SANM II 13:234–35 (T-1234); and Blackhawk, *Violence*, 55–87.

82. For food taboos, see Wallace and Hoebel, *Comanches*, 70. For feral horses, see Flores, "Bison Ecology," 481; and Richard White, "Animals and Enterprise," in *The Oxford History of the American West*, ed. Clyde A. Milner II, Carol A. O'Connor, and Martha A. Sandweiss (New York: Oxford University Press, 1994), 239.

83. For Lipan-Texas relations and the 1749 treaty, see Anderson, *Indian Southwest*, 111–20; and Barr, "From Captives to Slaves," 32–38. For a long-term view on Apache-Spanish relations in Texas, see John, *Storms*, 258–87. For early eighteenth-century Texas, see Jesús F. de la Teja, "Spanish Colonial Texas," in *New Views of Borderlands History*, ed. Robert H. Jackson (Albuquerque: University of New Mexico Press, 1998), 127. For early Comanche excursions to the Texas plains, see Juan Agustín de Morfí, *History of Texas, 1673–1779*, trans. Carlos Eduardo Castañeda, 2 vols. (Albuquerque: Quivira Society, 1935), 2:294.

84. For Wichita-French trade along the Red River, see Elizabeth Ann Harper, "The Taovayas Indians in Frontier Trade and Diplomacy, 1719–1768," *CO* 31 (Autumn 1953): 278–79; and Smith, *Wichita Indians*, 28.

85. For Taovayas, Tonkawas, and Hasinais, see Harper, "Taovayas Indians," 271–72; Kelly F. Himmel, *The Conquest of the Karankawas and Tonkawas, 1821–1859* (College Station: Texas A&M University Press, 1999), 23–25; and Anderson, *Indian Southwest*, 145–48. For Lipan expansion on the Texas plains, see, e.g., Isidro Félix de Espinosa, *Crónica de los Colegios de Propaganda Fide de la Nueva España*, ed. Lino Gómez Canedo (1764; reprint, Washington, D.C.: Academy of American Franciscan History, 1964), 692. For Spanish accusations of French manipulation, see Morfí, *History*, 2:374–76, 390.

86. For Lipan farming, see Morris E. Opler, "Lipan Apache," in *Handbook of North American Indians*, vol. 13, *The Plains*, ed. Raymond J. DeMallie, 2 parts (Washington, D.C.: Smithsonian Institution, 2001), 2:948. Quote is from "A Statement by Fray Francisco Aparicio to Colonel Parrilla," Apr. 5, 1758, in *San Sabá Papers: A Documentary Account of the Founding and Destruction of San Sabá Mission*, ed. Lesley Byrd Simpson, trans. Paul D. Nathan (1959; reprint, Dallas: Southern Methodist University Press, 2000), 127–28.

87. For San Sabá, see Robert S. Weddle, *The San Sabá Mission: Spanish Pivot in Texas* (1964; reprint, College Station: Texas A&M University Press, 1999), 35–60. For a contemporary Spanish view of San Sabá as a provocation for a Norteño attack, see Morfí, *History*, 2:376.

88. "Deposition of Joseph Gutiérrez," "Deposition of Andrés de Villareal," "Deposition of Juan Leal," and "Deposition of Father Fray Manuel Miguel de Molina," in *San Sabá Papers*, 43–45, 68–77, 84–92 (quotes are from pp. 43, 71, and 90); Morfí, *History*, 2:378–85 (the quote on painted faces is from p. 378); and Weddle, *San Sabá Mission*, 88.

89. "Deposition of Joseph Gutiérrez," "Deposition of Sergeant Joseph Antonio Flores," and "Memorandum by Colonel Diego Ortiz Parrilla," in *San Sabá Papers*, 44, 56, 98. Quotes are from Manuel de la Piscina to the viceroy, Mar. 24, 1758, and "Deposition of Father Fray Miguel de Molina," in ibid., 35, 90–91.

90. Henry Easton Allen, "The Parrilla Expedition to the Red River in 1759," *SHQ* 43 (July 1939): 53–71; Weddle, *San Sabá Mission*, 107–40; and Smith, *Wichita Indians*, 31–34. The loss of the cannons was a major blow to Texas because cannons were rare in the northern frontier and because they had considerable value as symbols of Spain's military might. Twenty years later Spaniards were still trying to recover the lost cannons, finally succeeding in 1779. See de Mézières to Teodoro de Croix, Apr. 19, 1778, and "Summary by Croix of the Reports of de Mézières," Sep. 23, 1778, *ADM*, 2:208, 228.
91. Curtis D. Tunnell and W. W. Newcomb, Jr., *A Lipan Apache Mission: San Lorenzo de la Santa Cruz, 1762–1771* (Austin: Texas Memorial Museum, 1969), 167–72; and John, *Storms*, 355.
92. "Itinerary of Señor Marqués de Rubí, Field Marshal of His Majesty's Armies, in the Inspection of the Interior Presidios that by Royal Order He Conducted in this New Spain, 1766–1768," and Cayetano María Pignatelli Rubí Corbera y San Climent, marqués de Rubí, "Dictamen of April 18, 1768," in *Imaginary Kingdom: Texas as Seen by the Rivera and Rubí Military Expeditions, 1727 and 1767*, ed. Jack Jackson (Austin: Texas State Historical Association, 1995), 111, 179, 181 (quote is from p. 111); Nicolás de Lafora, *Relación del viaje que hizo a los presidios internos situados en la frontera de la América septentrional perteneciente al Rey de España*, ed. Vito Alessio Robles (Mexico City: Editorial Pedro Robredo, 1939), 182; and Anderson, *Indian Southwest*, 124–26.
93. Rubí, "Dictamen," 178–81.
94. For the reception of Rubí's policies, see *Imaginary Kingdom*, ed. Jackson, 82–84.
95. For Apache raiding in northern New Spain, see David J. Weber, *Bárbaros: Spaniards and Their Savages in the Age of Enlightenment* (New Haven: Yale University Press, 2005), 74–75. For travel between San Antonio and Santa Fe, see *PV*, 262.
96. Quotes are from Kavanagh, *Comanche Political History*, 87; and Wheat, *Mapping the Trans-Mississippi West*, 1: facing 108.
97. For the 1726 estimate, see Rivera, *Diario*, 78. The estimate of Comanche population in 1750 is based on the following deductions. In that year Pierre Satren, a Frenchman who had lived in Comanchería for two months, reported that the rancherías in the upper Arkansas River valley could muster two thousand warriors. When women, children, and the elderly are added to this figure, it seems that between eight and ten thousand Comanches were living in the Arkansas River valley alone. To this figure should be added all the Comanche rancherías on the Llano Estacado. See "Declaration of Pedro Satren," Mar. 5, 1750, *PT*, 3:317. For Apache population decline, see Morfí, *History*, 2:272.
98. For the centrality of farming in Apache culture, see Dolores A. Gunnerson, *The Jicarilla Apaches: A Study in Cultural Survival* (DeKalb: Northern Illinois University Press, 1974), 242–43; Gunnerson, "Plains Village Tradition," 239–44; and J. Loring Haskell, *Southern Athapaskan Migration, A.D. 200–1750* (Tsaile, Ariz.: Navajo Community College Press, 1987), 85–92, 110–11.
99. De Mézières to Luis Unzaga y Amezaga, Oct. 29, 1770, *ADM*, 1:218–19.

CHAPTER 2. NEW ORDER

1. For an incisive analysis of these dynamics, see Gregory Evans Dowd, *War under Heaven: Pontiac, the Indian Nations and the British Empire* (Baltimore: Johns Hopkins University Press, 2002).
2. This reorganization of northern New Spain's frontier policies has received considerable attention from historians. For prominent examples, see Max L. Moorhead, *The Apache Frontier: Jacobo*

Ugarte and Spanish-Indian Relations in Northern New Spain, 1769–1791 (Norman: University of Oklahoma Press, 1968); David J. Weber, *Bárbaros: Spaniards and Their Savages in the Age of Enlightenment* (New Haven: Yale University Press, 2005), 204–35; Ross Frank, *From Settler to Citizen: New Mexican Economic Development and the Creation of Vecino Society, 1750–1820* (Berkeley: University of California Press, 2000); and Jeremy Adelman and Stephen Aron, "From Borderlands to Borders: Empires, Nation-States, and the Peoples in between in North American History," *American Historical Review* 104 (June 1999): 833–35.

3. Tomás Vélez de Cachupín to Joaquín de Montserrat, marqués de Cruillas, June 27, 1762, *PINM*, 150.

4. For the distribution of horses to the central and northern plains and on the difficulties the Indians in those regions faced in building viable horse cultures, see Pekka Hämäläinen, "The Rise and Fall of Plains Indian Horse Cultures," *JAH* 90 (Dec. 2003): 13–22.

5. For Pawnees, Kansas, Iowas, and Kiowas, see Pedro Vial and Francisco Xavier Chaves, Diary, in "Inside the Comanchería, 1785: The Diary of Pedro Vial and Francisco Xavier Chaves," ed. Elizabeth A. H. John, trans. Adán Benavides, Jr., *SHQ* 88 (July 1994): 50; Domingo Cabello y Robles, Responses Given by the Governor of the Province of Texas to Questions Put to Him by the Lord Commanding General of the Interior [Provinces] in an Official Letter of the 27th of January Concerning Various Conditions of the Eastern Comanches, Apr. 30, 1786, BA 17:418; and Zebulon Montgomery Pike, *The Expeditions of Zebulon Montgomery Pike*, ed. Elliott Coues, 2 vols. (1895; reprint, New York: Dover, 1987), 2:590. Pedro Vial, who lists the Kansas, Iowas, and Kiowas as Comanches' trading partners, wrote his account after spending the summer of 1785 in eastern Comanchería. The information on Comanche-Cheyenne and Comanche-Ponca horse trade is based on Cheyenne and Ponca folklore. See Alice Marriott and Carol K. Rachlin, *Plains Indian Mythology* (New York: Thomas Y. Crowell, 1975), 94–98; and Alice C. Fletcher and Francis La Flesche, *The Omaha Tribe*, Bureau of American Ethnology Bulletin 27 (Washington, D.C.: Smithsonian Institution, 1905–6), 79–80. For trails, see Donald J. Blakeslee and Robert Blasing, "Indian Trails in the Central Plains," *Plains Anthropologist* 33 (Feb. 1988): 24.

6. For Comanche trade in New Mexico and with the Wichitas, see Pedro Fermín de Mendinueta to Carlos Francisco de Croix, marqués de Croix, Sep. 3, 1768, *PINM*, 160–62. For British trade on the southern prairies and with the Wichitas, see *PV*, 11–12. For the 1776 report, see Francisco Atanasio Domínguez, *The Missions of New Mexico, 1776: A Description by Fray Francisco Atanasio Domínguez*, trans. and ed. Eleanor B. Adams and Angelico Chavez (Albuquerque: University of New Mexico Press, 1956), 252. Quote is from Nicolás de Lafora, *The Frontiers of New Spain: Nicolás de Lafora's Description, 1766–1768*, ed. and trans. Lawrence Kinnaird (Berkeley: Quivira Society, 1958), 94.

7. For the flow of commodities, see Vial and Chavez, Diary, 50; and Cabello, Responses, BA 17:418. Also see Pekka Hämäläinen, "The Western Comanche Trade Center: Rethinking the Plains Indian Trade System," *Western Historical Quarterly* 29 (Winter 1998): 492–93.

8. For Mandan and Hidatsa horse trade, see John C. Ewers, *Indian Life on the Upper Missouri* (1954; reprint, Norman: University of Oklahoma Press, 1968), 14–33; and John S. Milloy, *The Plains Cree: Trade, Diplomacy, and War, 1790 to 1870* (Winnipeg: University of Manitoba Press, 1988). Quote is from Estevan Rodriguez Miró to Antonio Rengel, Dec. 12, 1785, in *Before Lewis and Clark: Documents Illustrating the History of the Missouri, 1785–1804*, ed. A. P. Nasatir, 2 vols. (1952; reprint, Lincoln: University of Nebraska Press, 1990), 1:125. Miró also listed Apaches as the

distributors of horses to the Missouri valley, but this was an error: almost all Apaches had been pushed out of the plains by the 1760s.

9. Lafora, *Frontiers*, 93, 185. To preserve Spain's military hegemony in the Americas, the crown had prohibited the distribution of firearms among Indians since 1501. Fearful of losing the Indian trade and Indian allegiances to British contraband traders, Spanish officials frequently petitioned in the late eighteenth century for an exemption from the law, but the rigid regulations were not relaxed until the 1780s. See, e.g., Juan María Vicencio, barón de Ripperdá to the viceroy, Apr. 28, 1772, and José Areche to the viceroy, July 31, 1772, *ADM*, 1:269–71, 277–82.
10. Cabello, Responses, BA 17:418; and Pedro Tamarón y Romeral, *Bishop Tamarón's Visitation of New Mexico, 1760*, ed. Eleanor B. Adams (Albuquerque: University of New Mexico Press, 1954), 58. Quotes are from Domínguez, *Missions*, 252.
11. Frank, *From Settler to Citizen*, 37.
12. For Mendinueta's Indian policy, see, e.g., Mendinueta to Teodoro de Croix, June 18, 1768, *PINM*, 159–62 (quotes are from p. 159).
13. For drought, see Frank, *From Settler to Citizen*, 34–35, 38. For the 1771 truce and subsequent raids, see Hubert Howe Bancroft, *History of Arizona and New Mexico, 1530–1888* (San Francisco: History Company, 1889), 259; and *PINM*, 44, 169n70.
14. For the 1757 census, see John O. Baxter, *Las Carneradas: Sheep Trade in New Mexico, 1700–1860* (Albuquerque: University of New Mexico Press, 1987), 42. Quotes are from Mendinueta to Antonio María de Bucareli y Ursúa, Aug. 19, 1775, *PINM*, 184; and Antonio Bonilla, "Bonilla's Notes Concerning New Mexico [1776]," in *New Spain and the Anglo-American West: Historical Contributions Presented to Herbert Eugene Bolton*, ed. Charles W. Hackett, George P. Hammond, and J. Lloyd Mecham, 2 vols. (Lancaster, Pa., 1932), 1:195.
15. For Comanche horse wealth, see Mendinueta to Bucareli, Oct. 20, 1774, *PINM*, 175, and Juan Bautista de Anza, "Diary of the Expedition . . . against the Comanche Nation . . . ," Sep. 10, 1779, and Francisco Xavier Ortiz to Juan Bautista de Anza, May 29, 1786, *FF*, 139, 323. For minimum requirements, see John H. Moore, "The Dynamics of Scale in Plains Ethnohistory," *Papers in Anthropology* 23:2 (1982): 234.
16. For Comanche captive raiding in New Mexico, see Mendinueta to Croix, Nov. 10, 1769, and Aug. 4, 1770, AGN:PI 103:1, 88R,V, 114R,V; Mendinueta to Bucareli, Sep. 30, 1774, and Aug. 18, 1775, *PINM*, 169–73, 180–84; and Teodoro de Croix, "General Report of 1781," in *Teodoro de Croix and the Northern Frontier of New Spain, 1776–1783: From the Original Document in the Archives of the Indies, Seville*, ed. and trans. Alfred Barnaby Thomas (Norman: University of Oklahoma Press, 1941), 111. For Comanche captive trade in New Mexico and the almsgiving plan, see Mendinueta to Bucareli, Sep. 30, 1774, *PINM*, 170; Domínguez, *Missions*, 252; Croix to Anza, May 27, 1782, and Phelipe Neve to Anza, Apr. 28, 1784, SANM II 11:344, 723–24 (T-839, 894); and Oakah L. Jones, Jr., "Rescue and Ransom of Spanish Captives from the *indios bárbaros* on the Northern Frontier of New Spain," *Colonial Latin American Historical Review* 4 (Spring 1995): 143–44. For Comanche trade in New Mexican captives with the Wichitas, Pawnees, and French, see Juan Agustín de Morfí, *History of Texas, 1673–1779*, trans. Carlos Eduardo Castañeda, 2 vols. (Albuquerque: Quivira Society, 1935), 2:434; Athanase de Mézières to Croix, Apr. 19, 1778, *ADM*, 2:209; Jack B. Tykal, "From Taos to St. Louis: The Journey of María Rosa Villalpando," *NMHR* 65 (Apr. 1990): 161–74; and Angélico Cháves, *Origins of New Mexico Families: A Genealogy of the Spanish Colonial Period* (1954; reprint, Santa Fe: Museum of New Mexico Press, 1992), 281–82.

Juliana Barr has argued that during the eighteenth century Comanches seized captives with the intention of trading them rather than using them as laborers. See Juliana Barr, "From Captives to Slaves: Commodifying Indian Women in the Borderlands," *JAH* 92 (June 2005): 25–26.

17. For Lafora's plans, see Lafora, *Frontiers,* 95. For New Mexico's defenses, see Areche to Bucareli, Oct. 21, 1775, *PINM,* 185–86. For the 1777 and 1778 raids, see *PINM,* 51; and Croix, "General Report," 111. Quotes are from Domínguez, *Missions,* 124, 217; and Bonilla, "Notes," 195.
18. For Comanche raids in New Mexico, see Frank, *From Settler to Citizen,* 43–44, 49–50; Mendinueta to Croix, Apr. 27 and Nov. 10, 1769, and Aug. 4, 1770, and Mendinueta to Bucareli, July 23, 1773, AGN:PI 103:1, 51R–54R, 88R,V, 114R,V, 103:2, 230R–234V; "Extract of Reports from the Kingdom of New Mexico between September 17 and November 9 of the past year [1769]," and Mendinueta to Bucareli, Sep. 30, 1774, and May 12 and Aug. 18, 1775, *PINM,* 169–70, 179–183; Pedro Fermín de Mendinueta, Order for the Resettlement of Abiquiu, Nov. 2, 1770, SANM I 1:289–92 (T-36); Petition of Citizens of Nuestra Señora del Rosario de las Truchas, Mar. 6–10, 1772, SANM II 10:712–16 (T-666); Domínguez, *Missions,* 78, 83, 92, 112–113; Joseph Rubio to Mendinueta, Jan. 8, 1778, and Croix to Mendinueta, Jan. 8, 1778, SANM II 10:965, 970 (T-714, 716); Juan Agustín de Morfí, "Geographical Description of New Mexico," *FF,* 96; and Marc Simmons, "Settlement Patterns and Village Plans in Colonial New Mexico," *Journal of the West* 8:1 (1969): 15–16. Quotes are from Mendinueta to Bucareli, Feb. 8, 1775, *PINM,* 177; and E. Boyd, "Troubles at Ojo Caliente, a Frontier Post," *El Palacio* 64 (Nov. 1957): 353–54. The phrase "destroyed by hostile Comanches" is from a map prepared by Bernardo de Miera y Pacheco, which is reprinted in *FF,* 87. For Apache and Navajo raids, see Frank, *From Settler to Citizen,* 36–37; Domínguez, *Missions,* 254; and Bonilla, "Notes," 195.
19. For the 1779 map, see Domínguez, *Missions,* 2–3. For the effects of Comanche raids, see Mendinueta to Bucareli, Apr. 27, 1769, Jan. 18 and Aug. 8, 1771, Jan. 4 and Mar. 30, 1772, and July 23 and Oct. 16, 1773, AGN:PI 103:1, 51R–54R, 134R–135V, 155R–158R, 103:2, 177R–180R, 184R–186R, 230R–234V, 238R–239V; Mendinueta to Bucareli, Sep. 30, 1774, and May 12 and Aug. 18, 1775, Areche to Bucareli, Oct. 21, 1775, and Mendinueta to Croix, June 22, 1778, *PINM,* 170–73, 179–83, 185–86, 212; Domínguez, *Missions,* 143, 213–14, 254 (quotes are from p. 213); and Charles L. Lummis, *A New Mexico David and Other Stories and Sketches of the Southwest* (New York: Charles Scribner's Sons, 1891), 96–99. For Pecos, see Morfí, "Geographical Description," 93; and Domínguez, *Missions,* 214. In 1760, only sixteen years earlier, 168 families had lived in Pecos. See Tamarón, *Visitation,* 48.
20. Tamarón, *Visitation,* 53; and Frank, *From Settler to Citizen,* 42. Quote is from Domínguez, *Missions,* 217.
21. For Spanish punitive campaigns, see *PINM,* 38–51; and Croix to Mendinueta, Jan. 8, 1778, SANM II 10:970 (T-716). For a haunting account of the use of Indian ears as trophies in Santa Fe, see Ned Blackhawk, *Violence over the Land: Indians and Empires in the Early American West* (Cambridge: Harvard University Press, 2006), 16–18.
22. For the 1774 battle, see Mendinueta to Bucareli, Oct. 20, 1774, *PINM,* 174–75. For Bucareli's remark, see Bucareli to Mendinueta, Feb. 8, 1775, *PINM,* 177.
23. For the Apache wars of the 1770s, see Elizabeth A. H. John, *Storms Brewed in Other Men's World: The Confrontation of Indians, Spanish, and French in the Southwest, 1540–1795* (Norman: University of Oklahoma Press, 1975), 433–47. For New Mexico's defenses, see Mendinueta to Bucareli, Aug. 19, 1775, and Mendinueta to Croix, June 22, 1778, *PINM,* 184–83, 212–13; and *PINM,*

54n167. For New Mexico's settlement patterns, see Frank, *From Settler to Citizen*, 47–49. For Mendinueta's attempts to strengthen the frontier, see Mendinueta to Croix, Nov. 3, 1777, in "Governor Mendinueta's Proposals for the Defense of New Mexico, 1772–1778," ed. Alfred B. Thomas, *NMHR* 6 (Jan. 1931): 36–39.

24. For a copy of the Miera y Pacheco map and a translation of the legend, see Domínguez, *Missions*, 2–4. For Morfí's account, see Morfí, "Geographical Description," 92.

25. The following data on raids are from Mendinueta to Bucareli, Sep. 30, 1774, *PINM*, 169–72.

26. Frank, *From Settler to Citizen*, 33; and Mendinueta to Croix, Sep. 3, 1768, *PINM*, 160–61. Quotes are from Bucareli to Julián de Arriaga, Jan. 27, 1773, cited in *PINM*, 43; and Mendinueta to Croix, Sep. 3, 1768, *PINM*, 160.

27. For the variety and fluidity of exchange strategies on the Río Grande–Great Plains and Río Grande–Navajo borderlands, see Katherine A. Spielmann, "Interaction among Nonhierarchical Societies," in *Farmers, Hunters, and Colonists: Interaction between the Southwest and the Southern Plains*, ed. Katherine A. Spielmann (Tucson: University of Arizona Press, 1991), 7–13; Patricia Albers, "War, Merger, and Symbiosis: Contrasting Forms of Intertribal Relationship among Historic Plains Indians," in *Political Economy of North American Indians*, ed. John H. Moore (Norman: University of Oklahoma Press, 1993), 108–9; and James F. Brooks, *Captives and Cousins: Slavery, Kinship, and Community in the Southwest Borderlands* (Chapel Hill: University of North Carolina Press for the Omohundro Institute of Early American History and Culture, 2002), 86–88.

28. Domínguez, *Missions*, 59, 99, 111–13, 252; and Juan Agustín de Morfí, Desórdenes que se advierten en el Nuevo México [1778], AGN:HI 25, 132V. Quote is from Mendinueta to Bucareli, Oct. 20, 1774, *PINM*, 175.

29. Mendinueta to Bucareli, May 11, 1771, cited and translated in John L. Kessell, *Kiva, Cross, and Crown: The Pecos Indians and New Mexico, 1540–1840* (Washington, D.C.: National Park Service, 1979), 393–95.

30. Mendinueta to Croix, Jan. 28, 1769, AGN:PI 103:1, 60V–62V.

31. Domínguez, *Missions*, 251–52; and Max L. Moorhead, *New Mexico's Royal Road: Trade and Travel on the Chihuahua Trail* (Norman: University of Oklahoma Press, 1958), 43.

32. Domínguez, *Missions*, 252.

33. Mendinueta to Bucareli, Sep. 30, 1774, *PINM*, 172. The first reference to the "reverse" horse trade in Taos is from 1760. See Tamarón, *Visitation*, 58. That Comanches sold stolen New Mexican livestock at Taos is demonstrated by the fact that they often sold mules, which are sterile and were available to Comanches only in New Mexico. For mule trade at Taos, see Domínguez, *Missions*, 252. For aborted hunts, see Gary Clayton Anderson, *The Indian Southwest, 1580–1830: Ethnogenesis and Reinvention* (Norman: University of Oklahoma Press, 1999), 230–31. Quotes are from Morfí, "Geographical Description," 101; and Morfí, Desórdenes, AGN:HI 25, 132V.

34. For material destruction and starvation in New Mexico, see Mendinueta to Croix, Nov. 3, 1777, in "Mendinueta's Proposals," 35; Mendinueta to Croix, June 22, 1778, *PINM*, 212; Domínguez, *Missions*, 92, 213, 217; and Frank, *From Settler to Citizen*, 50–52. Maize is rarely mentioned in the contemporary accounts of Comanche-Taos trade, probably because it was so commonplace. For an account that portrays Taos as a food depot for Comanches, see Domínguez, *Missions*, 112. Quote is from Anza to Croix, May 26, 1780, *FF*, 177.

35. For the complex origins of "Los Comanches," see Thomas W. Kavanagh, "Los Comanches: Pieces

of an Historic, Folkloric Detective Story, Part I," *NMHR* 81 (Winter 2006): 1–37. Quote is from Domínguez, *Missions*, 112.

36. This depiction of "Los Comanches" draws on Brooks, *Captives and Cousins*, 1–10.
37. Gilberto Espinosa, trans., "Los Comanches," *New Mexico Quarterly* 1 (May 1931): 145.
38. Brooks, *Captives and Cousins*, 1–10. For other interpretations, see John, *Storms*, 478–79; and Frank, *From Settler to Citizen*, 63–64.
39. For the Ute–New Mexican alliance and Abiquiu trade, see Blackhawk, *Violence*, 70–93.
40. Francisco Atanasio Domínguez to Isidro Murillo, Nov. 25, 1776, in Domínguez, *Missions*, 286–87 (quote is from p. 286); and Angelico Chavez, trans., Ted J. Warner, ed., *The Domínguez-Escalante Journal: Their Expedition through Colorado, Utah, Arizona, and New Mexico in 1775* (Salt Lake City: University of Utah Press, 1995), 144–45. For Comanche range, see also Pedro Garrido y Duran, "An account of the events which have occurred in the provinces of New Mexico concerning peace conceded to the Comanche nation and their reconciliation with the Utes, since November 17 of last year and July of the current [1786]," *FF*, 295.
41. Chavez, trans., and Warner, ed., *Domínguez-Escalante Journal*, 47–48, 55–56, 65–69, 72 (the first two quotes are from pp. 67 and 69). The longer quote is from Silvestre Vélez de Escalante, *Pageant in the Wilderness: The Story of the Escalante Expedition to the Interior Basin, 1776*, ed. and trans. Herbert Eugene Bolton (Salt Lake City: Utah State Historical Society, 1950), 216.
42. Anderson, *Indian Southwest*, 128–37; and "Description of the most notable characteristics of the El Paso del Río del Norte, as given by one of its citizens, after seven years' residence there," Sep. 1, 1773, *HD*, 3:508.
43. John, *Storms*, 485; and *FF*, 16, 63–64.
44. Deborah Lamont Newlin, *The Tonkawa People: A Tribal History from the Earliest Times to 1893* (Lubbock: West Texas Museum Association, 1982), 15–18; and F. Todd Smith, *From Dominance to Disappearance: The Indians of Texas and the Near Southwest, 1786–1859* (Lincoln: University of Nebraska Press, 2005), 73–74. Quotes are from de Mézières to Ripperdá, July 4, 1772, *ADM*, 1:289–90; and Jean Louis Berlandier, *Journey to Mexico: During the Years 1826 to 1834*, trans. Sheila M. Ohlendorf, Josette M. Bigelow, and Mary M. Standifer, 2 vols. (Austin: Texas State Historical Association and University of Texas Press, 1980), 2:381.
45. The changes in the Hasinai-Comanche relations and the decreased political weight of the Hasinais became apparent in 1770, when Spanish officials decided to employ the Caddos as middlemen in an effort to negotiate peace with the Comanches. Spaniards sponsored a high-level meeting among the Kadohadachos instead of the Hasinais; indeed, the Hasinais were not even present. See Athanase de Mézières, "Official Relation . . . ," Oct. 29, 1770, *ADM*, 1:206–20. For the decline of the Hasinais and the commercial ascendancy of the Wichitas, see Daniel A. Hickerson, "Historical Processes, Epidemic Disease, and the Formation of the Hasinais Confederacy," *Ethnohistory* 44 (Winter 1997): 42–46.
46. For Comanche-Taovaya relations, see Declaration of Antonio Treviño, Aug. 13, 1765, BA 10:379; Carlos E. Castañeda, *Our Catholic Heritage in Texas, 1519–1936*, 7 vols. (Austin: Von Boeckmann-Jones, 1936–58), 4:194–96; and F. Todd Smith, *The Wichita Indians: The Traders of Texas and the Southern Plains, 1540–1845* (College Station: Texas A&M University Press, 2000), 42. For Taovaya farming, see Anderson, *Indian Southwest*, 162–63. For Texas's wealth in horses, see Dan Flores, *Horizontal Yellow: Nature and History in the Near Southwest* (Albuquerque: University

of New Mexico Press, 1999), 107–8; and Juan N. Almonte, "Statistical Report on Texas," trans. C. E. Castañeda, *SHQ* 28 (Jan. 1925): 191. For Louisiana's livestock markets, Daniel H. Usner, Jr., *Indians, Settlers, and Slaves in a Frontier Exchange Economy: The Lower Mississippi Valley before 1783* (Chapel Hill: University of North Carolina Press, 1992), 176–81.

47. Quote is from de Mézières, "Official Relation," 219. For Comanche raiding in Texas and its links to eastbound horse trade, see also Lafora, *Frontiers*, 149–50; and de Mézières to Luis Unzaga y Amezaga, July 3, 1771, Ripperdá to the viceroy, Aug. 2, 1772, Roque de Medina to Hugo O'Conor, Mar. 8, 1774, and de Mézières to Unzaga, Mar. 24 and Dec. 16, 1774, *ADM*, 1:253, 334, 2:32–34, 103, 115. For trade prohibitions, see O'Reilly to de Mézières, Jan. 23, 1779, *ADM*, 1:135–36; and Alejandro O'Reilly, "Proclamation," Dec. 7, 1769, in *Spain in the Mississippi Valley, 1765–94: Translations of Materials from the Spanish Archives in the Bancroft Library*, ed. Lawrence Kinnaird, 3 vols. (Washington, D.C.: GPO, 1946–49), 2:126. For slave traffic, see de Mézières to Croix, Apr. 19, 1776, *PT*, 2:247; and de Mézières to Croix, Apr. 19, 1778, *ADM*, 2:209.

48. For the Taovaya/Wichita trade system, Comanche participation in it, and the lack of European goods in Comanchería, see Declaration of Antonio Treviño, BA 10:379; Antonio de Ulloa to Hugo O'Conor, 1768, de Mézières to Unzaga, July 3, 1771, Ripperdá to the viceroy, Apr. 28, 1772, de Mézières to Ripperdá, July 4, 1772, Ripperdá to the viceroy, July 6, 1772, J. Gaignard, "Journal," and Croix to José de Gálvez, Sep. 23, 1778, *ADM*, 1:129, 251, 270, 301, 2:88–90, 222–23, and *PV*, 91–94. The quote "trifles" is from Gaignard, "Journal," 95.

49. For the impact of the British threat on Spain's Wichita policy, see Ulloa to O'Conor, 1768, and Ripperdá to the viceroy, Apr. 28, 1772, *ADM*, 1:127–30, 269–70. In 1773 Hugo O'Conor, the commanding general of the Interior Provinces, ordered Texas to implement Rubí's plans. Texas officials abandoned several presidios and missions in eastern Texas and began seeking friendly relations with the southern plains nations. In contrast to Rubí's recommendations, however, the colony did not focus its diplomatic efforts on the Comanches. For the implementation of Rubí's recommendations in Texas, see John, *Storms*, 448–64. For Osages, see de Mézières to Unzaga, May 20, 1770, *ADM*, 1:166–68 (quote is from p. 167); and Colin G. Calloway, *One Vast Winter Count: The Native American West before Lewis and Clark* (Lincoln: University of Nebraska Press, 2003), 364–65.

50. For the 1770 conference, see de Mézières, "Official Relation," 206–20 (quotes are from pp. 209–10). For Wichita-Spanish peace process, see Smith, *Wichita Indians*, 44–51. For Osage trade, see de Mézières to Unzaga, May 20, 1770, *ADM*, 1:166–67.

51. "Articles of Peace Granted to the Taouaïazés Indians," Oct. 27, 1771, and Ripperdá to the viceroy, Apr. 28, 1772, *ADM*, 1:256–59, 269–71. Betraying their anxiety, Comanches had begun "waging a most cruel war" against Wichitas upon learning about the Spanish-induced rapprochement between Wichitas and Lipans. See de Mézières "Official Relation," 212. Quotes are from de Mézières to Unzaga, July 3, 1771, *ADM*, 1:251; and "Articles of Peace," 257.

52. Ripperdá to Unzaga, May 26, 1772, *ADM*, 1:273–74. Also see Barr, "From Captives to Slaves," 42–43.

53. For Povea's visit, see Ripperdá to the viceroy, July 5, 1772, *ADM*, 1:320–21.

54. Gaignard, "Journal," 83–100 (quotes are from p. 94). Indicating just how effective the Wichita trade blockade was, one Comanche chief told Gaignard that it had been eight years since his followers had seen "Frenchmen." For Gaignard's instructions, see J. Gaignard to Unzaga, Jan. 6, 1774, *ADM*, 2:81–82. Quote is from Ripperdá to the viceroy, July 6, 1772, *ADM*, 1:331.

55. Quote is from de Mézières to Croix, Apr. 5, 1778, *ADM*, 2:195. For Comanche-Wichita aggression and Comanche expansion into Wichita range, see de Mézières to Unzaga, Dec. 16, 1774, and de Mézières to Croix, Apr. 8, 1778, and Sep. 13, 1779, *ADM*, 2:115, 198, 275.
56. For Osage and Lipan attacks, see de Mézières to Croix, Apr. 18, 1778, *ADM*, 2:203; and Willard H. Rollings, *The Osage: An Ethnohistorical Study of Hegemony on the Prairie-Plains* (Columbia: University of Missouri Press, 1992), 142–46. For the Lipan situation, see John, *Storms*, 403–4.
57. Morfí, *History*, 1:86, 2:434–35. Quote is from de Mézières to Croix, Apr. 18, 1778, *ADM*, 2:203.
58. For Comanche-Wichita trade in the early and mid-1780s, see Vial and Chavez, Diary, 50; and Cabello, Responses, BA 17:418. Quotes are from de Mézières to Croix, Sep. 13, 1779, *ADM*, 2:275; and Qui Te Sain to Bernardo de Gálvez, Nov. 4, 1780, in *Spain in the Mississippi Valley*, ed. Kinnaird, 1:392.
59. Ripperdá to B. de Gálvez, June 7, 1777, *ADM*, 2:131–32. Quotes are from de Mézières to the viceroy, Feb. 20, 1778, and Croix to J. de Gálvez, Sep. 23, 1778, *ADM*, 2:182, 222–23.
60. For de Mézières' plans and the Osage situation, see de Mézières to B. de Gálvez, Sep. 14, 1777, *ADM*, 2:141–47 (quote is from p. 146); and Gilbert C. Din, "The Spanish Fort on the Arkansas, 1763–1803," *Arkansas Historical Quarterly* 42 (Autumn 1983): 274–76. For Spanish losses to Apache raiders, see Barnard E. Bobb, *The Viceregency of Antonio María de Bucareli in New Spain, 1771–1779* (Austin: University of Texas Press, 1962), 151–52. For the council of war, see "Council of War, Chihuahua, June 9–15, 1778," *PINM*, 193–211. For de Mézières' activities, see de Mézières to Croix, Mar. 23, Apr. 5, 7, 18, and 19, and Nov. 15, 1778, *ADM*, 2:190–97, 200–1, 212–14.
61. De Mézières to Croix, Nov. 15, 1778, *ADM*, 2:232–33; and John, *Storms*, 529–30. For lack of gifts, see Croix, "General Report," 76, 79, and Domingo Cabello y Robles to Étienne Vaugine, Oct. 31, 1780, and Antonio Gil Ybarbo to B. de Gálvez, Nov. 1, 1780, in *Spain in the Mississippi Valley*, ed. Kinnaird, 1:389–91.
62. De Mézières to Croix, Apr. 19 and Nov. 15, 1778, and Teodoro de Croix, "Summary of the notices . . . ," Sep. 21, 1778, *ADM*, 2:212, 226, 229; Cabello to Croix, Feb. 12, July 4, Aug. 17, Sep. 19, Oct. 20, Nov. 17, 20, and 30, and Dec. 6, 1780, BA 13:911–13, 14:286–87, 370–76, 486–90, 613–22, 699–703, 709, 719–20; Cabello to Vaugine, Oct. 31, 1780, and Qui Te Sain to B. de Gálvez, Nov. 4, 1780, in *Spain in the Mississippi Valley*, ed. Kinnaird, 1:389, 392; Croix, "General Report," 74–89; Vial and Chavez, Diary, 51; Kelly F. Himmel, *The Conquest of the Karankawas and Tonkawas, 1821–1859* (College Station: Texas A&M University Press, 1999), 15–16; and Rollings, *Osage*, 150–52.
63. Oakah L. Jones, *Los Paisanos: Spanish Settlers on the Northern Frontier of New Spain* (Norman: University of Oklahoma Press, 1979), 46–47; and Croix, "General Report," 74, 77, 83, 97 (quotes are from pp. 74, 77, 97).
64. For livestock drives, see Cabello to Croix, July 10, 1780, BA 14:294–97; and Jack Jackson, *Los Mesteños: Spanish Ranching in Texas, 1721–1821* (College Station: Texas A&M University Press, 1986), 209–11. For continuing demand for stolen horses and mules in Louisiana, see, e.g., Cabello to Pedro Piernas, Jan. 13, 1783, and Cabello to B. de Gálvez, Dec. 15, 1783, in *Spain in the Mississippi Valley*, ed. Kinnaird, 2:69–70, 94.
65. De Mézières to Croix, Apr. 18, 1778, and Croix to J. de Gálvez, Sep. 23, 1778, *ADM*, 2:206, 221–22.
66. For eastern Comanche realm in the early 1780s, see Cabello, Responses, BA 17:418–19. For Comanche-Taovaya relations, see Cabello to Vaugine, Oct. 31, 1780, and Ybarbo to B. de Gálvez,

Nov. 1, 1780, in *Spain in the Mississippi Valley*, ed. Kinnaird, 1:389–91; Croix, "General Report," 75–80; and Cabello to Croix, Aug. 17, 1780, BA 14:370–73. For the hiatus in raiding and fear in Texas, see Odie B. Faulk, *The Last Years of Spanish Texas, 1778–1821* (London: Mouton, 1964), 63–64; Thomas W. Kavanagh, *Comanche Political History: An Ethnohistorical Perspective* (Lincoln: University of Nebraska Press, 1996), 95; and John, *Storms*, 632–33, 641–43.

67. For bison numbers, see William R. Brown, Jr., "Comancheria Demography, 1805–1830," *Panhandle-Plains Historical Review* 59 (1986): 9–11; and Dan Flores, "Bison Ecology and Bison Diplomacy: The Southern Plains from 1800 to 1850," *JAH* 78 (Sep. 1991): 470–71. For a groundbreaking study of the dangers of specialized hunting on the Great Plains, see Andrew C. Isenberg, *The Destruction of the Bison: An Environmental History, 1750–1920* (Cambridge: Cambridge University Press, 2000), esp. 63–92. For the concept of a dietary safety net, see William Cronon and Richard White, "Indians in the Land: A Conversation between William Cronon and Richard White," *American Heritage* 37 (Aug./Sep. 1986): 21.

68. Gaignard, "Journal," 94. Nicolas Ortiz toured among the western Kotsotekas and Jupes in 1786, counting seven hundred lodges with an average of eleven people in each, a total of some eight thousand people. Spaniards knew less about the third western Comanche division, the Yamparikas, but a 1786 report estimated that the western Comanches comprised about eighteen hundred lodges, which translates into an approximate total population of eighteen thousand. See Nicolas Ortiz to Anza, May 20, 1786, and "List of Comanches Who Came to Make Peace in New Mexico, 1786," *FF*, 323, 325–27. For mid-1780s figures for eastern Comanches, see Vial and Chavez, Diary, 37–38, 49. Vial and Chavez also gave an estimate for the western Comanches. In 1785, describing the *post*-epidemic situation in Comanchería, they noted that the western Comanches were "twice as numerous" as the eastern Comanches, suggesting a total western Comanche population of sixteen thousand. The New Mexico population was between seventeen and eighteen thousand in the 1770s, and the Texas population was estimated at thirty-seven hundred in the 1790. See Frank, *From Settler to Citizen*, 47–48; and Jesús F. de la Teja, "Spanish Colonial Texas," in *New Views of Borderlands History*, ed. Robert H. Jackson (Albuquerque: University of New Mexico Press, 1998), 127.

69. Quotes are from Bucareli to Mendinueta, Feb. 8, 1775, *PINM*, 178; Domínguez, *Missions*, 251; and de Mézières, "Official Relation," 219. Also see Francisco Marín del Valle, Description of the Province of New Mexico, 1758, AGN:CA 39:1, 21V; Cachupín to Juan Francisco de Güemes y Horcasitas, conde de Revillagigedo I, Mar. 8, 1750, *PT*, 3:328; Revillagigedo I to marqués de Ensenada, June 28, 1753, *PINM*, 111–12; and Mendinueta to the viceroy, May 11, 1771, cited in Kessell, *Kiva, Cross, and Crown*, 393. For modern scholarly interpretations, see E. Adamson Hoebel, *The Political Organization and Law-Ways of the Comanche Indians*, American Anthropological Association Memoir 54 (Menasha, Wis.: American Anthropological Association, 1940); T. R. Fehrenbach, *Comanches: The Destruction of a People* (New York: Da Capo, 1974), 185; and John, *Storms*, 307–8.

70. "Extract of reports from the kingdom of New Mexico between September 17 and November 9 of the past year [1769]," *PINM*, 167; and Anza, "Diary," 135–36.

71. For an excellent analysis of Comanche political culture before the reservation period, see Kavanagh, *Comanche Political History*, 28–62.

72. Quote is from Anza, "Diary," 135–36. It is possible that the elder Cuerno Verde was killed by Spaniards in 1774 in the battle that inspired one version of "Los Comanches." See Frank, *From*

Settler to Citizen, 63. Thomas Kavanagh, in contrast, believes that a Comanche chief who wore a headdress with green horns and was killed by Spaniards in 1768 near Ojo Caliente may have been Cuerno Verde the elder. See Kavanagh, "Los Comanches," 27–29.

73. Vial and Chavez, Diary, 33–39; and Cabello, Responses, 1786, BA 17:419.
74. Tellingly, Spaniards did not begin to distinguish between different Comanche divisions until the 1770s. See "Council of War, Chihuahua, June 9–15, 1778," *PINM*, 201.
75. Vial and Chavez, Diary, 50; Cabello, Responses, BA 17:418; and Hämäläinen, "Western Comanche Trade Center," 493–94.
76. Hämäläinen, "Western Comanche Trade Center," 494; and Miró to Rengel, Dec. 12, 1785, in *Before Lewis and Clark*, ed. Nasatir, 1:127.

CHAPTER 3. THE EMBRACE

1. Pedro Garrido y Duran, "An account of the events which have occurred in the provinces of New Mexico concerning peace conceded to the Comanche nation and their reconciliation with the Utes since November 17 of last year and July of the current [1786]," *FF*, 300.
2. David J. Weber, *The Spanish Frontier in North America* (New Haven: Yale University Press, 1992), 215–65; Ross Frank, *From Settler to Citizen: New Mexican Economic Development and the Creation of Vecino Society*, 1750–1820 (Berkeley: University of California Press, 2000), 65–70, 76–132; and Alfred Barnaby Thomas, ed. and trans., *Teodoro de Croix and the Northern Frontier of New Spain, 1776–1783: From the Original Document in the Archives of the Indies, Seville* (Albuquerque: University of New Mexico Press, 1941), 40–68. Rubí did not submit the report of his 1766–68 inspection tour until 1770, and the crown codified his recommendations into new regulations for frontier presidios and defenses in 1772. That same year Carlos III appointed Hugo O'Connor as commanding inspector of the Interior Provinces and ordered him to implement the new regulations. The monumental endeavor, which faced fierce local resistance, took more than four years to complete.
3. Pedro Galindo y Navarro to Teodoro de Croix, July 28, 1780, Juan Bautista de Anza, "Diary of the Expedition . . . against the Comanche Nation . . . ," Sep. 10, 1779, and Juan Bautista de Anza to Croix, Nov. 1, 1779, *FF*, 122–39 (quotes are from pp. 133, 135, 142); and Croix to Anza, July 14, 1780, SANM II 11:77–78 (T-799). For Anza, see Herbert E. Bolton, "Juan Bautista de Anza, Borderlands Frontiersman," in *Bolton and the Spanish Borderlands*, ed. John Francis Bannon (Norman: University of Oklahoma Press, 1964), 281–87. For Spanish views of the importance of Anza's victory, see H. Bailey Carroll and J. Villasana Haggard, trans., *Three New Mexico Chronicles: The Exposición of Don Pedro Bautista Pino 1812; the Ojeada of Lic. Antonio Barreiro 1832; and the Additions by Don José Agustín de Escudero, 1849* (Albuquerque: Quivira Society, 1942), 131–32. For similar modern views, see, e.g., Gary Clayton Anderson, *The Indian Southwest, 1580–1830: Ethnogenesis and Reinvention* (Norman: University of Oklahoma Press, 1999), 212.
4. For Kiowa migrations, see Pekka Hämäläinen, "The Rise and Fall of Plains Indian Horse Cultures," *JAH* (Dec. 2003): 839. For Comanche-Pawnee hostilities, see Francisco Xavier Ortiz to Anza, May 20, 1786, *FF*, 322; Fernando de la Concha to Jacobo Ugarte y Loyola, Sep. 7, 1790, SANM II 12:297 (T-1090); and Pedro Vial, "Diary of Pedro Vial from Santa Fe to St. Louis, May 21 to October 3, 1792," *PV*, 400.

5. For Kansas's situation, see Manuel Perez to Esteban Rodriguez Miró, Nov. 8, 1791, and Zenon Trudeau to governor, Jan. 15, 1798, in *Before Lewis and Clark: Documents Illustrating the History of the Missouri, 1785–1804*, ed. A. P. Nasatir, 2 vols. (1952; reprint, Lincoln: University of Nebraska Press, 1990), 1:149–50, 2:539; and Thomas F. Schilz and Jodye L. D. Schilz, "Beads, Bangles, and Buffalo Robes: The Rise and Fall of the Indian Fur Trade along the Missouri and Des Moines Rivers, 1700–1820," *Annals of Iowa* 49 (Summer/Fall 1987): 10–11. For the collapse of Mississippi valley markets and its effects in Comanchería, see Pekka Hämäläinen, "The Western Comanche Trade Center: Rethinking the Plains Indian Trade System," *Western Historical Quarterly* 29 (Winter 1998): 502–3. For shortages of trade goods in Comanchería in the mid-1780s, see Domingo Cabello y Robles, Responses Given by the Governor of the Province of Texas to Questions Put to Him by the Lord Commanding General of the Interior [Provinces] in an Official Letter of the 27th of January Concerning Various Conditions of the Eastern Comanches, Apr. 30, 1786, BA 17:418.
6. Elizabeth A. Fenn, *Pox Americana: The Great Smallpox Epidemic of 1775–1782* (New York: Hill and Wang, 2001), 146–66, 211–15; and Pedro Vial and Francisco Xavier Chaves, Diary, in "Inside the Comanchería, 1785: The Diary of Pedro Vial and Francisco Xavier Chaves," ed. Elizabeth A. H. John, trans. Adán Benavides, Jr., *SHQ* 88 (July 1994): 37–38, 49.
7. Fenn, *Pox Americana*, 211; and Croix to Anza, Feb. 24, 1783, SANM II 11:567–58 (T-858).
8. François Luis Hector, barón de Carondelet, "Military Report on Louisiana and West Florida," Nov. 24, 1794, in *Louisiana under the Rule of Spain, France, and the United States, 1785–1807: Social, Economic, and Political Conditions of the Territory represented in the Louisiana Purchase, as portrayed in hitherto unpublished contemporary accounts by Dr. Paul Alliot and various Spanish, French, English, and American Officials*, ed. and trans. James Alexander Robertson, 2 vols. (Cleveland: Arthur H. Clark, 1911), 1:297.
9. For the genesis of Spain's Indian policy, see Weber, *Spanish Frontier*, 227–30, 282–83.
10. Ibid., 279–83.
11. Elizabeth A. H. John, *Storms Brewed in Other Men's World: The Confrontation of Indians, Spanish, and French in the Southwest, 1540–1795* (Norman: University of Oklahoma Press, 1975), 660–66; and F. Todd Smith, *The Wichita Indians: Traders of Texas and the Southern Plains* (College Station: Texas A&M University Press, 2000), 75–79.
12. Vial and Chaves, Diary, 36–37 (quotes are from p. 37).
13. Ibid., 37–38. Each Comanche ranchería had its own camp crier, *tekwawapi̠*. See Jean Luis Berlandier, *The Indians of Texas in 1830*, ed. John C. Ewers, trans. Patricia Reading Leclercq (Washington, D.C.: Smithsonian Institution, 1969), 44; and Ernest Wallace and E. Adamson Hoebel, *The Comanches: Lords of the South Plains* (Norman: University of Oklahoma Press, 1954), 215.
14. Vial and Chaves, Diary, 38–39.
15. Ibid., 40, 43.
16. Ibid., 44.
17. Ibid., 44–45.
18. Ibid., 45.
19. Ibid., 45–46.
20. Cabello to Joseph Antonio Rengel, Nov. 25, 1785, BA 17:68–72. Quotes are from Vial and Chaves, Diary, 51; and "Treaty with the Eastern Comanches, October 1785, from the report of Pedro

de Nava Commandant General of the Interior Provinces, Chihuahua, July 23, 1799," in *Border Comanches: Seven Spanish Colonial Documents, 1785–1819*, ed. and trans. Marc Simmons (Santa Fe: Stagecoach, 1967), 21–22.

21. Cabello to Rengel, Nov. 25 and Dec. 9, 1785, and Jan. 10 and Mar. 14, 1786, and Cabello to Ugarte, July 31, 1786, BA 17:73–74, 88–92, 181–87, 324–25, 609–11; Garrido, "Account," 320; and John, *Storms*, 694–95. Quote is from Cabello, Responses, BA 17:420.
22. Rengel to José de Gálvez, Dec. 31, 1785, Archivo General de las Indias, Seville, Spain, Guadalajara, legajo 286, microfilm, Western History Collections, University of Oklahoma, Norman; and Garrido, "Account," 298–99.
23. Vial and Chaves, Diary, 46; and Garrido, "Account," 295.
24. For Ecueracapa as Cota de Malla, see Garrido, "Account," 295; and Ugarte to Cabello, Aug. 17, 1786, BA 17:707. The notion that Ecueracapa of the western Comanches was indeed Cota de Malla of the eastern Comanches is supported by Ecueracapa's detailed knowledge of the eastern Comanche-Texas peace process. In 1787 Pedro Vial encountered Ecueracapa in eastern Comanchería, which also supports the idea that he was attached to both eastern and western Comanche divisions. See Garrido, "Account," 320; and Pedro Vial, "Diary of Pedro Vial, Bexar to Santa Fe, October 4, 1786, to May 26, 1787," *PV*, 280. On the other hand, Ugarte later reported that Ecueracapa and Cota de Malla may have been two different men after all. See Ugarte to Anza, Oct. 5, 1786, *FF*, 341–42. For even more confusion regarding the identity of Camisa de Hierro/Cota de Malla, see Thomas W. Kavanagh, *Comanche Political History: An Ethnohistorical Perspective* (Lincoln: University of Nebraska Press, 1996), 120–21, 124. Both Elizabeth A. H. John and Gerald Betty identify Ecueracapa as Camisa de Hierro. See John, *Storms*, 668–69; and Gerald Betty, *Comanche Society: Before the Reservation* (College Station: Texas A&M University Press, 2002), 188–89. Quotes are from Garrido, "Account," 295, 299.
25. Quotes are from Garrido, "Account," 296.
26. Ibid., 297.
27. Ibid., 297–98.
28. Ibid., 300.
29. Garrido, "Account," and "The Spanish Comanche-Peace Treaty of 1786," *FF*, 300–1, 329–32. My interpretation differs from the traditional interpretation of the 1786 treaty as merely an outcome of Spain's Indian policy. For previous interpretations, see, e.g., Max L. Moorhead, *Apache Frontier: Jacobo Ugarte and Spanish Indian Relations in Northern New Spain, 1769–1791* (Norman: University of Oklahoma Press, 1968), 143–69; Charles L. Kenner, *The Comanchero Frontier: A History of New Mexican–Plains Indian Relations* (1969; reprint, Norman: University of Oklahoma Press, 1994), 51–60; and John, *Storms*, 583–92, 668–74.
30. Garrido, "Account," 300–1. For winter hunting west of the Pecos River, see ibid., 319–20.
31. Ibid., 301, 306.
32. Ibid., 302. This is the first mention of medals in Spanish-Comanche diplomacy. Spanish officials did not start distributing medals to Indian leaders until the late eighteenth century, but the practice quickly became a standard part of Bourbon Indian policy. Specially minted medals were routinely handed out in New Mexico, Texas, and Louisiana. See David J. Weber, *Bárbaros: Spaniards and Their Savages in the Age of Enlightenment* (New Haven: Yale University Press, 2005), 186–89.
33. For the importance of physical gestures and touching in Spanish-Indian diplomacy, see Juliana

Barr, "A Diplomacy of Gender: Rituals of First Contact in the 'Land of the Tejas,'" *William and Mary Quarterly* 61 (July 2004): 393–434.

34. For the Pecos council, see Garrido, "Account," 303–5 (quotes are from pp. 303–4).
35. Ibid., 305–6, 318–19 (quotes are from p. 306).
36. Ibid., 304, 306 (the quote "just rule" is from p. 304).
37. Pedro Garrido y Duran, "Account received of what was done in the Province of New Mexico by Governor Don Juan Bautista de Anza to break the secret alliance which the Navajo nation maintained with the Gila Apaches, their separation, and allegiance of the former to our side having been assured," *FF*, 345–48 (quote is from p. 348). See, too, James F. Brooks, *Captives and Cousins: Slavery, Kinship, and Community in the Southwest Borderlands* (Chapel Hill: University of North Carolina Press for the Omohundro Institute of Early American History and Culture, 2002), 114–15.
38. Garrido, "Account," 296–97; Concha to Juan Vicente de Güemes Padilla Horcasitas y Aguayo, conde de Revillagigedo II, May 6, 1793, in *Border Comanches*, ed. Simmons, 25–26; Fernando de la Concha, Instructions drawn up by Colonel Don Fernando de la Concha, former governor of the Province of New Mexico, so that his successor, the Lieutenant Colonel Don Fernando Chacón, may adapt what part of it that may seem to him suitable for the advantage, tranquility, and development of the aforesaid province, in "Notes and Documents: Advice on Governing New Mexico, 1794," ed. and trans. Donald E. Worcester, *NMHR* 24 (July 1949): 239–41; and Charles Bent to William Medill, Nov. 10, 1846, in *California and New Mexico: Message from the President of the United States Communicating Information Called For by a Resolution of the Senate* (New York: Arno, 1976), 183.
39. Bernardo de Gálvez, *Instructions for Governing the Interior Provinces of New Spain 1786*, trans. and ed. Donald E. Worcester (Berkeley: Quivira Society, 1951), 43, 79; Weber, *Spanish Frontier*, 231–32; and Kenner, *Comanchero Frontier*, 79.
40. Garrido, "Account," 311–12.
41. Ibid., 310–18 (quote is from pp. 317–18).
42. Ibid., 313–14. In colonial America, Native and colonial peoples often adopted children into communities as insurance of peace, but there is no evidence to suggest that Tahuchimpia's adoption stemmed from this logic. For adoptions in the Southwest, see Juliana Barr, "From Captives to Slaves: Commodifying Indian Women in the Borderlands," *JAH* 92 (June 2005): 23.
43. Garrido, "Account," and Ugarte to Anza, Oct. 5, 1786, *FF*, 319, 332–36, 340 (quotes are from pp. 335–36, 340).
44. Anza to Ugarte, Nov. 18, 1786, and Ugarte to José de Gálvez, Jan. 4, 1787, AGN:PI 65:2, 66R,V, 64R–65V; and Moorhead, *Apache Frontier*, 156–59.
45. For the San Carlos experiment, see Anza to Ugarte, Oct. 20, 1787, Ugarte to Concha, Jan. 22, 1788, and Concha to Ugarte, June 26, 1788, in "San Carlos: A Comanche Pueblo on the Arkansas River 1787: A Study in Comanche History and Spanish Indian Policy," ed. and trans. Alfred B. Thomas, *Colorado Magazine* 6 (May 1929): 86–99, 90–91 (quote "affection for their possession" is from p. 88); and Brooks, *Captives and Cousins*, 160–62. The longer quote is from Ronald J. Benes, "Anza and Concha in New Mexico, 1787–1793: A Study in New Colonial Techniques," in *The Spanish Borderlands: A First Reader*, ed. Oakah L. Jones (Los Angeles: Lorrin L. Morrison, 1974), 158–59.
46. Concha to Ugarte, Nov. 10, 1787, June 26, 1788, and July 6, 1789, AGN:PI 65:1, 50R–52V, 65:5,

1R–3R, 65:15, 2R,V; and John L. Kessell, *Kiva, Cross, and Crown: The Pecos Indians and New Mexico, 1540–1840* (Washington, D.C.: National Park Service, 1979), 407–9. Quotes are from Gálvez, *Instructions*, 72; Fernando de Chacón, Report, in "The Chacón Report of 1803," ed. and trans. Marc Simmons, *NMHR* 60 (Jan. 1985): 87; and Concha, Instructions, 251.

47. Quote is from Concha, Instructions, 246. For ciboleros, see Brooks, *Captives and Cousins*, 218.

48. For campaigns, see Garrido, "Account," and "Tally Sheet," *FF*, 307–9, 312, 316, 319–21, 324–25; Juan Bautista de Anza, Tarja, in Alfred Barnaby Thomas, "An Eighteenth-Century Comanche Document," *American Anthropologist* 31 (Apr.–June 1929): 294–98; Moorhead, *Apache Frontier*, 164–67; and Ugarte to Manuel Antonio Flórez, Mar. 13, 1788, in *Border Comanches*, ed. Simmons, 23. For captives, see Ugarte to Concha, Jan. 23, 1788, SANM II 12:22–23 (T-993); and Barr, "From Captives to Slaves," 45–46. For Apache capitulation, see Weber, *Bárbaros*, 193; and Moorhead, *Apache Frontier*, 200–69.

49. Cabello to Ugarte, July 30, 1786, BA 17:607–8; and Kavanagh, *Comanche Political History*, 110, 148–49.

50. Kavanagh, *Comanche Political History*, 185–89; and Elizabeth A. H. John, "Nurturing the Peace: Spanish and Comanche Cooperation in the Early Nineteenth Century," *NMHR* 59 (Oct. 1984): 345–52.

51. For Lipans, see Anderson, *Indian Southwest*, 137–38. For Taovaya relocation, see Cabello to Rengel, Apr. 16, 1786, BA 17:383–84.

52. Martínez Pacheco to Juan de Ugalde, Jan. 21, 1788, Pedro de Nava to Manuel Muñoz, Jan. 4, 1791, and Revillagigedo II to Muñoz, Jan. 5, 1791, BA 18:800–1, 21:92–93, 96; Fernando de la Concha, Ynforme, Apr. 20, 1791, AGN:PI 65:16, 2R,V; Nava to Concha, July 22, 1791, SANM II 12:604 (T-1135); F. Todd Smith, *From Dominance to Disappearance: The Indians of Texas and the Near Southwest, 1786–1859* (Lincoln: University of Nebraska Press, 2005), 40–46; and Anderson, *Indian Southwest*, 139–41.

53. Max L. Moorhead, *The Presidio: Bastion of the Spanish Borderlands* (Norman: University of Oklahoma Press, 1975), 256–66; and Weber, *Bárbaros*, 193–94.

54. For trails, see *PV*, 262–87, 316–68. For baptisms, see Kenner, *Comanchero Frontier*, 64. For missionization plans, see Richard E. Greenleaf, "The Nueva Vizcaya Frontier, 1787–89," in *Spanish Borderlands*, ed. Jones, 151–53.

55. Ortiz to Anza, May 20, 1786, *FF*, 324.

56. For a fascinating discussion of Spain's evolving Indian policy in the late eighteenth century and the *Nuevo sistema de gobierno económico para la Americ a*, see Weber, *Bárbaros*, chs. 4 and 5.

57. Gálvez, *Instructions*, 40–42.

58. Ibid., 48–49.

59. Garrido, "Account," 302, 317.

60. Gálvez, *Instructions*, 50; and Concha, Instructions, 240, 242. I have followed the slightly different translation of Concha's advice that David J. Weber provides in *Bárbaros*, 191.

61. Quote is from Nava to Concha, Dec. 31, 1793, in *Border Comanches*, ed. Simmons, 31. For the succession of western Comanche head chiefs, see Kavanagh, *Comanche Political History*, 5, 143–45, 292; Carroll and Haggard, *Three New Mexico Chronicles*, 130; and Alejo García Cónde to Facundo Melgares, Nov. 9, 1818, SANM II 19:438–40 (T-2771). For Comanche chiefs pledging loyalty and vassalage to Spain, see, e.g., Garrido, "Account," 306–7.

62. Quotes are from Concha, Instructions, 238; and José Cortés, *Views from the Apache Frontier:*

Report on the Northern Provinces of New Spain, ed. Elizabeth A. H. John, trans. John Wheat (Norman: University of Oklahoma Press, 1989), 82. Also see Carroll and Haggard, *Three New Mexico Chronicles*, 132, 135–36. For contemporary scholarly interpretations, see John, *Storms*, 735; and Jack August, "Balance-of-Power Diplomacy in New Mexico: Governor Fernando de la Concha and the Indian Policy of Conciliation," *NMHR* 56 (Spring 1981): 141–60.

63. For New Mexico's revitalization, see Frank, *From Settler to Citizen*, 119–76. For political changes among nomadic societies, see William Irons, "Political Stratification among Pastoral Nomads," in *Pastoral Production and Society*, ed. L'équipe écologie et anthropologie des sociétés pastorales (Cambridge: Cambridge University Press, 1979), 362; and Thomas J. Barfield, "The Shadow Empires: Imperial State Formation along the Chinese-Nomad Frontier," in *Empires: Perspectives from Archaeology and History*, ed. Susan E. Alcock, Terence N. D'Altroy, Kathleen D. Morrison, and Carla M. Sinopoli (Cambridge: Cambridge University Press, 2001), 34.

64. For an illuminating ethnohistorical analysis that makes a clear distinction between Comanche leaders' authority in external and internal affairs, see Morris W. Foster, *Being Comanche: A Social History and an American Indian Community* (Tucson: University of Arizona Press, 1991), esp. 54–69. Also see Kavanagh, *Comanche Political History*, 125–26.

65. For glimpses into the political roles and actions of Ecueracapa's followers, see Fernando de Chacón to Nava, Nov. 18, 1797, SANM II 14:233 (T-1404); Alfred Barnaby Thomas, ed.,"Documents Bearing upon the Northern Frontier of New Mexico," *NMHR* 4 (Apr. 1929): 156; and José Antonio Arce, Message to Chihuahua Legislature, Feb. 1, 1826, MANM 5:451. For Ugarte's prediction, see Ugarte to Anza, Feb. 8, 1787, AGN:PI 65:2, 67V–68R.

66. Joaquín Real Alencaster to Nemesio Salcedo, Nov. 20, 1805, SANM II 15:1028 (T-1925). This document has been translated in *Border Comanches*, ed. Simmons, 33–34. Somiquaso hardly became a pliant tool for Spanish imperialism. When a New Mexican interpreter named Alejandro Martín visited the newly elected Yamparika general's ranchería in 1806, his party was mistreated and robbed, and Martín failed "in getting the general to make the Indians return what was stolen." See Alencaster to N. Salcedo, Jan. 4, 1806, *PV*, 441.

67. See, e.g., Nava to Concha, Dec. 31, 1793, and Alencaster to the commanding general of the Interior Provinces, Nov. 20, 1805, in *Border Comanches*, ed. Simmons, 31, 33; and Chacón to Nava, Nov. 18, 1797, SANM II 14:233 (T-1404).

68. For fluid band membership, see Vial and Chaves, Diary, 49; David G. Burnet, "David G. Burnet's Letters Describing the Comanche Indians with an Introduction by Ernest Wallace," *West Texas Historical Association Year Book* 30 (1954): 124; and Kavanagh, *Comanche Political History*, 125–26. For the centrality of the consensus principle in Comanche politics, see Vial and Chavez, Diary, 38–45; and Garrido, "Account," 295. Also see Martha McCollough, *Three Nations, One Place: A Comparative Ethnohistory of Social Change among the Comanches and Hasinais during Spain's Colonial Era, 1689–1821* (New York: Routledge, 2004), 104.

69. Comanches' political evolution in the late eighteenth century is a revealing example of what Marshal Sahlins has called "the structure of the conjucture": it is a case of culture change that was triggered by external forces and yet indigenously orchestrated. See Sahlins, *Islands of History* (Chicago: University of Chicago Press, 1985), viii.

70. Rudolph C. Troike, "A Pawnee Visit to San Antonio in 1795," *Ethnohistory* 11 (Autumn 1964): 383–87; Frank, *From Settler to Citizen*, 132–36; Ugarte to Anza, Oct. 5, 1786, *FF*, 342; and Kavanagh, *Comanche Political History*, 148–49, 181–82.

71. For the rhetoric and language of the alliance, see, e.g., Vial, "Diary, Béxar to Santa Fe, Oct. 4, 1786–May 26, 1787," 277–78; and Cabello to Rengel, Nov. 25, 1785, and Testimony Given by Chief Cordero, Oct. 25, 1810, BA 17:72–73, 47:6–7.
72. For ransoming, see, e.g., José Mares, "Itinerary and Diary of José Mares, Bexar to Santa Fe, January 18 to April 27, 1788," *PV*, 307–8. For attacks, see Odie B. Faulk, *The Last Years of Spanish Texas, 1778–1821* (London: Mouton, 1964), 70; and Robert S. Weddle, *The San Sabá Mission: Spanish Pivot in Texas* (1964; reprint, College Station: Texas A&M University Press, 1999), 190. For slave traffic, see Barr, "From Captives to Slaves," 44–46. For Sabinal, see Concha to Ugarte, July 13, 1789, and Concha to Revillagigedo II, July 12, 1791, SANM II 12:289–91, 559–63 (T-1086), 1132; and Concha, Instructions, 240.
73. Juan de Dios Peña, Diary, June 12–Aug. 8, 1790, and Chacón to Nava, Nov. 19, 1797, SANM II 12:262–65, 14:234 (T-1089, 1090, 1200, 1405). Quote is from Concha to Nava, Nov. 1, 1791, in *Before Lewis and Clark*, ed. Nasatir, 1:148.
74. John, *Storms*, 754–55; Concha to Ugarte, Nov. 18. 1789, SANM II 12:211–12 (T-1064); and Concha to Revillagigedo II, May 6, 1793, in *Border Comanches*, ed. Simmons, 25–26 (quote "Regrettable are the consequences" is from p. 26). Quote "hate the Comanches" is from Concha, Instructions, 241.

CHAPTER 4. THE EMPIRE OF THE PLAINS

1. Fernando de la Concha, Instructions drawn up by Colonel Don Fernando de la Concha, former governor of the Province of New Mexico, so that his successor, the Lieutenant Colonel Don Fernando Chacón, may adapt what part of it that may seem to him suitable for the advantage, tranquility, and development of the aforesaid province, in "Notes and Documents: Advice on Governing New Mexico, 1794," ed. and trans. Donald E. Worcester, *NMHR* 24 (July 1949): 238; and H. Bailey Carroll and J. Villasana Haggard, trans., *Three New Mexico Chronicles: The Exposición of Don Pedro Bautista Pino 1812; the Ojeada of Lic. Antonio Barreiro 1832; and the Additions by Don José Agustín de Escudero, 1849* (Albuquerque: Quivira Society, 1942), 129, 135.
2. For the revival of the ranching industry, see Jack Jackson, *Los Mesteños: Spanish Ranching in Texas, 1721–1821* (College Station: Texas A&M University Press, 1986), chs. 9, 10, and 11. For Louisiana, see David J. Weber, *The Spanish Frontier in North America* (New Haven: Yale University Press, 1992), 280–82, 290.
3. Quote is from Jacobo Ugarte y Loyola to Juan Bautista de Anza, Oct. 5, 1786, *FF*, 339–40.
4. For Nolan, see Maurine T. Wilson, "Philip Nolan and His Activities in Texas" (M.A. thesis, University of Texas, Austin, 1932); and Dan L. Flores, ed., *Journal of an Indian Trader: Anthony Glass and the Texas Trading Frontier, 1790–1810* (College Station: Texas A&M University Press, 1985), 10–15. For Nacogdoches, see Weber, *Spanish Frontier*, 222; and Daniel H. Usner, Jr., *Indians, Settlers, and Slaves in a Frontier Exchange Economy: The Lower Mississippi Valley before 1783* (Chapel Hill: University of North Carolina Press, 1992), 134.
5. For American traders on the southern plains and in Comanchería, see Flores, ed., *Journal*, 15–18; *PV*, 206–28; F. Todd Smith, *The Wichita Indians: Traders of Texas and Southern Plains, 1540–1845* (College Station: Texas A&M University Press, 2000), 89–90; and J. Villasana Haggard, "The Neutral Ground between Louisiana and Texas, 1806–1821," *Louisiana Historical Quarterly* 28 (Oct. 1945): 1084–89.

6. For Texas trading frontier, see Flores, ed., *Journal*, 15–18. For Wichitas' revival, see, e.g., José Cortés, *Views from the Apache Frontier: Report on the Northern Provinces of New Spain*, ed. Elizabeth A. H. John, trans. John Wheat (Norman: University of Oklahoma Press, 1989), 84–85. For Comanche-Wichita trade, see Pedro Vial, "Diary of Pedro Vial, Bexar to Santa Fe, October 4, 1786, to May 26, 1787," and José Mares, "Journal of José Mares, Santa Fe to Bexar, July 31 to October 8, 1787," *PV*, 277, 296–97.
7. Reflecting the impact Wichitas' trading policies in Comanchería, in 1807 a Comanche chief complained to the Americans in Natchitoches how the Wichitas sold them U.S. goods "at a very great profit, they would demand of them a Horse or a Mule for a Narrow Strip of Scarlet Cloth, or a Small Parcel of Vermillion." See John Sibley, *A Report from Natchitoches in 1807*, ed. Annie Heloise Abel (New York: Museum of the American Indian, 1922), 75. For the Osage situation, see Colin G. Calloway, *One Vast Winter Count: The Native American West before Lewis and Clark* (Lincoln: University of Nebraska Press, 2003), 379–82; and Kathleen DuVal, *The Native Ground: Indians and Colonists in the Heart of the Continent* (Philadelphia: University of Pennsylvania Press, 2006), 164–205.
8. For the restored Comanche-Wichita alliance, see, e.g., Vial, "Diary," 276–77. For the Natchitoches talks, see Sibley, *Report*, 49–75 (quotes are from pp. 56–58).
9. Sibley, *Report*, 61–62.
10. John Sibley to Henry Dearborn, Nov. 20, 1808, in "Dr. John Sibley and the Louisiana-Texas Frontier, 1803–1814," ed. Julia Kathryn Garrett, *SHQ* 47 (July 1943): 50; and Sibley, *Report*, 74.
11. For Comanche range, see Sibley, *Report*, 78. Quotes are from Sibley, *Report*, 55; and James Wilkinson to Dearborn, July 27, 1805, in *The Territorial Papers of the U.S.*, vol. 13, *The Territory of Louisiana-Missouri, 1803–1806*, ed. Clarence E. Carter, 28 vols. (Washington, D.C.: GPO, 1948), 169. Also see Wilkinson to Zebulon Montgomery Pike, June 24, 1806, in Zebulon Montgomery Pike, *The Journals of Zebulon Montgomery Pike*, ed. Donald Jackson, 2 vols. (Norman: University of Oklahoma Press, 1966), 1:285–86.
12. For the Glass expedition, see Anthony Glass, "Life among the Indians, August–October, 1808," in *Journal*, ed. Flores, 47–79. For rumors and reports of American commercial activities among the Comanches, see Bernardo Bonavía to Nícolas Benítez, Oct. 20, 1809, Testimony of Chief Cordero, Oct. 25, 1810, and Manuel María de Salcedo, Questioning of a Comanche Indian, 1810 [n.d.], BA 43:215–16, 47:6–7, 701–2.
13. Sibley to William Eustice, Dec. 31, 1811, in "Dr. John Sibley," *SHQ* 49 (Apr. 1946): 403; David G. Burnet, "David G. Burnet's Letters Describing the Comanche Indians with an Introduction by Ernest Wallace," *West Texas Historical Association Year Book* 30 (1954): 138; and Smith, *Wichita Indians*, 112–13.
14. Quotes are from W. A. Trimble to John C. Calhoun, Aug. 7, 1818, in Jedidiah Morse, *Report to the Secretary of War of the United States on Indian Affairs* (New Haven: S. Converse, 1822), 259; *National Intelligencer*, Sep. 15, 1820; and Antonio Martínez to Joaquín de Arredondo, May 31, 1818, in *The Letters of Antonio Martínez, The Last Spanish Governor of Texas, 1817–1822*, ed. and trans. Virginia H. Taylor (Austin: Texas State Library, 1957), 136. Also see Bernardo Claudio de Luna to José Menchaca, Feb. 23, 1811, and Ignacio Pérez to Martínez, June 1, 1818, BA 48:107, 61:125–26.
15. Bonavía to Pedro Maria de Allande, Aug. 13, 1816, SANM II 18:682–83 (T-2667); Gary Clayton Anderson, *The Indian Southwest, 1580–1830: Ethnogenesis and Reinvention* (Norman: University of Oklahoma Press, 1999), 254; and Nemesio Salcedo, *Instrucción reservada de don Nemesio*

Salcedo y Salcedo, comandante general de Provincias Internas a su sucesor, ed. Isidro Vizcaya Canales (Chihuahua: Centro de Información del Estado de Chihuahua, 1990), 67. Quote is from Juan Antonio Padilla, Report on the Barbarous Indians of the Province of Texas, Dec. 27, 1819, in "Texas in 1820," trans. Mattie Austin Hatcher, *SHQ* 23 (July 1919): 55.

16. Stephen F. Austin to [Anastasio Bustamante?], May 10, 1830, in *The Austin Papers*, ed. Eugene C. Barker, 2 vols. (Washington, D.C.: GPO, 1924), 2:508; and F. Todd Smith, *From Dominance to Disappearance: The Indians of Texas and the Near Southwest, 1786–1859* (Lincoln: University of Nebraska Press, 2005), 106.
17. Anderson, *Indian Southwest*, 256–57; James Michael McReynolds, "Family Life in a Borderland Community: Nacogdoches, Texas, 1779–1861" (Ph.D. diss., Texas Tech University, 1978), 25–27; and Thomas W. Kavanagh, *Comanche Political History: An Ethnohistorical Perspective* (Lincoln: University of Nebraska Press, 1996), 483–84.
18. Quote is from Jean Louis Berlandier, *The Indians of Texas in 1830*, ed. John C. Ewers, trans. Patricia Reading Leclercq (Washington, D.C.: Smithsonian Institution, 1969), 48. Also see David J. Weber, "American Westward Expansion and the Breakdown of Relations between *Pobladores* and '*Indios Bárbaros*' on Mexico's Far Northern Frontier, 1821–1846," *NMHR* 56 (July 1981): 225; and Dan Flores, *Horizontal Yellow: Nature and History in the Near Southwest* (Albuquerque: University of New Mexico Press, 1999), 107–8.
19. T. B. Wheelock, "Journal of Colonel Dodge's Expedition from Fort Gibson to the Pawnee Pict Village," Aug. 26, 1834, in *American State Papers*, Class 5, *Military Affairs*, 5:381; and Sam Houston to Henry Ellsworth, Dec. 1, 1832, and Feb. 13, 1833, in *The Writings of Sam Houston*, ed. Amelia W. Williams and Eugene C. Barker, 8 vols. (Austin: University of Texas Press, 1938–43), 1:269–70, 273. Quotes are from Berlandier, *Indians*, 103, 114, 119; and José Francisco Ruíz, *Report on Indian Tribes of Texas in 1828*, ed. John C. Ewers (New Haven: Yale University Press, 1972), 14.
20. For Mexico's relations with removed eastern Indians, see Alexander Cummings to R. Jones, Jan. 18, 1826, in *The Territorial Papers of the United States*, vol. 20, *The Territory of Arkansas, 1825–1829*, ed. Clarence E. Carter and John P. Bloom (Washington, D.C.: GPO, 1954), 184–85; Lucas de Palacio to comisario particular of Béxar, Apr. 30, 1827, BA 102:928–29; Dianna Everett, *The Texas Cherokees: A People between Two Fires, 1819–1840* (Norman: University of Oklahoma Press, 1990), 36–48, 61–67; and H. Allen Anderson, "The Delaware and Shawnee Indians and the Republic of Texas, 1820–1845," *SHQ* 94 (Oct. 1990): 231–38.
21. David LaVere, *Contrary Neighbors: Southern Plains and Removed Indians in Indian Territory* (Norman: University of Oklahoma Press, 2000), 63–72; and Elizabeth A. H. John, "Documentary Evidence and Historical Context Bearing upon Possible Explanations of a Brief, Specialized Settlement on the Eastern Plains of New Mexico," in *Investigations at Sites 48 and 77, Santa Rosa Lake, Guadalupe County, New Mexico: An Inquiry into the Nature of Archaeological Reality*, ed. Frances Levine and Joseph C. Winter (Albuquerque: Office of Contract Archeology, University of New Mexico, 1987), 546.
22. Wheelock, "Journal," 375–81; "Treaty with Comanche and Witchetaw Indians," in *Indian Affairs: Laws and Treaties*, ed. Charles J. Kappler, 5 vols. (Washington, D.C.: GPO, 1904), 2:435–39 (quote is from p. 435); C. C. Rister, "Federal Experiment in Southern Plains Indian Relations, 1835–1845," *CO* 14 (Dec. 1936): 451–54; and M. Stokes and M. Arbuckle, Journal of the Proceedings of M. Stokes, M. Arbuckle, and F. W. Armstrong, in "The Journal of the Proceedings at

Our First Treaty with the Wild Indians, 1835," ed. Grant Foreman, *CO* 14 (Dec. 1936): 406–16. The landmark diplomatic treaty of Camp Holmes has traditionally been seen as the result of U.S. intervention—as well as the fact that the U.S. Senate had dispatched five hundred dragoons under Colonel Henry Dodge to the southern plains to display American power to the Indians. This view ignores the compelling commercial interests that drew removed Indians and plains nomads together and reduces Native American diplomacy to a derivative of American initiatives.

23. For an illuminating report on the economic conditions in Indian Territory in the early 1840s, see W. M. Armstrong to T. Heartley Crawford, Sep. 30, 1841, 27th Cong., 2d sess., S. Ex. Doc. 1, 333–39.

24. For exchange between Comanches and removed nations, see Grant Foreman, *Advancing the Frontier, 1830–1860* (Norman: University of Oklahoma Press, 1933); 172; Robert A. Irion to Sam Houston, Mar. 14, 1838, A. M. M. Upshaw to Mirabeau B. Lamar, June 18, 1840, and "Statement of J. G. Jowett in Relation to the Difficulties between the Indians of the United States, and the Citizens of Texas," May 7, 1842, *IPTS*, 1:43, 114, 128; *Arkansas State Gazette*, May 4, 1840; M. Duval to William L. Marcy, May 31, 1847, LR:OIA, Seminole Agency, 801:147–48; Randolph B. Marcy, *Adventure on Red River: Report on the Exploration of the Headwaters of the Red River by Captain Randolph B. Marcy and Captain G. B. McClellan*, ed. Grant Foreman (Norman: University of Oklahoma Press, 1937), 173; LaVere, *Contrary Neighbors*, 117, 122–26, 138–39; Victor Tixier, *Tixier's Travels on the Osage Prairies*, ed. John Francis McDermott, trans. Albert J. Salvan (Norman: University of Oklahoma Press, 1940), 151; Grant Foreman, *Pioneer Days in the Southwest* (1926; reprint, Lincoln: University of Nebraska Press, 1994), 226–27; Wilson T. Davidson, "A Comanche Prisoner in 1841," *SHQ* 45 (Apr. 1942): 339; A. W. Whipple, Report of Explorations for a Railway Route, Near the Thirty-fifth Parallel of North Latitude, from the Mississippi River to the Pacific Ocean, 1853–54, 33d Cong., 2d sess., S. Ex. Doc. 78, pt. 3, 16; Sarah Ann Horn, *An Authentic and Thrilling Narrative of the Captivity of Mrs. Horn, and Her Two Children, with Mrs. Harris, by the Camanche Indians* (1851; reprint, New York: Garland, 1977), 25–27; Rachel Plummer, "Narrative of the Capture and Subsequent Sufferings of Mrs. Rachel Plummer, Written by Herself," in *Held Captive by Indians: Selected Narratives, 1642–1836*, ed. Richard VanDerBeets (Knoxville: University of Tennessee Press, 1973), 360–62; James F. Brooks, *Captives and Cousins: Slavery, Kinship, and Community in the Southwest Borderlands* (Chapel Hill: University of North Carolina Press for the Omohundro Institute of Early American History and Culture, 2002), 307–8; and Susan Miller, *Coacoochee's Bones: A Seminole Saga* (Lawrence: University of Kansas Press, 2003), 99, 112.

25. Brad Agnew, *Fort Gibson: Terminal on the Trail of Tears* (Norman: University of Oklahoma Press, 1980), 144–48; Leonard McPhail, "The Diary of Assistant Surgeon Leonard McPhail on His Journey to the Southwest in 1835," ed. Harold W. Jones, Jr., *CO* 18 (Sep. 1940): 288–89; and "Treaty with Comanche and Witchetaw Indians," 435. Quotes are from Tixier, *Travels*, 150; and Stokes and Arbuckle, Journal, 413. For Osage loss of power, see also DuVal, *Native Ground*, 195–26.

26. Tixier, *Travels*, 150–51.

27. *Arkansas Intelligencer*, July 1845, 1; and W. Gilpin to R. Jones, Aug. 1, 1848, and John M. Richardson to Samuel M. Rutherford, Sep. 1, 1848, 30th Cong., 2d sess., H. Ex. Doc. 1, 138, 541. Quote is from J. C. Eldredge to Houston, Dec. 8, 1843, *IPTS*, 1:259. For Santa Fe trade, see Thomas D. Hall, *Social Change in the Southwest, 1350–1880* (Lawrence: University of Kansas Press, 1989), 155.

28. Josiah Gregg, *Commerce of the Prairies*, ed. Max L. Moorhead (Norman: University of Oklahoma Press, 1954), 234, 250–51; Foreman, *Pioneer Days*, 157–58, 225–26; James Bowie to Henry Rueg, Aug. 3, 1835, in *The Papers of the Texas Revolution, 1835–1836*, ed. John H. Jenkins, 10 vols. (Austin: Presidial, 1973), 1:301–2; and W. H. Clift, "Warren's Trading Post," *CO* 2 (June 1924): 129, 138–39.
29. For hide trade in Comanchería, see, e.g., *Telegraph and Texas Register*, June 12, 1837; James Mooney, *Calendar History of the Kiowa Indians* (1898; reprint, Washington, D.C.: Smithsonian Institution, 1979), 171–72; and Clift, "Warren's Trading Post," 134–35. For the commodification of the Great Plains bison in general, see Richard White, "Animals and Enterprise," in *The Oxford History of the American West*, ed. Clyde A. Milner, II, Carol A. O'Connor, and Martha A. Sandweiss (New York: Oxford University Press, 1994), 243–49; and Andrew C. Isenberg, *The Destruction of the Bison* (Cambridge: Cambridge University Press, 2000), 93–122.
30. Luis Deblanc to Francisco Luis Hector, barón de Carondelet, Feb. 22, 1796, and Carondelet to Miguel de la Grúa Talamanca y Branciforte, marqués de Branciforte, June 7, 1796, in *Before Lewis and Clark: Documents Illustrating the History of the Missouri, 1785–1804*, ed. A. P. Nasatir, 2 vols. (1952; reprint, Lincoln: University of Nebraska Press, 1990), 1:365, 2:439. Nasatir identifies the Ambaricas as Arikaras, but it is clear from the context that they were Yamparikas.
31. For reports and rumors of American commercial activities in western Comanchería, see José Manrique to Nemesio Salcedo, Mar. 27 and 29, 1810, N. Salcedo to Manrique, May 2, 1810, Manrique to N. Salcedo, Oct. 6, 1810, Bonavía to Pedro Maria de Allande, Aug. 13, 1816, Juan Lobato to Melgares, Sep. 22, 1818, Juan de Dios Peña to Facundo Melgares, Nov. 4, 1818, and Examination of Manuel Rivera, Oct. 8, 1819, SANM II 17:61–63, 66, 90–92, 196–200, 18:682–83, 19:302–4, 433–34, 19:987–90 (T-2308, 2310, 2016, 2363, 2667, 2750, 2768, 2850); John Jamison to the secretary of war, Aug. 19, 1817, LR, Secretary of War, Main Series, RG 107, Records of the Office of the Secretary of War, M221, NAMP, 74:J129(10); Julius De Mun to William Clark, Nov. 25, 1817, *American State Papers*, Class 1, *Foreign Relations*, 4:211–13; Pérez to Martínez, June 1, 1818, BA 61:126; Anonymous, Notes Concerning the Province of New Mexico Collected on My Mission to the West, in "Anonymous Description of New Mexico, 1818," ed. Alfred B. Thomas, *SHQ* 33 (July 1929): 58–59; and David J. Weber, *Taos Trappers: The Fur Trade in the Far Southwest, 1540–1846* (Norman: University of Oklahoma Press, 1968), 45–47. Quote is from Manuel Merino y Moreno, Report on the tribes of pagan Indians who inhabit the borderlands of the Interior Provinces of the kingdom of New Spain . . . , in "Views from a Desk in Chihuahua: Manuel Merino's Report on Apaches and Neighboring Nations, ca. 1804," ed. Elizabeth A. H. John, trans. John Wheat, *SHQ* 85 (Oct. 1991): 171.
32. Alberto Maynez, Journal of Events, Apr. 1–Dec. 1, 1815, SANM II 18:29–32 (T-2585); Kavanagh, *Comanche Political History*, 180–89; Concha, Instructions, 242; John, "Documentary Evidence," 543; and David J. Weber, *Bárbaros: Spaniards and Their Savages in the Age of Enlightenment* (New Haven: Yale University Press, 2005), 185.
33. Carroll and Haggard, *Three New Mexico Chronicles*, 135–36.
34. Melgares to Alexo Garcia Conde, Oct. 8, 1818, in "Documents Bearing upon the Northern Frontier of New Mexico, 1818–1819," ed. Alfred B. Thomas, *NMHR* 4 (Apr. 1929): 156. Quotes are from Anonymous, Notes, 58–59.
35. Thomas James, *Three Years among the Indians and Mexicans*, ed. Milo Milton Quaife (1846; reprint, New York: Citadel, 1966), 100–35, 220–56. For a different interpretation of James's visit, see

Charles L. Kenner, *The Comanchero Frontier: A History of New Mexican–Plains Indian Relations* (1969; reprint, Norman: University of Oklahoma Press, 1994), 70.

36. James, *Three Years*, 213–56 (quote is from pp. 227–28); and *Arkansas State Gazette*, Feb. 28, 1838, cited in Ralph A. Smith, "Mexican and Anglo-Saxon Traffic in Scalps, Slaves, and Livestock, 1835–1841," *West Texas Historical Association Year Book* 36 (1960): 102–3. Also see Douglas C. Comer, *Ritual Ground: Bent's Old Fort, World Formation, and the Annexation of the Southwest* (Berkeley: University of California Press, 1996), 92; José María Ronquillo to ayudante inspector, June 28, 1833, MANM 14:930; and Stephen G. Hyslop, *Bound for Santa Fe: The Road to New Mexico and the American Conquest, 1806–1848* (Norman: University of Oklahoma Press, 2002), 175.

37. Zenon Trudeau to Carondelet, July 4, 1796, in *Before Lewis and Clark*, ed. Nasatir, 1:329–30; Joaquin del Real Alencaster to N. Salcedo, June 13, 1807, and Summary of Recent Events in New Mexico, July 1–Sep. 13, 1808, SANM II 16:247, 556–61 (T-2056, 2134); James, *Three Years*, 245; José María Ronquillo, Report, Sep. 17, 1831, MANM 13:559–79; Charles Augustus Murray, *Travels in North America during the Years 1834, 1835, 1836*, 2 vols. (London: R. Bentley, 1839), 365; Gregg, *Commerce*, 246; James William Abert, *Expedition to the Southwest: An 1845 Reconnaissance of Colorado, New Mexico, Texas, and Oklahoma* (1846; reprint, Lincoln: University of Nebraska Press, 1999), 63; and David J. Wishart, *An Unspeakable Sadness: The Dispossession of Nebraska Indians* (Lincoln: University of Nebraska Press, 1994), 31.

38. Mooney, *Calendar History*, 162–64 (quote is from p. 163); Elizabeth A. H. John, "An Earlier Chapter of Kiowa History," *NMHR* 60 (Oct. 1985): 387; and Kavanagh, *Comanche Political History*, 146–47.

39. For Kiowas and Naishans and their move into Comanchería, see Mooney, *Calendar History*, 164; and Morris W. Foster and Martha McCollough, "Plains Apache," in *Handbook of North American Indians*, vol. 13, *The Plains*, ed. Raymond J. DeMallie, 2 parts (Washington, D.C.: Smithsonian Institution, 2001), 2:926–27. For Kiowas' and Naishans' trade with the Missouri villagers and their role as middlemen, see Pierre Antoine Tabeau, *Tabeau's Narrative of Loisel's Expedition to the Upper Missouri*, ed. Annie Heloise Abel, trans. Rose Abel Wright (Norman: University of Oklahoma Press, 1939), 154–55, 158 (quote is from p. 158); Gary E. Moulton, ed., *The Journals of the Lewis and Clark Expedition*, 13 vols. (Lincoln: University of Nebraska Press, 1983–2001), 3:403, 422; Zebulon Montgomery Pike, *The Expeditions of Zebulon Montgomery Pike*, ed. Elliott Coues, 2 vols. (1895; reprint, New York: Dover, 1987), 2:746; George E. Hyde, *Life of George Bent: Written from His Letters*, ed. Savoie Lottinville (Norman: University of Oklahoma Press, 1968), 31–32; and Pekka Hämäläinen, "The Western Comanche Trade Center: Rethinking the Plains Indian Trade System," *Western Historical Quarterly* 29 (Winter 1998): 506.

40. For the Cheyenne-Arapaho migration, see Pekka Hämäläinen, "The Rise and Fall of Plains Indian Horse Cultures," *JAH* 90 (Dec. 2003): 839–40. For fairs, see Edwin James, *James' Account of S. H. Long Expedition, 1819–20*, vols. 14–17 of *Early Western Travels, 1748–1846*, ed. Reuben Gold Thwaites (Cleveland: Arthur H. Clark, 1905), 16:55; and Jacob Fowler, *The Journal of Jacob Fowler*, ed. Elliott Coues (1898; reprint, Minneapolis: Ross and Haines, 1965), 51–59, 71–72. For Cheyennes as middlemen, see Joseph Jablow, *The Cheyenne in Plains Indian Trade Relations, 1795–1840*, Monographs of the American Ethnological Society 19 (New York: J. J. Augustin, 1951), 58–60; John Milloy, *The Plains Cree: Trade, Diplomacy, and War, 1790 to 1870* (Winnipeg: University of Manitoba Press, 1988), 35; and Hyde, *Life of George Bent*, 32.

41. Theodore Binnema, *Common and Contested Ground: A Human and Environmental History of*

the Northwestern Plains (Norman: University of Oklahoma Press, 2001), 137, 182–83; George E. Hyde, *Indians of the High Plains: From the Prehistoric Period to the Coming of Europeans* (Norman: University of Oklahoma Press, 1959), 182–83; James, *Account*, 16:55; John R. Bell, *The Journal of Captain John R. Bell, Official Journalist for the Stephen H. Long Expedition to the Rocky Mountains, 1820*, ed. Harlin M. Fuller and LeRoy R. Hafen (Glendale, Calif.: Arthur H. Clark, 1957), 180; and Fowler, *Journal*, 5. Berlandier, too, mentioned Shoshones ("Sonsores") visiting Comanche rancherías. See Berlandier, *Indians*, 142. Quote is from Charles Le Raye, "The Journal of Charles LeRaye," *South Dakota Historical Collections* 4 (1908): 174. For Shoshone weaponry, see also Moulton, ed., *Journals*, 5:122. For Crows, see Edwin Thompson Denig, *Five Indian Tribes of the Upper Missouri: Sioux, Aricaras, Assiniboines, Crees, Crows*, ed. John C. Ewers (Norman: University of Oklahoma Press, 1961), 164.

42. John H. Moore, *The Cheyenne Nation: A Social and Demographic History* (Lincoln: University of Nebraska Press, 1987), 235; Hyde, *Life of George Bent*, 37–41, 68; and Comer, *Ritual Ground*, 123.
43. For casualties, see, e.g., Foreman, *Pioneer Days*, 238; and Janet Lecompte, "Bent, St. Vrain, and Company among the Comanche and Kiowa," *Colorado Magazine* 49 (1972): 275; and *National Intelligencer*, Apr. 16, 1839. The description of the 1840 peace draws on Mooney, *Calendar History*, 276; and George Bird Grinnell, *The Fighting Cheyennes* (Norman: University of Oklahoma Press, 1915), 63–69 (quote is from p. 69). Both these works draw heavily on Native oral traditions.
44. For territorial arrangements, see George F. Ruxton, *Adventures in Mexico and the Rocky Mountains* (London: John Murray, 1861), 291–92; Hyde, *Life of George Bent*, 37; John W. Whitfield to C. E. Mix, Jan. 5, 1856, LR:OIA, Upper Arkansas Agency, 878:104; and John W. Abert, *Through the Country of the Comanche Indians in the Fall of the Year 1845: The Journal of a U.S. Army Expedition Led by Lieutenant James W. Abert*, ed. John Calvin (San Francisco: John Howell, 1970), facing 68. For strategic considerations, see Elliott West, *The Contested Plains: Indians, Goldseekers, and the Rush to Colorado* (Lawrence: University of Kansas Press, 1998), 77.
45. West, *Contested Plains*, 83, 192–96; and Comer, *Ritual Ground*, 125.
46. For Bent's Fort in American history, see, e.g., Comer, *Ritual Ground*, 246–50. For Comanche trade at Bent's Fort, see Hyde, *Life of George Bent*, 68–70; Ruxton, *Adventures*, 283–85, 291–92; Lecompte, "Bent," 281–85; and Comer, *Ritual Ground*, 154–56.
47. For intra-Comanche interactions, see chapter 6.
48. For the intersections of gifts, kinship, and trade in Comanche foreign relations, see Hämäläinen, "Western Comanche Trade Center," 492–93, 509–10; and David LaVere, "Friendly Persuasions: Gifts and Reciprocity in Comanche-Euroamerican Relations," CO 71 (Fall 1993): 322–37. For the Iroquois Great League of Peace and Power, see Daniel K. Richter, *The Ordeal of the Longhouse: The Peoples of the Iroquois League in the Era of European Colonization* (Chapel Hill: University of North Carolina Press for the Omohundro Institute of Early American History and Culture, 1992), 30–49.
49. For northern plains, see Patricia Albers, "Symbiosis, Merger, and War: Contrasting Forms of Intertribal Relationship among Historic Plains Indians," in *Political Economy of North American Indians*, ed. John H. Moore (Norman: University of Oklahoma Press, 1993), 93–132.
50. Alice Marriott and Carol K. Rachlin, *Plains Indian Mythology* (New York: Thomas Y. Crowell, 1975), 96–98. See also Mooney, *Calendar History*, 160–65.
51. For Ponca legends, see Ernest Wallace and E. Adamson Hoebel, *The Comanches: Lords of the South*

Plains (Norman: University of Oklahoma Press, 1954), 39. For Shoshones, see Colin G. Calloway, "Snake Frontiers: The Eastern Shoshones in the Eighteenth Century," *Annals of Wyoming* 63 (Summer 1991): 85–86.

52. For religious ceremonies, military societies, clothing accessories, hairstyles, and weaponry, see Merino, Report, 173; George Catlin, *Letters and Notes on the Manners, Customs, and Conditions of the North American Indians*, 2 vols. (1844; reprint, New York: Dover, 1973), 2:73; Whipple, Report, 34; William C. Meadows, *Kiowa, Apache, and Comanche Military Societies: Enduring Veterans, 1800 to the Present* (Austin: University of Texas Press, 1999), 276, 320; and Thomas W. Kavanagh, "Comanche," in *Encyclopedia of North American Indians: Native American History, Culture, and Life from Paleo-Indians to the Present*, ed. Frederick E. Hoxie (Boston: Houghton Mifflin, 1996), 132. For the Comanche language, see Berlandier, *Indians*, 103; Manuel García Rejón, comp., *Comanche Vocabulary: Trilingual Edition*, trans. and ed. Daniel J. Gelo (Austin: University of Texas Press, 1995), 5; Captain Frederick Marryat, *Travels and Adventures of Monsieur Violet* (Upper Saddle River, N.J.: Literature House, 1970), first page of ch. 26; W. P. Clark, *The Indian Sign Language* (Philadelphia: L. R. Hamersley, 1885), 120; John L. Kessell, *Kiva, Cross, and Crown: The Pecos Indians and New Mexico, 1540–1840* (Washington, D.C.: National Park Service, 1979), 439; Howard Meredith, *Dancing on Common Ground: Tribal Cultures and Alliances on the Southern Plains* (Lawrence: University Press of Kansas, 1995), 65; and Kavanagh, *Comanche Political History*, 180–81. This is not to suggest that the spread of language had become a one-way proposition. Early nineteenth-century sources are filled with references to Comanches who understood and spoke Spanish.

53. For Comanche-Kiowa-Naishan relations, see Alencaster to N. Salcedo, Aug. 30, 1806, SANM II 16:212 (T-2006); Mooney, *Calendar History*, 164–65, 171; Nancy P. Hickerson, "Ethnogenesis in the South Plains: Jumano to Kiowa?" in *History, Power, and Identity: Ethnogenesis in the Americas: 1492–1992*, ed. Jonathan D. Hill (Iowa City: University of Iowa Press, 1996), 87–88; Hämäläinen, "Western Comanche Trade Center," 506; Gerald Betty, *Comanche Society: Before the Reservation* (College Station: Texas A&M University Press, 2002), 119, 142; Thomas W. Kavanagh, "Comanche," in *Handbook of North American Indians*, vol. 13, *The Plains*, ed. DeMallie, 2:893; García Rejón, comp., *Comanche Vocabulary*, 5; and Robert S. Neighbors to William Medill, Sep. 14, 1847, 30th Cong., 1st sess., S. Ex. Doc. 1, 901. For the Comanche Sun Dance, see Meadows, *Kiowa, Apache, and Comanche Military Societies*, 318–23. Quotes are from Berlandier, *Indians*, 108, 135. For Comanches speaking for Kiowas and Naishans at diplomatic meetings with European colonial powers, see, e.g., Bartolomé Baca to commanding general, May 18, 1825, MANM 3:936; and Stokes and Arbuckle, Journal, 407.

54. José María Sánchez, "A Trip to Texas in 1828," trans. Carlos E. Castañeda, *SHQ* 29 (Apr. 1926): 261–62; Manuel de Mier y Terán, "Noticia de las tribus de salvajes conocidos que habitan en el Departamento de Tejas, y el número de Familias de que consta cada tribu, puntos en que habitan y terrenos en que acampan," *Sociedad de Geografía y Estadística de la Republica Mexicana Boletín* 2 (1870): 265; Berlandier, *Indians*, 109–11 (quotes are from pp. 109–10); Ruíz, *Report*, 16; García Rejón, comp., *Comanche Vocabulary*, 5; and W. O. Tuggle, *Shem, Ham and Japheth: The Papers of W. O. Tuggle Comprising His Indian Diary, Sketches and Observations, Myths and Washington Journal in the Territory and at the Capital, 1879–1882*, ed. Eugene Current-Garcia and Dorothy B. Hatfield (Athens: University of Georgia Press, 1973), 143. Melburn D. Thurman has identified the "Chariticas" and "Sarritechas" mentioned by Ruíz, Berlandier, and Terán as Lipan Apaches.

While it is possible that those ethnonyms were sometimes used to refer to Apaches, it seems clear that Ruíz, Berlandier, and Terán meant the Arapahoes: all three write that the Sarritechas/Chariticas came to Texas from the United States or "North America," that is, north of the Arkansas and Red rivers, which marked the boundary line between Mexico and the United States. Lipan Apaches, in contrast, had lived since the 1760s in southern Texas and northern Mexico below the Río Grande and would have entered the southern plains from the south. See Melburn D. Thurman, "On the Identity of the Chariticas: Dog Eating and Pre-Horse Adaptation on the High Plains," *Plains Anthropologist* 33 (May 1988): 159–70.

55. For shifting Wichita locations, see Smith, *Wichita Indians*, 29, 113, 137. For Comanche-Wichita cooperation, see Rafael Gonzáles to Juan de Castañeda, June 5, 1824, and Cayetano Andrado to Antonio Elozúa, Dec. 16, 1825, BA 77:224–25, 86:792–93; and Matthew Babcock, "Transnational Raid and Trade Routes: Comanche Expansion from the Rio Grande to Durango, 1821–1846" (unpublished paper in author's possession). For Pahayuko's statement, see "Talk of Pah-Hah-Yoco and Roasting Ear," Jan. 19, 1845, *IPTS*, 1:174. For Wichitas' reputation in Texas, see Austin to Mateo Ahumada, May 18, 1826, in *Austin Papers*, ed. Barker, 2:1338–40; Jean Louis Berlandier, *Journey to Mexico: During the Years 1826 to 1834*, trans. Sheila M. Ohlendorf, Josette M. Bigelow, and Mary M. Standifer, 2 vols. (Austin: Texas State Historical Association and University of Texas Press, 1980), 2: 313; and David G. Burnet to Henry R. Schoolcraft, Sep. 29, 1847, *IPTS*, 3:97. Quote is from "Minutes of Council at Tehuacana Creek," May 13, 1844, *IPTS*, 2:40.

56. Quotes are from Sibley to Eustice, Dec. 31, 1811, in "Dr. John Sibley," SHQ 49 (Jan. 1946): 403; Berlandier, *Indians*, 122; "Delegation from the Comanche Nation," in *Papers Concerning Robertson's Colony in Texas*, comp. and ed. Malcolm McLean, 18 vols. (Austin: University of Texas Press, 1974–93), 4:428; Gregg, *Commerce*, 437; and Thomas J. Farnham, *Travels in the Great Western Prairies*, vols. 28 and 29 of *Early Western Travels, 1748–1846*, ed. Reuben Gold Thwaites (Cleveland: Arthur H. Clark, 1906), 28:151. See also José Francisco Ruíz to Elozúa, Aug. 1, 1830, in *Robertson's Colony*, 4:334–35; Neighbors to Medill, Mar. 2, 1848, 30th Cong., 1st sess., S. Rpt. 171, 17; Gary Clayton Anderson, *The Conquest of Texas: Ethnic Cleansing in the Promised Land, 1820–1875* (Norman: University of Oklahoma Press, 2005), 48–49; Ruíz to Elozúa, Aug. 1, 1830, BA 133:31; and Sánchez, "Trip to Texas," 261, 265–66.

57. For voluntary immigrants, see "Delegation from the Comanche Nation," 428; R. B. Marcy, *Thirty Years of Army Life on the Border* (New York: Harper and Bros., 1866), 89; Susan Miller, "Those Homelands That You Call the Louisiana Purchase," in *The Louisiana Purchase and Its Peoples: Perspectives from the New Orleans Conference*, ed. Paul E. Hoffman (Lafayette: Louisiana Historical Association and the Center for Louisiana History, 2004), 84; Anderson, *Indian Southwest*, 224–26; and Brooks, *Captives and Cousins*, 194. Quotes are from Sibley, *Report*, 80; and Robert S. Neighbors, "The Na-Ü-Ni, or Comanches of Texas; Their Traits and Beliefs, and Divisions and Intertribal Relations," *IPTS*, 3:350.

58. Quotes are from Brooks, *Captives and Cousins*, 193; and Padilla, Report, 55.

59. Quote is from Sánchez, "Trip to Texas," 262. Also see Lila Wistrand Robinson and James Armagost, *Comanche Dictionary and Grammar* (Arlington: University of Texas at Arlington, 1990), 102; and Ladonna Harris, Stephen M. Sachs, and Benjamin J. Broome, "Wisdom of the People: Potential and Pitfalls in Efforts by the Comanches to Recreate Traditional Ways of Building Consensus," *American Indian Quarterly* 25 (Winter 2001): 117.

60. Catlin, *Letters*, 2:67–68.

61. For epidemics, see Mooney, *Calendar History*, 168, 172–73; and John C. Ewers, "The Influence of Epidemics on the Indian Populations and Cultures of Texas," *Plains Anthropologist* 18 (May 1973): 104–15. For population numbers, see David Dickson to Henry Clay, July 1, 1827, Despatches from United States Consuls in Texas, 1825–44, RG 59, General Records of the Department of the State, T153, NAMP, reel 1 (no frame number); J. C. Clopper, "Journal [1828]," in *Texas by Terán: The Diary Kept by General Manuel de Mier y Terán on His 1828 Inspection of Texas*, ed. Jack Jackson, trans. John Wheat (Austin: University of Texas Press, 2000), 25; José Francisco Ruíz, "'Comanches': Customs and Characteristics," in *The Papers of Mirabeau Buonaparte Lamar*, ed. Charles Adams Gulick, Jr., et al., 6 vols. (1920–27; reprint, Austin: Pemberton, 1968), 4:222; Houston to Ellsworth, Dec. 1, 1832, in *Writings of Sam Houston*, ed. Williams and Barker, 1:268; Report of G. W. Bonnell, reprinted in 30th Cong., 1st sess., S. Rpt. 171, 42; Foreman, *Advancing the Frontier*, 148–49; Hall, *Social Change*, 145; David J. Weber, *The Mexican Frontier, 1821–1846: The American Southwest Under Mexico* (Albuquerque: University of New Mexico Press, 1982), 177, 195; and LaVere, *Contrary Neighbors*, 64.
62. For Wichitas' and Kiowas' losses as front-line communities, see Foreman, *Advancing the Frontier*, 113; and Willard H. Rollings, *The Osage: An Ethnohistorical Study of Hegemony on the Prairie-Plains* (Columbia: University of Missouri Press, 1992), 269. For diplomatic settings, see, e.g., Baca to commanding general, May 18, 1825, MANM 3:936; "Treaty with the Comanche," Oct. 8, 1826, in *Documents of American Indian Diplomacy: Treaties, Agreements, and Conventions, 1775–1979*, comp. Vine Deloria, Jr., and Raymond DeMallie (Norman: University of Oklahoma Press, 1999), 154; Stokes and Arbuckle, Journal, 407; and "A Treaty Signed in Council at Tehuacana Creek, Oct. 9, 1844," *IPTS*, 2:113–14. Quote is from Neighbors, "Na-Ü-Ni," 349.
63. Manuel de Mier y Terán to Guadalupe Victoria, Mar. 28, 1828, in *Texas by Terán*, ed. Jackson, trans. Wheat, 30; and Sánchez, "Trip to Texas," 263.

CHAPTER 5. GREATER COMANCHERÍA

1. For raids and violence, see William H. Oberste, *History of Refugio Mission* (Refugio, Tex.: Refugio Timely Remarks, 1942), 217, 249–50; F. Todd Smith, *From Dominance to Disappearance: The Indians of Texas and the Near Southwest, 1786–1859* (Lincoln: University of Nebraska Press, 2005), 52–53; and Pedro de Nava to Manuel Muñoz, Jan. 27 and June 4, 1795, Miguel Músquiz to Juan Bautista de Elguézabal, Nov. 8, 1801, Elguézabal to Manuel Antonio Cordero y Bustamante, Jan. 6, 1802, Nava to Elguézabal, Jan. 19, 1802, Elguézabal to Nava, Apr. 14, 28, and 29, 1802, Nava to Elguézabal, Oct. 28, 1802, and Cuaderno Borrador, certified copy of Francisco Xavier de Uranga to Nava, Sep. 29, 1802, BA 25:269–70, 541–42, 30:406–7, 477–78, 494–500, 536–37, 873–75, 824–26. For the council, see Elguézabal to Cordero, Mar. 30, 1803, and Nemesio Salcedo to Elguézabal, Apr. 26, 1803, BA 31:157, 211–12.
2. For Spanish vulnerability and fears of American influence in Comanchería, see N. Salcedo to Elguézabal, Nov. 14, 1802, Sep. 13, 1803, and Aug. 14, 1804, Elguézabal to N. Salcedo, Sep. 11, 1805, and Testimony of Chief Cordero, Oct. 25, 1810, BA 30:899, 31:609, 32:607, 33:528–82, 47:6–7; N. Salcedo to Fernando Chacón, May 8, 1804, in *Before Lewis and Clark: Documents Illustrating the History of the Missouri, 1785–1804*, ed. A. P. Nasatir, 2 vols. (1952; reprint, Lincoln: University of Nebraska Press, 1990), 2:734–35; and Julia Kathryn Garrett, *Green Flag over Texas: A Story of the Last Years of Spain in Texas* (New York: Cordova, 1939), 10.

3. For gift distributions, see Miguel Díaz de Luna to Manuel María de Salcedo, Dec. 1, 1810, BA 47:419–33. For "lust for lucre," see Gary Clayton Anderson, *The Indian Southwest, 1580–1830: Ethnogenesis and Reinvention* (Norman: University of Oklahoma Press, 1999), 213. For a differing interpretation of gifting in Comanche-Spanish relations in Texas, see Raúl Ramos, "Finding the Balance: Béxar in the Mexican/Indian Relations," in *Continental Crossroads: Remapping U.S.-Mexico Borderlands History*, ed. Samuel Truett and Elliott Young (Durham: Duke University Press, 2004), 47–50.
4. For attacks, see Odie B. Faulk, "The Comanche Invasion of Texas, 1743–1836," *Great Plains Journal* 9 (Fall 1969): 33–34; and N. Salcedo to Elguézabal, Mar. 28, 1803, Elguézabal, Report, Aug. 31, 1803, and N. Salcedo to Elguézabal, Oct. 11, 1803, BA 31:155, 535–36, 712–13. For gifts, accommodation, and peaceful interactions, see N. Salcedo to Elguézabal, Aug. 14 and Sep. 10, 1804, Cordero to N. Salcedo, Sep. 11 and Oct. 5, 1805, Cordero to N. Salcedo, Mar. 12, 1806, N. Salcedo to Cordero, June 3, 1806, Cordero to N. Salcedo, June 20 and 27, 1806, Conference with Comanche Chief Cordero, July 31, 1810, and Bernardo Bonavía to N. Salcedo, Aug. 8, 1810, BA 32:606–7, 656–67, 33:584, 703–4, 34:419–22, 720–22, 821, 46:233–35, 312–13; Thomas W. Kavanagh, *Comanche Political History: An Ethnohistorical Perspective* (Lincoln: University of Nebraska Press, 1996), 186; J. Villasana Haggard, "The Neutral Ground between Louisiana and Texas, 1806–1821," *Louisiana Historical Quarterly* 28 (Oct. 1945): 1085; and Francisco Amangual, "Diary of Francisco Amangual from San Antonio to Santa Fe, March 30–May 19, 1808," *PV*, 467–74. For a panoramic and uniquely comparative analysis of Spanish tribute payments to independent Indians, see David J. Weber, *Bárbaros: Spaniards and Their Savages in the Age of Enlightenment* (New Haven: Yale University Press, 2005), 190–92.
5. For the lack of presents in Texas, see M. Salcedo to N. Salcedo, Sep. 18, 1811, and Simón de Herrera to N. Salcedo, Sep. 29, 1811, BA 49:202–5, 245–46. For attempts to increase gifts and maintain peace, see Herrera to N. Salcedo, Aug. 7 and 21, 1811, and N. Salcedo to Herrera, Sep. 17, 1811, BA 48:989–90, 49:73–74, 195–96. For attacks, see N. Salcedo to Bonavía, Aug. 27, 1810, Bernardo Bonavía, Manuel María de Salcedo, and Símon de Herrera, War Council, Oct. 1810 [n.d.], José Miguel Arcos to commanders of San Marcos, Colorado, and Brazos, Aug. 4, 1811, Herrera to N. Salcedo, Aug. 13, 1811, Herrera to Joaquín de Arredondo, Aug. 16, 1811, and N. Salcedo to Herrera, Dec. 18, 1811, BA 46:511–15, 47:122–27, 48:64–66, 49:47–48, 53–54, 756–57. For the El Sordo incident, see Proceedings Concerning the Capture of Comanche Chief Sordo and His Followers, Dec. 15, 1811, BA 729–47. For Sargento-Cordero, see John Jamison to the secretary of war, June 10, 1817, LR, Secretary of War, Main Series, RG 107, Records of the Office of the Secretary of War, M221, NAMP, 74:J186(10); and Thomas James, *Three Years among the Indians and Mexicans*, ed. Milo Milton Quaife (1846; reprint, New York: Citadel, 1966), 136.
6. For the San Marcos raid, see M. Salcedo to N. Salcedo, Aug. 5, 1812, BA 52:151–55. For troops, see Nemesio Salcedo, *Instrucción reservada de don Nemesio Salcedo y Salcedo, Comandante General de Provincias Internas a su sucesor*, ed. Isidro Vizcaya Canales (Chihuahua: Centro de Información del Estado de Chihuahua), 17. Quotes are from Juan Antonio Padilla, Report on the Barbarous Indians of the Province of Texas, Dec. 27, 1819, in "Texas in 1820," trans. Mattie Austin Hatcher, *SHQ* 23 (July 1919): 55; and Faulk, "Comanche Invasion," 36.
7. For the 1812–13 revolt and its aftermath, see David J. Weber, *The Mexican Frontier, 1821–1846: The American Southwest under Mexico* (Albuquerque: University of New Mexico Press, 1982), 9–10; and Salcedo, *Instrucción*, 37. For Comanche raids, see Benito de Armiñán to Arredondo, Mar.

22, 1814, Ignacio Pérez to Armiñán, Apr. 15, 1814, Armiñán to Arredondo, Apr. 16 and Aug. 1 and 15, 1814, and Proceedings Concerning the Investigation of Damages Caused by the Comanche Indians around Béxar, BA 53:584–85, 680–83, 715, 54:87–88, 122–23, 126–31; David G. Burnet, "David G. Burnet's Letters Describing the Comanche Indians with an Introduction by Ernest Wallace," *West Texas Historical Association Year Book* 30 (1954): 132; and Juan N. Almonte, "Statistical Report on Texas," trans. C. E. Castañeda, *SHQ* 28 (Jan. 1925): 181, 195. For the condition of Texas, see Arredondo to Armiñán, Jan. 31, 1814, Armiñán to Arredondo, Apr. 16, 1814, Anonymous to Arredondo, May 22, 1814, Arredondo to Armiñán, June 29 and 30, 1814, and Armiñán to Arredondo, Aug. 1 and 15, 1814, BA 53:510, 726–27, 924–25, 1027–36, 54:87–90, 122–23. The 1812–13 revolt was preceded, in early 1811, by the Casas Revolt, a Hidalgo Revolt-inspired coup directed against local *penisulares*, European-born Spaniards, and *mal gobierno* (bad government). The Casas Revolt seems to have had little impact on Comanche-Texas relations.

8. For Comanche-Lipan peace, see José Francisco Ruíz, *Report on Indian Tribes of Texas in 1828*, ed. John C. Ewers (New Haven: Yale University Press, 1972), 7; and Jean Louis Berlandier, *The Indians of Texas in 1830*, ed. John C. Ewers, trans. Patricia Reading Leclercq (Washington, D.C.: Smithsonian Institution, 1969), 132. Quotes in the following paragraph are from Berlandier, *Indians*, 133; and Antonio Martínez to Arredondo, June 26, 1818, in *The Letters of Antonio Martinez, Last Spanish Governor of Texas, 1817–1822*, ed. Virginia H. Taylor (Austin: Texas State Library, 1957), 150.
9. For raids and Spanish responses, see Juan Ignacio Flores to Martínez, July 23, 1817, Martínez to Antonio García de Tejada, Aug. 9, 1817, Tejada to Martínez, Aug. 25 and 27, 1817, and Martínez to Juan de Castañeda, Aug. 29 and Sep. 10, 1817, BA 59:11–13, 184–85, 340, 365–66, 387, 511–12; Omar Valerio-Jiménez, "*Indios Bárbaros*, Divorcées, and Flocks of Vampires: Identity and Nation on the Rio Grande" (Ph.D. diss., University of California, Los Angeles, 2001), 35–36; Instructions Which the Constitutional Ayuntamiento of the City of San Fernando de Bexar Draws . . . , Nov. 15, 1820, in "Texas in 1820," trans. Mattie Austin Hatcher, *SHQ* 23 (July 1919): 62–63; and Martínez to Arredondo, Oct. 4, 1819, in *Letters of Antonio Martinez*, 269.
10. Armiñán to Arredondo, Aug. 19, 1814, and José Félix Pérez to Armiñán, Aug. 22, 1814, BA 54:136–39, 151–52; Anderson, *Indian Southwest*, 254–55; Martínez to Arredondo, June 25, 1818, Apr. 5, 1819, and Mar. 2, 1820, in *Letters of Antonio Martinez*, 149, 219, 307; Instructions . . . of the City of San Fernando de Bexar, 61; Jack Jackson, *Los Mesteños: Spanish Ranching in Texas, 1721–1821* (College Station: Texas A&M University Press, 1986), 544–50; and David J. Weber, *The Spanish Frontier in North America* (New Haven: Yale University Press, 1992), 299.
11. Martínez to Arredondo, June 26 and Oct. 20, 1818, and Apr. 1, 1819, in *Letters of Antonio Martinez*, 150, 185, 218; and Almonte, "Statistical Report," 181.
12. For contemporary explanations of raiding, see, e.g., M. Salcedo to N. Salcedo, Sep. 11, 1805, Testimony of Chief Cordero, Oct. 25, 1810, and Manuel María de Salcedo, Questioning of a Comanche Indian, 1810 [n.d.], BA 33:582–83, 47:6–7, 701–2. Quote is from Stephen F. Austin to Anastasio Bustamante [?], May 10, 1830, in *The Austin Papers*, ed. Eugene C. Barker, 2 vols. (Washington, D.C.: GPO, 1924), 2:508–9. The idea that American borderland agents used Plains Indians as a tool to weaken and eventually conquer the Mexican Far North is also a well-entrenched theme in Mexican historiography. See James F. Brooks, "Served Well by Plunder: La Gran Ladronería and Producers of History Astride the Río Grande," *American Quarterly* 52 (Mar. 2000): 34.
13. Amangual, "Diary," 473.

14. Salcedo, *Instrucción*, 46; and Dan L. Flores, ed., *Journal of an Indian Trader: Anthony Glass and the Texas Trading Frontier, 1790–1810* (College Station: Texas A&M University Press, 1985), 11, 92–93. Quotes are from Bonavía, M. Salcedo, and Herrera, War Council, BA 47:123. For Comanches' need for guns in the early nineteenth century, see, e.g., John Sibley, *A Report from Natchitoches in 1807*, ed. Annie Heloise Abel (New York: Museum of the American Indian, 1922), 74.
15. For an illuminating example of the dynamics of Comanche-American trade, see Anthony Glass, "Life among the Indians, August–October, 1808," and "On the Winter Hunt, October, 1808–March, 1809," in *Journal*, ed. Flores, 47–60, 61–80. Also see the previous chapter for Thomas James's blundering first visit to Comanchería.
16. As George Bent noted, wild mustangs "made the best mount for hunting buffalo" but their breaking and training took months of careful and intensive labor. See George E. Hyde, *Life of George Bent: Written from His Letters*, ed. Savoie Lottinville (Norman: University of Oklahoma Press 1968), 34–37.
17. According to one early nineteenth-century observer, Comanches' "wealth consisted of horses and mules; those raised by themselves are generally of superior order. . . . Their fine horses they could scarcely be induced to sell, but those which they had stolen from the Mexicans they would dispose of almost at any cost." See *Houston Telegraph and Texas Register*, June 16, 1838. Quote is from Randolph B. Marcy, *Adventure on Red River: Report on the Exploration of the Headwaters of the Red River by Captain Randolph B. Marcy and Captain G. B. McClellan*, ed. Grant Foreman (Norman: University of Oklahoma Press, 1937), 158. Marcy's remark is echoed by Josiah Gregg who wrote that Comanches "dote upon their steeds: one had as well undertake to purchase a Comanche's child as his favorite riding-horse." See Josiah Gregg, *Commerce of the Prairies*, ed. Max L. Moorhead (Norman: University of Oklahoma Press, 1954), 435.
18. For American squatters, see Randolph B. Campbell, *Gone to Texas: A History of the Lone Star State* (New York: Oxford University Press, 2003), 97–98.
19. Juan Cortés to Martínez, Oct. 23, 1821, and Manuel Barrera to José Angel Navarro, Dec. 3, 1821, BA 68:664–65, 69:284–85; "Delegation from the Comanche Nation to the Mexican Congress," in *Papers Concerning Robertson's Colony*, comp. and ed. Malcolm McLean, 18 vols. (Austin: University of Texas Press, 1974–93), 4:428; Martha Rodríguez, *La guerra entre bárbaros y civilizados: el exterminio del nómada en Coahuila, 1840–1880* (Saltillo: Centro de Estudios Sociales y Humanísticos, 1998), 145–46; and Juan Mora-Torres, *The Making of the Mexican Border: The State, Capitalism, and Society in Nuevo Leon, 1848–1910* (Austin: University of Texas Press, 2001), 37.
20. Quotes are from "Treaty between the Mexican Empire and the Comanche Nation," Dec. 13, 1822, in *Documents of American Indian Diplomacy: Treaties, Agreements, and Conventions, 1775–1979*, comp. Vine Deloria, Jr., and Raymond DeMallie (Norman: University of Oklahoma Press, 1999), 150–52; and "Delegation from the Comanche Nation," 431.
21. Ohland Morton, *Terán and Texas: A Chapter in Texas-Mexican Relations* (Austin: Texas Historical Association, 1948), 68; and José Rafael González to Castañeda, Mar. 1, 1825, BA 79:663–64. Quotation is from Berlandier, *Indians*, 47–48.
22. Berlandier, *Indians*, 31.
23. Gómez Pedraza to Antonio Elozúa, Nov. 10, 1825, Cayetano Andrade to Elozúa, Nov. 10, 1825, and Elozúa to Andrade, Dec. 16, 1825, BA 85:733–34, 739–40, 86:799–800; Berlandier, *Indians*, 120; and José María Sánchez, "A Trip to Texas in 1828," trans. Carlos E. Castañeda, *SHQ* 29 (Apr. 1926): 262. Quotes are from González to Castañeda, Mar. 3, 1824, BA 76:939; and Gutierrez

de Lara to the governor of San Luis Potosi, July 1824, cited in Rupert Norval Richardson, *The Comanche Barrier to South Plains Settlement: A Century and a Half of Savage Resistance to the Advancing Frontier* (Glendale, Calif.: Arthur H. Clark, 1933), 74.

24. *Natchitoches Courier*, May 15, 1826, and Sebastián Camacho to Joel R. Poinsett, June 15, 1826, cited in David J. Weber, *The Mexican Frontier, 1821–1846: The American Southwest under Mexico* (Albuquerque: University of New Mexico Press, 1982), 95, 97. Also see David J. Weber, "American Westward Expansion and the Breakdown of Relations between *Pobladores* and '*Indios Bárbaros*' on Mexico's Far Northern Frontier, 1821–1846," *NMHR* 56 (July 1981): 224–26.

25. "Colonization Law of the State of Coahuila and Texas, March 25, 1825," in *Robertson's Colony*, 2:276; Weber, *Mexican Frontier*, 158–65; and Andrés Reséndez, *Changing National Identities at the Frontier: Texas and New Mexico, 1800–1850* (New York: Cambridge University Press, 2005), 28–29, 64–68.

26. Stephen F. Austin to José Antonio Saucedo, Aug. 26, 1824, Baron de Bastrop to Austin, Mar. 19, 1825, and Austin to Bustamante [?], May 10, 1830, in *Austin Papers*, ed. Barker, 2:507–8, 1058, 1181–82 (quote is from p. 507); Faulk, "Comanche Invasion," 39; and José Francisco Ruíz to Elozúa, Aug. 1, 1830, BA 133:30–32.

27. For the growth of Austin's colony, see Gregg Cantrell, *Stephen F. Austin, Empresario of Texas* (New Haven: Yale University Press, 1999), 146–49, 195–96, 210, 232, 236–39; and Manuel de Mier y Terán to Guadalupe Victoria, Mar. 28, 1828, in *Texas by Terán: The Diary Kept by General Manuel de Mier y Terán on His 1828 Inspection of Texas*, ed. Jack Jackson, trans. John Wheat (Austin: University of Texas Press, 2000), 33–34. For the distribution of Anglo colonies, see Reséndez, *Changing National Identities*, 38. For Wichita villages as Comanche staging areas and for the ethnic composition of Comanche war parties, see Anderson, *Indian Southwest*, 259–60.

28. Elozúa to Mateo Ahumada, Nov. 12, 1825, Andrade to Elozúa, Nov. 20, 1825, BA 85:860–61, 86:792–93; Gary Clayton Anderson, *The Conquest of Texas: Ethnic Cleansing in the Promised Land, 1820–1875* (Norman: University of Oklahoma Press, 2005), 49; Lester G. Bugbee, "The Texas Frontier, 1820–1825," *Publications of the Southern History Association* 4 (Mar. 1900): 119 and n34; Austin to Ahumada, Sep. 8, 1825, Austin to Saucedo, July 17 and Aug. 14, 1826, James Kerr to Austin, Feb. 26, 1827, and Bustamante to Austin, June 19, 1827, in *Austin Papers*, ed., Barker, 2:1196–97, 1374, 1424 1607, 1660; Berlandier, *Indians*, 66, 120; and Kavanagh, *Comanche Political History*, 231–34. Quote is from Jean Louis Berlandier, *Journey to Mexico: During the Years 1826 to 1834*, trans. Sheila M. Ohlendorf, Josette M. Bigelow, and Mary M. Standifer, 2 vols. (Austin: Texas State Historical Association and University of Texas Press, 1980), 2:343.

29. Elozúa to Ruíz, July 21, 1831, José María García to Elozúa, May 5, 1832, Juan José Hernández to José Antonio de la Garza, Sep. 22, 1832, Ramón Músquiz to Eca y Músquiz, Sep. 22 and Nov. 19, 1832, and Placido Benavides to Juan Nepomuceno Seguín, Aug. 22, 1834, BA 143:82, 149:789–90, 153:307–11, 349–50, 154:21–22, 162:932; Matthew McLaurine Babcock, "Trans-national Trade Routes and Diplomacy: Comanche Expansion, 1760–1846" (M.A. thesis, University of New Mexico, 2001), 99, 101; Domingo de Ugartechea to Martin Perfecto de Cos, Aug. 8, 1835, in *The Papers of the Texas Revolution, 1835–1836*, ed. John H. Jenkins, 10 vols. (Austin: Presidial, 1973), 1:321; and J. B. Wilkinson, *Laredo and the Rio Grande Frontier* (Austin: Jenkins, 1975), 147. Quotes are from "Fight between Lind and the Comanchees," in *The Papers of Mirabeau Buonaparte Lamar*, ed. Charles Adams Gulick, Jr., et al., 6 vols. (1920–27; reprint, Austin: Pemberton, 1968), 3:460; and Tadeo Ortiz de Ayala, Report to the President on the Conditions in Texas, Feb. 2, 1833,

in "Tadeo Ortiz de Ayala and the Colonization of Texas, 1822–1833," ed. Louise Kelly and Mattie Austin Hatcher, *SHQ* 29 (Apr. 1929): 331.

30. For the revival of ranching, see Weber, *Mexican Frontier,* 209. For raids, see Terán to Elozúa, Aug. 2, 1830, Principal commander of Coahuila and Texas to the commanders of the companies of Río Grande, Aguaverde, Bavia, Bahía, the major at the Plaza of Béxar, and the commander at Tenoxtitlan, Sep. 4, 1830, Mariano Cosío to Elozúa, Aug. 17, 1831, and Elozúa to Ruíz, Sep. 14, 1831, BA 133:37–39, 134:134, 143:548–49, 857–59. Quotes are from Berlandier, *Indians,* 122–23.

31. Sánchez, "Trip to Texas," 283; Alone Howren, "Causes and Origin of the Decree of April 6, 1830," *SHQ* 16 (Apr. 1913): 378–422; Almonte, "Statistical Report," 184, 192–93; Edward L. Miller, *New Orleans and the Texas Revolution* (College Station: Texas A&M University Press, 2004), 19–36; Weber, *Mexican Frontier,* 166–67, 228; and Reséndez, *Changing National Identities,* 38–40, 105. For the failure of Anglo colonies as a barrier against Comanche incursions, see Ortiz, Report, 330–34.

32. Berlandier, *Journey to Mexico,* 1:270, 2:412–13, 440, 542; Weber, *Mexican Frontier,* 89, 92; William Kennedy, *Texas: The Rise, Progress, and Prospects of the Republic of Texas,* 2 vols. (London: William Cloves and Sons, 1841), 2:44; Ortiz, Report, 314, 326; and Gilberto Miguel Hinojosa, *A Borderlands Town in Transition: Laredo, 1755–1870* (College Station: Texas A&M University Press, 1983), 38–46, 123. Quotes are from Sánchez, "Trip to Texas," 257; Anonymous, *Texas in 1837: An Anonymous, Contemporary Narrative,* ed. Andrew Forest Muir (1958; reprint, Austin: University of Texas Press, 1988), 110; Berlandier, *Journey to Mexico,* 2:429; Ortiz, Report, 314; and Berlandier, *Indians,* 119.

33. "Petition Addressed by the Illustrious Ayuntamiento of the City of Béxar to the Honorable Legislature of the State: To Make Known the Ills Which Afflict the Towns of Texas and the Grievances They Have Suffered since Their Union with Coahuila," in *Troubles in Texas, 1832: A Tejano Viewpoint from San Antonio,* ed. and trans. David J. Weber and Conchita Hassell Winn (Dallas: DeGolyer Library, 1983), 17.

34. For discussions on Tejanos' interests and shifting loyalties, see Jesús F. de la Teja, ed., *A Revolution Remembered: The Memoirs and Selected Correspondence of Juan N. Sequín* (Austin, Tex.: State House, 1991), 12–25; Andrés Tijerina, "Under the Mexican Flag," in *Tejano Journey,* ed. Gerald E. Poyo (Austin: University of Texas Press, 1996), 36–37; Stephen L. Hardin, "Efficient in the Cause," in ibid., 51; Weber, *Mexican Frontier,* 176, 251–55; and Reséndez, *Changing National Identities,* 158–59. Tellingly, the mounting Indian raids and the national government's inability to stop them also motivated Laredo's belated decision in 1838 to join the federalist revolutionary movement. See Hinojosa, *Borderlands Town,* 53.

35. For the assumed Mexican failure to form functioning governmental systems as a justification for the Anglo-driven revolt, see T. R. Fehrenbach, *Lone Star: A History of Texas and Texans* (1968; reprint, New York: Collier, 1980), 155–61. For a comprehensive analysis of Anglo-Texan views of the Mexicans, see James Ernest Crisp, "Anglo-Texan Attitudes toward the Mexican, 1821–1845" (Ph.D. diss., Yale University, 1976). See also James E. Crisp, *Sleuthing the Alamo: Davy Crockett's Last Stance and Other Mysteries of the Texas Revolution* (New York: Oxford University Press, 2004), esp. 38–42. For a study emphasizing the racist, vitriolic nature of the Anglo-Texan attitudes toward Mexicans and Indians, see Anderson, *Conquest of Texas,* esp. 33–42. Quote is from William H. Wharton, *Texas: A Brief Account of the Origin, Progress and Present State of the Colo-*

nial Settlements of Texas; Together with an Exposition of the Causes which have induced the Existing War with Mexico (1836; reprint, Austin: Pemberton, 1964), 3–5.

36. For an incisive analysis of how Anglo-Texans used Mexican weakness in the face of Indian power as a means to invalidate Mexico's claims to Texas soil, see Brian DeLay, "Independent Indians and the U.S.–Mexican War," *American Historical Review* 112 (Feb. 2007): 48–53. For Houston, see Anderson, *Conquest of Texas*, 112. Quote is from Mary Austin Holley, *Texas* (Lexington, Ky.: Clarke, 1836), 299. The idea that the supposed underutilization of Texas by Mexicans legitimized the Anglo takeover has proved remarkably resilient among Holley's successors. See Gerald E. Poyo and Gilberto M. Hinojosa, "Spanish Texas and Borderlands Historiography in Transition: Implications for United States History," *JAH* 75 (Sep. 1988): 400.

37. For Spanish plans, see, e.g., François Luis Hector Carondelet, barón de Carondelet to Duque de Alcudia, Jan. 8, 1796, in *Before Lewis and Clark*, ed. Nasatir, 2:392–93; and N. Salcedo to Joaquín Real del Alencaster, Jan. 16, 1806, *PV*, 443–45.

38. Charles Dehault Delassus to Sebastián Nicolás de Bari Calvo de la Puerta, marqués de Casa Calvo, Aug. 10, 1804, in *Before Lewis and Clark*, 2:742–45 (quote is from p. 744). Also see David J. Weber, *Taos Trappers: The Fur Trade in the Far Southwest, 1540–1846* (Norman: University of Oklahoma Press, 1968), 35. Spain's thin presence in the interior became an acute problem for Spanish officials when Spain and the United States were drawn into a bitter dispute over the extent of the Louisiana Purchase. Unable to claim any effective rule over Texas beyond San Antonio and Nacogdoches, Spanish administrators relied on history, commissioning José Antonio Pichardo to prepare a detailed study of the historical boundary between Texas and Louisiana. Pichardo's massive 5,127-page treatise helped bolster Spanish claims to Texas, but the argument was based on a past and largely vanished presence and was a poor compensation for the lack of a present one on the ground. In 1819, after tortured negotiations, Spain and the United States agreed on a boundary in the Adams-Onís Treaty. Spain retained Texas—the border traced the Sabine, Red, and Arkansas rivers to the Rockies—but only by ceding the Floridas to the United States. See Weber, *Spanish Frontier*, 295, 299–300.

39. For New Mexico's recovery, see Ross Frank, *From Settler to Citizen: New Mexican Economic Development and the Creation of Vecino Society, 1750–1820* (Berkeley: University of California Press, 2000), 119–56. This innovative study of New Mexico's late eighteenth- and early nineteenth-century economic growth emphasizes the role of the Bourbon Reforms, but it also underscores the crucial significance of the Comanche alliance.

40. For Comanche visits to Santa Fe, see Kavanagh, *Comanche Political History*, 180. Quote is from Fernando Chacón, Report, in "The Chacón Economic Report of 1803," ed. Marc Simmons, *NMHR* 60 (Jan. 1985): 87.

41. For new border villages, *genízaros*, and Spanish plans, see Juan Agustín de Morfí, "Desórdenes que se advierten en el Nuevo México [1778]," AGN:HI 25, 47R–48V; Russell M. Magnaghi, "The Genízaro Experiment in Spanish New Mexico," in *Spain and the Plains: Myths and Realities of Spanish Exploration and Settlement on the Great Plains*, ed. Ralph H. Vigil, Frances W. Kaye, and John R. Wunder (Niwot: University Press of Colorado, 1994), 119–20; Frances Levine, "Historical Settlement Patterns and Land-Use Practices on the Pecos Frontier," in *Investigations at Sites 48 and 77, Santa Rosa Lake, Guadalupe County, New Mexico: An Inquiry into the Nature of Archeological Reality*, ed. Frances Levine and Joseph C. Winter (Albuquerque: Office of Con-

tract Archeology, University of New Mexico, 1987), 556–75; John L. Kessell, *Kiva, Cross, and Crown: The Pecos Indians and New Mexico, 1540–1840* (Washington, D.C.: National Park Service, 1979), 434–59; Charles L. Kenner, *The Comanchero Frontier: A History of New Mexican–Plains Indian Relations* (1969; reprint, Norman: University of Oklahoma Press, 1994), 63–66; Richard L. Nostrand, *The Hispano Homeland* (Norman: University of Oklahoma Press, 1996), 71–97; and Brooks, *Captives and Cousins*, 195–98, 221. The eastward shift of New Mexico's commercial focus contributed to the decline and fall of Pecos, which became complete in 1838 when the remaining inhabitants abandoned the village.

42. For comanchero trade, see Alencaster to N. Salcedo, Jan. 4, 1806, *PV*, 441; José Manrique to N. Salcedo, Mar. 27, 1810, Manuel Baca to Manrique, June 1, 1813, Case against Josef Manuel González and Juan Domingo Cordero, June 8–Aug. 18, 1814, Alberto Maynez, Journal of Events, Apr. 1–Dec. 1, 1815, Pablo Lucero to Maynez, Aug. 16, 1815, and Examination of Manuel Rivera, Oct. 8, 1819, SANM II 17:61–63, 731–33, 992–1034, 18:29–32, 137–38, 19:987–90 (T-2308, 2492, 2542, 2585, 2619, 2850); Jacob Fowler, *The Journal of Jacob Fowler*, ed. Elliott Coues (1898; reprint, Minneapolis: Ross and Haines, 1965), 64; and Paul D. Friedman, *Final Report of History and Oral History Studies of the Fort Carson Piñon Canyon Maneuver Area, Las Animas County, Colorado* (Denver: Colorado State Office, Bureau of Land Management, 1985), 38.
43. Burnet, "Letters," 122.
44. Chacón, Report, 87. New Mexico's trade with other Mexican provinces, too, may have been heavily dependent on Comanche commerce, for buffalo robes and other animal skins constituted one of the colony's chief exports. See Weber, *Taos Trappers*, 30–31.
45. For the use of the Comanche language in New Mexico's eastern border, see Kavanagh, *Comanche Political History*, 180–81; and Kessell, *Kiva, Cross, and Crown*, 439. For ciboleros, see H. Bailey Carroll and J. Villasana Haggard, trans., *Three New Mexico Chronicles: The Exposición of Don Pedro Bautista Pino 1812; the Ojeada of Lic. Antonio Barreiro 1832; and the additions by Don José Agustín de Escudero, 1849* (Albuquerque: Quivira Society, 1942), 101–2; and Kenner, *Comanchero Frontier*, 100–7. Quote is from Chacón, Report, 84.
46. Gregg, *Commerce of the Prairies*, 67; and Fowler, *Journal*, 72. Also see Curtis Marez, "Signifying Spain, Becoming Comanche, Making Mexicans: Indian Captivity and the History of Chicana/o Performance," *American Quarterly* 53 (June 2001): 274–75.
47. Fernando de la Concha, Instructions drawn up by Colonel Don Fernando de la Concha, former governor of the Province of New Mexico, so that his successor, the Lieutenant Colonel Don Fernando Chacón, may adapt what part of it that may seem to him suitable for the advantage, tranquility, and development of the aforesaid province, in "Notes and Documents: Advice on Governing New Mexico, 1794," ed. and trans. Donald E. Worcester, *NMHR* 24 (July 1949): 243.
48. Concha, Instructions, 243–44, 250 (emphasis mine). See also Joaquín Real del Alencaster's report that the "residents of the Río Arriba and jurisdiction of La Cañada . . . continually, in spite of the restriction, live among them [Comanches], and are ones of worst conduct in all the province." See Alencaster to N. Salcedo, Jan. 4, 1806, *PV*, 441.
49. Proceedings into the Conduct of Vecinos of the Districts of Pecos and Cañada [1805], Maynez to the alcaldes, June 14, 1808, N. Salcedo to Maynez, Aug. 10, 1808, and Manrique to N. Salcedo, Mar. 27, 1810, SANM II 15:1043–98, 16:531, 592–93, 17:61–63 (T-1930, 2114, 2144, 2308); Frances Levine, "Economic Perspectives on the Comanchero Trade," in *Farmers, Hunters, and Colonists: Interaction between the Southwest and the Southern Plains*, ed. Katherine A. Spielmann (Tucson:

University of Arizona Press, 1991), 158–62; and Frances Levine and Martha Doty Freeman, *A Study of Documentary and Archaeological Evidence for Comanchero Activity in the Texas Panhandle* (Austin: Texas Historical Commission, 1982), 6.

50. Juan Lobato to Facundo Melgares, Sep. 22, 1818, and Juan de Dios Peña to Melgares, Nov. 4, 1818, SANM II 19:302–4, 433–34 (T-2750, 2768); and Melgares to Alexo Garcia Conde, Oct. 8, 1818, in "Documents Bearing upon the Northern Frontier of New Mexico, 1818–1819," ed. Alfred B. Thomas, *NMHR* 4 (Apr. 1929): 156.

51. Anonymous, Notes Concerning the Province of New Mexico Collected on My Mission to the West, in "Anonymous Description of New Mexico, 1818," ed. Alfred B. Thomas, *SHQ* 33 (July 1929): 62.

52. Manuel Durán to Melgares, Aug. 21, 1821, and Melgares to the alcaldes, Aug. 25, 1821, SANM II 20:735–36, 740–41 (T-3008, 3010); and Kavanagh, *Comanche Political History*, 201.

53. Weber, *Mexican Frontier*, 243; Kenner, *Comanchero Frontier*, 72–73; Manuel Martínez to Manuel Armijo, Sep. 22, 1827, Mariano Martín to Armijo, Sep. 23, 1827, Juan José Arocha, José Francisco Ruíz, and José Cavallero to José Antonio Chávez, Aug. 31, 1828, Chavéz, Diary, Aug. 2, 1829, Chavéz to José Antonio Vizcarra, Jan. 15, 1830, and Manuel Antonio Baca to Chavéz, Aug. 27, 1830, NMA 1827/1145, 1827/1175, 1828/943, 1829/463, 1830/99, 1830/636; Chavéz, Arocha, and Ruíz, Report, July 26, 1829, José J. Calvo, Circular, Oct. 16, 1831, and Chavéz to Vizcarra, Oct. 23, 1831, MANM 9:866–68, 13:483, 488; and Carroll and Haggard, *Three New Mexico Chronicles*, 77–78.

54. José María Ronquillo, Report, Sep. 17, 1831, Chávez to Vizcarra, Oct. 23, 1831, Ronquillo to ayudante inspector, Oct. 31, 1832, and June 28, 1833, and Mariano Martínez to departmental assembly, June 27, 1845, MANM 13:559–79, 13:488, 14:914, 930–31, 38:740–45; and Charles Bent to William Medill, Nov. 10, 1846, in *California and New Mexico: Message from the President of the United States Communicating Information Called For by a Resolution of the Senate* (New York: Arno, 1976), 184–85. For the importance of Comanche trade for New Mexico's subsistence economy during the Mexican period, see Antonio Narvona, "Report," Apr. 8, 1827, in Carroll and Haggard, *Three New Mexico Chronicles*, 90. For Navajo raids, see Gregg, *Commerce*, 200. For the impact of Santa Fe trade in New Mexico, see Weber, *Mexican Frontier*, 122–46; and Reséndez, *Changing National Identities*, 93–123. Quote is from jefe politico to comandante principal, Sep. 23, 1831, cited in Kenner, *Comanche Frontier*, 80.

55. For the Mexican nation-building project and the Chimayó Rebellion, see Weber, *Mexican Frontier*, 242–72; Reséndez, *Changing National Identities*, 56–92, 171–96; "An Account of the Rebellion," in Janet Lecompte, *A Rebellion in Río Arriba* (Albuquerque: University of New Mexico Press, 1985), 91–104; and James F. Brooks, "'This Evil Extends Especially . . . to the Feminine Sex': Negotiating Captivity in the New Mexico Borderlands," *Feminist Studies* 22 (Summer 1996): 293–94.

56. Albert Pike, *Prose Sketches and Poems*, ed. David J. Weber (College Station: Texas A&M University Press, 1987), 37, 40–42; Gregg, *Commerce*, 257; and James William Abert, *Expedition to the Southwest: An 1845 Reconnaissance of Colorado, New Mexico, Texas, and Oklahoma* (1846; reprint, Lincoln: University of Nebraska Press, 1999), 51, 71. Quote is from Gregg, *Commerce*, 436–37.

57. Armijo to Ministerio de Guerra y Marina, Sep. 7, 1840, NMA 1840/140; Armijo to Juan Almonte, Mar. 3, 1841, MANM 27:1116–20; Isidro Vizcaya Canales, ed., *La invasión de los indios bárbaros*

al noreste de Mexico en los años de 1840 y 1841 (Monterrey: Instituto Technológico y de Estudios Superiores de Monterrey, 1968), 257; and Weber, *Mexican Frontier*, 114–15. For an illuminating account of New Mexico's economic dependence on Comanche trade, see Donaciano Vigil, *Arms, Indians, and the Mismanagement of New Mexico*, ed. and trans. David J. Weber (El Paso: University of Texas at El Paso, 1986), 5.

58. List of Indians who Arrived in This Capital of Santa Fe, July 31, 1844, and Martínez to departmental assembly, June 27, 1845, MANM 37:651–52, 38:740–45; and Kavanagh, *Comanche Political History*, 208. Also see Reséndez, *Changing National Identities*, 225n77.

59. Howard Roberts Lamar, *The Far Southwest, 1846–1912: A Territorial History* (New Haven: Yale University Press, 1966), 42–55 (the quote "unconscious process of economic conquest" is from p. 47); Weber, *Mexican Frontier*, 190–95; and Reséndez, *Changing National Identities*, 81–83, 124–45, 171–96. Like Mexican Texas, Mexican New Mexico did eventually hand out massive land grants to foreign-born residents, but that process did not start until the early 1840s, and most of the lands remained unoccupied during the Mexican era. Quote "mongrel race" is from *Telegraph and Texas Register*, Mar. 23, 1842.

60. For the Texas Revolution and the Republic of Texas in general, see Weber, *Mexican Frontier*, 242–55; Reséndez, *Changing National Identities*, 146–70; and Fehrenbach, *Lone Star*, 247–67.

61. For Houston's scheme, see Anderson, *Conquest of Texas*, 122–23. Quote is from Sam Houston to the Comanche chiefs, Dec. 3, 1836, in *The Writings of Sam Houston, 1813–1863*, ed. Amelia W. Williams and Eugene C. Barker, 8 vols. (Austin: University of Texas Press, 1938–43), 7:5.

62. T. R. Fehrenbach, *Comanches: The Destruction of a People* (New York: Da Capo, 1974), 283–92, 305–9; *Telegraph and Texas Register*, July 21, 1838; R. A. Irion to Houston, Mar. 4, 1838, and "Treaty between Texas and the Comanche Indians," May 29, 1838, *IPTS*, 1:42–45, 50–52 (quote is from p. 44); and William Preston Johnston, *The Life of Albert Sidney Johnson, Embracing His Services in the Armies of the United States, the Republic of Texas, and Confederate States* (New York: D. Appleton, 1878), 89.

63. H. Allen Anderson, "The Delaware and Shawnee Indians and the Republic of Texas, 1820–1845," *SHQ* 94 (Oct. 1990): 243–46; John H. Jenkins and Kenneth Kesselus, *Edward Burleson, Texas Frontier Leader* (Austin: Jenkins, 1990), 183, 211; Anderson, *Conquest of Texas*, 173–81; J. W. Benedict, "Diary of a Campaign against the Comanches," *SHQ* 32 (Apr. 1929): 306; and Crisp, "Anglo-Texan Attitudes," chs. 2, 3, and 4.

64. H. W. Karnes to Albert Sidney Johnston, Jan. 10, 1840, and Johnston to W. S. Fisher, *IPTS*, 1:101, 105–6 (quotes are from pp. 101 and 105); and *Journals of the House of Representatives of the Republic of Texas, Fifth Congress, Appendix* (Austin: Gazette Office, 1841), 136–39.

65. Donaly E. Brice, *The Great Comanche Raid: Boldest Indian Attack of the Texas Republic* (Austin: Eakin, 1987), 27–48; and Anderson, *Conquest of Texas*, 183–91.

66. For the costs and the impact of Comanche war on Texas economy, see W. Eugene Hollon, *The Southwest: Old and New* (Lincoln: University of Nebraska Press, 1961), 128. For Mexican agents in Comanchería and rumors of a Mexican–Plains Indian alliance, see H. W. Karnes to Johnston, Jan. 10, 1840, *IPTS*, 1:43; and Crisp, "Anglo-Texan Attitudes," 116–17, 121. For peace sentiment among Texans, see, e.g., Johnston, *Life*, 88. For Houston's policies, see Anna Muckleroy, "The Indian Policy of the Republic of Texas," *SHQ* 25 (Jan. 1923): 200–2; Kavanagh, *Comanche Political History*, 256–78, 284–85; and Anderson, *Conquest of Texas*, 195–211. For captive exchanges,

see Michael L. Tate, "Comanche Captives: People between Two Worlds," *CO* 72 (Fall 1994): 247–51.

67. J. C. Eldredge to Houston, Dec. 8, 1843, and Mopechucope to Houston, Mar. 21, 1843, *IPTS*, 1:268–73, 2:6–9 (quote "from thence" is from p. 8). Quote "bones of their brothers" is from Pierce Mason Butler, "Report," Apr. 29, 1843, cited in Anderson, *Conquest of Texas*, 203.
68. "Minutes of Council at the Falls of the Brazos," Oct. 7, 1844, *IPTS*, 2:103–14 (quotes are from pp. 109–11).
69. "A Treaty Signed in Council at Tehuacana Creek," Oct. 9, 1844, *IPTS*, 2:114–19. Texas officials later treated the trading house line as effective border line. See, e.g., Thomas G. Western to Neighbors, July 18, 1845, *IPTS*, 2:292–93.
70. Western to Benjamin Sloat and L. H. Williams, Apr. 9, 1845, Western to Williams, Apr. 29, 1845, Western to A. Coleman, May 11, 1845, Western to Williams, May 12, 1845, Western to Sloat, May 12, 1845, "List of Invoices of Goods Sent to Trading House on Tehuacana Creek," Feb. 23–Dec. 25, 1844, Jan. 29–May 16, 1845, "Minutes of a Council Held at Tehuacana Creek and Appointment of Daniel D. Gulp as Secretary," Aug. 27, 1845, "Report of a Council with the Comanche Indians," Nov. 23, 1845, and "Treaty with the Comanche Indians," May 15, 1846, *IPTS*, 2:217, 225, 236–40, 242–48, 334–44, 410–12, 3:43–51; Fehrenbach, *Comanches*, 361; and Neighbors to Medill, Nov. 18, 1847, 30th Cong., 1st sess., S. Rpt. 171, 9–10. Several Lipan bands did move in the late 1840s into Comanchería, where they fell under Comanche control. See Neighbors to Medill, Oct. 23, 1848, 30th Cong., 1st sess., H. Ex. Doc. 1, 598.
71. "Report of Standing Committee on Indian Affairs," Oct. 12, 1837, *IPTS*, 1:24; and Anonymous, *Texas in 1837*, 110–11.
72. For early raids and Apache captives, see Pedro Vial and Francisco Xavier Chaves, Diary, in "Inside the Comanchería, 1785: The Diary of Pedro Vial and Francisco Xavier Chaves," ed. Elizabeth A. H. John, trans. Adán Benavides, Jr., *SHQ* 88 (July 1994): 51; David B. Adams, "Embattled Borderland: Northern Nuevo León and the Indios Bárbaros, 1686–1870," *SHQ* 95 (Oct. 1991): 211–13; N. Salcedo to Herrera, Dec. 18, 1811, BA 49:756–57; and Fernando de la Concha to Jacobo Ugarte y Loyola, Nov. 20, 1788, SANM II 12:108 (T-1024).
73. Babcock, "Trans-national Trade Routes," 65–71; Berlandier, *Indians*, 133–34 (quote on "bitter warfare" is from p. 134); and García Conde to Melgares, May 11, 1819, SANM II 19:711–13 (T-2819). The longer quote is from Anonymous, Notes, 64.
74. The escalation of the Comanche raiding has been pieced together from the following sources: Severino Martinez to Bartolomé Baca, June 10, 1825, in Ralph Emerson Twitchell, *The Spanish Archives of New Mexico*, 2 vols. (New York: Arno, 1976), 1:347; Baron de Bastrop to Austin, Mar. 19, 1825, in *Austin Papers*, ed. Barker, 2:1058; Cuauhtémoc José Velasco Avila, "La amenaza comanche en la frontera mexicana, 1800–1841" (Ph.D. diss., Universidad Nacional Autonóma de México, 1998), 133, 178, 267; Berlandier, *Journey to Mexico*, 2:542, 580–81; Vizcaya Canales, ed., *La invasión*, 40, 43–53; William B. Griffen, *Utmost Good Faith: Patterns of Apache-Mexican Hostilities in Northern Chihuahua Border Warfare, 1821–1848* (Albuquerque: University of New Mexico Press, 1988), 138–46; Wilkinson, *Laredo*, 117–21, 127–28, 144–47; David M. Vigness, "Indian Raids on the Lower Rio Grande, 1836–1837," *SHQ* 59 (July 1955): 14–23; Ralph A. Smith, "The Comanche Bridge between Oklahoma and Mexico, 1843–1844," *CO* 39 (Spring 1961): 54–69; Ralph A. Smith, "Indians in American-Mexican Relations before the War of 1846," *Hispanic*

American Historical Review 43 (Feb. 1963): 35–36, 40–42; Ralph A. Smith, *Borderlander: The Life of James Kirker, 1793–1862* (Norman: University of Oklahoma Press, 1999), 106; Weber, *Mexican Frontier,* 86; Isidro Vizcaya Canales, *Incursiones de indios al noreste en el México independiente, 1821–1885* (Monterrey: Archivo General del Estado de Nuevo León, 1995), 10–20; Martha Rodríguez, *Historias de resistencia y exterminio: los indios de Coahuila durante el siglo XIX* (Tlalpan: Centro de Investigaciones y Estudios Superiores en Antropología Social, 1995), 88–92; and Rodríguez, *La guerra,* 112–29. Quotes are from Berlandier, *Indians,* 123; and Gregg, *Commerce,* 436. For territorial claims, see Irion to Houston, Mar. 14, 1838, *IPTS,* 1:44. Quote is from Report of G. W. Bonnell, Nov. 3, 1838, reprinted in 30th Cong., 1st sess., S. Rpt. 171, 43.

75. For the importance of distance and distinctive zones of conflict and peace for empires, see Charles S. Maier, *Among Empires: American Ascendancy and Its Predecessors* (Cambridge: Harvard University Press, 2006), esp. 20–23.

76. Marcy, *Adventure,* 173.

77. Miguel Ramos Arizpe to Lucas Alamán, Aug. 1, 1830, Herbert E. Bolton Papers, Carton 40, no. 673, no page, Bancroft Library, University of California at Berkeley; Smith, "Comanche Bridge," 63–69; and Gregg, *Commerce,* 436. Quote is from Thomas J. Farnham, *Travels in the Great Western Prairies,* vols. 28 and 29 of *Early Western Travels, 1748–1846,* ed. Reuben Gold Thwaites (Cleveland: Arthur H. Clark, 1906), 28:151.

78. For traders promoting raids, see Comer, *Ritual Ground,* 14. For Comanche war parties collecting supplies in Texas, see Western to Coleman, May 11, 1845, and Sloat to Western, July 24, 1845, *IPTS,* 2:236–37, 298–99. For Mexican views, see Valerio-Jiménez, "*Indios Barbaros,*" 37. For New Mexicans in Comanche war parties, see Griffen, *Utmost Good Faith,* 139, 159. Quotes are from James Bowie to Henry Rueg, Aug. 3, 1835, in *Papers of the Texas Revolution,* ed. Jenkins, 1:302; Smith, "Indians in American-Mexican Relations," 46; and Sloat to Western, Aug. 18, 1845, *IPTS,* 2:325.

79. For the Comanche trail system, see Smith, "Comanche Bridge," 54–56; and Smith, "Indians in American-Mexican Relations," 35–36.

80. Marcy, *Adventure,* 160; Smith, *Borderlander,* 68, 106; and Smith, "Comanche Bridge," 59. Quote is from John Russell Bartlett, *Personal Narrative of Explorations and Incidents in Texas, New Mexico, California, Sonora, and Chihuahua,* 2 vols. (New York: D. Appleton, 1854), 2:386.

81. For the planning and execution of raids, see Neighbors to Medill, Sep. 14, 1847, 30th Cong., 1st sess., S. Ex. Doc. 1, 902; Bartlett, *Personal Narrative,* 2:447–48; Smith, "Comanche Bridge," 54–69; Rodríguez, *La guerra,* 121, 129; Velasco Avila, "La amenaza comanche," 130–31; and Babcock, "Trans-national Trade Routes," 82–83. Quote is from Berlandier, *Indians,* 82.

82. *El Fanal de Chihuahua,* Jan. 25, 1835, 67; Griffen, *Utmost Good Faith,* 143; Gregg, *Commerce,* 250; Valerio-Jiménez, "*Indios Barbaros,*" 37–40, 185; Joseph Milton Nance, *After San Jacinto: The Texas-Mexican Frontier, 1836–1841* (Austin: University of Texas Press, 1963), 45; Hinojosa, *Borderlands Town,* 50–53; Vigness, "Indian Raids," 16–23; Mora-Torres, *Mexican Border,* 39; and Juan Manuel Maldonado to Arista, Nov. 12, 1840, comandancia general de Nuevo León to minister of war and marine, Dec. 6, 1840, and Maldonado to comandancia general e inspección de Nuevo León, Dec. 13, 1840, in *La invasión,* ed. Vizcaya Canales, 141–43, 156–59, 165–66. Quotes are from Gregg, *Commerce,* 250; and Valerio-Jiménez, "*Indios Barbaros,*" 38.

83. Rodríguez, *La guerra,* 111; Smith, "Comanche Bridge," 63–68; Smith, "Indians in American-

Mexican Relations," 49; James Hobbs, *Wild Life in the Far West: Personal Adventures of a Border Mountain Man* (1873; reprint, Glorieta, N. Mex.: Rio Grande, 1969), 32, 37; and John Miller Morris, *El Llano Estacado: Exploration and Imagination of the High Plains of Texas and New Mexico, 1513–1860* (Austin: Texas State Historical Association, 1997), 301, 303.

84. DeLay, "Independent Indians," 53–55; Smith, "Comanche Bridge," 59–68; Velasco Avila, "La amenaza comanche," 169–72; Víctor Orozco, comp., *Las Guerras indias en la historia de Chihuahua: Antología* (Ciudad Juárez: Universidad Autónoma de Ciudad Juárez, 1992), 201–73; and Weber, *Mexican Frontier*, 50.

85. Rodríguez, *La guerra*, 111; "Circular del Gobierno acerca de la guerra con los bárbaros," Oct. 31, 1831, in *Reseñas históricas del estado de Chihuahua*, ed. José M. Ponce de León (Chihuahua: Imprenta del Gobierno, 1910), 261–62; Smith, "Comanche Bridge," 61; Weber, *Mexican Frontier*, 109–15; Adams, "Embattled Borderland," 215–16; Berlandier, *Indians*, 30; and George F. Ruxton, *Adventures in Mexico and the Rocky Mountains* (London: John Murray, 1861), 102.

86. Anonymous, *Texas in 1837*, 110. Quote is from Gregg, *Commerce*, 203n10.

87. Ralph A. Smith, "The Bounty Wars of the West and Mexico," *Great Plains Journal* 28 (1989): 102–21; Smith, *Borderlander*, 75–171, 225–34; Kavanagh, *Comanche Political History*, 201–10, 328–31; and L. R. Bailey, *Indian Slave Trade in the Southwest* (1966; reprint, Los Angeles: Westernlore, 1973), 50–51.

88. For Mexico City's responses, see, e.g., Valerio-Jiménez, "*Indios Bárbaros*," 37–38.

89. Ibid., 36–38.

90. Rodríguez, *La guerra*, 148.

91. "Treaty with the Comanche," Oct. 8, 1826, in *Documents*, comp. Deloria and DeMallie, 153–55 (quote is from p. 154); Ramón Músquiz to Béxar ayuntamiento, May 1834, and Navarro Angel to Béxar ayuntamiento, Aug. 27, 1835, BA 161:779–80, 166:470; Matthew Babcock, "Trans-national Raid and Trade Routes: Comanche Expansion from the Rio Grande to Durango, 1821–1846" (manuscript in author's possession); Rodríguez, *La guerra*, 148; and "Convenios celebrados por este Estado y los Generales de las Nacion Comanche y la Caihua, in *Reseñas históricas*, 270–72.

92. For treaties, see Rodríguez, *La guerra*, 151–55; and Martha Rodríguez, "Los tratados de paz en la guerra entre 'bárbaros' y 'civilizados' (Coahuila 1840–1880)," *Historia y Grafía* 10 (Jan.–June 1998): 73–77. For Arista's decree, see Babcock, "Trans-national Trade Routes and Diplomacy," 114. Quote is from "Report of a Council," 412. The treaty violation Santa Anna referred to may have been a fight near Matamoros in late 1844 or early 1845 in which Santa Anna's band "had been whipped by the Mexicans." See Neighbors to Western, Jan. 14, 1845, *IPTS*, 2:167.

93. Comanches often carried stolen Mexican stock directly to Bent's Fort and other market outlets in the north. See, e.g., G. Cooke, Journal of an expedition of a detachment of U.S. Dragoons from Fort Leavenworth to protect the Annual Caravan of traders, from Missouri to the Mexican boundary on the road to Santa Fe . . . Commencing May 27th, and ending July 21st, 1843, in "Journal of the Santa Fe Trail," ed. William E. Connelly, *Mississippi Valley Historical Review* 12 (Sep. 1925): 240. Quote is from Marcy, *Adventure*, 173.

94. For escalating raiding, see Smith, "Comanche Bridge," 57–68; Ralph A. Smith, "The Comanches' Foreign War: Fighting Head Hunters in the Tropics," *Great Plains Journal*, 24–25 (1985–86): 22–27; Adams, "Embattled Borderland," 208–11, 215–16; Nance, *After San Jacinto*, 189, 443; and Vito Alessio Robles, *Coahuila y Texas: Desde la consumacion de la independencia hasta el*

tratado de paz de Guadalupe Hidalgo, 2 vols. (Mexico, 1946), 2:235–36; William Bollaert, *William Bollaert's Texas*, ed. W. Eugene Hollon and Ruth Lapham Butler (Norman: University of Oklahoma Press for the Newberry Library, 1956), 360; Vizcaya Canales, ed., *La invasión;* and Western to Coleman, May 11, 1845, and Sloat to Western, Aug. 18, 1845, *IPTS*, 2:236, 325. Quote is from Bent to Medill, Nov. 10, 1846, in *California and New Mexico*, 184.

95. Quotes are from James Josiah Webb, *Adventures in the Santa Fe Trade, 1844–1847*, ed. Ralph P. Bieber (Lincoln: University of Nebraska Press, 1995), 241; and Ruxton, *Adventures*, 78, 101–2, 117, 125.

96. Rodríguez, *Historias de resistencia*, 92; and Max L. Moorhead, *New Mexico's Royal Road: Trade and Travel on the Chihuahua Trail* (Norman: University of Oklahoma Press, 1958), 147–48. Quotes are from Gregg, *Commerce*, 203; *El Registro Oficial, periodico del gobierno del departamento de Durango*, IV, no. 301, Dec. 29, 1844, cited in Smith, "Comanche Bridge," 69; José Fuentes Mares, . . . *Y México se refugio en el desierto* (Mexico City: Editorial Jus, S. A., 1954), 137, cited in Smith, "Indians in American-Mexican Relations," 62; and Ruxton, *Adventures*, 102.

97. For trade, see Ugartechea to the governor of Monclova, Feb. 8, 1835, and secretary of relations to Agustin Viesca, June 10, 1835, in *Papers of the Texas Revolution*, ed. Jenkins, 1:18, 149; Smith, *Borderlander*, 47–48, 106–8; and Kavanagh, *Comanche Political History*, 201–10.

98. For Apache raiding, see Weber, *Mexican Frontier*, 86; Samuel Truett, *Fugitive Landscapes: The Forgotten History of the U.S.-Mexico Borderlands* (New Haven: Yale University Press, 2006), 28–30; and Gregg, *Commerce*, 202–3.

99. For decades after the loss of Texas, Mexico pointed to Comanche raids in northern Mexico as a critical factor that prevented the reconquest of the province. See *Informe de la comisión pesquisidora de la frontera del norte al Ejecutivo de la Unión* . . . (Mexico City: Imprenta del Gobierno en Palacio, 1877), 267–68. For the debilitating impact of Comanche raiding on Mexico's plans of reconquest, see Nance, *After San Jacinto*, 396–97. For Canales's republic, see Milton Lindheim, *The Republic of the Rio Grande: Texans in Mexico, 1839–40* (Waco, Tex.: W. M. Morrison, 1964); and Vigness, "Indian Raids," 23.

100. Quotes are from Ulysses S. Grant, *Memoirs and Selected Letters: Personal Memoirs of U. S. Grant, Selected Letters, 1839–1865* (New York: Library of America, 1990), 41; and "La Diputación Permanente de la Honorable Legislatura de Chihuahua á sus comitentes," Apr. 6, 1848, in *Reseñas históricas*, ed. Ponce de León, 344. Traditional accounts of the Mexican-American War and the Mexican Cession rarely discuss the impact of Comanche raiding. See, e.g., K. Jack Bauer, *The Mexican War* (1974; reprint, Lincoln: University of Nebraska Press, 1992); and Douglas V. Meed, *The Mexican War, 1846–1848* (New York: Routledge, 2003). But there are exceptions: Smith, "Indians in American-Mexican Relations"; Weber *Mexican Frontier;* José de la Cruz Pacheco Rojas, "Durango entre dos guerras, 1846–1847," in *México al tiempo de su guerra con Estados Unidos, 1846–1848*, comp. Josefina Zoraida Vázquez (Mexico City: El Colegio de México, Secretaría de Relaciónes Exteriores, and Fondo de Cultura Económica, 1998), 197–203; Mora-Torres, *Mexican Border*, 11–51; Pekka Hämäläinen, "The Rise and Fall of Plains Indian Horse Cultures," *JAH* 90 (Dec. 2003): 842–43; and DeLay, "Independent Indians."

101. For Mexico's defensive plans and continuing problems with Comanche raiders in the months leading up to the war with the United States, see Smith, "Indians in American-Mexican Relations," 55–61. In early 1845, only a year before Taylor's push to the Río Grande, Comanches were still raiding the few remaining settlements in the Nueces Strip. See H. L. Kinney to Anson Jones,

Feb. 11, 1845, in Anson Jones, *Memoranda and Official Correspondence Relating to the Republic of Texas, Its History and Annexation* (1859; reprint, Chicago: Rio Grande, 1966), 432.

102. Bauer, *Mexican War*, 147–48; Weber, *Mexican Frontier*, 107–21; Smith, "Indians in American-Mexican Relations," 61–64; Griffen, *Utmost Good Faith*, 120–21; Neighbors to Medill, Sep. 14, 1847, 30th Cong., 1st sess., S. Ex. Doc. 1, 902; Neighbors to Medill, Nov. 18, 1847, 30th Cong., 1st sess., S. Rpt. 171, 9; Samuel Chester Reid, *The Scouting Expeditions of McCulloch's Texas Rangers* (Philadelphia: Keystone, 1890), 66; and Napoleon Jackson Tecumseh Dana to Susan Sanford Dana, July 29, 1846, in Napoleon Jackson Tecumseh Dana, *Monterrey Is Ours! The Mexican War Letters of Lieutenant Dana, 1845–1847*, ed. Robert H. Ferrell (Lexington: University Press of Kentucky, 1990), 103. Quote is from Smith, "Indians in American-Mexican Relations," 60.

103. For the lack of national response, the sense of abandonment in the Mexican North, and the subsequent fragmentation of common Mexican identity, see Weber, *Mexican Frontier*, 240; Luis Aboites Aguilar, "Poblamiento y estado en el norte de México, 1830–1835," in *Indio, nación y comunidad en el México del siglo XIX*, ed. Antonio Escobar Ohmstede (Mexico City: Centro de Estudios Mexicanos y Centroamericanos/Centro de Investigaciones y Estudios Superiores en Antropología Social, 1993), 303–13; Mora-Torres, *Mexican Border*, 38–40; and DeLay, "Independent Indians," 54–55. Quote is from Rachel Plummer, "Narrative of the Capture and Subsequent Sufferings of Mrs. Rachel Plummer, Written by Herself," in *Held Captive by Indians: Selected Narratives, 1642–1836*, ed. Richard VanDerBeets (Knoxville: University of Tennessee Press, 1973), 352. Northern provinces did not manage to agree on a unified Indian policy until 1852, and even that effort was aborted the next year when Santa Anna returned to power. See Mora-Torres, *Mexican Border*, 40–41.

104. For weak local resistance in northern Mexico and Mexicans cooperating with U.S. troops, see Army of Occupation, Orders, No. 115, Sep. 11, 1846, Army of Occupation, Orders, No. 123, Sep. 27, 1846, and Army of Occupation, Special Orders, No. 78, June 4, 1846, 30th Cong., 1st sess., H. Ex. Doc. 60, 504–5, 507, 522–23; Valerio-Jiménez, "*Indios Barbaros*," 213, 218–21; Bauer, *Mexican War*, 149–51, 157, 225; N. J. T. Dana to S. S. Dana, Sep. 4, 1846, in Dana, *Monterrey Is Ours!* 114–15; Gregg to the editors of the *Louisville Journal*, Dec. 29, 1846, in Josiah Gregg, *Diary and Letters of Josiah Gregg*, ed. Maurice Garland Fulton, 2 vols. (Norman: University of Oklahoma Press, 1941–44), 1:322; and Weber, *Mexican Frontier*, 275.

105. Translation of a Proclamation by the General Commanding the Army of the U.S. of America, 30th Cong., 1st sess., H. Ex. Doc. 60, 166–67; and Vigil, *Arms*, 7.

106. For American attempts to justify the conquest through racial stereotypes, see David J. Weber, "'Scarce more than apes': Historical Roots of Anglo-American Stereotypes of Mexicans in the Border Region," in *New Spain's Far Northern Frontier: Essays on Spain in the American West, 1540–1821*, ed. David J. Weber (Dallas: Southern Methodist University Press, 1979), 295–307; Elliott West, "Reconstructing Race," *Western Historical Quarterly* 34 (Spring 2003): 10–11; and DeLay, "Independent Indians," 62–66. The notion that the officials of the invading U.S. Army saw and represented themselves as liberators of Mexico from Indian menace has survived in folktales and fiction, most famously in Cormac McCarthy's *Blood Meridian: Or, the Evening Redness in the West* (New York: Random House, 1985), 33–34. For a penetrating look into one of the most famous postoccupation insurgencies, the Taos Revolt of 1847, see Reséndez, *Changing National Identities*, 254–63.

107. "Narrative of Julio Carrillo . . . ," *Antepasados* I (Fall 1970), cited in Weber, *Mexican Frontier*,

275. Juan Mora-Torres speculates that the beleaguered settlers of Nuevo León, like those of New Mexico, might have accepted occupation peacefully had the United States attempted it. See Mora-Torres, *Mexican Border*, 40.

CHAPTER 6. CHILDREN OF THE SUN

1. For Comanche horse ownership, see Pedro Fermín de Mendinueta to Antonio María de Bucareli y Ursúa, Sep. 30, 1774, *PINM*, 175; Juan Bautista de Anza, "Diary of the Expedition . . . against the Comanche Nation . . . ," Sep. 10, 1779, and Francisco Xavier Ortiz to Juan Bautista de Anza, May 20, 1786, *FF*, 139, 323; John Sibley, A *Report from Natchitoches in 1807*, ed. Annie Heloise Abel (New York: Museum of the American Indian, 1922), 41; Anthony Glass, "On the Winter Hunt, October, 1808–March, 1809," in *Journal of an Indian Trader: Anthony Glass and the Texas Trading Frontier, 1790–1810*, ed. Dan L. Flores (College Station: Texas A&M University Press, 1985), 67; Jacob Fowler, *The Journal of Jacob Fowler*, ed. Elliott Coues (1898; reprint, Minneapolis: Ross and Haines, 1965), 65; Jean Louis Berlandier, *Journey to Mexico: During the Years 1826 to 1834*, trans. Sheila M. Ohlendorf, Josette M. Bigelow, and Mary M. Standifer, 2 vols. (Austin: Texas State Historical Association and University of Texas Press, 1980), 2:343–44; Albert Pike, *Prose Sketches and Poems*, ed. David J. Weber (College Station: Texas A&M University Press, 1987), 47, 50; T. B. Wheelock, "Journal of Colonel Dodge's Expedition from Fort Gibson to the Pawnee Pict Village," Aug. 26, 1834, *American State Papers*, Class 5, *Military Affairs*, 5:376; Ralph P. Bieber, *Southern Trails to California in 1849* (Cleveland: Arthur H. Clark, 1937), 302–5; Report of Exploration and Survey from Fort Smith, Arkansas, to Santa Fe, Made in 1849, by First Lieutenant James H. Simpson, and Report of Captain R. B. Marcy's Route from Fort Smith to Santa Fe, Nov. 20, 1849, 31st Cong., 1st sess., H. Ex. Doc. 45, 16, 45; and John W. Whitfield to Charles E. Mix, Jan. 5, 1856, LR:OIA, Upper Arkansas Agency, 878:107. The figures are averages. If only the number of tipis is given in the source, the number of people has been derived by multiplying the number of lodges by ten. For minimum requirements, see John H. Moore, "The Dynamics of Scale in Plains Indian Ethnohistory," *Papers in Anthropology* 23 (Summer 1982): 234.
2. For horse eating, see Juan Antonio Padilla, Report on the Barbarous Indians of the Province of Texas, Dec. 27, 1819, in "Texas in 1820," trans. Mattie Austin Hatcher, *SHQ* 23 (July 1919): 54; José Francisco Ruíz, *Report on Indian Tribes of Texas in 1828*, ed. John C. Ewers (New Haven: Yale University Press, 1972), 8; Victor Tixier, *Tixier's Travels on the Osage Prairies*, ed. John Francis McDermott, trans. Albert J. Salvan (Norman: University of Oklahoma Press, 1940), 266; and Randolph B. Marcy, *Adventure on Red River: Report on the Exploration of the Headwaters of the Red River by Captain Randolph B. Marcy and Captain G. B. McClellan*, ed. Grant Foreman (Norman: University of Oklahoma Press, 1937), 175. For losses caused by climatic and weather conditions, see Gary Clayton Anderson, *The Indian Southwest, 1580–1830: Ethnogenesis and Reinvention* (Norman: University of Oklahoma Press, 1999), 227; and James Sherow, "Workings of the Geodialectic: High Plains Indians and Their Horses in the Region of the Arkansas River Valley, 1800–1870," *Environmental History Review* 16 (Summer 1992): 61–84.
3. For an imaginative analysis of the dynamics and dilemmas of hunting and herding, see Elliott West, *The Way to the West: Essays on the Central Plains* (Albuquerque: University of New Mexico Press, 1995), chs. 1 and 2. Also see Pekka Hämäläinen, "The Rise and Fall of Plains Indian Horse Cultures," *JAH* 90 (Dec. 2003): 833–62.

4. Sibley, *Report*, 78; Padilla, Report, 54; and Rachel Plummer, "Narrative of the Capture and Subsequent Sufferings of Mrs. Rachel Plummer, Written by Herself," in *Held Captive by Indians: Selected Narratives, 1642–1836*, ed. Richard VanDerBeets (Knoxville: University of Tennessee Press, 1973), 355. Quotes are from "Declaration of Felipe de Sandoval," *PT*, 3:324; Pedro Vial and Francisco Xavier Chaves, Diary, in "Inside the Comanchería, 1785: The Diary of Pedro Vial and Francisco Xavier Chaves," ed. Elizabeth A. H. John, trans. Adán Benavides, Jr., *SHQ* 88 (July 1994): 49; Glass, "Winter Hunt," 67–68; John P. Sherburne, *Through Indian Country to California: John P. Sherburne's Diary of the Whipple Expedition, 1853–1854*, ed. Mary McDougall Gordon (Stanford: Stanford University Press, 1988), 91; and Francisco Atanasio Domínguez, *The Missions of New Mexico: A Description by Francisco Atanasio Domínguez*, trans. and ed. Eleanor B. Adams and Angélico Chávez (Albuquerque: University of New Mexico Press, 1956), 111.
5. Sherow, "Workings of the Geodialectic," 69; and West, *Way to the West*, 21–22.
6. For the size of Comanche rancherías, see Vial and Chavez, Diary, 49; Report of G. W. Bonnell, reprinted in 30th Cong., 1st sess., S. Rpt. 171, 42; D. G. Burnet to H. R. Schoolcraft, Sep. 29, 1847, *IPTS*, 3:87; and Thomas W. Kavanagh, *Comanche Political History: An Ethnohistorical Perspective* (Lincoln: University of Nebraska Press, 1996), 42.
7. Athanase de Mézières to Juan Maria Vicencio, barón de Ripperdá, July 4, 1772, *ADM*, 1:297.
8. Marcy's Route, 45. Also see Ernest Wallace and E. Adamson Hoebel, *The Comanches: Lords of the South Plains* (Norman: University of Oklahoma Press, 1954), 55–57.
9. Marcy, *Adventure*, 60–61 (quote is from p. 61); and Wallace and Hoebel, *Comanches*, 263.
10. Quote is from Sibley, *Report*, 79. For labor division between sexes, see Wallace and Hoebel, *Comanches*, 92–96.
11. Marcy, *Adventure*, 159–60; Josiah Gregg, *Commerce of the Prairies*, ed. Max L. Moorhead (Norman: University of Oklahoma Press, 1954), 437–38; David G. Burnet, "David G. Burnet's Letters Describing the Comanche Indians with an Introduction by Ernest Wallace," *West Texas Historical Association Year Book* 30 (1954): 132; and Wallace and Hoebel, *Comanches*, 250–67. Quote is from Berlandier, *Journey to Mexico*, 2:345.
12. Wallace and Hoebel, *Comanches*, 46; and Sibley, *Report*, 77. Quotes are from de Mézières to the viceroy, Feb. 20, 1778, *ADM*, 2:175; *Telegraph and Texas Register*, June 16, 1838; and Theodore Ayrault Dodge, "Some American Riders," *Harper's New Monthly Magazine* (May 1891): 862. Comanche lore states that Comanches began to breed their own horses almost immediately after they had acquired their first animals. See Alice Marriott and Carol. K. Rachlin, *Plains Indian Mythology* (New York: Thomas Y. Crowell, 1975), 93.
13. Wallace and Hoebel, *Comanches*, 46–50; Anderson, *Indian Southwest*, 227–28; and Dan Flores, *Horizontal Yellow: Nature and History in the Near Southwest* (Albuquerque: University of New Mexico Press, 1999), 106.
14. George Catlin, *Letters and Notes on the Manners, Customs, and Conditions of the North American Indians*, 2 vols. (1844; reprint, New York: Dover, 1973), 2:62; and John C. Ewers, *The Horse in the Blackfoot Indian Culture: With Comparative Material from Other Western Tribes*, Bureau of American Ethnology Bulletin 159 (Washington, D.C.: Smithsonian Institution, 1955), 341–42.
15. For such tensions, see West, *Way to the West*, 20–37; and Dan Flores, "Bison Ecology and Bison Diplomacy: The Southern Plains from 1800 to 1850," *JAH* 78 (Sep. 1991): 481.
16. Contrary to the conventional view, the bison did not migrate in large masses over great distances along established trails but instead moved short distances from one source of grass to another.

See Frank Gilbert Roe, *The North American Buffalo: A Critical Study of the Species in Its Wild State* (Toronto: University of Toronto Press, 1970), 84, 188. Comanches seem to have been unique among other Plains Indian tribes, which typically organized only one great hunt, in the summer. See the various articles in Raymond J. DeMallie, ed., *Handbook of North American Indians*, vol. 13, *The Plains* (Washington, D.C.: Smithsonian Institution, 2001).

17. Domingo Cabello y Robles, Responses Given by the Governor of the Province of Texas to Questions Put to Him by the Lord Commanding General of the Interior [Provinces] in an Official Letter of the 27th of January Concerning Various Conditions of the Eastern Comanches, Apr. 30, 1786, BA 17:418; H. Bailey Carroll and J. Villasana Haggard, trans., *Three New Mexico Chronicles: The Exposición of Don Pedro Bautista Pino 1812; the Ojeada of Lic. Antonio Barreiro 1832; and the additions by Don José Agustín de Escudero, 1849* (Albuquerque: Quivira Society, 1942), 130; Padilla, Report, 54; Gregg, *Commerce*, 433–34; and Robert S. Neighbors, "Na-Ü-Ni, or Comanches of Texas; Their Traits and Beliefs, and Divisions and Intertribal Relations," *IPTS*, 3:355.

18. Manuel Merino y Moreno, Report on the tribes of pagan Indians who inhabit the borderlands of the Interior Provinces of the kingdom of New Spain . . . , in "Views from a Desk in Chihuahua: Manuel Merino's Report on Apaches and Neighboring Nations, ca. 1804," ed. Elizabeth A. H. John, trans. John Wheat, *SHQ* 85 (Oct. 1991): 171; Burnet, "Letters," 128–29; and Jean Louis Berlandier, *The Indians of Texas in 1830*, ed. John C. Ewers, trans. Patricia Reading Leclercq (Washington, D.C.: Smithsonian Institution, 1969), 36.

19. José María Sánchez, "A Trip to Texas in 1828," trans. Carlos E. Castañeda, *SHQ* 29 (Apr. 1926): 262; and Burnet to Schoolcraft, Sep. 29, 1847, *IPTS*, 3:91.

20. Gregg, *Commerce*, 434; Burnet to Schoolcraft, Sep. 29, 1847, and Neighbors, "Na-Ü-Ni," *IPTS*, 3:91, 355; Marcy, *Adventure*, 167; and Richard Irving Dodge, *Our Wild Indians: Thirty-three Years' Personal Experience among the Red Men of the Great West* (1882; reprint, New York: Archer House, 1959), 216. For sororal polygyny, see Wallace and Hoebel, *Comanches*, 138. Quote is from Berlandier, *Indians*, 118.

21. Wallace and Hoebel, *Comanches*, 47, 141, 225–26, 241; Lila Wistrand Robinson and James Armagost, *Comanche Dictionary and Grammar* (Arlington: University of Texas at Arlington, 1990), 76; Noah Smithwick, *The Evolution of a State or Recollections of Old Texas* (Austin: Gammel, 1900), 178; Thomas James, *Three Years among the Indians and Mexicans*, ed. Milo Milton Quaife (1846; reprint, New York: Citadel, 1966), 227–28; and E. Adamson Hoebel, *The Political Organization and Law-ways of the Comanche Indians*, American Anthropological Association Memoir 54 (Menasha, Wis.: American Anthropological Association, 1940), 49, 73. Quote is from Gregg, *Commerce*, 436.

22. The cultural and ideological underpinnings of indigenous and colonial slave systems in the Southwest borderlands have been explicated most forcefully by James Brooks, who draws on the works of Claude Meillasoux, Suzanne Miers, Igor Kopytoff, and Patricia Albers. See James F. Brooks, "'This Evil Extends Especially . . . to the Feminine Sex': Negotiating Captivity on the New Mexico Borderlands," *Feminist Studies* 22 (Summer 1996): 218, 300; and James F. Brooks, *Captives and Cousins: Slavery, Kinship, and Community in the Southwest Borderlands* (Chapel Hill: University of North Carolina Press for the Omohundro Institute of Early American History and Culture, 2002), 16–18, 30–37.

23. Quotes are from Ruíz, *Report*, 9; "Delegation from the Comanche Nation," in *Papers Concerning Robertson's Colony in Texas*, comp. and ed. Malcolm McLean, 18 vols. (Austin: University of

Texas Press, 1974–93), 4:428–29; Berlandier, *Indians*, 76; George Archibald McCall, *New Mexico in 1850: A Military View*, ed. Robert W. Frazier (Norman: University of Oklahoma Press, 1968), 103; George E. Hyde, *Life of George Bent: Written from His Letters*, ed. Savoie Lottinville (Norman: University of Oklahoma Press, 1968), 69; and Waddy Thompson, *Recollections of Mexico* (New York: Wiley and Putnam, 1846), 172. Also see James, *Three Years*, 244.

24. Berlandier, *Indians*, 76; and Michael L. Tate, "Comanche Captives: People between Two Worlds," *CO* 72 (Fall 1994): 242–44. Quote is from Ruíz, *Report*, 13.
25. Quotes are from Berlandier, *Indians*, 75–76.
26. Plummer, "Narrative," 340; Sarah Ann Horn, *An Authentic and Thrilling Narrative of the Captivity of Mrs. Horn, and Her Two Children, with Mrs. Harris, by the Camanche Indians* (1851; reprint, New York: Garland, 1977), 22–23; Bianca Babb, A True Story of My Capture by, and Life with the Comanche Indians, in "Every Day Seemed to be a Holiday: The Captivity of Bianca Babb," ed. Daniel J. Gelo and Scott Zesch, *SHQ* 107 (July 2003): 60; Theodore Adolphus Babb, *In the Bosom of the Comanches: A Thrilling Tale of Savage Indian Life, Massacre, and Captivity Truthfully Told by a Surviving Captive* (Dallas: Hargreaves, 1923), 39–40; and Hugh D. Corwin, *Comanche and Kiowa Captives in Oklahoma and Texas* (Lawton, Okla.: Cooperative, 1959), 7. Quotes are from Gregg, *Commerce*, 436; and Marcy's Route, 44. For resistance to disease, see Brooks, *Captives and Cousins*, 70.
27. For literate captives, see Berlandier, *Indians*, 83. For slaves used in special industries, see Ralph Linton, "The Comanche Sun Dance," *American Anthropologist* 37 (July–Sep. 1935): 421. Quotes are from Berlandier, *Indians*, 75; and Hyde, *Life of George Bent*, 69.
28. Tixier, *Travels*, 270; and Plummer, "Narrative," 340.
29. Quotes are from Berlandier, *Indians*, 75–76. Also see Smithwick, *Evolution*, 176; Berlandier, *Journey to Mexico*, 2:345; Wilson T. Davidson, "A Comanche Prisoner in 1841," *SHQ* 45 (Apr. 1942): 336–38; Ole T. Nystel, *Lost and Found, or Three Months with the Wild Indians* (Dallas: Wilmans Brothers, 1888), 6–7; Horn, *Authentic and Thrilling Narrative*, 15; Anderson, *Indian Southwest*, 240; Tate, "Comanche Prisoners," 239; and Berlandier, *Indians*, 76n76. For natal alienation, see Orlando Patterson, *Slavery and Social Death* (Cambridge: Harvard University Press, 1982), esp. 5.
30. Here I am in perfect accordance with James Brooks, who sees borderlands slavery as a fluid and multifaceted social institution embedded in kinship networks and economies. Where my view differs from Brooks's is the emphasis on economic motives. Whereas Brooks is more interested in captives as cultural and social persons than as workers, I see Comanche slavery primarily (although not exclusively) as a system of labor exploitation geared around exchange-oriented surplus production. See Brooks, *Captives and Cousins*, esp. 6, 180–81. Quote is from Burnet, "Letters," 130.
31. For blood bondsmen, see Wallace and Hoebel, *Comanches*, 241. For Is-sa-keep, see Marcy's Route, 46. See also Corwin, *Comanche and Kiowa Captives*, 39; Tate, "Comanche Captives," 237–41; and Brooks, *Captives and Cousins*, 188–90. Comanche slavery was a distinctively patriarchal institution, but some Comanche women could gain possession of slaves as gifts from men. See Curtis Marez, "Signifying Spain, Becoming Comanche, Making Mexicans: Indian Captivity and the History of Chicana/o Performance," *American Quarterly* 53 (June 2001): 282. Quotes are from Smithwick, *Evolution*, 183; and Horn, *Authentic and Thrilling Narrative*, 23.
32. Wallace and Hoebel, *Comanches*, 241–42; Robinson and Armagost, *Comanche Dictionary*, 39;

and Thomas Gladwin, "Comanche Kin Behavior," *American Anthropologist* 50 (Jan.–Mar. 1948): 82.

33. For Hekiyan'i, see Wallace and Hoebel, *Comanches,* 260–63 (quote is from p. 262). For captive Euro-American women considered as pure Comanches, see John Sibley, "Character of the Hietan Indians," in *Journal,* ed. Flores, 81. Quotes are from Gregg, *Commerce,* 436; Neighbors, "Na-Ü-Ni," 355; Brooks, *Captives and Cousins,* 187; and Berlandier, *Indians,* 76, 83.
34. Berlandier, *Indians,* 83; Neighbors, "Na-Ü-Ni," 356; Corwin, *Comanche and Kiowa Captives,* 168; and Brooks, "'This Evil Extends,'" 284, 290. Quotes are from Berlandier, *Indians,* 76; and Ruíz, *Report,* 15.
35. For kin terminology, see Robinson and Armagost, *Comanche Dictionary,* 68. For the legal rights of slaves, see Wallace and Hoebel, *Comanches,* 241. Quotes are from Burnet, "Letters," 130; Tixier, *Travels,* 270; and Berlandier, *Indians,* 119–20.
36. Quotes are from Burnet, "Letters," 130; Berlandier, *Indians,* 76; and Sánchez, "Trip to Texas," 263. Also see Hyde, *Life of George Bent,* 69; Burnet to Schoolcraft, Sep. 29, 1847, *IPTS,* 3:87; John Holland Jenkins, *Recollections of Early Texas: Memoirs of John Holland Jenkins,* ed. John Holmes Jenkins III (Austin: University of Texas Press, 1958), 231; and Corwin, *Comanche and Kiowa Captives,* 105–6.
37. Quotes are from Gregg, *Commerce,* 249–50. More theoretical distinctions can be slippery when applied to the Comanche slavery. For example, the early nineteenth-century Comanches seemed to be in the process of slowly transforming themselves from a "society with slaves," where slavery was one of many labor sources, into a "slave society," where the slavery institution formed the very core of economic production, but such possible trajectory was aborted by the collapse of Comanche power in the 1850s and 1860s.
38. Wallace and Hoebel, *Comanches,* 39–40; Catlin, *Letters,* 2:67; J. C. Eldredge to Sam Houston, Dec. 8, 1843, *IPTS,* 1:267; Marcy, *Adventure,* 164; and Kavanagh, *Comanche Political History,* 147. Also see Sibley, *Report,* 80.
39. Quotes are from Burnet to Schoolcraft, Sep. 29, 1847, *IPTS,* 3:87; and Marcy, *Adventure,* 158. Also see Wallace and Hoebel, *Comanches,* 39; and Ralph Linton, *The Study of Man: An Introduction* (New York: D. Appleton, 1936), 297.
40. For horse names, see Robinson and Armagost, *Comanche Dictionary,* 88; and Colin G. Calloway, *One Vast Winter Count: The Native American West before Lewis and Clark* (Lincoln: University of Nebraska Press, 2003), 284. For bride price, see Ruíz, *Report,* 14; and Berlandier, *Indians,* 118. See also Brooks, *Captives and Cousins,* 177–78.
41. For slave numbers, see Lester G. Bugbee, "The Texas Frontier, 1820–1825," *Publications of the Southern History Association* 4 (Mar. 1900): 119n35. Quote is from Marcy, *Adventure,* 159.
42. Wallace and Hoebel, *Comanches,* 134; and Jane Fisburne Collier, *Marriage and Inequality in Classless Societies* (Stanford: Stanford University Press, 1988), 32–43.
43. For clothing and adornments, see Francisco Amangual, "Diary of Francisco Amangual from San Antonio to Santa Fe, March 30–May 19, 1808," *PV,* 482; and Gregg, *Commerce,* 435. Quote is from Sibley, *Report,* 79–80.
44. In piecing together these strategies of distinction, I have relied especially on Wallace and Hoebel, *Comanches,* 146–47; and Collier, *Marriage and Inequality,* 35–43.
45. Ortiz to Anza, May 20, 1786, *FF,* 322; and Antonio Elozúa, Affidavit, Mar. 3, 1829, BA 120:513. For band names, see Burnet, "Letters," 124.

46. Wallace and Hoebel, *Comanches*, 131, 255, 272; and Ruíz, *Report*, 13.
47. Collier, *Marriage and Inequality*, 32–34.
48. Ibid., 38; Robinson and Armagost, *Comanche Dictionary*, 124; Anderson, *Indian Southwest*, 237; Wallace and Hoebel, *Comanches*, 132–33, 145; and Babb, True Story, 57.
49. Quote is from Marcy, *Adventure*, 157. Gregg noted that although chiefs often had eight to ten wives, three was considered the "usual number" for "common warriors." See Gregg, *Commerce*, 433–34.
50. Quote is from Neighbors, "Na-Ü-Ni," 353. Also see Hoebel and Wallace, *Comanches*, 211. For sons following their fathers to leadership positions, see Gregg, *Commerce*, 433.
51. For the uncertainty of male status, see Collier, *Marriage and Inequality*, 48–57; and Marcy, *Adventure*, 158–59. For well-off polygynous former slaves, see, e.g., Corwin, *Comanche and Kiowa Captives*, 95, 101; and Wallace and Hoebel, *Comanches*, 261.
52. Wallace and Hoebel, *Comanches*, 225–28, 234; Ruíz, *Report*, 14; Berlandier, *Indians*, 118; Neighbors, "Na-Ü-Ni," 355; and Robinson and Armagost, *Comanche Dictionary*, 56. Face challenging can be seen as an example of what some historians have called cultural strategies of navigating or managing emotions. See, e.g., William M. Reddy, *The Navigation of Feeling: A Framework for a History of Emotions* (New York: Cambridge University Press, 2001). More broadly, the practice of face challenging illustrates how the Comanches balanced between conflict and consensus on a societal level: their society had deep in-built contradictions and conflicts that were offset—but never eliminated—by enduring and partly reinvented traditions of social bonding and solidarity.
53. Quote is from Marcy, *Adventure*, 159. For *tekwʉniwapi̲s*, see Robinson and Armagost, *Comanche Dictionary*, 107.
54. Cabello, Responses, BA 17:418. For Comanche coup system, see Wallace and Hoebel, *Comanches*, 246–50.
55. Ruíz, *Report*, 10–11.
56. Quotes are from, Ruíz, *Report*, 11; and Berlandier, *Indians*, 71.
57. Marcy, *Adventure*, 156.
58. For marital residence, see Wallace and Hoebel, *Comanches*, 140.
59. Wallace and Hoebel, *Comanches*, 210–12; Kavanagh, *Comanche Political History*, 36–38; and Morris W. Foster, *Being Comanche: A Social History of an American Indian Community* (Tucson: University of Arizona Press, 1991), 58–59. Quote is from Neighbors, "Na-Ü-Ni," 357.
60. Quotes are from Burnet to Schoolcraft, Sep. 29, 1847, *IPTS*, 3:87; Marcy, *Adventure*, 158–59; and Report of G. W. Bonnell, 42. See also Berlandier, *Indians*, 39; Wallace and Hoebel, *Comanches*, 212–13; Kavanagh, *Comanche Political History*, 38–39; and Robinson and Armagost, *Comanche Dictionary*, 107.
61. Wallace and Hoebel, *Comanches*, 213–15. Quote is from José Francisco Ruíz, "'Comanches': Customs and Characteristics," in *The Papers of Mirabeau Buonaparte Lamar*, ed. Charles Adams Gulick, Jr., et al., 6 vols. (1920–27; reprint, Austin: Pemberton, 1968), 4:223.
62. Quotes are from Wallace and Hoebel, *Comanches*, 213, 215; Marcy, *Adventure*, 157; and L. H. Williams to Thomas G. Western, Nov. 23, 1845, *IPTS*, 2:415. See also Neighbors, "Na-Ü-Ni," 353.
63. M. C. Fisher, "On the Arapahoe, Kiowa, and Comanche," *Journal of the Ethnological Society of London* 1 (1869): 284; and Gregg, *Commerce*, 250–51.
64. For Comanche abstinence, see Sánchez, "Trip to Texas," 262; Burnet to Schoolcraft, Sep. 29, 1847, *IPTS*, 3:90; and Gregg, *Commerce*, 432. For Pawnees, see Richard White, *The Roots of*

Dependency: Subsistence, Environment, and Social Change among the Choctaws, Pawnees, and Navajos (Lincoln: University of Nebraska Press, 1983), 191–92, 204. For connections between alcohol use and loss of economic and political autonomy among various Native North American groups, see Peter C. Mancall, *Deadly Medicine: Indians and Alcohol in Early America* (Ithaca: Cornell University Press, 1995).

65. James, *Three Years*, 243–44. For *paraibo* control, see also José Cortés, *Views from the Apache Frontier: Report on the Northern Provinces of New Spain*, ed. Elizabeth A. H. John, trans. John Wheat (Norman: University of Oklahoma Press, 1989), 82; and Eldredge to Houston, Dec. 8, 1843, *IPTS*, 1:268.

66. For the organization of Comanche war parties, see Ruíz, *Report*, 9–10; Berlandier, *Indians*, 70; and Wallace and Hoebel, *Comanches*, 216, 223–24, 250.

67. Quotes are from Tomás Vélez de Cachupín to Don Juan Francisco de Güemes y Horcasitas, Mar. 8, 1750, *PT*, 3:328; Burnet to Schoolcraft, Sep. 29, 1847, *IPTS*, 3:87; Report of G. W. Bonnell, 43; and H. G. Catlett to W. Medill, May 12, 1849, *ARCIA*, 1849, 967. See also Kavanagh, *Comanche Political History*, 151; and Martha McCollough, *Three Nations, One Place: A Comparative Ethnohistory of Social Change among the Comanches and Hasinais during Spain's Colonial Era, 1689–1821* (New York: Routledge, 2004), 102–3.

68. This challenges the traditional—and still prevailing—view that the Comanches never managed to offset the deepening fragmentation on a local level. Ernest Wallace and E. Adamson Hoebel, for example, wrote in 1952 that the Comanches "consisted of a people who had a common way of life. But that way of life did not include political institutions or social mechanisms by which they could act as a tribal unit." Mirroring Wallace and Hoebel, William C. Meadows has recently concluded that division was "the highest level of consistent sociopolitical integration" among the nineteenth-century Comanches: "the Comanche of the nineteenth century were exhibiting an evolutionary stage of pandivisional tribal sodality . . . which was prematurely inhibited prior to reaching fruition due to the collapse of the Comanche and larger Plains economy." Meadows's interpretation is influenced by his simplified notion of the Comanches as a one-dimensional warrior society whose political existence was conditioned by martial matters: "Territorial divisions developed incipient 'tribelike' structures which did not encompass the entire pan-Comanche ethnic or linguistic population, but remained division-based, perhaps owing to an increasing reliance on warfare and raiding, which was generally division-based." Quotes are from Wallace and Hoebel, *Comanches*, 22; and William C. Meadows, *Kiowa, Apache, and Comanche Military Societies: Enduring Veterans, 1800 to the Present* (Austin: University of Texas Press, 1999), 332–33, 336.

69. Burnet, "Letters," 122–24.

70. See Vial and Chaves, Diary, 36; Pedro de Nava to Fernando de la Concha, Dec. 31, 1793, in *Border Comanches: Seven Spanish Colonial Documents, 1785–1819*, ed. and trans. Marc Simmons (Santa Fe: Stagecoach, 1967), 31; Manuel de Salcedo, Questioning of a Comanche Indian, 1810 [n.d.], BA 47:701–2; Josef Manrique to Nemesio Salcedo, Mar. 27, 1810, SANM II 17:61–63 (T-2308); Pike, *Prose Sketches*, 48; Neighbors to Medill, Jan. 20, 1848, 30th Cong., 1st sess., H. Ex. Doc. 1, 574; Neighbors to Medill, Mar. 2, 1848, 30th Cong., 1st sess., S. Rpt. 171, 17; Berlandier, *Indians*, 121; Marcy, *Adventure*, 141–42; Catlett to Medill, May 12, 1849, *ARCIA*, 1849, 967; Robert S. Neighbors, "Texas Indians in 1849," *IPTS*, 3:109; Daniel J. Gelo, "'Comanche Land and Ever Has Been': A Native Geography of the Nineteenth-Century Comanchería," *SHQ* 103 (Jan. 2000): 285;

Nancy A. Kenmotsu, Timothy K. Perttula, Patricia Mercado-Allinger, Thomas R. Hester, James E. Bruseth, Sergio Iruegas, and Curtis Tunnell, "Medicine Mounds Ranch: The Identification of a Possible Comanche Traditional Cultural Property in the Rolling Plains of Texas," *Plains Anthropologist* 40 (1995): 240–48; Meadows, *Kiowa, Apache, and Comanche Military Societies*, 310–11, 336–37; Anderson, *Indian Southwest*, 229; and Gerald Betty, *Comanche Society: Before the Reservation* (College Station: Texas A&M University Press, 2002), 21–23.

71. For elections, see, e.g., Cabello, Responses, BA 17:419; Fernando Chacón, Report on the Election of a Comanche General, Nov. 18, 1797, SANM II 14:233 (T-1404); and Report of G. W. Bonnell, 42. For the controlling function of divisional councils, see Foster, *Being Comanche*, 67.

72. Vial and Chaves, Diary, 38–44; Neighbors, "Na-Ü-Ni," 353; and Grant Foreman, "The Texas Comanche Treaty of 1846," *SHQ* 51 (Apr. 1948): 323–24. Quote is from J. Cameron, "Comanche Indians; the Country West of the Colorado," in *Lamar Papers*, ed. Gulick et al., 1:475.

73. Eldredge to Houston, Dec. 8, 1843, *IPTS*, 1:272.

74. Burnet, "Letters," 125.

75. For religion and ritual life as integrative forces, see Daniel Joseph Gelo, "Comanche Belief and Ritual" (Ph.D. diss., Rutgers University, 1986). For societies, see Kavanagh, *Comanche Political History*, 48–49; Meadows, *Kiowa, Apache, and Comanche Military Societies*, 276–82, 318; and Juliana Barr, "Beyond Their Control: Spaniards in Native Texas," in *Choice, Persuasion, and Coercion: Social Control on Spain's North American Frontiers*, ed. Jesús F. de la Teja and Ross Frank (Albuquerque: University of New Mexico Press, 2005), 161. Quote is from E. Adamson Hoebel, *The Law of Primitive Man: A Study in Comparative Legal Dynamics* (Cambridge: Harvard University Press, 1954), 129.

76. Quote is from Ruíz, *Report*, 15. For sun worship, see also Wallace and Hoebel, *Comanches*, 195. For the Comanche Sun Dance, see Meadows, *Kiowa, Apache, and Comanche Military Societies*, 318–23.

77. Merino, Report, 170; and Burnet to Schoolcraft, Sep. 29, 1847, and Neighbors, "Na-Ü-Ni," *IPTS*, 3:85, 88, 349. For contrasting, more symbolic meaning of national gatherings among the Cheyennes, see Elliott West, *The Contested Plains: Indians, Goldseekers, and the Rush to Colorado* (Lawrence: University of Kansas Press, 1998), 85.

78. Berlandier, *Indians*, 67; and Ruíz, *Report*, 10.

79. Berlandier, *Indians*, 69–70. For national wars and multidivisional armies, see Fernando de la Concha, Instructions drawn up by Colonel Don Fernando de la Concha, former governor of the Province of New Mexico, so that his successor, the Lieutenant Colonel Don Fernando Chacón, may adapt what part of it that may seem to him suitable for the advantage, tranquility, and development of the aforesaid province, in "Notes and Documents: Advice on Governing New Mexico, 1794," ed. and trans. Donald E. Worcester, *NMHR* 24 (July 1949): 238; Nava to Concha, July 26, 1791, and Joaquín del Real Alencaster to commanding general, June 13, 1807, SANM II 12:617, 16:347–48 (T-1137, 2056); Gregg, *Commerce*, 246; Ruíz, *Report*, 9; John Sibley to William Eustice, May 10, 1809, in "Dr. John Sibley and the Louisiana-Texas Frontier, 1803–1814," ed. Julia Kathryn Garrett, *SHQ* 47 (Jan. 1944): 323; and Berlandier, *Indians*, 73, 117. This is not how historians have seen Comanche warfare. In a typical—and influential—passage, E. Adamson Hoebel wrote that "so far as it [war] was a national policy, it was not explicitly directed by a governing or political body. It was a matter of individual motivation." See Hoebel, *Law of Primitive Man*, 132.

See, too, Ralph Linton's view of the Comanches as overly "individualistic, too reliant on visions and dreams, to take concerted action for long," and of their society as one of "low in content but high in efficiency." See Linton, *Study of Man*, 89.

80. Berlandier, *Indians*, 72–73, 80. See also Ruíz, *Report*, 11–12; and Meadows, *Kiowa, Apache, and Comanche Military Societies*, 295, 303, 312–17, 332.
81. "Delegation from the Comanche Nation," 428. The report is partly based on Ruíz's eyewitness account. See also ch. 5, above. For Big Horses, see Meadows, *Kiowa, Apache, and Comanche Military Societies*, 280–81.
82. Daniel K. Richter, *The Ordeal of the Longhouse: The Peoples of the Iroquois League in the Era of European Colonization* (Chapel Hill: University of North Carolina Press for the Omohundro Institute of Early American History and Culture, 1992), 40–41.
83. For a long-term historical view of the Comanche political organization that emphasizes the flexibility and change of divisional configurations, see Kavanagh, *Comanche Political History*, esp. 292–93, 478–91.
84. Concha, Instructions, 238.
85. For the evolution of nomadic empires, see Nikolay N. Kradin, "Nomadism, Evolution, and World-Systems: Pastoral Societies in Theories of Historical Development," *Journal of World-Systems Research* 8 (Fall 2002): 373; and Thomas J. Barfield, *The Perilous Frontier: Nomadic Empires and China* (Cambridge: Basil Blackwell, 1989).
86. Berlandier, *Indians*, 45–46, 67n67; Fowler, *Journal*, 59, 62; James Hobbs, *Wild Life in the Far West: Personal Adventures of a Border Mountain Man* (1873; reprint, Glorieta, N. Mex.: Rio Grande, 1969), 37–38; and Pedro Vial, "Diary, Bexar to Santa Fe, October 4, 1786, to May 26, 1787," and Amangual, "Diary," *PV*, 279–81, 466–67.
87. Amangual, "Diary," 467 (quote is from p. 501); Ortiz to Anza, May 29, 1786, *FF*, 322–23; Marcy, *Adventure*, 141–42, 175; Berlandier, *Indians*, 37, 43; and Gelo, "Comanche Land," 279–82, 297, 302–3.
88. Francisco Amangual, the Spanish officer, stayed among the Comanches as they made a transition from riverine winter camp to more mobile existence on the open plains. See Amangual, "Diary," 467–508. See also Cabello, Responses, BA 17:419; Juan de Dios Peña, Diary, June 12–Aug. 8, 1790, SANM II 12:263 (T-1089); and Houston to Henry Ellsworth, Dec. 1, 1832, in *The Writings of Sam Houston*, ed. Amelia W. Williams and Eugene C. Barker, 8 vols. (Austin: University of Texas Press, 1938–43), 1:269.
89. For war and the extension of hunting ranges, see Peña, Diary, SANM II 12:263; Berlandier, *Indians*, 67–69; and Marcy, *Adventure*, 172. For sentinels, see Jefferson Morgenthaler, *The River Has Never Divided Us: A Border History of La Junta de los Rios* (Austin: University of Texas Press, 2004), 31–32.
90. See, e.g., John Miller Morris, *El Llano Estacado: Exploration and Imagination on the High Plains of Texas and New Mexico, 1536–1860* (Austin: Texas State Historical Association, 1997), 188.
91. Catlin, *Letters*, 2:61.
92. Ibid., 2:60–61, 64–66. For large summer villages, see also Santiago Fernández, "Diary of Santiago Fernández from Santa Fe to the Taovayas and Return to Santa Fe, June 24–July 21, 1788, and July 24–December (August?) 17, 1788," and Francisco Xavier Fragoso, "Diary of Francisco Xavier Fragoso, Santa Fe to Natchitoches to San Antonio to Santa Fe, June 24, 1788–August 20, 1789," *PV*, 321, 332, 337; and James, *Three Years*, 127.

93. Hobbs, *Wild Life*, 35–36; Wallace and Hoebel, *Comanches*, 55–62; and Kavanagh, *Comanche Political History*, 59–60. Berlandier traveled in fall 1828 with a Comanche ranchería that was on its way to a large fall village near the abandoned presidio of San Sabá. See Berlandier, *Journey to Mexico*, 2:351. For bear hunting, see Berlandier, *Indians*, 46n23.
94. There is another way to put this: empires tend to replicate their hierarchical structures in both their internal and external dynamics. For this kind of dual stratification, see, e.g., Charles S. Maier, *Among Empires: American Ascendancy and Its Predecessors* (Cambridge: Harvard University Press, 2006), esp. 10–11.

CHAPTER 7. HUNGER

1. For Marcy's comments, see Randolph B. Marcy, *Adventure on Red River: Report on the Exploration of the Headwaters of the Red River by Captain Randolph B. Marcy and Captain G. B. McClellan*, ed. Grant Foreman (Norman: University of Oklahoma Press, 1937), 162–64 (quote is from p. 162). For Comanche population, see Pierce M. Butler and M. G. Lewis to William Medill, Aug. 8, 1846, Documents Relating to the Negotiation of Ratified and Unratified Treaties with Various Tribes of Indians, RG 75, Records of the Bureau of Indian Affairs, T494, NAMP, 4:270–71; and Robert S. Neighbors to W. J. Worth, Mar. 7, 1849, *ARCIA*, 1849, 963. In 1854 William B. Parker reported that the Comanches and Kiowas combined numbered 20,000. See William B. Parker, *Notes Taken during the Expedition Commanded by Capt. R. B. Marcy, U.S.A., Through Unexplored Texas, in the Summer and Fall of* 1854 (Philadelphia: Hayes and Zell, 1856), 231. For Mexican slaves, see W. Gilpin to R. Jones, Aug. 1, 1848, 30th Cong., 2d sess., H. Ex. Doc. 1, 139; and Neighbors to Medill, Nov. 21, 1853, LR:OIA, Texas Agency, 859:303.
2. For carrying capacity, see Tom McHugh, *The Time of the Buffalo* (Lincoln: University of Nebraska Press, 1972), 16–17; William R. Brown, Jr., "Comancheria Demography," *Panhandle-Plains Historical Review* 59 (1986): 9–10; and Dan Flores, "Bison Ecology and Bison Diplomacy: The Southern Plains from 1800 to 1850," *JAH* 78 (Sep. 1991): 470–71. McHugh's figures suggest that the Comanchería could have supported 6.2 million bison, Brown puts the figure at 7 million, and Flores at 8 million. For annual reproduction rates, see Flores, "Bison Ecology," 476–77; and Andrew C. Isenberg, *The Destruction of the Bison: An Environmental History, 1750–1920* (Cambridge: Cambridge University Press, 2000), 27–28. Flores's figures suggest that modern protected herds have a 6 percent natural mortality rate. In early nineteenth-century Comanchería, however, two factors—wolf predation and accidental deaths caused by uncontrolled fires and floods—upped this percentage considerably. According to Isenberg, the annual toll of wolf predation was between 30 and 40 percent of the calf crop, which for Comanchería's bison population would have meant an average annual loss of nearly 7 percent of total numbers. According to William R. Brown, Jr., the historic bison herds' annual losses to fires, floods, and other calamities can be estimated at 2.5 percent of herd totals. See Isenberg, *Destruction*, 28; and Brown, "Comancheria Demography," 10.
3. For minimum requirements, see Brown, "Comancheria Demography," 10–11. For hunting practices, see William A. Dobak, "Killing the Canadian Buffalo: 1821–1881," *Western Historical Quarterly* 27 (Spring 1996): 46; Flores, "Bison Ecology," 479–80; and Douglas B. Bamforth, *Ecology and Human Adaptation on the Great Plains* (New York: Plenum, 1988), 81.
4. For the hunting activities of Osages and immigrant tribes in Comanchería in the late 1830s and

1840s, see W. M. Armstrong to T. Heartley Crawford, Sep. 30, 1841, 27th Cong., 2d sess., S. Ex. Doc. 1, 338; Willard H. Rollings, *The Osage: An Ethnohistorical Study of Hegemony on the Prairie-Plains* (Columbia: University of Missouri Press, 1992), 20–21, 257–85; Dianna Everett, *The Texas Cherokees: A People between Two Fires, 1819–1840* (Norman: University of Oklahoma Press, 1990), 114; and David LaVere, *Contrary Neighbors: Southern Plains and Removed Indians in Indian Territory* (Norman: University of Oklahoma Press, 2000), 79–118. Some Comanches complained soon after the Treaty of Camp Holmes that the removed Indians killed too many buffalos, and one Comanche chief reportedly tore up his copy of the treaty agreement in disgust. See C. C. Rister, "Federal Experiment in Southern Plains Indian Relations, 1835–1845," *CO* 14 (Dec. 1936): 451–52.

5. For the growth of cibolero hunting activities on the Llano Estacado, see H. Bailey Carroll and J. Villasana Haggard, trans., *Three New Mexico Chronicles: The Exposición of Don Pedro Bautista Pino 1812; the Ojeada of Lic. Antonio Barreiro 1832; and the additions by Don José Agustín de Escudero, 1849* (Albuquerque: Quivira Society, 1942), 101–2. For the cataclysmic impact of the 1840 peace on the bison ecology, see Elliott West, *The Way to the West: Essays on the Central Plains* (Albuquerque: University of New Mexico Press, 1995), 61–63. For Cheyenne and Arapaho bison harvest, see John W. Whitfield to Charles E. Mix, Jan. 5, 1856, LR:OIA, Upper Arkansas Agency, 878:104.
6. For dietary overlap, see Flores, "Bison Ecology," 481. For Comanche camps and their ecological impact, see George E. Hyde, *Life of George Bent: Written from His Letters*, ed. Savoie Lottinville (Norman: University of Oklahoma Press, 1968), 37, 42; A. W. Whipple, Report of Explorations for a Railway Route, Near the Thirty-fifth Parallel of North Latitude, from the Mississippi River to the Pacific Ocean, 1853–54, 33d Cong., 2d sess., S. Ex. Doc. 78, 35; and Thomas W. Kavanagh, *Comanche Political History: An Ethnohistorical Perspective* (Lincoln: University of Nebraska Press, 1996), 133–39.
7. Human predation could have profound effects on bison's migration and settlement patterns: when pressured, the herds migrated more erratically, aggregated into larger and more mobile herds, and sometimes even shifted their core home range. See Douglas B. Bamforth, "Historical Documents and Bison Ecology on the Great Plains," *Plains Anthropologist* 32 (Feb. 1987): 1–16. For wild horses, see Flores, "Bison Ecology," 481. For *pastores*, see James H. Simpson, Report of Exploration and Survey Route from Fort Smith, Arkansas, to Santa Fe, New Mexico, Made in 1849, and Report of Captain R. B. Marcy's Route from Fort Smith to Santa Fe, Nov. 20, 1849, 31st Cong., 1st sess., H. Ex. Doc. 45, 17–18, 46–48; and Whipple, Report, 38–39. For the Santa Fe trade and bovine diseases, see West, *Way to the West*, 54–79.
8. Antonio José Martínez, Esposición que el Presbítero Antonio José Martínez, Cura de Taos en Nuevo México, dirije al Gobierno del Exmo. Sor. General D. Antonio López de Santa-Anna. Proponiendo la civilisación de las Naciones bárbaras que son al canton del departamento de Nuevo-México (Taos: J. M. B., 1843), 4, facsimile in *Northern Mexico on the Eve of the United States Invasion: Rare Imprints Concerning California, Arizona, New Mexico, and Texas, 1821–1846*, ed. David J. Weber (New York: Arno, 1976). Quote is from George F. Ruxton, *Adventures in Mexico and the Rocky Mountains* (London: John Murray, 1861), 266.
9. David W. Stahle and Malcolm K. Cleaveland, "Texas Drought History Reconstructed and Analyzed from 1698 to 1980," *Journal of Climate* 1 (Jan. 1988): 65; Kevin Sweeney, "Thirsting for War, Hungering for Peace: Drought, Bison Migrations, and Native Peoples on the Southern Plains,

1845–1859," *Journal of the West* 41 (Summer 2002): 71–75; Flores, "Bison Ecology," 482; and West, *Way to the West*, 79–80. Quotes are from Neighbors to Medill, Oct. 12, 1847, 30th Cong., 1st sess., S. Ex. Doc. 1, 905; and Marcy, *Adventure*, 172. In the massive hunts of the 1870s, American hide hunters slaughtered an estimated 3.3 million bison on the southern plains. It seems probable that the bulk of the other half of the estimated peak number of 7 million bison had disappeared from the southern plains by 1860. As will be shown below, Comanches' population dropped in the 1850s and 1860s from around 20,000 to below 5,000, a collapse that may have eased the pressure enough for the bison to establish new ecological equilibrium for those two decades. For the toll of Anglo-American hunting, see Frank Gilbert Roe, *North American Buffalo: A Critical Study of the Species in Its Wild State* (Toronto: University of Toronto Press, 1970), 436–41. Seen from a macroscale perspective, the long drought that began in 1845 marked the end of the Little Ice Age, a global cooling period from the mid-sixteenth to the mid-nineteenth century. On the southern plains, then, the Little Ice Age ended with exceptional abruptness, putting enormous stress on the bison herds.

10. For the restrictions on ciboleros' hunting, see Charles L. Kenner, *The Comanchero Frontier: A History of New Mexican–Plains Indian Relations* (1969; reprint, Norman: University of Oklahoma Press, 1994), 108. For Comanche hunting, see Whitfield to Mix, Jan. 5, 1856, LR:OIA, Upper Arkansas Agency, 878:104. Quote is from Whitfield to George W. Manypenny, Sep. 4, 1855, 34th Cong., 1st sess., S. Ex. Doc. 1, 437.
11. For fluctuations of bison numbers and droughts, see West, *Way to the West*, 80; and Gary Clayton Anderson, *The Indian Southwest, 1580–1830: Ethnogenesis and Reinvention* (Norman: University of Oklahoma Press, 1999), 185–86, 199–200, 252. For social taboos and waste, see Isenberg, *Destruction*, 65, 84; and Shepard Krech III, *The Ecological Indian: Myth and History* (New York: W. W. Norton, 1999), 142–43.
12. Flores, "Bison Ecology," 484–85; Dobak, "Killing the Canadian Buffalo," 49–50; and Ernest Wallace and E. Adamson Hoebel, *The Comanches: Lords of the South Plains* (Norman: University of Oklahoma Press, 1954), 200–1. Quote is from Richard Irving Dodge, *Our Wild Indians: Thirty-three Years' Personal Experience among the Red Men of the Great West* (1883; reprint, New York: Archer House, 1959), 286.
13. For Native American conceptions of nature, animals, and conservation, see Krech, *Ecological Indian*, 149.
14. Quotes are from Capron Horace to George T. Howard, Sep. 30, 1852, LR:OIA, Texas Agency, 858:1068, 1071; and Whitfield to Manypenny, Sep. 4, 1855, 34th Cong., 1st sess., S. Ex. Doc. 1, 437.
15. W. H. Clift, "Warren's Trading Post," CO 2 (June 1924): 135–36; Hyde, *Life of George Bent*, 93–95, 104–8; and Lewis H. Garrard, *Wah-to-yah and the Taos Trail*, ed. Ralph P. Bieber (1850; reprint, Glendale, Calif.: Arthur H. Clark, 1938), 330. For the bison decline on the central plains, see West, *Way to the West*, 51–83.
16. John H. Moore, *The Cheyenne Nation: A Social and Demographic History* (Lincoln: University of Nebraska Press, 1987), 197–203; Elliott West, *The Contested Plains: Indians, Goldseekers, and the Rush to Colorado* (Lawrence: University of Kansas Press, 1998), 198–200, 285; Morris W. Foster and Martha McCollough, "Plains Apache," in *Handbook of North American Indians*, vol. 13, *The Plains*, ed. Raymond J. DeMallie, 2 parts (Washington, D.C.: Smithsonian Institution, 2001), 2:928; Andrews to Manypenny, Sep. 6, 1855, LR, Southern Superintendency, RG 75, Records of

the Bureau of Indian Affairs, M640, NAMP, 833:379–80; A. H. McKisick to Elias Rector, Oct. 21, 1855, LR:OIA, Wichita Agency, 928:22–23; and F. Todd Smith, *The Caddos, the Wichitas, and the United States, 1846–1901* (College Station: Texas A&M University Press, 1996), 42–59.

17. For the 1854 treaties, see "Treaty with the Delawares, 1854," "Treaty with the Shawnee, 1854," "Treaty with the Sauk and Foxes of Missouri, 1854," and "Treaty with the Kickapoo, 1854," in *Indian Affairs: Laws and Treaties,* ed. Charles J. Kappler, 5 vols. (Washington, D.C.: GPO, 1904), 2:614–26, 634–36; and Francis Paul Prucha, *The Great Father: The United States Government and the American Indians,* 2 vols. (Lincoln: University of Nebraska Press, 1984), 118–19. For the 1854 battle, see James Bordeaux to Alfred Cumming, Sep. 27, 1854, 33d Cong., 2d sess., S. Ex. Doc. 1, 297–98 (quote is from p. 298). For subsequent hostilities between Comanches and immigrant Indians, see Whitfield to Manypenny, Sep. 4, 1855, 34th Cong., 1st sess., S. Ex. Doc. 1, 437. For Comanche-Osage relations, see Manypenny to R. McClelland, Nov. 26, 1855, and C. W. Dean to Manypenny, Sep. 1, 1855, 34th Cong., 1st sess., S. Ex. Doc. 1, 330–31, 441–42.

18. For Calhoun's actions, see James S. Calhoun to Orlando Brown, Jan. 25, Mar. 31, and July 15, 1850, and Calhoun to Luke Lea, July 28, 1851, in *The Official Correspondence of James S. Calhoun While Indian Agent at Santa Fé and Superintendent of Indian Affairs in New Mexico,* ed. Annie Heloise Abel (Washington, D.C.: GPO, 1915), 104–5, 181–83, 226, 390–91. Some Mexican writers have argued that U.S. officials deliberately refrained from suppressing cross-border raids in order to weaken northern Mexican provinces and prepare them for future incorporation. See David B. Adams, "Embattled Borderland: Northern Nuevo León and the Indios Bárbaros, 1686–1870," *SHQ* 95 (Oct. 1991): 217.

19. Quote is from John Greiner to Lea, Apr. 30, 1852, in *Correspondence of James S. Calhoun,* 529. Also see Greiner to E. V. Sumner, Apr. 4, 1852, in ibid., 519–20; and John Greiner, "The Journal of John Greiner," ed. Annie Heloise Abel, *Old Santa Fe Magazine of History, Archaeology, Genealogy and Biography* 3 (July 1916): 192–93.

20. Kenner, *Comanchero Frontier,* 107–12; John Ward, Journal, June 6, 1853, in "Indian Affairs in New Mexico under the Administration of William Carr Lane," ed. Annie Heloise Abel, *NMHR* 46 (Apr. 1941): 345–46; Greiner, "Journal," 199; and Whipple, Report, 31, 33.

21. For epidemics, see Rupert Norval Richardson, *The Comanche Barrier to South Plains Settlement: A Century and a Half of Savage Resistance to the Advancing Frontier* (Glendale, Calif.: Arthur H. Clark, 1933), 159, 259n523; Albert G. Boone to W. P. Dole, Feb. 2, 1862, LR:OIA, Upper Arkansas Agency, 878:625; and James Mooney, *Calendar History of the Kiowa Indians* (1898; reprint, Washington, D.C.: Smithsonian Institution, 1979), 173, 176, 311.

22. For food raiding, see Christopher Carson to David Meriwether, July 26, 1855, LR:OIA, New Mexico Superintendency, reel 547 (no frame number); and A. H. Blake to W. T. Magruder, July 20, 1855, and R. Johnson to R. Williams, Sep. 26, 1855, Registers of Letters Received and Letters Received by Headquarters, Department of New Mexico, RG 393, Records of United States Army Continental Commands, M1120, NAMP, 4:594, 614–15. For demands to restrict hunting, see Clint Padgitt, interviewed by William V. Ervin, WPA Federal Writers' Project Collection, Manuscript Division, Library of Congress; and Kavanagh, *Comanche Political History,* 345. For deer, elk, and bear hunting and horse eating, see Whitfield to Mix, Jan. 5, 1856, LR:OIA, Upper Arkansas Agency, 878:104–5; Robert G. Carter, *On the Border with Mackenzie* (New York: Antiquarian, 1961), 279; William Bollaert, *William Bollaert's Texas,* ed. W. Eugene Hollon and Ruth Lapham Butler (Norman: University of Oklahoma Press, 1956), 361; and Robert S. Neighbors, "The Na-

Ü-Ni, or Comanches of Texas; Their Traits and Beliefs, and Divisions and Intertribal Relations," *IPTS*, 3:356. For sheep and goats, see Simpson, Report, 16. According to Whitfield, thirty-two hundred Comanches living in the upper Arkansas basin used two thousand deer, one thousand elk, and five hundred bear a year. The large number of killed deer is particularly revealing, for Comanche traditions state that deer hunting was an emergency measure used only when whole camps were out of food. For deer hunting and food taboos, see Wallace and Hoebel, *Comanches*, 67, 70. For population, see W. B. Parker, "Census of the Tribes of Southwestern Texas in 1854," *IPTS*, 3:217; and Whitfield to Mix, Jan. 5, 1856, LR:OIA, Upper Arkansas Agency, 878:106–8. Quotes are from Thomas Fitzpatrick to A. Cumming, Nov. 19, 1853, 33d Cong., 1st sess., S. Ex. Doc. 1, 363; and Wallace and Hoebel, *Comanches*, 70.

23. Ralph P. Bieber, "The Southwestern Trails to California," *Mississippi Valley Historical Review* 12 (Dec. 1925): 359–62; and Walker Wyman, "Freighting: A Big Business on the Santa Fe Trail," *Kansas Historical Quarterly* 1 (Nov. 1931): 17–27.
24. "Treaty with the Comanche, Kiowa, and Apache, 1853," in *Indian Affairs*, ed. Kappler, 2:600–2; Fitzpatrick to Cumming, Nov. 19, 1853, 33d Cong., 1st sess., S. Ex. Doc. 1, 361–64 (quotes are from p. 363); and Kavanagh, *Comanche Political History*, 348–50.
25. For Comanches along the Arkansas, see Whitfield to commissioner of Indian Affairs, Sep. 4, 1855, 34th Cong., 1st sess., S. Ex. Doc. 1, 435–38; Robert C. Miller, "Report," *ARCIA*, 1857, 141–43; Whitfield to Cumming, Aug. 15, 1855, LR:OIA, Upper Arkansas Agency, 878:17; and Miller, Invoices of Goods Received for Comanche, Kiowa, and Apache Indians of the Arkansas River, May 12, 1858, RCS 5:198–221. For the Colorado gold rush, see West, *Contested Plains*, 145–70.
26. Whitfield to Manypenny, Sep. 4, 1855, 34th Cong., 1st sess., S. Ex. Doc. 1, 437; and Meriwether to Manypenny, Sep. 1855, LR:OIA, New Mexico Superintendency, reel 547 (no frame number).
27. Whipple, Report, 38–40; Kenner, *Comanchero Frontier*, 120–37; and Kavanagh, *Comanche Political History*, 370–73.
28. T. R. Fehrenbach, *Lone Star: A History of Texas and the Texans* (New York: Collier, 1968,) 279–324.
29. Rudolph Leopold Biesele, "The Relations between the German Settlers and the Indians in Texas, 1844–1860," *SHQ* 31 (Oct. 1927): 116–29; J. Pinckney Henderson to W. L. Marcy, Aug. 22, 1847, IPTS, 5:33–34; and Terry G. Jordan, *German Seed in Texas Soil: Immigrant Farmers in Nineteenth-Century Texas* (Austin: University of Texas Press, 1966), 40–54, 118–91.
30. Neighbors to Medill, Mar. 2, 1848, 30th Cong., 1st sess., S. Rpt. 171, 16–19; and Robert M. Utley, *Frontiersmen in Blue: The United States Army and the Indian, 1848–1865* (Lincoln: University of Nebraska Press, 1967), 61, 71–73. Quote is from *Telegraph and Texas Register*, Dec. 10, 1845.
31. Quotes are from Bordeaux to Cumming, Sep. 27, 1854, 33d Cong., 2d sess., S. Ex. Doc. 1, 299; and Russell Bartlett, *Personal Narrative of Explorations and Incidents in Texas, New Mexico, California, Sonora, and Chihuahua*, 2 vols. (New York: D. Appleton, 1854), 2:424. For Nuevo León, see Adams, "Embattled Borderland," 220.
32. For Comanche raids in Texas and Mexico, see P. H. Bell to U.S. Congress, Feb. 7, 1850, G. M. Brooke to W. Scott, May 28, 1850, J. H. Rollings to Brooke, Sep. 25, 1850, Bell to the Legislature, Feb. 12, 1852, H. Redmond to W. Mann, Apr. 16, 1852, and "Report of Indian Commissioners H. W. Berry and W. J. Moore," Jan. 1, 1857, *IPTS*, 3:114–20, 155–56, 158–59, 264–65; George Archibald McCall, *New Mexico in 1850: A Military View*, ed. Robert W. Frazer (Norman: University of Oklahoma Press, 1968), 103; Kevin Mulroy, *Freedom on the Border: The Seminole Maroons in Florida,*

the Indian Territory, Coahuila, and Texas (Lubbock: Texas Tech University Press, 1993), 67–73; Ralph A. Smith, "The Comanches' Foreign War: Fighting Head Hunters in the Tropics," *Great Plains Journal* 24–25 (1985–1986): 31–41; J. Fred Rippy, "The Indians of the Southwest in the Diplomacy of the United States and Mexico, 1848–1853," *Hispanic American Historical Review* 2 (Feb. 1919): 384–90; and Juan Mora-Torres, *The Making of the Mexican Border: The State, Capitalism, and Society in Nuevo León, 1848–1910* (Austin: University of Texas Press, 2001), 36–51. Quotes are from Neighbors to Medill, Nov. 21, 1853, LR:OIA, Texas Agency, 859:304, 306; and Julius Fröebel, *Seven Years' Travel in Central America, Northern Mexico, and the Far West of the United States* (London: R. Bentley, 1859), 22.

33. For Texas Rangers, see Brooke to Bell, Jan. 30, 1850, and Bell to M. Fillmore, Aug. 20, 1852, *IPTS*, 3:75, 179. For army officials' views on Comanches, see, e.g., Brooke to Scott, May 28, 1850, *IPTS*, 3:120. For the army and garrisons, see T. R. Fehrenbach, *Comanches: The Destruction of a People* (New York: Da Capo, 1974), 402–3, 417–18.

34. For the dispersal, see William J. Hardee to George Deal, Aug. 29, 1852, LR:OIA, Texas Agency, 858:890; and Kavanagh, *Comanche Political History*, 385. Quote is from R. B. Marcy, *Thirty Years of Army Life on the Border* (New York: Harper and Brothers, 1866), 210.

35. For Ketumsee's petition, see "Negotiations between the United States and the Comanche, Lipan, and Mescalero Tribes of Indians," Oct. 26, 1851, *IPTS*, 3:145. For rations, captives, and disputes, see Howard to Lea, Feb. 27 and June 1, 1852, and John A. Rogers, Report, June 28, 1852, LR:OIA, Texas Agency, 858:966–68, 999–1007, 1129; and "Report of R. B. Marcy and R. S. Neighbors to P. H. Bell," Sep. 30, 1854, *IPTS*, 3:189. Quotes are from Horace Capron to Howard, Sep. 30, 1852, and Hamilton W. Merrill to Rogers, Mar. 29, 1852, LR:OIA, Texas Agency, 858:1069, 1119.

36. For the land policies of Texas, see Fehrenbach, *Lone Star*, 282–83.

37. For negotiations, see Parker, *Notes*, 199–201 (quote is from pp. 199–200). For the reservation, see George W. Manypenny, "Report," *ARCIA*, 1856, 14–15; and Neighbors to Manypenny, Feb. 20 and Mar. 19, 1856, John A. Baylor to Neighbors, Mar. 1, 1856, John A. Baylor, Census Roll of Comanche Indians, Apr. 30, 1856, and Neighbors to Manypenny, May 14, 1856, LR:OIA, Texas Agency, 860:509–10, 533–34, 623–25, 637, 640–41.

38. For raids, see Neighbors to Mix, Oct. 20, 1854, LR:OIA, Texas Agency, 859:874; E. M. Pease to P. F. Smith, June 20, 1855, W. E. Jones to Pease, July 5 and 7, 1855, Bexar County committee to Pease, Sep. 1, 1855, "Petition to E. M. Pease for Rangers in Goliad County," Sep. 13, 1855, "Petition from Bandera to E. M. Pease," Sep. 21, 1855, Jones to Pease, Sep. 22, 1855, "Petition from Medina to E. M. Pease," Oct. 5, 1855, "Statement of Rufus Doane and J. F. Crosby," Nov. 13, 1855, and "Report of Indian Commissioners H. W. Berry and W. J. Moore," Jan. 1, 1857, *IPTS*, 3:219, 222–23, 231–33, 238–46, 248–49, 259–60, 264–65; Douglas Cooper to Rector, May 26, 1858, LR, Southern Superintendency, RG 75, Records of the Bureau of Indian Affairs, M640, NAMP, 834:422–23; and A. Montgomery to Samuel Cooper, Mar. 13, 1858, 35th Cong., 2d sess., H. Ex. Doc. 2, 415–16. For trade, see Neighbors to Manypenny, Sep. 18, 1856, *ARCIA*, 1856, 175. For white "Indian raiders," see Doyle Marshall, "Red-Haired 'Indian' Raiders on the Texas Frontier," *West Texas Historical Association Year Book* 61 (1985): 88–105. Quote is from Ross to Neighbors, Oct. 7, 1855, *IPTS*, 3:250–51.

39. Pease to citizens of Bexar county, July 25, 1855, Pease to J. H. Callahan, July 25, 1855, "Newspaper Item Concerning Indian Depredations," Aug. 6, 1855, Ross to Neighbors, Oct. 7, 1855, and H. R. Runnels to the Senate, Jan. 22, 1858, *IPTS*, 3:228–31, 250–51, 270–71; and Gary Clayton Ander-

son, *The Conquest of Texas: Ethnic Cleansing in the Promised Land* (Norman: University of Oklahoma Press, 2005), 264–68. Quotes are from D. C. Buell to Captain W. J. Newton, Jan. 30. 1855, cited in Anderson, *Conquest of Texas,* 266; and Neighbors to J. W. Denver, Sep. 16, 1857, 35th Cong., 1st sess., S. Ex. Doc. 11, 551–52.

40. For a Comanche war of extermination in Texas, see John Smiley to Neighbors, Nov. 3, 1857, LR: OIA, Texas Agency, 860:1159. For connections between raiding parties and reservation bands, see John S. Ford to Runnels, Feb. 27, 1858, TSA:RR, box 301–27, folder 3; and Robert C. Millar to A. M. Robinson, Aug. 17, 1858, 35th Cong., 2d sess., S. Ex. Doc. 1, 450. Ketumsee and other reservation chiefs repeatedly tried to prevent the raiding parties from entering the reservation. See, e.g., Baylor to Neighbors, Oct. 7, 1858, *IPTS,* 3:251–52. Quotes are from Neighbors to Denver, Sep. 16, 1857, 35th Cong., 1st sess., S. Ex. Doc. 11, 551; and Ford to Runnels, Feb. 27, 1858, TSA:RR, box 301–27, folder 3.

41. For the cancellation of annuities, see Kavanagh, *Comanche Political History,* 394. For new military policy, see D. E. Twiggs to L. Thomas, July 6, 1858, 35th Cong., 2d sess., S. Ex. Doc. 1, pt. 2, 258. For the Battle of Little Robe Creek, see Ford to Runnels, May 22, 1858, 35th Cong., 2d sess., H. Ex. Doc. 27, 17–20.

42. Earl Van Dorn, Report, Oct. 5, 1858, 35th Cong., 2d sess., S. Ex. Doc. 1, 272–74; and Utley, *Frontiersmen in Blue,* 134–35.

43. William Bent, Report, Oct. 5, 1859, 36th Cong., 1st sess., S. Ex. Doc. 2, pt. 2, 506. For the merger, see Charles Bogy and W. R. Irvin to Lewis Bogy, Dec. 8, 1866, Documents Relating to the Negotiation of Ratified and Unratified Treaties with Various Tribes of Indians, RG 75, Records of the Bureau of Indian Affairs, T494, NAMP, 7:709–12.

44. Anderson, *Conquest of Texas,* 307–24. For campaigns to exterminate the reservation Indians in Texas, see George Barnard to Runnels, May 4, 1859, TSA:RR, box 301–29, folder 18; and *Southern Intelligencer,* May 25, 1859.

45. For the spread of Texas ranching, see Terry G. Jordan, *North American Cattle-Ranching Frontiers: Origins, Diffusion, and Differentiation* (Albuquerque: University of New Mexico Press, 1993), 218–20. That the removal of Texas reservations so obviously overlapped with the expansion of the ranching system was not a coincidence; some army officers who were involved with the obliteration of Texas reservations were also involved in ranch development along the Brazos valley. See, e.g., Ty Cashion, *A Texas Frontier: The Clear Fork Country and Fort Griffin, 1849–1887* (Norman: University of Oklahoma Press, 1996), 50–52.

46. Anderson, *Conquest of Texas,* 327–42; Kenner, *Comanchero Frontier,* 141–44, 147–49, 155–56; Nicholas S. Davis to James H. Carleton, Oct. 30, 1864, Carleton to Michael Steck, Oct. 29, 1864, and Compact made and entered into between the Confederate Indian tribes and the Prairie tribes of Indians, made at Camp Napoleon, on Washita River, May 26, 1865, in *The War of the Rebellion: A Compilation of the Official Records of the Union and Confederate Armies,* 70 vols. (Washington, D.C.: GPO, 1880–1901), series 1, vol. 41, pt. 1, 212–13, pt. 4, 319–20, vol. 48, pt. 2, 1102–4.

47. For climate, see Stahle and Cleaveland, "Texas Drought History," 65.

48. John B. Sanborn, Report, Oct. 16, 1865, *ARCIA,* 1865, 528–35 (Eagle Drinking's statement is from p. 535); and "Treaty with the Comanche and Kiowa, 1865," in *Indian Affairs,* ed. Kappler, 2:892–95. The two Penateka signatories, Potsanaquahip and Tosawa, had only fleeting attachments to the supposedly ceded lands: Potsanaquahip's band had been shifting toward northern Comanchería since the late 1850s, while Tosawa already resided in a reservation in Indian Territory.

49. Richard White, "Animals and Enterprise," in *The Oxford History of the American West*, ed. Clyde A. Milner II, Carol A. O'Connor, and Martha A. Sandweiss (New York: Oxford University Press, 1994), 252–53; and Wallace and Hoebel, *Comanches*, 307–8.
50. A. B. Norton to D. N. Cooley, Sep. 28, 1866, *ARCIA*, 1866, 151; J. W. Throckmorton to E. M. Stanton, Aug. 5, 1867, *IPTS*, 4:235–36; Lorenzo Labadi to Norton, Aug. 28, 1867, in U.S. Department of the Interior, *Report of the Secretary of the Interior communicating . . . information in relation to the Indian tribes of the United States*, 2 vols. (Washington, D.C.: GPO, 1867), 2:214; and LaVere, *Contrary Neighbors*, 177–82.
51. For pastoralism, see Whitfield to Mix, Jan. 5, 1856, LR:OIA, Upper Arkansas Agency, 878:107; and Pekka Hämäläinen, "The Rise and Fall of Plains Indian Horse Cultures," *JAH* 90 (Dec. 2003): 844–45. For Labadi's account, see Labadi to Norton, Aug. 28, 1867, U.S. Department of the Interior, *Report*, 2:214–15 (quote is from p. 215).
52. For beef eating, see Wallace and Hoebel, *Comanches*, 69. Quote is from Hyde, *Life of George Bent*, 37.
53. For Texas longhorns, see Don Worcester, *The Texas Longhorn: Relic of the Past, Asset for the Future* (College Station: Texas A&M University Press, 1987), 3–24.
54. For American and *rico* involvement, see Kenner, *Comanchero Frontier*, 156–61, 173–74; and Brooks, *Captives and Cousins*, 317–18, 321.
55. Quotes are from Philip McCusker to Thomas Murphy, Sep. 7, 1866, LR:OIA, Kiowa Agency, 375:391; and Norton to Cooley, July 31, 1866, *ARCIA*, 1866, 151.
56. For comanchero trade, see J. Evetts Haley, "The Comanchero Trade," *SHQ* 38 (Jan. 1935): 161–64; Kenner, *Comanchero Frontier*, 178–79; Norton to Cooley, Sep. 28 and July 31, 1866, *ARCIA*, 1866, 145, 151; Patrick Henry Healy to Cooley, July 31, 1867, LR:OIA, New Mexico Superintendency, reel 554 (no frame number); Carter, *On the Border with Mackenzie*, 32; and Michael L. Tate, "Comanche Captives: People between Two Worlds," *CO* 72 (Fall 1994): 250. Quote is from Vicente Romano, "Los Comanches," interviewed by Lorin W. Brown, Apr. 6, 1937, WPA Federal Writers' Project Collection, Manuscript Division, Library of Congress.
57. For rituals, see Romano, "Los Comanches"; and Jonathan H. Jones, *A Condensed History of the Apache and Comanche Indian Tribes for Amusements and General Knowledge: Prepared from the General Conversation of Herman Lehmann, Willie Lehmann, Mrs. Mina Keyser, Mrs. A. J. Buckmeyer and Others* (San Antonio: Johnson Brothers, 1899), 38 (quote is from pp. 198–99). For inflated prices, see J. Marvin Hunter, *The Boy Captives: Life among the Indians* (1927; reprint, New York: Garland, 1977), 58; and Rafael Chacon, *Legacy of Honor: The Life of Rafael Chacón, a Nineteenth-Century New Mexican*, ed. Jacqueline Dorgan Meketa (Albuquerque: University of New Mexico Press, 1982), 105–6.
58. For annuities, see Jesse Leavenworth to Cooley, June 5, 1866, Leavenworth to L. V. Bogy, Feb. 26, 1867, and Leavenworth to N. G. Taylor, June 18, 1867, LR:OIA, Kiowa Agency, 375:250–51, 505–6, 604–5; and H. Douglas to assistant adjutant general, Jan. 13, 1867, 40th Cong., 1st sess., S. Ex. Doc. 13, 52–54. For ransoming and the controversy over the practice, see Throckmorton to Cooley, Nov. 5, 1866, M. Walker to C. McKeever, May 14, 1867, and G. Salmon to J. P. Newcomb, June 23, 1867, *IPTS*, 4:124–25, 209, 314–15; Leavenworth to Murphy, Dec. 14, 1866, LR:OIA, Kiowa Agency, 375:398–401; Labadi to Norton, Aug. 28, 1867, U.S. Department of the Interior, *Report*, 2:214–15; John DuBois to Cyrus H. De Forrest, July 12, 1867, Letters Received by Headquarters, District of New Mexico, RG 393, Records of United States Army Continental Com-

mands, M1088, NAMP, 5:356–57; and Leavenworth to Taylor, May 21, 1868, 41st Cong., 2d sess., H. Misc. Doc. 139, 6. Quotes are from J. B. Barry to Throckmorton, Mar. 16, 1867, *IPTS*, 4:177; and I. C. Taylor to Cooley, Sep. 30, 1866, *ARCIA*, 1866, 281.

59. William Tecumseh Sherman's endorsement on M. Walker's report, June 25, 1867, *IPTS*, 4:210. For the clash between the captive trade and slave economies of the Southwest and U.S. modernization policies, see Brooks, *Captives and Cousins*, ch. 8.

60. For the retreat of the Texas frontier, see W. Fanning to Throckmorton, Feb. 7, 1867, H. I. Richards to Throckmorton, Feb. 25, 1867, Barry to Throckmorton, Mar. 16, 1867, Richards to Throckmorton, Mar. 19, 1867, H. Secrest to Throckmorton, Apr. 8, 1867, I. Mullins to Throckmorton, Apr. 20, 1867, Throckmorton to Stanton, Aug. 5, 1867, and Jones to Pease, Aug. 7, 1867, *IPTS*, 4:154–55, 167, 177–80, 183–84, 196, 236–38. Quotes are from Barry to Throckmorton, Mar. 16, 1858, and W. C. Billingsly to D. R. Curley, June 24, 1867, *IPTS*, 4:177, 224.

CHAPTER 8. COLLAPSE

1. For Sand Creek and the central plains, see Elliott West, *The Contested Plains: Indians, Goldseekers, and the Rush to Colorado* (Lawrence: University of Kansas Press, 1998), 290–310. For Lakotas, see Robert M. Utley, *The Indian Frontier of the American West, 1846–1890* (Albuquerque: University of New Mexico Press, 1984), 103–5.
2. For the Peace Commission's work and designs, see Francis Paul Prucha, *The Great Father: The United States Government and the American Indians*, 2 vols. (Lincoln: University of Nebraska Press, 1984), 1:488–92; and Ray Allen Billington, *Westward Expansion: A History of the American Frontier*, 4th ed. (New York: Macmillan, 1974), 570–71.
3. William T. Hagan, *United States–Comanche Relations: The Reservation Years* (1976; reprint, Norman: University of Oklahoma Press, 1990), 27–43; and "Treaty with the Kiowa and Comanche, 1867," in *Indian Affairs: Laws and Treaties*, ed. Charles J. Kappler, 5 vols. (Washington, D.C.: GPO, 1904), 2:977–82.
4. For traditional interpretations, see, e.g., Billington, *Westward Expansion*, 571; Hagan, *United States–Comanche Relations*, 37; and Dee Brown, *Bury My Heart at Wounded Knee: An Indian History of the American West* (1970; reprint, London: Vintage, 1991), 241–42, 258.
5. All quotes of Paruasemena's speech are from "Proceedings of Council with the Comanches, Kiowas, Arapahoes, and Apaches at Medicine Lodge Creek, Kansas," Oct. 19, 1867, in Nathaniel G. Taylor, John B. Henderson, Samuel F. Tappan, John B. Sanborn, William S. Harney, Alfred H. Terry, William T. Sherman, and Christopher C. Augur, *Papers Relating to Talks and Councils Held with the Indians in Dakota and Montana in the Years 1866–1869* (Washington, D.C.: GPO, 1910), 59–60.
6. For the stipulations, see "Treaty with the Kiowa and Comanche," 977–81 (quote is from p. 980). For Native American ideas of territoriality and land ownership in general, see Patricia Albers and Jeanne Kay, "Sharing the Land: A Study in American Indian Territoriality," in *A Cultural Geography of North American Indians*, ed. Thomas E. Ross and Tyrel G. Moore (Boulder: Westview, 1987), 47–91. For Comanches in particular, see Daniel J. Gelo, "'Comanche Land and Ever Has Been': A Native Geography of the Nineteenth-Century Comanchería," *SHQ* 103 (Jan. 2000): 273–307. Arrell Morgan Gibson provided a traditional—and typical—interpretation that the Medicine Lodge Treaty became, in the end, an unqualified American victory. "Despite these rhapsodic utter-

ances" by Paruasemena and Satanta, he wrote, "the will of the commissioners prevailed, and before the council closed, the chiefs had assented to drastically reduced ranges." See Gibson, *The West in the Life of the Nation* (Lexington, Mass.: D. C. Heath, 1976), 433. The Commission's interpretation was also complicated by the fact that Kwahadas, who controlled most of the "ceded" lands, were not represented at the talks. Here, however, the commissioners departed from the standard U.S. agenda of denying Indians' external sovereignty and treated Comanche signatories as representatives of sovereign polities who could negotiate for the whole of the Comanche community.

7. Quotes are from "Treaty with the Kiowa and Comanche," 980–81. See also Andrew C. Isenberg, *The Destruction of the Bison: An Environmental History, 1750–1920* (Cambridge: Cambridge University Press, 2000), 124; and Henry M. Stanley, "A British Journalist Reports the Medicine Lodge Council of 1867," *Kansas Historical Quarterly* 33 (Autumn 1967): 289.
8. O. H. Browning to Nathaniel G. Taylor, Dec. 19, 1867, Leavenworth to Taylor, May 21, 1868, Philip McCusker to Leavenworth, Apr. 10, 1868, McCusker to Taylor, June 5, 1868, Taylor to Browning, July 1, 1868, and L. S. Walkley to W. B. Hazen, Dec. 28, 1868, LR:OIA, Kiowa Agency, 375:476, 859–62, 866–71, 873–75, 376:525–28; and Hagan, *United States–Comanche Relations*, 52–55. Quote is from McCusker to Hazen, Dec. 21, 1868, LR:OIA, Kiowa Agency, 376:520.
9. Prucha, *Great Father*, 1:479–606; and Utley, *Indian Frontier*, 129–55, 164–65.
10. For reservation and off-reservation bands and relations between them, see Benjamin Grierson to W. G. Mitchell, Apr. 12 and July 10, 1870, and Lawrie Tatum to Enoch Hoag, Feb. 11, 1870, LR: OIA, Kiowa Agency, 376:572–74, 612–13, 798–99; Tatum to Hoag, May 20 and July 13, 1871, Tatum to Grierson and Ranald Mackenzie, Aug. 4, 1871, and Tatum to Francis A. Walker, May 1, 1872, RCS 34:418, 471–72, 486–87, 41:592–97; and Tatum to Hoag, Sep. 1, 1871, *ARCIA*, 1871, 503.
11. For intertribal bands, see George Getty to C. McKeever, Mar. 13, 1869, Letters Sent by the 9th Military Department, the Department of New Mexico, and the District of New Mexico, RG 393, Records of United States Army Continental Commands, M1072, NAMP, 4:455–56; Grierson to assistant adjutant general, Department of the Missouri, June 14, 1870, LR:OIA, Kiowa Agency, 376:591–92; George E. Hyde, *Life of George Bent: Written from His Letters*, ed. Savoie Lottinville (Norman: University of Oklahoma Press, 1968), 137; and Thomas W. Kavanagh, *Comanche Political History: An Ethnohistorical Perspective* (Lincoln: University of Nebraska Press, 1996), 429.
12. For Tatum's policies, see Lawrie Tatum, *Our Red Brothers and the Peace Policy of President Ulysses S. Grant* (1899; reprint, Lincoln: University of Nebraska Press, 1970), 38–45. For Comanche strategies, see J. Marvin Hunter, *The Boy Captives: Life among the Indians* (1927; reprint, New York: Garland, 1977), 57–58; Tatum to Hoag, May 20, 1871, and Oct. 10, 1872, RCS 41:611, 779; and Hagan, *United States–Comanche Relations*, 68–73. When the governor of Texas demanded that stricter measures be adopted to suppress Comanche raiding into Texas, he specifically insisted that Comanche men should be forced to collect their annuities personally rather than through chiefs. See "Negotiations Concerning Big Tree and Satanta," Oct. 6, 1873, *IPTS*, 4:352. For ransoming, see Tatum to Hoag, Aug. 19, 1870, and Mar. 31, 1873, LR:OIA, Kiowa Agency, 376:995–96, 378:235–36; and Tatum to Hoag, May 12, 1871, RCS 34:410–11.
13. Utley, *Indian Frontier*, 164–66; and Tatum, *Our Red Brothers*, 33–34. Quote is from P. H. Sheridan to E. D. Townsend, Nov. 1, 1869, 41st Cong., 2d sess., H. Ex. Doc. 1, pt. 2, 38.
14. See Tatum to E. S. Parker, July 24, 1869, LR:OIA, Kiowa Agency, 376:291–94; and Hagan, *United States–Comanche Relations*, 63–67.

15. Quotes are from Rupert Norval Richardson, *The Comanche Barrier to South Plains Settlement: A Century and a Half of Savage Resistance to the Advancing Frontier* (Glendale, Calif. Arthur H. Clark, 1933), 352; and Cyrus Beede to Hoag, Aug. 13, 1872, LR:OIA, Central Superintendency, 61:760.
16. Charles L. Kenner, *The Comanchero Frontier: A History of New Mexican–Plains Indian Relations* (1969; reprint, Norman: University of Oklahoma Press, 1994), 167–69, 174; William Steele, "Report of Indian Depredations," Nov. 1, 1875, *IPTS*, 4:388–91; Hagan, *United States–Comanche Relations*, 75; Tatum to Hoag, Mar. 31, 1873, LR:OIA, Kiowa Agency, 378:240; and C. C. Augur to assistant adjutant general, Aug. 14, 1872, 42d Cong., 3d sess., S. Ex. Doc. 7, 1.
17. Kenner, *Comanchero Frontier*, 183–87; and Vicente Romano, "Los Comanches," interviewed by Lorin W. Brown, Apr. 6, 1937, WPA Federal Writers' Project Collection, Manuscript Division, Library of Congress. Quotes are from Herman Lehmann, *Nine Years among the Indians, 1870–1879: The Story of the Captivity and Life of a Texan among the Indians*, ed. J. Marvin Hunter (1927; reprint, Albuquerque: University of New Mexico Press, 1993), 92; and John Hatch to assistant adjutant general, Apr. 15, 1872, cited in Kavanagh, *Comanche Political History*, 469.
18. Quote is from "Proceedings of Council with the Comanches," 60.
19. For estimates of Comanche population, see Kavanagh, *Comanche Political History*, 471–73.
20. For the situation in Kansas, see West, *Contested Plains*, 323–26.
21. For federal officials and slave traffic, see, e.g., William L. Cady to Hoag, Sep. 9, 1870, cited in Carl Coke Rister, *Border Captives: The Traffic in Prisoners by Southern Plains Indians, 1835–1875* (Norman: University of Oklahoma Press, 1940), 175. For military elite and Peace Policy, see James L. Haley, *The Buffalo War* (1976; reprint, Austin: State House, 1998), 99–100; and Utley, *Indian Frontier*, 164–65.
22. Utley, *Indian Frontier*, 143–48; Hagan, *United States–Comanche Relations*, 76–77; and Tatum to Grieson and Mackenzie, Aug. 4, 1871, RCS 34:486–87.
23. For the post–Civil War U.S. Army and its strategic options on the plains, see Sherry Marker, *Plains Indian Wars*, 2d ed. (New York: Facts on File, 2003), 72–79; and David D. Smits, "The Frontier Army and the Destruction of the Buffalo, 1865–1883," *Western Historical Quarterly* 25 (Autumn 1994): 314–18.
24. For the distinctiveness of the Anglo-American frontier among the expanding colonial frontiers in the West, see John Mack Faragher, "Americans, Mexicans, and Métis," in *Under an Open Sky: Rethinking America's Western Past*, ed. William Cronon, George Miles, and Jay Gitlin (New York: W. W. Norton, 1992), 90–105.
25. For the situation in Texas, the 1871 campaign, and the patrol system, see T. R. Fehrenbach, *Comanches: The Destruction of a People* (New York: Da Capo, 1974), 496–513, 518. For the September 1872 attack, see Mackenzie to assistant adjutant general, Oct. 12, 1872, LR:OIA, Central Superintendency, 62:110–14; and Tatum, *Our Red Brothers*, 134–35. For the Comanche move onto the reservation, see Tatum to Hoag, Dec. 9, 1872, RCS 41:839–40; Tatum to Hoag, Jan. 11, 1873, LR:OIA, Kiowa Agency, 378:129–31; and Hagan, *United States–Comanche Relations*, 89–90.
26. Kenner, *Comanchero Frontier*, 192–202.
27. Thomas C. Battey, *The Life and Adventures of a Quaker among the Indians* (1875; reprint, Norman: University of Oklahoma Press, 1968), 82, 105, 114, 138, 161–62 (quote is from p. 164); Hagan, *United States–Comanche Relations*, 93–94; and Kavanagh, *Comanche Political History*, 434–37.
28. "Negotiations Concerning Big Tree and Satanta," 352–57.

29. William Cronon, *Nature's Metropolis: Chicago and the Great West* (New York: W. W. Norton, 1991), 216–17; Isenberg, *Destruction*, 130–34; and Smits, "Frontier Army," 326–27. Quote in the following paragraph is from Smits, "Frontier Army," 332.
30. Smits, "Frontier Army," 328–32; Ty Cashion, *A Texas Frontier: The Clear Fork Country and Fort Griffin, 1849–1887* (Norman: University of Oklahoma Press, 1996), 157–76; Haley, *Buffalo War*, 23–28, 35–36; and Lehmann, *Nine Years*, 171.
31. For Isatai, see J. M. Haworth to Hoag, May 6, 1874, LR:OIA, Kiowa Agency, 379:218–19; Battey, *Life and Adventures*, 302–3; and Wallace and Hoebel, *Comanches*, 319.
32. For reservation problems, see E. P. Smith to Haworth, Nov. 24, 1873, Letters Sent by the Office of Indian Affairs, RG 75, Records of the Bureau of Indian Affairs, M21, NAMP, 114:474; Haworth to Beede, Dec. 8, 1873, and Haworth to C. Delano, Dec. 15, 1873, RCS 47:1062–69, 1080–96; and Beede to Smith, Mar. 10, 1874, and Haworth to Hoag, Mar. 10, 1874, LR:OIA, Central Superintendency, 63:1110–11. For the Elk Creek gathering, see James Mooney, *Calendar History of the Kiowa Indians* (1898; reprint, Washington, D.C.: Smithsonian Institution, 1979), 201–3; Battey, *Life and Adventures*, 307–8; and Wallace and Hoebel, *Comanches*, 319–25.
33. For internal disputes, see Haworth to Hoag, June 8, 1874, LR:OIA, Kiowa Agency, 379:297–99; Haworth to Smith, Sep. 1, 1874, 43d Cong., 2d sess., H. Ex. Doc. 1, pt. 5, 527–28; Kavanagh, *Comanche Political History*, 49–51; and William T. Hagan, *Quanah Parker, Comanche Chief* (Norman: University of Oklahoma Press, 1993), 12.
34. G. Derek West, "The Battle of Adobe Walls," *Panhandle-Plains Historical Review* 36 (1963): 16–29; and Mooney, *Calendar History*, 203.
35. For raids, see Haley, *Buffalo War*, 78; and Richardson, *Comanche Barrier*, 382–83. For Fort Griffin, see Smits, "Frontier Army," 332; and Isenberg, *Destruction*, 138. For drought, see Hagan, *Quanah Parker*, 13.
36. G. K. Sanderson to post adjutant, Aug. 5 and 8, 1874, LR:OIA, Kiowa Agency, 379:856–57, 870–73. For the U.S. Army attacks, which later became known as the Red River War, see William H. Leckie, "The Red River War: 1874–1875," *Panhandle-Plains Historical Review* 29 (1956): 83–91.
37. For the battle of the Palo Duro Canyon, see Robert G. Carter, *On the Border with Mackenzie, or Winning West Texas from the Comanches* (New York: Antiquarian, 1961), 487–95; and Mooney, *Calendar History*, 210–11.
38. Haley, *Buffalo War*, 181; and Haworth to Smith, Sep. 20, 1875, *ARCIA*, 1875, 275.
39. J. W. Davidson to assistant adjutant general, Oct. 10, 1874, Augur to W. D. Whipple, Nov. 17, 1874, Davidson to Augur, Dec. 23, 1874, and Nelson A. Miles, "Report," Mar. 4, 1875, in "The Indian Campaign on the Staked Plains, 1874–1875: Military Correspondence from War Department, Adjutant General's Office, File 2815–1874," ed. Joe F. Taylor, *Panhandle-Plains Historical Review* 34 (1961): 69–73, 106–7, 141, 209–13; Hagan, *Quanah Parker*, 14; and Hagan, *United States-Comanche Relations*, 112–14.

CONCLUSION. THE SHAPE OF POWER

1. The best study of the envisioning and realization of this new American empire in the West is William Cronon, *Nature's Metropolis: Chicago and the Great West* (New York: W. W. Norton, 1991), esp. 41–93.
2. See Walter Prescott Webb, *The Great Plains* (Boston: Ginn, 1931); and Rupert Norval Richardson,

The Comanche Barrier to South Plains Settlement: A Century and a Half of Savage Resistance to the Advancing Frontier (Glendale, Calif.: Arthur H. Clark, 1933).

3. Walter Prescott Webb, "History as High Adventure," *American Historical Review* 64 (Jan. 1959): 274; and Cormac McCarthy, *Blood Meridian: Or, the Evening Redness in the West* (New York: Random House, 1985), 54.
4. T. R. Fehrenbach, *Comanches: The Destruction of a People* (New York: Da Capo, 1974), xiv, 191, 496.
5. For Iroquois, see Daniel K. Richter's incisive analysis in *The Ordeal of the Longhouse: The Peoples of the Iroquois League in the Era of European Colonization* (Chapel Hill: University of North Carolina Press, 1992), esp. 2–3; and Alan Taylor, *The Divided Ground: Indians, Settlers, and the Northern Borderland of the American Revolution* (New York: Vintage, 2005), esp. 3–7.
6. See, e.g., Richter, *Ordeal*, 133–61; Gregory Evans Dowd, *A Spirited Resistance: The North American Indian Struggle for Unity, 1745–1815* (Baltimore: Johns Hopkins University Press, 1992), 51–56; Tom Hatley, *The Dividing Paths: Cherokees and South Carolinians through the Era of Revolution* (Oxford: Oxford University Press, 1993), 217–18; John H. Moore, *The Cheyenne Nation: A Social and Demographic History* (Lincoln: University of Nebraska Press, 1987), 191–204; and Richard White, *The Roots of Dependency: Subsistence, Environment, and Social Change among the Choctaws, Pawnees, and Navajos* (Lincoln: University of Nebraska Press, 1983), 250–314.
7. The most telling example of such paralyzing internal divisions is, once again, the Iroquois, who splintered in the late seventeenth and early eighteenth centuries into three contending factions: Anglophiles, Francophiles, and neutrals. See Richter, *Ordeal*, 105–213.
8. For Mongol frontier strategies, see Thomas J. Barfield, "The Shadow Empires: Imperial State Formation along the Chinese-Nomad Frontier," in *Empires: Perspectives from Archaeology and History*, ed. Susan E. Alcock, Terence N. D'Altroy, Kathleen D. Morrison, and Carla M. Sinopoli (Cambridge: Cambridge University Press, 2001), 15–17, 24–28. For broader discussions of nomadic empires and their limitations, see Thomas D. Hall, "Role of Nomads in Core-Periphery Relations," in *Core/Periphery Relations in Precapitalist Worlds*, ed. Christopher Chase-Dunn and Thomas D. Hall (Boulder: Westview, 1991), 212–39; and Nikolay N. Kradin, "Nomadism, Evolution, and World-Systems: Pastoral Societies in Theories of Historical Development," *Journal of World-Systems Research* 8 (Fall 2002): 368–88.
9. This view corresponds with Michael Mann's notion that imperial powers are better understood as intersecting, often shifting networks of power than as rigidly structured polities. It is also compatible with Terence N. D'Altroy's observation of empires: "The outstanding feature of preindustrial empires was the continually metamorphosing nature of relations between the central powers and the societies drawn under the imperial aegis." See Michael Mann, *The Sources of Social Power*, vol. 1, *A History of Power from the Beginning to A.D. 1760* (Cambridge: Cambridge University Press, 1986); and Terence N. D'Altroy, "Empires in a Wider World," in *Empires*, 125.
10. For an illuminating treatise of this historiographical tradition, see Gerald E. Poyo and Gilberto M. Hinojosa, "Spanish Texas and Borderlands Historiography in Transition: Implications for United States History," *JAH* 75 (Sep. 1988): 393–402.
11. For Texas's and New Mexico's peripheral status in the Spanish imperial system as a function of their retarded economic development, see, e.g., Thomas D. Hall, "The Río de la Plata and the Greater Southwest," in *Contested Ground: Comparative Frontiers on the Northern and Southern*

Edges of the Spanish Empire, ed. Donna J. Guy and Thomas E. Sheridan (Tucson: University of Arizona Press, 1998), 156–57. My argument here has been strongly influenced by Ross Frank, *From Settler to Citizen: New Mexican Economic Development and the Creation of Vecino Society, 1750–1820* (Berkeley: University of California Press, 2000), esp. 119–39.

12. These social dynamics in New Mexico have been touched upon in the first three chapters of this book. For the dreams and failures of New Mexico's elite, see also Ramón A. Gutiérrez, *When Jesus Came, the Corn Mothers Went Away: Marriage, Sexuality, and Power in New Mexico, 1500–1846* (Stanford: Stanford University Press, 1991), 101–8, 176–206, 303–6; and Oakah L. Jones, Jr., *Los Paisanos: Spanish Settlers on the Northern Frontier of New Spain* (Norman: University of Oklahoma Press, 1979), 163–65.
13. For the first in-depth study of Spanish-Ute relations and the Great Basin slave system, see Ned Blackhawk, *Violence over the Land: Indians and Empires in the Early American West* (Cambridge: Harvard University Press, 2006).
14. David J. Weber, *The Spanish Frontier in North America* (New Haven: Yale University Press, 1992), 305–11; and Alfred Crosby, *Ecological Imperialism: The Biological Expansion of Europe, 900–1900* (Cambridge: Cambridge University Press, 1986), 182–84.
15. I have made this point of Lakotas' exceptional durability before. See Pekka Hämäläinen, "The Rise and Fall of Plains Indian Horse Cultures," *JAH* 90 (Dec. 2003).
16. For Osages, see Willard H. Rollings, *The Osage: An Ethnohistorical Study of Hegemony on the Prairie-Plains* (Columbia: University of Missouri Press, 1992); and Kathleen DuVal, *The Native Ground: Indians and Colonists in the Heart of the Continent* (Philadelphia: University of Pennsylvania Press, 2006).
17. Two profoundly important studies have retold the story of the U.S. expansion into the Southwest through the reactions and choices of local communities, thus challenging the conventional top-down models and showing how the identity choices, loyalty decisions, and active and passive resistance of ordinary frontier residents influenced the process of annexation. See David J. Weber, *The Mexican Frontier, 1821–1846: The American Southwest under Mexico* (Albuquerque: University of New Mexico Press, 1982); and Andrés Reséndez, *Changing National Identities at the Frontier: Texas and New Mexico, 1800–1850* (New York: Cambridge University Press, 2005). The role of Native peoples in the Americanization of the Southwest, by contrast, has received only meager coverage.
18. The fallacy of thinly occupied, semi-empty North America informs even Niall Ferguson's much-debated *Colossus*, which is explicitly framed as an antidote to the myth of American exceptionalism. See Niall Ferguson, *Colossus: The Rise and Fall of the American Empire* (London: Penguin, 2004), esp. 35–41.
19. For a brilliant analysis of these dynamics, see Curtis Marez, "Signifying Spain, Becoming Comanche, Making Mexicans: Indian Captivity and the History of Chicana/o Performance," *American Quarterly* 53 (June 2001): 267–307.
20. Dan Flores, *The Natural West: Environmental History of the Great Plains and Rocky Mountains* (Norman: University of Oklahoma Press, 2001), 53. The still persisting academic and nonacademic tendency to gloss over the negative effects of Native Americans' actions on their environments and economies generates similar distortions as the tendency to depict the Indians as victimized innocents of European aggression. By granting Indians only partial agency, both lines of reasoning

oversimplify the historical experience of American Indians and, by extension, deny their histories and cultures. For a similar argument, see Richard White and William Cronon, "Ecological Change and Indian-White Relations," in *Handbook of North American Indians*, vol. 4, *History of Indian-White Relations*, ed. Wilcomb E. Washburn (Washington, D.C.: Smithsonian Institution, 1989), 417.

21. For national consolidation, see D. W. Meinig, *The Shaping of America: A Geographic Perspective on 500 Years of History*, vol. 3, *Transcontinental America, 1850–1915* (New Haven: Yale University Press, 1998), pts. 2 and 3; and Elliott West, "Reconstructing Race," *Western Historical Quarterly* 34 (Spring 2003): 7–26.

BIBLIOGRAPHY

ARCHIVAL SOURCES

Archivo General de la Nación. Mexico City, Mexico. Photostatic copy. Zimmerman Library. University of New Mexico, Albuquerque.
Archivo General de las Indias. Seville, Spain. Guadalajara. Microfilm copy. Western History Collections. University of Oklahoma, Norman.
Ramo de Californias.
Ramo de Historias.
Ramo de Provincias.
Bancroft Library. University of California at Berkeley.
Herbert E. Bolton Papers.
Béxar Archives. University of Texas at Austin. Microfilm copy. Zimmerman Library. University of New Mexico, Albuquerque.
General Manuscript Series, 1717–1836.
Library of Congress. Manuscript Division. Washington, D.C.
WPA Federal Writers' Project Collection.
Mexican Archives of New Mexico. Microfilm copy. New Mexico State Records Center and Archives, Santa Fe.
New Mexico State Archives. Center for Southwest Research. University of New Mexico, Albuquerque.
Spanish Archives of New Mexico. New Mexico State Records Center and Archives, Santa Fe.
Series I, land grant records.
Series II, provincial records.
Texas State Archives. Austin, Texas.
Texas Governor Hardin Richard Runnels Records.
U.S. National Archives. Microfilm Publications. Washington, D.C.
Record Group 59. General Records of the Department of the State.
Despatches from United States Consuls in Texas, 1825–44. Microcopy T153.

Record Group 75. Records of the Bureau of Indian Affairs.
Documents Relating to the Negotiation of Ratified and Unratified Treaties with Various Tribes of Indians. Microcopy T494.
Letters Received by the Office of Indian Affairs. Central Superintendency. Microcopy 234.
Letters Received by the Office of Indian Affairs. Kiowa Agency. Microcopy 234.
Letters Received by the Office of Indian Affairs. New Mexico Superintendency. Microcopy 234.
Letters Received by the Office of Indian Affairs. Seminole Agency. Microcopy 234.
Letters Received by the Office of Indian Affairs. Texas Agency. Microcopy 234.
Letters Received by the Office of Indian Affairs. Upper Arkansas Agency. Microcopy 234.
Letters Received by the Office of Indian Affairs. Wichita Agency. Microcopy 234.
Letters Received by the Office of the Secretary of War Relating to Indian Affairs. Microcopy 271.
Letters Received by the Southern Superintendency. Microcopy 640.
Letters Sent by the Office of Indian Affairs. Microcopy 21.
Records of the Central Superintendency. Microcopy 856.
Record Group 107. Records of the Office of the Secretary of War.
Letters Received by Secretary of War. Main Series. Microcopy 221.
Record Group 393. Records of United States Army Continental Commands.
Letters Received by Headquarters. District of New Mexico. Microcopy 1088.
Letters Sent by the 9th Military Department, the Department of New Mexico, and the District of New Mexico. Microcopy 1072.
Registers of Letters Received and Letters Received by Headquarters. Department of New Mexico, 1854–1865. Microcopy 1120.

PERIODICALS

Arkansas Intelligencer
Arkansas State Gazette
El Fanal de Chihuahua
Natchitoches Courier
National Intelligencer
Southern Intelligencer
Telegraph and Texas Register

GOVERNMENT DOCUMENTS

Carter, Clarence E., ed. *The Territorial Papers of the U.S.* Vol. 13, *The Territory of Louisiana-Missouri, 1803–1806.* 28 vols. Washington, D.C.: GPO, 1948.
Carter, Clarence E., and John P. Bloom, eds. *The Territorial Papers of the United States.* Vol. 20, *The Territory of Arkansas, 1825–1829.* Washington, D.C.: GPO, 1954.

Kappler, Charles J., ed. *Indian Affairs: Laws and Treaties.* 5 vols. Washington, D.C.: GPO, 1904.

Morse, Jedidiah. *Report to the Secretary of War of the United States on Indian Affairs.* New Haven: S. Converse, 1822.

Taylor, Nathaniel G., John B. Henderson, Samuel F. Tappan, John B. Sanborn, William S. Harney, Alfred H. Terry, William T. Sherman, and Christopher C. Augur. *Papers Relating to Talks and Councils Held with the Indians in Dakota and Montana in the Years 1866–1869.* Washington, D.C.: GPO, 1910.

U.S. Congress. *American State Papers.* Class 1, *Foreign Relations,* 1789–1828.

———. *American State Papers.* Class 5, *Military Affairs,* 1789–1838.

———. House of Representatives.

24th Cong., 1st sess., Doc. 181.
30th Cong., 1st sess., Ex. Doc. 1.
30th Cong., 1st sess., Ex. Doc. 60.
30th Cong., 2d sess., Ex. Doc. 1.
31st Cong., 1st sess., Ex. Doc. 45.
35th Cong., 2d sess., Ex. Doc. 2.
35th Cong., 2d sess., Ex. Doc. 27.
41st Cong., 2d sess., Ex. Doc. 1.
41st Cong., 2d sess., Misc. Doc. 139.
43d Cong., 2d sess., Ex. Doc. 1.

———. Senate.

27th Cong., 2d sess., Ex. Doc. 1.
30th Cong., 1st sess., Ex. Doc. 1.
30th Cong, 1st sess., Rpt. 171.
33d Cong., 1st sess., Ex. Doc. 1.
33d Cong., 2d sess., Ex. Doc. 1.
33d Cong., 2d sess., Ex. Doc. 78.
34th Cong., 1st sess., Ex. Doc. 1.
35th Cong., 1st sess., Ex. Doc. 11.
35th Cong., 2d sess., Ex. Doc. 1.
36th Cong., 1st sess., Ex. Doc. 2.
40th Cong., 1st sess., Ex. Doc. 13.
42d Cong., 3d sess., Ex. Doc. 7.

U.S. Department of the Interior. *Report of the Secretary of the Interior communicating . . . information in relation to the Indian tribes of the United States.* 2 vols. Washington, D.C.: GPO, 1867.

U.S. Office of Indian Affairs. *Annual Report of the Commissioner of Indian Affairs,* 1849.

———. 1856.

———. 1857.

———. 1865.

———. 1866.

———. 1871.

———. 1875.

U.S. President. *California and New Mexico: Message from the President of the United States Communicating Information Called For by a Resolution of the Senate.* New York: Arno, 1976.

The War of the Rebellion: A Compilation of the Official Records of the Union and Confederate Armies. 70 vols. Washington, D.C.: GPO, 1880–1901.

PRINTED PRIMARY SOURCES

Abel, Annie Heloise, ed. *The Official Correspondence of James S. Calhoun While Indian Agent at Santa Fé and Superintendent of Indian Affairs in New Mexico.* Washington, D.C.: GPO, 1915.

Abert, James William. *Expedition to the Southwest: An 1845 Reconnaissance of Colorado, New Mexico, Texas, and Oklahoma.* 1846. Reprint, Lincoln: University of Nebraska Press, 1999.

———. *Through the Country of the Comanche Indians in the Fall of the Year 1845: The Journal of a U.S. Army Expedition Led by Lieutenant James W. Abert,* edited by John Calvin. San Francisco: John Howell, 1970.

"Account of the Rebellion, An." In Janet Lecompte, *A Rebellion in Río Arriba,* 91–104. Albuquerque: University of New Mexico Press, 1985.

Almonte, Juan N. "Statistical Report on Texas," translated by C. E. Castañeda. *SHQ* 28 (Jan. 1925): 177–202.

Anonymous. Notes Concerning the Province of New Mexico Collected on My Mission to the West. In "Anonymous Description of New Mexico, 1818," edited by Alfred B. Thomas. *SHQ* 33 (July 1929): 57–66.

Anonymous. *Texas in 1837: An Anonymous, Contemporary Narrative,* edited by Andrew Forest Muir. 1958. Reprint, Austin: University of Texas Press, 1988.

Anza, Juan Bautista de. Tarja. In Alfred B. Thomas, "An Eighteenth Century Comanche Document." *American Anthropologist* 31 (Apr.–June 1929): 274–98.

Babb, Bianca. A True Story of My Capture by, and Life with the Comanche Indians. In "Every Day Seemed to Be a Holiday: The Captivity of Bianca Babb," edited by Daniel J. Gelo and Scott Zesch. *SHQ* 107 (July 2003): 49–67.

Babb, Theodore Adolphus. *In the Bosom of the Comanches: A Thrilling Tale of Savage Indian Life, Massacre, and Captivity Truthfully Told by a Surviving Captive.* Dallas: Hargreaves, 1923.

Barker, Eugene C., ed. *The Austin Papers.* 2 vols. Washington, D.C.: GPO, 1924.

Bartlett, John Russell. *Personal Narrative of Explorations and Incidents in Texas, New Mexico, California, Sonora, and Chihuahua.* 2 vols. New York: D. Appleton, 1854.

Benedict, J. W. "Diary of a Campaign against the Comanches." *SHQ* 32 (Apr. 1929): 300–10.

Berlandier, Jean Louis. *The Indians of Texas in 1830,* edited by John C. Ewers and translated by Patricia Reading Leclercq. Washington, D.C.: Smithsonian Institution, 1969.

———. *Journey to Mexico: During the Years 1826 to 1834,* translated by Sheila M. Ohlendorf, Josette M. Bigelow, and Mary M. Standifer. 2 vols. Austin: Texas State Historical Association and University of Texas Press, 1980.

Bieber, Ralph P. *Southern Trails to California in 1849*. Cleveland: Arthur H. Clark, 1937.

Bollaert, William. *William Bollaert's Texas*, edited by W. Eugene Hollon and Ruth Lapham Butler. Norman: University of Oklahoma Press for the Newberry Library, 1956.

Bolton, Herbert Eugene, ed. and trans. *Athanase de Mézières and the Louisiana-Texas Frontier, 1768–1780*. 2 vols. Cleveland: Arthur H. Clark, 1914.

Bonilla, Antonio. "Bonilla's Notes Concerning New Mexico." In *New Spain and the Anglo-American West: Historical Contributions Presented to Herbert Eugene Bolton*, edited by Charles W. Hackett, George P. Hammond, and J. Lloyd Mecham, 191–209. 2 vols. Lancaster, Pa., 1932.

Burnet, David G. "David G. Burnet's Letters Describing the Comanche Indians with an Introduction by Ernest Wallace." *West Texas Historical Association Year Book* 30 (1954): 115–40.

Cachupín, Tomás Vélez de. Brief Description of the Province and Territory of New Mexico in the Kingdom of New Spain. In "New Mexico in the Mid-Eighteenth Century: A Report Based on Governor Vélez Cachupín's Inspection," translated and edited by Robert Ryal Miller. *SHQ* (Oct. 1975): 169–81.

Candelaria, Juan. "Noticias que da Juan Candelaria vecino de esta villa de San Francisco Xauier de Alburquerque de edad de 84 años," edited by Isidro Armijo. *NMHR* 4 (July 1929): 274–97.

Carroll, H. Bailey, and J. Villasana Haggard, trans. *Three New Mexico Chronicles: The Exposición of Don Pedro Bautista Pino 1812; the Ojeada of Lic. Antonio Barreiro 1832; and the additions by Don José Agustín de Escudero, 1849*. Albuquerque: Quivira Society, 1942.

Carter, Robert G. *On the Border with Mackenzie*. New York: Antiquarian, 1961.

Catlin, George. *Letters and Notes on the Manners, Customs, and Conditions of the North American Indians*. 2 vols. 1844. Reprint, New York: Dover, 1973.

Chacón, Fernando de. Report. In "The Chacón Report of 1803," edited and translated by Marc Simmons. *NMHR* 60 (Jan. 1985): 83–88.

Chavez, Angelico, trans., and Ted J. Warner, ed. *The Domínguez-Escalante Journal: Their Expedition through Colorado, Utah, Arizona, and New Mexico in 1775*. Salt Lake City: University of Utah Press, 1995.

Concha, Fernando de la. Instructions drawn up by Colonel Don Fernando de la Concha, former governor of the Province of New Mexico, so that his successor, the Lieutenant Colonel Don Fernando Chacón, may adapt what part of it that may seem to him suitable for the advantage, tranquility, and development of the aforesaid province. In "Notes and Documents: Advice on Governing New Mexico, 1794," edited and translated by Donald E. Worcester. *NMHR* 24 (July 1949): 236–54.

Cooke, G. Journal of an expedition of a detachment of U.S. Dragoons from Fort Leavenworth to protect the Annual Caravan of traders, from Missouri to the Mexican boundary on the road to Santa Fe . . . Commencing May 27th, and ending July 21st, 1843. In "Journal of the Santa Fe Trail," edited by William E. Connelly. *Mississippi Valley Historical Review* 12 (June, Sep. 1925): 72–98, 227–55.

Cortés, José. *Views from the Apache Frontier: Report on the Northern Provinces of New*

Spain, edited by Elizabeth A. H. John and translated by John Wheat. Norman: University of Oklahoma Press, 1989.

Crespo, Benito. "Documents Concerning Bishop Crespo's Visitation, 1730." *NMHR* 28 (July 1953): 222–33.

Croix, Teodoro de. "General Report of 1781." In *Teodoro de Croix and the Northern Frontier of New Spain, 1776–1783: From the Original Documents in the Archives of the Indies, Seville*, edited and translated by Alfred Barnaby Thomas, 69–243. Albuquerque: University of New Mexico Press, 1941.

Dana, Napoleon Jackson Tecumseh. *Monterrey Is Ours! The Mexican War Letters of Lieutenant Dana, 1845–1847*, edited by Robert H. Ferrell. Lexington: University Press of Kentucky, 1990.

Davidson, Wilson T. "A Comanche Prisoner in 1841." *SHQ* 45 (Apr. 1942): 335–42.

Deloria, Vine, Jr., and Raymond DeMallie, comps. *Documents of American Indian Diplomacy: Treaties, Agreements, and Conventions, 1775–1979*. Norman: University of Oklahoma Press, 1999.

Denig, Edwin Thompson. *Five Indian Tribes of the Upper Missouri: Sioux, Aricaras, Assiniboines, Crees, Crows*, edited by John C. Ewers. Norman: University of Oklahoma Press, 1961.

Dodge, Richard Irving. *Our Wild Indians: Thirty-three Years' Personal Experience among the Red Men of the Great West*. 1882. Reprint, New York: Archer House, 1959.

Dodge, Theodore Ayrault. "Some American Riders." *Harper's New Monthly Magazine* (May 1891): 849–62.

Domínguez, Francisco Atanasio. *The Missions of New Mexico, 1776: A Description by Fray Francisco Atanasio Domínguez*, translated and edited by Eleanor B. Adams and Angelico Chavez. Albuquerque: University of New Mexico Press, 1956.

Espinosa, Gilberto, trans. "Los Comanches." *New Mexico Quarterly* 1 (May 1931): 133–46.

Espinosa, Isidro Félix de. *Crónica de los Colegios de Propaganda Fide de la Nueva España*, edited by Lino Gómez Canedo. 1764. Reprint, Washington, D.C.: Academy of American Franciscan History, 1964.

Farnham, Thomas J. *Travels in the Great Western Prairies*. Vols. 28 and 29 of *Early Western Travels, 1748–1846*, edited by Reuben Gold Thwaites. Cleveland: Arthur H. Clark, 1906.

Fisher, M. C. "On the Arapahoe, Kiowa, and Comanche." *Journal of the Ethnological Society of London* 1 (1869): 274–87.

Flores, Dan L., ed. *Journal of an Indian Trader: Anthony Glass and the Texas Trading Frontier, 1790–1810*. College Station: Texas A&M University Press, 1985.

Fowler, Jacob. *Journal of Jacob Fowler*, edited by Elliott Coues. 1898. Reprint, Minneapolis: Ross and Haines, 1965.

Fröebel, Julius. *Seven Years' Travel in Central America, Northern Mexico, and the Far West of the United States*. London: R. Bentley, 1859.

Gálvez, Bernardo de. *Instructions for Governing the Interior Provinces of New Spain 1786*, translated and edited by Donald E. Worcester. Berkeley: Quivira Society, 1951.

García Rejón, Manuel, comp. *Comanche Vocabulary: Trilingual Edition,* translated and edited by Daniel J. Gelo. Austin: University of Texas Press, 1995.

Garrard, Lewis H. *Wah-to-yah and the Taos Trail,* edited by Ralph P. Bieber. 1850. Reprint, Glendale, Calif.: Arthur H. Clark, 1938.

Garrett, Julia Kathryn, ed. "Dr. John Sibley and the Louisiana-Texas Frontier, 1803–1814." *SHQ* 47, 49 (July 1943, Jan. 1944, Apr. 1946): 48–51, 319–24, 399–430.

Grant, Ulysses S. *Memoirs and Selected Letters: Personal Memoirs of U. S. Grant, Selected Letters, 1839–1865.* New York: Library of America, 1990.

Gregg, Josiah. *Commerce of the Prairies,* edited by Max L. Moorhead. Norman: University of Oklahoma Press, 1954.

———. *Diary and Letters of Josiah Gregg,* edited by Maurice Garland Fulton. 2 vols. Norman: University of Oklahoma Press, 1941–44.

Greiner, John. "The Journal of John Greiner," edited by Annie Heloise Abel. *Old Santa Fe: Magazine of History, Archaeology, Genealogy and Biography* 3 (July 1916): 189–243.

Gulick, Charles Adams, Jr., et al., eds. *The Papers of Mirabeau Buonaparte Lamar.* 6 vols. 1920–27. Reprint, Austin: Pemberton, 1968.

Hackett, Charles Wilson, ed. *Historical Documents Relating to New Mexico, Nueva Vizcaya, and Approaches Thereto, to 1773.* 3 vols. Washington, D.C.: Carnegie Institution, 1923–37.

———, ed. *Pichardo's Treatise on the Limits of Texas and Louisiana.* 4 vols. Austin: University of Texas Press, 1931–46.

Harpe, Bernard de La. "Account of the Journey of Bénard de La Harpe: Discovery Made by Him of Several Nations Situated in the West," translated and edited by Ralph A. Smith. *SHQ* 62 (Apr. 1959): 75–86.

———. "La Harpe's First Expedition in Oklahoma," translated by Anna Lewis. *CO* 2 (Dec. 1924): 332–49.

Hobbs, James. *Wild Life in the Far West: Personal Adventures of a Border Mountain Man.* 1873. Reprint, Glorieta, N. Mex.: Rio Grande, 1969.

Holley, Mary Austin. *Texas.* Lexington, Ky.: Clarke, 1836.

Horn, Sarah Ann. *An Authentic and Thrilling Narrative of the Captivity of Mrs. Horn, and Her Two Children, with Mrs. Harris, by the Camanche Indians.* 1851. Reprint, New York: Garland, 1977.

Informe de la comisión pesquisidora de la frontera del norte al Ejecutivo de la Unión . . . Mexico City: Imprenta del Gobierno en Palacio, 1877.

Instructions which the Constitutional Ayuntamiento of the City of San Fernando de Bexar Draws . . . , Nov. 15, 1820. In "Texas in 1820," translated by Mattie Austin Hatcher. *SHQ* 23 (July 1919): 61–68.

Jackson, Jack, ed. *Imaginary Kingdom: Texas as Seen by the Rivera and Rubí Military Expeditions, 1727 and 1767.* Austin: Texas State Historical Association, 1995.

James, Edwin. *Account of an Expedition from Pittsburgh to the Rocky Mountains, Performed in the Years 1819, 1820.* Vols. 14–17 of *Early Western Travels, 1748–1846,* edited by Reuben Gold Thwaites. Cleveland: Arthur H. Clark, 1906.

James, Thomas. *Three Years among the Indians and Mexicans,* edited by Milo Milton Quaife. 1846. Reprint, New York: Citadel, 1966.

Jenkins, John H., ed. *The Papers of the Texas Revolution, 1835–1836*. 10 vols. Austin: Presidial, 1973.

Jenkins, John Holland. *Recollections of Early Texas: Memoirs of John Holland Jenkins*, edited by John Holmes Jenkins III. Austin: University of Texas Press, 1958.

Jones, Anson. *Memoranda and Official Correspondence Relating to the Republic of Texas, Its History and Annexation*. 1859. Reprint, Chicago: Rio Grande, 1966.

Journals of the House of Representatives of the Republic of Texas, Fifth Congress, Appendix. Austin: Gazette Office, 1841.

Kennedy, William. *Texas: The Rise, Progress, and Prospects of the Republic of Texas*. 2 vols. London: William Cloves and Sons, 1841.

Kinnaird, Lawrence, ed. *Spain in the Mississippi Valley, 1765–94: Translations of Materials from the Spanish Archives in the Bancroft Library*. 3 vols. Washington, D.C.: GPO, 1946–49.

Lafora, Nicolás de. *The Frontiers of New Spain: Nicolás de Lafora's Description, 1766–1768*, edited and translated by Lawrence Kinnaird. Berkeley: Quivira Society, 1958.

———. *Relación del viaje que hizo a los presidios internos situados en la frontera de la América Septentrional perteneciente al Rey de España*, edited by Vito Alessio Robles. Mexico City: Editorial Pedro Robredo, 1939.

Lehmann, Herman. *Nine Years among the Indians, 1870–1879: The Story of the Captivity and Life of a Texan among the Indians*, edited by J. Marvin Hunter. 1927. Reprint, Albuquerque: University of New Mexico Press, 1993.

LeRaye, Charles. "The Journal of Charles Le Raye." *South Dakota Historical Collections* 4 (1908): 150–80.

Loomis, Noel M., and Abraham P. Nasatir. *Pedro Vial and the Roads to Santa Fe*. Norman: University of Oklahoma Press, 1967.

McCall, George Archibald. *New Mexico in 1850: A Military View*, edited by Robert W. Frazier. Norman: University of Oklahoma Press, 1968.

McLean, Malcolm, comp. and ed. *Papers Concerning Robertson's Colony in Texas*. 18 vols. Austin: University of Texas Press, 1974–93.

McPhail, Leonard. "The Diary of Assistant Surgeon Leonard McPhail on His Journey to the Southwest in 1835," edited by Harold W. Jones, Jr. CO 18 (Sep. 1940): 283–302.

Marcy, Randolph B. *Adventure on Red River: Report on the Exploration of the Headwaters of the Red River by Captain Randolph B. Marcy and Captain G. B. McClellan*, edited by Grant Foreman. Norman: University of Oklahoma Press, 1937.

———. *Thirty Years of Army Life on the Border*. New York: Harper and Bros., 1866.

Margry, Pierre, ed. *Découvertes et établissements des français dans l'ouest et dans le sud de L'Amérique Septentrionale, 1614–1754: Mémoires et documents originaux*. 6 vols. Paris: D. Jouaust, 1879–88.

Marriott, Alice, and Carol K. Rachlin. *Plains Indian Mythology*. New York: Thomas Y. Crowell, 1975.

Marryat, Captain Frederick. *Travels and Adventures of Monsieur Violet*. Upper Saddle River, N.J.: Literature House, 1970.

Martínez, Antonio José. Esposición que el Presbítero Antonio José Martínez, Cura de Taos en Nuevo México, dirije al Gobierno del Exmo. Sor. General D. Antonio López de

Santa-Anna. Proponiendo la civilisación de las Naciones bárbaras que son al canton del departamento de Nuevo-México (Taos: J. M. B., 1843). In *Northern Mexico on the Eve of the United States Invasion: Rare Imprints Concerning California, Arizona, New Mexico, and Texas, 1821–1846*, edited by David J. Weber. New York: Arno, 1976.

Merino y Moreno, Manuel. Report on the tribes of pagan Indians who inhabit the borderlands of the Interior Provinces of the kingdom of New Spain . . . In "Views from a Desk in Chihuahua: Manuel Merino's Report on Apaches and Neighboring Nations, ca. 1804," edited by Elizabeth A. H. John and translated by John Wheat. *SHQ* 85 (Oct. 1991): 148–75.

Mier y Terán, Manuel de. Noticia de las tribus de salvajes conocidos que habitan en el Departamento de Tejas, y el número de Familias de que consta cada tribu, puntos en que habitan y terrenos en que acampan." *Sociedad de Geografía y Estadística de la Republica Mexicana Boletín* 2 (1870): 264–69.

———. *Texas by Terán: The Diary Kept by General Manuel de Mier y Terán on His 1828 Inspection of Texas*, edited by Jack Jackson and translated by John Wheat. Austin: University of Texas Press, 2000.

Miera y Pacheco, Bernardo de. "Miera's Report," edited by Herbert S. Auerbach. *Utah Historical Quarterly* 11 (1943): 114–22.

Morfí, Juan Agustín de. *History of Texas, 1673–1779*, translated by Carlos Eduardo Castañeda. 2 vols. Albuquerque: Quivira Society, 1935.

Moulton, Gary E., ed. *The Journals of the Lewis and Clark Expedition*. 13 vols. Lincoln: University of Nebraska Press, 1983–2001.

Murray, Charles Augustus. *Travels in North America during the Years 1834, 1835, 1836*. 2 vols. London: R. Bentley, 1839.

Nasatir, A. P., ed. *Before Lewis and Clark: Documents Illustrating the History of the Missouri, 1785–1804*. 2 vols. 1952. Reprint, Lincoln: University of Nebraska Press, 1990.

Nystel, Ole T. *Lost and Found, or Three Months with the Wild Indians*. Dallas: Wilmans Brothers, 1888.

Ortiz de Ayala, Tadeo. Report to the President on the Conditions in Texas, Feb. 2, 1833. In "Tadeo Ortiz de Ayala and the Colonization of Texas, 1822–1833," edited by Louise Kelly and Mattie Austin Hatcher. *SHQ* 29 (Apr. 1929): 311–42.

Padilla, Juan Antonio. Report on the Barbarous Indians of the Province of Texas, Dec. 27, 1819. In "Texas in 1820," translated by Mattie Austin Hatcher. *SHQ* 23 (July 1919): 47–60.

Parker, William B. *Notes Taken during the Expedition Commanded by Captain R. B. Marcy through Unexplored Texas*. Philadelphia: Hayes and Zell, 1856.

"Petition Addressed by the Illustrious Ayuntamiento of the City of Béxar to the Honorable Legislature of the State: To Make Known the Ills Which Afflict the Towns of Texas and the Grievances They Have Suffered since Their Union with Coahuila." In *Troubles in Texas, 1832: A Tejano Viewpoint from San Antonio*, edited and translated by David J. Weber and Conchita Hassell Winn, 15–32. Dallas: DeGolyer Library, 1983.

Pike, Albert. *Prose Sketches and Poems*, edited by David J. Weber. College Station: Texas A&M University Press, 1987.

Pike, Zebulon Montgomery. *The Expeditions of Zebulon Montgomery Pike,* edited by Elliott Coues. 2 vols. 1895. Reprint, New York: Dover, 1987.

———. *The Journals of Zebulon Montgomery Pike,* edited by Donald Jackson. 2 vols. Norman: University of Oklahoma Press, 1966.

Plummer, Rachel. "Narrative of the Capture and Subsequent Sufferings of Mrs. Rachel Plummer, Written by Herself." In *Held Captive by Indians: Selected Narratives, 1642–1836,* edited by Richard VanDerBeets, 333–66. Knoxville: University of Tennessee Press, 1973.

Ponce de León, José M., ed. *Reseñas históricas del estado de Chihuahua.* Chihuahua: Imprenta del Gobierno, 1910.

Rivera, Pedro de. *Diario y derrotero de lo caminado, visto y observado en la visita que hizo a los presidios de la Nueva España Septentrional el Brigadier Pedro de Rivera,* edited by Vito Alessio Robles. Mexico City: Secretaría de la Defensa Nacional, 1946.

Robertson, James Alexander, ed. and trans. *Louisiana under the Rule of Spain, France, and the United States, 1785–1807: Social, Economic, and Political Conditions of the Territory represented in the Louisiana Purchase, as portrayed in hitherto unpublished contemporary accounts by Dr. Paul Alliot and various Spanish, French, English, and American Officials.* 2 vols. Cleveland: Arthur H. Clark, 1911.

Ruíz, José Francisco. *Report on Indian Tribes of Texas in 1828,* edited by John C. Ewers. New Haven: Yale University Press, 1972.

Ruxton, George F. *Adventures in Mexico and the Rocky Mountains.* London: John Murray, 1861.

Salcedo, Nemesio. *Instrucción reservada de don Nemesio Salcedo y Salcedo, comandante general de Provincias Internas a su sucesor,* edited by Isidro Vizcaya Canales. Chihuahua: Centro de Información del Estado de Chihuahua, 1990.

Sánchez, José María. "A Trip to Texas in 1828," translated by Carlos E. Castañeda. *SHQ* 29 (Apr. 1926): 249–88.

Sherburne, John P. *Through Indian Country to California: John P. Sherburne's Diary of the Whipple Expedition, 1853–1854,* edited by Mary McDougall Gordon. Stanford: Stanford University Press, 1988.

Sibley, John. *A Report from Natchitoches in 1807,* edited by Annie Heloise Abel. New York: Museum of the American Indian, 1922.

Simmons, Marc, ed. and trans. *Border Comanches: Seven Spanish Colonial Documents, 1785–1819.* Santa Fe: Stagecoach, 1967.

Simpson, Lesley Byrd, ed., and Paul D. Nathan, trans. *San Sabá Papers: A Documentary Account of the Founding and Destruction of San Sabá Mission.* 1959. Reprint, Dallas: Southern Methodist University Press, 2000.

Smithwick, Noah. *The Evolution of a State or Recollections of Old Texas.* Austin: Gammel, 1900.

Stanley, Henry M. "A British Journalist Reports the Medicine Lodge Council of 1867." *Kansas Historical Quarterly* 33 (Autumn 1967): 249–320.

Stokes M., and M. Arbuckle. Journal of the Proceedings of M. Stokes, M. Arbuckle, and F. W. Armstrong. In "The Journal of the Proceedings at Our First Treaty with the Wild Indians, 1835," edited by Grant Foreman. *CO* 14 (Dec. 1936): 398–418.

Tabeau, Pierre Antoine. *Tabeau's Narrative of Loisel's Expedition to the Upper Missouri*, edited by Annie Heloise Abel and translated by Rose Abel Wright. Norman: University of Oklahoma Press, 1939.

Tamarón y Romeral, Pedro. *Bishop Tamarón's Visitation of New Mexico, 1760*, edited by Eleanor B. Adams. Albuquerque: University of New Mexico Press, 1954.

Tatum, Lawrie. *Our Red Brothers and the Peace Policy of President Ulysses S. Grant.* 1899. Reprint, Lincoln: University of Nebraska Press, 1970.

Taylor, Joe F., ed. "The Indian Campaign on the Staked Plains, 1874–1875: Military Correspondence from War Department, Adjutant General's Office, File 2815-1874." *Panhandle-Plains Historical Review* 34 (1961).

Taylor, Virginia H., ed. and trans. *The Letters of Antonio Martínez, The Last Spanish Governor of Texas, 1817–1822.* Austin: Texas State Library, 1957.

Thomas, Alfred Barnaby, ed. and trans. *After Coronado: Spanish Exploration Northeast of New Mexico, 1696–1727.* Norman: University of Oklahoma Press, 1935.

———, ed. "Documents Bearing upon the Northern Frontier of New Mexico." *NMHR* 4 (Apr. 1929): 146–64.

———, ed. and trans. *Forgotten Frontiers: A Study of the Spanish Indian Policy of Don Juan Bautista de Anza, Governor of New Mexico, 1777–1787.* Norman: University of Oklahoma Press, 1942.

———, ed. "Governor Mendinueta's Proposals for the Defense of New Mexico, 1772–1778." *NMHR* 6 (Jan. 1931): 21–39.

———, ed. *The Plains Indians and New Mexico, 1751–1778: A Collection of Documents Illustrative of the History of the Eastern Frontier of New Mexico.* Albuquerque: University of New Mexico Press, 1940.

———, ed. and trans. "San Carlos: A Comanche Pueblo on the Arkansas River, 1787: A Study in Comanche History and Spanish Indian Policy." *Colorado Magazine* 6 (May 1929): 79–91.

Thwaites, Reuben Gold, ed. *The French Regime in Wisconsin.* Madison: Wisconsin Historical Society, 1908.

Tixier, Victor. *Tixier's Travels on the Osage Prairies*, edited by John Francis McDermott and translated by Albert J. Salvan. Norman: University of Oklahoma Press, 1940.

Tuggle, W. O. *Shem, Ham and Japheth: The Papers of W. O. Tuggle Comprising His Indian Diary, Sketches and Observations, Myths and Washington Journal in the Territory and at the Capital, 1879–1882*, edited by Eugene Current-Garcia and Dorothy B. Hatfield. Athens: University of Georgia Press, 1973.

Twitchell, Ralph Emerson. *The Spanish Archives of New Mexico.* 2 vols. New York: Arno, 1976.

Vélez de Escalante, Silvestre. *Pageant in the Wilderness: The Story of the Escalante Expedition to the Interior Basin, 1776*, edited and translated by Herbert Eugene Bolton. Salt Lake City: Utah State Historical Society, 1950.

Vial, Pedro, and Francisco Xavier Chaves. Diary. In "Inside the Comanchería, 1785: The Diary of Pedro Vial and Francisco Xavier Chaves," edited by Elizabeth A. H. John and translated by Adán Benavides, Jr. *SHQ* 88 (July 1994): 30–52.

Vigil, Donaciano. *Arms, Indians, and the Mismanagement of New Mexico*, edited and translated by David J. Weber. El Paso: University of Texas at El Paso, 1986.

Vizcaya Canales, Isidro, ed. *La invasión de los indios bárbaros al noreste de Mexico en los años de 1840 y 1841*. Monterrey: Instituto Technológico y de Estudios Superiores de Monterrey, 1968.

Ward, John. Journal. In "Indian Affairs in New Mexico under the Administration of William Carr Lane," edited by Annie Heloise Abel. *NMHR* 16 (Apr. 1941): 328–58.

Webb, Josiah. *Adventures in the Santa Fe Trade, 1844–1847*, edited by Ralph P. Bieber. Lincoln: University of Nebraska Press, 1995.

Wharton, William H. *Texas: A Brief Account of the Origin, Progress and Present State of the Colonial Settlements of Texas; Together with an Exposition of the Causes which have induced the Existing War with Mexico*. 1836. Reprint, Austin: Pemberton, 1964.

Wheat, Carl I., ed. *Mapping the Trans-Mississippi West, 1540–1861*. 6 vols. San Francisco: Institute of Historical Cartography, 1957–63.

Williams, Amelia W., and Eugene C. Barker, eds. *The Writings of Sam Houston*. 8 vols. Austin: University of Texas Press, 1938–43.

Winfrey, Dorman H., and James M. Day, eds. *The Indian Papers of Texas and the Southwest, 1825–1916*. 5 vols. Austin: Pemberton, 1966.

SECONDARY SOURCES

Aboites Aguilar, Luis. "Poblamiento y estado en el norte de México, 1830–1835." In *Indio, nación y comunidad en el México del siglo XIX*, edited by Antonio Escobar Ohmstede, 303–13. Mexico City: Centro de Estudios Mexicanos y Centroamericanos/Centro de Investigaciones y Estudios Superiores en Antropología Social, 1993.

Abu-Lughod, Janet L. *Before European Hegemony: The World System, A.D. 1250–1350*. New York: Oxford University Press, 1989.

Adams, David B. "Embattled Borderland: Northern Nuevo León and the Indios Bárbaros, 1686–1870." *SHQ* 95 (Oct. 1991): 205–20.

Adelman, Jeremy, and Stephen Aron. "From Borderlands to Borders: Empires, Nation-States, and the Peoples in between in North American History." *American Historical Review* 104 (June 1999): 814–41.

Agnew, Brad. *Fort Gibson: Terminal on the Trail of Tears*. Norman: University of Oklahoma Press, 1980.

Albers, Patricia C. "Symbiosis, Merger, and War: Contrasting Forms of Intertribal Relationship among Historical Plains Indians." In *Political Economy of North American Indians*, edited by John H. Moore, 93–132. Norman: University of Oklahoma Press, 1993.

Albers, Patricia, and Jeanne Kay. "Sharing the Land: A Study in American Indian Territoriality." In *A Cultural Geography of North American Indians*, edited by Thomas E. Ross and Tyrel G. Moore, 47–91. Boulder: Westview, 1987.

Alessio Robles, Vito. *Coahuila y Texas: Desde la consumacion de la independencia hasta el tratado de paz de Guadalupe Hidalgo*. 2 vols. Mexico, 1946.

Anderson, Gary Clayton. *The Conquest of Texas: Ethnic Cleansing in the Promised Land, 1820–1875*. Norman: University of Oklahoma Press, 2005.

———. *The Indian Southwest, 1580–1830: Ethnogenesis and Reinvention.* Norman: University of Oklahoma Press, 1999.

Anderson, H. Allen. "The Delaware and Shawnee Indians and the Republic of Texas, 1820–1845." *SHQ* 94 (Oct. 1990): 231–60.

Aquila, Richard. *The Iroquois Restoration: Iroquois Diplomacy, 1701–1754.* 1983. Reprint, Lincoln: University of Nebraska Press, 1997.

Aron, Stephen. *American Confluence: The Missouri Frontier from Borderland to Border State.* Bloomington: Indiana University Press, 2006.

August, Jack. "Balance-of-Power Diplomacy in New Mexico: Governor Fernando de la Concha and the Indian Policy of Conciliation." *NMHR* 56 (Spring 1981): 141–60.

Axtell, James. *After Columbus: Essays in the Ethnohistory of Colonial North America.* New York: Oxford University Press, 1988.

———. *Natives and Newcomers: The Cultural Origins of North America.* New York: Oxford University Press, 2001.

———. *The Rise and Fall of the Powhatan Empire: Indians in the Seventeenth-Century Virginia.* Williamsburg: Colonial Williamsburg Foundation, 1995.

Baerreis, David A., and Reid A. Bryson. "Historical Climatology of the Southern Plains: A Preliminary Survey." *Oklahoma Anthropological Bulletin* 13 (Mar. 1963): 70–75.

Bailey, L. R. *Indian Slave Trade in the Southwest.* Los Angeles: Westernlore, 1966.

Bamforth, Douglas B. *Ecology and Human Adaptation on the Great Plains.* New York: Plenum, 1988.

———. "Historical Documents and Bison Ecology on the Great Plains." *Plains Anthropologist* 32 (Feb. 1987): 1–16.

Bancroft, Hubert Howe. *History of Arizona and New Mexico, 1530–1888.* San Francisco: History Company, 1889.

Barfield, Thomas J. *The Perilous Frontier: Nomadic Empires and China.* Cambridge: Basil Blackwell, 1989.

———. "The Shadow Empires: Imperial State Formation along the Chinese-Nomad Frontier." In *Empires: Perspectives from Archaeology and History,* edited by Susan E. Alcock, Terence N. D'Altroy, Kathleen D. Morrison, and Carla M. Sinopoli, 10–41. Cambridge: Cambridge University Press, 2001.

Barr, Juliana. "Beyond Their Control: Spaniards in Native Texas." In *Choice, Persuasion, and Coercion: Social Control on Spain's North American Frontiers,* edited by Jesús F. de la Teja and Ross Frank, 149–77. Albuquerque: University of New Mexico Press, 2005.

———. "A Diplomacy of Gender: Rituals of First Contact in the 'Land of the Tejas.'" *William and Mary Quarterly* 61 (July 2004): 393–434.

———. "From Captives to Slaves: Commodifying Indian Women in the Borderlands." *JAH* 92 (June 2005): 19–46.

Battey, Thomas C. *The Life and Adventures of a Quaker among the Indians.* 1875. Reprint, Norman: University of Oklahoma Press, 1968.

Bauer, K. Jack. *The Mexican War.* 1974. Reprint, Lincoln: University of Nebraska Press, 1992.

Baxter, John O. *Las Carneradas: Sheep Trade in New Mexico, 1700–1860.* Albuquerque: University of New Mexico Press, 1987.

Bell, John R. *The Journal of Captain John R. Bell, Official Journalist for the Stephen H. Long Expedition to the Rocky Mountains, 1820*, edited by Harlin M. Fuller and LeRoy R. Hafen. Glendale, Calif.: Arthur H. Clark, 1957.

Benes, Ronald J. "Anza and Concha in New Mexico, 1787–1793: A Study in New Colonial Techniques." In *The Spanish Borderlands: A First Reader*, edited by Oakah L. Jones, 156–69. Los Angeles: Lorrin L. Morrison, 1974.

Betty, Gerald. *Comanche Society: Before the Reservation*. College Station: Texas A&M University Press, 2002.

Bieber, Ralph P. "The Southwestern Trails to California." *Mississippi Valley Historical Review* 12 (Dec. 1925): 342–75.

Biesele, Rudolph Leopold. "The Relations between the German Settlers and the Indians in Texas, 1844–1860." *SHQ* 31 (Oct. 1927): 116–29.

Billington, Ray Allen. *Westward Expansion: A History of the American Frontier*. 4th ed. New York: Macmillan, 1974.

Binnema, Theodore. *Common and Contested Ground: A Human and Environmental History of the Northwestern Plains*. Norman: University of Oklahoma Press, 2001.

Blackhawk, Ned. *Violence over the Land: Indians and Empires in the Early American West*. Cambridge: Harvard University Press, 2006.

Blakeslee, Donald J., and Robert Blasing. "Indian Trails in the Central Plains." *Plains Anthropologist* 33 (Feb. 1988): 17–25.

Bobb, Barnard E. *The Viceregency of Antonio María de Bucareli in New Spain, 1771–1779*. Austin: University of Texas Press, 1962.

Bolton, Herbert E. "Juan Bautista de Anza, Borderlands Frontiersman." In *Bolton and the Spanish Borderlands*, edited by John Francis Bannon, 281–87. Norman: University of Oklahoma Press, 1964.

Boyd, E. "Troubles at Ojo Caliente, a Frontier Post." *El Palacio* 64 (Nov. 1957): 347–62.

Bradley, J. Parker, and Lars Rodseth, eds. *Untaming the Frontier in Anthropology, Archaeology, and History*. Tucson: University of Arizona Press, 2005.

Brice, Donaly E. *The Great Comanche Raid: Boldest Indian Attack of the Texas Republic*. Austin: Eakin, 1987.

Brooks, James F. *Captives and Cousins: Slavery, Kinship, and Community in the Southwest Borderlands*. Chapel Hill: University of North Carolina Press for the Omohundro Institute of Early American History and Culture, 2002.

———. "Served Well by Plunder: La Gran Ladronería and Producers of History Astride the Río Grande." *American Quarterly* 52 (Mar. 2000): 23–58.

———. "'This Evil Extends . . . Especially to the Feminine Sex': Negotiating Captivity on the New Mexico Borderlands." *Feminist Studies* 22 (Summer 1996): 279–309.

Brown, Dee. *Bury My Heart at Wounded Knee: An Indian History of the American West*. 1970. Reprint, London: Vintage, 1991.

Brown, William R. Jr. "Comancheria Demography, 1805–1830." *Panhandle-Plains Historical Review* 59 (1986): 1–17.

Brugge, David M. *Navajos in the Catholic Church Records of New Mexico, 1694–1875*. Tsaile, Ariz.: Navajo Community College Press, 1985.

Bugbee, Lester G. "The Texas Frontier, 1820–1825." *Publications of the Southern History Association* 4 (Mar. 1900): 102–21.

Calloway, Colin G. *New Worlds for All: Indians, Europeans, and the Remaking of Early America.* Baltimore: Johns Hopkins University Press, 1997.

———. *One Vast Winter Count: The Native American West before Lewis and Clark.* Lincoln: University of Nebraska Press, 2003.

———. "Snake Frontiers: The Eastern Shoshones in the Eighteenth Century." *Annals of Wyoming* 63 (Summer 1991): 82–92.

Campbell, Randolph B. *Gone to Texas: A History of the Lone Star State.* New York: Oxford University Press, 2003.

Cantrell, Gregg. *Stephen F. Austin, Empresario of Texas.* New Haven: Yale University Press, 1999.

Cashion, Ty. *A Texas Frontier: The Clear Fork Country and Fort Griffin, 1849–1887.* Norman: University of Oklahoma Press, 1996.

Castañeda, Carlos E. *Our Catholic Heritage in Texas, 1519–1936.* 7 vols. Austin: Von Boeckmann-Jones, 1936–58.

Cayton, Andrew R. L., and Fredrika J. Teute, eds. *Contact Points: American Frontiers from the Mohawk Valley to the Mississippi, 1750–1830.* Chapel Hill: University of North Carolina Press for the Omohundro Institute of Early American History and Culture, 1998.

Chacon, Rafael. *Legacy of Honor: The Life of Rafael Chacón, a Nineteenth-Century New Mexican,* edited by Jacqueline Dorgan Meketa. Albuquerque: University of New Mexico Press, 1982.

Cháves, Angélico. *Origins of New Mexico Families: A Genealogy of the Spanish Colonial Period.* 1954. Reprint, Santa Fe: Museum of New Mexico Press, 1992.

Clark, W. P. *The Indian Sign Language.* Philadelphia: L. R. Hamersley, 1885.

Clift, W. H. "Warren's Trading Post." CO 2 (June 1924): 129–40.

Collier, Jane Fishburne. *Marriage and Inequality in Classless Societies.* Stanford: Stanford University Press, 1988.

Comer, Douglas C. *Ritual Ground: Bent's Old Fort, World Formation, and the Annexation of the Southwest.* Berkeley: University of California Press, 1996.

Cordain, Loren, et al. "Plant-Animal Subsistence Ratios and Macronutrient Energy Estimations in Worldwide Hunter Gatherer Diets." *American Journal of Clinical Nutrition* 71 (Mar. 2000): 682–92.

Corwin, Hugh D. *Comanche and Kiowa Captives in Oklahoma and Texas.* Lawton, Okla.: Cooperative, 1959.

Crisp, James E. *Sleuthing the Alamo: Davy Crockett's Last Stance and Other Mysteries of the Texas Revolution.* New York: Oxford University Press, 2004.

Cronon, William. *Nature's Metropolis: Chicago and the Great West.* New York: W. W. Norton, 1991.

Cronon, William, George Miles, and Jay Gitlin. "Becoming West: Toward a New Meaning for Western History." In *Under an Open Sky: Rethinking America's Western Past,* edited by William Cronon, George Miles, and Jay Gitlin, 3–27. New York: W. W. Norton, 1992.

Cronon, William, and Richard White. "Indians in the Land: A Conversation between William Cronon and Richard White." *American Heritage* 37 (Aug.–Sep. 1986): 18–25.

Crosby, Alfred. *Ecological Imperialism: The Biological Expansion of Europe, 900–1900*. Cambridge: Cambridge University Press, 1986.

D'Altroy, Terence N. "Empires in a Wider World." In *Empires: Perspectives from Archaeology and History*, edited by Susan E. Alcock, Terence N. D'Altroy, Kathleen D. Morrison, and Carla M. Sinopoli, 125–27. Cambridge: Cambridge University Press, 2001.

DeLay, Brian. "Independent Indians and the U.S–Mexican War." *American Historical Review* 112 (Feb. 2007): 35–68.

Deloria, Vine, Jr. *We Talk, You Listen: New Tribes, New Turf*. New York: Macmillan, 1970.

DeMallie, Raymond J., ed. *Handbook of North American Indians*. Vol. 13, *The Plains*. Washington, D.C.: Smithsonian Institution, 2001.

Dennis, Matthew. *Cultivating a Landscape of Peace: Iroquois-European Encounters in Seventeenth-Century America*. Ithaca: Cornell University Press, 1993.

Din, Gilbert C. "The Spanish Fort on the Arkansas, 1763–1803." *Arkansas Historical Quarterly* 42 (Autumn 1983): 270–93.

Dobak, William A. "Killing the Canadian Buffalo: 1821–1881." *Western Historical Quarterly* 27 (Spring 1996): 33–52.

Dowd, Gregory Evans. "'Insidious Friends': Gift Giving and the Cherokee-British Alliance in the Seven Years' War." In *Contact Points: American Frontiers from the Mohawk Valley to the Mississippi, 1750–1830*, edited by Andrew R. L. Cayton and Fredrika J. Teute, 114–50. Chapel Hill: University of North Carolina Press for the Omohundro Institute of Early American History and Culture, 1998.

———. *A Spirited Resistance: The North American Indian Struggle for Unity, 1745–1815*. Baltimore: Johns Hopkins University Press, 1992.

———. *War under Heaven: Pontiac, the Indian Nations and the British Empire*. Baltimore: Johns Hopkins University Press, 2002.

Dunn, William Edward. "Apache Relations in Texas, 1718–1750." *Texas State Historical Association Quarterly* 14 (Jan. 1911): 198–269.

Dunn-Chase, Christopher, and Thomas D. Hall. *Rise and Demise: Comparing World-Systems*. Boulder: Westview, 1997.

DuVal, Kathleen. *The Native Ground: Indians and Colonists in the Heart of the Continent*. Philadelphia: University of Pennsylvania Press, 2006.

Elliott, J. H. *Empires of the Atlantic World: Britain and Spain in America, 1492–1830*. New Haven: Yale University Press, 2006.

Everett, Dianna. *The Texas Cherokees: A People between Two Fires, 1819–1840*. Norman: University of Oklahoma Press, 1990.

Ewers, John C. *The Horse in Blackfoot Indian Culture: With Comparative Material from Other Western Tribes*. Bureau of American Ethnological Bulletin 159. Washington, D.C.: Smithsonian Institution, 1955.

———. *Indian Life on the Upper Missouri*. 1954. Reprint, Norman: University of Oklahoma Press, 1968.

———. "The Influence of Epidemics on the Indian Populations and Cultures of Texas." *Plains Anthropologist* 18 (May 1973): 104–15.

Faragher, John Mack. "Americans, Mexicans, and Métis." In *Under an Open Sky: Rethinking America's Western Past,* edited by William Cronon, George Miles, and Jay Gitlin, 90–109. New York: W. W. Norton, 1992.

Faulk, Odie B. "The Comanche Invasion of Texas, 1743–1836." *Great Plains Journal* 9 (Fall 1969): 10–50.

Fehrenbach, T. R. *Comanches: The Destruction of a People.* New York: Da Capo, 1974.

———. *Lone Star: A History of Texas and Texans.* 1968. Reprint, New York: Collier, 1980.

Fenn, Elizabeth A. *Pox Americana: The Great Smallpox Epidemic of 1775–1782.* New York: Hill and Wang, 2001.

Ferguson, Niall. *Colossus: The Rise and Fall of the American Empire.* London: Penguin, 2004.

Fernández-Armesto, Felipe. *The Americas: The History of the Hemisphere.* London: Phoenix, 2004.

Fletcher, Alice C., and Francis La Flesche. *The Omaha Tribe.* Bureau of American Ethnology Bulletin 27. Washington, D.C.: Smithsonian Institution, 1905–06.

Flores, Dan. "Bison Ecology and Bison Diplomacy: The Southern Plains from 1800 to 1850." *JAH* 78 (Sep. 1991): 465–85.

———. *Caprock Canyons: Journeys into the Heart of the Southern Plains.* Austin: University of Texas Press, 1990.

———. *Horizontal Yellow: Nature and History in the Near Southwest.* Albuquerque: University of New Mexico Press, 1999.

———, ed. *Journal of an Indian Trader: Anthony Glass and the Texas Trading Frontier, 1790–1810.* College Station: Texas A&M University Press, 1985.

———. *The Natural West: Environmental History of the Great Plains and Rocky Mountains.* Norman: University of Oklahoma Press, 2001.

Foreman, Grant. *Advancing the Frontier, 1830–1860.* Norman: University of Oklahoma Press, 1933.

———. *Pioneer Days in the Southwest.* 1926. Reprint, Lincoln: University of Nebraska Press, 1994.

———. "The Texas Comanche Treaty of 1846." *SHQ* 51 (Apr. 1948): 313–32.

Foster, Morris W. *Being Comanche: A Social History of an American Indian Community.* Tucson: University of Arizona Press, 1991.

Foster, Morris W., and Martha McCollough. "Plains Apache." In *Handbook of North American Indians.* Vol. 13, *The Plains,* edited by Raymond J. DeMallie, pt. 2, 926–40. 2 parts. Washington, D.C.: Smithsonian Institution, 2001.

Frank, Andre Gunder, and Barry K. Gillis, eds. *The World System: Five Hundred Years or Five Thousand?* London: Routledge, 1994.

Frank, Ross. *From Settler to Citizen: New Mexican Economic Development and the Creation of Vecino Society, 1750–1820.* Berkeley: University of California Press, 2000.

Friedman, Paul D. *Final Report of History and Oral History Studies of the Fort Carson Piñon Canyon Maneuver Area, Las Animas County, Colorado.* Denver: Colorado State Office, Bureau of Land Management, 1985.

Gallay, Alan. *The Indian Slave Trade: The Rise of the English Empire in the American South, 1670–1717.* New Haven: Yale University Press, 2002.

Garrett, Julia Kathryn. *Green Flag over Texas: A Story of the Last Years of Spain in Texas.* New York: Cordova, 1939.

Gelo, Daniel J. "'Comanche Land and Ever Has Been': A Native Geography of the Nineteenth-Century Comanchería." *SHQ* 103 (Jan. 2000): 272–307.

Gibson, Arrell Morgan. *The West in the Life of the Nation.* Lexington, Mass.: D. C. Heath, 1976.

Gladwin, Thomas. "Comanche Kin Behavior." *American Anthropologist* 50 (Jan.–Mar. 1948): 73–94.

Goss, James A. "The Yamparika—Shoshones, Comanches, or Utes—or Does It Matter?" In *Julian Stewart and the Great Basin: The Making of an Anthropologist,* edited by Richard O. Clemmer, L. Daniel Myers, and Mary Elizabeth Rudden, 74–84. Salt Lake City: University of Utah Press, 1999.

Greenleaf, Richard E. "The Nueva Vizcaya Frontier, 1787–89." In *The Spanish Borderlands: A First Reader,* edited by Oakah L. Jones, 144–55. Los Angeles: Lorrin L. Morrison, 1974.

Greiser, Sally T. "Late Prehistoric Cultures on the Montana Plains." In *Plains Indians, A.D. 150–1550: The Archaeological Past of Historic Groups,* edited by Karl H. Schlesier, 34–55. Norman: University of Oklahoma Press, 1994.

Griffen, William B. *Utmost Good Faith: Patterns of Apache-Mexican Hostilities in Northern Chihuahua Border Warfare, 1821–1848.* Albuquerque: University of New Mexico Press, 1988.

Grinnell, George Bird. *The Fighting Cheyennes.* Norman: University of Oklahoma Press, 1915.

Gump, James O. *The Dust Rose Like Smoke: The Subjugation of the Zulu and the Sioux.* Lincoln: University of Nebraska Press, 1994.

Gunnerson, Dolores A. *The Jicarilla Apaches: A Study in Cultural Survival.* DeKalb: Northern Illinois University Press, 1974.

Gunnerson, James H. "Plains Village Tradition: Western Periphery." In *Handbook of North American Indians.* Vol. 13, *The Plains,* edited by Raymond J. DeMallie, pt. 1, 234–44. 2 parts. Washington, D.C.: Smithsonian Institution, 2001.

Gutiérrez, Ramón A. *When Jesus Came, the Corn Mothers Went Away: Marriage, Sexuality, and Power in New Mexico, 1500–1846.* Stanford: Stanford University Press, 1991.

Hagan, William T. *Quanah Parker, Comanche Chief.* Norman: University of Oklahoma Press, 1993.

———. *United States–Comanche Relations: The Reservation Years.* 1976. Reprint, Norman: University of Oklahoma Press, 1990.

Haggard, Villasana. "The Neutral Ground between Louisiana and Texas, 1806–1821." *Louisiana Historical Quarterly* 28 (Oct. 1945): 1001–28.

Haley, J. Evetts. "The Comanchero Trade." *SHQ* 38 (Jan. 1935): 157–76.

Haley, James L. *The Buffalo War.* 1976. Reprint, Austin: State House, 1998.

Hall, Thomas D. "The Río de la Plata and the Greater Southwest." In *Contested Ground: Comparative Frontiers on the Northern and Southern Edges of the Spanish Empire,* edited by Donna J. Guy and Thomas E. Sheridan, 150–66. Tucson: University of Arizona Press, 1998.

———. "Role of Nomads in Core-Periphery Relations." In *Core/Periphery Relations in Precapitalist Worlds,* edited by Christopher Chase-Dunn and Thomas D. Hall, 212–39. Boulder, Westview, 1991.

———. *Social Change in the Southwest, 1350–1880.* Lawrence: University Press of Kansas, 1989.

Hämäläinen, Pekka. "The Rise and Fall of Plains Indian Horse Cultures." *JAH* 90 (Dec. 2003): 833–62.

———. "The Western Comanche Trade Center: Rethinking the Plains Indian Trade System." *Western Historical Quarterly* 29 (Winter 1998): 485–513.

Hamell, George R. "Strawberries, Floating Islands, and Rabbit Captains: Mythical Realities and European Contact in the Northeast during the Sixteenth and Seventeenth Centuries." *Journal of Canadian Studies* 21 (Winter 1987): 72–94.

Hardin, Stephen L. "Efficient in the Cause." In *Tejano Journey,* edited by Gerald E. Poyo, 49–71. Austin: University of Texas Press, 1996.

Harper, Elizabeth Ann. "The Taovayas Indians in Frontier Trade and Diplomacy, 1719–1768." CO 31 (Autumn 1953): 268–89.

Harris, Ladonna, Stephen M. Sachs, and Benjamin J. Broome. "Wisdom of the People: Potential and Pitfalls in Efforts by the Comanches to Recreate Traditional Ways of Building Consensus." *American Indian Quarterly* 25 (Winter 2001): 114–34.

Haskell, Loring. *Southern Athapaskan Migration, A.D. 200–1750.* Tsaile, Ariz.: Navajo Community College Press, 1987.

Hatley, Tom. *The Dividing Paths: Cherokees and South Carolinians through the Era of Revolution.* Oxford: Oxford University Press, 1993.

Hendricks, Rick, and John P. Wilson, eds. and trans. *The Navajos in 1705: Roque Madrid's Campaign Journal.* Albuquerque: University of New Mexico Press, 1996.

Hickerson, Daniel A. "Historical Processes, Epidemic Disease, and the Formation of the Hasinais Confederacy." *Ethnohistory* 44 (Winter 1997): 31–52.

Hickerson, Nancy P. "Ethnogenesis in the South Plains: Jumano to Kiowa?" In *History, Power, and Identity: Ethnogenesis in the Americas, 1492–1992,* edited by Jonathan D. Hill, 70–89. Iowa City: University of Iowa Press, 1996.

———. *The Jumanos: Hunters and Traders of the South Plains.* Austin: University of Texas Press, 1994.

Hijiya, James A. "Why the West Is Lost." *William and Mary Quarterly* 51 (Apr. 1994): 276–92.

Himmel, Kelly F. *The Conquest of the Karankawas and Tonkawas, 1821–1859.* College Station: Texas A&M University Press, 1999.

Hinderaker, Eric. *Elusive Empires: Constructing Colonialism in the Ohio Valley, 1673–1800.* New York: Cambridge University Press, 1997.

Hine, Robert V., and John Mack Faragher. *The American West: A New Interpretive History.* New Haven: Yale University Press, 2000.

Hinojosa, Gilberto Miguel. *A Borderlands Town in Transition: Laredo, 1755–1870.* College Station: Texas A&M University Press, 1983.

Hoebel, E. Adamson. *The Law of Primitive Man: A Study in Comparative Legal Dynamics.* Cambridge: Harvard University Press, 1954.

———. *The Political Organization and Law-Ways of the Comanche Indians.* American Anthropological Association Memoir 54. Menasha, Wis.: American Anthropological Association, 1940.

Hollon, W. Eugene. *The Southwest: Old and New.* Lincoln: University of Nebraska Press, 1961.

Howren, Alone. "Causes and Origin of the Decree of April 6, 1830." *SHQ* 16 (Apr. 1913): 378–422.

Hoxie, Frederick. "Ethnohistory for a Tribal World." *Ethnohistory* 44 (Fall 1997): 603–12.

———. "The Problem of Indian History." *Social Science Journal* 25 (1988): 389–99.

Hunter, J. Marvin. *The Boy Captives: Life among the Indians.* 1927. Reprint, New York: Garland, 1977.

Hyde, George E. *Indians of the High Plains: From the Prehistoric Period to the Coming of Europeans.* Norman: University of Oklahoma Press, 1959.

———. *Life of George Bent: Written from His Letters,* edited by Savoie Lottinville. Norman: University of Oklahoma Press 1968.

Hyslop, Stephen G. *Bound for Santa Fe: The Road to New Mexico and the American Conquest, 1806–1848.* Norman: University of Oklahoma Press, 2002.

Irons, William. "Political Stratification among Pastoral Nomads." In *Pastoral Production and Society,* edited by L'équipe écologie et anthropologie des sociétés pastorales, 221–34. Cambridge: Cambridge University Press, 1979.

Irwin, J. E. *Photographs of Kiowa and Comanche Indians.* Chickasha, I.T.: Irwin, ca. 1898.

Isenberg, Andrew C. *The Destruction of the Bison: An Environmental History, 1750–1920.* Cambridge: Cambridge University Press, 2000.

Jablow, Joseph. *The Cheyenne in Plains Indian Trade Relations, 1795–1840.* Monographs of the American Ethnological Society 19. New York: J. J. Augustin, 1951.

Jackson, Jack. *Los Mesteños: Spanish Ranching in Texas, 1721–1821.* College Station: Texas A&M University Press, 1986.

Jenkins, John H., and Kenneth Kesselus. *Edward Burleson, Texas Frontier Leader.* Austin: Jenkins, 1990.

Jennings, Francis. *The Ambiguous Iroquois Empire: The Covenant Chain Confederation of Indian Tribes with English Colonies.* New York: W. W. Norton, 1984.

———. *The Invasion of America: Indians, Colonialism, and the Cant of Conquest.* Chapel Hill: University of North Carolina Press for the Institute of Early American History and Culture at Williamsburg, 1975.

John, Elizabeth A. H. "Documentary Evidence and Historical Context Bearing upon Possible Explanations of a Brief, Specialized Settlement on the Eastern Plains of New Mexico." In *Investigations at Sites 48 and 77, Santa Rosa Lake, Guadalupe County, New Mexico: An Inquiry into the Nature of Archaeological Reality,* edited by Frances Levine and Joseph C. Winter, 539–49. Albuquerque: Office of Contract Archeology, University of New Mexico, 1987.

———. "An Earlier Chapter of Kiowa History." *NMHR* 60 (Oct. 1985): 379–97.

———. "Nurturing the Peace: Spanish and Comanche Cooperation in the Early Nineteenth Century." *NMHR* 59 (Oct. 1984): 345–69.

———. *Storms Brewed in Other Men's Worlds: The Confrontation of Indians, Spanish, and French in the Southwest, 1640–1795.* Norman: University of Oklahoma Press, 1975.

Johnston, William Preston. *The Life of Albert Sidney Johnson, Embracing His Services in the Armies of the United States, the Republic of Texas, and Confederate States.* New York: D. Appleton, 1878.

Jones, Jonathan H. *A Condensed History of the Apache and Comanche Indian Tribes for Amusements and General Knowledge: Prepared from the General Conversation of Herman Lehmann, Willie Lehmann, Mrs. Mina Keyser, Mrs. A. J. Buckmeyer and Others.* San Antonio: Johnson Brothers, 1899.

Jones, Oakah L., Jr. *Los Paisanos: Spanish Settlers on the Northern Frontier of New Spain.* Norman: University of Oklahoma Press, 1979.

———. "Rescue and Ransom of Spanish Captives from the *indios bárbaros* on the Northern Frontier of New Spain." *Colonial Latin American Historical Review* 4 (Spring 1995): 129–48.

Jordan, Terry G. *German Seed in Texas Soil: Immigrant Farmers in Nineteenth-Century Texas.* Austin: University of Texas Press, 1966.

———. *North American Cattle-Ranching Frontiers: Origins, Diffusion, and Differentiation.* Albuquerque: University of New Mexico Press, 1993.

Kavanagh, Thomas W. "Comanche." In *Encyclopedia of North American Indians: Native American History, Culture, and Life from Paleo-Indians to the Present,* edited by Frederick E. Hoxie, 131–32. Boston: Houghton Mifflin, 1996.

———. "Comanche." In *Handbook of North American Indians.* Vol. 13, *The Plains,* edited by Raymond J. DeMallie, pt. 2, 886–906. 2 parts. Washington, D.C.: Smithsonian Institution, 2001.

———. *Comanche Political History: An Ethnohistorical Perspective.* Lincoln: University of Nebraska Press, 1996.

———. "Los Comanches: Pieces of an Historic, Folkloric Detective Story, Part I." *NMHR* 81 (Winter 2006): 1–37.

Kehoe, Alice Beck. *America before European Invasions.* London: Longman, 2002.

Kenmotsu, Nancy A., Timothy K. Perttula, Patricia Mercado-Allinger, Thomas R. Hester, James E. Bruseth, Sergio Iruegas, and Curtis Tunnell. "Medicine Mounds Ranch: The Identification of a Possible Comanche Traditional Cultural Property in the Rolling Plains of Texas." *Plains Anthropologist* 40 (1995): 237–50.

Kenner, Charles L. *The Comanchero Frontier: A History of New Mexican–Plains Indian Relations.* 1969. Reprint, Norman: University of Oklahoma Press, 1994.

Kessell, John L. *Kiva, Cross, and Crown: The Pecos Indians and New Mexico, 1540–1840.* Washington, D.C.: National Park Service, 1979.

Khazanov, Anatoly M. *Nomads and the Outside World.* 1983. Reprint, Madison: University of Wisconsin Press, 1994.

Kicza, John E. "Patterns in Early Spanish Overseas Expansion." *William and Mary Quarterly* 49 (Apr. 1992): 229–53.

Kradin, Nikolay N. "Nomadism, Evolution, and World-Systems: Pastoral Societies in Theories of Historical Development." *Journal of World-Systems Research* 8 (Fall 2002): 368–88.

Krech, Shepard, III. *The Ecological Indian: Myth and History.* New York: W. W. Norton, 1999.

Lamar, Howard Roberts. *The Far Southwest, 1846–1912: A Territorial History.* New Haven: Yale University Press, 1966.

LaVere, David. *Contrary Neighbors: Southern Plains and Removed Indians in Indian Territory.* Norman: University of Oklahoma Press, 2000.

———. "Friendly Persuasions: Gifts and Reciprocity in Comanche-Euroamerican Relations." *CO* 71 (Fall 1993): 322–37.

Leckie, William H. "The Red River War: 1874–1875." *Panhandle-Plains Historical Review* 29 (1956): 78–100.

Lecompte, Janet. "Bent, St. Vrain, and Company among the Comanche and Kiowa." *Colorado Magazine* 49 (1972): 273–93.

Lepore, Jill. *The Name of War: King Philip's War and the Origins of American Identity.* New York: Vintage, 1998.

Levine, Frances. "Economic Perspectives on the Comanchero Trade." In *Farmers, Hunters, and Colonists: Interaction between the Southwest and the Southern Plains,* edited by Katherine A. Spielmann, 155–69. Tucson: University of Arizona Press, 1991.

———. "Historical Settlement Patterns and Land-Use Practices on the Pecos Frontier." In *Investigations at Sites 48 and 77, Santa Rosa Lake, Guadalupe County, New Mexico: An Inquiry into the Nature of Archeological Reality,* edited by Frances Levine and Joseph C. Winter, 551–75. Albuquerque: Office of Contract Archeology, University of New Mexico, 1987.

Levine, Frances, and Martha Doty Freeman. *A Study of Documentary and Archaeological Evidence for Comanchero Activity in the Texas Panhandle.* Austin: Texas Historical Commission, 1982.

Levine, Frances, and Anna LaBauve. "Examining the Complexity of Historical Population Decline: A Case Study of Pecos Pueblo, New Mexico." *Ethnohistory* 44 (Winter 1997): 75–112.

Limerick, Patricia Nelson. *The Legacy of Conquest: The Unbroken Past of the American West.* New York: W. W. Norton, 1987.

Lindheim, Milton. *The Republic of the Rio Grande: Texans in Mexico, 1839–40.* Waco, Tex.: W. M. Morrison, 1964.

Linton, Ralph. "The Comanche Sun Dance." *American Anthropologist* 37 (July–Sep. 1935): 420–28.

———. *The Study of Man: An Introduction.* New York: D. Appleton, 1936.

Loomis, Noel M., and Abraham P. Nasatir. *Pedro Vial and the Roads to Santa Fe.* Norman: University of Oklahoma Press, 1967.

Lummis, Charles L. *A New Mexico David and Other Stories and Sketches of the Southwest.* New York: Charles Scribner's Sons, 1891.

Magnaghi, Russell M. "The Genízaro Experiment in Spanish New Mexico." In *Spain and the Plains: Myths and Realities of Spanish Exploration and Settlement on the Great Plains,* edited by Ralph H. Vigil, Frances W. Kaye, and John R. Wunder. Niwot: University Press of Colorado, 1994.

Maier, Charles S. *Among Empires: American Ascendancy and Its Predecessors*. Cambridge: Harvard University Press, 2006.

Mancall, Peter C. *Deadly Medicine: Indians and Alcohol in Early America*. Ithaca: Cornell University Press, 1995.

Mann, Michael. *The Sources of Social Power*. Vol. 1, *A History of Power from the Beginning to A.D. 1760*. Cambridge: Cambridge University Press, 1986.

Marez, Curtis. "Signifying Spain, Becoming Comanche, Making Mexicans: Indian Captivity and the History of Chicana/o Performance." *American Quarterly* 53 (June 2001): 267–307.

Marker, Sherry. *Plains Indian Wars*. 2d ed. New York: Facts on File, 2003.

Marshall, Doyle. "Red-Haired 'Indian' Raiders on the Texas Frontier." *West Texas Historical Association Year Book* 61 (1985): 88–105.

Martin, Calvin, ed. *The American Indian and the Problem of History*. New York: Oxford University Press, 1987.

McCarthy, Cormac. *Blood Meridian: Or, the Evening Redness in the West*. New York: Random House, 1985.

McCollough, Martha. *Three Nations, One Place: A Comparative Ethnohistory of Social Change among the Comanches and Hasinais during Spain's Colonial Era, 1689–1821*. New York: Routledge, 2004.

McHugh, Tom. *The Time of the Buffalo*. Lincoln: University of Nebraska Press, 1972.

McNitt, Frank. *Navajo Wars: Military Campaigns, Slave Raids, and Reprisals*. Albuquerque: University of New Mexico Press, 1972.

Meadows, William C. *Kiowa, Apache, and Comanche Military Societies: Enduring Veterans, 1800 to the Present*. Austin: University of Texas Press, 1999.

Meed, Douglas V. *The Mexican War, 1846–1848*. New York: Routledge, 2003.

Meinig, D. W. *The Shaping of America: A Geographic Perspective on 500 Years of History*. Vol. 1, *Atlantic America, 1492–1800*. New Haven: Yale University Press, 1986.

———. *The Shaping of America: A Geographic Perspective on 500 Years of History*. Vol. 3, *Transcontinental America, 1850–1915*. New Haven: Yale University Press, 1998.

Meredith, Howard. *Dancing on Common Ground: Tribal Cultures and Alliances on the Southern Plains*. Lawrence: University Press of Kansas, 1995.

Merrell, James H. *The Indians' New World: Catawbas and Their Neighbors from European Contact to the Era of Removal*. Chapel Hill: University of North Carolina Press, 1989.

———. *Into the American Woods: Negotiators on the Pennsylvania Frontier*. New York: W. W. Norton, 1999.

———. "Shamokin, 'the very seat of the Prince of Darkness': Unsettling the Early American Frontier." In *Contact Points: American Frontiers from the Mohawk Valley to the Mississippi, 1750–1830*, edited by Andrew R. L. Cayton and Fredrika J. Teute, 16–59. Chapel Hill: University of North Carolina Press for the Omohundro Institute of Early American History and Culture, 1998.

Merritt, Jane T. *At the Crossroads: Indians and Empires on a Mid-Atlantic Frontier, 1700–1763*. Chapel Hill: University of North Carolina Press for the Omohundro Institute of Early American History and Culture, 2003.

Miller, Edward L. *New Orleans and the Texas Revolution.* College Station: Texas A&M University Press, 2004.

Miller, Susan. *Coacoochee's Bones: A Seminole Saga.* Lawrence: University of Kansas Press, 2003.

———. "Those Homelands That You Call the Louisiana Purchase." In *The Louisiana Purchase and Its Peoples: Perspectives from the New Orleans Conference,* edited by Paul E. Hoffman, 75–87. Lafayette: Louisiana Historical Association and the Center for Louisiana History, 2004.

Milloy, John S. *The Plains Cree: Trade, Diplomacy, and War, 1790 to 1870.* Winnipeg: University of Manitoba Press, 1988.

Mooney, James. *Calendar History of the Kiowa Indians.* 1898. Reprint, Washington, D.C., Smithsonian Institution, 1979.

Moorhead, Max L. *The Apache Frontier: Jacobo Ugarte and Spanish-Indian Relations in Northern New Spain, 1769–1791.* Norman: University of Oklahoma Press, 1968.

———. *New Mexico's Royal Road: Trade and Travel on the Chihuahua Trail.* Norman: University of Oklahoma Press, 1958.

———. *The Presidio: Bastion of the Spanish Borderlands.* Norman: University of Oklahoma Press, 1975.

Moore, John H. *The Cheyenne Nation: A Social and Demographic History.* Lincoln: University of Nebraska Press, 1987.

———. "The Dynamics of Scale in Plains Ethnohistory." *Papers in Anthropology* 23:2 (1982): 225–46.

Mora-Torres, Juan. *The Making of the Mexican Border: The State, Capitalism, and Society in Nuevo León, 1848–1910.* Austin: University of Texas Press, 2001.

Morgenthaler, Jefferson. *The River Has Never Divided Us: A Border History of La Junta de los Rios.* Austin: University of Texas Press, 2004.

Morris, John Miller. *El Llano Estacado: Exploration and Imagination of the High Plains of Texas and New Mexico, 1513–1860.* Austin: Texas State Historical Association, 1997.

Morton, Ohland. *Terán and Texas: A Chapter in Texas-Mexican Relations.* Austin: Texas Historical Association, 1948.

Muckleroy, Anna. "The Indian Policy of the Republic of Texas." *SHQ* 25 (Jan. 1923): 184–206.

Mulroy, Kevin. *Freedom on the Border: The Seminole Maroons in Florida, the Indian Territory, Coahuila, and Texas.* Lubbock: Texas Tech University Press, 1993.

Nance, Joseph Milton. *After San Jacinto: The Texas-Mexican Frontier, 1836–1841.* Austin: University of Texas Press, 1963.

Newcomb, W. W., Jr. *The Indians of Texas: From Prehistoric to Modern Times.* Austin: University of Texas Press, 1961.

Newlin, Deborah Lamont. *The Tonkawa People: A Tribal History from the Earliest Times to 1893.* Lubbock: West Texas Museum Association, 1982.

Nostrand, Richard L. *The Hispano Homeland.* Norman: University of Oklahoma Press, 1996.

Oberste, William H. *History of Refugio Mission.* Refugio, Tex.: Refugio Timely Remarks, 1942.

Opler, Marvin K. "The Origins of Comanche and Ute." *American Anthropologist* 45 (Jan.–Mar. 1943): 155–58.

———. "The Southern Ute of Colorado." In *Acculturation in Seven American Indian Tribes*, edited by Ralph Linton, 119–203. New York: D. Appleton-Century, 1940.

Opler, Morris E. "Lipan Apache." In *Handbook of North American Indians*. Vol. 13, *The Plains*, edited by Raymond J. DeMallie, pt. 2, 941–52. 2 parts. Washington, D.C.: Smithsonian Institution, 2001.

Orozco, Víctor, comp. *Las Guerras indias en la historia de Chihuahua: Antología*. Ciudad Juárez: Universidad Autónoma de Ciudad Juárez, 1992.

Pacheco Rojas, José de la Cruz. "Durango entre dos guerras, 1846–1847." In *México al tiempo de su guerra con Estados Unidos (1846–1848)*, compiled by Josefina Zoraida Vázquez, 189–212. Mexico City: El Colegio de México, Secretaría de Relaciones Exteriores, and Fondo de Cultura Económica, 1998.

Parks, Douglas R. "Enigmatic Groups." In *Handbook of North American Indians*. Vol. 13, *The Plains*, edited by Raymond J. DeMallie, pt. 2, 965–73. 2 parts. Washington, D.C.: Smithsonian Institution, 2001.

Patterson, Orlando. *Slavery and Social Death*. Cambridge: Harvard University Press, 1982.

Peregrine, Peter N., and Gary M. Feinman, eds. *Pre-Columbian World-Systems*. Madison, Wis.: Prehistory, 1996.

Poyo, Gerald E., and Gilberto M. Hinojosa. "Spanish Texas and Borderlands Historiography in Transition: Implications for United States History." *JAH* 75 (Sep. 1988): 393–416.

Pritchard, James. *In Search of Empire: The French in the Americas, 1670–1730*. New York: Cambridge University Press, 2004.

Prucha, Francis Paul. *The Great Father: The United States Government and the American Indians*. 2 vols. Lincoln: University of Nebraska Press, 1984.

Ramos, Raúl. "Finding the Balance: Bexar in the Mexican/Indian Relations." In *Continental Crossroads: Remapping U.S.–Mexico Borderlands History*, edited by Samuel Truett and Elliott Young, 35–65. Durham: Duke University Press, 2004.

Ray, Arthur J., and Donald Freeman. *Give Us Good Measure: An Economic Analysis of Relations between the Indians and the Hudson's Bay Company before 1763*. Toronto: University of Toronto Press, 1978.

Reddy, William M. *The Navigation of Feeling: A Framework for a History of Emotions*. New York: Cambridge University Press, 2001.

Reher, Charles A. "Adaptive Process on the Shortgrass Plains." In *For Theory Building in Archaeology*, edited by Lewis R. Binford, 13–40. New York: Academic, 1977.

Reher, Charles A., and George C. Frison. "The Vore Site, 48CK302, A Stratified Buffalo Jump in the Wyoming Black Hills." *Plains Anthropologist* 25, Memoir 16 (1980).

Reid, Samuel Chester. *The Scouting Expeditions of McCulloch's Texas Ranger*. Philadelphia: Keystone, 1890.

Reséndez, Andrés. *Changing National Identities at the Frontier: Texas and New Mexico, 1800–1850*. New York: Cambridge University Press, 2005.

Rhode, David, and David B. Madsen. "Where Are We?" In *Across the West: Human Popu-*

lation Movement and the Expansion of the Numa, edited by David B. Madsen and David Rhode, 213–22. Salt Lake City: University of Utah Press, 1994.

Richardson, Rupert Norval. *The Comanche Barrier to South Plains Settlement: A Century and a Half of Savage Resistance to the Advancing Frontier.* Glendale, Calif.: Arthur H. Clark, 1933.

Richter, Daniel K. *Facing East from Indian Country: A Native History of Early America.* Cambridge: Harvard University Press, 2001.

———. *The Ordeal of the Longhouse: The Peoples of the Iroquois League in the Era of European Colonization.* Chapel Hill: University of North Carolina Press for the Omohundro Institute of Early American History and Culture, 1992.

———. "Whose Indian History?" *William and Mary Quarterly* 50 (Apr. 1993): 379–93.

Rippy, J. Fred. "The Indians of the Southwest in the Diplomacy of the United States and Mexico, 1848–1853." *Hispanic American Historical Review* 2 (Feb. 1919): 363–96.

Rister, Carl Coke. *Border Captives: The Traffic in Prisoners by Southern Plains Indians, 1835–1875.* Norman: University of Oklahoma Press, 1940.

———. "Federal Experiment in Southern Plains Indian Relations, 1835–1845." *CO* 14 (Dec. 1936): 434–55.

Robinson, Lila Wistrand, and James Armagost. *Comanche Dictionary and Grammar.* Arlington: University of Texas at Arlington, 1990.

Rodríguez, Martha. *La guerra entre bárbaros y civilizados: el exterminio del nómada en Coahuila, 1840–1880.* Saltillo: Centro de Estudios Sociales y Humanísticos, 1998.

———. *Historias de resistencia y exterminio: los indios de Coahuila durante el siglo XIX.* Tlalpan: Centro de Investigaciones y Estudios Superiores en Antropología Social, 1995.

———. "Los tratados de paz en la guerra entre 'bárbaros' y 'civilizados' (Coahuila 1840–1880)." *Historia y Grafía* 10 (Jan.–June 1998): 67–90.

Roe, Frank Gilbert. *The North American Buffalo: A Critical Study of the Species in Its Wild State.* Toronto: University of Toronto Press, 1970.

Rollings, Willard H. *The Osage: An Ethnohistorical Study of Hegemony on the Prairie-Plains.* Columbia: University of Missouri Press, 1992.

Sahlins, Marshall. *Islands of History.* Chicago: University of Chicago Press, 1985.

Salisbury, Neil. "The Indians' New World: Native Americans and the Coming of Europeans." *William and Mary Quarterly* 53 (July 1996): 435–58.

———. *Manitou and Providence: Indians, Europeans, and the Making of New England, 1500–1643.* New York: Oxford University Press, 1982.

Schilz, Thomas F., and Jodye L. D. Schilz. "Beads, Bangles, and Buffalo Robes: The Rise and Fall of the Indian Fur Trade along the Missouri and Des Moines Rivers, 1700–1820." *Annals of Iowa* 49 (Summer/Fall 1987): 4–25.

Schlesier, Karl H. "Commentary: A History of Ethnic Groups in the Great Plains, A.D. 150–1550." In *Plains Indians, A.D. 150–1550: The Archaeological Past of Historic Groups*, edited by Karl H. Schlesier, 308–81. Norman: University of Oklahoma Press, 1994.

Secoy, Frank Raymond. *Changing Military Patterns on the Great Plains.* Monographs of the American Ethnological Society 21. New York: J. J. Augustin, 1952.

Sherow, James. "Workings of the Geodialectic: High Plains Indians and Their Horses in the Region of the Arkansas River Valley, 1800–1870." *Environmental History Review* 16 (Summer 1992): 61–84.

Shimkin, Demitri B. "Introduction of the Horse." In *Handbook of North American Indians.* Vol. 11, *Great Basin,* edited by Warren L. d'Azevedo, 517–24. Washington, D.C.: Smithsonian Institution, 1986.

———. "Shoshone-Comanche Origins and Migrations." In *Proceedings of the Sixth Pacific Science Congress of the Pacific Science Association,* 17–25. 6 vols. Berkeley: University of California Press, 1940.

Simmons, Marc. *Coronado's Land: Essays on Daily Life in Colonial New Mexico.* Albuquerque: University of New Mexico Press, 1991.

———. "Settlement Patterns and Village Plans in Colonial New Mexico." *Journal of the West* 8:1 (1969): 7–21.

Smith, F. Todd. *The Caddos, the Wichitas, and the United States, 1846–1901.* College Station: Texas A&M University Press, 1996.

———. *From Dominance to Disappearance: The Indians of Texas and the Near Southwest, 1786–1859.* Lincoln: University of Nebraska Press, 2005.

———. *The Wichita Indians: The Traders of Texas and the Southern Plains, 1540–1845.* College Station: Texas A&M University Press, 2000.

Smith, Ralph A. *Borderlander: The Life of James Kirker, 1793–1862.* Norman: University of Oklahoma Press, 1999.

———. "The Bounty Wars of the West and Mexico." *Great Plains Journal* 28 (1989): 102–21.

———. "The Comanche Bridge between Oklahoma and Mexico, 1843–1844." CO 39 (Spring 1961): 54–69.

———. "The Comanches' Foreign War: Fighting Head Hunters in the Tropics." *Great Plains Journal* 24–25 (1985–1986): 21–44.

———. "Indians in American-Mexican Relations before the War of 1846." *Hispanic American Historical Review* 43 (Feb. 1963): 34–64.

———. "Mexican and Anglo-Saxon Traffic in Scalps, Slaves, and Livestock, 1835–1841." *West Texas Historical Association Year Book* 36 (1960): 98–115.

Smits, David D. "The Frontier Army and the Destruction of the Buffalo: 1865–1883." *Western Historical Quarterly* 25 (Autumn 1994): 313–38.

Speth, John D., and Katherine A. Spielmann. "Energy Source, Protein Metabolism, and Hunter-Gatherer Subsistence Strategies." *Journal of Anthropological Archaeology* 2:1 (1983): 1–31.

Spielmann, Katherine A. "Interaction among Nonhierarchical Societies." In *Farmers, Hunters, and Colonists: Interaction between the Southwest and the Southern Plains,* edited by Katherine A. Spielmann, 1–17. Tucson: University of Arizona Press, 1991.

———. *Interdependence in the Prehistoric Southwest: An Ecological Analysis of Plains-Pueblo Interaction.* New York: Garland, 1991.

Stahle, David W., and Malcolm K. Cleaveland. "Texas Drought History Reconstructed and Analyzed from 1698 to 1980." *Journal of Climate* 1 (Jan. 1988): 59–74.

Sweeney, Kevin. "Thirsting for War, Hungering for Peace: Drought, Bison Migrations, and

Native Peoples on the Southern Plains, 1845–1859." *Journal of the West* 41 (Summer 2002): 71–78.

Tate, Michael L. "Comanche Captives: People between Two Worlds." *CO* 72 (Fall 1994): 228–63.

Taylor, Alan. *American Colonies*. New York: Viking, 2001.

———. *The Divided Ground: Indians, Settlers, and the Northern Borderlands of the American Revolution*. New York: Vintage, 2006.

Teja, Jesús F. de la, ed. *A Revolution Remembered: The Memoirs and Selected Correspondence of Juan N. Sequín*. Austin: State House, 1991.

———. "Spanish Colonial Texas." In *New Views of Borderlands History*, edited by Robert H. Jackson, 107–30. Albuquerque: University of New Mexico Press, 1998.

Thompson, Leonard, and Howard Lamar. "Comparative Frontier History." In *The Frontier in History: North America and South America Compared*, edited by Howard Lamar and Leonard Thompson. New Haven: Yale University Press, 1981.

Thurman, Melburn D. "On the Identity of the Chariticas: Dog Eating and Pre-Horse Adaptation on the High Plains." *Plains Anthropologist* 33 (May 1988): 159–70.

Tijerina, Andrés. "Under the Mexican Flag." In *Tejano Journey*, edited by Gerald E. Poyo, 33–47. Austin: University of Texas Press, 1996.

Trigger, Bruce. "Early Native North American Responses to European Contact: Romantic versus Rationalistic Interpretations." *JAH* 77 (Mar. 1991): 1195–1215.

Troike, Rudolph C. "A Pawnee Visit to San Antonio in 1795." *Ethnohistory* 11 (Autumn 1964): 380–93.

Truett, Samuel. *Fugitive Landscapes: The Forgotten History of the U.S.–Mexico Borderlands*. New Haven: Yale University Press, 2006.

Tunnell, Curtis D., and W. W. Newcomb, Jr. *A Lipan Apache Mission: San Lorenzo de la Santa Cruz, 1762–1771*. Austin: Texas Memorial Museum, 1969.

Tykal, Jack B. "From Taos to St. Louis: The Journey of María Rosa Villalpando." *NMHR* 65 (Apr. 1990): 161–74.

Usner, Daniel H., Jr. *Indians, Settlers, and Slaves in a Frontier Exchange Economy: The Lower Mississippi Valley before 1783*. Chapel Hill: University of North Carolina Press, 1992.

Utley, Robert M. *Frontiersmen in Blue: The United States Army and the Indian, 1848–1865*. Lincoln: University of Nebraska Press, 1967.

———. *The Indian Frontier of the American West, 1846–1890*. Albuquerque: University of New Mexico Press, 1984.

Vehik, Susan C., and Timothy G. Baugh. "Cultural Continuity and Discontinuity in the Southern Prairies and Cross Timbers." In *Plains Indians, A.D. 150–1550: The Archaeological Past of Historic Groups*, edited by Karl H. Schlesier, 239–63. Norman: University of Oklahoma Press, 1994.

———. "Prehistoric Plains Trade." In *Prehistoric Exchange Systems in North America*, edited by Timothy G. Baugh and Jonathon E. Ericson, 249–74. New York: Plenum, 1994.

Vigness, David M. *Incursiones de indios al noreste en el México independiente (1821–1885)*. Monterrey: Archivo General del Estado de Nuevo León, 1995.

———. "Indian Raids on the Lower Rio Grande, 1836–1837." *SHQ* 59 (July 1955): 14–23.
Wallace, Ernest, and E. Adamson Hoebel. *The Comanches: Lords of the South Plains*. Norman: University of Oklahoma Press, 1954.
Webb, Walter Prescott. *The Great Plains*. Boston: Ginn, 1931.
———. "History as High Adventure." *American Historical Review* 64 (Jan. 1959): 265–81.
Weber, David J. "American Westward Expansion and the Breakdown of Relations between *Pobladores* and '*Indios Bárbaros*' on Mexico's Far Northern Frontier, 1821–1846." *NMHR* 56 (July 1981): 221–38.
———. *Bárbaros: Spaniards and Their Savages in the Age of Enlightenment*. New Haven: Yale University Press, 2005.
———. *The Mexican Frontier, 1821–1846: The American Southwest under Mexico*. Albuquerque: University of New Mexico Press, 1982.
———. "'Scarce more than apes': Historical Roots of Anglo-American Stereotypes of Mexicans in the Border Region." In *New Spain's Far Northern Frontier: Essays on Spain in the American West, 1540–1821*, edited by David J. Weber, 295–307. Dallas: Southern Methodist University Press, 1979.
———. *The Spanish Frontier in North America*. New Haven: Yale University Press, 1992.
———. *Taos Trappers: The Fur Trade in the Far Southwest, 1540–1846*. Norman: University of Oklahoma Press, 1968.
Weddle, Robert S. *The San Sabá Mission: Spanish Pivot in Texas*. 1964. Reprint, College Station: Texas A&M University Press, 1999.
Wedel, Waldo R. *Central Plains Prehistory: Holocene Environments and Culture Change in the Republican River Basin*. Lincoln: University of Nebraska Press, 1986.
West, Elliott. *The Contested Plains: Indians, Goldseekers, and the Rush to Colorado*. Lawrence: University of Kansas Press, 1998.
———. "Reconstructing Race." *Western Historical Quarterly* 34 (Spring 2003): 7–26.
———. *The Way to the West: Essays on the Central Plains*. Albuquerque: University of New Mexico Press, 1995.
West, G. Derek. "The Battle of Adobe Walls." *Panhandle-Plains Historical Review* 36 (1963): 16–29.
White, Richard. "Animals and Enterprise." In *The Oxford History of the American West*, edited by Clyde A. Milner II, Carol A. O'Connor, and Martha A. Sandweiss, 237–73. New York: Oxford University Press, 1994.
———. "Creative Misunderstandings and New Understandings." *William and Mary Quarterly* 63 (Jan. 2006): 9–14.
———. *The Middle Ground: Indians, Empires, and Republics in the Great Lakes Region, 1650–1815*. New York: Cambridge University Press, 1991.
———. *The Roots of Dependency: Subsistence, Environment, and Social Change among the Choctaws, Pawnees, and Navajos*. Lincoln: University of Nebraska Press, 1983.
———. "The Winning of the West: The Expansion of the Western Sioux in the Eighteenth and Nineteenth Centuries." *JAH* 65 (Sep. 1978): 319–43.
White, Richard, and William Cronon. "Ecological Change and Indian-White Relations." In *Handbook of North American Indians*. Vol. 4, *History of Indian-White Relations*,

edited by Wilcomb E. Washburn, 417–29. Washington, D.C.: Smithsonian Institution, 1989.

Wilkinson, J. B. *Laredo and the Rio Grande Frontier.* Austin: Jenkins, 1975.

Wishart, David J. *An Unspeakable Sadness: The Dispossession of Nebraska Indians.* Lincoln: University of Nebraska Press, 1994.

Worcester, Don. *The Texas Longhorn: Relic of the Past, Asset for the Future.* College Station: Texas A&M University Press, 1987.

Wyman, Walker. "Freighting: A Big Business on the Santa Fe Trail." *Kansas Historical Quarterly* 1 (Nov. 1931): 17–27.

THESES, DISSERTATIONS, AND UNPUBLISHED PAPERS

Babcock, Matthew McLaurine. "Trans-national Raid and Trade Routes: Comanche Expansion from the Rio Grande to Durango, 1821–1846." Unpublished paper.

———. "Trans-national Trade Routes and Diplomacy: Comanche Expansion, 1760–1846." M.A. thesis, University of New Mexico, 2001.

Crisp, James Ernest. "Anglo-Texan Attitudes toward the Mexican, 1821–1845." Ph.D. diss., Yale University, 1976.

Gelo, Daniel Joseph. "Comanche Belief and Ritual." Ph.D. diss., Rutgers University, 1986.

Magnaghi, Russell M. "The Indian Slave Trade in the Southwest: The Comanche, a Test Case." Ph.D. diss., University of Nebraska–Lincoln, 1979.

McReynolds, James Michael. "Family Life in a Borderland Community: Nacogdoches, Texas, 1779–1861." Ph.D. diss., Texas Tech University, 1978.

Valerio-Jiménez, Omar. "*Indios Bárbaros,* Divorcées, and Flocks of Vampires: Identity and Nation on the Rio Grande." Ph.D. diss., University of California, Los Angeles, 2001.

Velasco Avila, Cuauhtémoc José. "La amenaza comanche en la frontera mexicana, 1800–1841." Ph.D. diss., Universidad Nacional Autonóma de México, 1998.

Wilson, Maurine T. "Philip Nolan and His Activities in Texas." M.A. thesis, University of Texas, Austin, 1932.

INDEX